THE GOOD WALKS GUIDE

ABOUT THE GUIDE AND ITS AUTHOR

The Good Walks Guide is a compilation of 150 walks throughout Britain, many of which appeared for the first time in two earlier Consumers' Association publications, the *Holiday Which? Good Walks Guide* and the *Holiday Which? Town and Country Walks Guide*. Although all walks have been completely checked or rechecked and newly mapped for this ringbound edition, please bear in mind when following our walk directions that the countryside is always changing.

TIM LOCKE, who compiled and wrote these guides, is a travel researcher and writer of long standing, with particular expertise in Britain, Europe, New England and the Far East. He has also written guides to the Lake District, the West Country and Yorkshire and the Peak District for Consumers' Association; other publications include *The Thomas Cook Guide to Munich and Bavaria* and *The AA Explorer Guides* to Britain, Thailand, Germany and to Boston and New England.

THE
GOOD WALKS GUIDE

EDITED BY TIM LOCKE

WHICH?
BOOKS

CONSUMERS' ASSOCIATION

ACKNOWLEDGEMENTS

Thanks to all those who helped to check the walks, especially:

Brian Allingham, Ann Apps, R. Ashton, Graham Avery, Susi Bailey, Ellen Barr, Philip Belgeonne, Norma Benathan, Roberta Boyd, Alyson Brownhill, Margaret Bullock, Ron Bussell, Bob Carpenter, Ray Carver, E.G. Chandler, Roger Chick, Barbara and Brian Coates, John Cripps, Marianne Croll, B. Cusack, J. Davidson, Ron Davies, Gwyneth Ellery, Geoff Elliott, Arthur Fasler, A.A.J. Fluck, M. Given, John Goodwin, W. Grace, Anthony J. Green, Gwenda Gofton, P. Hanley, Peter Harwood, Brenda Horwill, V. Jelkin, Dr H.D. Johnstone, Delia King, Tim Kirby, The Kirby-Harris family, B.R. Lee, Anne Locke, Stephen Locke, John Lillie, W.B.H. and H. Lord, Andrew McIlwraith, Alec Malkinson, Jo Marsh, R. Miles, Liz More O'Ferrall, John Pearson, Richard Phillips, Hilary Potts, Mike and Mel Powell, Tessa Rashford, Geoffrey Rawlinson, Chris Regan, Bruce Riddell, Graeme Robertson, Rosemary Rosher, Frank Skelcey, L.H. Smaje, Jacqueline Smith, Paul Smith, Andrea Tarr, James Tims, Nick Trend, Tony and Anna Wakeling, M.J. Walden, R. Walden, P.R. Ward, Dorothea Whitworth, G.N. Williams, Joan Williams, T. Wilsher, Mrs W. Wilson, Harold Wiseman and the many others who sent valuable comments

Warm thanks also to the Countryside Commission, various branches of the Ramblers' Association, Rebecca Folland, Hugh Morgan and Elaine Pollard

Which? Books are commissioned and researched by Consumers' Association and published by Which? Ltd, 2 Marylebone Road, London NW1 4DF

Distributed by The Penguin Group:
Penguin Books Ltd, 27 Wrights Lane, London W8 5TZ

First edition April 1995
Copyright © 1995 Which? Ltd

British Library in Cataloguing in Publication Data
Good Walks Guide: 150 Great Walks in Outstanding Locations Throughout Britain
I. Locke, Tim
796.510941

ISBN 0 85202 543 2

Cover and typographic design by Paul Saunders
Maps by Jillian Luff, Bitmap Graphics
Key map (inside front cover) by David Perrott Cartographics

Typeset by Litho Link Ltd, Welshpool, Powys
Printed and bound in Great Britain by Scotprint Ltd, Musselburgh, Lothian

CONTENTS

WALKS

PHOTOGRAPHS

With thanks to the following people and agencies for the use of their photographs. For each walk, the credits are given in the order that the photos appear.

Front cover Spectrum Colour Library (Seven Sisters, East Sussex – Walk 31); Cephas (woodland scene in north Devon)
Spine Spectrum Colour Library (Ullswater, Cumbria – near Walk 130)
Title page Spectrum Colour Library (Blea Tarn, Cumbria – Walk 126)

Walk 1 Spectrum Colour Library (both) **2** Tim Locke; J. Allan Cash **3** Holiday Which? (both) **4** Holiday Which?; Spectrum **5** Spectrum (both) **6** Spectrum (both) **7** Clare Pawley; Cephas/David Barnett **8** Spectrum (both) **9** Tim Locke; Cephas/Mike Herringshaw **10** Spectrum **11** Spectrum; Cephas/Mike Herringshaw **12** Spectrum (both) **13** J. Allan Cash; Cephas/David Barnett **14** Spectrum (both) **15** Spectrum (both) **16** Spectrum **17** Spectrum (both) **18** Spectrum (both) **19** Spectrum (both) **20** Spectrum (both) **21** Spectrum (both) **22** Spectrum (both) **23** Spectrum **24– 25** Holiday Which? **26** Cephas/Martin Walls (both) **27** Cephas/Martin Walls (both) **28** Tim Locke (both) **29– 30** J. Allan Cash **31** Spectrum (both) **32** Cephas/John Heinrich **33** Cephas/Martin Walls **34** Spectrum (both) **35** Cephas/Nigel Blythe (both) **36** Spectrum (both) **37** Spectrum (both) **38** Spectrum **39** J. Allan Cash (both) **40** Spectrum (both) **41** Spectrum (both) **42** Spectrum **43** Tim Locke **44** Spectrum **45** Spectrum (both) **46** J. Allan Cash (both) **47** Spectrum (both) **48** Spectrum (both) **49** Cephas/Martin Walls; Tim Locke **50** Cephas/Martin Walls (both) **51** Spectrum **52** R.P. Curson **53– 54** Spectrum **55** Spectrum (both) **56** Tim Locke (both) **57** Cephas/Martin Walls; Cephas/Graham Wicks **58** Tim Locke; Cephas/Martin Walls **59** Spectrum; Tim Locke **60** Spectrum (both) **61– 62** Spectrum (both) **63** Spectrum (both) **64** Spectrum **65** Spectrum; Tim Locke **66** Spectrum **67** From a postcard of Quenby Hall by English Life Publications Ltd, Derby **68** Spectrum; Tim Locke **69– 70** Spectrum (both) **71** Spectrum (both) **72** Tim Locke; Spectrum **73** Jan McMillan (both) **74** Tim Locke (both) **75** Spectrum **76– 77** Spectrum; J. Allan Cash **78** The National Trust (Severn Regional Office) (both) **79** Tim Locke; Spectrum **80** Spectrum **81** J. Allan Cash (all three photos) **82** Spectrum; J. Allan Cash **83** Spectrum (both) **84** Spectrum; Jeremy Moore **85** Laurence Main; Janet and Colin Bord/Fortean Picture Library **86** Janet and Colin Bord/Fortean Picture Library (both) **87** Llangoed Hall, Llyswen; J. Allan Cash **88** Tim Locke **89** Laurence Main; ffotograff/Patricia Aithie **90** Janet and Colin Bord/Fortean Picture Library (both) **91** Spectrum (both) **92** Spectrum (both) **93** Janet and Colin Bord/Fortean Picture Library (both) **94** Spectrum (both) **95** Tim Locke; Spectrum **96** Spectrum; J. Allan Cash **97** Spectrum **98** The Copper Mine Inn; J. Allan Cash **99** J. Allan Cash; Quarry Bank Mill Trust Ltd **100** Mike Williams (both) **101** Spectrum; Tim Locke **102** J. Allan Cash (both) **103** J. Allan Cash; Spectrum **104** Spectrum (both) **105** Spectrum (both) **106** Spectrum (both) **107** Mike Williams (both) **108** Spectrum **109** Spectrum **110** Spectrum **111** Spectrum (both) **112** Spectrum (both) **113** Cephas/Dorothy Burrows; Cephas/P.A. Broadbent **114** Cephas/Dorothy Burrows; J. Allan Cash **115** Tim Locke; Spectrum **116** Holiday Which?; Spectrum **117** Spectrum **118** Holiday Which? **119** Spectrum (both) **120** Spectrum **121** Holiday Which?; Keith Routledge **122** Spectrum (both) **123** Spectrum (both) **124** J. Allan Cash (both) **125** Spectrum (both) **126** Holiday Which?; Spectrum **127** Spectrum (both) **128** Spectrum; illustration from *The Tale of Tom Kitten* copyright © Frederick Warne & Co., 1907, 1987 **129** Tim Locke; Spectrum **130** Spectrum (both) **131** Holiday Which?; Spectrum **132** Holiday Which?; Spectrum **133** Spectrum **134** Spectrum (both) **135** Spectrum (both) **136** The Still Moving Picture Company/S.J. Whitehorne; Spectrum **137** Spectrum; Tim Locke **138** Spectrum **139** Spectrum; The Still Moving Picture Company/Distant Images **140** The Still Moving Picture Company/STB/Paul Tomkins **141** Scotland in Focus (both) **142** The Still Moving Picture Company; The Still Moving Picture Company/STB/Paul Tomkins **143** Scotland in Focus (both) **144** Spectrum (both) **145** Scotland in Focus (all three photos) **146** Spectrum (both) **147** The Still Moving Picture Company/Robert Lees; Spectrum **148** The Still Moving Picture Company/STB; The Still Moving Picture Company/Angus Johnston **149** Spectrum (both) **150** The Still Moving Picture Company/STB/Paul Tomkins; The Still Moving Picture Company/STB

INTRODUCTION

IT was one of the ever-recurring wonders of the whole incredibly compressed island – a nest of countries, as they put it – that for the production of its effects so little of a given quality went so far: that so few miles made a distance, and so short a distance a difference.

EDITH WHARTON, *Afterward (1909)*

THE GOOD WALKS GUIDE draws together some of the best walks in Britain: some are famous classics, but many are relatively unknown gems. In every case, when walking the route, we have applied our special tests for its inclusion. First, would we enjoy repeating the walk (at our own pace, and without the need to take notes all the time)? Secondly, would we recommend a friend to travel some distance to undertake it?

In seeking out the super-special, we have tramped literally thousands of miles, making notable finds as well as enduring some heroic failures, and firmly establishing our lists of likes and dislikes.

THREE CHEERS FOR...

Scenic variety

Blessed with a superb network of footpaths and bridleways, and endowed with an astonishing diversity of natural and man-made features, much of Britain is at an ideal scale for exploration on foot. No other method of travel provides for such an intimate acquaintance with the countryside. Our favourite walks have changing views and a variety of landscapes, keeping the walker's interest going until the very last step.

Not all of Britain's countryside offers the kind of walks we have been seeking: much depends on local topography and the network of walkers' routes. Some coastal areas have nothing to offer inland, and so don't merit anything other than a straightforward there-and-back walk along the coast path (if there is one). Many upland areas are so vast in scale that you would need to hike 20 miles to get a change in view. And we've endeavoured to exclude walks that are merely pleasant strolls and pretty much indistinguishable from all else in the region.

Clear waymarking

It can take feats of map-reading to find your way across fields, especially large ones with several gates at different points. The path often isn't defined on the ground and you can't see where to exit. There's now a legal requirement for landowners to show the line of the path on the ground where it crosses arable land, by not covering it with crops. But this doesn't always happen. Furthermore, paths across pasture are unlikely to be well trodden except in very well-walked areas. The potential for confusion is often even greater in woodland, where there may be no landmarks to guide you.

To counter this problem, waymarkers – small, coloured arrow motifs – are placed prominently. Yellow indicates a public footpath, blue a public bridleway, and red a byway open to all traffic. By careful positioning they can give very precise directions.

Waymarkers make obvious sense: the walker is less likely to stray, so the landowner should have little reason to fear unintentional trespass. Even expert map-readers can get it wrong, especially where field boundaries shown on maps have been added or removed, and in forests where the precise course of the path may be difficult to identify. Where paths have been diverted, waymarkers ought to be placed as a matter of course. But some landowners might feel that if they don't install waymarkers, then walkers are less likely to come on to their land; we fervently hope this kind of attitude is well on the wane.

Caring landowners

Considerate landowners keep paths unobstructed, maintain their stiles and gates and generally welcome walkers on rights of way across their land. Super-considerate landowners have been known to install special dog-gates by stiles (many dogs are unable to cross a stile); one of the most thoughtful touches we've seen was on the Offa's Dyke Path, where a farmer penned a poem inviting walkers to help themselves to drinking water from a specially provided tap. We found a spectacular example of landscape beautification near Penshurst in Kent, where the farmer had transformed some functional barns into a pink *trompe l'oeil* resembling a neat country mansion as we approached it through the fields (Walk 35).

Conscientious highway authorities

District or county councils are responsible for ensuring that paths and bridleways are usable, for erecting signposts where the path leaves a public road, and for erecting footbridges. It's a mammoth task, needing the co-operation of walkers and landowners; many highway authorities have pulled the stops out to make paths easy and pleasant to use, although clearly there is still much work to be done.

Bed and breakfast

B&B is a great British institution. On the whole the standard is very acceptable, and on our travels the vast majority of the breakfasts have set us up for the day. Some owners proved themselves founts of local knowledge about paths and places. The wide availability of B&B is a boon to long-distance walking. *The Good Bed and Breakfast Guide*, also published by Consumers' Association, is useful for those planning to spend some days walking. And many local tourist offices operate a book-a-bed-ahead scheme.

Welcoming pubs that are actually open when you arrive

Publicans who welcome walkers don't mind hikers in flapping cagoules, make provision for children and serve decent food (or let you eat your sandwiches in the garden). The law about pub opening times has been eased in recent legislation but in practice the traditional sport of walking at six miles an hour to make it to the pub on time is still alive and well on Sunday afternoons.

The best of Britain's pubs feature in another Consumers' Association publication, *The Which? Guide to Country Pubs* (many of the selected pubs are on the routes of walks in this guide).

Ordnance Survey (OS) Pathfinder, Outdoor Leisure and Explorer Maps

These maps, published at 1:25,000 scale, show field boundaries, rights of way, buildings and a huge amount of topographical detail. Britain just about leads the way in walkers' maps, and we're very lucky as a nation to have them.

Walker-friendly dogs

As most of them are.

THREE BROKEN BOOTLACES FOR...

Gates (across public rights of way) tied up with ridiculous bits of baler twine

Likewise, stiles that are festooned with barbed wire; paths that have been deliberately blocked; farmyards full of oozy slurry and with no obvious way out; paths that start confidently, then suddenly peter out miles from anywhere; signs that announce 'dangerous animals' or 'private land' where there is a public right of way; landowners (emphatically in the minority) who remove waymarkers in the hope that people won't walk paths they can't follow; public rights of way over arable fields that are invisible and involve crossing a sea of heavy-duty, extra-adhesive ploughed mud. Many of these features are illegal, but they are found all too often.

Walkers who don't treat the countryside properly

...and give the rest of us a bad name. Particular culprits are those who find gates shut and leave them open, who leave souvenirs of their memorable picnic for all to see (and for livestock to choke on), who let their dogs off leads when crossing farmland or moorland, who park in front of farm gates and who knowingly stray from the right of way when the route is obvious.

Empty plastic fertiliser sacks adorning the countryside

There's nothing illegal about a farmer littering his own land, but why should the countryside look like a dump?

The loss of treasured landscapes

We've painstakingly sifted out the best areas for walking in this guide, but overall much of our landscape has suffered devastating losses. The twentieth century has inflicted huge damage on the rural landscape. Since 1945 the countryside of England and Wales has lost 40 per cent of its broad-leaved woods, 95 per cent of its traditional herb-rich hay meadows, 80 per cent of its chalk down pastures, 60 per cent of its heathlands and over half its marshes.

In their stead have appeared vast arable prairies, unsightly sheds, monotonous blanket coverings of conifer plantations, new roads, buildings, golf courses, quarries and pylons. Changes in agriculture and forestry planting are largely exempt from planning controls. Large areas of countryside have already been transformed by modern farming practices. Until recently, financial incentives for farmers to produce as much as possible have led to the replacement of water-meadows, rough grazing and moorland with arable fields. Road and house-building have eaten into the countryside too.

Sometimes, the very beauty of the landscape has contributed to its own downfall. Shelley, Coleridge and Wordsworth admired the Valley of Rocks in Exmoor, Devon (Walk 11). It's still a wonderful place, but marred by an over-prominent car park and turning-point used by visitors who drive out here and wish they didn't have to look at these twentieth-century embellishments (fortunately, the only eyesore on an otherwise perfect walk).

Irrational path networks

Public rights of way were registered mostly in the 1950s (following the National Parks and Access to the Countryside Act 1949), being charted by highway authorities on the Definitive Map (see page xviii). Ramblers' groups collected much of the evidence that went into its creation.

Many of these routes were presented on a parish-by-parish basis, and included ancient routes, such as paths to churches and between farms and villages. The fact that the network exists at all is to be treasured, but paths don't always go where landowners and walkers want them to. Public rights of way sometimes reach dead ends at parish boundaries, where the adjacent parish decided forty or fifty years ago not to register the section of path that fell in its area. Other paths lead to main roads with no way of continuing a walk without an unpleasant encounter with heavy traffic. Others don't make the best of the scenery, or indulge in inexplicable minor detours and little loops where it seems common sense to cut a corner (although to do so would be trespassing). Many paths go straight through farmyards – not a treat for anyone who is frightened by dogs or dislikes being ankle-deep in mud – where perhaps both farmer and walker would prefer the routes bypassed instead. Agreements between landowners and highway authorities can solve this problem. There has been a lot of talk about rationalising the path network. Ramblers' groups shudder at the idea, quite rightly, of any reduction of rights of way. Landowners don't want to fork out for the appreciable costs of path diversions.

Situations where it's practically impossible to know whether you have the right to walk

In theory, it should be easy to find out where you can walk. In practice, it is quite easy to trespass innocently, or to fail to realise that you have access to a particular path or area (though trespassers would generally not get prosecuted – see page xvii). Instances are:

- *The OS map is out of date and paths have been closed, diverted or opened* If a landowner tells you that your map is out of date and you have no right to be on a certain right of way, what do you do? The only way of checking is to consult the Definitive Map kept by the highway authority – but that is kept in an office, closed at weekends, when most people walk. We have come across this precise problem (in Clwyd, Cornwall and Dorset), and on each occasion it turned out that the farmer was either misinformed or bluffing.

  To mitigate the confusion, there should be a sign and/or waymarking explaining any discrepancies with the OS map. If there isn't any such marking, then the walker should follow what the map says.

- *The right of way does not appear on the OS map at all* Sometimes, there are discrepancies between the OS map and the Definitive Map prepared by the highway authority. Occasionally, the OS map contains errors, such as marking a public right of way on the wrong side of a field boundary.

- *The right of way is correctly mapped but only prodigiously gifted map-readers would be able to find it* In particular, there are lots of moorland paths which are quite unmarked (and the course of them has probably never been evident). Again, waymarks seem to be the answer.

- *There is another path marked on the map, not as a right of way* A curiously large number of paths do not follow quite the same course on the ground as they do on the map. In the Lake District, for example, many of the routes across the fells are not quite aligned with the green dashes (showing rights of way) on the OS maps. However, small black dashes (representing other paths, not necessarily rights of way) are the routes walkers use. If you try climbing Helvellyn and stick closely to the map you will find that this is exactly what happens. Fortunately, there's pretty free access to much of the Lakeland fell area anyway, but in other regions there is scope for confusion and accidental trespass.

- *Roads are not mapped as rights of way* There's clearly no confusion when the road is maintained by the highway authority and is coloured in on the map. OS maps often show lesser roads as two parallel black lines, broken or unbroken. The status of these 'white roads' is woolly in the extreme. Some are private driveways; others are impenetrable thickets between two field boundaries (which, because they are marked on OS maps by black lines, can look just like a road); others are surfaced roads used by all traffic; others are actually signposted as rights of way; while others are ancient green lanes with no indication of whether you can or cannot walk along them. The last category can be frustrating if you are trying to devise your own route. It doesn't even help looking at the Definitive Map. There is a good chance they may be unclassified country roads (open to all traffic); usually the transport department of the county or district council can help identify these, but it's a cumbersome business trying to extract the information, which may well not be shown on the Definitive Map.

Walker-eating dogs

Found lurking in farmyards or gardens, tied up all day by a chain that is just long enough to give Fido the chance of a morsel of tasty walker.

ENCOURAGING SIGNS

Improving the paths

More and more people are walking in the countryside. OS maps showing rights of way and field boundaries now cover the whole of Britain. Hiking guides and self-guided trails have mushroomed. Walking boots have got more user-friendly. Even the Ministry of Defence has published a booklet of walks on its lands.

Allied to increased mobility and awareness in our rural surroundings, there are distinct signs that things are improving for the walker. Between 1986 and 1991 annual expenditure on rights of way doubled from £12.3 million to £24.8 million, a hefty increase even in real terms. But progress is piecemeal, much dependent on the efficiency of the relevant highway authority.

The Countryside Commission aims to have all of England's 120,000 miles of rights of way in usable condition by the year 2000, to get paths legally defined and promoted and publicised. This may sound a tall order, but when we started researching walks in 1985, ploughed-out paths and missing stiles were a fact of life; now these are not so common, at least in certain parts of the country (such as in the countryside within 50 miles of London). Better maps (showing precise routes of public footpaths and bridleways), a heartier public appetite for walking, and (in lots of areas) more walker-aware highway authorities keen to recognise the needs of walkers have each played a part.

The Countryside Commission carried out nationwide surveys in 1987 and 1994 to give an overview of the state of the network of rights of way and to vet the progress that highway authorities are making in this matter. The Adopt-a-Path scheme, pioneered in South Yorkshire, is one success story: residents and parish councils are encouraged to adopt a path, walk it frequently and report any problems to the highway authority. Another successful initiative has been the Parish Paths Partnership scheme, through which the Countryside Commission has encouraged local communities to take care of footpaths in their parishes; grants are given to enable surveys and maintenance, while the highway authority is able to concentrate on more complicated legal issues concerning rights of way.

Protecting the countryside

English Nature, the Countryside Council for Wales, and Scottish Natural Heritage have replaced the national-based Nature Conservancy Council; these and the Countryside Commission (and its Scottish equivalent) advise the government and help administer protected areas. The Countryside Commission is also responsible for the establishment of National Trails, such as the Pennine Way, South Downs Way and Offa's Dyke Path. International conventions, European legislation and British Acts of Parliament provide the legal framework for countryside protection.

UK protection

The most scenically important areas of England and Wales are the *National Parks* (these are the Brecon Beacons, the Broads, Dartmoor, Exmoor, the Lake District, the North York Moors, Northumberland, the Peak District, the Pembrokeshire Coast, Snowdonia and the Yorkshire Dales; the New Forest is a Special Protected Area). They are managed by the National Park Authorities to preserve the landscape for recreation and conservation.

When the National Park Authorities were set up, there was no control over agriculture, the major use to which land was put. Therefore the Parks were as subject as anywhere else to environmental vandalism – disappearing hedgerows, unsightly factory-like farm buildings, overgrazing and so on. However, planning control within the National Parks now covers farm buildings.

The Parks themselves have helped plug the gap: each Park has a Farm Conservation Officer, who advises farmers on conservation matters. Sometimes, management agreements are made whereby the Parks compensate a farmer for abstaining from agricultural 'improvements', such as draining moorland. A clear assurance that damage will not be done is given for a specified price.

Conservation measures in National Parks are very varied. In the Yorkshire Dales, grants are given for repairing dry-stone walls and barns (Swaledale has 750 barns, most in poor repair), which are such an integral part of the Pennine landscape. On Exmoor and the North York Moors regeneration projects have been carried out with the aim of re-establishing moorland;

bracken is a particular problem on the grouse moors, as resident ticks transmit a virus harmful to both grouse and sheep. Meanwhile, pony-owners on Dartmoor are offered financial incentives to continue grazing traditional Dartmoor ponies on the commons.

Areas of Outstanding Natural Beauty and Heritage Coasts cover 85 areas of England, Wales and Northern Ireland. No major industrial or commercial development is allowed within them, unless it is of vital importance. The Scottish equivalents are *National Scenic Areas*.

National Nature Reserves are maintained by English Nature, the Countryside Council for Wales and Scottish Natural Heritage. The primary purpose is to conserve wildlife and geological features, and to give opportunities for research. *Local Nature Reserves* are owned by highway authorities in consultation with these bodies. Additionally, there are many conservation trusts and wildlife organisations that own reserves.

Over 5,000 areas (some very small) designated as *Sites of Special Scientific Interest (SSSIs)* have some outstanding feature, such as rare flora or fauna, which is worth protecting. However, current legislation is inadequate to safeguard SSSIs for posterity: nearly 200 a year are damaged by development or other causes. Highway authorities can also set up their own *country, forest or metropolitan parks*.

A notable success has been the introduction of thousands of *Countryside Stewardship Schemes*. These offer incentives to landowners to restore valued landscapes and habitats such as chalk downland, coastal areas and lowland heath. Additional payments may be made to give public access; many new paths have been created.

International protection

International protection is limited to a handful of sites of worldwide importance. *World Heritage Sites* are natural and cultural treasures of exceptional interest, designated by UNESCO; the UK's natural sites are the island of St Kilda's, 40 miles west of the Western Isles, and the Giant's Causeway in Northern Ireland. UNESCO also designates *Biosphere Reserves*, of significant wildlife value. *Ramsar Sites* are wetland habitats protected by international convention.

Additionally, European Community Protection includes *Special Protection Areas* designated for the protection of bird species. *Environmentally Sensitive Areas* have been selected to encourage farmers to farm in a traditional way for the benefit of the landscape and wildlife. There are over 20 such areas in the UK (see the feature box in Walk 122).

The *Hedgerow Incentive Scheme*, launched by the Countryside Commission in 1992, provides aid for improved management of environmentally important hedges. Government research identified a net loss of 53,000 miles of hedgerows in Great Britain between 1984 and 1990; lack of long-term management rather than deliberate removal was the main factor.

HOW THE WALKS ARE PRESENTED

Each walk is introduced by a **summary** outlining why we have included it in the *Guide*, together with an idea of the terrain and ease of route-finding. **Length** and **time** (for an average walking pace, excluding stops) are stated for the full walk and any variants.

Difficulty is graded 1 to 3 (see below). For the **start,** we assume that readers have a standard road atlas and give further directions where needed. Note that in order to achieve the best sequence of the walk we have not always started routes at the most obvious car park in the area; for example Walk 47 in Bedfordshire could have started on the Dunstable Downs, which has a large car park, but then the walk would begin by following the escarpment, which is the highlight of the route.

Grid references are given, enabling the starting point to be pinpointed to within 100 metres for those with OS maps; these references are simply given for further clarification and are not essential for finding where to begin the walk. Because of the way we have broken up the directions into numbered sections, it is often possible to join the walk halfway round, or walk only a short section of it. Some walks start from railway stations, which have been mentioned accordingly.

Ordnance Survey (OS) map numbers are given for Landranger maps (scale 1:50,000, or about 1¼ inches to the mile) and Pathfinder maps (scale 1:25,000, or about 2½ inches to the mile). Pathfinder maps also have a further reference number based on the National Grid (e.g. TF 34/44); these are given too. In some areas (particularly National Parks) 1:25,000-scale mapping is published in the form of Outdoor Leisure and Explorer maps, which are like the Pathfinder sheets but which cover bigger areas. Again, it shouldn't be necessary to carry these maps for the purpose of following our walks, but we have listed them for those who want the information and perhaps wish to extend or adapt the routes.

Refreshments covers pubs, cafés, restaurants, tearooms and even reasonably permanent ice-cream vans. Where no refreshments are listed, we found none. Readers might like to cross-refer to *The Which? Guide to Country Pubs*, which features a number of outstanding pubs found on these walks. A really good pub can make a delightful focus for a country walk.

Feedback from checkers encouraged us to make the **walk directions** very detailed. We have broken up the text into numbered sections which refer to the map. If you feel confident of finding the way for one section, skip the text for a bit and pick it up later. As well as telling you where to turn left and right, we have peppered the directions with features confirming you're on the correct path – field boundaries, buildings, street names, pub names, landscape features, ascents, descents, and so on. Sometimes, particularly in woodland where there may be no obvious landmarks, we have resorted to giving short distances in yards; we have paced these out, so they won't be correct to the nearest inch, but should give you a rough idea of what to expect. But we have also tried to be reasonably succinct, knowing the reader won't want to wade through long sentences and miles of text. On the whole we have perhaps erred on the side of too much detail (e.g. if a path is well waymarked, we have still described the route, field by field, stile by stile, in case any of the waymarks goes missing), but we hope you will understand why. Always read the next sentence ahead so you know what you're looking for. In order to keep the directions reasonably manageable, we have tried to keep to routes that don't involve too much description and that have many identifiable and permanent landmarks to guide you.

On the route lists points of interest, using letters which are inserted into the walk directions and are shown on the map. Although the directions do not include compass bearings, a compass can be useful for picking out landmarks from viewpoints.

Feedback welcome!

Please bear in mind that things can change, and it is virtually impossible for every detail to be up to date. Gates are replaced by stiles, signposts by waymarks – and *vice versa* – field boundaries disappear or are added. Rather more rarely, land use changes: a field becomes woodland, and housing estates get built.

We would very much like to hear from you if you have any difficulties with following the walk, or if you have any other comments. Please write to Which? Books, Consumers' Association, 2 Marylebone Road, London NW1 4DF so that we can amend our directions for any future editions.

DIFFICULTY

In the text, the walks are graded as follows, taking into account conditions underfoot, any steep slopes and length. Grading sometimes straddles two categories.

1 Easy Mostly on the level; suitable for anyone who can manage a few miles, such as families with small children. Wear stout shoes or wellingtons.

2 Middling Within the capabilities of most occasional walkers; be prepared for stiles, gentle slopes and occasional rough terrain. Wear stout shoes or walking boots.

3 Energetic Within the capabilities of a reasonably experienced walker, but be prepared for some sizeable ascents and descents. Walking boots and suitable clothing essential.

WHAT MAKES A GOOD WALK: OUR HOUSE RULES

A walk should be like a good novel: keeping you interested until the very end, unravelling a bounty of surprises and being pleasurable enough to justify a later re-acquaintance. A series of connecting paths in a scenic area is not enough. The walk must follow a pleasing sequence, so finding the most appropriate starting point is important.

The walk must be legal and physically manageable
To the best of our knowledge, none of the walks in the *Guide* involves trespass: they are all along public paths, bridleways, roads or permitted paths (see page xvi).

Although it's possible to turn an ankle on even the gentlest stroll, none of these rambles should present an unacceptable degree of danger, so we have excluded any route requiring climbing and scrambling, such as the bridgeless ravines and slithery scree slopes of the great high-level routes on the Scottish munroes, high Lakeland fells and in Snowdonia.

A general snag is that stiles may go missing and paths become overgrown. There is a legal duty in England and Wales for local authorities to ensure that paths are not blocked. None of these routes was obstructed at the time of checking: if you find a path blocked, write to the local county council (see How to complain on page xvii). The start should be easy to find, and there must be some car parking near the start (sometimes simply by the roadside).

The sequence of the walk should make the outing memorable
Opening stages should get you into the right mood straight away, and not be along a noisy main road or crunching over flat ploughed fields fringed by housing estates. There should, ideally, be a pub or café halfway along the walk so that you can continue your walk feeling refreshed. The climax of the walk should not be too early: in this way, interest should be sustained throughout. Walk 143 on the isle of Lismore, Strathclyde, reaches a dramatically situated ruined castle after the toughest part of the walk, then towards the end offers views to the mainland from an ancient stone tower. Walk 103 in the Peak District has a splendid finale high up on Froggatt Edge. The very end of the walk should not be too demanding on the feet or too difficult to follow.

Road-walking should generally be avoided
This applies particularly to busy roads. Quiet lanes are often pleasant for a distance, but can become monotonous after a while. Nevertheless, some lanes are actually preferable to fiddly routes across fields or through forests. Road-walking should never account for more than about a third of the total length (or time).

There should be plenty of attractions to sustain interest
These might include ridge walks, castles, stately homes, viewpoints, nature reserves, rivers, cliff-tops and attractive villages. The terrain should be as varied as possible: some of the best walks derive distinction from continuous changes of landscape. Fortunately, the British landscape lends itself admirably to varied short walks. Above all, the walk should have a sense of purpose, and give the walker a feeling of achievement.

The walk shouldn't demand great feats of navigation
We have been at pains to ensure that route-finding problems are kept to a minimum. Compass-reading is not necessary for any of the walks in this book (although it is sensible to carry a compass to guide you through mist on upland walks, and we often refer to compass directions when describing views). Ways through forests and over moorland often pose difficulties, and we have spent many hours re-walking sections to make sure you have some landmark or a good path to guide you.

Obvious walks are excluded
Waymarked circuits, organised trails and there-and-back walks up mountains or along long-distance paths may be splendid in their own right but hardly need a guide to locate them; we have, however, incorporated parts of ready-made walks in our own routes.

The walker should be walking into the view, not away from it
A gradual descent can be a glorious way of savouring views. At Rhossili Down (Walk 83) in Glamorgan, a sharp haul up to the summit is rewarded by a marvellous stroll along a gently descending moorland track with the whole of the Gower peninsula stretched out ahead.

CLOTHING AND EQUIPMENT

Footwear Comfortable walking boots are essential for walks graded 3, and they also make the going noticeably easier on less demanding routes. Even if you plan to do walks only three or four times a year, it might be worthwhile to invest in a pair of walking boots. Providing they are cleaned after use, they should last for years.

Some advantages are:
- *Ankle support* Rough ground is not confined to scree and boulders: it is quite possible to turn an ankle walking across a ploughed field.
- *Protection* Boots should keep out most water. They also protect you against mud, rock, scree, wire and rough terrain; thicker and more rigid soles give extra protection.
- *Comfort* Boots that fit you properly will make walking far less tiring than will ordinary shoes. Wellington

boots are quite good for wet, level walks of up to about three miles, but thereafter can become uncomfortable. Stout shoes are generally fine for short lowland strolls, although the suction effect of mud can prise off shoes completely.

- *Fitting* Finding the right boot to fit you can be quite an art: the boots should have enough room for your toes not to hit the front of them when you descend (kick the floor to try this out), but should also fit snugly around the heel. Try them on wearing two pairs of socks. There should be just enough space for you to squeeze two fingers in the boot behind your heel.

Socks Wear a thin pair next to the skin, then a thicker woollen pair (ideally loopstitch type) over the top. Take a spare pair of each in case the others get soaked.

Trousers Corduroy or woollen trousers (or, even better, breeches) are the best; jeans restrict knee movement too much when wet. Overtrousers keep out the wind effectively; some brands are waterproof without causing the wearer to sweat. They are also a good means of keeping the mud off your trousers. Shorts and skirts can be pleasant in warmer months, but put walkers' legs at the mercy of stinging nettles.

Jackets There is a wide range of anoraks, cagoules (nylon or 'breathable' man-made materials) and waxed cotton jackets on the market; which you use is largely a matter of taste. For hill walks take two woollen sweaters – one thick and one thin – to help maintain your body heat in case the weather changes rapidly.

Gloves Take a pair that will not get soaked through in the rain; waxed wool, 'breathable' man-made material or leather are best.

Hat A substantial amount of body heat is lost through the head: a woollen hat or balaclava, coupled with the hood of your jacket (in case of rain) should prove effective.

Other equipment Essential for hill and mountain expeditions (can be useful on less ambitious outings, too):

- *Compass* Many of the upland routes in this book are easy to find in reasonably clear weather, but in thick mist all the landmarks can vanish; if you have no compass you will have to rely on your sense of direction. This can quickly fail even experienced walkers.
- *Whistle* For emergency use only; the distress signal is six blasts, repeated every minute.
- *Torch* Useful for all types of walks in case you are benighted; can also be used for signalling. Take spare batteries.
- *Food and drink* Water-purifying tablets will enable you to drink spring water safely. Otherwise, emergency rations should include chocolate, mint cake or

anything with plenty of sugar, to give you quick energy. Take some food with you for long lowland walks too (especially those where no pubs or tea-rooms are listed in the text).
- *Survival bag* To get inside to avoid exposure.
- *Rucksack* Even the cheapest day sack will be much more satisfactory (and safer, as it is easier to balance yourself) than a bag slung over your shoulder or carried in your hand.
- *OS maps* Our sketch-maps and painstaking directions should (we hope) make it difficult for you to get lost on lowland routes, but in accordance with what we have said about the need to take a compass, an OS map for hill and mountain walks is essential in case of mist or if you have to leave the route (for example, in an emergency).
- *First-aid kit* Include plasters for blisters; antiseptic cream; sunscreen; massage cream for cramp or other muscular discomfort.

In addition
Map-case – protect your map from the elements – take the one supplied at the front of the *Guide*. A *folding pocket lens* (about 8x or 10x magnification; available at some optical shops) can add greatly to the enjoyment of wild flowers. A pair of *lightweight binoculars* is useful for bird-watching. The contents of a *vacuum flask* can warm you up on a cold hilltop. You might also like to carry a *towel* so that you can refresh your feet in a stream or in the sea.

SENSE AND SAFETY ON FOOT

Although we have not included in this guide walks that require great feats of navigation or an unacceptably high degree of physical danger, some of the hill and mountain walks could cause problems for anyone who isn't sensibly prepared. Even on the most innocuous-looking day, the weather on high ground can surprise you with a sudden change for the worse – mist, gale-force winds, blizzards or driving rain and so on. Also, while serious risks on a lowland walk are fairly unlikely, suitable clothing will make the outing more comfortable, and you should be able to cover greater distances without getting tired.

Walking safely on the hills
Allow plenty of time and attempt only walks that are well within your capability. Our grading system for standard of difficulty (see page xiii) and rough timings are designed to help you choose the walks that suit you.

Time yourself carefully
The timings are rough ones, based on an average rate; you will need to add on some time for refreshments and looking at features of interest. Generally, two miles per

hour is an average speed for lowland walking; quite a lot of time is spent crossing stiles and reading directions. Types of terrain that can be crossed easily include downland tracks, gentle descending mountain tracks, firm sandy beaches and old railway lines, where an average speed of three miles per hour is likely. Much slower are shingle beaches, mountain ascents, steep mountain descents, scree, boulders and boggy moorland, where you should reckon on an average speed of one mile per hour. Always choose walks well within your capabilities and level of experience.

Slow and steady wins the mountain race

A useful rule for mountain ascents is to walk at a slow but rhythmic plod, a rate so gentle that you won't need to stop too often on the way and can therefore gain some momentum. A brisk pace can be exhausting and, except for the fittest and most experienced fell-walkers, is nearly always slower than the rhythmic plod over a long distance.

Learn some elementary first aid. If bad weather conditions suddenly develop, huddle against a wall, boulder or anything else at hand, put on all the clothes in your rucksack and improvise a shelter with a survival bag or whatever is available. Do not rub to keep warm, or take alcohol, as both encourage blood to the surface, which reduces the core body temperature.

Look after your feet

If your boot is rubbing unpleasantly, take it off immediately and put a plaster over the sore part before it develops into a blister.

Check the weather

Before setting out, check the local weather forecast. In National Parks, information centres should be able to help you; otherwise pre-recorded weather forecasts are provided by weather centres over the telephone.

Leave messages

If you are venturing into wild or remote areas, leave a note of where you are going with a hotel, youth hostel, tourist office or a friend. Be sure to tell them when you get back – otherwise a search party may be sent out.

Take the right equipment

See page xiv.

Consideration in the countryside

On the whole the relationship between landowners and walkers is a happy one. However, friction does sometimes occur, and it may be the fault of the inconsiderate walker. Livestock may stray when gates are left open, or get injured by contact with dogs or with litter left by picnickers. Crops may be damaged when walkers do not keep to the path.

Wherever you go, follow the Country Code – see page xix.

WALKING IN THE COUNTRYSIDE: LAW AND PRACTICE

To the best of our knowledge, none of the walks in this book involves trespassing or following obstructed footpaths. But if you're walking in the countryside it is useful to have an understanding of the rights and duties of visitors to it. The countryside is not an open playground through which we can wander at will, but the law in England and Wales (see page xviii for Scotland) gives you specific rights of access to parts of it. And even where there are no such rights, many landowners are happy to allow you on part of their property.

Paths for the walker

Public rights of way On these, you have a legal right of passage, and no one can stop you using it. Most rights of way are marked on Ordnance Survey (OS) maps. You can walk along a public right of way, whether it's a public footpath, a public bridleway (where you can also ride or cycle) or a byway (or 'road used as a public path', which you can often drive along). Such paths should, by law, be signposted where they leave a road, but in practice signs may be missing. On the way, a landowner, local authority, local footpath group or private individual may have waymarked the route, but waymarkings are far from universal. The conventional symbols are yellow arrows for public rights of way, blue ones for bridleways and acorn motifs for Countryside Commission Long-Distance Paths.

There is no obligation to waymark paths after they leave the road, but a farmer must make the line of the path apparent after ploughing, within 14 days if it is the first disturbance for that crop or within 24 hours of any subsequent disturbance (unless a longer period has been agreed with the highway authority).

Forestry Commission tracks and paths i.e. those that are not public rights of way. You have permissive access – which means that you are generally welcome, but that you cannot insist on any legal rights of access. This is so that the farmer has the right to close off the tracks, notably during tree-felling.

Canal towpaths Unless there is a sign to the contrary, you can usually use them.

Other tracks and paths If you find a well-trodden path or track but an OS map does not show it as a right of way, it is not safe to assume you can use it. However, some landowners, including some private ones as well as, for example, local councils and water authorities, give permissive access to parts of their land (signposts or waymarks will confirm if this is so), and occasionally a new public right of way may have been created.

Land you are allowed on

Some commons A common is simply an area of land over which local people have various rights, such as to graze cattle. There is not necessarily any legal right for the public to walk or picnic. But some privately owned common land is open to the public, and any local authority-owned common will have been set aside for public use.

Areas where 'access agreements' have been made Occasionally, a local authority will have made a formal agreement with a landowner to allow public access (except in some cases in the lambing or shooting seasons). These have occurred in some National Parks, but otherwise are rather uncommon. Notices are usually displayed where public access is permitted.

Moorland Much moorland is owned privately, often for the purpose of raising game birds, and you should not assume you have access to it. But out of the shooting season the public is permitted access to many moorland paths and tracks.

Country parks and picnic sites The public has access if they are owned by a local authority.

Beaches Access is allowed if they are owned by a local authority, and usually if privately owned, too.

National Trust land including open land, beaches and woodland, often marked by signs and shown on OS maps. The public is allowed access unless there are notices to the contrary.

HOW TO COMPLAIN

If you want to complain about missing or broken stiles, ploughed-out paths, impenetrable vegetation, bulls, fierce dogs, missing signposts or other problems hindering your use of a public right of way, contact the rights of way section of the county council. The council holds the *County Definitive Map*, a record of rights of way, including the latest footpath diversions, closures and creations. It also has a legal duty to see that public rights of way are usable; it should also provide signposts where a public right of way leaves a public road and is responsible for maintaining the surface of the right of way. Where necessary, it has a duty to put pressure on landowners to erect stiles and remove obstructions. Do report problems (we do), because otherwise the path may deteriorate further and fall into disuse. Local authorities welcome reports (and may even rely on them), and though they may not have the resources to act immediately they should look into the matter in due course. A brief telephone call should be enough.

SOME QUESTIONS ANSWERED

The path I want to use has a sign saying 'Trespassers Will Be Prosecuted' and there's an irate landowner advancing towards me. What should I do?

If you are simply going about the innocent activity of walking, it is most unlikely that such a sign is anything more than a meaningless threat; trespassers might get sued for damages, but would not generally get prosecuted. The exceptions to the rule are if you are trespassing on Ministry of Defence or railway land, or are committing the offence of 'aggravated trespass' under the Criminal Justice Act 1994, which, controversially, makes it a criminal offence if you are on someone's land with intent to cause damage or to disrupt any lawful outdoor activity (such as fox-hunting), but it is possible that walkers might unwittingly find themselves falling foul of the criminal law.

The Ordnance Survey map shows a public path crossing a field, but I can see no trace of it. Am I entitled to follow the route?
Usually, yes – but make sure you follow the precise and legal route. By walking the route you are quite within your rights, and are doing a service to others by marking the line of the path, and making the landowner aware that people want to use it. A path might be obscured by crops: you have a right to follow the route through them, but if they are really impenetrable you are entitled to skirt the field. There's a chance that the path may have been closed or diverted; if so, you could expect signs to that effect. By law, within two weeks of ploughing, farmers must indicate the line of a public path which crosses a field, and must not plough paths which skirt fields. Unfortunately this law is often flouted.

I can see where the path goes, but I can't get to it. What should I do?
It's all too common for paths to be obstructed by rubbish, thick vegetation, fallen trees or barbed wire. You may remove just enough of an obstruction to allow you to pass, but be sure not to cause any unnecessary damage and ensure that no livestock can stray as a result of your action. It may be more practical to find a way round the obstacle, but if this takes you on to someone else's land, you are trespassing. By law, a landowner must not keep a fierce dog which deters people from using a right of way. On the other hand, a farmer can quite legally put a bull in a field crossed by a right of way, provided the bull is either of a non-dairy breed and is accompanied by cows or heifers, or is less than 11 months old. If such a bull (or indeed any bull) charges you, the farmer would be liable for damages if the bull injured you and he knew that the bull was dangerous.

Can the dog come with us wherever we go?
Generally, yes, and certainly on rights of way, provided you keep it under close control at all times. It is advisable to put the dog on a lead if you are crossing a field with livestock in it. A farmer is quite within his rights to shoot a dog that is worrying livestock – and the dog-owner could face prosecution. A dog can do untold

damage to birds during the nesting season, and to other wildlife, even if it is doing no more than hunting along a hedgerow. It may also be unwelcome on moorland: some moorland areas display notices expressly prohibiting dogs.

There's an unfenced field with a pretty view: may we have a picnic there?

Do not assume that an unfenced field is intended as an open invitation, but provided you take your litter with you, you can normally picnic anywhere to which you're allowed access (see above). But you don't have any legal rights to do so, and you may have to move on if a landowner asks you to.

May I pick wild flowers and wild fruit?

As a general rule, leave wild flowers well alone. Some species are protected, and picking them is a criminal offence. In many areas it is permissible by consent or custom, although not by legal right, to gather fruit that is growing wild (particularly blackberries), provided you

do not stray from the public right of way or area to which you are allowed access.

Scotland

The law and practice differ in two main ways. First, you do not have legal rights of access to much of the countryside or along many of its paths. But there is a tradition of relatively free access to moorland and mountain areas (subject to closure at certain times, principally deer-stalking and shooting seasons). And if a path is defined on the ground you may usually assume that you may follow it. In fields, keep to the edges. Secondly, such public rights of way as exist are not distinguished from others paths on OS maps, although they are normally signposted. Black dashed lines on OS maps can denote anything from a right of way to an unfollowable route across moorland, and plenty of clear paths (sometimes even signposted ones) do not appear on OS maps at all. For further information on rights of way, contact the Planning Department of the district or regional council.

COUNTRYSIDE ACCESS CHARTER

Your rights of way are:
- public footpaths – on foot only
- bridleways – on foot, horseback and pedal cycle
- byways (usually old roads), most 'roads used as public paths' and, of course, public roads – all traffic.

Use maps and signs – Ordnance Survey Pathfinder and Landranger maps show most public rights of way – or look for paths that have coloured waymarking arrows – yellow on footpaths, blue on bridleways, red on tracks that can be legally used by vehicles.

On rights of way you can:
- take a pram, pushchair or wheelchair if practicable
- take a dog (on a lead or under close control)
- take a short route round an illegal obstruction or remove it sufficiently to get past.

You have a right to go for recreation to:
- public parks and open spaces – on foot
- most commons near older towns and cities – on foot and sometimes on horseback
- private land where the owner has a formal agreement with the local authority.

In addition you can use the following by local or established custom or consent – ask for advice if you're unsure:
- many areas of open country like mountain, moorland, fell and coastal areas, especially those of the National Trust, and most commons
- some woods and forests, especially those owned by the Forestry Commission
- country parks and picnic sites
- most beaches
- towpaths on canals and rivers
- some land that is being rested from agriculture, where notices allowing access are displayed
- some private paths and tracks.

Consent sometimes extends to riding horses and pedal cycles.

For your information:
- county and metropolitan district councils and London boroughs have a duty to protect, maintain and record rights of way, and hold registers of commons and village greens – report problems you find to them
- obstructions, dangerous animals, harassment and misleading signs on rights of way are illegal
- if a public path runs along the edge of a field, it must not be ploughed or disturbed
- a public path across a field can be ploughed or disturbed to cultivate a crop, but the surface must be quickly restored and the line of the path made apparent on the ground
- crops (other than grass) must not be allowed to inconvenience the use of a right of way, or prevent the line of the path from being apparent on the ground
- landowners can require you to leave land to which you have no right of access
- motor vehicles are normally permitted only on roads, byways, and some 'roads used as public paths'
- follow any local byelaws.

And, wherever you go, follow the Country Code
- Enjoy the countryside and respect its life and work
- Guard against all risk of fire
- Fasten all gates
- Keep dogs under close control
- Keep to public paths across farmland
- Use gates and stiles to cross fences, hedges and walls
- Leave livestock, crops and machinery alone
- Take your litter home
- Help to keep all water clean
- Protect wildlife, plants and trees
- Take special care on country roads
- Make no unnecessary noise.

Reproduced by permission of the Countryside Commission

INDEX OF WALKS BY COUNTY

WHEAL COATES AND ST AGNES BEACON

FROM St Agnes the walk leads out along the side of a valley to the cliff-tops, then round St Agnes Head before climbing gently on to one of Cornwall's best-known viewpoints. Relics of tin and copper mining are evident in the rugged landscape of moorland cliffs. Route-finding is generally easy, but a little complicated around the Beacon.

LENGTH 5 miles (8 km), 3 hours
DIFFICULTY 2–3
START St Agnes (on B3277 north-west of Truro); start at car park which is signposted in centre of village. Grid reference 720505
OS MAPS Landranger 203 and 204; Pathfinder 1352 (SW 75); also tiny part of Pathfinder 1360 (SW 74/84)
REFRESHMENTS Pubs, cafés and shops in St Agnes; also hotel bar and café at ⑤.

WALK DIRECTIONS

① Turn right out of the car park to the main street in St Agnes, along which you turn left Ⓐ, soon passing St Agnes Hotel. After the church, fork right downhill (signposted Perranporth) down Town Hill. ② After 80 yards fork left on to a steep path called Stippy Stappy, descending with a terrace of cottages on your left; at the end of the terrace the path bends left and then immediately fork right.

The path drops to cross a stream and rises to a road. Turn right on road. ③ After 50 yards turn sharp left on to a driveway signposted as footpath to the Cliffs. After 40 yards keep forward ignoring a turn to the right Ⓑ. When the path bends right by bench above the sea, ignore left turn (too steep for comfort) but continue to the next junction by a marker-post for coast path where ④ you turn left down to the road and

houses. Turn right on road ⑤ and take the first left, just after 30 mph speed derestriction sign and just before a small car park. Beyond the end of the road, continue for 2½ miles along the cliff path (keep

Kittiwakes nest in dense colonies on cliffs, and rarely venture far inland

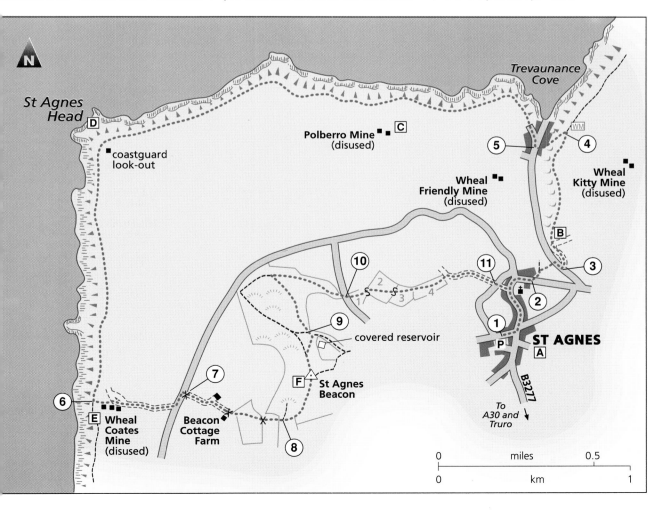

to seaward side wherever the path forks) [C] [D]. ⑥ Eventually you reach the spectacular mine ruins of Wheal Coates [E], and turn left in front of them on to a stony track leading inland towards the right end of St Agnes Beacon.

Turn left on the road and immediately after first house on right (called Blue Hills) ⑦ turn right on a driveway between walls. Ignore side turns (keep right after 100 yards where left goes into a small caravan site), to enter a farmyard at the end of the driveway by a gate. Keep to the right, between barns then soon into a field with St Agnes Beacon up ahead. Head on up towards the right end of the Beacon; field walls taper outwards – leave left-hand wall and keep up across the middle of field to a stile and gateway 90 yards to the right of top left-hand corner.

In second field, carry on up the left edge to a gate beside stile to emerge on to the corner of a path at edge of rough moorland ⑧. Keep forward and 50 yards later fork left up to the trig point on the summit [F]. From the summit go forward, taking right fork ahead (not turning 90° right, which heads to outskirts of St Agnes).

When you come close to a small covered reservoir on the right, and just before a field ahead, fork left. ⑨ 50 yards later bear half left at four-way junction, initially close to the field fence on right but soon diverging from it. 100 yards later, fork right (concrete platforms of old buildings are seen by path); the path soon swings round to the left and just as a road comes into view a short distance below, turn sharp right at an oblique path junction.

⑩ Emerge on to a road, cross and take the stile opposite, follow the left edge of (first) field to where field tapers in narrowly: here, take the stile on right into second field, where you proceed quarter left to another stile. In third and fourth fields keep to left edge (partly on enclosed paths) then forward on an enclosed track which soon bends to the right.

⑪ When you reach the road (Beaconsfield Place) at edge of St Agnes, cross to the tarmacked path opposite (not grassy path just to right of it) leading into the main street. Turn right to reach the car park.

ON THE ROUTE

[A] **St Agnes** is a former tin and copper mining community, now a retirement town and resort. The mines have closed but the ruined mine buildings have survived. On the left as you go along main street, **St Agnes Miners' and Mechanics' Institute** (1893) was founded by John Passmore Edwards, a Victorian philanthropist who was responsible for the setting up of many colleges, orphanages and hospitals in England. Stippy Stappy is the town's quaintest street name, and is thought to mean merely 'very steep'.

[B] New buildings on the outskirts of St Agnes have recently changed this valley's appearance, but two abandoned mine buildings dominate the scene: to the left is **Wheal Friendly** and to the right **Wheal Kitty**: the latter was worked 1834–1930.

[C] The coast path passes close to **Polberro Mine**, which is briefly seen to the left as you gain the cliff-top; this was once the richest mine in Cornwall.

[D] **St Agnes Head** is a noted place for sea-birds with 900 pairs of kittiwakes representing the largest colony in the area, and there are also herring gulls, fulmars and guillemots breeding here. Migrants include gannets, skuas, petrels and shearwaters; out to sea you may catch a glimpse of a grey seal or the (entirely harmless) basking shark. In view are **Bowden Rocks**, sometimes called Man and His Man; as you round the Head, the coastline southwards to **Godrevy Point** (on the east side of St Ives Bay) is revealed.

[D] **Wheal Coates** Perched on a cliff-top, this tin mine was worked for most of the 19th century and for a few years before the First World War, but was never especially productive. Its ruins are among the most evocative industrial relics in Cornwall, and have recently been restored by the National Trust.

[F] **St Agnes Beacon** (630ft) From this modest moorland summit a panorama extends over the whole of this walk and inland too. **St Michael's Mount** may be seen to the south-west, while southwards are the uplands beyond Redruth, and shipping may be observed in Falmouth harbour to the south-east. The hill has man-made lumps on it, possibly ancient burial mounds, and an enclosure which may be of Roman origin.

Ruins like these, the remains of Wheal Coates tin mine, are particular to Cornwall

GILLAN CREEK AND HELFORD RIVER

WOODED combes dotted with wild flowers, a complex landscape of estuaries and small boats in sheltered creeks contribute to what is possibly the best round walk on the Lizard Peninsula. It is easy to find the way, and there are no steep gradients. Dogs are not allowed in Bosahan Estate (between St Anthony-in-Meneage and Helford).

LENGTH 5 miles (8km), 3 hours
DIFFICULTY 1
START Manaccan (east of Helston); roadside parking opposite the turn for Gweek.
Grid reference 764250
OS MAPS Landranger 204; Pathfinder 1370 (SW 72/82)
REFRESHMENTS Pub and shop in Manaccan; pub, shop and tea-room in Helford

---

WALK DIRECTIONS

① A With the Gweek turning behind you, take the path by the restored well (passing to the right of thatched cottage) leading beside a

Helford's pub and its neighbours with their rival thatches

row of cottages up to the right side of church, reaching the road by post office. Keep right on the road and opposite the church gate turn right on to unmade lane (signposted as a

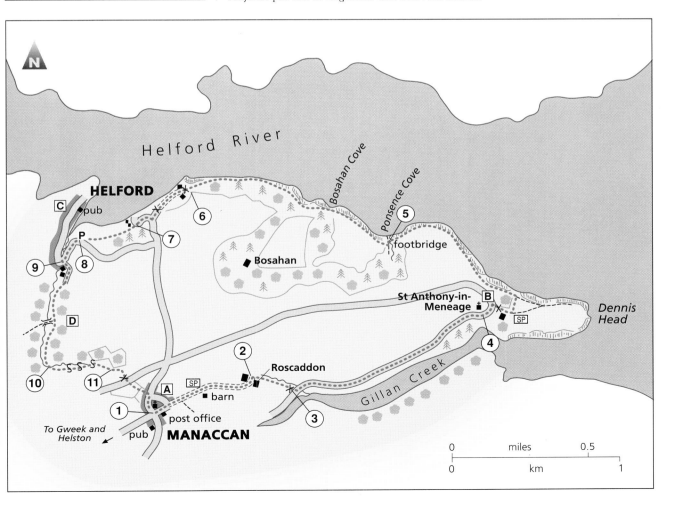

The tidal Helford River meanders through some of Cornwall's most beautiful pastoral countryside

footpath); keep forward after 100 yards, ignoring the path on right to Carne.

The track soon bends slightly right by a barn, signposted St Anthony, and continues as a concrete track to a house (Roscaddon), where ② you bear slightly left as signposted downhill on a grassy path, initially between garden hedges and then entering woodland. The path proceeds to reach a road ③. Turn left on the road.

④ At the church of St Anthony B, the road bends left uphill. Just after passing the gate at the top of churchyard, fork right on to a path up towards a kissing-gate by signpost and Bosahan Estate sign, which briefly leads through woods. On emerging into the open, fork left at signpost (right fork detours to Dennis Head and returns), proceeding uphill along edge of field.

At the end of field turn left again through kissing-gate and follow the coast path. ⑤ At next small bay (Ponsence Cove) cross the stream and keep left on the other side and almost immediately right as waymarked. ⑥ Join track by buildings, then proceed until reaching the corner of the road. Turn right downhill on the road.

⑦ Just before Treath Cottage, turn left up signposted steps. The path leads through woods, then along edge of field (ignore a kissing-gate on right when level with Sailing Club), to reach a car park by road and former chapel ⑧. Turn right downhill into Helford, past a footbridge (do not cross except for detour to village and pub) C. ⑨ Where the road is about to cross the river, keep left steeply uphill on a concrete driveway (signposted Manaccan).

By a thatched house this proceeds as a broad path into woods D. Soon ignore a right fork (over footbridge), but continue with the stream always to your right. ⑩ The path and stream make a major left turn; 50 yards later the path crosses the stream and soon continues as a sunken path with fields up on your right. Emerge into a field by a stone stile. Keep slightly right up across field to a projecting corner of woodland ⑪.

Keep forward with the woodland fence on your left, then after only 20 yards turn right up to the top of field to find a small gate in the hedgerow which lines the top of the field. Turn left on the road and immediately right by a signpost over the stile. Follow the left edge of field and proceed on to road at the edge of Manaccan, where you turn to the right.

ON THE ROUTE

A **Manaccan** occupies a sloping site amid a green, unspoilt landscape of steep lanes, pastoral farmland, neatly rounded hills and secluded wooden combes. At the bottom of the village is a covered well and pub, the New Inn. This rustic thatched cottage is a genuinely unspoilt country pub and something of a rarity in the county. The walls are hung with local paintings and the atmosphere is one of casual friendliness. In the upper part of the village, palms grow in the churchyard, and a fig tree is set in the church's south wall.

B **St Anthony-in-Meneage** A beautifully sited church which overlooks Gillan Creek, with a handsome granite and sturdy 15th-century oak roof; look for a German carving in the east wall of the same period as the roof, depicting the Last Supper.

C **Helford** is a sheltered village of lush blooms and thatched cottages, set beside a wooded creek, with much boating activity in summer. The Shipwrights Arms is idyllically sited by the banks of the river. The thatched building dates from the 18th century and its interior has a distinctly nautical atmosphere, with model ships, maritime pictures, navigational lamps, and sketches of Cornish fishermen. This pub also has a delightful terraced garden.

D The walk through these **woods** is a particular delight in early spring when daffodils and primroses give a blaze of colour.

ST ANTHONY IN ROSELAND

A ROUND walk of considerable distinction on a beautiful peninsula, first along cliffs and then looking over the harbour to Falmouth before the final section along the wooded Porthcuel river. No problems with route-finding and the going is easy all the way. Nettles can be a problem in high summer for short sections along the coast.

LENGTH 5 miles (8km), 2½ hours
DIFFICULTY 1
START Towan Beach car park by Porth Farm, on Roseland Peninsula east of Falmouth; car park is on right just after Porthcuel river appears on right, and then Towan Beach villas sign is seen on left; follow signs for St Anthony from Gerrans. Grid reference 868329
OS MAPS Landranger 204; Pathfinder 1366 (SW 83)

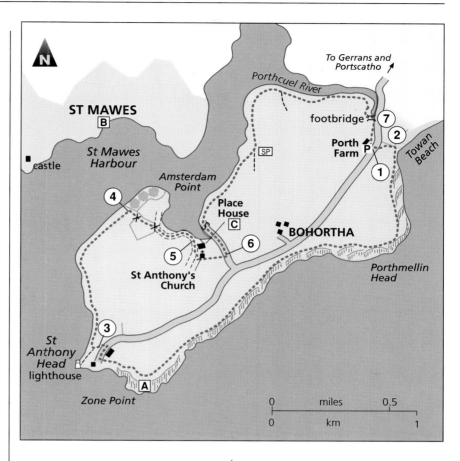

WALK DIRECTIONS

① Cross the road from the car park and take the path opposite and slightly to the left, signposted to the beach. ② Just before the beach, turn right on to cliff path, past Porthmellin Head and later emerging on to the road after Zone Point (near toilets) Ⓐ. ③ When level with the end of the cottages on your right (ex-Captain's and Lieutenant's quarters) turn left on a path signposted to lighthouse, dropping abruptly.

At the bottom (before you reach the lighthouse) turn sharp right at a path junction. The path follows the coast until woods near Amsterdam Point ④ Ⓑ, where the path turns right uphill (waymarked) along a field edge with woods on the left. Cross a stile at the top and continue down to left of next field and emerge on to a track. Turn right.

⑤ Fork right at entrance to Place House (left goes into grounds which are private) Ⓒ. When you are past the church at back of the house, fork left and immediately left again as waymarked, down steps past

church entrance, and go forward through churchyard to road ⑥.

Turn left on the road, to reach a quay where you take signposted stile on right. The path follows the riverside all the way, until crossing a bridge at the end of the creek ⑦. Turn right on the other side of bridge on a path parallel to road

then around the right-hand side of a field to a farm building, where you emerge just below the car park.

ON THE ROUTE

Ⓐ **View** from Zone Point and St Anthony Head over **Carrick Roads**, a broad estuary providing superb natural anchorage for vessels of all

The church at St Anthony, mainly 13th century, is unusual in having a central belfry

sizes. **Falmouth** lies to the west, the town dominated on its seaward aspects by the impressive **Pendennis Castle**, one of the chain of forts built by Henry VIII against a possible French invasion. The castle's outer curtain wall was added in the 16th century; inside it lies a 16-sided rampart encompassing a circular keep. Falmouth was a particularly prosperous port after 1688 until the 19th century when it flourished as a base for Mail Packets which operated from here to Spain, Portugal, the West Indies and North and South America. The **lighthouse** at St Anthony Head is *open to the public*.

B Across the water is **St Mawes**, an old port which has expanded into a busy yachting centre. The **castle** 1540–43 was built by Henry VIII, and has a round tower and bastions on three sides; this allows guns to fire round a wide arc. Carrick Roads (see **A**) was never attacked and the guns are still in place in their original condition.

C **Place House** The manor house is on the site of a 13th-century monastery, and the **church** dates from then but has been substantially restored; inside the latter are memorials to the Spry family (who own Place House), including Admiral Thomas Spry and nautical Commander-in-Chief, Richard Spry.

Carrick Roads, one mile across from St Anthony's Head over to St Mawes, is one of Europe's largest natural harbours

PONT PILL AND LANTIC BAY

FROM Polruan quay the route snakes up narrow steps between precariously stacked-up terraced cottages, then follows two contrasting scenic sections – first along the Pont Pill (a deep river valley), then back along the coast from Lantic Bay. Easy route-finding; some brief steep sections.

WALK DIRECTIONS

① Ⓐ From the quay follow road past the Lugger Inn, after which the road soon bends right. Immediately turn left into East Street, following signposts for The Hills: at end of the street keep right up steps (signposted); at top of steps ② fork left (signposted). This becomes an

earthy path and is generally level.

③ After ½ mile fork right, passing National Trust sign for North Downs 30 yards later. ④ Join and keep forward on track coming in sharply from left, but 20 yards later fork left on to a waymarked path (still keeping level). ⑤ On reaching a gate on to a road, do not pass through the gate but keep left (signposted to Pont and Hall Walk) over a stile and following the path

The view of Polruan at the very start of the walk

LENGTH 5½ miles (9km), 3 hours
DIFFICULTY 2
START Polruan (east and across river from Fowey). Grid reference 126510. Start by Polruan quay. Parking at top of town or at top of Fowey, passenger ferry from Fowey every 15 minutes, all year (*note last ferry times as you leave*)
OS MAPS Landranger 200; Pathfinder 1354 (SX 05/15)
REFRESHMENTS Full range in Polruan

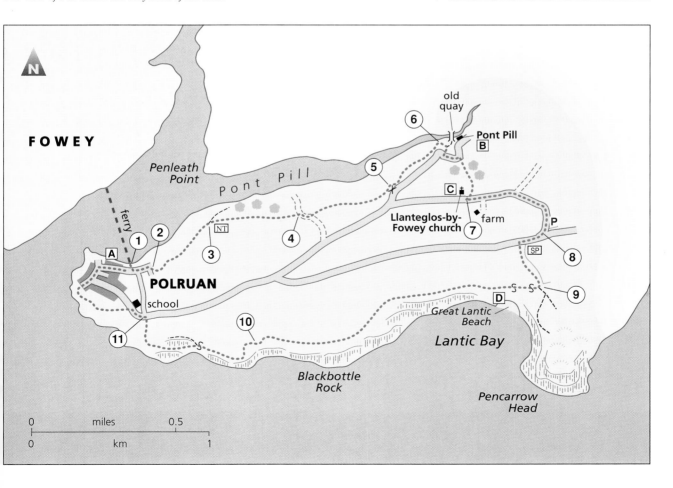

Polruan seen from Fowey, its equally picturesque neighbour across the water

closely parallel to the road which is beyond the hedge; the path drops abruptly.

⑥ At T-junction with a track at bottom of steps, turn right up to the road (or left for detour to Pont Quay B). Turn left on road and immediately right at a hairpin bend on to a grassy track just to the right of the entrance to Pont Poultry Farm: follow this up to Llanteglos-by-Fowey churchyard C and on to a surfaced lane ⑦.

Turn left on the lane (immediately ignore a minor track forking to right by farmhouse) and follow the lane down and then up (ignoring left fork to Carne Farm). ⑧ At a T-junction with road, turn right towards Polruan. After 150 yards take a gate beside a stile on

the left by National Trust sign for Pencarrow Head. Follow left edge of field towards the sea and where the field boundary on left bends left, follow it around to a gate giving on to Pencarrow Head ⑨: cross the stile immediately on right to continue along the cliff-top coast path (the next stile on the left can be taken for a detour on to Great Lantic Beach) D.

You pass Blackbottle Rock National Trust sign; later ⑩ the path drops into undercliff; ignore a later right fork (which peters out). ⑪ The path reaches a gate and goes on to the road at the edge of Polruan. Turn left on the road past the primary school then fork left on to a signposted track on to the cliff again and later reaching a narrow

road, which you follow down to Polruan Quay.

ON THE ROUTE

A **Polruan** Connected to the neighbouring port of Fowey by passenger ferry; both towns cling to their respective hillsides. Blockhouse forts guard the harbour mouth and there are mazes of double-yellow-lined streets, old inns, narrow steps between huddled terraces, and spectacular views across the harbour. Ships from the nearby china clay works, located half a mile up the river, wend their way past the small boats in the harbour. Fowey was Sea Rat's 'little grey town' in *The Wind in the Willows*. The town received its charter in 1245 to supply ships to the Navy; in the 15th century the Fowey Gallants attacked the French coast so persistently that Edward IV agreed to stop them, and, when they refused, he organised his Dartmouth men to steal the Fowey ships.

B **Pont Pill** The quay has been restored by the National Trust. A notice dated 1894 posted on the farmhouse gives dues for discharging and shipping.

C **Llanteglos-by-Fowey** The tower dominates the scene for miles around; just outside the porch a 12-ft lantern cross, lichen-covered, is of great antiquity. The Perpendicular church is, despite some restoration, one of Cornwall's finest and the endearingly drunken angles of the arches and the roofs have not been straightened out.

D **Great Lantic Beach** A sandy beach at the foot of rugged cliffs in a crescent-shaped bay. The cliffs have been degraded into rounded slopes by the forces of erosion to create the profile seen today. There are **views** inland of the strange moonscape uplands of the china clay country over near St Austell.

THE WEBBURN VALLEY AND DR BLACKALL'S DRIVE

A PLEASANT riverside and field-path walk, with some sections along roads as far as Bel Tor Corner, but the drama begins in the second half, with grand views from Dr Blackall's Drive. The field-path sections need some care; otherwise the route is easily found.

LENGTH 5½ miles (9km), 3 hours
DIFFICULTY 2
START New Bridge car park, on the Two Bridges–Ashburton road (B3357) (do not confuse with Dartmeet Bridge which is 4 miles north-west). Grid reference 711709
OS MAPS Landranger 191 and 202; Outdoor Leisure 28
REFRESHMENTS Leusdon Lodge near Leusdon church after ⑥

WALK DIRECTIONS

① Ⓐ From car park, walk to river, just to right of New Bridge and follow riverside path under the bridge; the path continues just above the river; where the path nearly meets road, do not emerge on to road but continue down hill, still beside river, through woods and open ground.

② Path later emerges on to road, along which turn right. Ignore private driveway on left by lodge but ③ take next left (signposted Lowertown) leading uphill.

④ Where after 300 yards this road is about to bend right across stream, keep forward on track signposted Poundsgate. This track goes through double gates and enters woods proceeding with stream on right and later emerging into field.

Keep forward, along right edge of field; then take left-hand of two gates and go forward with hedgerow on right in the second and third fields, to join road ⑤. Turn right along road. Just after red-brick bungalow on left, take signposted gate on right and follow left edge of field for 100 yards, until taking narrow gate on left (ignore broad gate just before this).

Proceed along left edge of two more fields to reach houses at Lowertown, where a track takes you on to a road ⑥. Turn left to follow road uphill. Past church on right, ignore a left turn, then ⑦ turn right at T-junction with more major road.

⑧ Just after Ponsworthy village sign, as road bends left, take signposted gate on left into Sweaton Farm.

In farmyard, take gate directly ahead and slightly uphill, leading on to rising track between walls. After ¼ mile, this reaches gate into field ahead where you keep forward along left edge until ⑨ crossing stile on left near end of field. Immediately turn right along right edge of next field to cross stile and turn left on to

road next to road junction, where turn right (signposted Dartmeet).

⑩ After ⅓ mile, as soon as open land appears on left, turn left on to

The shapely New Bridge makes a delightful scene by the River Dart

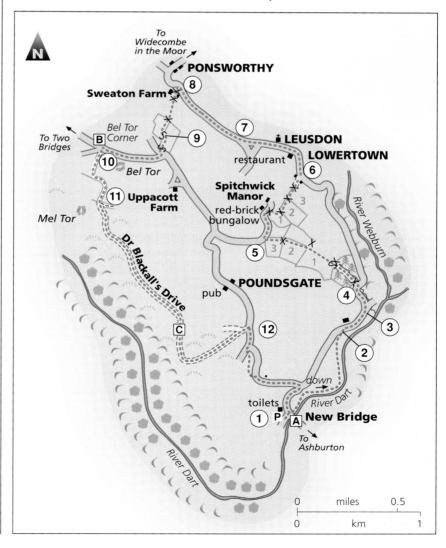

Dartmoor, the largest of the five granite uplands in the South-West, is dominated by expanses of wild moor dotted with gnarled tors

ADOPTING TRIG POINTS

The familiar British trig point is now redundant with today's cartographic surveying methods. The Ordnance Survey invited the public to adopt these important landmarks, so that someone would maintain the structures and keep them in the landscape. The scheme caught the public imagination: response was overwhelming, and virtually all the most visible trig points were adopted.

NEW RIGHTS OF WAY

Most rights of way are created by 'dedication' – either expressly by the landowner, or implicitly, where it can be shown that the public has been using a path without interruption or challenge for at least 20 years. The use must have been open and frequent, so that the landowner knew or ought to have known about it. County and district councils have powers to establish new rights of way by agreement with landowners, who receive compensation. Parish councils cannot offer compensation but may also make such agreements.

Orders may be made by highway authorities or district councils to create, divert or extinguish public rights of way. Such paths cannot be extinguished merely because they are obstructed or inconvenient to the landowner; they must be no longer needed for public use.

it, keeping alongside wall on left B. Where wall ends at a corner, continue to the left on track between walls. ⑪ At end of section between walls, keep right at fork of tracks (or ascend Mel Tor on right for detour) and follow this spectacular and well-defined route for one mile C until reaching road ⑫.

Turn right on road, immediately keeping left on major road towards Ashburton, to descend to New Bridge (it is best to walk along the open land on right-hand side of the road until road makes bend to left).

ON THE ROUTE

A **New Bridge** New in 1413, the granite bridge spans the Dart at a beauty spot on a very attractive wooded section of the river.

B **Bel Tor Corner** An impressive viewpoint, looking west to the television mast on North Hessary Tor and Dartmoor prison, south to Venford Reservoir and east to Haytor Rocks.

C The track is **Dr Blackall's Drive**, created for Dr Joseph Blackall of Spitchwick Manor (the house after ⑤) in the 1870s as a scenic carriage ride across the edge of the moorland, looking into the magnificent wooded Dart gorge. It is one of the finest high-level walks in the National Park, and yet is quite easily managed.

HOUND TOR AND HONEYBAG TOR

TORS provide natural waymarking and splendid focal points for much of the way. The walk starts by climbing on to one of Dartmoor's most exciting features, Hound Tor, then follows a superb ridge route to Honeybag Tor, via easy moorland paths: there is one steep descent. This walk is equally enjoyable in the reverse direction.

LENGTH 5½ miles (9km), 3 hours
DIFFICULTY 2
START Hound Tor car park, north-east of Widecombe in the Moor (signposted off Widecombe in the Moor–Bovey Tracey road). Grid reference 739791
OS MAPS Landranger 191; Outdoor Leisure 28

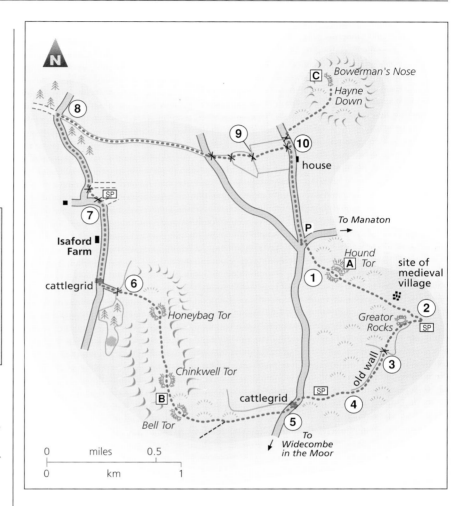

WALK DIRECTIONS

① Make your own way from car park up to summit of Hound Tor Ⓐ, then continue to left-hand side of next group of rocks (Greator Rocks). Just before the rocks are reached, you pass remains of a medieval village (which appears as a series of tiny stone enclosures).

② Do not take signposted gate at left end of Greator Rocks, but turn right along the rocky ridge. At end of ridge keep forward and roughly level (there is a wall down on left

Bowerman's Nose, one of many granite outcrops on Dartmoor

and the Becka Brook beyond it at the bottom of the valley) to find gate signposted Bonehill Down in the wall ahead ③

Continue forward alongside wall on right (keeping alongside it as it bends slightly right) and just before wall ends at a corner ④ bear right to cross the wall and walk 100 yards to signpost from where you proceed to stile beside gate giving on to road.

Turn left on road, over cattle-grid, then ⑤ turn right on to open land on rough path (which becomes well defined) with wall initially close away to right: you are heading for rocks on Bell Tor; where the wall away to right reaches a corner, fork right to Bell Tor. At the Tor Ⓑ continue right along dramatic ridge, past Chinkwell Tor, then dropping and rising to Honeybag Tor (where ridge ends).

Here turn left, descending carefully on uneven ground and aiming for gate just to right of

woodland below ⑥. Beyond the gate follow a track between walls down to reach surfaced lane. Turn right on lane, soon past Isaford Farm on left, then ⑦ when lane bends left you can cut off a small corner by continuing forward through signposted gate and walking along right-hand side field to re-emerge on to lane, which you follow up past small wood.

⑧ Immediately after wood ends turn right through gate (signposted Hayne Down and Manaton), on enclosed track. Cross next road and take signposted gate opposite. Go forward, following left edge of first and second fields. ⑨ In third field proceed down to gate in far left-hand corner on to lane ⑩.

From here it is a short walk back to Hound Tor along the lane to the right but first you can turn left along the lane for a few yards then ascend slope on the right to detour to the unmistakable Bowerman's Nose Ⓒ.

ON THE ROUTE

A **Hound Tor** Without doubt one of Dartmoor's most impressive rock groups, with resistant rocks surviving weathering to leave a complex of jointed rock and pinnacles. The **medieval village** between this and Greator Rocks comprises 11 buildings, including longhouses and outbuildings; entrances and fireplaces can be made out. The Black Death of 1348 probably ended the village's life. A fine view extends south-east (ahead as you look towards Greator Rocks) to the pyramidal form of Haytor Rocks, and east across the deep wooded valley of the River Bovey in the vicinity of Lustleigh Cleave.

B **Bell Tor, Chinkwell Tor and Honeybag Tor** A trio of mini-summits with the last being the most dramatic. To the left (west) is the East Webburn valley, lined on its far side by the bulky form of Hamel Down, with Widecombe in the Moor on the valley floor; Hound Tor can be seen to the right.

C **Bowerman's Nose** The most prominent of a sizeable rock group, sprawling over Hayne Down. There should be no difficulty picking out this much-photographed 30-foot high feature. Its name immortalises John Bowerman, a local man who died in 1663 and is buried in North Bovey. There is a good view north to Easdon Tor and north-east to Manaton church.

'As I was going to Widecombe Fair' the singer encountered 'Old Uncle Tom Cobbleigh and all'

WAYMARKS

Footpaths are sometimes marked with yellow arrows; bridleways (for walkers, cyclists and horse-riders) are shown by blue arrows; red arrows indicate byways (open to all traffic). National Trails are waymarked with acorn motifs.

SEASONAL HAZARDS

Summer walking in shorts or a skirt can be delightful, but be aware of the possibility of stinging nettles. The problem is often worst along paths in between fences. It may pay to take a pair of secateurs with you to deal with high-summer vegetation. July and August bring out the midges, notably around the lochs of Scotland.

In autumn, woodland paths often get obscured by fallen leaves. Mud can be a problem at any time of year, especially along bridleways where horses may churn up the path surface.

WOODCOMBE POINT AND PRAWLE POINT

PLEASANT and easily followed tracks between hedges form the inland link sections to this exploration of one of the finest parts of the South Devon seaboard, located to the east of Salcombe Harbour. At the coast, the path runs above low sandstone cliffs and at the foot of craggy slopes of gorse and bracken; there is a small secluded beach at the foot of the cliffs near the end.

LENGTH 5½ miles (9km), 2½ hours

DIFFICULTY 2

START East Prawle, 9 miles south-east of Kingsbridge. Car parking by village green, opposite Pig's Nose Inn. Grid reference 781364

OS MAPS Landranger 202; Outdoor Leisure 20

REFRESHMENTS Pig's Nose Inn and Providence Inn, both in East Prawle

---

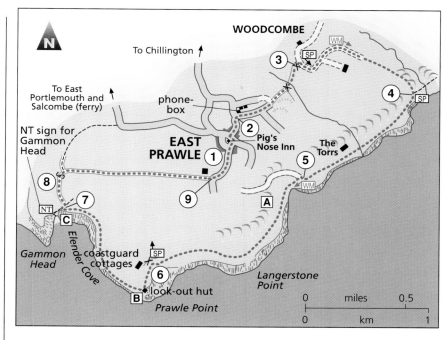

WALK DIRECTIONS

① With the Pig's Nose Inn on your left, follow the road down to the T-junction, at which you turn left then take first right. ② After 200 yards turn right on lane in front of the phone-box. Ignore the right turn to Maelcombe House after 250 yards and ignore the left turn 100 yards later. After a further 100 yards, the track narrows to a path, at first between hedges, then through bracken with hedge on the left, then forward along left edge of field (well waymarked).

③ At the end of field you emerge on the corner of a track and turn right, signposted Woodcombe Sand. Track bends left after 100 yards; 100 yards later keep forward on grassy track where main (stony) track turns right. Grassy track itself bends right shortly by marker post and descends towards sea.

④ After ½ mile, you reach a T-junction with the coast path (signposted). Turn right. The path is obvious and well waymarked as it passes a farm, then keeps slightly inland, making for a craggy headland (Langerstone Point) Ⓐ.

⑤ Two fields before Langerstone

Point turn sharp left, waymarked on post on left (ahead is a track between hedges which soon ascends). Follow the left edge of field to regain cliff-top.

⑥ Just before the coastguard cottages, avoid turning inland, the signposted East Prawle, but follow the fence below cottages to reach look-out hut at Prawle Point Ⓑ. Continue to the end of next bay, Elender Cove. ⑦ In the recess of the cove Ⓒ, turn sharp right on path. 75 yards later, turn sharp left.

⑧ Cross stile after 400 yards and 100 yards later turn right on to track between hedges. ⑨ After 1 mile, turn left on road, and follow this back to the start.

ON THE ROUTE

Ⓐ The **moorland slope** on your right was once a cliff, but has been eroded, and the material washed down to its base to form a less steep slope, separated from the sea by the present low cliffs.

Ⓑ **Prawle Point** The southernmost

In the centre of East Prawle – a favourite pub for walkers exploring this southernmost tip of the Devon coast

point in Devon. An 11th-century record refers to vessels stopping here on their way from Denmark to the Holy Land. **View** west across the mouth of the Salcombe Estuary to Bolt Head; east to Great Sleaden Rock, near Start Point.

c A flight of steps down on the left leads to a **small sandy beach**. Two Spanish galleons were driven ashore here, and doubloons were found in the nineteenth century.

Prawle Point, for centuries an important marker for seamen navigating the English Channel. Part of this walk features dog-gates by stiles, and near here you may find vegetables such as cauliflowers being cultivated on the steep slopes

HARTLAND POINT AND QUAY

THIS is a remote area, but one worth the pilgrimage, not just for Stoke church but also for some of England's most exciting cliff scenery. The inland sections at the start are along easily managed green lanes dipping and rising between hedges; the coast is tough going and includes several quite tiring ascents; the wind can make it even more demanding. There should be no difficulty in finding the way. The walk can be extended along the coast south of Hartland Quay to take in the waterfalls at Speke's Mill Mouth.

LENGTH 6 miles (9.5km), 3 hours
DIFFICULTY 3
START Stoke village (west of Hartland), by church; roadside parking in the village. Grid reference 235247
OS MAPS Landranger 190; Pathfinder 1253 (SS 22/32)
REFRESHMENTS Hotel at Hartland Quay

WALK DIRECTIONS

① Ⓐ Facing the church lych-gate by toilets where the main road bends to the left towards Hartland Quay, take the minor road to the right which is signposted Unsuitable For Motors. This drops to the valley floor Ⓑ and then rises. ② Past a farm, where the road bends right, keep straight on taking a track between hedges, which drops and then rises.

③ Fork right in front of the next farm; the track heads up to the right of the rightmost barn, to reach a road along which you turn right. ④

Hartland Point is vintage and remote walking territory

After 300 yards turn sharp left on a signposted bridleway (a track, narrowing to a path, between hedges). This drops (ignore

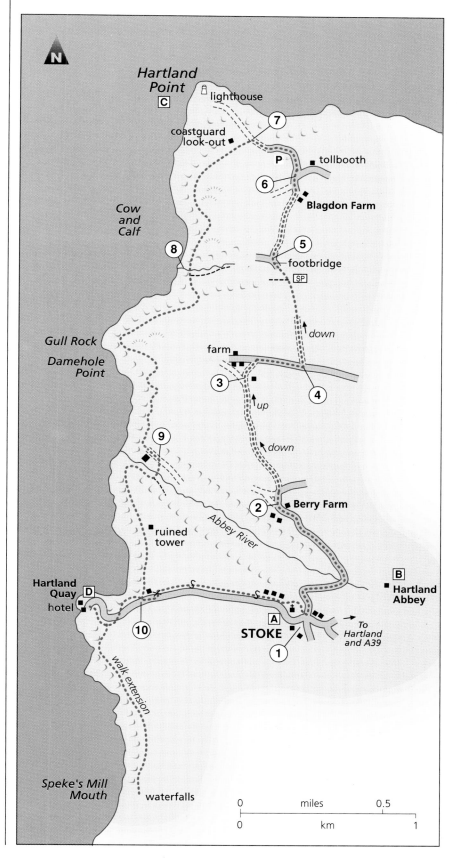

signposted stile on the left at bottom) and crosses a footbridge, and then has a stream on the left for a few yards until reaching a gate.

Just beyond this ⑤ turn right at track T-junction by a signpost. Follow this to a farm, at end of which the track bends left; 50 yards later ignore the track on your left and ⑥ another 50 yards later at track junction (by a silo on the left and with a tollbooth away to the right) go straight ahead. You are now following a surfaced track leading past a car park; keep to the surfaced track, through a gate towards the look-out hut on Hartland Point ⒸC, then ⑦ fork left 50 yards after the gate (just before pillars on either side of track; a permissive path can be followed for an optional detour to the lighthouse) on to the signposted coast path which you follow to Hartland Quay along the cliff-tops. ⑧ After 1 mile, cross a minor valley by footbridge and skirt a field on the seaward side.

⑨ After a further 1 mile the coast path drops through a valley by a cottage; the continuation is to the left of the cottage to regain the cliff-top. ⑩ Eventually you reach a road (Hartland Quay ⒹD is reached by a detour down to the right; use the path to the right of the road: the path then crosses the road and continues on the other side). Turn left on the road but immediately take a signposted gate on your left into a field and turn right along field edge closely parallel to the road leading to Stoke church. At the edge of the village, the path still avoids the road all the way to the churchyard which is then crossed.

ON THE ROUTE

ⒶA **Stoke** The highest church tower

Before the lighthouse at Hartland Point could be built, a road had to be cut in the cliff to make the site accessible by land

in the county soars 128 feet, and was built as a landmark for sailors. There is an extensive view from the top. This is one of the most absorbing country churches in Devon, with a notable delicate medieval screen (the oak tie-beam above it was taken from the wooden battleship *Revenge*), well-preserved wagon roofs and an intricately carved Norman font.

ⒷB View of **Hartland Abbey** on the right, a castellated mansion on the site of a 12th-century abbey (*open April to September, 2 to 5.30, Wednesday, Sunday and bank holiday Monday*).

ⒸC **Hartland Point** Boasts some of the most spectacular cliffs in the South-West. The Point has a view of the Isle of Lundy, which is 11 miles out to sea, and the Glamorgan coast. A coastguard look-out is perched high on the cliff,

with the lighthouse (briefly glimpsed after you head round the headland) far below. To the south the view opens out along Bude Bay. Vertical tilting and uplifting of strata, combined with the forces of the sea, have created some bizarre coastal landforms.

ⒹD **Hartland Quay** The hotel is created from the former harbour buildings, which includes stables for donkeys that carried cargo up the hill from the quay; the quay functioned for 400 years, dealing with the movement of grain and building materials before being washed away in storms in the 19th century. A small **museum** here has displays about shipping and the coastline. A mile south of the quay, the coast path reaches a series of waterfalls at **Speke's Mill Mouth**, where a stream tumbles 160 feet to the beach (return the same way).

HOLDSTONE HILL AND THE LADIES' MILE

EXMOOR'S remarkable landscape variety is neatly encapsulated in this stunningly beautiful walk, beginning on a gentle downhill track through moorland, with patchwork fields and green hills in the distance, then along the side of an incised combe. The finale is the coast path from above Heddon's Mouth to the 360-degree panorama on Holdstone Hill. The route is quite easy to find and ascents are gentle.

WALK DIRECTIONS

① Turn left out of the car park, along the road. After 300 yards turn right, signposted Trentishoe Mill (site of), by metal posts. The track drops gently. ② 100 yards before reaching the corner of wall keep straight on (ignoring right fork). The wall is then close by on your right; the track narrows to path width and soon bends left leaving the wall and dropping into trees.

③ At an oblique path T-junction, turn left on the level 'Ladies' Mile' path A . ④ Eventually you reach a four-way signpost where the valley is about to swing to the right; keep to the level path, signposted Rhydda Bank Corner. ⑤ Emerge on to a road,

> **LENGTH** 7 miles (11km), 3 hours
> **DIFFICULTY** 2
> **START** Holdstone Hill car park, between Combe Martin and Hunter's Inn; turn off A399 opposite London Inn at south end of Combe Martin on the road heading east (signposted Buzzacott Manor); at crossroads keep forward, signposted Trentishoe and Hunter's Inn; the car park is on the left by a group of houses after 1 mile. Grid reference 624474
> **OS MAPS** Landranger 180; Outdoor Leisure 9

turn right then after 50 yards you reach a crossroads where you turn left signposted Trentishoe Church.

Turn right at the next T-junction, soon past Trentishoe church B , where the road bends to the right. ⑥ One field after the last house on the left in Trentishoe, turn left by a National Trust sign for Headon Valley Estate and signpost for the coast path C . The path is soon joined by a field boundary on the left and leads to the sea, then bending left alongside the field boundary.

⑦ The path drops down six steps to a signposted stile on the left and leaves the cliff to cross moorland, over another stile beside a gate: follow the main path (ignore left fork just after). ⑧ When you reach a signpost at a four-way junction, keep straight on, soon through a breach in a low overgrown wall, to reach an oblique junction with a

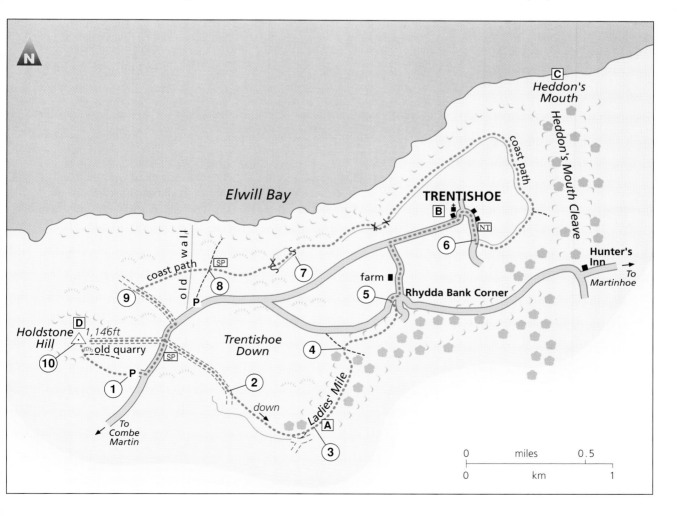

broad track, with bungalows visible to the left ⑨.

Turn sharp left towards the bungalows, at which you turn right along a road. Either follow the road back to the car park, or when you have passed two bungalows on the right, turn right (opposite the track on which you started the walk) to follow a track to the top of Holdstone Hill D. ⑩ At the summit turn sharp left, descending past a small abandoned quarry on the left; 50 yards later fork right and descend to the car park.

ON THE ROUTE

A **The Ladies' Mile** A path specially created to enjoy wonderful views along a terrace halfway up the slope of this deep and steep-sided valley, which includes attractive woodlands and moorland features.

B **Trentishoe** A tiny village with a diminutive church to match. Its tower may well have been a hiding-place for contraband. The church contains a musicians' gallery of 1731; a chunk cut out of the parapet enabled the double-bass player to have enough room to bow!

C **Heddon's Mouth**, just to the east, was once a tiny port, from which lime fertiliser used to be shipped across the Bristol Channel. The stony beach retains the remains of an old lime-kiln. A popular walk begins from the Hunter's Inn, a mile or so south, and follows the floor of the wooded valley known as Heddon's Mouth Cleave. From the Cleave, before it reaches the beach, it is possible to follow either of two paths around the cliff eastwards to Woody Bay, from which quiet country lanes can be taken past Martinhoe church

The Exmoor pony wandering in the open expanses of moorland has come to symbolise this National Park

to the Hunter's Inn.

D The **views** from **Holdstone Hill** (1,146ft) are not that different from those already seen but the extra height gives added exhilaration. The Glamorgan coast may be visible.

INLAND EXMOOR

Today moorland is the exception and enclosed pasture the rule, but the landscape is still strikingly empty, sparsely superimposed by villages in deep vales and by vestiges of prehistoric habitation high up, with humps of Bronze Age barrows discernible. Driving over inland Exmoor involves close-up views of hedgerows until a cattlegrid brings you out on to open unfenced land of bare and expansive horizons, where ponies and sheep spill on to the road. Exmoor ponies are not wild in that they are all owned by someone, but they roam freely all year round. They are descended from a herd of just 20, the Anchor Herd from Ashway Farm, west of Dulverton. The National Park Authority occasionally tops up the stock when numbers dwindle.

Red deer are Exmoor's natural and most magnificent species of deer, but roe deer (migrants from Dorset and Hampshire), and fallow and sika deer (descended from escapees from deer parks), can also be seen.

The central moor has a covering of coarse purple moor grass and whortleberries (bilberries) for the most part, with blue heath speedwell, heath-spotted orchids and bog pimpernel also putting in an appearance. Traditional purple-flecked heathery uplands are found more around the edges, in the Dunkery area, along the coast, and on Holdstone and Winsford Hills.

WATERSMEET, LYNMOUTH AND THE VALLEY OF ROCKS

THE route emerges, after a short climb, in dramatic fashion – high above the oak and whitebeam woodlands of the Lyn Valley – then follows the river along the valley bottom to Lynmouth, where the ascent to Lynton can be made by path or cliff railway. A short and easy (optional) western loop leads along the cliffs, into the Valley of Rocks and back over Hollerday Hill. Because the walk is a figure-of-eight, it can be treated as two shorter circuits instead. Paths are well defined; route-finding is made easy by thorough signposting. Can be slippery after rain.

WALK DIRECTIONS

① Standing with Lynton town hall behind you, turn left and take second right, downhill (Queen Street). After 150 yards fork left uphill past the Crown Hotel and 100 yards later turn left on a tarmac path (signposted Lyn Bridge) opposite Alford Terrace. Follow this for 500 yards to merge into side road and continue 100 yards down to main road ②. Cross road, take the path to right of Olde Cottage Inne

LENGTH *Full walk* 7 miles (11km), 3½ hours
Two short walks 4½ miles (4km), 1½ hours
DIFFICULTY 2–3
START *Both walks* Lynton, on B3234, just off A39 (Minehead to Barnstaple). Grid reference 719495
OS MAPS Landranger 180; Outdoor Leisure 9
REFRESHMENTS Plenty in Lynton and Lynmouth. NT café beautifully sited at Watersmeet

opposite, cross a bridge, then turn left on path signposted Watersmeet. The path ascends between the trees, soon emerging with views of Lynmouth and Lynton. The path is easy to follow, as it runs along fence/bank on the right, high above Lyn Valley; avoid side turnings.

The path zigzags down after ¼ mile, crosses a stream and zigzags up to rejoin fence on right. ③ 250 yards after the fence on right ends, fork left downhill, signposted Watersmeet, to a road. Cross road, take the path opposite to reach rivers at Watersmeet A. Cross two bridges ④.

Turn left in front of café. Avoid crossing first bridge (signposted Lynmouth) but keep straight on (signposted Countisbury). Then follow signs to Lynmouth along side of valley. ⑤ After 1 mile, cross bridge at National Trust sign to Watersmeet, pointing the way you have come. Follow the riverside path into Lynmouth B ⑥.

Cross the road and follow the seafront at Lynmouth as far as the funicular railway C, then *either* take path (which avoids Lynton town centre) 20 yards before the cliff

The razorbill can propel itself powerfully under water when diving for fish

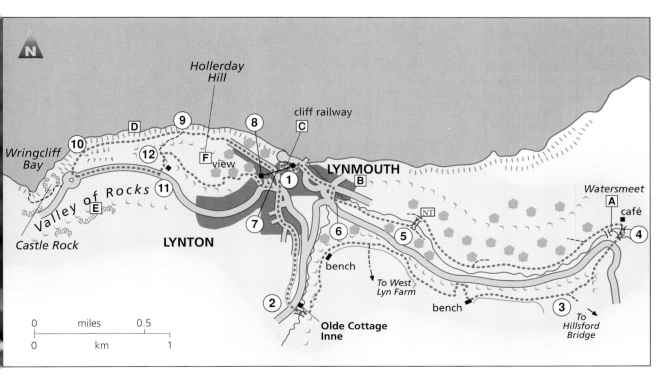

railway (signposted Lynton), ascending the coast path to reach a narrow residential road (turn left to finish at Lynton) *or* take the cliff railway into the centre of Lynton.

⑦ *From path route* Turn right on residential road, following signs to Valley of Rocks.

⑧ *From cliff railway* Continue to town centre. Standing with Lynton town hall behind you, turn left and take the third turning on the left, signposted to Valley of Rocks.

Both routes lead on to a surfaced cliff path D. ⑨ Ignore left fork where crags begin on left. ⑩ Turn left where the slope ends on left, to reach a road and turning-circle. E Here you can turn right to detour to Wringcliff Bay (path signposted, about 5 minutes). Turn left on the road to continue up Valley of Rocks ⑪. 400 yards after the car park, turn left by stone shelter (opposite second entrance to picnic site). Immediately fork right (signposted Lynton). The path zigzags uphill. ⑫ Keep right at T-junction (signposted again Lynton) after 200 yards, and follow back to Lynton. (After ¼ mile, the sharp left turn signposted to viewpoint only is an optional detour F. Ignore side paths.

ON THE ROUTE

A **Watersmeet** marks the meeting of the West Lyn and East Lyn Rivers; after the first bridge you can detour ¼ mile to the right to view the waterfalls of the right-hand river. The idyllically sited café was built by the Halliday family in 1830 for use as a hunting- and fishing-lodge. Irish spurge, a botanical rarity found only in a few sites on the South-West Peninsula, grows in these woods.

B **Lynmouth** A small, restrained Victorian resort with one or two reminders of its days as a fishing village. It was devastated in the 1952 floods, when 9 inches of rain fell in 24 hours on to an already saturated subsoil, and 90 million tons of water surged down the Lyn Valley, carrying houses and some inhabitants right out to sea.

C **Cliff railway** (frequent services;

small fee) When built by Sir George Newnes in 1890 it was the steepest railway in the world, rising 400ft over just 860ft horizontal distance. It operates on water gravity, the weight of the water-tank in the car at the top providing the haulage for the car at the bottom (the water emptying out of the top car as it descends).

D **Coast path Views** across to Wales, especially the cliffs at Nash Point in Glamorgan. **Birds:** guillemots, razorbills, fulmars. **Mammals:** feral horned goats (both on coast path and in the Valley of Rocks).

E **Valley of Rocks** A dry valley – probably the course of the Lyn before it cut through to the sea at Lynmouth – of striking sedimentary Devonian rock formations and open moorland. Immediately ahead, above the coast as you leave the cliff path, is Castle Rock; two of the inhabitants of its cave appear to have been Aggie Norman, a madwoman who became Mother Meldrum in *Lorna Doone*, and a 'white lady' whose ghost returned to haunt the Black Abbot of Lynton, who wronged her. **View** west to Jennifred's Leap, a folly, prominent on the cliff-top on other side of Wringcliff Bay, and Woody Bay beyond. The valley's romantic charm appealed strongly to Shelley, Coleridge and Wordsworth; now it is somewhat marred by a road and too-prominent car park.

F **Hollerday Hill** offers a **view** of the whole walk: Valley of Rocks, the Lyn Valleys and Lynton.

Understandably, the Valley of Rocks made a strong impression on Shelley, Coleridge and Wordsworth: its quintessentially romantic nature is undeniable

HURLSTONE POINT AND SELWORTHY BEACON

THIS walk takes in an outstanding viewpoint and a picturesque thatched village. Deciduous woodlands after the start soon lead to gentle grassy cliffs, then a steep, sharp haul, rewarded by the views from Selworthy Beacon. The route descends gently across grassland, then more steeply down a partially wooded combe to reach Selworthy, where a track leads back to the start. Good signposting most of the way on defined paths and tracks.

LENGTH 5½ miles (9km), 2½ hours

DIFFICULTY 2–3

START Allerford, just of A39, 1 mile east of Porlock. Small car park in village centre (free).
Grid reference 904469

OS MAPS Landranger 181; Outdoor Leisure 9

REFRESHMENTS Cross Lane Restaurant in Allerford, by main road; tea and coffee at West Somerset Museum of Rural Life, opposite car park in Allerford

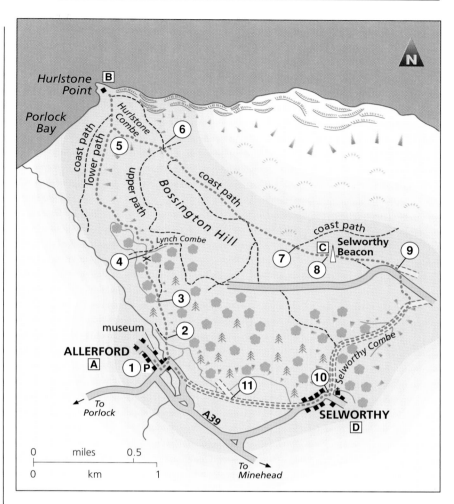

Allerford's picturesque double-arched packhorse bridge

WALK DIRECTIONS

① Ⓐ Turn right out of cark park, then left after 50 yards, over packhorse bridge. Follow road uphill for 50 yards, then left over a stile (signposted Bossington). Bear half right up to a gate by woods. ② Pass immediately through a second gate to enter woods. Ignore left fork after 30 yards, but follow path to next junction ③. Continue forward on level (signposted Hurlstone Point Lower Path) for 500 yards to gate.

④ Beyond gate, at the junction, take a half left and follow gently rising path until it leaves the woods. Path continues towards Hurlstone Point Ⓑ (optional detour) through open ground along the hillside with the sea visible to the left. ⑤ 250 yards before Hurlstone Point turn right, steeply uphill along Hurlstone Combe (path signposted by acorn marker denoting coast path). ⑥ Continue forward at the crossing of paths at the top of a steep slope, following coast path markers. 130 yards later keep right at T-junction of tracks (signposted with acorn marker). Follow the coast path signs for another ¾ mile. ⑦ Leave the coast path for track ahead (where coast path is signposted to left), leading to a prominent cairn on Selworthy Beacon Ⓒ ⑧. Continue forward from the beacon, forking left after 250 yards, then following track downhill. Where the road comes into view just a few

yards to your right, fork right on to a path leading to it ⑨. Cross the road, take track opposite, slightly to the left. 200 yards later this is joined by another track coming in from the left; after another 100 yards turn right (signposted Selworthy). Track descends into valley, through woods and into Selworthy village Ⓓ ⑩. Descend through Selworthy, take the first right near the bottom of village (signposted Allerford), passing between barns, then go forward on the track between hedges. ⑪ After ½ mile ignore the forest track half right; continue down between the hedges. Continue forward at the corner of lane, following this into Allerford.

ON THE ROUTE

Ⓐ **Allerford** A straggly village, but with some pleasant old cottages around its picturesque packhorse bridge. The **West Somerset Museum of Rural Life** houses a

THE EXMOOR COAST

The thin coastal strip, with its immediate hinterland, from Minehead west to Combe Martin, has the monopoly of Exmoor's most distinctive scenery, with moorland hills coming right down to the cliffs, while close by are some delectable inland combes with shady rivers. Seaward bluffs are bold and assertive, windswept and excitingly rugged, sea level only reached at a few shingly or rocky bays and coves; the absence of bathing beaches has precluded resort development, and the cliffs are mostly the preserve of sea-birds and walkers. From the road you get some fine glimpses of the best of the coast, notably on Porlock Hill, at County Gate, in the Valley of Rocks (see Walk 11) and by Holdstone Down.

One of Selworthy's chocolate-box thatched cottages

dairy and a Victorian kitchen, and there are craft displays.

B **Hurlstone Point** A craggy headland and look-out. From here you can look westwards along coast to Foreland Point near Lynton. The path east of here is signposted dangerous (immediately around the corner, before the path ascends, there is a fine **view** of the cliffs).

C **Selworthy Beacon** Offers a view north across the Bristol Channel to Cardiff, the Glamorgan uplands, Gwent and the Wye Valley, south to Dunkery Hill and west to Porlock Hill.

D **Selworthy** A tiny village, beautifully sited and one of the most enchanting spots in Exmoor. The white-painted **church**, the first building you see, is famous for its south aisle, which has a wagon roof

ornamented by wall-plates with angels bearing shields and by bosses with symbols of the Passion and the face of Christ. Down the street are a group of thatched cottages and a handsome tithe barn with 14th-century moulding depicting a sheep, pig and corn sheaf.

WAYMARKS

Footpaths are sometimes marked with yellow arrows; bridleways (for walkers, cyclists and horse-riders) are shown by blue arrows; red arrows indicate byways (open to all traffic). National Trails are marked with acorn motifs.

AROUND CHEDDAR GORGE

BRITAIN'S most famous limestone land-form is often viewed from the road which follows its floor, but the Gorge is remarkable when seen from the high-level path on this route. Earlier sections of this walk lead through the farmland of the Mendip plateau and a fine nature reserve. There are two fairly steep ascents.

LENGTH 3 or 4½ miles (5 or 7km), 2 or 3 hours
DIFFICULTY 2–3
START Cheddar (town); turn off the A371 in Cheddar town centre by the market cross on to the B3135 signposted to the Gorge. Follow the road until car park on right immediately before the Butchers Arms pub. Grid reference 461536
OS MAPS Landranger 182; Pathfinder 1198 (ST 45/55)
REFRESHMENTS Full range in Cheddar

WALK DIRECTIONS

① Ⓐ Follow the road towards Cheddar Gorge, passing the Galleries Inn on your right then take second bridge on left, signposted as path to Gorge and toilets; bear right in front of the White Hart Inn, then, just after the path bends left in front of waterworks gate, fork left (signposted). ② The path rejoins the road.
For 3-mile walk via Gorge Follow the Gorge road to beyond the end of the Gorge, then take signposted stile on right for Draycott 3½ and West Mendip Way, and pick up walk directions at ⑧.

For 4-mile walk As soon as you rejoin the road take signposted ascending track sharp left. Initially you pass trees on your left, then a field appears down on your left. ③ At the end of the field, turn right on a signposted enclosed path just before a house.

The path bends left to pass behind the house and just before the next house (with iron balconies) turn sharp right on to a rising path, up into woodland and through

The huge variety of formations in the Cheddar Showcaves increase by one cubic inch every 400 years

kissing-gate in the wall. ④ Cross the stile into the open scrubby land and keep forward and slightly to the right, uphill alongside a dilapidated wall.

The scrubland later gives way to open grassland, where you cross a wide track with a sign for Piney Sleight. Keep forward alongside wall; on re-entering more woodland, the path is clear again and reaches a solid wall at edge of farmland ⑤. Cross the wall via a stile and proceed along left edge of three fields to pass immediately left of Piney Sleight Farm. After the farm proceed on an enclosed track between high hedge and fence.
⑥ Where, after a cattlegrid, the track ceases to be enclosed, turn right by signpost for Cheddar Ⓑ to continue with wall on right along edge of two large fields. ⑦ At the end, pass through a gate beside stile into woodland and follow track gently down, entering a nature reserve at the bottom by a gate and proceeding forward on track along bottom of valley Ⓒ. This leads to a gate on to the road. Cross road and take stile opposite and slightly to right, signposted Draycott 3½, West Mendip Way ⑧.

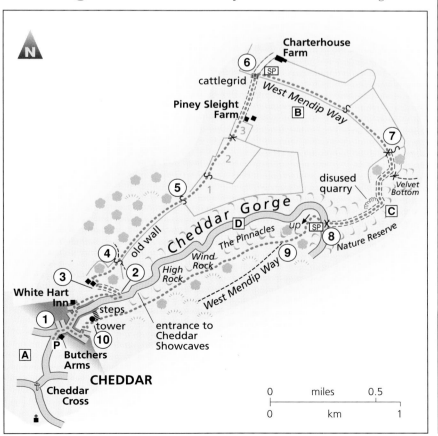

The path leads steeply up through woods. ⑨ 50 yards after emerging into the open, fork right and follow the path, keeping as close to edge of cliff as possible to enjoy the remarkable sequence of views to the Gorge ꞮDꞮ.

⑩ At Prospect Tower, you can either take steps ('Jacob's Ladder') down on the right in front of the Tower or continue to the left of the Tower on path dropping to the road at the edge of Cheddar, where you proceed downhill to reach the starting point.

ON THE ROUTE

ꞮAꞮ **Cheddar** The world-renowned cheese was made in local farmhouses as early as the 12th century but has more or less disappeared as a local cottage industry. At the town centre is a famous hexagonal market cross, of medieval origin.

ꞮBꞮ **West Mendip Way** A 30-mile long-distance path developed by local Rotary Clubs, from the cathedral city of Wells, to Uphill on the Bristol Channel, passing Wookey Hole cave and Bladon Hill on the way. The scenery here gives a good idea of the Mendip plateau, with no hint of the nearby drama of Cheddar Gorge.

ꞮCꞮ **Black Rock and Velvet Bottom Nature Reserves** Limestone valley and woods, strongly resembling the Derbyshire Dales, with carboniferous limestone overlaid with glacial loess giving a rich flora; the presence until the 19th century of lead mining has meant that species have adapted to the high lead content of the soil. **Trail leaflets** are available at a dispenser near the road.

ꞮDꞮ **Cheddar Gorge** For one mile, grey limestone cliffs rise 450ft on either side of the road, to make one of the most enthralling landscapes in the country. A primeval river gouged out a tunnel through the rock, and the collapse of its roof creates the canyon we see today. The Cheddar Showcaves are open to the public. The high-level path used on this section of the walk gets the most remarkable **views** of all – both into the Gorge, and westwards across the fenlands of the Somerset Levels and Cheddar Reservoir to the Quantock Hills. 274 steps lead up **Jacob's Ladder** to the **Prospect Tower** (opened 1908), a tinny structure which is something between a lighthouse and a helter-skelter ride.

The two-mile chasm of Cheddar Gorge conceals a remarkable series of chambers that follow the course of underground streams. There was no carriage road through the Gorge until 1800: until then access would have been by horse or pack-mule or on foot

BURRINGTON COMBE AND DOLEBURY WARREN

A RICHLY diverse route beginning along a wooded valley, then crossing open moorland before encountering the dramatic limestone gorge of Burrington Combe. Near the end, before the final descent, the walk takes in one of the best viewpoints in the whole of the Mendip Hills. Paths are reasonably well defined; route-finding is a little involved, but not difficult.

Bluebells carpet parts of the Mendips in spring

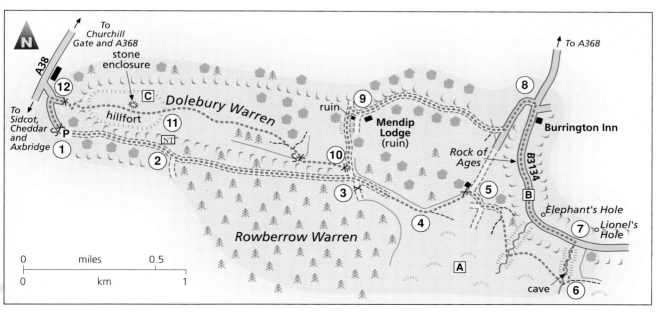

WALK DIRECTIONS

① Pass over stile by gate and follow level track along bottom of wooded combe. ② After ½ mile, 100 yards after passing NT sign for Dolebury Warren on your left, fork left. ③ ¼ mile later keep straight on at a crossing of tracks (avoiding turnings half right to forest gate and sharp left). ④ Where open moorland [A] appears on right, continue on track alongside woodland on left for ¼ mile.

⑤ Turn right (across moorland) on broad track, opposite gate with private footpath sign, in front of large wooden cabin hidden among the trees. Turn left at crossing of tracks after 200 yards; track now makes towards Burrington Combe, a deep rocky valley ahead. Fork right after 50 yards, and 50 yards later

fork left. Track leads down to small combe, across stream, then left up other side.

⑥ At next (even smaller) combe, track descends to bottom – a waterfall where the stream disappears underground can be heard away to right – then bends left up other side. 30 yards later turn left on steep path descending along edge of bracken, then soon along right side of stream. Step across stream just as it disappears into cavern, then continue down bottom of combe to road ⑦.

Turn left on road, along bottom of Burrington Combe [B]. You can avoid walking along parts of the road by taking a parallel path to the left. ⑧ 150 yards after Burrington Inn, turn left at crossroads. Road ascends, soon bending sharp left,

LENGTH 6½ miles (10.5km), 3½ hours
DIFFICULTY 2
START Small car park at foot of Dolebury Warren. From Churchill Gate (junction of A38 and A368) continue south on A38 towards Cheddar for 600 yards, then take first fork left (cul-de-sac called Dolberrow), just after terrace of brick cottages. Immediately keep right (parallel to main road) and follow lane to end; parking space by gate. Grid reference 446588
OS MAPS Landranger 172 or 182; Pathfinder 1198 (ST 45/55 or Explorer 4)
REFRESHMENTS Crown Inn, Churchill, near start; Burrington Inn just before ⑧

and 30 yards after hedge on your right ends, fork right on to track between hedges, soon entering woods. Ignore any turnings to the left and follow for ¼ mile. ⑨ Pass ruins of Mendip Lodge on your left and continue straight on, avoiding fork to left; after 75 yards, when main track swings right, carry straight on, to right of ruined building. Past wooden barrier, turn left up sunken track, soon between walls.

View across Chew Valley Lake

⑩ After ¼ mile turn right through gate into field by National Trust sign for Dolebury Warren. Proceed alongside fence on left to its corner, then maintain direction along line of hedgerow trees to reach fence. Here, take gate/stile on right to enter scrubby woodland; bear half left to gain top of ridge, keeping right at first fork. At top of ridge, make for grassy summit ahead [c] ⑪.

Summit itself is encircled by large grassy bank (ramparts of hillfort). Continue forward, on track, keeping just to left of/below small stone enclosure. On passing between grassy banks turn left on track to descend to lane ⑫. Left on lane, and keep left at next junction to return to start.

ON THE ROUTE

[A] Carpets of **bluebells** on this moorland in spring indicate that it was once covered with forest.

[B] **Burrington Combe** A deep limestone gorge honeycombed with caves and underground streams. Like its more famous neighbour, Cheddar Gorge, the combe was cut in the Ice Age by the action of streams that could not sink through the permeable rock while it was frozen. As you round the corner along the bottom of the combe you pass a large outcrop, immortalised in 1762 by the Revd Augustus Toplady of Blagdon, who wrote the words for the hymn 'Rock of Ages' while sheltering from a storm in a crevice in the rock. Opposite is Aveline's Hole, a cave in which human skeletal remains dating back 10,000 years were found. Tway-blade orchids can be seen in spring .

[C] **Dolebury Warren** This grassy ridge, partially covered with commercial forest, has well-preserved ramparts of a 20-acre Iron-Age hillfort at the west end. Views extend north-east to Dundry Hill; north-west over the Severn Estuary towards South Wales; south-west to the Quantock Hills; south over the Mendips; east across Chew Valley Lake, and towards Bath.

BARRIERS TO PROGRESS

Never climb a gate that you can open. Gates across rights of way that are locked or impossible to open should be climbed at the hinges to minimalise damage to the gate and gatepost.

ADOPTING TRIG POINTS

The familiar British trig point is now redundant with today's cartographic surveying methods. The Ordnance Survey invited the public to adopt these important landmarks, so that someone would maintain the structures and keep them in the landscape. The scheme caught the public imagination: response was overwhelming, and virtually all the most visible trig points were adopted.

CASTLE COMBE AND BY BROOK

A route through a pleasing landscape of soft green hills and intricate woodlands, entering Castle Combe through an archway. The walk passes some of the mills which contributed to the village's medieval textile industry. Route-finding is somewhat complicated at the start, but then becomes easy.

LENGTH 5 miles (8km), 2½ hours

DIFFICULTY 2

START Lay-by by telephone opposite church in Ford, on A420 5 miles west of Chippenham. Grid reference 841739

OS MAPS Landranger 173; Pathfinder 1168 (ST 87/97)

REFRESHMENTS Pub and shop in Ford; pubs, shop, tea-room in Castle Combe

WALK DIRECTIONS

① With the church on your left, follow A420 downhill (towards Chippenham); take the first left after 100 yards before bus shelter, and immediately fork right on to track. After 90 yards, just before the track reaches gate to last house, take a stile on the left into an open area, turn right on a path along the bottom edge. The path soon enters woods; 100 yards later, it goes down a small slope on right (at yellow waymarker on tree) and continues in an open area initially alongside trees on left then cuts half right across field to bridge and stile together ②.

Path then ascends a slope, soon through a small wood and out again on the far side where you continue diagonally left uphill (away from woods; look for waymarker), on main path to a hedgerow along the top of slope. Turn left alongside the hedgerow, soon past a waymark and over a stile by a gate into woods.

The path continues inside edge of woods, with a fence on your right initially. ③ When you reach road junction at gate, turn left (towards West Kington). ④ After ½ mile, where the road bends left (just after going downhill), take a signposted

woodland track on right. Branch right by gate on path to take path running between fields which then later descends to cross a river at bridge. ⑤ Turn right on the other side of the bridge, on a track alongside valley close to the stream and soon go over a stile by a gate (ignore path on left just before this).

You reach a restored mill on right (with chimney), and turn right just after it to take a metal gate (gate itself is usually locked, but there is a concealed kissing-gate on its right).

Follow the track through woods, with stream on left; leave woods and emerge on to golf course; follow track to right, over a stone

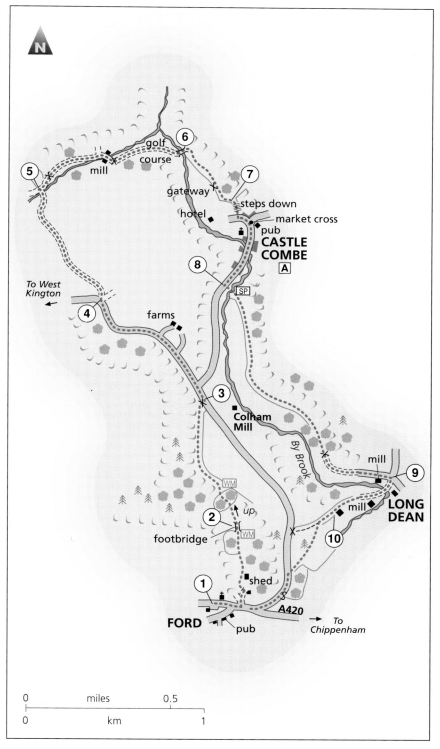

footbridge ⑥. Turn right on other side of bridge; on passing an ornamental gateway (to right of, but separate from, path), the path enters woods with a wall on right.

⑦ 70 yards after path and wall bend left take stile and steps down on your right to enter Castle Combe village Ⓐ. Go through the centre of the village past Market Cross on left (ignoring left turn here) and along the main street.

⑧ After the end of the village, take second footbridge on left over the river (the first bridge is obviously private; the second one is walled on one side and has a signpost on the far side).

Go over stile to pick up a well-defined path, initially uphill, but soon levelling out with a fence and hedgerow on the right most of the way as it goes in and out of woods and eventually reaches houses at the hamlet of Long Dean ⑨. Here turn right at lane junction, then as soon as you cross a bridge over a small channel keep right at fork, now on a level track; soon you pass over By Brook and rise past a house on your left now on a narrower path to reach a gate.

Go forward along the fence on your right to enter open downland ⑩; here *either* continue along top edge alongside hedgerows to reach a

The bridge over By Brook with the church beyond: Castle Combe is rich in delectable views

gate on to the road *or* cut off a corner by taking a path halfway across the downland keeping at the same level and bearing half left to a stile in recessed corner of wood giving on to the road. *Both routes* Turn left on the road to reach main road at Ford; and turn right to reach the starting place.

ON THE ROUTE

Ⓐ **Castle Combe** is rightly regarded as one of England's most beautiful villages. It grew rich in the Middle Ages from the wool trade, and had the great added bonus of honey-coloured Cotswold stone as building material. The **church tower** is 15th century, built 'at the expense of the clovers of the district'. In the 1960s, the village was temporarily transformed into a seaport as a setting for the film of *Dr Doolittle*, with a jetty and harbour wall constructed alongside the brook.

Castle Combe from the market cross: a film-maker's dream

PATH PROBLEMS

It is illegal to obstruct a public right of way. If you find an obstruction, such as impenetrable crops or barbed wire, across such a path you are entitled to remove it/them (or in the case of crops, walk over them). If the problem is bad, you can take an alternative route providing you do not trespass or cause damage.

It is illegal to put up a sign on a right of way that deters potential users, such as Private or Path Closed, when it refers to that route.

Waymarks and signposts have the same status as any other traffic sign, and it is an offence to remove them. If you come across hindrances like these, write to the relevant highway authority, which has the duty to sort out problems relating to rights of way. Give exact locations, with grid references, and a sketch map if possible.

AVEBURY: AN ARCHAEOLOGICAL TOUR

A PLEASANT country walk in its own right, over cultivated chalkland, but the concentration of major archaeological sites makes this route well worth seeking out.

LENGTH 6½ miles (10.5km), 3½ hours

DIFFICULTY 2

START West Overton (just off A4 west of Marlborough). Park on roadside in village centre near bus shelter and telephone-box. Grid reference 132680

OS MAPS Landranger 173; Pathfinder 1185 and 1169 (SU 06/16 and SU 07/17)

REFRESHMENTS Pub (just off route) and shop at West Overton; pub, shop and restaurant in Avebury; tea-room on A4 between ④ and ⑤)

WALK DIRECTIONS

① With telephone and bus shelter on your right, follow the main village street past shop. The street bends left, then right, and continues to East Kennett.

② At the edge of East Kennett, road bends left in front of wall (minor road joins on right). Where the wall ends take enclosed path on right. At the road turn right, then take the next left (just after telephone-box and opposite gate to big house) into the main part of the village.

After the church, the lane becomes an unsurfaced track, bends right then left past a house called Fortwitchen and soon bends right again. ③ After 250 yards take a grassy track on the right at staggered crossroads down to reach a T-

junction of tracks where you take the stile ahead. Keep alongside left edge of three fields over a series of stiles (if stiles are missing, there may be an alternative route immediately to the left).

Avebury's stone circle, one of the major archaeological sites in Britain

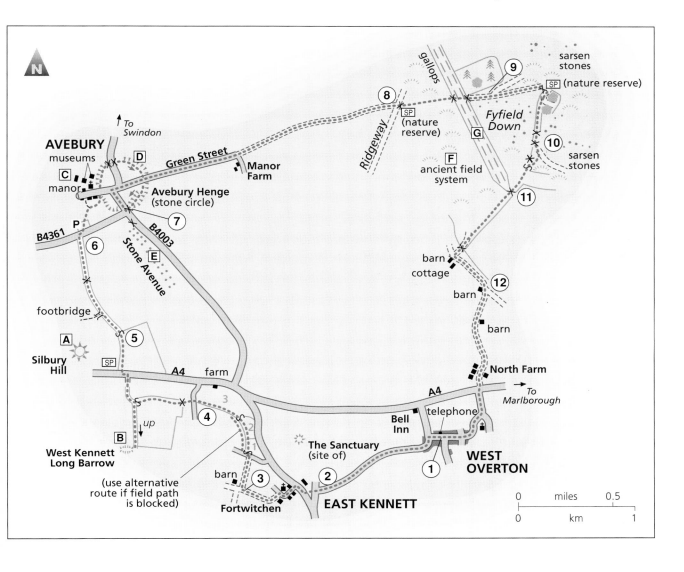

④ Emerge on to a surfaced lane and take track opposite, soon reaching a gate where you keep forward, along right edge of field Ⓐ. At the far end of field join a fenced path: detour left uphill to West Kennett Long Barrow Ⓑ. Return to the fenced path and follow it down to the A4. Turn left on A4 but after 30 yards take signposted stile on the right.

Go forward away from the A4 and along left edge of field ⑤ to reach a stile on to a path running along enclosed strip. Cross further stiles and ignore footbridge on left; follow the path to reach the road ⑥. Cross into the car park opposite and go slightly to right to take surfaced path in far right-hand corner (between litter bin and information board). The path soon bends right between sports fields and through rampart of Avebury stone circle and into road at Avebury village Ⓒ.

Go forward following signs for Museums but before you reach the first museum take steps up on the right and turn left on the ramparts which fringe the stone circle Ⓓ. Soon cross a major road and later a minor road but still continue along the ramparts and follow to reach a road junction where the ramparts bend right ⑦: here you can detour left to cross the road and take the gate opposite to view the Stone Avenue Ⓔ.

Return to ramparts, heading to the village and reaching the road in front of the Red Lion pub. Turn right on road and immediately keep forward as the main road bends left in the Swindon direction; you are now on Green Street (with No Through Road sign). Keep straight on for 1¼ miles (road becomes a track at a farm after ½ mile).

⑧ Reach a junction by a signpost with ridgeway to left and right. Here take the gate ahead (signposted Fyfield Down) Ⓕ and follow a faint grassy path towards the right corner of woodland ahead (shortly before reaching the wood, cross broad grassy 'gallops' by gates) Ⓖ.

⑨ 200 yards after passing start of woodland, fork right on to a grassy track (may be invisible in summer), aiming for left and end of woodland

strip ahead. Take a gate to enter the strip of woodland and turn right on track but immediately leaving it for a grassy track alongside a fence on right as the chalky track bends left. Descend on the path through a sequence of gates close together (care needed as the route is not obvious here); ⑩ by the last of the gates keep alongside right-hand fence, now walking across rough downland.

After 160 yards take a stile alongside a gate on right (avoiding gate just before this). Proceed up to the corner of fence and hedgerow 150 yards away ⑪, then go forward with fence on your left, eventually going through a gate at end of gallops; then continue with fence on your left to reach a gate at bottom of field. Proceed down on to a well-defined track to cottage and barns.

Turn left at T-junction of tracks in front of the cottage. ⑫ 400 yards later just after a big barn on right, turn right at junction eventually to reach a big farm where you go forward, just to the left of thatched barn, and continue down to A4. Take turning opposite signposted West Overton and take first right to reach the village centre.

ON THE ROUTE

Ⓐ **Silbury Hill** First seen here on the right and passed later; it has been called 'a great, green plum-pudding'. This is the largest man-made prehistoric mound in Europe, its origin and purpose a mystery. No burial has been found here, and it may have served some astronomical or religious function.

Ⓑ **West Kennett Long Barrow** A mound of chalk 100 yards long and 8 feet high, accessible at its east end, with glass covers providing natural illumination and enabling visitors to walk right into the depth of the barrow. Excavated 1859 and 1956. At least 46 individuals are buried in the tomb; an unknown number of bodies which were removed in the 17th century. Pottery finds suggest the barrow was used for burial for a very long period, perhaps 1,000 years; in the course of excavation a scatter of objects was found, which might have been funeral gifts. The

great blocking stone at the entrance was placed to seal the burial chambers.

Ⓒ **Avebury** has a pleasant village street of stone and brick cottages, some under thatch. **Avebury Manor** was built on the site of a Benedictine cell; the gardens (NT; fee) are *open* from Easter to the end of October. Close by are two **museums:** the **Great Barn** has a main collection of rustic bygones, and the adjacent English Heritage **Alexander Keiller Museum** is concerned with the archaeology of Avebury. The Red Lion, an immaculately thatched L-shaped pub, complete with a 17th-century well, stands at the heart of the village.

Ⓓ **Avebury Henge Stone Circle** John Aubrey said in 1663 that Avebury 'does so much exceed in greatness the so renowned Stonehenge as a cathedral does a parish church'. The site probably dates from about 2600 BC and was largely lost to view until 1939 when Alexander Keiller cleared it of trees and undergrowth. The area is roughly circular and covers 11.5 hectares (4½ acres), enclosed by a ditch. Within this lies an outer circle of 98 sarsen stones (from nearby Fyfield Down), with two smaller inner circles.

Ⓔ **Stone Avenue** Sited on a strip parallel to the modern road, 2,000 stones, thought to predate Avebury Henge by 1,000 years. The avenue led to the Sanctuary, another stone circle, destroyed by farmers in the early 18th century, as one observer put it, 'for dirty little profits'. It is worth going over the brow of the hill to get the best impression of the site.

Ⓕ **Fyfield Down** A National Nature Reserve, famous for the surviving traces of Celtic field systems, whose divided lynchets (or banks) stand up to 10 feet high. The sarsen stones used to construct the circles at Avebury probably came from here. Many other stones are scattered through the reserve.

Ⓖ **Marlborough Downs** One of the foremost areas in England for race-horse training. There are numerous gallops such as this one.

ABBOTSBURY

A FIGURE-OF-EIGHT route round a much-visited village. The first circuit leads up to the downs north of Abbotsbury; this requires a little effort, but is recommended for the exhilarating views. The more leisurely, second circuit tours the village's famous sights – the church, tithe barn, Swannery, Chesil Beach and St Catherine's Chapel. Care is needed to find the way on first circuit, but route-finding on the second circuit is quite easy.

LENGTH 6 miles (9.5km), 3 hours (can be split into two walks of 2½ and 3½ miles)
DIFFICULTY 2
START Abbotsbury village centre, on B3157 between Bridport and Weymouth. Grid reference 577853
OS MAPS Landranger 194; Pathfinder 1331 (SY 58)
REFRESHMENTS Pubs, tea-rooms and shop in Abbotsbury

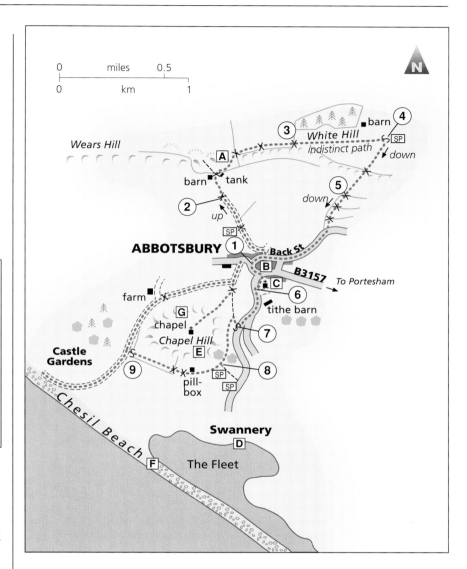

WALK DIRECTIONS

For first circuit ① Take Back Street, by Toilets sign opposite Ilchester Arms. After 150 yards turn left on track (signpost bollard to White Hill was on the verge of collapse at time of inspection, but may have been reinstated). Ignore right fork after 30 yards (leading into field) and ascend. Soon emerge into open ground and then pass signpost: ignore the half right direction it gives to Lime Kiln car park but continue uphill to gate ②.

Beyond this, proceed towards top of ridge, finding gate to the right of open-sided barn and then bear half right as signposted over hummocky area to reach the top Ⓐ. Follow ridge, soon reach signpost for Hardy Monument: here take the left-hand of two gates and walk along ridge with fence on right. ③ ¼ mile later reach another signpost by gate, with woods beginning away to left: keep alongside fence on right for 80 yards, but where it veers half right keep straight on, walking parallel to woods away to your left.

④ Reach signpost in front of fence ahead, and turn sharp right (leaving fence immediately); Chapel Hill (with chapel on top) comes into view – head for it. Shortly, pick up defined track, through gate and descending, still heading for the chapel. Further down, near signpost, is a gate ⑤: beyond it follow right edge of two fields, then turn right on road into Abbotsbury.

For second circuit Ⓑ, start with Ilchester Arms on right and follow main street, then turn right into Church Street, turning left into churchyard and passing to right of church Ⓒ. ⑥ Leave churchyard by far gate, turn right on road, through gateway, then left on road at T-junction. After passing tithe barn, fork right, signposted Swannery Pedestrians, No Cars Please.

⑦ After 200 yards take stile on right signposted St Catherine's Hill (or detour ahead to see Swannery Ⓓ). Path follows right edge of small field, to emerge at base of Chapel Hill. Path proceeds to right for

The mellow stone thatched cottages of Abbotsbury's main street

50 yards to cross stream, where turn sharp left, signposted West Bexington (coast path). Path leads into woods, on far side of which keep forward, skirting base of hill without losing height, soon past signpost bollard ⑧ to Chapel Hill Ⓔ and later past pill-box, eventually reaching gate in corner of fence. Go forward, still skirting hill, with fence on left until stile gives on to enclosed track ⑨.

Detour left to Chesil Beach Ⓕ; right, to Abbotsbury, is the continuation. Fork right when level with farms on your left, and fork right again ¼ mile later. Just after passing stone barn on your right, detour right to St Catherine's Chapel (on hill-top) via gate Ⓖ; left into Abbotsbury is the continuation.

ON THE ROUTE

Ⓐ This superb **view** extends over Abbotsbury, with a great sweep of the Dorset coast, including Chesil Beach, Portland Bill (the island joined on to the south-east end of the Beach) and (to the west) its highest point at Golden Cap, beyond which are the cliffs near Sidmouth. The top of the ridge is dotted with **prehistoric burial mounds**, and one mile west is the ancient earthwork of Abbotsbury Castle.

Ⓑ **Abbotsbury** Mellow orange ironstone and a preponderance of thatch make the main village street one of Dorset's most memorable.

Ⓒ **Church of St Nicholas** Mostly 15th century, but with 17th- and 18th-century touches; plaster barrel ceiling and a Jacobean pulpit (look for the bullet holes in its canopy, made by the Parliamentarians in a Civil War attack). At the back of the churchyard is a labelled fragment of the wall of the

Benedictine abbey (founded in the 11th century by Ore, a member of King Canute's household), which gives Abbotsbury its name. Below is the huge medieval **tithe barn**, 272ft long. One tenth of local produce was stored here, paid as tax to the abbey. It now houses a country museum of rural life.

Ⓓ The **Swannery** (*open* mid-May to mid-September and Sunday afternoons in winter), at the west end of the lagoon enclosed by Chesil Beach (known as the Fleet), has existed since at least 1393 and was created by the abbey; over 500 swans, some wild geese and varieties of duck live here. If detouring ahead on the road to the Swannery you can either return to this point or leave the road a little further towards the Swannery, past the cluster of houses, where a plank footbridge is signposted to sub-tropical gardens: cross field to stile then turn left at signpost bollard, at ⑧.

Ⓔ Grassy terraces on the steep-sided Chapel Hill are good examples of **Anglo-Saxon field systems.**

Ⓕ **Chesil Beach** (or Chesil Bank) From here you can look down the length of this extraordinary natural feature, a 16-mile long shingle bank culminating at Portland Bill; the orange cliff of Golden Cap lies in the other direction. The pebbles get larger as you proceed towards Portland Bill. A unique place, sadly vulnerable to the whims of pirate gravel extractors who have recently removed chunks of it. Walking even a few hundred yards along the beach is a stiff challenge; swimming is dangerous, because of undercurrents.

The Fleet is a narrow tidal lake, eight miles long, and hemmed in by Chesil Beach. It is the second oldest nature reserve in Britain (Wicken

Fen in Cambridgeshire is the oldest) and is noted for its **flora** and **marine life**, including 150 species of seaweed, and eelgrass (harbouring eels and stickleback). Among the **bird-life** are mute swans, but there is also a sizeable population of waders and diving birds (notably around the mudflats at Herbury), including dunlin, reed warbler and shelduck. This shallow lagoon, known as the Fleet, was the testing ground for the 'bouncing bomb' used in the famous dam-buster raid in the Second World War. It was also the setting for J. Meade Faulkner's classic smuggling story, *Moonfleet*, first published in 1898.

Ⓖ The **chapel** belonged to the Benedictine abbey, dedicated (like several other such buildings on hilltop sites) to St Catherine, and built about 1400. It has not been used since the Reformation, but it still has an ornate ceiling (partly restored); the floor is of bare earth. (English Heritage, *open* mid-March to mid-October, 9.30 to 6.30 weekdays, 2 to 6.30 Sundays; mid-October to mid-March, 9.30 to 4 weekdays, 2 to 4 Sundays.)

Abbotsbury's famous swannery is over 600 years old

HARDY MONUMENT AND BRONKHAM HILL

ONE ascent through grassy fields and woodland at the start, then all the rest is effortless walking along grassy ridges, with views all round, and gorse providing colour.

LENGTH 5 miles (8km), 2½ hours

DIFFICULTY 2

START Portesham, just north of B3157 and 5 miles north-west of Weymouth. Roadside parking. Grid reference 603858

OS MAPS Landranger 194; Pathfinder 1332 (SY 68/78)

REFRESHMENTS Pubs, tea-room and shop in Portesham

WALK DIRECTIONS

① From main street with Portesham church on left, take road uphill signposted Hardy Monument. 75 yards after village store, take bridleway on right (signposted Hardy Monument), rising and soon entering field, where you keep left along hawthorn trees. ② At field corner, turn right now with wall on left, to leave field by next corner on track which runs between walls. Where walls taper outwards after only 30 yards, keep along right-hand wall in this and the next field (Hardy Monument, which you soon reach, is visible ahead), at end of which ③ turn left on enclosed track. Fork right after 50 yards and descend to pass between barn (on your left) and walled enclosure (right), just after which fork left, again signposted to Hardy Monument. Follow this rising woodland path ④, forking right after 400 yards by another signpost, to leave woods and reach the Hardy Monument ⑤ Ⓐ.

Beyond monument, turn right (downhill) on road. Where woods on right end, take second track on right (first track goes into woods), signposted Corton Hill; follow this along the ridge for 1¼ miles Ⓑ, ignoring left turn signposted Martinstown after ¾ mile. ⑥ On reaching pylons, turn right on farm track (left is 'private road') and follow down to road ⑦.

Turn right along road, and at next junction ⑧ take gate on right (actually just on the Portesham road). Ascend grassy ridge Ⓒ, and follow the top – soon over stile, then with wall on right. Soon, turn right on track for a few yards, but leave it where it goes through a gate,

The spectacular splash of gorse along Bronkham Hill in late summer

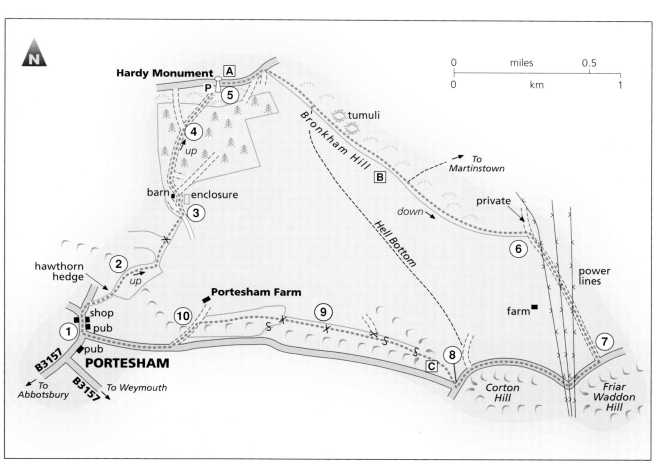

and continue along top of ridge with fence on right. ⑨ At end of field take left-hand of two gates, continue with fence on right to next gate where proceed still along top of

ridge to reach farm track with farm away to right ⑩. Turn left and follow the farm track down to the road where you turn to the right into Portesham.

The Hardy Monument is one of the area's best view points

ON THE ROUTE

A **The Hardy Monument** Commemorates not the writer but Admiral Sir Thomas Masterman Hardy, Nelson's flag captain at Trafalgar, who lived in Portesham. The monument itself, erected 1844, is a landmark for miles around.

The **view** of the coast extends from White Nothe (near Lulworth) to the east as far as Golden Cap to the west, with the Isle of Portland in the middle. The adjacent heathland is a designated Site of Special Scientific Interest for its heath vegetation.

B **Bronkham Hill** is lined with ancient burial mounds. The gorse-clad ridge, with elevated views on both sides, offers very enjoyable walking.

C This nameless ridge is covered with **strip lynchets** (remains of ancient field systems). There are more good **views** too, with the Hardy Monument to the north and over Waddon Vale to the coast to the south.

PATH PROBLEMS

It is illegal to obstruct a public right of way. If you find an obstruction, such as impenetrable crops or barbed wire, across such a path you are entitled to remove it/them (or in the case of crops, walk over them). If the problem is bad, you can take an alternative route providing you do not trespass or cause damage.

It is illegal to put up a sign on a right of way that deters potential users, such as Private or Path Closed, when it refers to that route.

Waymarks and signposts have the same status as any other traffic sign, and it is an offence to remove them. If you come across hindrances like these, write to the relevant highway authority, which has the duty to sort out problems relating to rights of way. Give exact locations, with grid references, and a sketch map if possible.

HIGHWAY AUTHORITIES' DUTIES AND POWERS

Highway authorities have the main responsibility for rights of way, and have discretionary powers too.

Important statutory duties are:

- asserting and protecting the public's rights to use and enjoy rights of way
- ensuring that farmers comply with the law that paths over cultivated land are restored after they have been ploughed or otherwise disturbed, and thereafter remain visible on the ground, and ensuring that farmers do not allow growing crops to inconvenience right of way users
- maintaining bridges used by rights of way (landowners are responsible for gates and stiles, but highway authorities can put pressure on landowners to keep gates and stiles in usable condition)
- maintaining the surface of most rights of way
- preparing and keeping up to date a 'definite map and statement' giving a legal record of all rights of way
- signposting rights of way where they leave metalled highways and providing additional signs and waymarks along a path whenever they are necessary.

Discretionary powers include:

- creating new paths by agreement with the landowner
- improving rights of way, for instance by providing seats and lighting
- providing footpath wardens.

LULWORTH COVE, FOSSIL FOREST AND MUPE BAY

A WILD coast of great geological interest. Involves a steep climb up Bindon Hill (this can be avoided, as described) for fine views. The route crosses part of Lulworth army ranges, but these are open to the public most weekends and daily in August and at the Easter holiday period (to check times, telephone (01929) 462721 and ask for the range office); waymarked with yellow posts and signposted. Keep to the paths; there are unexploded shells about. Easy route-finding.

WALK DIRECTIONS

① Follow the road to the cove A and make your way round the pebbly beach to the left side of the cove, where steps lead up to lowest point of cliffs (at very high tide this will not be possible; instead take the path rising steeply from behind the café and around the top of the rim of the cove until you reach the point where steps come up from the beach). Continue away from the cove at the signpost, and follow, ignoring right turn to Pepler Point, to enter Lulworth Ranges by a gate B ②.

Beyond the gate turn right to reach the cliff-top; a hurdle gives access to Fossil Forest C, but at the

LENGTH 3½ miles (5.5km), 2 hours; extension to Durdle Door adds 2 miles (3km), 1 hour
DIFFICULTY 3
START Lulworth Cove (large car park), 17 miles south of Dorchester. Grid reference 822800
OS MAPS Landranger 194; Outdoor Leisure 15
REFRESHMENTS Café and restaurants in Lulworth Cove and West Lulworth; Castle Inn in West Lulworth

time of writing this was closed. (If it is open, you can continue along rocky cleft for a short distance, but there is no way out at the far end. Return to the cliff-top.) Follow a grassy path marked by yellow posts along the edge of the cliffs.

③ At Mupe Bay D, steps on the right give access to a sandy beach. If you are tired, fork left, signposted Little Bindon, and follow an easy track back to Lulworth Cove. Otherwise, keep right along the cliff-top; at the next stile, coast path climbs Bindon Hill, very steeply – follow yellow marker posts. ④ At top turn sharp left E, signposted Lulworth, on a track along the ridge, soon passing a flagpole and then reaching a radar station.

Continue forward beyond the radar station, signposted West Lulworth, on a track between fences. ⑤ 100 yards later pass through a gate (track ends) and turn right along fence for 75 yards, then left along a grassy bank, an ancient earthwork. Follow the bank around the hill until Lulworth Cove comes into view; cross a stile and descend steeply to the bottom.
Extension to Durdle Door
On returning to the starting point, take the prominent path rising from the car park and heading westwards. It soon joins the coast and later passes above Durdle Door F, a

Durdle Door, perhaps the most spectacular natural arch on Britain's coast

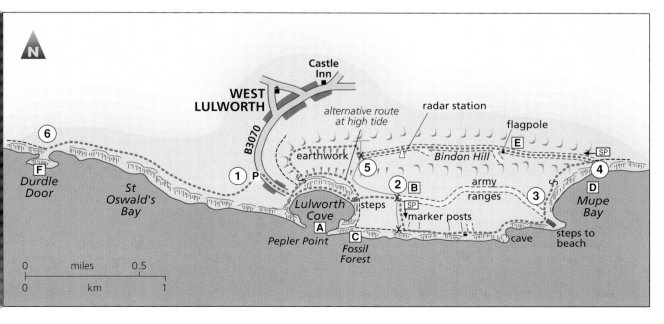

natural arch beneath the cliffs ⑥. Return the same way.

ON THE ROUTE

[A] **Lulworth Cove** The great Alpine earth movement, which crossed Europe and pushed up what are now the Alps, is seen at its westernmost extent here, with the folding of the layers of chalk, sandstone and hard Portland limestone exposed. The circular bay was formed when a 400ft breach in the Portland stone along the coast allowed the sea to cut into the weak rock behind.

[B] **Little Bindon** Just on the right on entering the ranges are the remains of a small chapel and cottage built by monks in the 12th century.

[C] **Fossil Forest** Petrified algae that surrounded stumps of trees some 135 million years ago are exposed just under the edge of the cliff. The 'forest' is designated a Site of Special Scientific Interest; chipping with hammers is prohibited.

[D] **Mupe Bay** Huge chalk and sandstone cliffs flank the bay; there is an unspoilt sandy beach below. In unrulier days this was one of the biggest centres for smuggling in Dorset; there is a smugglers' cave at the near end of the first (smaller) bay. The land here has not been farmed for half a century, and the absence of insecticides and pesticides makes this a haven for wild flowers. Numerous shags and cormorants can be seen. Butterflies on this coast include the rare Lulworth skipper, which has orange wings, edged with brown.

[E] **Bindon Hill** The view westwards extends to the Isle of Portland, a peninsula much-quarried for its Portland limestone, which has been used to front many great public buildings in London and Dublin.

[F] **Durdle Door** This magnificent natural arch was created by the action of the waves, which will one day cause its destruction.

Sergeant Troy in Hardy's Far from the Madding Crowd *was thought to have drowned in Lulworth Cove*

SWYRE HEAD AND KIMMERIDGE LEDGES

A COASTAL walk at two levels, making it an absorbing route throughout: high along the grassy ridge past Swyre Head, following an easy farm-track skirting the top edge of the slope, then a cliff-top walk eventually ascending Hounstout Cliff. Easy route-finding.

LENGTH 7 miles (11km), 3 hours

DIFFICULTY 2

START Kingston car park, 1½ miles south of Corfe Castle. Turn off B3069 at Kingston, by Scott Arms, fork right in front of church (with big tower); car park is ¼ mile down this lane, on left immediately after driveway on left to Encombe House (signposted path for Hounstout Cliff). Grid reference 954795

OS MAPS Landranger 195; Outdoor Leisure 15

REFRESHMENTS Pub in Kingston; tea-room in Kimmeridge

WALK DIRECTIONS

① Turn left out of main car park entrance on the lane by which you arrived from Kingston; soon lane leaves woods Ⓐ. ② ½ mile later, fork left by sign to Encombe Farm, taking track between gate pillars, but immediately leaving it for gate on right: follow the track across a field, soon forking right and reaching gate. Keep forward on track, with wall and belt of trees on right.

③ Bear sharp right in front of stile (which leads to grassy mound and Swyre Head) Ⓑ, and follow track along top edge of hillside (signposted Kimmeridge), with fence on left. ④ After 1½ miles, track descends to road: turn left, then at road junction immediately after, take signposted stile for Kimmeridge church. Path descends to churchyard.

Beyond, go forward on road through village ⑤, and follow for ¾ mile to the sea. Fork left by houses, then ⑥ take track on right 50 yards later (signposted Toilets). Where track bends left, take path straight ahead, soon reaching coast and turn

left on coast path, down steps, then up steps and past tower Ⓒ. Walk along cliff-top path. After 3 miles, coast path makes major ascent of Hounstout Cliff, with undercliff down to right Ⓓ. ⑦ Turn left at top by stone seat, over stile, leaving coast path. Follow path by wall overlooking Encombe House along top of ridge Ⓔ.

⑧ After one mile, enter woods, passing house on your right, then turn right at T-junction, avoiding immediate right turn (private) but, just after, taking the right-hand of three tracks, signposted Kingston.

⑨ Opposite signpost to Hounstout you can turn left into car park.

ON THE ROUTE

Ⓐ The village of **Kingston** has two churches, both built in the 19th century. The disused 'old' church, on the main road, is undistinguished; the 'new' one, built in 1880 of Purbeck stone, is considered the best church design of G E Street, the architect of the Strand Law Courts in London.

At the start of the walk there is a view of **Corfe Castle** and the **Purbeck Ridge** on the right (north). Corfe Castle is a very pretty Purbeck-stone village, dominated by

its ruined 12th- to 16th-century castle standing on a detached part of the Purbeck ridge (NT; *open to the public*). In AD978 King Edward the Martyr was murdered here by his stepmother, so that her own son could succeed to the throne. It was besieged by Parliamentary forces in 1646. Stones from the castle were used for building much of the village centre.

Ⓑ **Swyre Head** (666ft) gives an impressive view along the wildest part of the Purbeck coast looking west into the army training area

The coast near Kimmeridge yields both fossils and oil

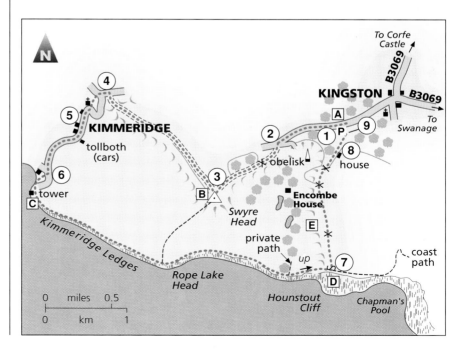

The spiky ruins of Corfe Castle occupy a hillock in a breach in the whaleback Purbeck Ridge and can be seen from far around

original purpose, probably either a beacon for sailors or an oratory for a priest to pray for lost sailors' souls. There is no electricity, no organ, not even an altar, just a stone pier for its centrepiece.

Bird-watchers might see guillemots, kittiwakes, razorbills, puffins and shags, and flora-lovers spotted orchid, yellow rattle, black bryony, goatsbeard, lords and ladies. Butterflies include the rare Lulworth Skipper: it has orange wings edged with brown, and it flits quickly from plant to plant.

E At the bottom of the valley nestles **Encombe House**, built *c* 1735; still the seat of the Earls of Eldon. It is *open to the public.*

around Worbarrow Tout. The **grassy mound** is a tumulus, on a site obviously chosen for its natural position.

C The **cliffs** here are formed of fossiliferous Kimmeridge clay, comprising alternate bands of crumbly dark shale and harder yellow limestone; the rock is almost horizontal here, forming the Kimmeridge ledges. A 'nodding donkey' on the west side of the bay was the first onshore oil well in Britain, installed by BP in 1959. Earlier schemes to exploit the shale were largely abortive: Sir William Clavell in the 17th century boiled seawater, using energy from the shale, to make salt, and also tried to set up an alum and glass industry here. An ambitious plan in 1847 to use the shale to provide (among

other things) gas for street lighting in Paris failed because of the strong sulphur odour that was created. A seven-foot dinosaur head found here is now in the museum in Dorchester. The **tower** was built in 1831 by Revd John Clavel as a garden feature for nearby Smedmore House and was later used as a coastguard look-out post.

D **Hounstout Cliff** towers 500 feet above the sea and has a tumbled undercliff. The coast path continues in roller-coaster fashion past **St Aldhelm's Head**, site of the first radar station; radar pioneering experiments took place here in the Second World War. The Head is capped by **St Catherine's Chapel** (formerly the Devil's Chapel), a simple 12th-century building whose square plan betrays a different

ADOPTING TRIG POINTS

The familiar British trig point is now redundant with today's cartographic surveying methods. The Ordnance Survey invited the public to adopt these important landmarks, so that someone would maintain the structures and keep them in the landscape. The scheme caught the public imagination: response was overwhelming, and virtually all the most visible trig points were adopted.

COMMON LAND

There are 8,675 registered commons in England and Wales, covering an area about the size of Surrey, Berkshire and Oxfordshire put together. There are none in Scotland.

Despite the popular belief to the contrary, there is no automatic public right of access to all of these.

Common land is a legacy from the time when much of the country was wild and not owned by anyone, and used communally. The manorial system gave it legal owners, but the peasantry retained rights to share the land's produce, such as for grazing or for firewood. The enclosure of much of England and Wales reduced the number of commons. Of those that survive, some may be used only by commoners (who may be the residents of a village or hamlet); others have public access for all, such as the commons of London. Many commons are important wildlife sites; over one-third have been designated Sites of Special Scientific Interest (SSSIs).

Common land registers and maps are held by the relevant county council, metropolitan district council or London borough. Unfortunately, many of the common rights were not recorded when registers were assembled and legal loopholes have appeared that give means of deregistering commons so they can be used like any other private land.

BULBARROW HILL AND MILTON ABBAS

THE best of the Dorset downs, leading along the unspoilt valley of Heath Bottom and emerging at one of the grand viewpoints of the country. A gentle descent leads through Green Hill Down Nature Reserve, followed by an exploration of Milton Abbey, a secret Norman chapel tucked away in the woods, and Milton Abbas – the epitome of the English estate village. The route-finding is quite easy, with nearly all the going along defined paths, tracks and peaceful lanes.

WALK DIRECTIONS

① With the church on your left follow 'no through road' ahead, signposted Higher Houghton.

Proceed out of the village then turn right where road bends right at junction of road and track, signposted Ibberton. ② After passing a farm, the road becomes unmetalled; continue past two more

> **LENGTH** 6 miles (9.5km), 3 hours
> **DIFFICULTY** 2
> **START** Winterbourne Houghton, 5 miles west of Blandford Forum. Roadside parking near church and phone-box. Grid reference 820045
> **OS MAPS** Landranger 194; Pathfinder 1299 and 1300 (ST 60/70 and ST 80/90)
> **REFRESHMENTS** Tea Clipper tea-room and Hambro Arms in Milton Abbas

houses to reach a gate into a field. Proceed along the bottom of the valley, climbing slowly.

③ After ¾ mile, the track enters woods by a gate. At the far end emerge into a field and continue forward (no path) to a small gate in the hedgerow up on your right. Beyond the gate turn left on the road. Keep forward at the next junction, signposted Bulbarrow. ④ Where the road reaches a viewpoint on Bulbarrow Hill Ⓐ continue forward, taking the left turn, signposted Ansty and Hilton. Turn left shortly before a mast, on to a track immediately to the left of Bulbarrow Farm entrance; the track is signposted Milton Abbey. Do not enter area of Nissen huts. Where the

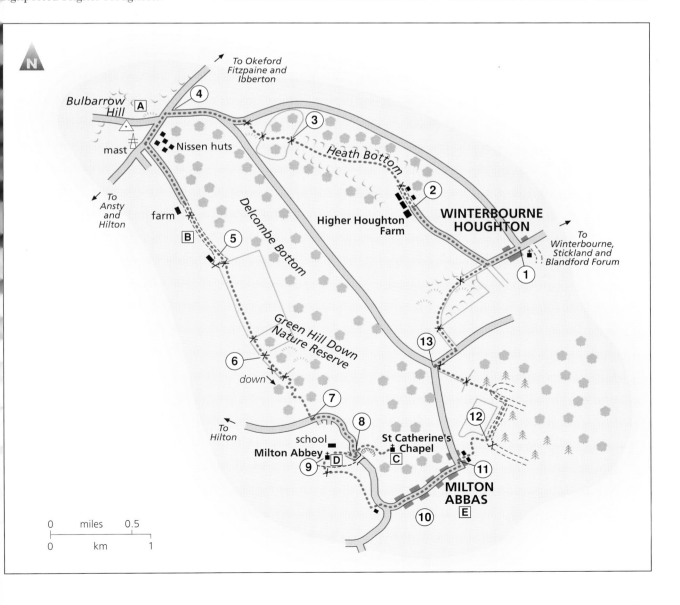

Milton Abbas' main street curves down to an artificial lake

track becomes unsurfaced by a farm, continue forward and descend steadily B.

⑤ At the next barn, the track forks; take left-hand fork, through a gate, and proceed with the hedge on your right along the top of two large fields. ⑥ Enter Green Hill Down Nature Reserve by a gate and sign, and continue with hedge on your right through scrubby land, ignoring left turns and ignoring a gate/stile on right by overhead cable. Proceed to a small gate, leaving the reserve and continuing on a twisty narrow path, through scrub and coppice, which gradually descends to the road ⑦. Turn left on the road, follow it to houses, then fork left slightly uphill, on road.

⑧ Where the road descends, continue sharp right (signposted Milton Abbey car park) but first detour left up steps leading around the top of a chalk pit to the chapel C. Retrace your steps (down towards the abbey, then first path on the right) to the road and cross into the school grounds. Take first left turn, and follow signs to abbey D ⑨. Turn left out of the abbey door and 100 yards later cross a surfaced path for the path opposite which is hedged on the left-hand side. Follow this to lodge, then turn right on the road to enter Milton Abbas village E ⑩.

Proceed up the main street of village, turn left at the top. ⑪ Take first right turn, signposted Forestry Commission private road. Ignore side turnings; the road soon becomes a track and enters a wood at a sign for Milton Park Wood. The track then curves round to left. ⑫ Just before a gate across the track, turn

left on to a narrower track which rises along the edge of woods, then descends to a T-junction with forest track. Turn left, then 100 yards later keep forward where the main track bends to the right. Ascend to a gate, into field, then go forward with a fence on your left, to the road ⑬.

Turn right on the road and, 250 yards later, left on a track between fences. Follow this for ¼ mile to enter a scrubby area by a gate, and turn half right on to a grassy track leading downhill to a corner of the lane. Continue forward to the starting-point.

ON THE ROUTE

A **Bulbarrow Hill** has one of the biggest panoramas in inland Dorset, looking far into Somerset and Wiltshire. From left to right the principal landmarks are the Quantock Hills, Glastonbury Tor, the Mendips, White Sheet Hill and Salisbury Plain.

B **Views** extend south-eastwards towards Corfe Castle, the most memorable medieval castle ruin in Dorset, and to Poole Harbour.

C **St Catherine's Chapel** Hidden deep in the woods and reached only by a path, this Norman chapel seems like a time-warp survival. In former years the building was used as a pigeon loft and as a labourer's cottage. Just below it, some 100 grass steps enclosed by a yew hedge form a magical vista of Milton Abbey.

D **Milton Abbey** The abbey was built on the site of a college of canons founded in 932 by King Athelstan; this later became a Benedictine monastery. Only the

choir, crossing and transepts of the 14th- and 15th-century church were built; the Dissolution arrived before the nave could be added. However its interior has an effect of airiness and height, accentuated by the lightness of the stonework. The adjacent mansion, which now houses a prestigious public school, was built as a house in 1771 by Sir William Chambers for Lord Milton.

E **Milton Abbas** In the late 18th century Lord Milton wanted more privacy around his house, so he cleared the old village and moved it here. The result is all of a piece: identical detached, thatched cottages flank the grass verges on both sides of a broad sloping street. Opposite the church, the group of brick almshouses date from 1674 but were re-erected here in 1779. The Hambro Arms is set in the middle of the village street and has an open-plan interior and a comfortable lounge adorned with old prints and a collection of pub water-jugs.

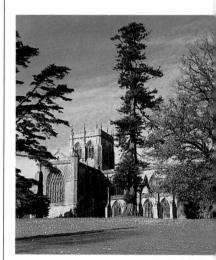

Milton Abbas church

TWO FURTHER WALKS IN DORSET

Studland The village adjoins strongly contrasting landscapes, which can all be enjoyed in a 6-mile walk. Head east along the coast path to Old Harry Rocks, representing Old Harry and Old Harry's Wife: these chalk pinnacles, battered by wave action, are detached from the crumbling cliff head along the coast, then as the path is about to drop, follow the ridge of Ballard Down inland to the west. This is a marvellous high-level path, with views over Poole Harbour and Swanage Bay. Beyond the obelisk at the end you drop to the road, which can be followed back to Studland. Alternatively, and better, follow paths north and east across the golf course and Studland Heath – the latter being the largest of Dorset's surviving heathlands. A curious rock outcrop known as the Agglestone has attracted more than a century's worth of graffiti.
Powerstock lies amid glorious downlands, and invites a village-to-village walk along valleys linking West Milton and North Poorton, from where the minor road can be followed back for a 3½-mile circuit. The paths are not particularly well defined. The Three Horseshoes at Powerstock is a nicely placed lunch spot.

BREAMORE HOUSE AND THE MIZMAZE

AN exploration in an unspoilt corner of the country, traversing gentle farmland and woodland, and taking in a considerable bounty of architectural and historic interest. Easy route-finding; nearly all on clearly defined tracks.

WALK DIRECTIONS

① With the Cartwheel Inn on your right, walk up the main street of Whitsbury for ½ mile, ignoring a turning on your right to Whitsbury Manor Stud (signed). 30 yards later, where the road bends left, take a surfaced track on the right (not sharp right through gate of Manor House). 50 yards later follow the track as it bends to the right behind stables, then fork left on to an

unmetalled track Ⓐ. Follow this downhill for ½ mile. ② At the bottom cross the track, take the gate ahead and follow a grassy track

LENGTH	5 miles (8km), 2½ hours
DIFFICULTY	1
START	Village of Whitsbury, 4 miles north-west of Fordingbridge. There is car parking space by the phone-box opposite the Cartwheel Inn, otherwise park further up the street in the village. Grid reference 129188
OS MAPS	Landranger 184; Pathfinder 1262 and 1282 (SU 02/12) and SU 01/01)
REFRESHMENTS	Cartwheel Inn, Whitsbury; tea-room at Countryside Museum near Breamore House

along the edge of two fields before it enters woods, then continue forward ignoring cross-tracks ③. The track soon emerges into the open, following the right edge of a field to the gate/stile by the next group of trees. Beyond the gate/stile turn

Take a very minor detour at point ⑤ to visit Breamore church

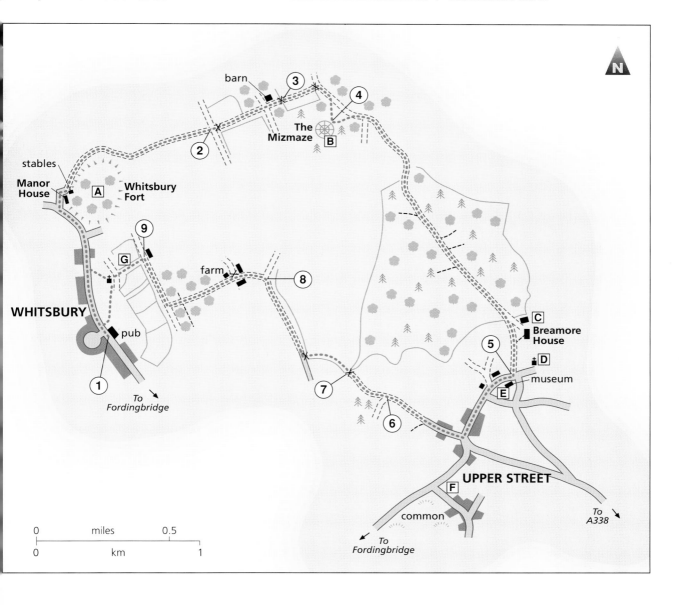

right on the track, and shortly bear right up towards wood. Walk along the edge of the wood until you reach a sign to the Mizmaze (Mizmaze itself is hidden in the woods) B.

④ From Mizmaze return to the track, which soon bends left and runs between hedges. Shortly, the track enters woods; avoid side turns, and proceed to the bottom, emerging into parkland and passing just to the right of the entrance to Breamore House, where the driveway is picked up C. ⑤ Just after passing between gateposts capped by stone lions turn right D, past the Countryside Museum E. Keep left 200 yards later and emerge on to road. Turn right on the road, through the hamlet of Upper Street F, then take next road turning on the right, by a grassy triangle.

⑥ Where the road ends, continue forward on a track between hedges, forking right after 250 yards. ⑦ Where the track reaches a gate/stile, continue forward along the left side of field to pass through a gate, then turn right on the track. ⑧ After ¼ mile, just as the track begins to bend right, take a track on your left leading to a farm. Pass through the farmyard (avoiding right turn in centre of farmyard), picking up a track at the far end

COMMON LAND

There are 8,675 registered commons in England and Wales, covering an area about the size of Surrey, Berkshire and Oxfordshire put together. There are none in Scotland.

Despite the popular belief to the contrary, there is no automatic public right of access to all of these. Common land is a legacy from the time when much of the country was wild and not owned by anyone, and used communally. The manorial system gave it legal owners, but the peasantry retained rights to share the land's produce, such as for grazing or for firewood. The enclosure of much of England and Wales reduced the number of commons. Of those that survive, some may only be used by commoners (who may be the residents of a village or hamlet); others have public access for all, such as the commons of London. Many commons are important wildlife sites; over one-third have been designated Sites of Special Scientific Interest (SSSIs)

Common land registers and maps are held by the relevant county council, metropolitan district council or London borough. Unfortunately many of the common rights were not recorded when registers were assembled and legal loopholes have appeared that give means of deregistering commons so they can be used like any other private land.

marked by a line of trees on its right-hand side. The track leads up to woods, at the far side of which you turn right.

⑨ Where the track reaches the end of a surfaced road by the first house, turn left on track between fences G heading for Whitsbury church, half-hidden in trees. Turn left at the T-junction of tracks, then right through a gate to enter the churchyard. In front of the church, with Whitsbury in view below, *either* take the gate and proceed down to a gate by a thatched building to emerge close to the pub; *or*, if you parked further up in the village, take the gate at the far end of the

churchyard which leads on to a fenced path and down into the village.

ON THE ROUTE

A On the right is the overgrown 16-acre site of **Whitsbury Iron Age camp**, with three lines of ramparts and ditches. Excavation has revealed the outline of a circular timber house.

B **Mizmaze** An enigmatic cobweb-like turf maze 87ft across, cut in the grass and surrounded by yew trees. Its origin is uncertain; it may be Anglo-Saxon.

C **Breamore House** (*open* to public; 2 to 5.30; closed Mondays and Fridays) Elizabethan mansion, home of the Hulse family since 1748, containing a collection of paintings and furniture. The house was partially rebuilt after fire damage in 1856.

D Just to the left is **Breamore church**. Partly Saxon, with some 'long and short' work on the quoins of the tower, alternating horizontal and vertical stones at the corner of the building, typical of the period. Several windows and all of the south transept date from this time; otherwise the church is mostly Norman and 14th century.

E **Countryside and Carriage Museum** A farm museum with workshops, smithy, carriages and old steam engines.

F **Upper Street** is a particularly well-preserved hamlet of thatched cottages. The next left turn leads to a common, flanked by scattered cottages.

Despite being rebuilt in the 19th century, Breamore House retains Elizabethan-style features such as mullions and tall brick chimneystacks

BROCKENHURST AND SETLEY POND

ONE of the finest circular walks in the New Forest, through a nature reserve of ancient woodland and across pasture fields to the Hobler Inn, then emerging suddenly on to wide, open heathland with belts of woodland in the distance. In the middle of the heath is Setley Pond, used for model-boat sailing (or skating in deep winter). Returns to Brockenhurst station by footpaths; the walk is rural in character until the very end. Paths are undefined across fields, and directions need care over the heath.

LENGTH 6½ miles (10km), 3 hours
DIFFICULTY 1–2
START Brockenhurst station (south side), on A337 (Lymington to Lyndhurst). Grid reference 301019
OS MAPS Landranger 195 and 196; Outdoor Leisure 22
REFRESHMENTS Pubs and cafés in Brockenhurst; Hobler Inn at ⑧

WALK DIRECTIONS

① From station car park on south side of station, walk to main road, turn right and after 30 yards turn left on road signposted to St Nicholas Parish Church. After church, continue on road half right for 200 yards. ② Turn left opposite stables through wicket gate and walk between fences through Brockenhurst Park and into Brockenhurst Woods nature reserve. The path is undulating and marked with yellow waymarks at regular intervals.

③ After 1 mile, join large track coming in from right and after 100 yards pass isolated cottage known as The Lodge, keeping straight on at junction of tracks just after. Ignore left turn at bottom of slope, but continue uphill for 200 yards on the same track. ④ Look out carefully for a yellow marker post indicating small path on right, which leads up through woods then passes through a gate ⑤. Pass through the gate and carry straight on across the turf, with fence on left, heading for houses and the road. Cross the road and take

the path between fences (signposted) directly opposite, soon to reach another road ⑥.

Again cross road, to path opposite, leading down to cross a footbridge. Continue uphill across left edge of two fields to enter left-hand edge of woods by a stile. ⑦ Follow the path running on edge of woods and where path emerges into fields follow the right edge of field to a stile to the right of rear of pub (Hobler Inn). Cross two further stiles to reach main road ⑧.

Cross road and turn left on it. After 30 yards, opposite pub sign, turn right over stile on path immediately to right of cottage. Path runs between hedges and after ¼ mile crosses stile and emerges at corner of heathland ⑨. Make towards red-brick house in front of you, and just beyond it take right track at junction of tracks. After

30 yards cross gravel cross-track and continue direction on path which soon runs alongside Setley Pond.

⑩ At the end of the pond continue half right, keeping to left of car park, to reach a wooden barrier. Turn left on gravel roadway after 10 yards by Setley Pond sign, and turn half left on path across heath. This soon runs parallel to road and merges with it just before a railway bridge. ⑪ Pass under railway bridge and, 50 yards beyond it, bear half right on path next to a height-restriction road-sign (which faces away from you; avoid path immediately after railway bridge which runs parallel to railway). This rises gently, and after ¼ mile crosses railway by footbridge ⑫.

After bridge, bear quarter left on path (not immediately obvious) making for a road-sign showing mileages and destinations. At the

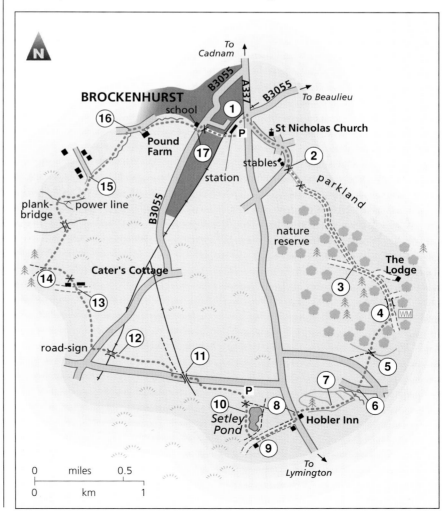

Ponies grazing in the pastures are part of the New Forest scene

to power lines, at which you turn left to pass a gabled house, where direction is continued on a gravel track. Follow this for 300 yards.

⑮ Where main track bends left, take track straight on, passing another house and go through kissing-gate. Path at first runs between fences and soon runs alongside a stream. Ignore side turns by bridge and cross final stile to emerge on road ⑯. Turn right on road for 100 yards and, just before a small road-bridge, turn right on driveway to Pound Farm. Just across stream, before farm, turn left past hurdle and make for distant red-brick buildings (no path), with stream on left. After 100 yards, by footbridge on left, turn half right on path which emerges on road (school on left) ⑰.

Turn left and after 30 yards turn right through kissing-gate on path between fences. Cross stile at end of path, and turn left along residential road, near end of which a small gate on right leads down to station.

road, continue opposite on path which bears half right, and follow this, making for a white house with shutters and lodge, ¼ mile distant. ⑬ At house (Cater's Cottage) and lodge, pick up gravel track which leads between them to a wooden barrier; track narrows to become a path leading across open heath.

⑭ ¼ mile after barrier, immediately before prominent group of trees, turn sharp right on path. This path bends 90 degrees left after ¼ mile and then, after 200 yards, crosses a stream by a footbridge, after which it briefly becomes indistinct and crosses another stream by a plank-bridge. Turn immediately right

THE NEW FOREST

The New Forest is one of Europe's largest lowland heathlands, a type of landscape that has rapidly dwindled in this country in the last half-century. Despite its name, it is not all tree cover: large expanses are open, undulating heath, remarkably remote and primeval in character. Red deer and ponies wander through the Forest. The ponies are now wild but belong to Commoners who own grazing rights. A number of scattered hamlets, typically of thatched cottages, exist; many of these came into being by the existence of squatters' rights, which enabled common land to be settled.

From 1079 the area was established as a royal hunting forest; William Rufus, son of William the Conqueror, met his death in a hunting accident in the Forest.

The flora of the New Forest is considerably varied; the acidic heathlands support a range of plants, such as the insect-eating sundews. Woodlands are particularly rich in fungi.

For walkers, there is general access along the paths and tracks, although very few of these are actually mapped as rights of way. In addition to the route described here, there is a good deal of excellent and varied walking, particularly on the western side of the New Forest. Fritham is a recommended starting point for walks into delightful deciduous woodlands and on to open heaths; the lone High Corner Inn is usefully placed to the south-west.

SELBORNE AND NOAR HILL

A RAMBLE in the countryside of naturalist Gilbert White (see C), taking in much of the best landscape in eastern Hampshire: grassy fields, downland, orchards and deciduous woodlands, clinging to steep escarpments. Beyond Selborne, the route ascends two hills, with good views. Route-finding is involved but signposting and waymarking is thorough.

LENGTH   10 miles (16km), 5 hours
DIFFICULTY   2
START   Hawkley village green, 2½ miles west of Liss. Grid reference 746291
Short walk, omitting Hawkley
LENGTH   5 miles (8km), 2½ hours
DIFFICULTY   2
START   Selborne, on B3006 between Alton and Liss. Start walk at ⑩. Grid reference 741337
OS MAPS   Landranger 186; Pathfinder 1265 and 1244 (SU 62/72 and SU 63/73)
REFRESHMENTS   Pub in Hawkley; pubs, shop and tea-room in Selborne

---

WALK DIRECTIONS

① From the village green take the road signposted West Liss, passing pub. At T-junction, go straight on, on a signposted path between fences. ② At the end turn left on the road, past Uplands, then where the road bends left take a signposted path on right, enter the field and follow the right edge.

③ At the end take signposted gate, then turn right on a surfaced lane. At farm Ⓐ, take the centre of three tracks, initially level but soon descending gently. You soon reach a large field, and cross in the same direction to find a gate at the far end ④. Continue on track beyond, crossing a stream and ascending gently to reach a surfaced lane. Turn right on lane (ignore an immediate left turn), down to T-junction where you take the signposted woodland path opposite and slightly to the right (do not confuse with a broader track just to the left of this); the path skirts a garden fence on your

right and soon reaches a stile ⑤.
Cross the field to a kissing-gate and turn left on lane (the driveway to Le Court), ignoring immediate left turn by grassy triangle. 100 yards later, turn left on a signposted track which passes close to Le Court (on your right) and skirts around an orchard. After Le Court, it bends left as it enters the orchard, soon passing a brick barn: keep on the level (soon with a fence on left).

⑥ When you reach a signpost by a water-tank, turn left then immediately left again over a stile into woods. The path climbs for 40

yards, then turn right over stile to enter a field, and follow the left edge – soon houses come into view, when you cross a stile to join a track which leads to road. Turn left on road Ⓑ, then after 300 yards (opposite signpost and sign for Wildwood Antiques) take a track on your right to enter a field ⑦.

Keep along the fence on your right until crossing a stile on right, beyond which the path begins to descend and doubles back to another stile, then goes sharp left, down along the left edge of the field to reach a stile into woods and to a

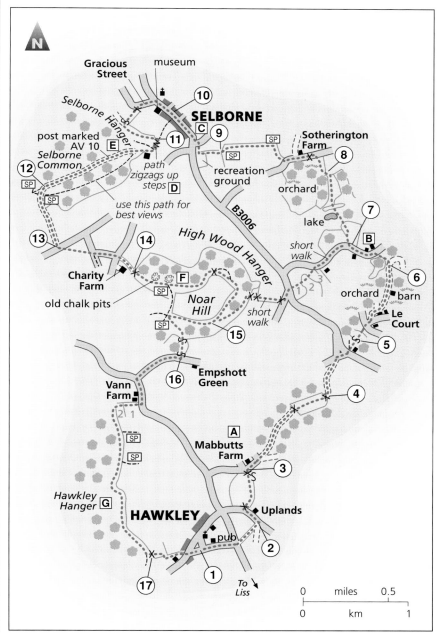

lake. Go over the stile near the lake, keep lake close to your left and walk along edge of (often boggy) field: soon further stiles ahead indicate the route ahead – up the centre of a small valley, at the far end of which ⑧ you cross a stile (slightly to left) up into woods, to reach an orchard. Go through gate half right, finding a track between a tall hedge (right) and an orchard (left). At end of hedge turn left, soon after which you take a gate on right on to the road.

Turn left on the road; after 300 yards where road bends left, take a signposted track on right (not the track immediately after a farm: it's a little further on than this), to enter a large field and follow right edge as signposted. In field corner turn left (signposted), still along field edge.

⑨ At the end of the field, the route is ahead and slightly to the left (signposted) with a ditch and line of trees on your right. Soon continue forward by signpost along the right edge of recreation field until taking a path on the right. You reach a road and turn left, then right at the next junction through Selborne ☐C☐.

⑩ Pass Selborne Arms and museum on your left, then after a church turn left into Gracious Street. Just after the houses end and where the road bends right, take gate ahead and follow the left edge of field to reach a stile into woods, where you turn left on a woodland path skirting the base of wooded hill, with a fence on your left.

⑪ After ¼ mile, at a National Trust sign for Selborne Common, take path ahead which zigzags up steps ☐D☐. At the top (marked by a boulder and a bench) turn right along hedge, keeping to left along a broader woodland path (right fork goes along the top edge of the slope; *note* there is a left turn you can take 70 yards later which gives views to the south – see map) ☐E☐. Follow the path through woods and semi-open areas. ⑫ After ¾ mile, do not pass through posts out of woods ahead (near National Trust sign which faces other way), but turn left just before it by a four-way signpost, and go straight on at the next signpost a few yards later: the track descends, leaving woods, soon to reach a road.

⑬ Cross the road to a gate

opposite and bear half left across the field, leaving by a signpost in the diagonally opposite corner, keeping woods to your right and turn right on the road (*note* if this field is ploughed or cropped, it is easier to omit it by turning left on the road then right at next junction). Follow the road to a T-junction, take the wide signposted bridleway between hedges opposite and slightly to the left. At farm gate, bear left up a narrow track. This soon enters a semi-wooded area by gate and sign for Noar Hill Nature Reserve ⑭ ☐F☐.

Follow the track, keeping straight on at a signpost after ¼ mile (ignoring right turn used as a short cut). The track leads through woods and a semi-open area and reaches a gate; go straight on along the path around the top of the hill, with the woods just to your right. Path narrows and runs between trees. ⑮ Reach a T-junction.
For short walk Turn left and descend to the bottom; take a gate into a field. Head to the next gate then forward, with a fence on your right to reach the road. Turn left on road and at main road take signposted path opposite (if ploughed or cropped it is easier to turn left along main road, then first right): head across first field to a waymark post just to the left of corner of hedge then cut across second field corner to the next signpost, where you continue in third field towards a house, emerging on the road by a signpost, and turn right on the road. Ignore driveway on right to Le Court. ¼ mile later, turn left on the track opposite a signpost and sign for Wildwood Antiques, to enter field. This is ⑦.
For full walk Turn right at T-junction ⑮. After ¼ mile, turn left at signpost for Hangers Way, descending through woods. At the bottom take a stile into a field, cross to the stile in bottom corner then go forward (with fence on left) to a surfaced lane. ⑯ Turn right on lane and left at T-junction. Pass Vann House and Vann Farm on your right, then take a signposted stile on the right, follow the right edge of two fields towards a wooded hill, and turn left (signposted) in the corner of second field, still skirting

the field. Follow this path along bottom of hillside for one mile ☐G☐, ignoring signposted footpath and (later) a bridleway to left. ⑰ When you are level with Hawkley away to the left, a gate on the left gives access to a field path, back to village. Turn left at road T-junction to reach the village green.

ON THE ROUTE
☐A☐ **Mabbutts Farm** Half-timbered, with a thatched roof, in a traditional landscape.
☐B☐ **View** over the Hampshire–Surrey borders.
☐C☐ **Selborne** Gilbert White, naturalist and author of *The Natural History and Antiquities of Selborne* (published 1789), was born in 1720 in the Vicarage. His home and death-place (1793), The Wakes, is now a museum to him and Captain Lawrence Oates, who accompanied Scott to the South Pole, 1911–12, and died on the return journey (*open* 11 to 5.30, last admission 5, daily mid-March to mid-October; weekends during rest of year). White's grave is signposted in the churchyard. Also in the village is a restorer of gypsy caravans and horse-drawn carts (workshop sometimes open weekends). National Trust owns 275 acres of nearby common, woodland and meadows.
☐D☐ In 1853 Gilbert White and his brother John cut this **zigzag path** to the top of Selborne Hanger.
☐E☐ The beech woods clinging to these escarpments are known as hangers. On top of **Selborne Hill** is a plateau with an area of old commonland. This is a fine example of a woodland habitat on the clay-capped Hampshire chalk, supporting a rich variety of woodland species. **View** from the top of the zigzag path over Selborne; 1½ miles east of the village is a farm on the site of an Augustinian priory.
☐F☐ **Noar Hill Nature Reserve** Chalk pits and scrub. The disturbed land is a good site for chalkland **flora** (including autumn gentian), which attracts a variety of **butterflies** such as marbled white and Duke of Burgundy.
☐G☐ This pleasant final section skirts the bottom of **Hawkley Hanger**, where there are more beech woods.

THE NEEDLES, TENNYSON DOWN AND THE YAR

A MAGNIFICENT coastal walk, memorable for its views and scenic diversity. The coastal sections include beach, woodland and scrub-covered cliffs. A descent to Alum Bay is followed by West High Down and Tennyson Down, a long grassy ridge with a variety of chalk-loving plants and sea views on three sides. The finale takes a level route inland along a former railway track along the River Yar (of botanical interest for its reed and marsh plants). The walk can be shortened by making it into a series of strolls; Freshwater Bay (serviced by buses) is a good starting-point for a there-and-back walk along Tennyson Down to the Needles. Route-finding is made quite easy by thorough signposting; all on clearly defined paths and tracks.

WALK DIRECTIONS

① Ⓐ From ferry terminal, with the sea on your right, cross bridge over River Yar. 400 yards later, where the road veers left, turn right on signposted coast path. Ⓑ ② Where the seawall ends, after 400 yards, and 200 yards before jetty, turn left up wooden steps (marked Fort Victoria) into woods and follow for 50 yards to a tarmac lane. Turn right along the lane and fork left after 100 yards along a track signposted to the coast path ③. Follow the track Ⓒ for 200 yards, then continue on path ahead (ignoring a track to the right).

④ After ½ mile the path climbs up steps and leaves woods, passing between fences to reach a road on the fringes of Colwell. Turn left on the road, then ¼ mile later turn right at a junction, signposted as footpath.

⑤ After 200 yards the road gives out. Continue past houses on signposted coast path on the left. After 200 yards emerge from between hedges. Unless it is low tide (in which case you can walk along the shore to pick up the seawall – see map) do not take the path on the right signposted coast path. Instead, continue straight on for ¼ mile to a road and turn right ⑥.

LENGTH 11 miles (17.5km), 5½ hours	returning to Totland by bus
DIFFICULTY 3	**OS MAPS** Landranger 196; Outdoor Leisure 29
START Yarmouth ferry terminal (train to Lymington for ferry to Yarmouth). *Or* start at Totland pier (point ⑦) and finish at Freshwater Bay,	**REFRESHMENTS** You will find a wide range at Yarmouth, Alum Bay and Freshwater Bay; there is also a café at the south end of Headon Warren (see map)

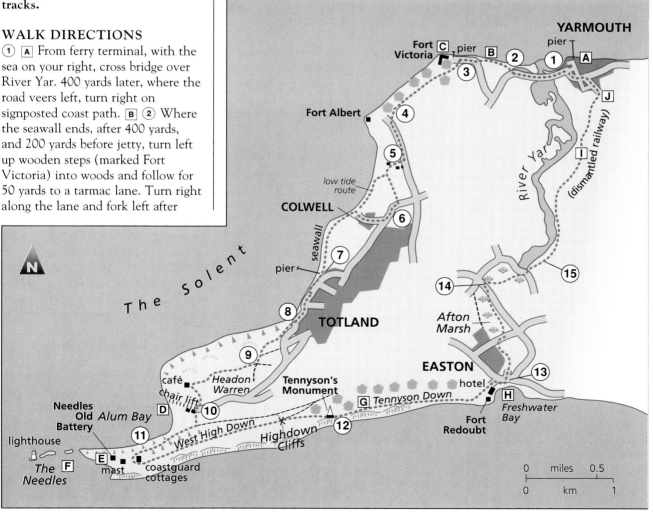

Follow the road for ¼ mile and turn right down Colwell Chine Road. Follow this to the end and turn left along the seawall for ½ mile to a pier ⑦. From the pier continue along seawall. After 300 yards, and just past Old Totland lifeboat house, take steep steps up on the left. Turn right at the top, and follow the road for 200 yards. ⑧ Where the road veers left take a path half right, signposted Alum Bay, to Headon Warren (you now follow the coast path markers until dropping to Alum Bay). After 400 yards emerge at open gorse heath-land; keep straight on uphill at the junction of paths (following coast path).

⑨ After 150 yards, just beyond where a path comes in sharp left, take the right fork and ¼ mile later keep right where left fork leads to summit. Continue past a bench on your left and follow the path on to the ridge to descend to Alum Bay. Before a bunker, take track on left for 200 yards passing pitch-and-putt course on the right. Pass through a gate and turn left to reach a road ⑩. Turn right on road and follow signs on road to Needles Headland.

Follow the surfaced track for 500 yards round the edge of the cliffs D, E, then ⑪ take the path half left up to West High Down. After 100 yards turn across a stile to emerge on a road, just below coastguards' cottages. Turn left on the road which curves left (or take detour to Needles viewpoint F via metalled track on the right). Between coastguards' cottages (left) and mast (right), head half right to a gate.

Proceed along the middle of the ridge G (path is undefined) for 1 mile to reach a gate. Turn half right up to Tennyson's monument (signposted Freshwater Bay). Beyond the monument keep close to cliffs ⑫. After ¾ mile leave Tennyson Down and follow a fence on the left down to a track. Turn left on the track, ignoring immediate right fork to Fort Redoubt. At the road turn right into Freshwater Bay H ⑬. After 75 yards turn left along Coastguard Lane. At the end of the lane continue on path straight on. Take kissing-gate and, 100 yard after

next kissing-gate, fork right and follow the path to a road.

Turn right along the road for 50 yards, then left just before a bridge on the path into Afton Marsh nature reserve. After 50 yards the path crosses to the other side of the stream and Yarmouth signs should be followed; in ½ mile you reach a road ⑭. Turn left along the road for 50 yards, then turn right on a path signposted Yarmouth. After 50 yards the path makes a right turn. ⑮ After ¼ mile cross a road and then follow the track of an old railway (with River Yar on left) all the way back to Yarmouth I, J. Turn left on the road, back to the starting-place.

ON THE ROUTE

A **Yarmouth** An attractive port dominated by the yachting on the Yar Estuary. On its seafront is one of a chain of castles built by Henry VIII as a defence against a French invasion; its design was based on the use of cannon (the first generation of English castles to be so built) and the tower was dispensed with. Nearby is a crenellated house with bogus gun-ports to fool the French.

B **View** On the mainland, Hurst Castle, another of Henry VIII's protective chain.

C Just off to the right is **Fort Victoria country park.** Two forts,

The lighthouse (1858) marking the Needles sends out a beam visible for 15 miles

Fort Victoria and Fort Albert, were built in 1840 as part of the defences of the Solent. Fort Albert, which is quite remarkably hideous, has been recently used for torpedo testing. A small **museum** at Fort Victoria gives the history.

D **View** of **Alum Bay**. The cliffs are brilliantly coloured, like those a few miles over to the west, on the mainland at Studland in Dorset (to which the Isle of Wight was once connected). The sands are coloured white by quartz, red by iron oxide, grey by carbonaceous remains and yellow by limonite. On the downs above Alum Bay is a **monument to Marconi**, who made experimental wireless transmissions here in 1897.

E Detour ahead to **the Needles Old Battery** (National Trust; *open to public*), part of the Solent defences, built in 1862. This is the best viewpoint for the Needles.

F **The Needles** Five chalk pinnacles, gradually being destroyed by the sea. A sixth, Lot's Wife, collapsed in 1764 with a crash that was heard on the mainland.

G **West High Down** and **Tennyson Down View** east and south-east over much of the island, including Bonchurch Down near Ventnor and Brighstone Forest; to the north you can see over the Solent into Hampshire. On Tennyson Down is a **monument** to the poet Alfred Lord Tennyson, who lived for 40 years at Farringford House in Freshwater.

H **Freshwater Bay** Residential and holiday area with a natural rock arch on its sandy beach and some caves on its eastern side. Artist George Morland stayed here in 1799 when the bay had an inn and nothing else; while at Yarmouth he was arrested by the Isle of Wight Defensibles because they thought his pen and ink drawing of a spaniel was a spy map.

I **Dismantled railway line** is the former Freshwater, Yarmouth and Newport railway, the only line to have been built in the western part of the island, although there was a dense network further east.

J The three-storey brick building on the right at the end of the dyke path is an old **tide-mill**.

THE DEVIL'S PUNCH BOWL AND GIBBET HILL

FOLLOWING the rim of the Devil's Punch Bowl, one of Surrey's most striking natural features, the route later emerges from woods into the open, with charming rural views; Thursley is the halfway point and the view from wooded Gibbet Hill the final climax. There is one ascent, near the end.

WALK DIRECTIONS

① Take the track to the left of Hillcrest Café, past toilets. Proceed on the level, around the top edge of the Devil's Punch Bowl (with back gardens away to the left), ignoring any descending forks to the right. ② After ½ mile, fork right by National

Trust sign for Highcombe (left is private to Packways), immediately avoiding a right descending fork; you are now following power lines. Just after going under the power

> **LENGTH** 6 miles (9.5km), 3 hours
> **DIFFICULTY** 2
> **START** National Trust car park, Hindhead, on north side of A3 at east end of village, immediately east of filling station and Devil's Punchbowl Hotel. Grid reference 890357
> **OS MAPS** Landranger 186; Pathfinder 1245 (SU 83/93)
> **REFRESHMENTS** Hotel and cafés in Hindhead; pub in Thursley

lines, take the rightmost of three paths by a wooden post with blue waymarker arrows.

This path leads out to a viewpoint and bench A; then take path just to the right of the memorial stone, and 50 yards later turn right on a broad path. ③ ⅓ mile later, keep straight on at cross-junction by a waymarker post where the main path bends sharp right. The path gradually descends, eventually leaving the woods and reaching a junction of lanes. Turn right here, soon passing to the right of a farm B and continuing on track between hedges, which soon descends to cross a footbridge, immediately after which ④ you take a signposted stile into field and turn left. Follow the edge of field, soon uphill to cross a stile, and follow the path between fence and hedge C until you reach a tarmacked lane.

Turn left on lane, then ⑤ after 30 yards take signposted driveway for Hedge Farm on left (or to cut out the following section across fields, continue along the lane to Thursley church at ⑦). Almost immediately fork right on to path between fences (waymarked by yellow arrow), soon enter field by stile and proceed along left edge of it and next two fields.

At the end of the third field, cross stile on left and follow enclosed path, which bends right by a house and soon joins the lane. Continue forward along lane, then ⑥ turn right after 100 yards, opposite Smallbrook, taking the signposted gate. Cross the field to a stile (which soon comes into view), then follow

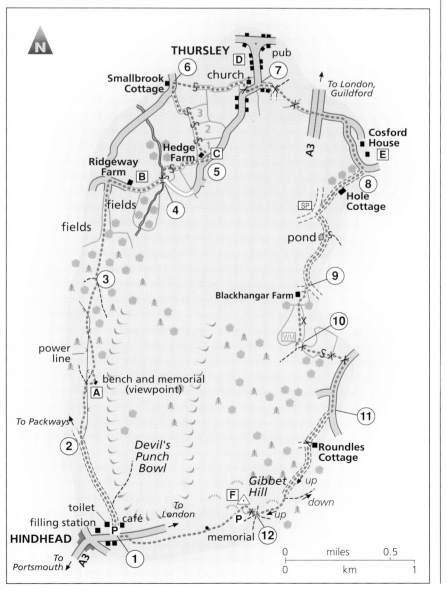

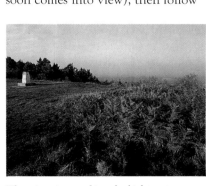

The trig point marking the highest spot on Gibbet Hill

path between fences to Thursley church ⒟.

In the churchyard, keep to the right of the church, turn left on lane then 50 yards later ⑦, where the lane bends left, keep forward on track (signposted Footpath) (or continue on lane to centre of Thursley; turn right at T-junction to reach pub). Where the track bends right (by Rack Close), take gate into field ahead and bear half right across field (blue arrow on top of gatepost indicates the direction), eventually joining end of hedgerow away to your right, then beyond the gate go forward on path to reach A3. Cross the road and take the lane opposite, which soon bends right (ahead is private, to Cosford House) ⒠.

⑧ ¼ mile later, where lane bends left, take signposted track on right. This soon passes Hole Cottage away to your left and later reaches a staggered cross-junction by a signpost: turn left here for Upper Valley Farm (avoid a driveway on right 50 yards later). The track soon passes a small pond on your right (ignore stile on left just after), then ⑨ ¼ mile later fork right towards Blackhangar Farm. Just after crossing the stream, and just before the farm itself, take stile on left and follow to top of field, close to garden fence, to find a stile into woods, beyond which you emerge into a field.

Follow left (bottom) edge of field, along power lines, until yellow waymarker arrow on post (near to end of field) points left into next field, which you cross to a gate beside a stile into woodland ⑩. Follow woodland path: it is clear at the beginning, but may be obscured later by fallen branches (but a ramshackle fence on your right is a useful waymarker); on reaching the corner of fence, cross slab footbridge on left, go over stile and follow left edge of woods (with field on left) until you cross a stile into field. Continue in the same direction along edge of field to a gate and stile

in the corner, then follow woodland track to road. Turn right on road, then keep left at next junction, along cul-de-sac to High Button. ⑪ 120 yards later, fork right on to track (wooded Gibbet Hill, which you will soon ascend, is ahead). Follow this track to reach corner of driveway, then go forward past Roundles Cottage, on ascending track.

After ¼ mile, bear right at oblique T-junction (still ascending).

⑫ Reach 7-way path junction, bear half right (through barrier) and go to trig point (summit pillar) on top of Gibbet Hill ⒡. Turn left at the trig point (in the Petersfield direction, as marked on top of the trig point itself) towards a low wooden fence enclosing car park and follow the broad track on right side of car park; ignore minor forks. Soon the A3 is audible down to right. Follow the track back to Hindhead, emerging on A3 opposite National Trust car park.

ON THE ROUTE

⒜ **View** over the **Devil's Punch Bowl**, a huge natural amphitheatre surrounded by mixed woods (Scots pines, birch, oak and others) and patches of heathland (bracken, gorse and heather) on the elevated sandy ground.

⒝ **Ridgeway Farm**, a fine example of the vernacular style, with a steeply sloping roof, and part timber construction; the first of a number of old farmhouses and cottages to look out for on this walk; others include **Smallbrook**, **Hole Cottage** and **Blackhangar Farm.**

⒞ The sudden emergence from woodland into the open is marked by good **views** north to the Hog's Back ridge.

⒟ **Thursley** Unspoilt and rural, with cottages scattered around the central green and its back lane. The **church** has an unusual wooden structure beneath the belfry in its centre (installed in Henry VIII's

time), a font thought to be of Saxon origin, and England's only surviving wooden Saxon windows. In the churchyard, by the war memorial cross, is a tombstone and epitaph to an unknown sailor murdered in 1786 on Hindhead Common by three men he encountered on his way on foot from London to Portsmouth.

⒠ **Cosford House**, with its artificial lakes, can be seen down to the left. There follows a particularly pleasant section of the walk, with a mixture of woods and views into more open country.

⒡ **Gibbet Hill** (894ft, the second highest hill in Surrey, after Leith Hill). Extensive **view** from the heathy summit over a complex landscape of rolling woodland, heath and distant hills, north over the Devil's Punch Bowl and towards the Hog's Back, and south over the broad, wooded vale of the Sussex Weald. Here stood the gibbet from which the three murderers of the sailor buried in Thursley churchyard (see above) were hanged; their bodies were kept hanging for years afterwards as a warning to others. A memorial stone to the incident is seen on the right between the trig point and the return to Hindhead (with a curse inscribed on the back against anyone who removes the stone). The broad track followed back to Hindhead is the old Portsmouth road, the stagecoach and packhorse route over the top of Gibbet Hill towards Petersfield.

The Devil's Punch Bowl, one of Surrey's most striking natural features

St Martha's Hill

A SHORT but varied walk, on a section of wooded greensand escarpment above the Tilling Bourne Valley. Views open out at the summit by St Martha's Chapel, before a descent to mill-ponds. Mostly on defined paths and tracks, but directions should be followed carefully; there is one steep climb, just after ④.

LENGTH 5 miles (8km), 2½ hours
DIFFICULTY 2
START Chilworth railway station (east end of Chilworth on A248), 4 miles east of Guildford. Park by phone-box outside station or along main road. Grid reference 031473
OS MAPS Landranger 186; Pathfinder 1226 (TQ 04/14)
REFRESHMENTS Percy Arms, Chilworth

WALK DIRECTIONS

① Ⓐ From the phone-box by the station make your way to main road ahead and turn left along it, passing the Percy Arms and then a primary school on your right. Immediately after the primary school, turn right on path (signposted No Cycling, No Horses) leading to a footbridge in woods ②. After the footbridge turn left at junction of paths and follow

to road. Turn right on road, then left after 100 yards by the corner of road on a signposted footpath (next to Halfpenny Lane sign) leading up between fences.

③ At the top, turn left on road and, after 20 yards, where road bends right, pass through gate ahead to follow track along left (bottom) side of field. After 400 yards it passes a barn; the track then rises between banks and descends. Just before it is about to ascend again (400 yards after barn), cross the stile on the right to follow a path leading to the projecting left-hand corner of wood ahead.

④ Cross stile into wood, and then climb steeply up, to reach a T-junction of earthy paths after 30 yards. Here keep straight on up (very steep) on grassy area between bushes. At the top bear half right to edge of woods, and turn right (with woods on left) along grassy track leading between posts. ⑤ After 100 yards ignore gate on left, leading into woods, but continue forward on track which enters woods by next gate/stile. Avoid side turns; proceed to the road ⑥.

Left on road and, after 30 yards (just after house on right), right on to track signposted North Downs Way. Avoid side turns and follow

A public footpath along the Tilling Bourne Valley

the path for ½ mile uphill to St Martha's Chapel ⑦ Ⓑ. Pass through the churchyard and leave by the gate on other side to descend on path with wooden railings. After 400 yards avoid North Downs Way, which forks off to left, but continue forward, soon passing a concrete pill-box on left.

⑧ 200 yards after pill-box look out for a notice-board displaying map on right of path; 10 yards beyond this, fork half right on a path leading downhill. After 50 yards turn right at T-junction of paths and descend steeply through

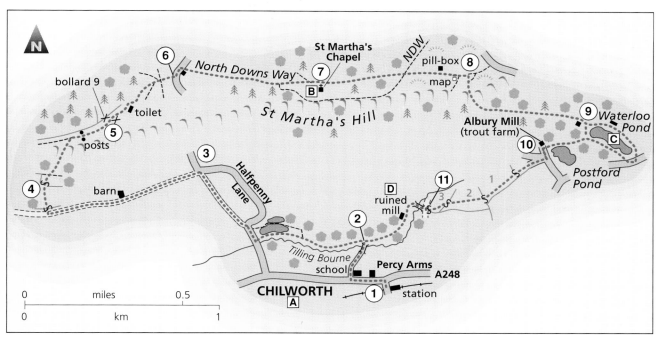

woods, with water visible away to right in later stages. After ½ mile, pass house at bottom of slope and reach lake ahead [c] [9]. Turn right to pass the end of lake and turn right at end (or, if you prefer, walk round the lake by continuing forward on path which leads through the garden of a house, then following the drive to road; turn right and immediately right again on signposted path leading along other side of lake).

Follow track through woods past an old water-mill on your right – now a trout farm – to reach the lane in front of the water-mill [10]. Turn left on lane and then immediately right on a signposted footpath leading alongside fence to stile.

Follow left edge of first field to next stile; in second field proceed with the stream on your left to next stile.

In the third field continue forward to a stile leading on to track [11]. Turn right on track to cross the brook, just after which you turn on the path alongside it. The brook is canalised and the remains of a lock and mill buildings are visible [D]; after passing these, the path forks half right away from the brook and shortly the footbridge you crossed at the beginning of walk is visible on left. Cross it and follow the path back.

ON THE ROUTE

[A] **Chilworth** Banknotes were produced here from the 16th century until recently.

[B] **St Martha's Chapel** The solitary parish **church** of Chilworth, which looks out over much of the best countryside in Surrey. The original 12th-century building was owned by the Prior of Newark from 1262, but it was later ruined. It was virtually rebuilt in 1848 in striking Norman style, using the old materials. Its dedication is obscure, either to St Martha, who reputedly came here with Joseph of Arimathea, or as a corruption of St Martyr's – an old legend tells of a massacre of Christians on this hill.

[C] The first of two **mill-ponds**.

[D] The shell of a **gunpowder mill**, standing among the alders and willows on the banks of the Tilling Bourne. In the 17th century this was an important area for manufacturing gunpowder; an ordnance factory existed here in the First World War. The bridge crossed at the start and end of the walk was originally for a railway that served the works.

St Martha's Chapel lies in solitary splendour overlooking some wonderful Surrey countryside

RANMORE COMMON AND DENBIES HILLSIDE

A peaceful and unspoilt tract of countryside within London's Green Belt. The going is easy and route-finding is straightforward, with well-defined paths and few junctions. Most of the walk is in woodland with a glorious opening-out at the end, along the escarpment of the North Downs, popular for kite-flying. This is a good walk to finish with a picnic: there is free access to the National Trust-owned field by the car park at the start and end of the route.

LENGTH 3½ miles (5.5km), 1½ hours
DIFFICULTY 1
START Denbies Hillside National Trust car park (pay and display for non-members), on Ranmore Common. From A24/A25 Deepdene roundabout in Dorking, take A24 north towards Leatherhead, then left opposite station signposted for Guildford/Business Park on A2033 (A25); at next roundabout go straight on (for Ranmore and Effingham), then right at next T-junction (for Ranmore and Effingham). After 1 mile, ignore right turn for Bookham and Westhumble; car park is on left 130 yards later, just after flint house on left.
Grid reference 143503
OS MAPS Landranger 187; Pathfinder 1206 (TQ 05/15)
REFRESHMENTS Ice-cream van in car park at start during summer weekends (and some weekdays); in winter this is replaced by a hot dog van

WALK DIRECTIONS

① Turn right out of cark park, along the road towards Dorking. After 130 yards take left turn, signposted to Bookham and Westhumble. Go past a church Ⓐ, then 50 yards later, opposite gabled flint house, ② turn left on a bridleway and follow this through the woodlands of Ranmore Common Ⓑ. (After ½ mile, ignore two minor turnings joining from the right, within 100 yards of each other.) On emerging into fields, the track continues (slightly to left) downhill between fences; 150 yards later, ignore gate on left by waymarks, but carry on between fences. Soon after, and ③ 50 yards before Bagden farmhouse, take a waymarked gate (in front of low barn) on your left. Beyond the farm, the path enters a field and follows the bottom of a valley. At the end of the field, go through a gate and turn left uphill to Tanner's Hatch Youth Hostel. Pass the small

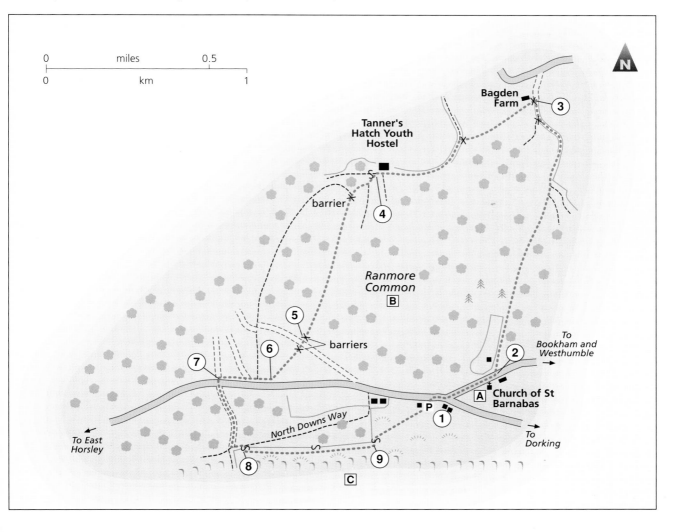

gateway to the youth hostel on the right; just 5 yards later, ignore a path ascending to the left, but ④ 20 yards later fork left (where path ahead crosses a stile), uphill on a broad path; 20 yards further, fork right (waymarked with blue arrow) on the more level path. Follow this for 130 yards, then fork left through a barrier (marked Footpath Only). This path rises gently for ½ mile. ⑤ Go forward, by barrier, over cross-track, and follow path ahead to a road ⑥. Turn right on a path on near side of road; follow this for 220 yards (three tracks join the road from the right during the distance). ⑦ Cross road (opposite the third track passed on the right) and take a stony track opposite (there were No

Parking signs here when the walk was inspected). Follow this until the North Downs Way (the first path junction), marked with acorn waymarks and barriers, crosses; turn left on the North Downs Way, but in 30 yards ⑧ take a stile on right and follow path along top of a grassy slope [c]. Ignore the next stile on left into woodland. ⑨ Where the woods on left end, take a stile into field (Steer's Field, National Trust) and proceed to a gate beside a stile and into Denbies Hillside car park.

ON THE ROUTE

[A] **St Barnabas Church, Ranmore**
A spectacular Victorian church of 1859, designed by Sir George

A huge variety of butterflies can be found on these chalklands

Gilbert Scott, perhaps best known for the Albert Memorial (1863) and St Pancras Station (1865). The soaring octagonal tower, capped by a copper weather-vane, is a prominent landmark. The building is known as the Church on the North Downs.
[B] **Ranmore Common** Some 470 acres of woodland, owned by the National Trust and with free access along its paths and tracks, giving excellent opportunities for seeing wild deer. It is bounded to the south by the Polesden Lacey estate.
[C] **The North Downs** The National Trust owns five miles of chalk downs here, preserved as an important habitat. Chalkland flora such as bee orchids proliferate. This in turn attracts butterflies: over 40 species have been spotted here, including the marbled white, chalkhill blue, Adonis blue and green hair-streak. The **view** covers much of the Weald, with Dorking prominent to the fore. To the right are the Surrey upper greensand hills; in a notch in the skyline can be seen Leith Hill Tower, on the highest hill in South-East England. Leith Hill itself is 965 feet, but the tower takes it above the 1,000-foot mark, it is another excellent viewpoint and recommended area for walks. The ancient **Pilgrims' Way**, which led from Winchester to the shrine of St Thomas à Becket at Canterbury, follows the North Downs escarpment just below the modern North Downs Way.

A path winding its way over the North Downs of Surrey towards Dorking

RICHMOND AND HAM

EXPLORES Richmond's wealth of Georgian (and earlier) streets and follows the edge of Richmond Park where it slopes abruptly towards the Thames, whose towpath provides the return route.

WALK DIRECTIONS

① Turn left out of the station, along The Quadrant; keep right at the junction with The Square (ignoring left fork signposted to registry office), then soon turn left into Church Court by the signpost to Parish Church. Keep to left of church, cross main road and take Halford Road opposite. Turn right at T-junction, along The Vineyard A ;

keep straight on past the church where road markings indicate compulsory left turn for traffic, then turn left into Hill Rise (which becomes Richmond Hill; soon a walkway to right of pavement gives excellent views B).

Follow up to pass through the gates of Richmond Park, just beyond Star and Garter Home. ② Inside the park, take path to right of traffic roundabout, along top of slope, walking parallel to road; for the best views, drop down and follow the bottom of the slope C . Soon go through deer-gate into garden, taking any of several paths leading past Pembroke Lodge on your left

LENGTH   5 miles (8km), 2½ hours
Extension to Isabella Plantation adds
1½ miles (¾ hour)
DIFFICULTY   1
START   Richmond station (mainline
and District line); car parks in town
centre; or park in Richmond Hill or at
Pembroke Lodge car park in
Richmond Park
REFRESHMENTS   Full range in
Richmond; café in Pembroke Lodge
in Richmond Park; pubs in Ham and
along the river at Richmond

D , then exit by deer-gate; continue along top of slope.

③ Eventually, near the road junction and signpost, a pond and Ham Gate (a prominent large white lodge) are visible down on right. *For short walk* bear downhill on any path to reach these, and pick up walk directions at ⑥. *For extension further into Richmond Park* proceed to road junction, and take track opposite signposted Pen Ponds (any 'no admittance' signs refer to vehicles). Ignore side-turns (but a detour right after 200 yards to the Isabella Plantation E is recommended) and follow ¾ mile to reach road by car

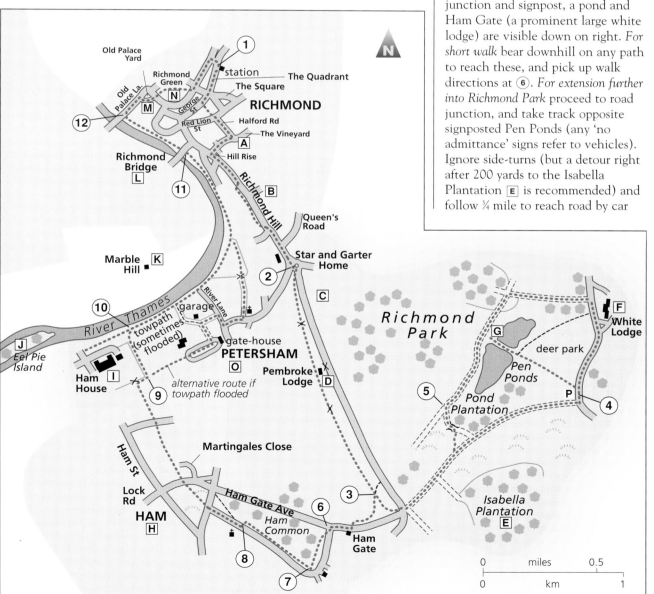

park ④. Turn left, up to White Lodge F, at which you turn left on a grassy track to Pen Ponds.

Take the causeway between the two ponds G; turn left on the far side. Ignore side-turns, and 600 yards later ⑤ join a broad horse track, which crosses a tiny brick bridge over channel; immediately after, bear right and soon join the track you were on earlier. Follow this back to road junction, and take road opposite to Ham Gate.

⑥ Just after Ham Gate, turn left into Church Road: find the path running just inside woods and parallel to road (or you can follow the road, keeping right along it at its next corner). ⑦ Where pillars for driveway to Wilmer House are still visible away to left, turn right, still inside woods and parallel with road; houses are visible away to left. ⑧ When you come level with the church, either follow the road or take any of several paths leading half right through woods; both routes soon lead to a large green flanked by houses (Ham village) H.

Follow the right edge of the green; 100 yards after Martingales Close (on right) take path on right leading towards Ham House. In front of Ham House gates I, turn right, then ⑨ left at corner of wall towards the river. ⑩ Join the towpath and then turn right J. At high tide the towpath may be flooded, in which case see below.

Follow towpath K beyond Richmond Bridge ⑪ L, then just before next bridge ⑫ turn right on road by sign for White Swan pub. Just after pub turn right into Old Palace Yard M, exit via archway, then cross Richmond Green N, aiming for Richmond Theatre (with prominent green copper domes). Continue past the theatre, over railway, then take signposted path on right into town centre, emerging opposite the station. *If river towpath is flooded* return to corner of wall at ⑨, turn left on long straight path to gatehouse, 50 yards before which you cross the school driveway on left and take track opposite. 200 yards later, turn right on path between fences, to reach River Lane in Petersham, where you turn right to join the main road. Turn left along

main road for 200 yards through Petersham village O, then left on path signposted to St Peter's church. Beyond the church continue forward by the remains of old lamp-post, on path. After crossing field, path reaches river, where you turn right and resume walk directions at ⑪.

ON THE ROUTE

A **The Vineyard** Its name is probably historically accurate; now this is a quiet side street with several good 17th-, 18th- and 19th-century houses and two sets of 19th-century almshouses.

B **Richmond Hill** The Richmond end of the hill has a pocket-handkerchief triangular village green and some fine 18th-century houses. The Queen's Terrace is a 17th-century feature; there is a grand prospect of Windsor, the Thames, the park, London airport and more. Numerous artists and poets, including Turner, have been attracted to record the view. No 116 (Downe House) was once leased to playwright Sheridan; by the junction with Nightingale Lane is Wick House, once the home of Joshua Reynolds.

C **Richmond Park** (note: *closes before dusk*). An area of 2,358 acres, enclosed in 1635 by Charles I as a hunting park, and encompassed by a 10-mile wall. Public access was gained in the 18th century after a vigorous campaign by brewer John Lewis, and remains one of London's largest semi-untamed expanses, with rough pasture, woodlands and ponds. Do not approach the deer, especially in summer.

D **Pembroke Lodge**, the 18th-century former home of Bertrand Russell, is now run as a refreshment room; fine Wedgwood ceilings, extensive view from tables outside.

E **Isabella Plantation** Fine azaleas and heathers in a plantation crossed by an attractive stream.

F Porticoed **White Lodge** is a splendid villa with its specially created vista down a broad ride; built in 1729 as a rural retreat; birthplace of Edward VIII in 1894, it now houses the Royal Ballet School.

G After you cross the causeway between Pen Ponds a surprise view appears of the **British Telecom Tower.**

H **Ham** Remains rural in feel, with mainly 18th- and 19th-century houses scattered around its large green, and a pond at its far end.

I **Ham House** (gardens *open* daily 10 to 6, free; **house** Tuesday to Sunday, 11 to 5). Jacobean mansion giving outstanding insight into fashionable living of the period.

J **The Thames** Seen first is **Eel Pie Island**, so called because a now demolished hotel on it used to sell eel pies to visitors.

K **Marble Hill**, a stucco Palladian mansion of 1729, is seen on the other side of the river.

L **Richmond Bridge** An elegant structure built in 1777 of Portland stone; now London's oldest bridge; **Heron Square** (1986), immediately after the bridge is Quinlan Terry's controversial neo-classical creation; loathed by some post-modernists as shameless pastiche, venerated by others for its period detail, variety and sensitive use of materials.

M **Old Palace** The gate-house and various brickwork now incorporated into adjacent houses are remains of the palace built by Henry VII, former Duke of Richmond (the Yorkshire town giving its name to this one), on the site of the priory of Shene, first occupied by Henry I in 1125. Edward III, Henry VII and Elizabeth I all died here. Much of the palace's destruction was wrought by Cromwell's men.

N **Richmond Green** A former knights' jousting ground belonging to the palace, and now a handsome green tucked round the back of Richmond's main thoroughfares. It is worth taking in each side, for the quality of its predominantly 17th- and 18th-century houses is exceptional. The **theatre** (built 1899) is a capricious piece of late Victoriana, with two mock burning torches at the entrance.

O **Petersham** has some outstanding houses, including 16th-century Montrose House with superb wrought-iron gates. **St Peter's church** is a Saxon foundation, rebuilt 1266 and altered every century since the 16th. Internally it is very much early 19th century in appearance, with late 18th-century box-pews. The gate-house near the school is 1898 mock-Jacobean.

PARHAM PARK AND AMBERLEY WILD BROOKS

THREE very different landscapes in the space of a few miles are on offer in this walk – a deer park, marshy levels and the chalk ridge of the South Downs, with an exceptionally picturesque village halfway round and a finely sited castle. Easy route-finding; Amberley Wild Brooks, between ⑦ and ⑧, may be boggy.

WALK DIRECTIONS

① With Crown Inn on your right, follow A283 out of Cootham and away from Storrington. After 300 yards where the road bends right go forward on estate drive by signs for Parham House (note you are allowed to walk on the path to Rackham even when house is closed to the public) Ⓐ.

Proceed past lodge, ignore sharp left turn shortly after, but ② 100

yards later fork right on grassy path signposted to Rackham and proceed with the fence on your right until reaching junction of tarmacked estate drives: keep forward, leaving estate at the lodge ½ mile later. Turn left on road, and keep straight on at next road junction (signposted Amberley).

③ 100 yards later (where the woods on your right end), turn right by the buildings, on a broad track leading past Pine Cottage and skirting the edge of woods Ⓑ. Soon avoid the footbridge on your left, but bear right (signposted), still along edge of woods, avoiding a right turn 100 yards later; shortly

LENGTH   9 miles (14.5km), 4 hours
DIFFICULTY   2–3
START   Crown Inn, Cootham (hamlet is not named on all road maps), on A283 1 mile west of Storrington, and ½ mile west of junction of A283 and B2139; roadside parking in nearby cul-de-sacs off main road. Grid reference 074145
By train Amberley. Walk down station approach road, turn right along B2139, then next right into

High Titton (South Downs Way). ⅓ mile later turn right at junction near Highdown (house); start walk directions at ⑨.

OS MAPS   Landranger 197; Pathfinder 1287 (TQ 01/11)
REFRESHMENTS   Pub at Cootham; pub and shop at Amberley; pub and tea-room at Amberley station (off main route, but useful for those arriving by train); tea-room at Parham House (when house is open)

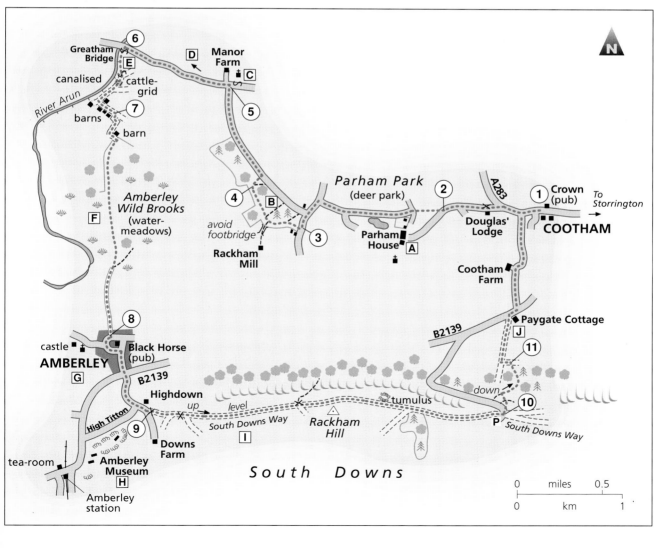

woodland appears on left of track for a while before being replaced by fields. ④ Just as the woods recommence on your left, bear right by a signpost (forking left after 30 yards). Join the tarmacked lane, and turn left along it.

⑤ After ½ mile you reach a T-junction with Greatham church C ahead and slightly to the right: turn left D. ⑥ After ¼ mile, immediately before the river bridge E, take the stile on left and walk along raised grassy dyke alongside river. Shortly after next stile, the dyke ends: bear right (signposted), soon joining farm track and keep right along it, with river down to right. After track crosses cattlegrid, ignore sharp left turn but proceed to reach modern house, where track bends left (signposted; ahead is private), and passes barns on your right, shortly after which ⑦ you fork right as signposted (ahead is private) and follow a snaking track to a wooden barn, where a signpost points left along the edge of a field.

In next field turn right (again signposted), with channel on right and maintain the same direction (soon crossing small footbridges) over Amberley Wild Brooks F for 1 mile until entering Amberley village. ⑧ Turn right at T-junction with village street G (or left for pub), then left at next T-junction (or right for church and castle), then right at next T-junction. Soon cross B2139 and take ascending lane opposite.

¼ mile later bear left at junction by Highdown (house) H (or turn right to return to station), then ⑨ 75 yards later take the rising path on left signposted South Downs Way. Follow South Downs Way signposts for 2 miles I: the route ascends between fences at first, then just after a track coming in sharp right it proceeds uphill with fence on left; 1 mile later a trig point (summit pillar) is seen close to the right, then 1 mile later you reach car park and end of road on your left ⑩.

Turn left on the road, immediately leaving it for a signposted bridleway on right, which descends through bushes (ignore left fork after 30 yards): descend steadily, soon through trees to bottom of slope where ⑪ you turn left at T-junction with chalky track (signposted); the track then bends right, soon reaching the road J. Turn right on road, then immediately left on minor road, and follow this to A283 near Cootham, where you turn right to return to Crown Inn or left to continue the walk if you started elsewhere.

ON THE ROUTE

A **Parham House** (*open* bank hols, Easter Sun to first Sun in Oct; Sun, Wed, Thur) In a fine site under the South Downs. The interior contains a great hall and a long gallery running the length of the house; notable furniture and portraits. Just south of the house, the 16th-century church is worth a look: Gothicised in the 1820s, it has box pews and an unusual 14th-century font.

B **Rackham Plantation** Fine woods despite the 1987 storm, with Scots pines, silver birch, some gorse.

C **Greatham church** No road leads to the restored Norman building. Inside is simple, with harmonium and oil lamps, a 17th-century communion rail, and an early 19th-century pulpit. Adjacent is the manor house, dated 1672.

D Half right shortly after passing a telephone-box, the grey-roofed farm whose farmhouse was the refectory for **Hardham Priory** (the remains of an Augustinian foundation) is visible in the middle distance. By it is the ruined chapter house.

E **Greatham Bridge** has a quaint piecemeal appearance, with ten stone arches of varying sizes and a more recent iron extension on the

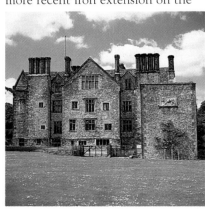

Parham House, an Elizabethan mansion set in a deer park, with a lake close by

near side. The River Arun is canalised at this point.

F **Amberley Wild Brooks** is an area of water-meadows (probably a shallow lake in medieval times, based on the principle of flooding meadows with a system of sluices so that the organic silt from the river would enrich the soil). Outstanding for birdlife: Bewick's swan, pintail, shoveller, teal and wigeon; and marsh-loving wild flowers. Among the many who have admired the quiet beauty of this place was composer John Ireland, who named a piano piece after it.

G **Amberley** A remarkably unspoilt village scattered around a rough square of lanes, all half-timbered or stone and much of it under thatch. Vestiges of a wall-painting in the **church**, which is most notable for its Norman work, and a huge chancel arch with palm-tree ornamentation; an iron hour-glass stand above the pulpit is a rarity. In a corner of the churchyard, a peep-hole in St Richard's Gate gives a view of Amberley **castle**. Continue down the lane by the church to the end of the village for close-ups of the castle's formidable curtain wall, towering above the water-meadows. It was once the home of the Bishop of Chichester; a licence to crenellate (or to fortify) was given in 1379. It has a large 16th-century house inside, half-timbered, with lovely gardens.

H **Amberley Museum** (*open* Easter to end October, 10 to 6 daily, last admission at 5) is between Highdown and Amberley station (entrance is at the latter). Visiting this as part of the walk would make a very long day, but there is a view over most of the site from High Titton, the lane to your right. Working displays, reconstructions, railway, history of chalk extraction and much more.

I **South Downs Way** After the ascent, there is an easy ridge section with views on both sides. As with most of the South Downs, there are numerous prehistoric antiquities on the way; one of the more visible is a grassy **burial mound** on the left by a small group of trees, shortly before woodland ahead is reached.

J **Old tollhouse** (Paygate Cottage) is on right as you reach the road.

FRISTON AND THE SEVEN SISTERS

ONE of the most attractive stretches of coastal scenery in South-East England, with a section of mixed woodland in Friston Forest and two smart, pretty villages. Some of the up and down along the cliffs can be omitted by taking the shorter route. This walk is recommended for wild flowers in spring. Route-finding is moderately easy, mostly on defined paths and tracks; keep well clear of the crumbly cliff edge.

WALK DIRECTIONS

① Leave the car park and turn right along the A259 for 60 yards Ⓐ. At bus stop, cross the road on to a track between buildings, cross a stile and ascend a steep grassy field straight ahead to a flint wall. Cross the wall and proceed into Friston Forest along path signposted West Dean. Descend steps to village Ⓑ ②.

At the corner of tarmac lane turn right and follow lane round past houses and then into Friston Forest. (Just before Friston Forest sign, lane on left leads 100 yards to church and rectory.) Keep forward to follow signs to Friston. ③ Bear right at fork just after the second white house. Continue straight along broad stony track, ignoring side turnings. After ¼ mile, where main track swings left, continue forward on grassy track. ④ After ¼ mile, track meets tarmac lane at T-junction with private drive opposite. Turn left and follow the lane which bends round to right. 40 yards before second vehicle passing-point, take a gate in wall on right to enter a field. Bear half left across the field and pass through a small gate in wall on the far side ⑤. Cross the lane and go over a stile into next field, making for the top far left corner. Cross stile and enter

wood. Emerge on to A259 at Friston ⑥. Cross A259, go down the lane opposite, signposted Crowlink.

For shorter walk Follow the lane through NT car park then to a cluster of houses at Crowlink. Carry

LENGTH	*Full walk* 7½ miles (12km), 4 hours
DIFFICULTY	3
	Shorter walk 6½ miles (10.5km), 3 hours
DIFFICULTY	2–3
START	Seven Sisters Country Park (car park; free) at Exceat on A259, 6 miles west of Eastbourne and 2 miles east of Seaford. Grid reference 518995
OS MAPS	Landranger 199; Pathfinder 1324 (TV 49/59/69)
REFRESHMENTS	Tiger Inn, East Dean; cafés at Seven Sisters Country Park and Birling Gap

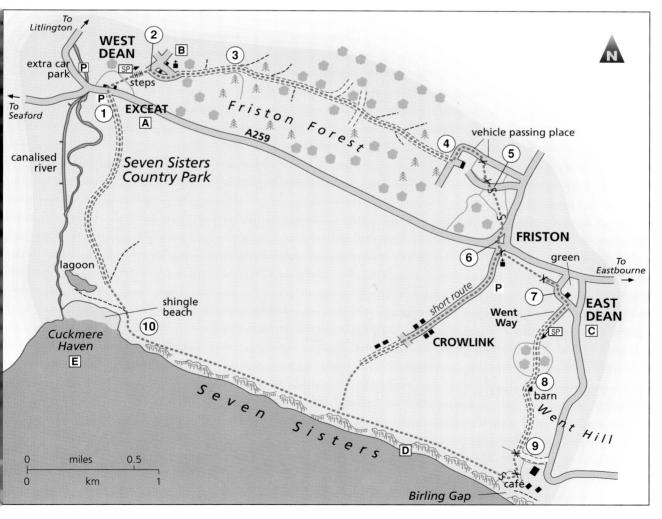

The common spotted orchid; other flora to spot along the cliffs include gentians and thistles

straight on, ignoring turning on the right signposted Crowlink House. The lane becomes a track and then, just beyond last house, a grassy footpath which leads on to path along the Seven Sisters D. Turn right here and continue directions from ⑩.

For full walk Follow lane for 40 yards, then enter the churchyard on left. Proceed through the churchyard and leave by the far right corner. Walk downhill to East Dean through a grassy combe. Go through gate on to surfaced lane. At T-junction turn right and in a few yards reach the village green C. ⑦ (To visit the church, fork left into Lower Street.)

Fork right into Went Way. At the end of the lane proceed straight on through a gate on to path signposted Birling Gap. At corner of garden go half left, ignoring cross-track. Ascend through a wood and emerge on to open downland (Went Hill) ⑧. Make for a prominent small barn. Head for prominent slightly sunken track to your right, which descends gradually towards sea. ⑨ When the track bends sharply to the left after ⅓ mile, proceed straight on through a gate to gate/stile. Cross the stile and bear half right to another gate. Go through this gate and turn right; you are now back on the path along the Seven Sisters D. Follow the coast for 2 miles.

⑩ When descending from last

'Sister' (above Cuckmere Haven E) bear half right downhill (signposted Exceat) and make for a prominent wide grassy track, later joining concrete track back to Exceat and the car park.

ON THE ROUTE

A **Exceat** Formerly a sizeable village, hit hard by the Black Death. The village now has an **Interpretation Centre** for the Seven Sisters Country Park.

B **West Dean** By the fine Norman **church** is the 13th-century **rectory**, one of the oldest continually inhabited houses in Britain. King Alfred is thought to have had a manor house here, quite possibly at the ruined house by the dovecote in the village centre.

C **East Dean** Attractive flint-walled cottages surround the village green; nearby is the simple Norman church with its Saxon tower.

D **Seven Sisters** A series of seven chalk spurs with dry valleys between, abruptly cut off to form sheer cliffs, just west of the culmination of the South Downs at Beachy Head. From here to Cuckmere Haven is good for **bird-watching.** Viper's Bugloss, a tall blue and pink flower, is a common sight on the cliffs, and is one of the most spectacular species of chalkland flora.

E **Cuckmere Haven** Near the river mouth a **Roman burial ground** and **mammoth's tusk** have been found. The lagoon marshland, alluvial grassland and shingle bank are a rich habitat for **wildlife** and **flora.** During the Second World War, the beach was lit up at night as a dummy town to trick enemy bombers and confuse them into thinking they were flying over Seaford.

Looking eastwards from the shingle of Cuckmere Haven along the magnificent Seven Sisters towards Beachy Head

LULLINGTON HEATH AND THE LONG MAN OF WILMINGTON

ONE of the finest short walks in the South Downs, leading out of picturesque Alfriston, along the Cuckmere River and up on to the Downs, later skirting their base and passing an extraordinary hill-carving. Route-finding is easy.

WALK DIRECTIONS

① Ⓐ Start in the main street in Alfriston with the George Inn on your left, and follow the street for 30 yards, then (just after Congregational Church on left) take a path on the left signposted to the church; this leads between walls; keep forward between walls where another path leads to the church and Clergy House to the right, and cross the bridge over the Cuckmere River. Turn right on the other side (this is the South Downs Way, marked with acorn motifs) and follow the path along the river for ¾ mile Ⓑ. ② After passing Litlington church, away to your left, and 50 yards before the next bridge over the river, turn left on a tarmacked path, leaving river to reach Litlington. Turn left along the village street. ③ Just after passing the church, take a track on the right signposted Jevington, and immediately bear left as signposted in the farmyard (ahead leads up to a house); this track almost immediately bends right and rises gently Ⓒ. ④ After ½ mile, keep

LENGTH 4 miles (6.5km), 3 hours	foot; limited roadside parking near
DIFFICULTY 1–2	the pub; head towards church and
START Alfriston (2 miles south of	start walk at ③. Grid reference
A27 Lewes–Eastbourne road); pay	524016
and display car park. Grid reference	**OS MAPS** Landranger 199;
521031	Pathfinder 1324 (TV 49/59/69)
Alternatively start at Litlington	**REFRESHMENTS** Pubs and tea-rooms
(¾ mile south-east), which adds the	in Alfriston; pub and tea-garden in
pleasure of arriving in Alfriston on	Litlington

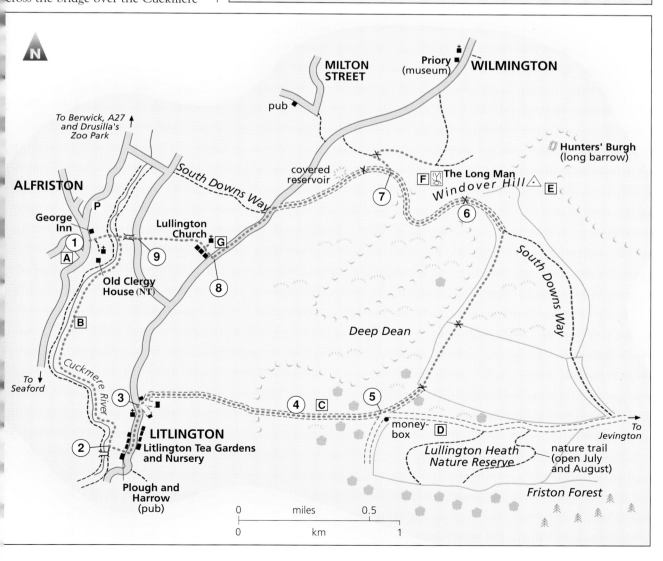

straight on, ignoring sharp left turn (downhill) but keep ascending. ⑤ ½ mile later turn left at track junction (signposted Long Man) by Lullington Heath Nature Reserve sign and a stone money-box D. Beyond the next gate (where you leave the nature reserve), the path continues in the same direction across farmland, with a steep slope down on your left, to the next gate; continue forward, alongside fence on left. As the path and fence curve left above the head of a valley, a well-defined track begins (you are now on part of the long-distance South Downs Way, waymarked with acorn motifs). ⑥ E Beyond the next gate (at the summit of Windover Hill), the track bears further to the left, then later swings right downhill. ⑦ ¼ mile later, where a fence joins on the right, detour to see the Long Man of Wilmington; fork right down alongside fence for 150 yards (hamlet of Milton Street comes into view below), then turn right through a gate; the Long Man is seen above the path a short distance along F. Return to point ⑦ and turn right, downhill.

The track drops past a small but prominent concrete building forming part of Windover covered reservoir, and proceeds down to a road. Turn left on the road (leaving the South Downs Way). ⑧ After ¼ mile, turn right on a path (signposted Lullington Church); detour right to the church after 100 yards G. Return to the main path and continue along it, soon entering a field and continuing along the right-hand edge towards Alfriston. Near the end of the field continue

Alfriston's 'cathedral' and its fellow 14th-century neighbour, the half-timbered Clergy House

forward between hedges (ignoring minor field–path to right). ⑨ At the road, turn right and immediately left on a path (South Downs Way), crossing over a bridge, then soon going over a larger bridge over the Cuckmere River (which you crossed at the start of the walk if you began from Alfriston). Proceed forward, between walls, into Alfriston.

ON THE ROUTE

A **Alfriston** This delightful old-world village has a narrow, winding main street lined with tile-hung houses. The ancient timbered **Star Inn** has a heavy roof of Horsham slabs, and a front adorned with wooden carvings, including St George and the dragon; at the corner of the inn is a figure-head taken from a Dutch ship washed ashore 300 years ago at nearby Cuckmere Haven. Opposite is the **George Inn**, which has Tudor wall-paintings. In the tiny square is the shaft of one of only two market crosses in Sussex (the other is at Chichester). The **museum and heritage centre** is in a former blacksmith's forge and contains displays of local history.

Off the main street, near the river, is the **church**, dubbed the 'cathedral of the South Downs', a spacious and regular building of c.1360, with fine tracery in its windows. Nearby is the half-timbered and thatched **Clergy House**, of the same age as the church, built as a priest's house. In 1896 it became the first building to be bought by the National Trust (*open* April to October 11 to 6 daily or sunset if earlier).

B The **Cuckmere River** has been canalised, to prevent tidal flooding; there are often fleets of swans and ducks present.

C The modest ascent is soon rewarded with views disproportionate to the effort expended. First comes a deep valley immediately down to the left, the slopes of which are too steep for ploughing and have thus remained as rugged grassland. Elsewhere, the impact of modern agriculture on the

landscape is very apparent.

D **Lullington Heath** (a nature reserve maintained by English Nature) is an untamed, rolling expanse, of botanical interest because of coinciding chalk and acid soils, with typical species of each co-existing, for example gorse and salad burnet.

E At **Windover Hill** there is an expansive view north across the Sussex Weald and the Ashdown Forest. Arlington Reservoir is prominent in the middle distance.

F **The Long Man of Wilmington** Seen at its best from this path, a 226ft figure cut in the chalk hillside, carefully done to avoid any distortion from foreshortening. The Long Man appears to have a staff in each hand but the precise origin and purpose of the figure are uncertain; one theory is that he represents Balder, Norse God of Spring. The earliest written record is 18th century but he is probably much older. At the top of the grassy spur to the left of the Long Man is **Hunters' Burgh**, a long barrow which is thought to be the burial place of a Neolithic hunter. **Wilmington** is the nearby village. One long street runs up from a green at the north end to the church and priory ruins. Outside the church is a great yew tree, reputedly 1,000 years old and Sussex's oldest tree. The church itself has a 12th-century chancel, a 14th-century nave, and a square, Jacobean font. The adjacent **priory** (*open* Monday to Saturday 11 to 5; closed Tuesday; Sunday 2 to 5) is an 11th-century Benedictine foundation which belonged to Grestrain Abbey in Normandy; this was the abbey's principal English possession. It was seized by the Crown during the war with France, and later became a farmhouse (hence 14th- and 16th-century modifications). Inside is an agricultural display.

G **Lullington church** stands isolated, reached only by a footpath. Only the chancel remains of a larger building, making the 13ft-square building one of England's smallest churches.

ASHDOWN FOREST AND POOH STICKS BRIDGE

FROM the typical Wealden landscapes around Hartfield, the route climbs on to Ashdown Forest, an area of unspoilt, elevated heathland unlike anywhere else in the South-East, and giving some of the finest walking in the region. The forest is instantly familiar to anyone who has read the Winnie-the-Pooh stories. For those who do not wish to tackle the full route, the path described from Gills Lap to the AA Milne Memorial is especially recommended.

WALK DIRECTIONS

① A From Hartfield village centre with the Hay Waggon pub and war memorial on your right, walk downhill along B2026 in the Edenbridge direction, keeping left along B2026 at road junction. Just before the road crosses bridge, take a path on the right into Forest Way Country Park (just to left of driveway to former station). Avoid path to left going under bridge but continue, 20 yards later taking the next path on the right, leading on to dismantled railway by the platform of the former Hartfield station B. Follow the railway line for ¾ mile, ignoring a path crossing after ½ mile (where there is a stile and footbridge to the left) but ¼ mile after this, ② take path over a stile on right, waymarked with WW sign denoting the Wealdway C, which you follow all the way to the top of Ashdown

Forest (but which is not always waymarked or signposted). The path crosses a field at 90 degrees to the direction of railway track, to take a

stile to the right of a gate at far end of field (and to left of derelict brick barn); in the next field maintain direction to reach a stile by a gate

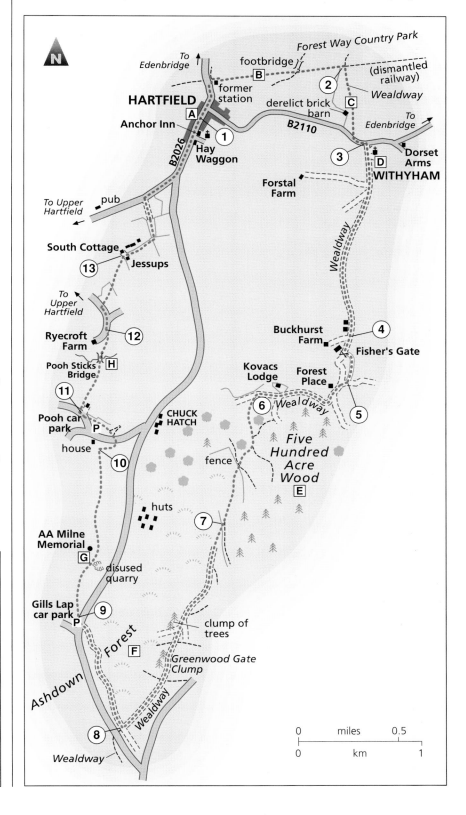

LENGTH 8 miles (13 km), 4 hours

DIFFICULTY 2

START Hartfield, on B2026 and B2110 south of Edenbridge and east of Forest Row; park in the village centre near the Hay Waggon public house. Grid reference 478357

OS MAPS Landranger 188; Pathfinder 1248 (TQ 43/53)

REFRESHMENTS Anchor, Hay Waggon, tea-room and shop, all in Hartfield; Dorset Arms, Withyham; ice-cream van often in Gills Lap car park ⑨ at weekends giving on to road. Turn left along road, then ③ take the first turning on the right signposted to Withyham Church. Ignore driveways to left leading to church D and houses but keep along this quiet lane; later, ignore farm roads to the right but continue towards Buckhurst Farm (Private notices refer to vehicles; there is no public vehicular access to this lane, but it is open to walkers). ④ At houses at Fisher's Gate, keep left at fork (over cattlegrid), then just after cottages and a partly weather-boarded house on the right, the path leaves the driveway to the left, as signposted, where the driveway ahead is gated and leads into farm. The path is enclosed by fences and leads into woodland, reaching a junction with track ⑤; to the right is marked as private, while to the left the track forks into two. Turn left to take the right-hand of these forks, and keep right at the end of the triangle enclosed by the tracks. 50 yards later fork right just after brick house (Forest Place) on right, then 100 yards later fork right again, taking the rightmost of three tracks; this bends right and descends. At the bottom, pass hedged garden of Kovacs Lodge on right, and keep right at track junction, alongside a fence. ⑥ 30 yards after a field appears on right, fork left on a path rising gently through Five Hundred Acre Wood E; keep to main path, rising all the time (soon, ignore a minor descending sharp left turn and keep right at a fork soon after). Go forward at a path crossing, taking path through break in fence; the path continues to rise. ⑦ Fork right as soon as open land appears on your right, into open heath F. Follow Wealdway marker posts (notches cut into top of posts indicate the direction), and ignore side paths (you are generally following the main track and maintaining the same direction). After ½ mile ignore a sharp left turn and fork right soon after, on the main path. At next junction (by a clump of trees on right; road may be audible to the left), keep forward, joining a broad track coming from left; fork right 80 yards later, and fork left 100 yards after that. ⑧

Reach T-junction with broad track (to the left this leads towards road and mast) 50 yards before the road: turn right (route now leaves the Wealdway) on this track, parallel to road away to the left. As the track descends, Gills Lap car park is in view ahead, half left; the track bends left; keep right at next fork to cross the road and enter the car park ⑨. Turn right on a path passing benches and following top of ridge with road parallel to right (but not visible). The path drops gently (ignore any side turns) and later passes a small abandoned quarry with pool on right and memorial to AA Milne on left just after G. ⑩ ½ mile later, just before a house with tiled roof, the path bends to the right and reaches a road. Cross over to a sandy bridleway opposite. Ignore all right forks and descend gently; later a field appears on the right, and ⑪ the path reaches road by Andbell House on right. Turn right on the road, then after 50 yards take a path on right which drops to Pooh Sticks Bridge H. Beyond the bridge, the path rises to reach the end of small road (coming from Ryecroft Farm from left) ⑫: keep right along it, ignoring first turning on right; 100 yards later, take a path over a stile by gate on right. Head across the field to a stile; cross next field keeping to the left of a prominent house, to find stile in top right-hand corner ⑬. Keep right, to take path between driveways to Jessups and Southbridge Cottage. Enter a field, follow left edge (just before house on left, ignore stile on left); as soon as you enter next field, turn left to cross stile and walk down narrow field to stile in middle at bottom (ignore gateway to the right), leading on to a track down to bottom of next field. Turn right on road, and keep left at next junction, into Hartfield.

ON THE ROUTE
A **Hartfield** An attractive Wealden village with timber-framed and pantile-hung cottages. The shop Pooh Corner offers a comprehensive range of Pooh memorabilia.
B **Dismantled railway** The Forest Way Country Park occupies part of the former railway line from Three

Bridges to Tunbridge Wells.
C **Wealdway** The 80-mile long-distance walkers' route traverses a varied cross-section of the Weald, from Gravesend to Eastbourne.
D **Withyham church**, rebuilt in 1663, contains monuments to the Sackvilles, the earls of Dorset.
E **Five Hundred Acre Wood** The wood was enclosed in 1693 and includes stands of oak and beech. This was the Forest (or Hundred Acre Wood) of the Winnie-the-Pooh stories. In the adjacent heathland, the sandy tracks leading to clumps of Scots pines are strongly reminiscent of the illustrations for the stories by EH Shepard.
F **Ashdown Forest** One of the major lowland heaths of southern England, created as a Royal Hunting Ground and disafforested in 1662; parts were subsequently enclosed and re-forested. The Forest is part woodland and part heath, with a substantial covering of heather. No buildings or pylons detract from the views; the land is maintained by the Conservators of Ashdown Forest. Somewhere in the valley down to the right where this walk emerges into the open was where Pooh and his friends mounted an 'expotition' to the North Pole.
G **AA Milne memorial** This is the 'enchanted place', or Galleon's Lap (Gills Lap in real life) of the stories; this fine viewpoint has a memorial to AA Milne, author of the stories and father of Christopher Robin.
H **Pooh Sticks Bridge** In *The House at Pooh Corner*, Pooh, Piglet and Christopher Robin played Pooh Sticks by dropping twigs into the brook and seeing which came out first on the other side of the bridge. The Milnes lived nearby at Cotchford Farm (not open).

Pooh Sticks Bridge, identical to the original of 1907

SHOREHAM AND LULLINGSTONE

A FAVOURITE Sunday escape for Londoners. This green-belt terrain lies close to the capital but is quite rural in character and gives scope for a walk taking in the River Darent, Shoreham and the North Downs. The golf course in Lullingstone Park is largely screened by woodland, through which the paths pass. Lullingstone Roman Villa and Lullingstone Castle are passed in the final stages. A charming riverside path concludes the walk. Paths are waymarked throughout.

LENGTH *Full walk* 6 miles (9.5km), 3 hours *Shortened version* (omitting Lullingstone Villa and Lullingstone Castle) 4½ miles (7km), 2½ hours

DIFFICULTY 2

START Lullingstone Park Visitor Centre, ½ mile (1km) south of Eynsford station, off A225. Free car park. Grid reference 526638

OS MAPS Landranger 188; Pathfinder 1192 (TQ 46/56)

REFRESHMENTS Pubs in Shoreham; teas at Lullingstone Castle (2 to 5pm, weekends and Bank Holidays March to September); cafeteria at Lullingstone Park Visitor Centre (open daily all year)

WALK DIRECTIONS

① Go out to the road and turn right along it A. Past a group of houses as

Part of the fine mosaics at Lullingstone Roman Villa

the road is about to bend right, take track on left with yellow arrow markers (Darent Valley Path), through field and follow all the way to Shoreham. ② Emerge on lane by houses, turn left and immediately right on to path by river, cross by footbridge and keep right on other side, along river to centre of village by bridge ③ B. Go right up village street, then turn right at T-junction.

④ After 60 yards, bear left by house number 13, on signposted path uphill, between hedges; chalk cross comes into view on right. Further up, emerge by stile on to downland C, go up alongside fence on right to next stile into Meenfield Wood, then right at cross-junction of paths. The path now goes along the level, with fine views of the valley, then drops slightly (beyond barrier, ignore

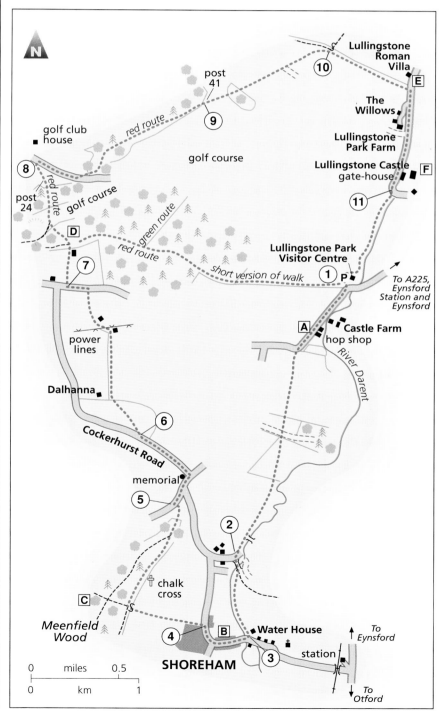

a sharp left turn), finally bending left to road ⑤. Turn right on road, follow Well Hill signs (ignore right turn for Shoreham at first junction, then turn left at second junction to go up Cockerhurst Road. ⑥ Take signposted path on right opposite bungalow gate; path goes up through rough land; then gets fainter (maintain direction uphill, finding a stile 100 yards to the right of red-roofed house, which comes into view). Follow field path along left edge of field to bungalow under power lines, where the path continues to the left, and is now enclosed; past the last bungalow it becomes a concrete track until the road. Turn left on road, then ⑦ right after 100 yards over stile (where overhead wires cross); the path goes along left edge of field, and then is enclosed; emerge by a stile in woods and reach signpost at four-way crossing Ⓓ.

For short walk turn right and follow red marker posts back to the start.

For full walk go forward and follow woodland path until emerging into open by fairway of golf course; turn right downhill and follow red marker posts carefully: the route crosses over another fairway, goes into woods and emerges, soon ⑧ joining park road (club house in view to left), going right along it and then bearing left, into woods, where you follow red or blue markers (which follow almost the same route, soon merging again). ⑨ Finally the red route emerges from woodland: go forward to find a marked barrier into a strip of woods, then proceed out into the open (down and up); the blue route then drops to the right but keep ahead on the red route, reaching a fence where ⑩ you turn right and follow path downhill (ignore a stile on right soon after).

At the bottom, you reach the estate road; Lullingstone Roman Villa is immediately to the left Ⓔ.

Go right on the road, past Lullingstone Castle gatehouse Ⓕ, then ⑪ as road bends left go forward to find riverside path leading to Lullingstone Park Visitor Centre.

ON THE ROUTE

Ⓐ **Hop fields** are seen on both sides of the road. On the left the Hop Shop (*open* daily except Sunday) has hop products, dried flowers and more.

Ⓑ **Shoreham** is an unspoilt village nestled among the North Downs and with a river along part of its street. The visionary artist Samuel Palmer lived at Water House (where the walk enters the village) from 1827 to 1834, the most productive years of his life (many of his paintings have a local setting). Palmer attracted a group of young disciples who called themselves The Ancients; sceptical and suspicious villagers called them the Extolagers. William Blake paid a visit to Palmer here in 1827.

The Kings Arms claims to have the last surviving Ostler Box, a kind of cubby hole giving access to the bar from the street for the convenience of horsemen. The late-Perpendicular **church** is restored but has some outstanding features,

The Church of St Botolph (open all year), in the grounds of Lullingstone Castle, was rebuilt in the 14th century along the lines of the Norman original. The Queen Anne porch is one of several later additions

notably the rood screen spanning the width of the building. Stained glass by the eminent Pre-Raphaelite Burne-Jones was installed in 1903, after the artist's death.

Ⓒ This fine **view** extends over the Shoreham and the Darent Valley. The **chalk cross** seen to the right was cut into the hillside as a memorial for those who died in the First World War. The **woodland** crowning the slope was partially destroyed in the great storm of 1987.

Ⓓ **Lullingstone Park** and golf course is managed by Sevenoaks District Council and is designated as a Site of Special Scientific Interest for its ancient pollard trees and other woodland supporting lichens, breeding birds and over 500 species of fungi (including some rarities). Trail leaflets are available from the Countryside Centre where this walk starts. The stile by which the park is entered is said to be the tallest in Kent!

Ⓔ **Lullingstone Roman Villa** (English Heritage; *open* Good Friday or 1 April, whichever is earlier, to 30 September daily; rest of year closed Monday). Protected from the elements by a large shed, this country villa was occupied for much of the Roman period and retains superb mosaics. A particular feature of the villa is that it has four very distinct periods of occupation by four owners; one had a room with a natural spring, intended for pagan worship of the water goddesses; another built a Christian chapel. The entrance fee includes an audio tour.

Ⓕ **Lullingstone Castle** (*open* April to September, 2 to 6 weekends and Bank Holidays) is a family mansion with great hall, library and state rooms, containing collections of porcelain, furniture and portraits. The castle estate formerly included Lullingstone Park. The 15th-century gate-house is one of the earliest all-brick buildings in the country.

PENSHURST AND CHIDDINGSTONE

AN attractive cross-country route linking two charming Wealden villages, with quintessential Kentish views. The terrain is low-lying but by no means flat, with enough changes in elevation to sustain interest. Paths are mostly defined or waymarked, but, because of the intricate nature of this landscape, the route is not always obvious. Some gentle ascents; stinging nettles are a slight problem on some sections in summer.

> **LENGTH** 6½ miles (10.5 km), 3 hours
> **DIFFICULTY** 2
> **START** Penshurst village, on B2176 south-west of Tonbridge; park on village street near Leicester Arms. Grid reference 526438
> **OS MAPS** Landranger 188; Pathfinder 1228 (TQ 44/54)
> **REFRESHMENTS** Leicester Arms, shop and two tea-rooms in Penshurst; Rock Inn, Hoath Corner; Castle Inn, Chiddingstone (open all day on Saturday)

WALK DIRECTIONS

① Ⓐ With the Leicester Arms on your left, walk along village street, passing village hall on your right and past village stores and filling station on left. Just after the primary school on right, turn right into a lane called The Warren; ignore a left turn to Redcot and continue past a row of cottages; ② at Warren Farm the lane ends: keep forward, entering a field by a stile and proceeding along the right-hand edge. In second field cross to footbridge ahead, from which an enclosed path leads to third field, which you cross diagonally right to a stile by a gate in corner (in line with oast-house in the distance), and go forward along the right edge of the next feld.

③ Emerge on a driveway, with a large house to the right, and take rising path between hedges to the right of field and to left of the two driveways that lead into the house. This later passes a vineyard on the left. At the top of main ascent, take a stile on left and continue forward along right edge of field. At the end of the field, a stile leads to a narrow path emerging over slab bridge on to a track ④; turn right along this

Penshurst village was almost entirely built in the 19th century, echoing earlier styles

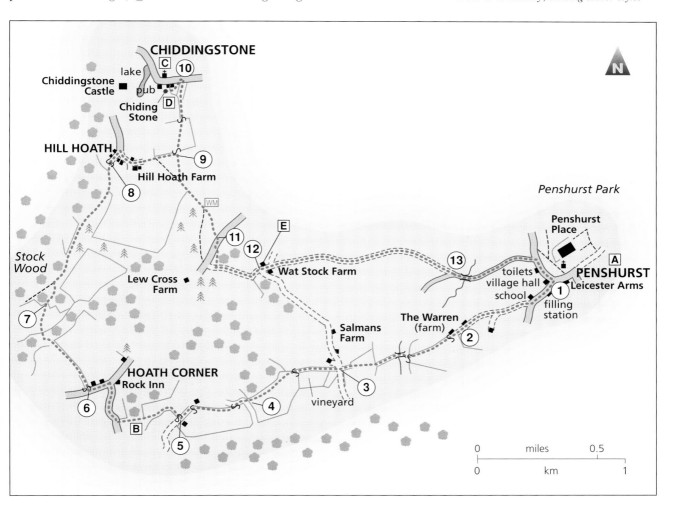

track which immediately bends left. Just before track enters field by gate, take the stile on the left and keep right to follow right edge of field. Just past pantile-hung house on right, take the stile on the right and follow path to end of driveway (emerging by a garage).

Follow driveway for 100 yards, then ⑤ take stile on right, opposite house. Follow the left edge of field; where hedge on left reaches a corner, turn left on a path between the hedge and a fence. At the end of field on right, keep forward, on a rising track B, to reach road. Turn right on the road, to hamlet of Hoath Corner. Take next road turning on left (towards Markbeech), to pass Cares Cross (house) and Pear Tree Cottage, then immediately ⑥ take a signposted stile on right by a telegraph post: this enclosed path descends, then beyond a footbridge soon goes along edge of field (with hedge on right), then into a woodland to the bottom of slope. On emerging into a field, keep right, up a rise, alongside woodland on the right until it reaches a corner, where you go forward across field to find a stile into woodland ⑦. A narrow path leads to T-junction with a broader one: turn right and in 80 yards ignore a right fork. ⑧ After ½ mile emerge by a stile at end of driveway by houses at Hill Hoath. Go forward, then turn right at T-junction. 70 yards later, after house on right, take the track on left, passing Hill Hoath Cottages on your left and a farm and barns on your right; past the last barn, pick up a path alongside a fence on your left. 30 yards beyond next stile ignore path waymarked to right (part of Eden Valley Walk) but keep forward close to the fence.

⑨ This reaches a path junction at a stile; the *continuation* of route is to the right (i.e. not crossing stile itself) but first *detour* to Chiddingstone by crossing the stile and following the field path to the left, later continuing as an enclosed path and passing football pitch on right, finally emerging on road at Chiddingstone ⑩ C. Return the same way to path junction

mentioned above (the Chiding Stone D signposted is worth a look as it's only a short walk from the village).

On rejoining the main walk, bear left E; on joining broader path (part of the Eden Valley Walk) lined with trees, turn left again, through a gate and keep left as waymarked at the next fork.

⑪ At the road, turn right and after 30 yards take gate on left and continue across the field to a stile beside a gate on to track. Turn left. ⑫ At farm, fork left, and 50 yards later keep straight on, ignoring track entering field to left. ⑬ After 1 mile this joins a road: keep left, over a bridge. Turn right at the main road to enter Penshurst village.

ON THE ROUTE

A **Penshurst** The village has a charming corner around the churchyard, entered by an archway beneath a picturesque half-timbered house. Next to the village is Penshurst Place, one of the great manor houses of the Weald (*open* Easter to September daily) and birthplace of Philip Sidney, the Elizabethan poet. The house dates back some 650 years and has a magnificent Great Hall; the **gardens** are noted for double herbaceous borders and clipped yew hedges. A public footpath just to the left (west) of the church, and heading northwards, enters the Penshurst Place estate, and gains some glorious views of the house.

On starting the walk, notice the quaint garage/filling station, with its horseshoe-shaped doorway, a legacy from its former days as the village blacksmith's shop.

Penshurst and Chiddingstone villages both give their names to local **vineyards**, one of which is passed on the early stages of this walk.

B This track passes along a ridge of the **upper greensand**, giving views northwards to the **North Downs**; a number of rock outcrops along the road which is encountered next serve to show the distinctly un-green nature of this rock.

C **Chiddingstone** A one-street village of rare perfection, with a

delightful group of 16th- and 17th-century half-timbered houses, built at the height of the Wealden iron industry, and the ancient Castle Inn under the ownership of the National Trust. The tile-hung inn has been a hostelry since 1370; it has numerous cosy corners, as well as a pretty garden. Opposite them the **church** dates from the 13th century and has a Perpendicular tower and a Jacobean font and pulpit. Continue along the street (i.e. with the church on your right) for a glimpse across the ornamental lake of **Chiddingstone Castle**, a Gothic revival manor house rebuilt in the early 19th century, and renowned for its collection of art and antiquities, including Egyptian and Oriental pieces (*open* Wednesday, Sunday and bank holidays April to October; Tuesday to Sunday during June to September).

D **The Chiding Stone** A sandstone outcrop, adorned with a good century's worth of graffiti, which has given its name to the village; in less civilised times this was the place to which men brought their nagging wives so that the assembled villagers could nag them back by way of retribution!

E As you cross the field, note a rather striking **pink house** prominent in the mid-distance, half left: all is not what it seems. When you reach this point at ⑫, the *trompe l'œil* reveals itself.

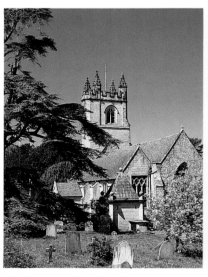

Chiddingstone Church harbours a grotesque carving of a head with two noses, two mouths and three eyes

ONE TREE HILL AND IGHTHAM MOTE

SOME of Kent's most rewarding walking is found in the greensand country, where the sandy soils give rise to a distinctive vegetation and the landscape is predominantly woodland and pasture. One of the crowning glories is the escarpment, notably between One Tree Hill and

Ightham Mote, the focus of the largest conservation project undertaken by the National Trust

Ightham Mote, which appears in the latter stages of this varied route. The beginning is an ascent from Ivy Hatch into woodland; mud is often a problem in these first stages. You need to look for the route with some care before dropping down to the Padwell Arms. Orchards and oast-houses follow, with another wooded section before One Tree Hill, from where the route is waymarked all the way back.

WALK DIRECTIONS

① Take the main village street, passing between the Plough on right, shop and bus stop on left, forking left at first junction, signposted Stone Street. Take the next right turn (Pine Tree Lane), then ② left after 30 yards on a path climbing through the woods Ⓐ. Ignore the path through gate on

| LENGTH 6 miles (9.5km), 3 hours |
| DIFFICULTY 2 |
| START Ivy Hatch (parking in village centre), by Plough public house. Grid reference 587546 |
| OS MAPS Landranger 188; Pathfinder 1208 (TQ 45/55) |
| REFRESHMENTS Plough, Ivy Hatch; shop at Ivy Hatch; Padwell Arms, Stone Street; tea-room at Ightham Mote for visitors to house |

right after ¾ mile. Turn right at road, past the school and church (ignore driveway to Cone Hill on left) then turn left on a signposted bridleway into woods where the road is about to bend right. ③ After 20 yards take the footpath on the left at signpost. This path is not defined at the start: go at right angles to the bridleway for 30 yards,

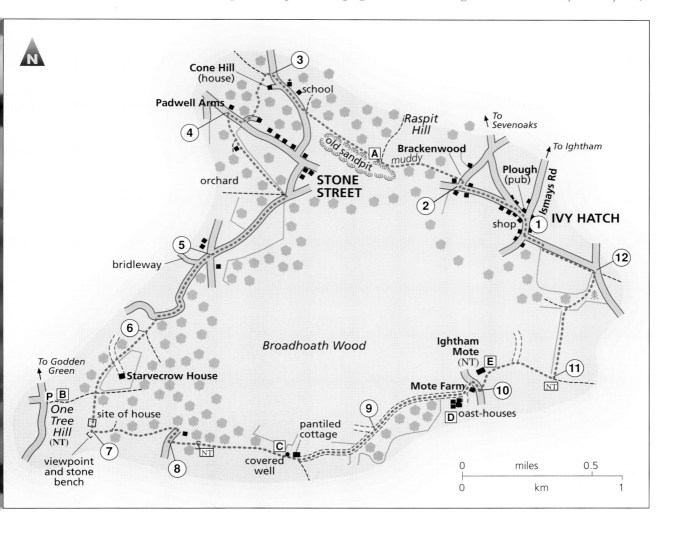

then as the slope steepens bear slightly left to pick up a narrow but defined path which hugs the slope and descends to an enclosed section between fences, past brick and stone houses to a driveway and on to a road. Turn right to the Padwell Arms. There is a nicely positioned terrace outside. ④ Take bridleway through the orchard opposite the Padwell Arms. This passes to the left of house in orchard. Turn right at road. ⑤ At junction keep forward (ignoring right turn to Seal and passing triangular green on left). After ¼ mile, as the road is about to bend right uphill, take a signposted footpath on left into woods. ⑥ After 200 yards, fork right, uphill, soon joined by a field fence on left; cross over track going to house to left, continue with fence on left. Where fence on left ends at corner, go forward at path junction, past National Trust sign for One Tree Hill, taking path with wooden

LOCAL STROLLS

The best stroll based on the walk described here is from One Tree Hill eastwards in the direction of Ightham Mote. The One Tree Hill car park (3 miles east of Sevenoaks) is rather tucked away on the east side of a minor road that leads south 1 mile from the Buck's Head at Godden Green.

Knole Park is a fine expanse of parkland dominated by the largest stately home in the country (365 rooms and 52 staircases). The park has a population of deer (not to be approached) and is crossed by public rights of way.

Further west, there are walks from Westerham into Squerries Park, where the signposted Tower Walk takes you to a ruined tower in the middle of the estate. There are more paths open to the public than are shown on OS maps here. Longer walks can extend to French Street and Toy's Hill (where the Fox and Hounds pub stands alone in the forest). Toy's Hill itself is an area of woodland owned by the National Trust but sadly devastated in the 1987 storm; however, the paths around it have been re-opened.

railings on left. Where path and railings bend right, go forward, under railings and across turf (site of old house) to a viewpoint with a stone bench at top of slope ⑦ Ⓑ. Turn left, taking the path level with the bench at top of slope (this is the Greensand Way, well signposted in this section, which you follow to Ightham Mote). Keep left in 50 yards (ignoring path descending to right), turn right at T-junction 40 yards later, and fork right after further 70 yards, over a stile and through trees. Reach the end of lane, turn right downhill along it for 70 yards, then ⑧ left on path. At cottage Ⓒ take track ahead (ignore stile to right, entering field). ⑨ Beyond gate, ignore track rising to the left. Track bends left at a group of oast-houses Ⓓ, to reach the road. Turn right along the road and ⑩ almost immediately left between the brick gateposts of Ightham Mote. Follow this estate road (which bends right in front of iron gates to Ightham Mote Ⓔ, then rises); as it bends left keep forward on a track between fields. ⑪ After passing below a converted oast-house, you reach National Trust sign for Ightham Mote (facing other way); take the gate on left and follow track up left side of field, into woods (ignore small path immediately on left) and follow it to road ⑫. Turn left to reach Ivy Hatch, using the path along left side of road.

ON THE ROUTE

Ⓐ The path climbs on to a **greensand ridge**. The sandy nature of the soil is apparent on the path. At its summit, an abandoned sandpit down on the left has created a precipitous cliff-like drop.
Ⓑ **One Tree Hill** is owned by the National Trust, and comprises an area of mixed woodland. There is alternative access from a car park. Paths lead to a fine viewpoint over Tonbridge and the Weald.
Ⓒ On the left, just before this pantiled cottage, a good example of

Wealden domestic architecture, is a covered **well**. In the distance at the 2 o'clock position and to the right of Shipbourne church is **Hadlow Tower**, a slender Gothic-revival folly erected in 1838 but sadly damaged by the 1987 storm.
Ⓓ This fine group of **oast-houses**, built as kilns for drying hops, at Mote Farm is a typical Kentish sight.
Ⓔ **Ightham Mote** (National Trust; *open* April to end October, daily except Tuesday and Saturday) is an outstanding example of a medieval moated manor house, with a brick and timber exterior. The Great Hall, the Old Chapel, 14th-century crypt and painted ceiling of the Tudor Chapel are among its glories.

WEATHER TILING

A feature of many Wealden houses is the tile-hung wall, a practice dating from the late 17th century in the region. This weatherproofing measure spread to other parts of England, but is essentially a speciality of Kent, Surrey and Sussex. In many cases, the same type of tile is used for the roof. Frequently, the tiles are hung on to wooden battens or affixed by pegs. Older tile-hung houses are commonly wooden framed and covered with pantiles. These are large tiles, known as Flanders Tiles before 1700 when they were imported from Holland. An Act of Parliament at the time of George I stipulated that their measurements should be at least 13½ × 9½ × ½ inches. Their design required only a single overlap, making them lighter; this in turn economised on the amount of roof timbers required.

Oast-houses, very much a component of the Kentish landscape, were built for drying hops

CHILHAM AND GODMERSHAM PARK

A ROUTE joining two interesting villages mostly by downland and field paths, with changing views for much of the way. Route-finding is a little complicated, but helped by good waymarking; sections ③–⑨ follow the Stour Valley Walk.

LENGTH 5½ miles (9km), 3 hours
DIFFICULTY 2
START Car park in Chilham village
Grid reference 066536
Alternatively start at Godmersham, on A28 6 miles north-east of Ashford; park by bus shelter and phone-box on main road (near signposted turning for Crundale and Waltham) and start walk directions at ⑩. Grid reference 066507
OS MAPS Landranger 179 or 189; Pathfinder 1211 (TR 05/15)
REFRESHMENTS Two pubs, shop, tea-room and castle tea-room in Chilham

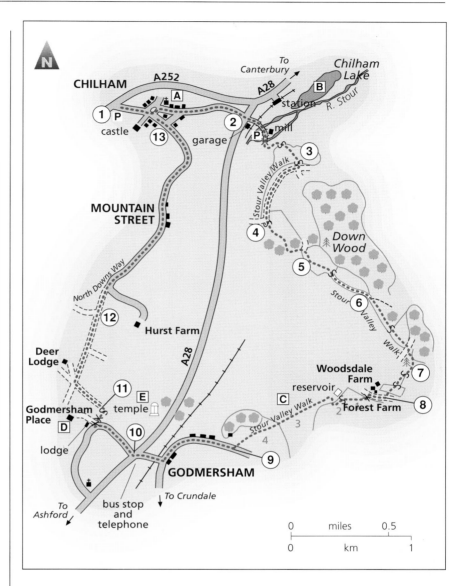

WALK DIRECTIONS

① Turn right out of car park into the main square. From village square Ⓐ, with castle gate behind you, take the far right exit from square (the road to the right of the church path), keeping left at next junction (by pub). (Ignore Branch Road on right and Felborough Close on left.) At the end of the village, road almost joins A252 (on your left); however turn right here crossing

The centre of Chilham, a picturebook start and finish to the walk

main road and taking cul-de-sac to left of garage ②; this leads over level-crossing. Cross bridge (it is however worth detouring a few yards left on path to Chilham Lake Ⓑ before you do this), keep right (left goes to mill house), then after second bridge keep left on main path passing between red-brick house and river to reach field: keep forward (signposted Stour Valley Walk Link Path), along hedgerow to reach track ③ where you turn right. You are now in the waymarked Stour Valley Walk, which is followed until ⑨.

Ignore left turn after only 20 yards. ④ After ⅓ mile reach junction with main track bending right downhill and narrow path proceeds ahead. Take the stile up on left here, and

cross the field diagonally, making for entrance in woods away to your right (halfway up the field). On the other side of the woods, turn left in field, following its edge uphill, then in next field turn right along bottom edge for 80 yards to reach a waymark post, where ⑤ bear half left across field, uphill, to reach stile in fence ahead.

Beyond it, the path drops, then continues between hedges with grassy slope up on left and field on right. ⑥ Where field on right ends, fork right on to waymarked path which runs along inside edge of woods, with fence on right. You soon reach a field; keep forward alongside fence (with farms visible to your right) and go forward into wood; the path snakes a little. ⑦

The seventeenth-century façade of Chilham's castle; allow time at least to wander in the fine gardens

ON THE ROUTE

A **Chilham** Perhaps the most handsome of all the Kent villages, with a central square surrounded by black and white houses, an ancient pub, the church and the castle entrance; narrow lanes slope downhill from each corner. The **castle** (*open* April to October, daily 11 to 5) was built in 1616 for an officer of James I, but its keep is Norman. The **gardens** (*open*, as for castle, to 6pm), with yew and box hedges, look out to the downs, and there are falconry displays; inside is a Kent Battle of Britain **museum**. Large **church**, with many monuments, and 15th-century flint chequerwork tower; to the north is the Queen Anne **rectory**.

B The permissive path to the left just before you reach the weatherboarded **water-mill** has been given over to public access by the Mid Kent Water Company. The path skirts reed-fringed **Chilham Lake**, created by the gravel extraction industry and now an attractive haunt for waterfowl, including swans and moorhens. As you begin to ascend, Great Water (another of the Stour Valley lakes) comes into view.

C **View** over the **Stour Valley** and **North Downs**. Oast-houses (for drying hops) in the distance complete a classically Kentish scene.

D 18th-century landscaped parkland surrounds **Godmersham Place**, built by Thomas Brodnax in 1732, and later inherited by his cousin Edward Knight, Jane Austen's brother. Jane used to stay here and look after the house. Her letters to her sister Cassandra described in great detail the boorish men and artless women whose company she was obliged to keep here, a society that provided some of the raw material of her novels. Half a mile south, further along the road is the **church**, which has a Norman carving of a bishop, very possibly St Thomas of Canterbury; it is a rare survival of the destruction wrought on such features in churches across the country.

E To the right, a **Grecian temple**, erected as a feature for the parkland, stands on a hillock.

Fork right just after waymark post, soon entering a field: stiles (to left of farms) are visible ahead, marking your route, which almost immediately enters a field on right, then follows its left edge down to the next stiles.

8 Turn right on track, then just after first house (Forest Farmhouse), take signposted stile on left and bear right in first field (initially parallel to road), heading up to a stile just to the left of a prominent triangular bank (which is a reservoir) on skyline. Beyond stile, keep forward (slightly uphill) along right edge of second field, turning right after 130 yards by waymark post to enter third field: turn left along the top of third field for 100 yards, then at waymark post bear half right diagonally across field (in line with church in far distance) **C**.

Continue same direction down across fourth field, to leave by the far corner on to the lane **9**. Turn right on lane, then right again after ½ mile at road junction (signposted Chilham), passing under railway and through Godmersham. **10** Cross main road to a turning with a weight limit sign, then keep forward after bridge where road bends left, taking estate gates to right of lodge **D**. Immediately take small gate on right, and cross parkland. As soon as you rejoin the wooden fence which is on left **E**, **11** turn left on a wide track between fences which heads towards estate farm (Deer Lodge).

Reach five-way track junction and turn right again, between fences, then soon forward along right edge of field. **12** Reach junction of tracks, with North Downs Way ahead and sharp left, and go forward. Soon reach corner of lane and go forward (right turn is a private road leading to Hurst Farm).

13 After ¾ mile fork left into School Hill at edge of Chilham, to reach village centre.

THE WARREN

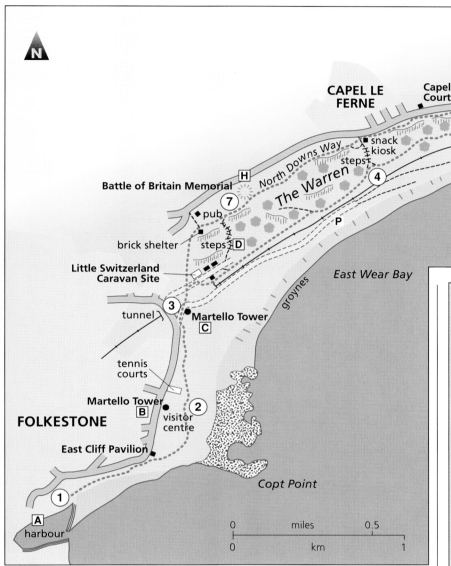

LENGTH *Full walk starting from Folkestone harbour* 5 miles (8km), 2½ hours. *Shorter walk starting from Martello Tower Visitor Centre* 4 miles (6km), 2 hours

DIFFICULTY 3

START *Full walk* The harbour, Folkestone (grid reference 235362). *Shorter walk* Martello Tower Visitor Centre, East Cliff, Folkestone (on the east side of the town; start walk at ② ; grid reference 240366)

OS MAPS Landranger 179; Pathfinder 1252 (TR 13/23)

REFRESHMENTS Full range in Folkestone; two pubs (predominantly serving caravan sites) at top cliffs at ⑥ . Bar and snack kiosk between ⑥ and ⑦ ; Valiant Sailor pub near Battle of Britain Memorial

ON the eastern side of Folkestone is the tumbled undercliff known as the Warren, a fascinating place for the naturalist and unlike anywhere else in the South-East. A maze of steep paths criss-crosses this wilderness. A bridge over the railway provides access to the shore. Steps lead steeply up on to the cliff-top, where the level North Downs Way provides an easy route back. The paths are well defined but can be very slippery after rain. Folkestone's harbour, still an active fishing centre, adjoins a sandy beach, with opportunities for reviving the feet after the walk. Easy route-finding.

WALK DIRECTIONS

① A From harbour, with the sea on your right, follow esplanade, until the end, where the path goes up steps. Carry on to right of East Cliff Pavilion (prominent mock-Tudor café); the path along the coast is possible but there have been landslips and it is better to proceed over the golf course. ② B At Martello Tower Visitor Centre carry on, on the seaward side of lawn tennis courts towards another martello tower (signposted to Warren). You reach this by turning off main road on to a little road by a car park sign for Roman Site C . ③ At the martello tower, where the road bends right downhill, carry forward on a narrow path uphill for

75 yards until a footbridge, where you take steps on right and turn right on a small road leading to Little Switzerland Caravan Site. Just before the site, take path on right down steps; shortly keep right at fork, descending via steps D . Ignore path to left at a small clearing (you join the railway fence just after). ④ At fork (with both paths waymarked), bear right. ⑤ At the railway bridge, the path ahead (along left side of railway) is the continuation, but first cross the bridge for views of the coast and access to the shore E . Recross bridge, and turn right on the above-mentioned path F . This later

climbs steeply up the cliff. ⑥ At the top, turn left on coast path Ⓖ. At a small lane, turn left and immediately right, following signposts for Coast Path. ⑦ After the Battle of Britain Memorial Ⓗ, there is a signposted path leading down steps to the left; you can either take these (they drop to Little Switzerland Caravan Site (restaurant/phone-box); turn right on the road at bottom) or go forward and almost immediately right (at end of caravan site on right) and left at path junction (if you reach a flat-topped brick structure, go back; the path beyond is badly eroded and steep). Both routes lead to the main road at point reached near the start of the walk.

ON THE ROUTE

Ⓐ **Folkestone Harbour** Although devastated by bombing in the Second World War, the harbour has retained an appreciable atmosphere, with fishing-boats and fresh-fish stalls. The Old High Street, winding up from the west side, hints at the higgledy-piggledy character which once prevailed. Beyond it lies the Bayle, Folkestone's village-like old quarter. In total contrast, the Leas (on the western cliff) is a genteel Victorian resort survival, with neat lawns and shrubberies overlooked by stucco villas.

At the end of the esplanade, where the walk ascends steps, is the point where electrical power is transported to and from France.

Ⓑ **Martello Tower** One of originally 74 such towers built between 1805 and 1808 along the Kent and Sussex coasts as a defensive measure against Napoleon. The towers were able to fire a 24-pound cannon ball one mile out to sea, and were manned by 24 soldiers and an officer. Some were subsequently used by coastguards. Many have been converted into private homes, but others stand empty. In addition to the visitor centre here, a martello tower at Dymchurch is also open to the public as a museum. By the tower, **Copt Point** was around 700BC a thriving centre for the production of querns (stones for grinding corn).

Ⓒ By the toilets and summer parking area is the vanished site of a

Roman villa, whose outlines can occasionally be discerned in extremely dry conditions.

Ⓓ **The Warren** did not exist in its present state until the 1840s. The cliffs are a fragile mixture of resistant greensand (a brown-coloured sandstone) underneath extremely unstable gault clay, which itself underlies chalk. The collapse of the whole area was triggered by the construction of Folkestone Harbour in the early 19th century, which stopped the natural easterly drift of shingle; a constantly renewed shingle bank had protected the unstable clay and chalk cliffs of the Warren, but after the harbour arm was built, the shingle bank was washed away and the cliff was attacked by the sea. Landslips now became bigger and more frequent than they had been. The railway line here is one of the costliest to maintain on the entire national network. There was a massive slip in the undercliff in 1915 when a train was passing through; miraculously there were no fatalities but the railway was dislodged and Warren Halt station went with it.

Once an area of pasture, the Warren is now several landscapes. Scrub and woodland has invaded, with hart's tongue ferns prevalent, as well as hawthorn and blackthorn. The area is a designated Site of Special Scientific Interest (SSSI). Over 50 species of birds breed here. Green woodpeckers, tree creepers, goldfinches and chaffinches are commonly seen, and blackcaps are summer migrants from Africa.

Ⓔ **The shore** gives good opportunities for fossil-hunting in the gault clay. The concrete aprons, or groynes, on the shore serve two purposes: they protect the coast from erosion and they act as 'toe-weighting' to prevent 'rotational slip' from occurring. The latter process is a tendency for the cliff to collapse and the shore to be uplifted.

Ⓕ The walk now enters **grassland**, a noted site for chalk grassland plants, including cowslips, milkwort, gentians, thyme and orchids.

Ⓖ On a clear day, **views** extend across the English Channel to France; Cap Gris-Nez is the most prominent feature.

Ⓗ **Battle of Britain Memorial** Grassy banks surrounding a propeller-shaped motif and statue of an airman looking out to sea commemorate the air battle that took place from 10 July to 31 October 1940, in which the RAF retained control of strategic air-space thanks largely to the planning of Air Chief Marshal Sir Hugh Dowding. It inspired Winston Churchill's immortal words: 'never in the field of human conflict was so much owed by so many to so few'. In all, 544 RAF air crew were lost.

Folkestone beach with the Warren beyond

COMBE WOOD AND INKPEN HILL

THE route passes through the game reserve of Combe Wood then, after a short stretch on tarmac lanes and farm tracks, reaches the edge of the chalk escarpment with views over the south Midlands. The conclusion is a delightful descent over rolling downland to Combe. All tracks are well defined and the route-finding is quite easy.

WALK DIRECTIONS

① Take the track up past the church Ⓐ. At the top (½ mile) continue forward as signposted at crossing of tracks, then drop down into Combe Wood. Avoid side turns (mostly marked Private) and follow the track for another mile to reach junction of tracks at bottom, with signposts pointing left and right ②. Turn right, following the track along the bottom of valley. After 500 yards this leaves woods ③.

For shorter walk Turn right uphill, with woodland fence on your right. After ¾ mile cross a stile. Continue forward, on a track bending round left to reach a prominent corner of woodland where a footpath sign points the way you have come. Keep right, at the corner, following the right edge of field. At a break in the hedge on the right, and as indicated by marker arrow, change to the other side of hedge. Follow this until

> **LENGTH** *Full walk* 7½ miles (12km), 3 hours
> *Shorter walk omitting Buttermere* 5½ miles (9km), 2 hours
> **DIFFICULTY** 2
> **START** Church at Combe village, between Inkpen and Netherton. Park by church. Grid reference 368607
> **OS MAPS** Landranger 174; Pathfinder 1186 and 1202 (SU 26/36 and SU 25/35)

reaching a junction of tracks with bridleway signpost pointing the way you have come. This is point ⑧. Turn right to continue.

For full walk Cross a gate on right but go ahead alongside a fence on left, following the track along the valley, soon joined by woods on your left. ④ After ½ mile, where woods

Harvest time in the rolling countryside of the Kennet Valley near Inkpen

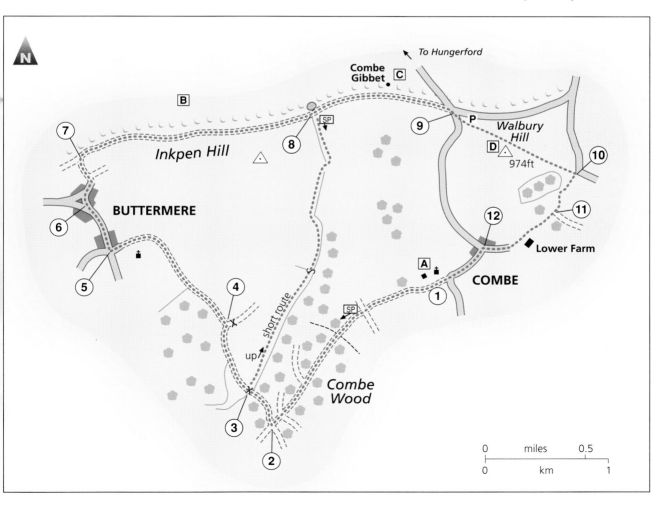

end on the left, reach a junction of tracks and turn left on track between fences. Follow this into the hamlet of Buttermere to reach a T-junction with a phone-box on right in the hamlet ⑤. Turn right on the road, avoid immediate left turn, but follow the road for 500 yards to cottages ⑥.

Turn right here, down No Through Road (road sign). At the end, 30 yards beyond last house, take the left fork, following the track on to escarpment. ⑦ At cross-track after 200 yards turn right B. After 1½ miles you reach crossing of tracks ⑧. With track marked bridleway on your right, continue forward. Follow track, past Combe Gibbet C and down to the road ⑨. Cross the road, continue through the car park and pick up a track at the far side. This leads over Walbury Hill D; after ¾ mile it reaches the corner of a road ⑩.

Turn sharp right through a gate at a signpost, go ahead and downhill through bushes and past horse jumps to join a path coming down from the left. Descend to Combe, avoiding left turn after 150 yards ⑪. The track becomes a tarmac lane; continue forward past cottages, avoiding left turn by a thatched cottage to reach Y-junction of lanes ⑫. Turn left along the road (signposted Linkenholt and Netherton) and follow it as far as the hairpin bend just below the church.

ON THE ROUTE

A Behind the 13th-century **church** is **Manor Farm**, an 18th-century

Combe Gibbet, a stark reminder to travellers in the days of capital punishment to keep on the straight and narrow

rebuilding of an older house in which Charles II stayed, *en route* to Marlborough. A pretty **gazebo** in the garden is dated 1667 and is visible from the walk.

B Here you have a good **view** over the Kennet Valley: north to Lambourn Downs; north-east to hills of the Thames Valley; east to Newbury and Greenham Common airfield.

C **Combe Gibbet** This is a replica of earlier gibbets that have variously been chopped down by anti-capital

punishment demonstrators and blown over by the wind. It was probably sited deliberately within view of the travellers along this track, for whom the bodies which hanged from it acted as a warning. This stands on a 200ft-long prehistoric burial mound.

D **Walbury Hill** At 974ft, this is the highest point in Berkshire. It is encircled by the just-discernible ramparts of Walbury Camp, which covers an 82-acre site, the largest **hillfort** in the county.

CULHAM COURT AND HENLEY REGATTA COURSE

THIS walk incorporates the towpath along the famous regatta course by the banks of a very beautiful stretch of the Thames, which though seen from the bridge at the start is reserved for the second half of the walk, crossing woodland and unspoilt farmland in the first half. Most paths are well defined; route-finding is quite easy.

LENGTH 7 miles (11km), 3½ hours
DIFFICULTY 1–2
START Road-bridge over river at Henley-on-Thames
OS MAPS Landranger 175; Pathfinder 1156 (SU 68/78)
REFRESHMENTS Full range in Henley; Five Horseshoes (after ④); Flower Pot Hotel, Aston

The annual Royal Regatta at Henley – but the river is the town's main focus all year round

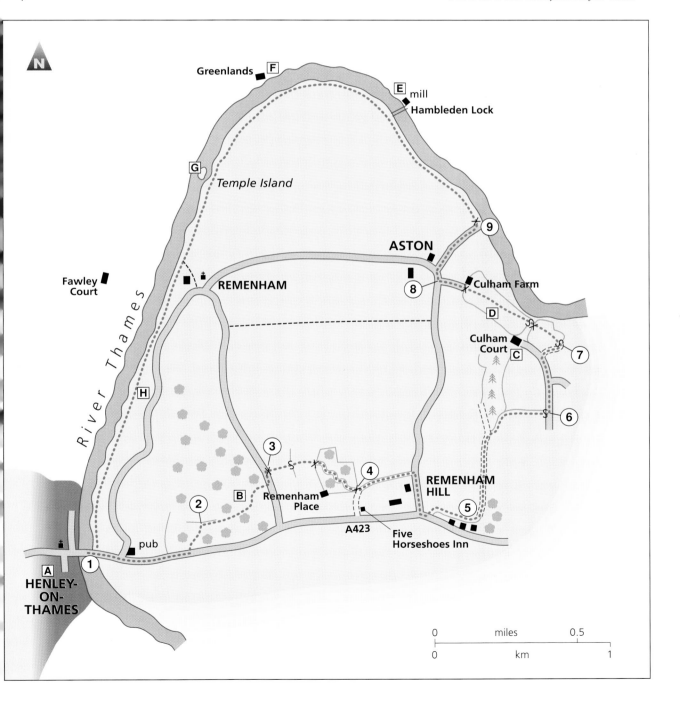

WALK DIRECTIONS

① Ⓐ From Henley Bridge walk along the left-hand footway of A423 over bridge (away from Henley), passing the Little Angel Inn and then allotments below on your left, to the end of footway; here turn left up a flight of steps into the woodland. Shortly cross over a track and continue climbing on path between iron railings. ② At wire-fenced plantation ahead bear right; cross over track and follow a well-defined woodland path Ⓑ, shortly bearing left and right past a house on left to reach stile. Turn left along the road for about 20 yards, then ③ turn right through a gate across field to a stile, and across a second field to go through gate. Follow enclosed path into well-defined winding woodland path.

④ On reaching a gate turn left to follow a track and then path with a fence on left and hedge on right, to arrive at a road. Turn right along Aston Lane to the junction with main road (A423); here turn immediately left into a field and follow edge of field with conifers and houses on right. ⑤ At the end of the houses, turn left into track along edge of a field with large trees and then a hedge on your right. Just before the copse ahead, turn right through a gap in the hedge and continue along edge of next field with the hedge on your left, and at signpost turn right along a line of trees, to reach a stile at a tarmac farm road ⑥.

Turn left along the road and, shortly after, fork left at a small clump of fenced trees; at the bottom of dip in drive up to Culham Court Ⓒ turn sharp right along gravel track. ⑦ Just before overhead wires converge, turn sharp left into a field at gates and continue along the edge of field with fence on right. At the end of the fence, go through middle of field to a gate just to the right of railings around Culham Court Ⓓ,

The recently refurbished Temple on Temple Island. The Regatta starts level with the far side, away from Henley

then, keeping iron railings on your left, pass through two iron gates and through another gate.

Go ahead through the middle of a long narrow field to an iron gate just to the left of a distant farm building, then follow tarmac track ahead down to road ⑧. Turn right at the T-junction. At the centre of Aston village, where the road bends left, fork right on a minor cul-de-sac down to the river ⑨. Turn left along the towpath, first passing Hambleden Lock Ⓔ; then the Greenlands estate, seen on the opposite bank Ⓕ; Temple Island Ⓖ; and Fawley Court, also opposite, to return, along the regatta course Ⓗ, to Henley.

ON THE ROUTE

Ⓐ **Henley** has a strong flavour of Edwardian elegance and comfort, and repays exploration. The first Oxford and Cambridge Boat Race was rowed here in 1829 (Oxford won).

Ⓑ This is a particularly rewarding walk in **spring**, in bluebell time:

they are here in great numbers.

Ⓒ **Culham Court** (1770–1) A pleasing example of neo-classical style.

Ⓓ The grass to either side of this stretch of path is full of daffodils in season.

Ⓔ A short detour across the river at **Hambleden Lock** is recommended; an attractive weather-boarded water-mill and mill house are on the opposite bank.

Ⓕ **Greenlands** is a Victorian mansion in the Italian style, which was formerly the home of Viscount Hambleden.

Ⓖ **The Temple** was designed by James Wyatt to improve the view from Fawley Court, which he classicised in 1771. The Court has gardens created by Capability Brown.

Ⓗ **Henley Royal Regatta** was established in 1839 as 'a source of amusement and gratification to the neighbourhood and the public in general'. It acquired the 'Royal' from the Prince Consort's patronage in 1851.

COOKHAM AND WINTER HILL

A THAMES VALLEY route full of interest, beginning over fields and through beech woods. The southern edge at Winter Hill adds drama, when the walk descends to join the Thames towpath into Cookham. Route-finding is intricate, but paths are signposted. Nettles can be a problem in summer.

WALK DIRECTIONS

① With your back to the road, leave the car park at the far left-hand corner by footpath signpost to cross a low footbridge over stagnant water, and crossing a stile to proceed along the right edge of field (with a tree-lined ditch on your right).

When the field narrows (50 yards before end) bear left up the slope to a stile then continue along a narrow enclosed path. Emerge on to gravel track, turn right to a stile 50 yards away (or left to return to the station; left on road then immediately right

along Poundcroft Lane), to enter the golf course ②. Follow the edge of the golf course; where the fence on the left ends, keep forward across a railway bridge.

On the other side continue straight ahead, slowly climbing through the middle of golf course, passing just to the right of a brown

The beech is the hallmark tree of the Chilterns

LENGTH 6½ miles (10.5km), 3½ hours
DIFFICULTY 2
START Cookham Moor National Trust car park, just west of Cookham (north of Maidenhead), opposite a small bridge (there is a National Trust sign for Footpath Cockmarsh at car park). Grid reference 893854
By train Cookham (limited Sunday service in summer). Leave the station on the side by shops, follow road ahead then left just before The Gate pub into Poundcroft Lane; proceed ahead along a gravel track to reach the road. Turn left then immediately right on to gravel track, 50 yards later cross a signposted stile on to the golf course at ②.
OS MAPS Landranger 175; Pathfinder 1157 (SU 88/98)
REFRESHMENTS Pubs in Cookham Dean; pubs, café and tea-rooms in Cookham

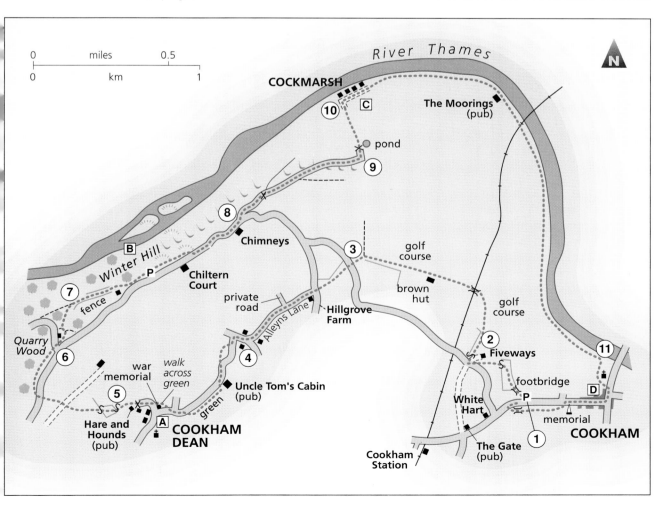

corrugated building, then soon with a hedge on left. Where the hedge ends, turn left on to the fenced path shortly to reach the road ③.

Cross the road and take the path opposite: proceed with the fence on your right, to reach a road by a stile beside gate, just to the right of white buildings (with red roof) of Hillgrove Farm. Continue ahead down Alleyns Lane to road T-junction at bottom, where you turn right along Dean Lane for 70 yards, then turn left steeply up Warners Hill, either by following the road or using a short parallel path on the right.

④ At T-junction at Uncle Tom's Cabin (pub), turn right (either along road or along grass of Hardings Green). After the green, the road bends right; at junction just after this bend, keep left, then immediately turn right across the middle of Cookham Dean village green in the direction of pub sign for Hare and Hounds Ⓐ.

On reaching the Hare and Hounds pub buildings turn right on a narrow signposted path, through a copse to reach a stile ⑤, where you continue slightly left in the field ahead, soon with a wire fence on your right to find a stile in far corner at edge of a small valley. Maintain direction down through the middle of next field to reach a track at valley bottom; proceed ahead up the other side to a double power-post.

Emerge on the road, take a narrow woodland path opposite, then right after 25 yards on path that runs closely parallel to road. ⑥ At the road junction cross Quarry Wood Road and take an enclosed path opposite, just to the right of house garden, and follow this to T-junction of paths where you turn left for 15 yards; then where iron fence on right ends, take the path on the right (*NB* if path from Quarry Bank Road is too overgrown, turn left along the road, then after 100 yards, just after last house, turn right on path, then left 70 yards later, just where the iron fence is about to begin on left). At this point there

was a metal post (remains of signpost) at time of inspection.

Follow the path through woods (there are white arrow-markers on trees); soon ⑦ you reach the top of the edge, where the path bends to right. A fence soon begins on your right; ignore a sharp left turn. Join a gravel drive for 20 yards, then just before the road turn left along a narrow path to emerge on top of Winter Hill Ⓑ.

Continue along the top of the hill, keeping off the road on your right for as long as possible, but rejoining the road near a house called Chiltern Court; ignore left road turn (Gibraltar Lane) soon after. ⑧ 30 yards beyond a house called Chimneys, fork left down a broad gravel track by National Trust sign for Cockmarsh Ⓒ.

30 yards after passing a gate beside a stile, ignore minor left fork (which descends) but keep along the level; 100 yards later ignore minor right fork (which ascends). Soon the main track gently drops. ⑨ At the bottom of slope bear left to a gate beside a stile and signpost, and follow path across field towards houses, to reach the corner of a concrete farm road. Keep forward towards the line of houses, where you ⑩ turn right, still along the track to join River Thames towpath at last bungalow (Ferry Cottage).

Keep beside the water's edge, continue along edge of field then soon along the well-defined towpath close to the river, with houses on your right. After passing under a railway bridge, continue on towpath for 1 mile. ⑪ 100 yards before the next bridge, turn right to enter Cookham churchyard.

Leave the churchyard by the far side opposite a house called Churchgate; turn left and continue ahead to reach the road; turn right then right again along the length of Cookham High Street Ⓓ. After the war memorial, walk along surfaced path (raised causeway). Just before the causeway crosses a brick bridge, turn right down steps and cross the road to return to the car park.

ON THE ROUTE

Ⓐ **Cookham Dean** Kenneth Grahame, author of *The Wind in the Willows*, used to stay here as a child with his grandmother. His uncle used to take him on the river, where he discovered the attractions of messing about in boats. In later life, when he became Secretary of the Bank of England, he came back to live at Mayfield, 1906–1910. *The Wind in the Willows* began as a series of bedtime stories for his son, Alastair, and was shaped into a book and published in 1908.

Ⓑ **Winter Hill** Fine **views** across the Thames Valley to the Chilterns.

Ⓒ **Cockmarsh** 130 acres of flat, marshy meadows and steep chalk slopes, preserved by the National Trust and designated as a Site of Special Scientific Interest. It had five ancient burial mounds, only one of which is now discernible. An excavation in the last century revealed two cremated bodies.

Ⓓ **Cookham** The artist Stanley Spencer was born here in 1891; throughout his life, Cookham was an essential source of his inspiration. Such paintings as his *Resurrection* (in the Tate Gallery), set in Cookham churchyard, are firmly rooted in the village scene. The Spencer Gallery is *open* Easter to October, daily: 10.30 to 5.30; November to Easter, Saturday, Sunday and public holidays: 11 to 1, 2 to 5.

The 15th-century inn, Bel and the Dragon, is named with reference to one of the books of Apocrypha. The inn stands on glebe land and was built as a house of refreshment for those attending church services.

Holy Trinity Church, Cookham, in springtime

COLESHILL AND BADBURY HILL

A ROUTE encompassing two small hills between the Vale of White Horse and the Thames valley with a number of features of interest, including Coleshill village, Badbury Hill, and the great barn at Great Coxwell. The walk follows well-waymarked field paths and gentle field tracks, and there are wide views for much of the way.

WALK DIRECTIONS

① With your back to the post office, turn left along the road for 30 yards, then turn left down Puddledock Lane, marked as no through road. After 250 yards, the road passes barns on the left and becomes an unmade track between hedges (avoid all side turns). ② After another ½ mile, the track enters a field by a gate; cross to the far corner on track, then go through

gate to the next field Ⓐ.

Continue on track through this second field, keeping the hedge on your right, to take the gate ahead. Emerge on to a farm track; immediately to your right are buildings of Colleymore Farm, but turn left along the track, for 200 yards. ③ Immediately after passing a cottage on the left, and just before the track enters field ahead, turn right through a gate into a field. Keep to the right-hand edge of field, then forward over double stiles into a second field, still with the hedge on your right.

Just before the buildings of Ashen Copse Farm, cross a stile to the right then immediately left, keeping farm buildings on your left (do not enter the farmyard). At the end of the second barn, continue forward on a concrete track (which comes from

the farmyard), and when 30 yards later this meets tarmac farm road cross this to take track in field ahead ④.

The track leads down slightly to the left to run alongside a wood on the left; at the end of first field, the track now has a woodland on right.

LENGTH 5½ miles (9km), 2½ hours
START Great Coxwell post office (from A420 follow signs for Great Coxwell; in village, turn left, signposted to church, and park 30 yards along the road, near post-box and post office); Great Coxwell is just off A420, Swindon–Oxford, west of Faringdon. Grid reference 270937
OS MAPS Landranger 163; Pathfinder 1135 (SU 29/39)
REFRESHMENTS Shop at Great Coxwell; shop and pub at Coleshill

⑤ When wood on right ends, do not continue forward on the obvious track, but follow the edge of the wood around to the right.

After 30 yards, as the woodland bends slightly right, go forward on the level across a field and to left side of nearest clump of oaks (this path was well marked at time of inspection, and waymark arrows were helpful), where you continue forward to cross the stile directly ahead.

Continue to a stile in the opposite fence; this is in fact a double stile, with a bridge across a ditch in between ⑥. Coleshill village is now visible ahead [B]; cross a wide field to a stile in line with the right-hand end of visible buildings, and then go forward to a gate to the right of buildings. Go through this gate on to a short section of driveway alongside a house, then forward through a gateway on to the road at a junction ⑦.

Go straight ahead, and continue along the road for 200 yards to emerge on main road at centre of Coleshill village, opposite church [C]. Turn right on the main street, passing the post office on your right, followed by Radnor Arms public house on the left. Immediately after the Radnor Arms, turn left on a minor road. ⑧ At next junction, after 150 yards, take signposted track opposite and slightly to the left, immediately forking left to enter a field. Follow left-hand edge of this and the next field [D].

At the end of second field, take path in corner (it may be obscured by vegetation) and enter a wood ⑨. Maintain direction along the side of the wood, and continue forward over a plank-bridge and stile into a field. Continue up the side of the field, with the hedge on your left, then over a stile on to a fenced path along the side of the next field. Cross plank-bridge between stiles, then turn left along edge of field to another plank-bridge between stiles 10 yards to the right of an electricity pole ⑩.

Bear half right across field ahead aiming for the stile near Brimstone Farm. Emerge on farm track and

turn right along it, keeping to the right of all farm buildings. After 75 yards cross a concrete track (which leads to the left of the farmhouse) and take the gate ahead, then go forward along the left side of a field.

Continue forward through field, keeping hedge on left, to bridge over ditch and gate at far corner. ⑪ In the next field, turn left but right after 10 yards, to stay within the field, and follow its left-hand edge. At the corner, enter woodland and continue forward on a path with hedge and field on your left. When the field on the left ends, continue ahead on a path uphill, which becomes better defined. Go directly uphill through the wood, ignoring all cross-tracks and following yellow waymarks.

⑫ As the path levels out, continue to avoid side turns, later passing an enclosure on left; the track starts to rise again, then runs alongside ramparts to the left [E], and over a stile beside a gate into Badbury Hill car park.

Continue through the car park, then proceed on track. Turn left on to the road for 200 yards. ⑬ Turn right over a stile on to a footpath signposted to Great Coxwell. Descend on a track across a field; after 200 yards, a fence comes in on the left and the track runs alongside with a plantation then small wood on the left. 50 yards before the end of the field, turn left over a stile into a wood, then half right across the corner of wood to a footbridge and stile into a field.

Once in the field, turn left along the edge of wood and follow edge of

Great Coxwell's Great Barn – almost cathedral-like in its majestic proportions

field round until a footpath sign directs you left over a gate beside a stile into enclosure around Great Barn [F]. Keeping to the right of the barn, continue forward to the road then turn right to return to the start of walk.

ON THE ROUTE

[A] Fine **views** southwards over the Vale of White Horse towards the Wiltshire downs.

[B] The field ahead used to contain **Coleshill House**, erected c.1650 but gutted by fire in 1952, and subsequently demolished. Inigo Jones contributed to its design, and the house was once described as the best Jonesian mid-17th-century house in England. All that remains are four lodges and traces of the park. A mile due south of Coleshill is Strattenborough Castle Farm, an ordinary farm whose rear, facing the great house, had two castellated sham towers erected in 1792 to add romance to the view.

[C] **Coleshill church** has a complex and obscure history, but the earliest part appears to be late Norman. The village also contains many attractive stone houses. In front of the church, on the green, is the stump of an ancient stone cross. The clockhouse, stable yard and huge walled garden (now a nursery) of Coleshill House, seen in the centre of the village, are part of a working estate owned by the National Trust.

[D] Good **views** over the Thames valley, with the woods around Buscot House visible in the middle distance.

[E] The ramparts are the remains of **Badbury Hillfort**, an Iron Age site.

[F] **Great Barn, Great Coxwell** (National Trust; pay fee into honesty box) This was built in or around the 13th century by Cistercian monks of Beaulieu Abbey in Hampshire, and remains one of the finest barns in Europe. It is of huge proportions, 152ft long, 44ft wide and 48ft high, and retains its original oak support-posts, surmounted on stone bases. William Morris, who lived nearby at Kelmscott, thought it 'as noble as a cathedral'. The barn continues to be used by the nearby farm.

DORCHESTER AND WITTENHAM CLUMPS

A FIGURE-OF-EIGHT route exploring a fine Thames valley village and taking in the unspoilt woodlands and impressive hillfort and viewpoints on Wittenham Clumps. The walk concludes with a delightful amble along the Thames towpath. Waymarking is thorough, and all of the walk is on well-tramped and visible paths. There are two very short ascents.

LENGTH 5 miles (8km), 2½ hours (or two separate walks of 2½ miles each)

DIFFICULTY 1

START Dorchester, just off A4074 (north-west of Wallingford and south-east of Oxford). Free car park by public toilets signposted from main street, near the abbey, in a side turning called Bridge End. Grid reference 579941

OS MAPS Landranger 164 or 174; Pathfinder 1136 (SU 49/59)

REFRESHMENTS Full range in Dorchester

WALK DIRECTIONS

① Turn left out of the car park and walk along the main street in village, passing Fleur de Lys Inn and George Hotel both on your left [A].
② Turn left opposite the White Hart Hotel, into Malthouse Lane; ignore a right turn into a garage, but turn right in front of a row of black-and-white thatched cottages: the lane here narrows to path width. Emerge on to a small road, turn left along it for 250 yards, then ③ fork right on to a signposted path (for Day's Lock), which passes just to the left of house No 50 (Sinodun), and between garden fences, then crosses a field. Turn right at T-junction with path in front of fence and Dyke Hills [B] (a prominent grass bank). After 150 yards cross over a track and continue forward, now on a path between fences. ④ At the end of the fenced section, go through a gate and cross a field, heading to Day's Lock on the River Thames. Turn left along the river, soon crossing it by bridges, then proceeding on the far bank on a

lane. As soon as you pass Little Wittenham church [C], take the gate on the left into Little Wittenham Nature Reserve, immediately forking left on a grassy path (marked by blue and yellow waymarks) across a large field known as Church Meadow (the right-hand path leads towards Round Hill, the prominent hill ahead: you will later return this way) [D]. ⑤ At the end of the field, take

the left-hand of two gates to enter Little Wittenham Wood. After 60 yards fork right through a wooden barrier; ignore left turn after 150 yards, but 100 yards later turn left at T-junction with a hard track, downhill along it. ⑥ Just after the track begins to rise, and as it is about to veer left, fork right on to a path rising to a stile leading into a field. Turn right on the path along

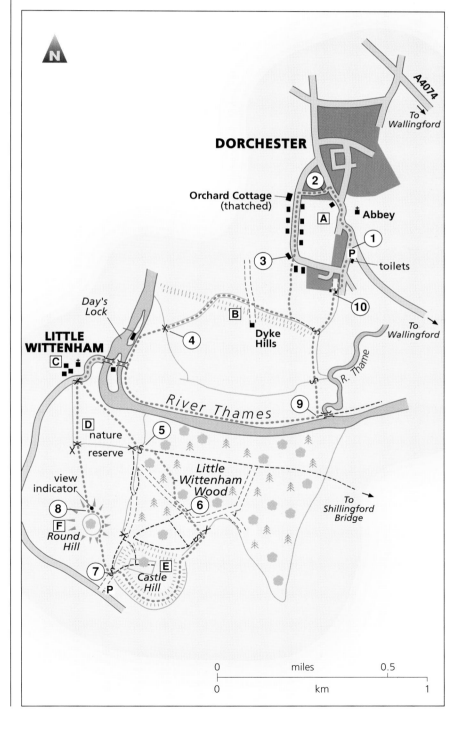

the field edge, uphill. The path crosses a stile: turn right and immediately left, on to a grassy bank (the outer rampart of Castle Hill fort) E. Follow the path along the top of this rampart until ⑦ taking a stile on the left; do not proceed on track that heads down to car park, but bear right up Round Hill, to join the fence that surrounds the woodland crowning its summit F. Turn right, alongside the fence, until reaching a bench and view indicator ⑧. From the view indicator, take the path down towards Little Wittenham church, through a gate at the bottom, then along the left edge of Church Meadow, to reach the gate passed through earlier. Turn right on the lane, to re-cross the bridges over the Thames. On the other bank, turn right along the river (you have to pass under the bridge to do this), in the other direction from Day's Lock. ⑨ After ¾ mile, just before the river path crosses a footbridge over tributary river (confusingly called the Thame), turn left, initially along the Thame, then forward as the Thame bends to the right, to take a stile. Proceed forward through a long strip-shaped field, passing a brick pill-box on the right (Dyke Hills are again seen to the left) and crossing another stile. Proceed forward, along the right edge of a field. ⑩ At the unmade lane at the edge of Dorchester, go forward (ignoring minor side turns) for 30 yards, then take the path between hedges on the right opposite a thatched cottage. Turn left at the end, passing a triangular green on your right, then go forward, to pass between Chequers Inn and Roman Catholic church, and reach the car park.

ON THE ROUTE

A **Dorchester** A handsome village that retains many thatched, tiled, half-timbered buildings. Now bypassed, this was formerly a busy staging-post on the London to Oxford road; the George and the White Hart are two imposing coaching-inns from this period. The 18th-century yellow coach standing outside the George is a reminder of the village's former importance as a stopping point; the interior of the pub is comfortably unpretentious in tone.

Dorchester **Abbey** is an Augustinian foundation, dating from the 12th century but greatly extended in the two centuries following. It has a lofty interior, with some magnificent arcades. Above all it is noted for its Norman lead front, its Jesse window with its stained glass and remarkable tracery embellished with stone figures, and the 14th-century sedilia beneath the south window. Adjacent to the abbey, the former abbey guest house and grammar school, dating from about 1400, houses a small **museum** (*open* in summer, except Mondays and Sunday mornings).

A Roman settlement was sited between modern-day Dorchester and the Thames, on a road linking Silchester and Alchester; nothing remains of it, but an altar to Jupiter and Augustus has been discovered, along with pavements and Roman coins.

B **Dyke Hills** These substantial grassy ramparts are the remains of an Iron Age town, sited on a strategic bend in the river. They consist of a double line of banks, with a ditch in between. Originally, wooden pallisades would have been built around them, protecting the community and its livestock.

C **Little Wittenham** The **church** in this tiny hamlet is largely Victorianised, but its tower is 14th and 15th century. Within the tower are memorials to the Dunch family. A brass plate of 1597 commemorates the older William Dunch, sheriff of the county, auditor to the mint and MP for Wallingford. His grandson (also William Dunch, and an MP) died 1611 or 1612 and is represented by an alabaster carving, together with that of his wife, who was related to Oliver Cromwell, and their children.

D **Little Wittenham Nature Reserve** An area of grassland and woodland, crisscrossed by public rights of way and permissive paths. The reserve includes Castle Hill and Round Hill (together forming Wittenham Clumps, each being capped by trees), over which there is open access. Some 30 species of butterflies and 120 species of bird have been seen here, and the flora includes orchids; there is a bird-watcher's hide. Some areas of the woodland are coppiced.

E **Castle Hill** These are the outer ramparts of a fort, which like Dyke Hills was an important Iron Age site; the two sites are very likely linked. In the middle of Castle Hill, a plaque identifies the Poem Tree, carved with a poem written by Joseph Tubb, 1844–45. The original inscription has, sadly, deteriorated.

F **Round Hill** The hill rises to only 393 feet but gives a fine view over the Thames valley, and across to Coombe Hill, the highest point in the Chilterns. The British Leyland Works at Cowley and Culham Laboratory are also prominent.

The view from Round Hill of Little Wittenham Church

TURVILLE AND STONOR PARK

A QUIET corner of the Chilterns, offering an enjoyable blend of mixed woods and open farmland; the route passes through the deer park of Stonor House. The rolling nature of the terrain gives changes of altitude, but there are no steep climbs.

LENGTH 8½ miles (13.5km), 4 hours

DIFFICULTY 2

START Turville, west of High Wycombe and south of M40. Grid reference 767912

OS MAPS Landranger 175; Pathfinder 1137 and 1156 (SU 69/79 and SU 68/78) or Explorer 3

REFRESHMENTS Pubs at Turville, Pishill and Stonor

WALK DIRECTIONS

① Start on the village green in Turville Ⓐ, between the church and the Bull and Butcher pub. Walk down village street to left of church; at end of village, by Turville village sign, turn left down track marked by public bridleway sign. Follow track through belt of trees and for 300 yards along left-hand edge of field,

ignoring turn to left half way down side.

② At field corner (which is not very clear-cut), turn left into wood on clear path, but after 10 yards turn sharp right and slightly uphill. After 20 yards, this path divides; take left-hand fork, as indicated by arrow on tree, and go diagonally up hill on narrow but clear path.

At top of slope turn right along woodland track, which continues to ascend and then runs along just inside top edge of wood, with field on left. After 500 yards, just before

Cobston Windmill, a fine example of a smock mill

end of wood, turn left at T-junction of tracks towards buildings of Turville Court. Turn right on surfaced farm road by house and continue down this to the road junction ③.

At the junction, go up bank to right and over stile into field, following public footpath sign. Cross field to closest point on far hedge; then turn left following hedge towards Turville Grange. Shortly before house, go right over stile and then turn left towards house. Soon cross another stile into garden and maintain direction down track to left of house. At end of wall on left, go through gate out on to Turville Heath then bear slightly right and emerge in front of the house Ⓑ.

Turn left on surfaced track, opposite wrought-iron gates to house, and follow to public road at junction. Turn right along road signposted to Northend and Watlington. ④ 70 yards later, at next road junction, continue forward on signposted footpath taking direction from signs to Saviours. Path goes to left of gate to Saviours and immediately enters

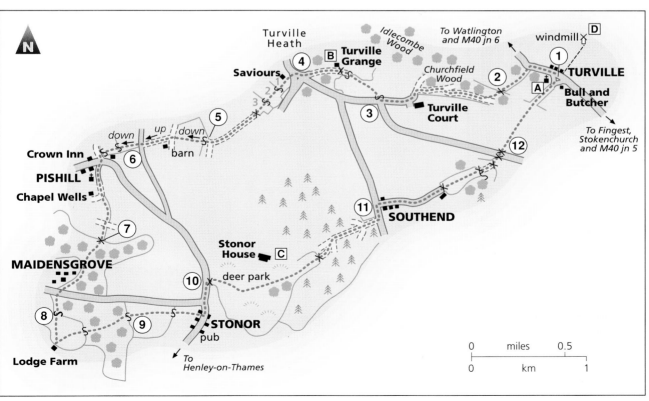

(first) field by gate. Keep to left of house keeping level and making for stile into second field. Continue forward to stile into third field, then maintain direction (diagonally) to reach kissing-gate and turn right on to fenced track.

Track soon enters field (but continues with fence on right). Follow track into next field; ⑤ after 100 yards, track divides (with left fork leading towards Stonor village, visible in its valley): take right-hand fork, marked by white arrows. Soon cross stile and descend to bottom of valley on well-defined field path to open-sided barn. Keep right of barn and then ascend to ridge, ignoring crossing path. Path becomes track.

⑥ At top of rise, cross the surfaced lane. Continue downhill alongside hedge on left to cross stile at corner of field and continue on broad path (past house and garden on left) to further stile. Turn left on track, soon reaching road where turn right. After 50 yards on road, turn left on surfaced lane signposted to Pishill church and marked as Oxfordshire Way (pub is 100 yards' detour to the right along road).

Pass Pishill church on your right then, at end of the lane, take footpath to left of entrance to Chapel Wells, on footpath marked 'PS22, OW'. After 75 yards, take left-hand fork marked OW, then down left edge of field. At bottom, ignore cross-track and continue up edge of field to enter wood ⑦. Continue forward into woods on footpath going uphill, and at top of rise maintain direction keeping field visible on right.

A ¼ mile into the woods, fork left (the right fork goes towards nearby house), now descending gently towards road. Cross road, and take right-hand path opposite (the narrower of two paths): this ascends through woods with edge of woods close on right.

After 200 yards, and shortly before end of woods, ignore stile on right but 20 yards later ⑧ take stile ahead to emerge into field. Continue straight ahead across field towards farm buildings, but at end of field do not leave field; instead turn sharp left on to path running diagonally across the field, keeping

just to the left of a pylon, to stile.

Cross this stile into woods and continue forward downhill on woodland path marked by white arrows, ⑨ to enter field by stile: continue forward and make for village of Stonor clearly visible at the bottom of the slope (crossing this and the next field, then following enclosed path into the village). Turn left on road (or detour 100 yards to right for pub).

⑩ After 300 yards, iron railings around Stonor Park start on right: here enter park through gate by sign Private Deer Park and take grassy path heading uphill and away from fence towards a line of trees. Follow the line of trees as path becomes better defined and marked by white arrows ⓒ.

After ½ mile, leave the deer park by a gate into wood. Ignore side turns (keep forward at first junction; ¼ mile later, near edge of woods, avoid left and right turns) and proceed up to road. Turn left along the road for 100 yards for minor junction at hamlet of Southend, where ⑪ turn right on surfaced track marked as public footpath, keeping small common on right. At end of common, keep to left of pair of brick houses and take farm road signposted to Southend Farm.

Follow this concrete track to end of farm buildings, and when track swings right around buildings continue forward over stile beside gate marked by white arrows. Cross field keeping just to the right of

pylons to gate beside stile in middle of far edge, then steeply down fenced track through wood. At end of wood, take gate beside stile directly ahead (ignore gate to left), then descend down left-hand edge of field to gate beside stile and road ⑫.

Cross road and enter field by gate beside stile, then forward across field; when inspected, this path was very well defined but if unclear take direction from windmill on hill ahead ⓓ. At end of field, enclosed path continues ahead, emerging after 200 yards on road by bungalows. Follow this down to main village street and starting point.

ON THE ROUTE

ⓐ **Turville** is a small village with a number of attractive half-timbered houses and a flint church of Norman origin with a 16th-century tower. The Bull and Butcher pub is a black and white timbered cottage with a garden.

ⓑ **Turville Grange** 18th century, with fine facade.

ⓒ View of **Stonor House**, its walled garden, and private chapel. Home of the Stonor family for 600 years, the original Tudor manor was extended in Tudor times, and a new roof and windows added in 1760. During the Elizabethan religious troubles, the Jesuit, Edmund Campion, had a secret printing-press here.

ⓓ **Cobston Windmill** This smock mill was constructed in the 18th century. Its top part was designed to rotate separately.

LONDON'S GREEN BELT

London is fortunate to have appreciable pockets of unspoilt countryside on its back doorstep. Without the Green Belt policy, it is likely that much of this would have been lost to the seemingly unstoppable surge of suburbanisation that crept outwards from the capital as it expanded dramatically in the 19th and 20th centuries. Rail travel made commuting a possibility for everyone; with the advent of the Metropolitan Line, speculative builders wasted no time in creating estates of suburban villas in the inter-war years.

In 1898 Ebenezer Howard published *Tomorrow*, in which he argued the case for living in garden cities, and for green belts; his vision became reality when seven years later Letchworth became the world's first garden city, with houses in a landscaped setting. Although his notions of communal land ownership have not survived, many of his ideals have had a profound effect on our lives. After the Second World War, a Green Belt was designated around London, halting further expansion. Beyond the Green Belt, a ring of New Towns (including Stevenage, Crawley, Basildon and Bracknell) were built to house a huge overspill population from London; these were designed very much like updated garden cities, with town centres and sub-neighbourhood centres.

London's Green Belt has still faced some major threats, not least by the construction of the M25 which destroyed some very fine countryside (particularly in the vicinity of the North Downs), and the hastily constructed New Towns have been criticised for their design; but the Green Belt is often cited as one of the outstanding planning success stories.

MARLOW AND THE THAMES

THE Thames towpath is the finale to a walk starting from the attractive riverside town of Marlow and heading out through fine Chilterns beech woods, which are particularly attractive in spring and autumn. Most unusually, the route follows a path that leads into a short tunnel at one point. Route-finding is a little intricate in the woodland sections, but the route takes defined paths and tracks.

LENGTH 6 miles (9.5km), 3½ hours
DIFFICULTY 2
START Marlow town centre, by obelisk and Crown public house in High Street. Grid reference 866848
OS MAPS Landranger 175; Pathfinder 1157 (SU 88/98)
REFRESHMENTS Full range in Marlow; Royal Oak at Bovingdon Green; refreshment kiosk at Temple Lock

WALK DIRECTIONS

① A From the obelisk in High Street, with Crown public house on left, turn left into West Street, then right into Oxford Road (signposted Bovingdon Green). Turn right into Queen's Road, then ② take the path on left by Duke of Cambridge pub (the path runs to the right of a concrete track); carry on into allotments, then between fields. ③ At a surfaced lane, with a house to right, turn left and fork right to reach main road. Bear right along it. Take next left turn into the hamlet of Bovingdon Green. Take the signposted stony track which leaves from the far right-hand corner of the green; immediately ignore a path on the left but keep on the track, which becomes a path between fences. Soon ignore a stile on the right but keep between fences. ④ The path enters woods: keep forward, initially with a fence on your left; at the first

Beeches are typical of the chalk hills of the Chilterns

path crossing, go forward, up a rise following arrows on trees (do not go too far right). The path is ill-defined but keeps fairly close to the left edge of woods. ⑤ Emerge by a road fork, keep left and immediately right to take right-hand road to T-junction, then proceed on the right-hand of two signposted paths: look for

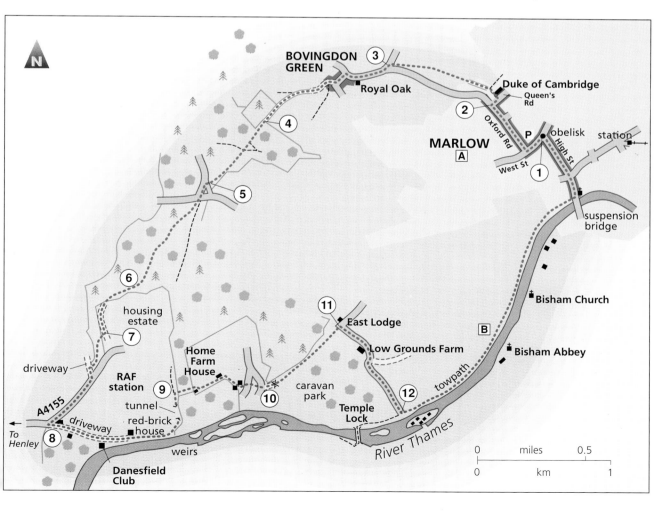

marker arrows. ⑥ After ½ mile this path bends right to skirt a housing estate, then joins a gravel track by houses; proceed (past glasshouses on left) until you reach a large multi-gabled white house on right, just before which ⑦ you take a paved path on right, down to the edge of woods, where you go left on path to reach a driveway, on which you keep left to reach a main road. Turn right. ⑧ Just before Medmenham village sign, by West Lodge, take driveway on left; beyond end of driveway find an enclosed path to right of last (red-brick) house, close

by river beneath chalky cliffs. The path eventually leaves the river, ascends and goes through a tunnel. ⑨ Where the wall on your right ends, turn right, with a fence on your right, on a woodland path, to a gate into open land: path is waymarked and continues to the right between fences, passing to the left of red-brick Home Farm House to enter a yard by farm cottages. From here, follow the lane for 50 yards, then take path on left leading down through workshop yard to road ⑩. Take the path opposite, skirting caravan park. ⑪ At gates by

East Lodge, turn right on lane, to pass Low Grounds Farm on your right, and fork right just beyond. ⑫ At the river, Temple Lock is to your right (for refreshments), but turn left along towpath B until reaching suspension bridge at Marlow, where you turn left to reach the start.

ON THE ROUTE

A **Marlow** A handsome riverside town approached from the Thames side by the suspension bridge of 1832, located next to All Saints church. Numerous houses date from around 1800, but the Old Parsonage dates from the 14th century. The Crown reputedly has counted Dick Turpin among its customers. The obelisk in the centre of Marlow commemorates the opening of the Hatfield–Bath road. At No 47 West Street is the house where the poet Percy Shelley lived from 1817 to 1818; Mary Shelley wrote *Frankenstein* here. At the Two Brewers pub, Jerome K. Jerome sketched out ideas for *Three Men in a Boat*, his comic story of three men and a dog making a trip along the Thames.

B The **Thames towpath** gains glorious views, passing Bisham Abbey (now a sports centre) and church on the opposite bank. The church contains the tomb of Lady Elizabeth Hoby, whose ghost is said to haunt the abbey. The Thames now forms the basis for a long-distance footpath, following close to the banks for much of the way.

The Thames at Marlow, a town full of literary resonances

SWAN-UPPING

Every year since the days of Elizabeth I a voyage has taken place on the Thames to mark the beaks of cygnets on the River Thames. All swans are royal property apart from some on the Thames, which belong to the Vintners and the Dyers, two ancient London livery companies. In the third week of July, the royal Keeper of Swans and the Swan Markers of the Vintners and Dyers row from Sunbury to Pangbourne, with the oarsmen colourfully attired in traditional livery and the boats festooned with flags. Roast swan forms the focus of an ensuing banquet.

THE CHESS VALLEY

THE walk takes in three attractive villages and varied and unspoilt country in and around the Chess Valley: green hills, patched with woodland, and two imposing houses. Paths are well walked but because of the intricate nature of the terrain the directions should be followed carefully.

WALK DIRECTIONS

① From the car park follow road downhill for 50 yards, then take the bridleway on left, which follows top edge of woods. After ¼ mile, ignore stile on left into playing field, but continue inside the edge of woods.

After ¼ mile pass close to a modern house, then 100 yards later turn sharp right to other side of fence on a descending woodland path ②.

At bottom of the woods, go through barrier (with Latimer House visible on hill ahead), follow the right edge of field, then cross road and take signposted gate opposite, along the left edge of small field to road junction, where you continue forward, over bridge Ⓐ, along road.

③ At T-junction, turn left, then opposite the path to church Ⓑ, take the waymarked path (Chess Valley walk) on right into field. Cross field

diagonally, making down to houses, then follow the path between hedges into main part of Latimer. Cross village green, turn right on road, then left 80 yards later by signpost, into field. Follow fence on left until it reaches a corner, then forward 80 yards to the corner of next fence, walking parallel with River Chess away to right; proceed alongside this fence. After the next field, continue on farm track, through farm, to reach the road ④. *For short walk* Turn right and follow road over river, then bear right where road divides, to reach T-junction, where you take the path opposite into woodland. Immediately fork left and follow path up the left edge of woods, then proceeding on path between hedges

Latimer's pump in the neat village green

LENGTH *Full walk* 6½ miles (10.5km), 3 hours
Short walk omitting Sarratt 3 miles (5km), 1½ hours

DIFFICULTY 2–3

START Car park (grid reference 005982), ¼ mile north of A404, 2½ miles north-west of Chorleywood; turn off A404 at east end of Little Chalfont into Stony Lane (signposted Latimer and Flaunden); car park is on left just where the woods begin
By train Chalfont and Latimer. Leave by the exit on London-bound platform, turn right outside station, left into Bedford Avenue, then right into Chenies Avenue, which you

follow to its end, ignoring side turns; where it becomes unsurfaced continue into woods, where you pass to far side of fence 20 yards away and take right-hand of two paths which descend through the woods: start walk at ②. To return to the station, follow the directions at ①, turning left through the barrier into Chenies Avenue 100 yards after the modern house.

OS MAPS Landranger 176, or 165 and 166; Pathfinder 1138 and 1139 (SU 89/99 and TQ 09/19)

REFRESHMENTS Pubs at Church End and Chenies; pub and shop at Sarratt

---

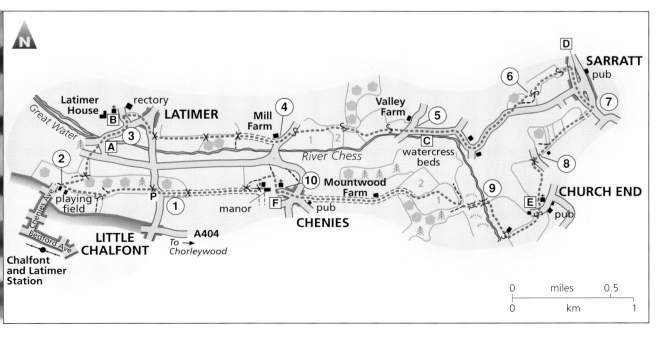

to reach Chenies church and manor house; this is point ⑩ (resume walk directions with church on right; the route will now return to the woods). *For full walk* Turn left on road, then right after 100 yards to take signposted stile: route is along the top of a pronounced grassy bank (marking old field boundary). Follow left edge of second field, then through woods, on other side of which keep right, soon joining river; in next field continue alongside river to reach corner of farm road ⑤ (left leads past Valley Farm), where keep forward for ¼ mile ⒸC, to join corner of another road. Turn right along this, then left at next junction (ahead is cul-de-sac), 50 yards after woods begin, take signposted footpath on left; keep left at fork, close to edge of woods.

⑥ Ignore gate beside stile on left leading out of woods but continue forward to stile into field: follow right edge of field, then at end take path into Sarratt ⒹD. Turn right along village green. ⑦ Just after pillar-box and post office, take lane on right, signposted Church End; after Forge Cottage cross stile and follow left edge of four fields, enter woods and fork left 20 yards later; path runs along ramshackle fence then in the same direction behind back gardens, before reaching lane ⑧.

Take kissing-gate opposite, turn left in field alongside woods, then forward to church. Emerge by church gate on to lane ⒺE, bear half right (over stile) towards signpost (for Chorleywood) 30 yards away, where you cross the driveway and take the stile into field. Turn right in field, along edge, to bottom corner, then go forward on track; turn right a few yards later to pass below cottage and over stile. Walk close to river.

⑨ At end of field, turn left, over footbridge. Path then crosses another footbridge (over channel); immediately after this avoid right fork. On entering woods, fork right, enter bottom of field and cross it diagonally (waymarked), uphill. On

Chenies, a manor house dating from the 14th century. Henry VIII stayed here with Anne Boleyn

reaching opposite hedgerow, follow it uphill, and in next field proceed along left edge to pick up farm track leading past left-hand side of farm, then on ⅓ mile to Chenies ⒻF.

Take the gravel driveway on opposite side of village green, to church ⑩, just after which turn right on path between walls. Descend into woods, where you turn left, along top edge. 120 yards later, fork left to continue along top edge. Emerge from woods just beyond house on left and continue straight ahead until path joins road at the car park.

ON THE ROUTE
ⒶA The first of a series of fine views over the **Chess Valley**; the Chess in this section has been dammed to create a landscaping effect for **Latimer House**, the grandiose 19th-century, Elizabethan-style mansion (now a National Defence College) on the hillside.
ⒷB **Latimer** A handsome early 18th-century rectory stands close to the **church**. The rest of the village surrounds a trim village green. Look out for the **wooden sheep** 'grazing' in the field crossed on the way from the church to the village.
ⒸC On the right are **watercress** beds.
ⒹD **Sarratt** has a half-mile-long

village green flanked by mostly 18th- and 19th-century cottages.
ⒺE The Norman **church**, early 19th-century **almshouses** and **pub** at **Church End** make an appealing group. The next section is one of the walk's visual highlights, with views over the Chess Valley, and a descent to the river, which is marshy and remote-feeling.
ⒻF **Chenies** has a triangular village green flanked by estate cottages built in the 1850s by the Earl of Bedford. The **church** is heavily restored, but worth a look for the spectacular array of 16th-century and 17th-century monuments in the **Bedford chapel**. Adjacent is the step-gabled and brick-turreted **Elizabethan manor house**, with a shell of one wing at the rear open to the elements. The main part of the manor is still a residence (*open* April to October, Bank Holidays and Wednesday and Thursday; afternoons only). It contains tapestries, a doll collection and a priest's hole, while in the grounds are a physic garden and a maze.

The **Red Lion**, has an L-shaped bar with old advertising signs, prints of traction engines, and a marked absence of piped music and fruit machines. It can get very crowded at weekends.

DUNSTABLE DOWNS AND THE TREE CATHEDRAL

AN excellent concentration of interesting features and varied scenery are offered by this walk. There is also a car park at Dunstable Downs, but we have started the walk at Whipsnade in order to keep the scenic highlight for the final stages. Route-finding is a little complex at times but made easier by good waymarking.

WALK DIRECTIONS

① Take the path through the barrier out of the car park, immediately fork right and go forward at a cross-junction near a bench 30 yards later A. Keep forward after 180 yards at the next cross-junction, to reach a barrier out of woods, where you take path with a fence and field on your left, for 200 yards.

② Cross the stile, go across the field towards stile (with house beyond), and turn right on the road.

LENGTH	5 miles (8km), 2½ hours
DIFFICULTY	2
START	Whipsnade Heath car park, at junction of B4540 and B4541 (south of Dunstable). Grid reference 016180
OS MAPS	Landranger 166; Pathfinder 1095 (TL 01/11)
REFRESHMENTS	Pubs at Whipsnade

After 80 yards (just after a barn on the left) take a signposted stile on the left, and follow an enclosed path until taking a stile on your left, on to a track along which you turn right. Soon, go over a cattlegrid and keep along the right edge of the field as waymarked, leaving the track but rejoining it a little further down; ignore another track forking left, but follow the main track which passes just to the right of a barn (the gate in front of barn is hard to open: access is via a concealed stile just to the left of it) ③.

Beyond the barn, continue forward to enter a field and go along its left edge. After 100 yards, take a

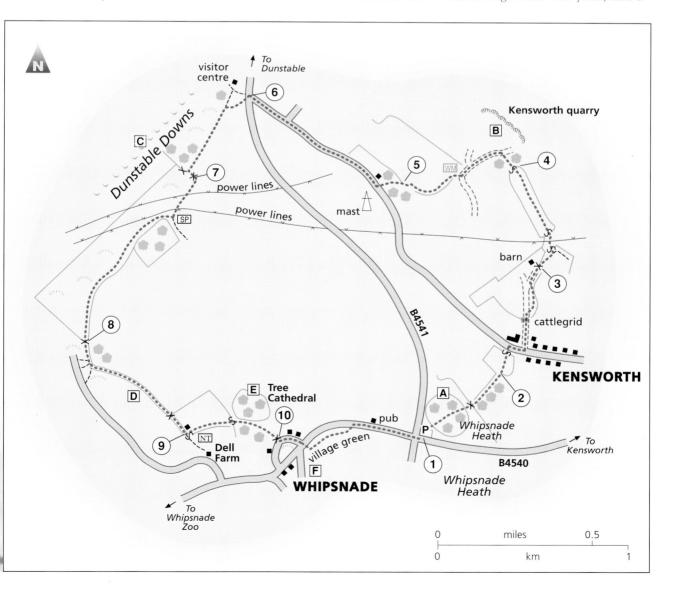

The Whipsnade Tree Cathedral, one of the National Trust's most unusual countryside properties

stile on the left and head up diagonally towards a stile by a signpost and wooden power post. Proceed along a long field, keeping level and midway up the slope (the top of which is on your right).

④ At the end, cross the stile and follow a woodland path to reach a field where you keep left Ⓑ on a track along the edge of the field. After 250 yards, leave the track where it bends left, and enter field on the right by waymark post, immediately keeping left along the left edge of field (roughly towards a mast).

⑤ 50 yards after passing under power lines, take a waymarked narrow path on the left into woods, then soon keeping along the right edge of a field to a road. Turn right on the road. ⑥ At T-junction with main road, go forward, across grass until you reach low scrubby trees (visitor centre is nearby to the right), in front of which you turn left along the level, on a path running closely to the top of the edge of Dunstable Downs escarpment, with view on the right Ⓒ. This is soon enclosed on both sides by scrub, and reaches a gate by a National Trust sign (leading into a big field crossed by pylons): do not go through the gate but turn left uphill to take the next gate ⑦.

Proceed along the top edge of this field. Just after passing under a second set of power lines ignore a bridleway signpost pointing left. ⑧ At the end of the field, go through a gate, keep alongside bushes at the top of slope, past a waymark post after 30 yards and 40 yards later bearing to the left (again waymarked) into bushes to follow an

enclosed path for ¼ mile Ⓓ to reach a signpost just beyond a modern house ⑨.

Turn left to take a stile by a National Trust sign for Whipsnade. Follow the right edge of the field towards woods; go over stile, then straight ahead for 100 yards to a waymark post. On the left is the Tree Cathedral Ⓔ. Go forward from the waymark post, with trees on your right for 150 yards, through a gate into a car park, giving access to a track ⑩. Go forward to the large green in Whipsnade village Ⓕ and turn left along the B4540 (or walk along the green) to reach the starting-point.

ON THE ROUTE

Ⓐ **Whipsnade Heath** A medieval clearing in the woods, with the trees now partly re-established; hollows here are chalk and flint excavations made by commoners in previous centuries. A circular path encompasses the heath.

Ⓑ To the right, **Kensworth quarry** is worked by a cement company, but it is designated a Site of Special Scientific Interest because of the opportunities its exposed faces present for the study of chalk formations and fossils.

Ⓒ **Dunstable Downs** This area of chalk downland, which is owned by the County Council, rises 800 feet above sea-level with a view over Ivinghoe Beacon, Totternhoe Knolls and the south-east Midlands. There may also be gliders to watch, from the nearby London Gliding Club. The chalk soil gives rise to diverse flora, birdlife and insect life.

Ⓓ This **green lane**, or 'holloway', is part of an ancient route from Whipsnade to Eaton Bray, superseded after 1800 by the present road to the west.

Ⓔ **Tree Cathedral** Created by Edmund Kell Blyth who planted a variety of species in the form of a cathedral, representing transepts, cloisters, chapels and nave. The dew pond commemorates two friends killed in the First World War. Blyth was inspired by the building of Liverpool's Anglican cathedral. An annual service is held, and explanatory maps are displayed. The Tree Cathedral is owned by the National Trust, but free access is always available.

Ⓕ **Whipsnade** is an attractive village with a huge green; houses around it date from the 17th century.

Dunstable Downs, an escarpment of the Chilterns, is considered by many to be Bedfordshire's best viewpoint. It is a popular place for flying kites and for gazing at the sunset

WILSTONE AND MARSWORTH RESERVOIRS AND THE GRAND UNION CANAL

AN unusual circuit, almost entirely on towpaths of the Grand Union Canal, its branches (including a derelict one) and the banks of its feeder reservoirs (good for bird-watching). There are short link sections across farmland and along roads. Easy route-finding, though a field path just after the start is undefined. You can start from Tring station, following the canal all the way to join the main walk.

WALK DIRECTIONS

① With the Half Moon pub on your left follow the street out of the village. Beyond the end of the village, reach T-junction with the busy B489; turn right along it for 100 yards, then cross the road carefully to the car park opposite ②. Climb steps on to Wilstone Reservoir embankment. Turn left and continue along the embankment for ½ mile. After the far corner of the reservoir, the track passes a belt of trees and reaches T-junction of tracks; turn right.

③ After 300 yards, at a gate signposted No Footpath, turn left on a path between hedges, leading up to a stile. Cross the stile, then go left along a derelict (drained) canal. ④ After 500 yards turn right on the road, follow it for 200 yards past houses (Little Tring), then ⑤ turn left, signposted Footpath, to pick up the drained canal. Just where the canal proper starts, cross to the left-hand towpath Ⓐ. ⑥ After ½ mile, cross at bridge to the right-hand towpath. Follow this for ½ mile to

A nesting great crested grebe; later, the chick will be transported on the parent's back

LENGTH 5 miles (8km), 2½ hours; 9 miles (14.5km), 3 hours if starting from Tring station **DIFFICULTY** 1 **START** Village centre, Wilstone (¼ mile off B489 and 8 miles east of Aylesbury). Grid reference 905140. Alternative start: Marsworth Reservoir car park (grid reference 919142); start walk at ⑧ *By train* Tring station. Turn left out of the station and follow the road past the hotel, and after 200 yards turn	right on the towpath along the right side of the canal. At the first bridge (¾ mile) cross to the other side of canal. Continue under second bridge ½ mile later. After 400 yards cross a footbridge to take the right branch of canals. Start at ⑦ **OS MAPS** Landranger 165; Pathfinder 1094 (SP 81/91) **REFRESHMENTS** Half Moon, Wilstone; Grand Junction Inn, near ⑦ (see map); Red Lion by bridge 130; White Lion Inn at ⑧

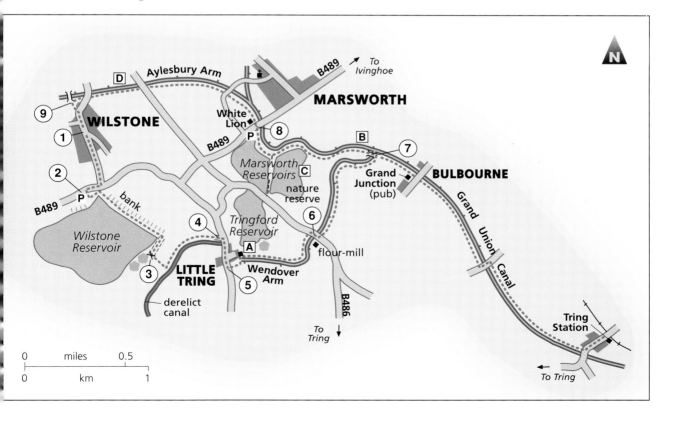

the junction with the main portion of the Grand Union Canal.

⑦ *For Tring station, turn right. To continue to Wilstone, cross the bridge to the left-hand towpath* B. Follow the towpath for ¾ mile, passing a reservoir on your left C, to bridge number 132 (the number is on a plaque above arch of bridge). ⑧ Cross the road and continue on the towpath opposite, passing the White Lion Inn. Take the left fork of canals after 300 yards. (You can detour here by taking the right canal fork to the **Red Lion** by bridge 130; a red-brick pub epitomising a village local and the occasional venue for

morris-dancing.) Follow left-hand towpath for 1 mile D.

⑨ 200 yards after passing under bridge 3, and just by a footbridge turn left to leave the canal for a footpath leading to houses at the edge of Wilstone village. Turn right on reaching the road; this leads to the village centre.

ON THE ROUTE

A **Tringford pumping station** Marks the navigable extent of the Wendover Arm. Built by the Grand Junction Canal company to pump water from the Marsworth, Wilstone and Tringford reservoirs.

B On the opposite bank are the **Bulbourne workshops**, where craftsmen make traditional wooden lock-gates.

C **Marsworth Reservoirs (nature reserve)** Divided by a dyke which you can walk along. **Birds** Wildfowl and waterside population, principally black tern and great crested grebe.

D **Birds** by and near the canal include reed and sedge warblers, little grebe, yellow wagtail, flycatchers, moorhen, coot, tufted duck, water rail, mistle thrush, kingfisher, tawny and barn owl, reed bunting and heron.

The locks at Marsworth; this walk is a must for all canal-lovers

ST PAUL'S WALDEN AND KING'S WALDEN

GRAND estates and country churches form the foci of this walk, which follows waymarked field paths and well-defined tracks for much of the way, although some sections require the walker to follow the directions carefully.

LENGTH 2½ miles (4km), 1½ hours, with optional extension to King's Walden making a total of 5 miles (8km), 2½ hours

DIFFICULTY 1

START Whitwell village centre (roadside parking), near Maiden's Head public house; on B651, south of Hitchin and east of Luton. Grid reference 184211

OS MAPS Landranger 166; Pathfinder 1072 (TL 02/12)

REFRESHMENTS Three pubs and shop at Whitwell; Strathmore Arms, St Paul's Walden

---

WALK DIRECTIONS

(1) With the Maiden's Head pub on your right, follow the main street in Whitwell, past shop, then just before the Eagle and Child pub [A], turn right into a lane called The Valley, soon crossing over the River Mimram. By the last house (Bury Hill Cottage) this lane becomes an unmade track. After 200 yards, bear right at a fork (left goes to a gate); Whitwell is soon seen to the right, then the track bends left; (2) 30 yards later take a kissing-gate on the right. Bear half left across the field (path not visible), to find a kissing-gate in the diagonally opposite corner; emerge on to a driveway leading to The Bury on the left [B], and turn right. Immediately ignore a minor track to the right; the driveway bends left. (3) At the next junction, keep forward (right turn goes to lodge), passing Gothic-style

Garden House on the right. At the next junction go straight on ignoring right fork. (4) When you reach a T-junction with the road

All Saints' Church, St Paul's Walden – the first of the churches on the walk

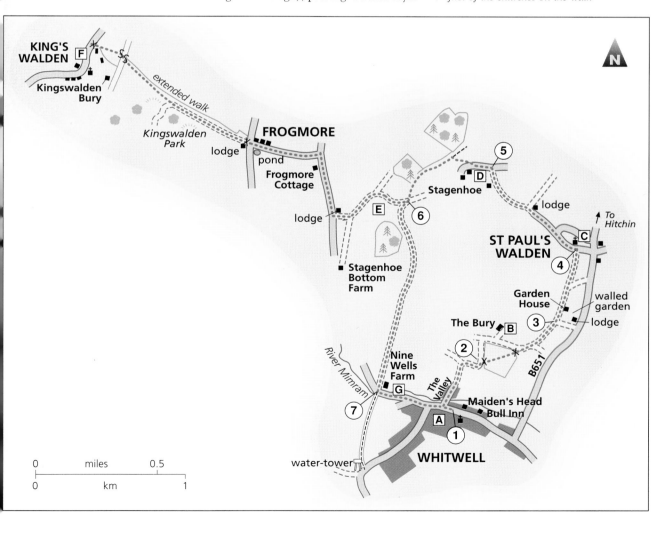

opposite St Paul's Walden church C, turn left. At a lodge, take the unmade track ahead (ignoring track to the right), leading past a castellated estate house on the left and on to a T-junction with a driveway ⑤. Turn left. After 70 yards, just before the gateway to the Sue Ryder Home (Stagenhoe) D, take the waymarked path on the right, alongside railings and along the left edge of field, initially closely parallel to driveway. At the corner of the field, as the driveway bends to the left, turn right and almost immediately bear half left through break in hedge, cutting briefly across the corner of next field to a waymarked path T-junction in front of a fence; turn left. The path drops. ⑥ Soon after woodland on the right ends, you reach a path junction at the bottom of a slight valley with houses visible to the right E.

For extended walk to King's Walden Turn right, heading for a distant double-gabled house with shutters: keep left at the first track junction, bending round to the left, then right at the next junction, on a track leading up to the left side of the lodge. Emerge on to a road, turn right along it, then left at next road junction. Soon you reach houses at the hamlet of Frogmore; just past the pond, keep forward at road T-junction to take the estate gate just to the right of the lodge. Follow the track for ⅓ mile until it bends left, where you keep forward as signposted, alongside fence on right (ignore stiles over the fence). Cross the driveway by taking stiles on either side, then cross a field, to a gate between rightmost houses and barn. Turn left on the road, to King's Walden church F. Retrace your steps to ⑥, and turn right to continue on the track uphill.

For short version of walk omitting King's Walden Go straight on (by turning left and immediately right) on the track uphill.

Both versions of walk As the track begins to descend, Whitwell comes into view. Proceed to reach the road ⑦; turn left G and follow the road back to the starting-point.

ON THE ROUTE

A The **Eagle and Child** at Whitwell derives its name from the badge of the Stanley family, the earls of Derby. Reputedly their ancestor Sir Thomas Latham had his illegitimate son placed under a tree in which an eagle had its nest; he brought his wife to the spot, where he pretended to see the infant for the first time and persuaded her to adopt the child as their heir. When he later changed his mind, the family altered the eagle crest to one bearing the eagle preying upon a child.

The **Bull Inn** was allegedly haunted by the ghost of a recruiting officer from the Napoleonic wars; a skeleton was found walled up in a cupboard here in the 1930s and was laid to rest in the churchyard, after which the ghostly happenings ceased.

B **The Bury** is the residence of the Bowes Lyon family and was the childhood home of the Queen

William Morris stained glass windows at King's Walden church

Mother. The house is a mixture of Georgian and neo-Elizabethan styles, having been substantially rebuilt in 1887. The woodland garden was laid out in 1730 with temples, statues and vistas.

C **Church of All Saints, St Paul's Walden** The church retains a medieval plan, but is memorable for its painted wooden ceiling and its baroque modifications when the lord of the manor, Edward Gilbert, 'repair'd and beautifi'd' the chancel, adding a vaulted ceiling, a screen and stucco wall decoration. A plaque commemorates the baptism of the Queen Mother here in 1900.

D **Stagenhoe** Now owned by the Sue Ryder Foundation for the Sick and Disabled, the imposing manor house is best seen from the track followed towards Whitwell at the end of the walk. It was for a period from 1488 held by the first Earl of Derby.

E In the enclosure ahead and to the right, **muntjac deer** may be seen.

F **King's Walden** Approached on this walk along a track through quintessential parkland, with mature oak trees. The **church** has some Early English arcades, a 15th-century carved screen and a stained-glass window (in the south wall, just to the right as you enter) by William Morris, the father of the Arts and Crafts movement. Look at the back of the church at the base of the tower for the church's celebrated – and enigmatic – medieval graffiti, which includes some semi-legible Latin scribblings and a jester-like figure playing what is thought to be a shawm (an early wind instrument). The image seems to be rather high up at first glance; but a look round the church reveals that the floor level has been appreciably lowered over the centuries.

G **Watercress beds** of Nine Wells Watercress Farm are seen on the left of the road; watercress may be on sale here.

ARDELEY AND BENINGTON

THIS route offers characteristic East Anglian landscape at its best, sufficiently undulating to sustain interest, with the villages of Ardeley and Benington the main focal points. Most of the going is along gentle farm tracks and the route is quite easy to follow.

WALK DIRECTIONS

① From the signpost on the grass triangle, with the direction for Great Munden on your left, turn right along a cul-de-sac, passing a post-box on your right. Keep to the principal road, which becomes an

unsurfaced track at the end of the village. Fork right at a major fork of tracks (just before a lone brick bungalow); 100 yards after the bungalow keep on the track as it bends left.

After ⅓ mile ②, fork left; 250

yards later ignore a sharp right turn. 500 yards later, bear right at a track junction by a waymarker post with a blue arrow, following a track along the right edge of the field towards Ardeley. Emerge at a housing estate, go forward to a T-junction with the

LENGTH 8½ miles (13.5km), 4 hours	centre of the hamlet. Grid reference 326255
DIFFICULTY 2	
START Wood End, on minor road signposted south-east from Ardeley and east of Walkern; limited roadside parking near small grass triangle with road signpost at the junction in the	**OS MAPS** Landranger 166; Pathfinder 1073 (TL 22/32)
	REFRESHMENTS Pub in Ardeley; pubs and shop in Benington

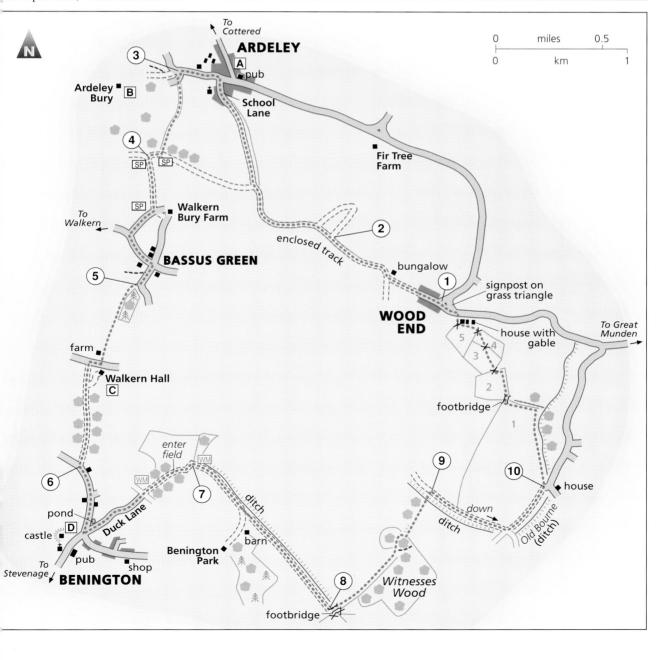

main village road A where you turn left, past the church.

③ Where the road bends right (after 400 yards) turn left (signposted Wood End) on a concrete track, keeping forward after 30 yards where it bends right through a gate, now on a path between hedgerow trees, and later with a hedgerow on the right only along the edge of a field B. At the end of the field, pass through a strip of woodland, then ④ turn right at a path T-junction.

After 80 yards, you reach a corner of the track by a signpost; turn left downhill, dipping then rising, to reach a farm road with the farm away to your left. Bear right along the farm road to T-junction with lane where you turn left. At houses (Bassus Green) turn right at the crossroads, towards Clay End. ⑤ After 150 yards, where trees begin, fork right on to a track signposted public bridleway, initially with woods on your left, then along the left edge of a field, dipping then rising to Walkern Hall Farm. Turn right on the road, then left after 50 yards by a signpost to Benington C, on a track which later merges into a concrete track, and proceeds along an avenue to reach a road ⑥. Left on road, into Benington D. At the road junction in the village centre, turn sharp left into Duck Lane (signposted Clay End). Where the lane becomes an unsurfaced track, go forward; 50 yards later, at a junction, keep forward by a blue waymarker post.

Benington in late autumn, with St Peter's Church

The track soon drops gently and bends left to enter a field with a ditch on the right. ⑦ After 80 yards, turn right by a waymark post, crossing the ditch and now on a track with a ditch alongside on the left, along the bottom of the valley. After ⅓ mile cross a track and keep forward alongside the ditch, soon merging into a better-defined track, still along the valley floor. 200 yards before going under a power line, ignore a left fork; keep the ditch on your left, go under the power line and ⑧ immediately cross a footbridge on the left and go uphill with a fence on your right and soon a wood on the right.

Enter the wood at a recessed corner, keep forward inside the woods (immediately ignoring a minor right fork) to reach a field after 100 yards. Turn right for 20 yards and then left along a grassy strip (old field Boundary) which soon becomes a hedgerow (walk along right-hand side of it), leading towards power lines. ⑨ At the end of the hedgerow, you reach a waymark post and ditch, and turn right at T-junction with track.

Follow this down to the bottom of the valley where you turn left at a junction, on a track with a ditch on the right. ⑩ Where a bridge and road appear on the right, ignore them and keep forward (or to avoid field route, if it is overgrown, you can turn left along the road, then left at next junction to return to Wood End), still with ditch on right. Soon you pass another bridge on your right, ignore a minor left fork, and turn left at the end of the field, with the hedgerow and ditch on your right.

At the next field corner, turn right over a low brick bridge to enter a second field, where you go forward up the right edge, turning left at the top right-hand corner, then after 50 yards take a gate on the right into a third field. Go diagonally left across to a gate in line with the nearest house (with dormer gables) in this

The brick well on Ardeley's village green was built in 1917 as a romantic feature

and the fourth field.

Enter the fifth field, proceed on the right edge (past the house on your right) and soon take a gate on the right by an open-sided barn (not through farmyard just before this) to follow a concrete track to the road. Turn left to the centre of Wood End.

ON THE ROUTE

A **Ardeley** A semi-circle of whitewashed thatched cottages are delightfully positioned around the green. The church opposite has interesting 15th-century roof tracery, ornate roof-bosses and angels bearing musical instruments.

B **Ardeley Bury** is seen away to the right. The house has a late-Tudor core, but what you see is a capricious indulgence of 1820, built for a Mr John Murray, with fanciful flint turrets, pinnacles, Gothicised windows, a baronial hall, a musicians' gallery and wedding-cake vaulting.

C **Walkern Hall** (on left) is early 19th century with a Greek Doric porch.

D **Benington** has an enchanting village green with a pond overhung by willows and surrounded by 16th-century plaster-rendered and half-timbered cottages, with the ancient Bell Inn close by. Near the church stands The Lordship, a Georgian house incorporating a strange mock-Norman folly made out of ruins of a castle demolished in 1212. With gate-house and portcullis, the effect is eye-opening.

BROCKET PARK AND AYOT ST LAWRENCE

THIS route begins on a path into the woods of the Brocket Estate, leading on to landscaped parkland and the miniature valley of the River Lea (here not much more than a brook), which winds its way between marshes to Waterend and is followed by the waymarked Lea Valley walk. A fine parkland avenue leads from Lamer House towards Ayot St Lawrence before the final sections along farmland tracks and the Ayot Way, a dismantled railway line. The short version of this walk follows the River Lea before returning along the Ayot Way. The views are much more extensive on the full version of the walk.

WALK DIRECTIONS

① A From the Waggoners' Inn take the stile opposite and slightly to left; follow waymarked path, soon into woods of Brocket Park.

② After ¼ mile, at junction of tracks near the edge of woods, fork right as waymarked, and proceed to emerge into golf course. Keep forward along path across golf course. At estate road turn right (or continue along estate road for view of lake from bridge, then retrace

steps) on path between fences waymarked Lea Valley Walk.

③ On reaching estate road again, cross it and turn left into field. Proceed initially alongside the fence on left, then maintain same direction over a rise where fence bears left (path is waymarked) B. Pass close to estate buildings and

LENGTH *Full walk* 8 miles (13km), 4 hours *Shorter walk* (omitting Ayot St Lawrence) 5 miles (8km), 2½ hours

DIFFICULTY 1 or 2

START Ayot Green, immediately west of A1(M), 3½ miles north of Hatfield. Take B197 (which runs closely parallel to A1(M) from Welwyn southwards), and turn off at signpost to Ayot St Lawrence and Ayot St Peter. After crossing the bridge over motorway, immediately

turn left (into Brickwall Close) and park on roadside by the Waggoners' Inn.

Grid reference 221140

OS MAPS Landranger 166; Pathfinder 1095 and 1096 (TL 01/11 and TL 21/31)

REFRESHMENTS Waggoners' Inn, Ayot Green, Brocket Arms (also serves teas at weekends and Bank Holiday Mondays, Easter to end of September), Ayot St Lawrence

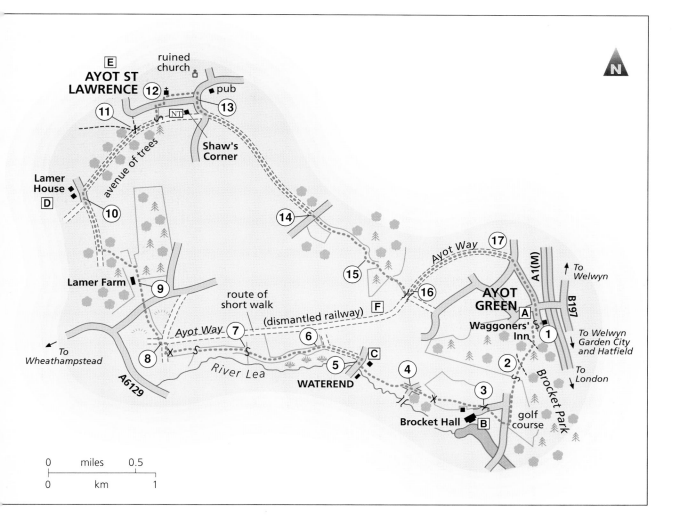

head across to a gate/stile visible on edge of woodland. Enter a wood, follow yellow marker arrows, ignoring any left turns, soon descending to a junction of tracks ④.

Continue forward on track following edge of the woods, then soon into fields. ⑤ After ⅓ mile, reach a road at Waterend Ⓒ; turn right on road, then left after 50 yards on a signposted bridleway (Lea Valley Walk). ⑥ After ¼ mile, where the main track bends right, continue ahead, parallel with a brook. The track soon enters a field, following left edge.

⑦ Beyond the stile, continue forward following power lines, and leave the field by a stile in far right-hand corner, just to the right of last power post. Beyond it, turn left on track, follow the gate at end of field, beyond which you turn right at T-junction of tracks (you cross over the Ayot Way, a dismantled railway line; *for short walk* turn right along it and follow 2 miles; ignore side turns until emerging at road junction; this is ⑰). ⑧ After 130 yards turn left at track junction, then 75 yards later turn right and ascend bank to a stile and follow path beyond. At the road, cross to the track opposite.

⑨ Shortly after trees begin on right, ignore left turn to farm but keep ahead on grassy track for 100 yards, then turn left (Footpath marked on tree). Keep along left side of the line of trees, then follow path into woods. Turn right, following woodland path until reaching a gate on to hard track, along which you turn right.

⑩ After ⅓ mile the track merges into a tarmac estate road: proceed along it for 100 yards, then fork right (left is Private, into Lamer House Ⓓ). The track runs along an avenue of trees. ⑪ Where the avenue ends, keep right on main track, ignoring signposted track to Ayot St Lawrence. Proceed just inside edge of woods, ignoring turnings to right, then at the end of second field on left, and 50 yards before track emerges into field, take a stile on left, and follow the right edge of field to a road. Turn right on road, then take next track on left, signposted St Lawrence's Church Ⓔ.

⑫ With the façade of the church behind you, turn left through ornate iron gates, then turn right on a grassy track and follow this to the road. Turn left for Ayot St Lawrence village, but to continue, turn right on road. ⑬ At Shaw's Corner ignore the right turn but keep forward, signposted Wheathampstead. Road soon bends left, then, where it bends right 20 yards later, keep forward on the signposted bridleway.

⑭ ¾ mile later cross the road and take a bridleway opposite alongside woods. Soon, the fence on right ends. ⑮ At the end of (large) field, track bends right (still alongside woods), then 100 yards later bears left to leave field and enter woods: keep forward, soon emerging into field. Track follows left edge of field for 50 yards, then bears left into next field, following the right edge in the same direction.

⑯ Where an old railway bridge crosses the track, take path on right up to it and turn left on to the old railway track Ⓕ (this is a permissive path only; in the unlikely event of it being closed, proceed under the railway bridge, and follow the track to road. Turn left on road, then take first right to Ayot Green). ⑰ When you reach the road junction, take signposted road ahead for Ayot Green and follow this to start.

ON THE ROUTE

Ⓐ **Ayot Green** Consists of about a dozen cottages flanking a tree-fringed triangular common.
Ⓑ **View** of Brocket Hall, an 18th-century red-brick mansion designed by George Paine; stands above the Broadwater, an ornamental lake crossed by a stone bridge.
Ⓒ **Waterend** A ford and a couple of houses. One is the West End House, a fine brick manor-house (1610); the other (across the brook) is the medieval White Cottage.
Ⓓ **Lamer House** Only a pretty stable-block is visible from the route. Apsley Cherry Garrard, co-traveller with Scott on the doomed Antarctic journey and author of *The Worst Journey in the World* (a title reputedly inspired by Shaw) lived here. Lamer Park has now lost some of its parkland feel but retains a fine

avenue along its north-eastern approach.
Ⓔ **Ayot St Lawrence** George Bernard Shaw lived at the new rectory, which he renamed Shaw's Corner, from 1906 until his death in 1950. Personal items inside include his walking sticks and notebooks. Shaw allegedly settled here because of an epitaph in the churchyard to a woman who died at 70, which said simply, 'Her life was short'; he thought that a village considering 70 a short life must be a good one to live in. The house is maintained by the National Trust and is *open to the public*.

The village has two **churches**: the first encountered on this walk is the new one, designed by Revett in 1778–9, its giant portico modelled on the Temple of Apollo at Delos; its position completes a vista from Lamer House. The second church is a Gothick, ivy-clad ruin. Other noteworthy buildings in the village include Ayot House (three-storey, early 18th century) and the half-timbered cottages adjoining the pub. **The Brocket Arms** dates from the 14th century and little has changed in this atmospheric old pub. The bar is beamed, with an inglenook at one end, and tales of hauntings abound featuring ghostly voices and mysterious footsteps.

The eye-catching Greek portico of Ayot St Lawrence's 'new' church

Ⓕ **Dismantled railway (Ayot Way)** Opened in 1860, linking Hatfield and Dunstable via Welwyn and Wheathampstead; closed to passenger traffic in 1965. When the gravel workings nearby were shut in 1971, it ceased operation completely.

ESSENDON AND STRATTON'S FOLLY

Surprisingly rural despite its proximity to suburban Hertfordshire, and justifiably one of the most walked parts of the country. The pub at Essendon is midway and the folly tower is seen in later stages. Route-finding moderately easy, but mud can be a problem.

WALK DIRECTIONS

① Proceed on the road (in direction from which you arrived, i.e.

continuing away from Goff's Oak), passing New Park Farm and house, and then on a farm track. After ½ mile the track bends right; ② 50 yards later, keep straight on (ignoring a minor track on left) to reach houses, then go forward to the road. Turn left on road and immediately right at junction signposted Essendon.

③ After ¼ mile, where the lane is about to bend right, fork left on to a

LENGTH 6½ miles (10.5 km), 3½ hours
DIFFICULTY 2
START At west end of village of Newgate Street (north of Cuffley), signposted from war memorial in centre of Goff's Oak (from which you keep left at next T-junction as signposted and left opposite Newgate Street church, by the Gable House Restaurant); park on roadside just before houses end. Grid reference 295052
OS MAPS Landranger 166; Pathfinder 1120 (TL 20/30)
REFRESHMENTS At Essendon; shop (open Sunday) and pub at Little Berkhamsted; Beehive Inn at ⑬

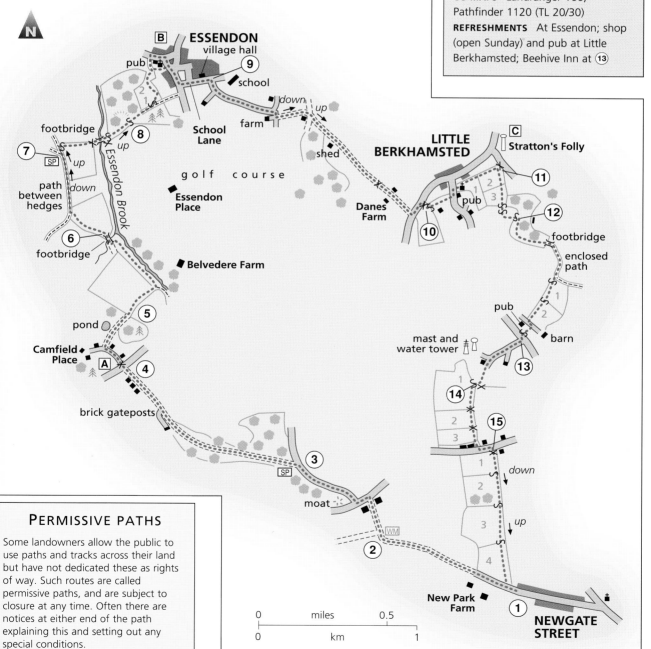

PERMISSIVE PATHS

Some landowners allow the public to use paths and tracks across their land but have not dedicated these as rights of way. Such routes are called permissive paths, and are subject to closure at any time. Often there are notices at either end of the path explaining this and setting out any special conditions.

woodland bridleway, which goes along the inside edge of woods; later views open up to your right as the track now runs in narrow woodland strip. Eventually keep forward on joining an unsurfaced driveway (at brick gateposts on left); finally, past houses on left, the track soon reaches a road ④.

Cross the road and take signposted driveway opposite. Follow this for 120 yards to a T-junction by signpost, where you bear right Ⓐ; 150 yards later ignore left turn, go forward on woodland track to enter the open ⑤. Enter the left-hand of two fields and continue in the same direction along right edge (in line with a distant tower on skyline), down to the bottom of valley. In the bottom corner of field, find a narrow path through the hedge and turn immediately left at junction of woodland paths (immediately past remains of kissing-gate at time of inspection).

The route proceeds inside woods with a stream away to the right, mostly on a sunken path with edge of woods on left. Cross a footbridge over a tributary coming in from left, picking up path on other side, and enter field ⑥. Go forward along left edge. Just before the end of the field (where boundary hedge curves right) go through break in hedgerow on left (this may be somewhat overgrown in summer) and immediately turn right on to a track between hedges.

⑦ After ⅓ mile, after the track rises, you reach a waymark at junction, and 20 yards later turn right at second waymark, and go down left edge of field to take the gate at the bottom. Cross the footbridge and go up into semi-open woodland, where the path rises, close to fence on right. Beyond the next stile there is a strip of cypresses and coppice on left; ⑧ 80 yards after a field begins on left, take stile on left and head across to a stile in line with Essendon church.

In the second field proceed along top (right) edge until stiles on the right give access to third field, where you head to a gate at left-hand end of churchyard. The pub is reached by enclosed path – or go through the churchyard Ⓑ.

Either way, turn right on village street to reach T-junction with main road. Turn right and take first left (School Lane). ⑨ 50 yards after the village hall on left, bear right on signposted farm road for Little Berkhamsted; ignore private driveway on right after 70 yards. Track now becomes a surfaced path and crosses golf course. It drops past a converted barn on the right and drops down to a mock-timbered house (Sandpit Lodge) at the edge of the golf course. With Sandpit Lodge on your right follow the farm track which rises through trees and later passes Danes Farm to reach a road. Turn left on road.

⑩ After 100 yards, take gates on right (by mains post marked 3 WO 10); follow the left edge of the field for 50 yards, then cross a stile on left and follow left edge of cricket pitch towards houses at Little Berkhamsted.

Turn left on road then take the signposted stile on right immediately before the church lych-gate. Enter the field, follow its left edge (with tower in view Ⓒ on left), proceed along left edge of second field (you can detour to the tower by taking gate at end, turn left on road and right at junction).

⑪ At the end of the second field, turn right (still inside the field, with hedge on left), and along the left edge of third field, entering trees at end of field and crossing a stile. The path proceeds inside edge of woodland for a short distance before entering next field, where you go forward along right edge for 30 yards: here do not cross stile on right, but turn left downhill to cross a stile into woodland ⑫. Immediately turn right by a waymark post (route 3; blue arrow) by path junction; the path leads round the woods, eventually curving left and later crossing a footbridge to leave the woods.

Where the main path bends markedly left, take the stile ahead into a field; go forward to follow the right edge of two fields, cross a track and follow the right edge of third field to reach a road (the Beehive Inn is on your right) ⑬. Turn left on road and after 20 yards turn right on to a minor road (signposted as bridleway to Little Berkhamsted). 50 yards before road ends by a mast (no access), bear left in front of house, and proceed with a brick garden wall on the right, then a water channel on right.

⑭ At the end of this field take stile on right, and turn left to proceed along left edge of three fields until a path by a house gives access to the road ⑮. Turn left on road and after 100 yards turn right by signpost, taking right-hand of two gates (left goes to house). Newgate Street is now visible on the rise ahead: go down left-hand side of two fields (at bottom, cross earth bridge with pond on right), then up left-hand side of two more fields to reach the starting-point.

The Five Horseshoes at Little Berkhamsted is one of three pubs along the walk

ON THE ROUTE

Ⓐ The lake on your left is part of the grounds of **Camfield Place**, where Beatrix Potter used to stay as a child and where she wrote her first rabbit story; the house, which she described as 'the place I love best in the world' was built by her grandfather, Edmund Potter. More recently it was acquired by novelist Barbara Cartland.

Ⓑ **Essendon** The **church** contains a shapely classical font made of black Wedgwood basalt-ware; given to the church in 1778 by Mary Whitbread, who also wove the Royal Arms hanging here. A fine cedar of Lebanon shades the churchyard.

Ⓒ **Stratton's Folly** Built 1789, by John Stratton; 150 spiral steps lead up to a former library.

THE WIMPOLE ESTATE

THE Wimpole Estate, owned by the National Trust, incorporates the largest continuous area of grassland in Cambridgeshire. The area is laced with rights of way and permissive paths, both of which feature on this walk; the terrain is mildly hilly. There are admission fees for Wimpole Hall and Home Farm, but not for the park, which is always open. The estate has a large number of rare breeds.

The main version of the walk has a surprise element, by reserving the view of the park and hall for the middle. The shorter version starts from Wimpole Hall itself and follows a course along tracks and across areas of farmland and grassland.

WALK DIRECTIONS

① Take Wimpole Road, opposite Hoops Inn, and follow it for 100 yards. Just after house number 18 on the right, take a track on the right (a signposted public footpath), leading past buildings; ignore a turn to the left and carry forward between hedges to a gate into a field. Cross the field half right to a stile in the diagonally opposite corner ②. Do not join the road beyond the stile but turn left through a gate (on a track leading towards barns of Manor Farm) and immediately take a stile on the left. The path continues along the right-hand fence; the field soon broadens; keep right, heading for a gate, giving on to a prominent rising track at the

LENGTH 4½ miles (7km), 2 hours
Short walk from Wimpole Hall 2½ miles (4km), 1½ hours

DIFFICULTY 1

START *Full walk* Hoops Inn, Great Eversden (south-west of Cambridge, on minor road off A603). Grid reference 364535
Short walk Wimpole Hall car park (by stable block; signposted off A603); start walk at ⑨. Grid reference 338510

OS MAPS Landranger 15; Pathfinder 1003 (TL 25/35)

REFRESHMENTS Hoop Inn, Great Eversden; refreshment room in Wimpole Hall (no admission charged if not visiting house)

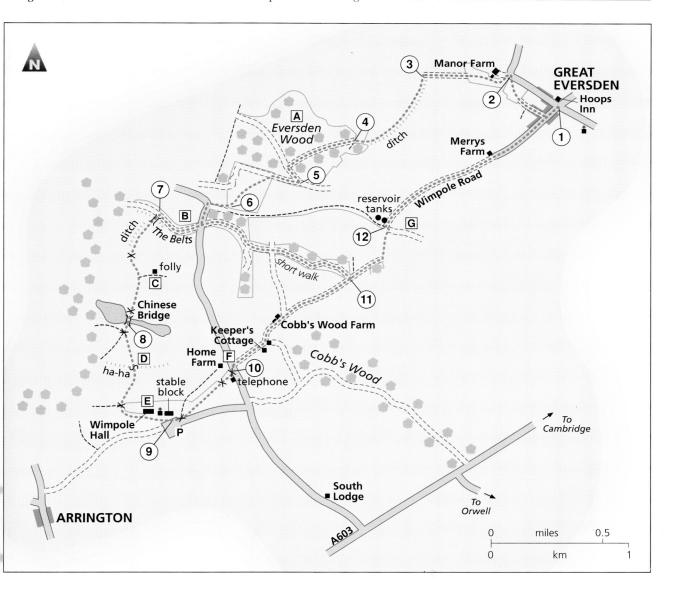

far end of the field. The track rises, then dips; ③ at the bottom of the dip, as the track ends, cross the ditch and turn left uphill, with the ditch alongside on your left. On reaching the corner of Eversden Wood, turn right. ④ In the next field, at the corner, enter woodland by taking the right-hand of two woodland tracks (going half left from previous direction) Ⓐ. Carry on until you reach a T-junction of tracks in woodland, where you go left. ⑤ After 150 yards, take a short path on the right, then almost immediately turn right on a track inside the edge of the wood. This soon leaves the wood and follows the edge of the field (at this point, the right of way should go half left to a gap in the diagonally opposite corner, by woodland, but if this is obstructed by deep ploughing or crops it may be easier to continue around the edge on the track). ⑥ From the point where the route goes through the gap into the next field, carry on along the edge of field, with woodland on your left, to reach a road. Turn left on the road. Just after woodland begins on the right, take a path (Wimpole Way) through a barrier on right, into woodland.

⑦ Ⓑ After ¼ mile, take the next path to the left, crossing a ditch by a footbridge and continuing down the right edge of field to the next gate. In the middle of the next field, there is an optional detour left to the folly Ⓒ. Return from the folly and carry on along the path you were following, leaving field by the next gate and crossing Chinese Bridge. ⑧ Beyond the next gate, head across the grass, towards Wimpole Hall, passing over a ditch by a ladder-stile Ⓓ, then keeping just to the right of the Hall, through kissing-gates. Turn left and pass in front of the Hall Ⓔ, chapel and stable block to reach a car park.

⑨ Ⓕ Leave the car park at the end furthest from the Hall and stable block, taking a gate on the north side of main access road and heading across a field towards a telephone-box in the middle distance and just to the right of large thatched barns of Home Farm;

The Italianate whimsy of Wimpole Hall's stable block, built in 1851

a kissing-gate just to the left of the telephone-box gives access to the estate road ⑩. Turn left and immediately right on a track (public footpath). At a brick lodge building (Keeper's Cottage), keep round to the left, then pass the buildings of Cobb's Wood Farm on your left (ignore a turning to the left). The track heads uphill and eventually passes woodland on the left ⑪.

For short walk Just before woodland on left ends, take woodland track on left and follow it, ignoring all side turns, until reaching a road. Cross and take the path beyond barrier opposite, into woodland and resume directions at ⑦.

For full walk Keep right as woodland ends (ignoring path into field on left). At the end of the field, keep forward as main track bends right, on a path to the left of a small woodland. Emerge at a field, where the view opens out ahead Ⓖ, and turn left. ⑫ At the next path junction, by reservoir tanks, take the track on the right and follow it down to Great Eversden; this track is Wimpole Road.

ON THE ROUTE

Ⓐ **Eversden Wood** is a patch of ancient woodland, a rare survival for Cambridgeshire, and consists of mixed deciduous trees and coppice.

Ⓑ The Wimpole estate was famous for its Dutch elms, but in the 1970s Dutch Elm Disease struck. This woodland, known as **The Belts**, was once victim; another was the 2¼-mile South Avenue, planted in 1720. Oak, ash and maple have been planted to remedy this loss.

Ⓒ The **folly** is an imposing mock-Gothic 'ruin' built in 1768 to grace the vista from Wimpole Hall. From the 19th century until the 1940s the tower was the living quarters for the head gamekeeper.

Nearby, the **Chinese Bridge** spans a neck of water leading into an attractive lily pond.

Ⓓ The path crosses the ditch over a ladder-stile; the ditch is a **ha-ha**, a landscaping contrivance whereby livestock could be contained within an area without the need for erecting a fence, which would have spoilt the view from the house.

Ⓔ **Wimpole Hall** (National Trust) The great mansion was built around 1640 by Sir Thomas Chicheley and later substantially enlarged and modified. James Gibbs, architect of St Martin-in-the-Fields in London, designed the chapel and library, while Sir John Soane, designer of the Bank of England, made further transformations in the late 18th century. In the latter part of the 18th century Capability Brown was employed to landscape the estate in the naturalistic manner that became such a hallmark of English garden design.

Adjacent to the Hall is the **Church of St Andrew**, a medieval church, classicised in 1749 and given Gothic touches in 1887. It possesses some fine monuments. The **stable block**, built in 1851, contains an exhibition on the estate, and visitor facilities.

Ⓕ Numerous rare breeds of farm animals are seen on the estate. There is a fascinating collection, together with an exhibition of bygone agricultural implements, in **Home Farm** (admission payable), signposted from the car park.

Ⓖ The view northwards encompasses the **radio telescopes** sited on the former Oxford–Cambridge railway line, and further to the left the **University Library** tower in Cambridge.

SHEPRETH AND BARRINGTON

NATURE reserves and thatched Cambridgeshire villages are the highlights of this level walk through pastoral countryside with a strong botanical interest.

LENGTH 3½ miles (5.5km), 1½ hours

DIFFICULTY 1

START Shepreth station. Grid reference 392482. *Alternatively* at car park by sign for Shepreth Riverside Walk, grid reference 385490, beginning the walk at ⑦

OS MAPS Landranger 154; Pathfinder 1026 (TL 24/34)

REFRESHMENTS Pubs at Shepreth and Barrington

WALK DIRECTIONS

① With Shepreth station on left walk along the road to the village, passing a sign pointing left to the Willers Mill Wildlife Park Ⓐ and then the village hall. When road junction is reached bear left past telephone box.

② Road passes weatherboarded mill house Ⓑ. Beyond the roadbridge in front of the mill, take Angle Lane bearing left and signposted Public Footpath to Barrington. This leads behind the Wildlife Park, and after 300 yards reaches railway at the gated crossing ③.

Beyond the crossing the route

continues as a wide farm track with a stream on left. Just short of derelict farm buildings, ignore track to right and keep straight ahead for 200 yards to Public Footpath signpost ④, indicating a route half across field, under line of electricity poles. On the far side of field, path turns left.

300 yards later, path crosses small stream by footbridge and passes entrance on left to nature reserve maintained by Cambridgeshire Wildlife Trust and occupying the area between the stream and the main river. The path continues with stream now on right for 60 yards to where it enters the River Rhee 100 yards below Barrington Mill ⑤

Cross the river via the footbridge and follow the footpath for a further 300 yards, past an old cemetery, then along Boot Lane. Continue to T-junction at Barrington high street and continue left through village for ½ mile, using paths along the green to the left of the road Ⓒ. The village cricket ground is passed away to the right Ⓓ, and then the Royal Oak on the near side.

⑥ At duck-pond and junction with road to Orwell, continue straight on along the road in the direction signposted to Shepreth, passing after 300 yards a modern bungalow on left incorporating the remains of a stone-built tower windmill Ⓔ. 200 yards later, the road turns sharply left, crossing the River Rhee and ⑦ reaches small car park on the right-hand side with sign for Shepreth Riverside Walk.

Leave the car park by kissing-gate in corner and take well-trodden path across pasture, with the river on the right and a narrow stream on the left-hand side of the field. After ½ mile, the path leaves the main river then later ⑧ crosses a stile and follows the small stream on the left into trees. Continue through the wood for ¼ mile.

When it leaves the trees, notice the man-made lake with islands for water birds on the right-hand side. The path skirts along the edge of arable land reaching a road (Malton

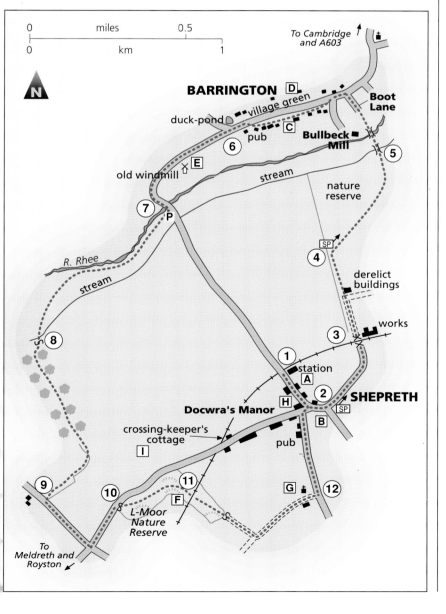

Lane) opposite a cottage. ⑨ Turn left to road junction where, turn left again at sign for North End, signposted Shepreth.

⑩ 150 yards past Stone Lane turning, cross footbridge with a stile (on right) leading into the Shepreth L-Moor Nature Reserve [F]. Take the path bearing left, faint at first but becoming clearer. It bears right, away from the road, to reach an area of disturbed ground. 10 yards later, fork right on to path leading towards clump of hawthorn trees with overhead wires of railway visible beyond. This leads to a stile beside gate with a low foot-tunnel under the line ⑪.

Go through the tunnel, then along path through field to another stile and on to a wide, grassy track. At T-junction with stonier path, turn left, passing Shepreth church [G] to emerge on to a road ⑫. Bear left along village street, passing pub, to the grass triangle opposite Docwra's Manor [H].

From here, Shepreth station is closely accessible, but a recommended diversion left for 400 yards will bring you to the former crossing-keeper's cottage [I].

ON THE ROUTE
[A] **Willers Mill Wildlife Park** has a collection of birds, animals and fish. *Open* throughout the year (free).
[B] **Shepreth Mill** is the last survivor of four mills in the village and was in use until the 1950s.

Kingfishers may be spotted in the L-Moor Nature Reserve

[C] **Barrington** has a number of ancient thatched houses and one of the longest village greens in England. The Royal Oak (on the green) is a lovely thatched pub adorned with hanging baskets. Its low-ceilinged, beamed interior is decorated with old beer jars and horse tack.

Barrington Mill, at the end of Mill Lane, was mentioned in the Domesday Book. In 1338 it passed to Michaelhouse, later Trinity College, Cambridge, and is now occupied by a company making scientific instruments.
[D] The U-shaped house at the rear of the green, to the left of the cricket pavilion, retains within its structure evidence that it was originally a medieval **aisled hall** of the 14th century.
[E] **The windmill**, originally known as Orwell Mill, was built in 1822 and was in use until 1890. An

earlier mill existed on this site in 1604.
[F] **L-Moor Nature Reserve** consists of about 20 acres of fen (one of the best such areas in south Cambridgeshire) and is managed by the Country Wildlife Trust. Birds found here include grasshopper warblers and kingfishers, and there is interesting flora. It is important that visitors do not stray from the rights of way and that great care is taken to avoid interference with plants and wildlife.
[G] **Shepreth church** is a small, simple early Gothic church with a Norman chancel arch and 18th-century memorials.
[H] **Docwra's Manor** Close inspection of what appears to be 18th-century brickwork reveals a sham facade, one brick thick, on an earlier timber-framed house. The garden (*open* Wednesday and Friday, April to October, 10 to 5) was created by celebrated botanist John Raven and is of remarkable quality: the walled garden between May and July presents a sea of silver and green spangled with colour.
[I] The former crossing-keeper's **cottage garden** is exceptionally well tended and has been featured on television and in national magazines. It is always freely *open to the public*, with a charmingly worded notice from the owner inviting one to enter it. There is a discreetly placed collection box in aid of the National Gardens Scheme.

SAFFRON WALDEN AND AUDLEY END

A SHORT walk with much to see, through the medieval streets of Saffron Walden and on grassy tracks through the parkland of Audley End House. Partly along country roads, with a pavement or wide grassy verge. Easy route-finding.

LENGTH 3 miles (5km), 1½ hours
DIFFICULTY 1
START Market Place, Saffron Walden. Pay-and-display car park on common; alleyway opposite is signposted to tourist information (in market place). Grid reference 538385
OS MAPS Landranger 154; Pathfinder 1050 (TL 43/53)
REFRESHMENTS Various in Saffron Walden; tea-room in Audley End House (when house is open)

Saffron Walden is a remarkably well-preserved East Anglian town; nearly all its plaster façades conceal ancient timber structures

WALK DIRECTIONS

① Ⓐ From Market Place, with tourist information/town hall on your left, take Market Hill (street ahead) leading to crossroads; turn left (Church Street) Ⓑ, then first right, a cul-de-sac leading into churchyard Ⓒ. Take tarmac path past left end of church, then continue right on main path (still beside church) to leave at opposite

side of churchyard, opposite museum entrance Ⓓ. Turn left along Museum Street and at T-junction turn left again into Castle Street.

② Take path on right, signposted Bridge End Gardens Ⓔ; this leads down between walls. Fork left, after 50 yards passing through gateway (to which you will return). Explore garden, return towards gateway, turning right just before it on to path leading to Bridge Street ③. Turn left into Bridge Street Ⓕ. The

Eight Bells pub was originally a 16th-century wool merchant's house; its interior is attractively beamed with a cosy fire and two roomy bars. ④ Turn right into Abbey Lane (opposite George Street), and where road turns right continue forward through estate gates; fork right, then 10 yards later take the right-hand path, leading across first field to gate, then between fences, past sewage works and to kissing-gate ⑤.

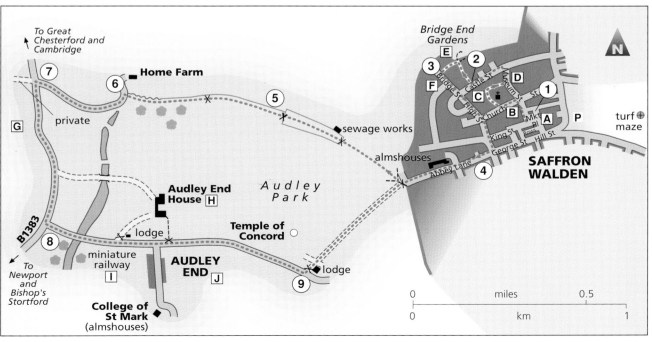

The turf maze on the common in Saffron Walden is something of an enigma

Enter next field and follow right-hand edge to next kissing-gate. Path then leads through trees, along stream, to estate road ⑥. Left on road, follow to main road ⑦. Left on main road ⑥, past front of Audley End House ⑭. ⑧ Take first road on left (signposted Audley End). This passes miniature railway ⑪ and Audley End village ⑫.

⑨ ½ mile after Audley End village turn left at gate-house. After 20 yards keep forward at crossing of tracks, and ignore faint left fork 50 yards later. Follow back to Abbey Lane gate-house, then proceed to town centre.

ON THE ROUTE

Ⓐ **Saffron Walden** Originally Cheyping Walden, the town prospered and grew in the Middle Ages as a centre of the saffron industry, the yellow pigment from the saffron crocus being used in cloth-making, food-colouring and medicine. The industry survived here until the 18th century. It has also been a wool- and cotton-weaving town. Many of its medieval streets are virtually intact, particularly in the north-west part of town, where there is barely a window out of place. There is much notable pargeting – the craft of decorating external plaster walls. Just south of Market Place is a small complex of lanes known as the Rows, whose names – Butcher, Market, Mercer – betray their origins as medieval market areas. On the far side of the common is an ancient, cobweb-like turf maze, of unknown date and purpose (possibly ornamental, or for monks or pilgrims to do penance, by crawling round); the common was used for a Royal Tournament in 1252.

Ⓑ **Sun Inn** (on left; no longer an inn) Boasts the best example of pargeting in the town, representing a fight between Tom Hickathrift, a carter of quite tremendous strength who could raise a haystack on his pitch-fork, and the Wisbech Giant, who is shielding himself with a wheel and axle. Cromwell may have stayed here while holding meetings in the church during the Civil War.

Ⓒ **St Mary the Virgin** The largest parish church in Essex, 200ft long, with a spacious nave; mainly Perpendicular (15th to early 16th century), partly restored later; its soaring tower was added in 1832.

Ⓓ **The museum** specialises in local and natural history.

Ⓔ **Bridge End Gardens** An elegant example of late 18th- to early 19th-century gardening, including a hedge maze, started in 1790 by Atkinson Francis Gibson.

Ⓕ **Youth Hostel** (on right) An early 16th-century half-timbered town house, with a carved dragon-post and two oriel windows. Formerly used as a malting; its oak-wheel sack-hoist is still in position.

Ⓖ Up on the right, just visible, is a **circular temple**, designed by Robert Adam to commemorate the British successes in the Seven Years War (1756–63).

Ⓗ On the left, stable block, and **Audley End House** (English Heritage; *open to the public*), a vast mansion purchased by Charles II and altered by Vanbrugh in the early 18th century. It was built on the site of the Benedictine Monastery of Walden, which was given by Henry VIII to Lord Audley after the Dissolution. The house as seen today is but a fraction of its original size. The grounds were designed by Capability Brown.

Ⓘ **Miniature railway** (runs Sundays and Bank Holidays) offers a 1½-mile ride through woods.

Ⓙ **Audley End** is a Georgian estate village to Audley End House. A fine group of Elizabethan almshouses (College of St Mark) are just visible at far end of street.

WIDDINGTON, DEBDEN AND NEWPORT

THREE distinctive East Anglian villages; rolling farmland with views all round and patches of woodland and parkland add variety to this walk. The final sections of the walk from Debden Hall Farm to Newport are the most attractive, with views over Debden Park and further, then the small-scale charm of the partly wooded valley of Debden Water. The route is mostly on defined tracks, but cross-field routes may be invisible.

WALK DIRECTIONS

① Cross the bridge over railway to London-bound platform, exit station, turn right on the road. Just before the chalk pits, take signposted path on the left, between hedges, then later along the left edge of a field. ② Ignore sharp left turn (leading to trig point),

continue forward to a road, where you turn left then keep straight on after 50 yards where road bends left, to take a track (for Waldegraves Farm) past barns.

The track soon crosses a field, with woods away to left. Just after joining woods you reach a junction of tracks by a barn. Turn right, heading across a field to right end of

woods 200 yards away, ③ where you continue forward alongside woods, then over a ditch by a plank; the tower of Widdington church (which you will soon reach) is visible half right. The path should be obvious as it heads quarter right across field, making towards the leftmost house.

On the far side of field, turn right along field edge, then at field corner

LENGTH *Full walk* 8 miles (13km), 4 hours	*Short walk* village green at Widdington (south-east of Newport; grid reference 538317): take the lane signposted to Widdington church, at which keep right, and begin the walk at ④
DIFFICULTY 2	
LENGTH *Short walk omitting Newport* 4 miles (6.5km), 2 hours	
DIFFICULTY 1–2	**OS MAPS** Landranger 167; Pathfinder 1050 (TL 43/53)
START *Full walk* Newport railway station (on B1383 south-west of Saffron Walden; at south end of village). Grid reference 523336.	**REFRESHMENTS** Pub and shop in Newport and Debden; pub in Widdington

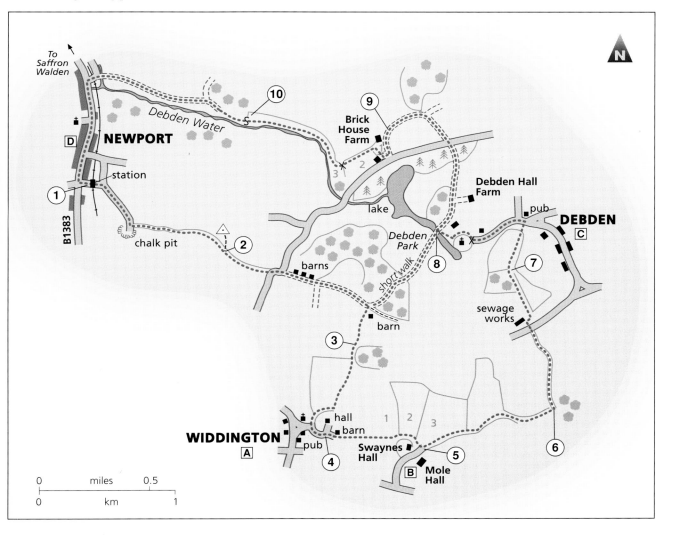

Many of the houses in Newport show fine examples of pargeting (ornamental plasterwork)

near the church bear left to reach the lane by church lych-gate. Turn right for Widdington village Ⓐ, or left to continue the route, which follows the lane. ④ 300 yards later, you pass driveway leading to triple-gabled house away to your left, then immediately after take a stile on the right into a field (as lane proceeds to converted weather-boarded barn); turn left in field, along the edge (continuing direction of lane, thus passing round to right of converted barn).

Where the hedgerow on left reaches a corner, continue the same direction across this (large) field; in winter months, the chimney stack of Swaynes Hall may be seen in trees ahead; make towards the left end of trees ahead, where you continue forward along the right edge of second and third fields Ⓑ. ⑤ At the end of third field turn left on a track enclosed on both sides by hedgerow trees.

After ¼ mile, the track continues ahead along right edge of field, then along the left edge of next (large) field. ⑥ 100 yards after entering small woodland, pass through a break in the hedgerow on your left to enter field, and descend along the left edge (Debden village is visible

on the hillside ahead); soon continue forward on a sunken path between hedges, and descend to a road. Cross the road to gates of sewage works (no entry), in front of which you turn right on a narrow path alongside fence; cross a stile, turn left, still alongside sewage works fence, then proceed on track ahead leading 30 yards to a field, where you go forward along the edge of the field to woods.

Keep forward, with woods on your left, then ⑦ forward along the right edge of the field ahead to Debden Ⓒ. Turn left on the road, then left again, signposted Debden church. Pass through the churchyard (if the gates are locked, which seems unlikely, turn right to skirt the churchyard), and proceed on the path on other side. ⑧ Reach T-junction with a track by lake.

For short walk Turn left to cross lake and follow track uphill (ignore signposted footpath on right after 50 yards), to and through woods, on other side of which you reach a barn and continue forward across field, heading for the right edge of woods 200 yards ahead; this is point ③.

For full walk Turn right on winding track (ignore minor side turns) and follow this for ½ mile to a road. Cross the road and take signposted track opposite, up to a corner of wood where you turn left (along power lines), descending to a farm ⑨. Turn left, downhill, on the surfaced farm track, then just before reaching road turn sharp right on driveway; after the driveway ends, cross the fence ahead (no stile at time of checking, but wooden fence is of a type that doubles as a stile), and proceed along bottom edge of field, at the end of which you turn left to enter a second field, and follow the right edge (which is slightly raised for ⅓ mile).

⑩ In the next field, shortly after fence bends markedly right, ignore left fork, but keep alongside fence until a stream comes into view on your left; now follow the stream. Enter woods by stile. Keep forward

all the way to Newport; the track enters a field and finally goes under a viaduct at the edge of the village. Turn left on the main road through the village Ⓓ, back to the starting-point.

ON THE ROUTE

Ⓐ **Widdington** Here there is a triple-gabled hall, with an older half-timbered portion at rear. The triangular village green is flanked by pleasant old cottages.

Ⓑ **Swaynes Hall** and **Mole Hall** Both fine farmhouses; continue right in corner of third field for a **view** over fence of Mole Hall, with duck-pond and flamingoes. A splendid example of a moated Elizabethan house (with wildlife park attached: continue down the road to T-junction where you go left; entrance is soon on left).

Ⓒ **Debden** Despite new development, the old centre with pond, pub and village pump retains its character. Debden Park has a semi-landscaped appearance. The artificial lake and estate church make a picturesque scene.

Ⓓ **Newport** is an outstandingly preserved village, retaining early buildings, many plastered with decorative pargeting; one fine street is on the right immediately before the viaduct, and the green close to the large Perpendicular church is worth taking in. The main concentration of buildings is the main street, including the exceptional brick and timber house, Monks Barn (with carved oriel window depicting the Virgin and Child) and the old toll-house (with board showing charges).

Waterfowl on the wintry moat of Mole Hall

GREAT BARDFIELD AND FINCHINGFIELD

TWO strikingly attractive villages, each with a village green, medieval church and wooden windmill. In between, the route follows brooks and tracks across gently rolling farmland, with wide skies and empty horizons lending an unmistakably East Anglian flavour. Stinging-nettles in summer make shorts or skirt unsuitable. There are some undefined routes across grassy and arable fields.

LENGTH 4½ miles (7km), 2½ hours
DIFFICULTY 1
START War memorial cross in Great Bardfield village centre near the Vine public house; on B1057, east of Thaxted. Grid reference 675305
OS MAPS Landranger 167; Pathfinder 1051 (TL 63/73)
REFRESHMENTS Pubs, tea-rooms and shops in Great Bardfield and Finchingfield

WALK DIRECTIONS

① Ⓐ Take the signposted track to the right of Vine pub, soon into (first) field. Go half left to find a stile in double hedgerow, emerging into a second field where you find a footbridge and stile in the opposite hedgerow, but a little down the slope to your right.

Proceed diagonally in third field to a gate, and turn half right in fourth field down to a stile near a brook. Keep right, along right edge of fifth field (with brook just to your right).

Cottages in Finchingfield set back from the picturesque village green

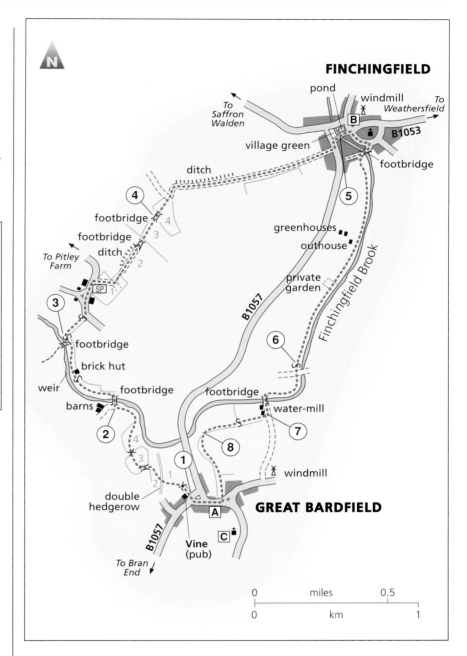

② Cross the footbridge over brook shortly before barns, and turn left on the other side, now alongside brook on the left.

By a weir and brick hut, the path is now enclosed. Ignore a footbridge on your left, but just after ③ cross a stile into field and turn right, up the field edge to a stile on to a road. Turn left on road, and go forward at junction, signposted Pitley Farm. After 80 yards, take the signposted gate on your right and follow the farm track in first field. After 100 yards, in middle of field (immediately after the hedgerow

away to left reaches a projecting corner), turn left and enter second field, proceeding along the left edge alongside a deep ditch.

After 250 yards, at the end of field, enter the right-hand of two fields ahead via a plank footbridge, to follow the left edge of third field for 150 yards until taking a plank footbridge on the left in field corner ④. Bear diagonally left across the middle of fourth field to yellow waymarker (roughly in line with direction given by the footbridge itself) to the far end of the left-hand hedgerow (if the field-path is obscured by crops, you are entitled to cross the field and will be doing a service to others by treading the correct route).

Emerge at the corner of well-defined farm track (leading ahead and to right), and turn right. The track immediately bends left, then right alongside a ditch on the left and heads for Finchingfield church, later with a fence on the right. Emerge into the village and turn left on the road to reach village green B.

⑤ Take either bridge by the pond and keep right. Take the first turn on right (just after red-brick Georgian house and before Finch Inn). This lane runs between walls for a short distance; 50 yards after left-hand wall ends, take the signposted path on the right. As soon as you cross a footbridge, fork left and follow the enclosed path, soon out of the woods and into a field. Continue always alongside Finchingfield Brook on your left.

After ¼ mile, in a field containing greenhouses, keep to the left of outhouse, still beside brook and soon across the end of a private garden. ⑥ 500 yards later, emerge on to a farm track and continue opposite and slightly to the right, to enter a field where you keep along the left edge (still alongside brook which has however disappeared from view).

⑦ After field and the route bend right, cross a footbridge on the left and go forward over field past a water-mill and cottage, then immediately turn right. Enter field, with the brook about 50 yards to your right: keep to the left edge of fields until ⑧ ditch is reached ahead, where the route continues to the left, now along the right edge of field with back gardens on the right and windmill away to the left. Keep

Finchingfield's village green; the church is somewhat nonchalantly capped by a comically undersized bell-turret but has an impressively grand interior

forward at the end of the field and join the road at Great Bardfield. Turn right and keep right at next junction (or left to detour to church C), to reach the war memorial.

ON THE ROUTE

A **Great Bardfield** The main street is wide and gently sloping, with village greens and a variety of medieval timber-framed and brick Georgian houses. Between the wars the village was home to several artists.

B **Finchingfield** The village centre makes a beautiful composition, with green, duck-pond and colour-washed cottages (the pargetted walls, adorned with decorative plasterwork, are very much the local style) leading the eye to the weather-boarded windmill. Opposite a group of almshouses, the churchyard is entered under an overhanging building that was the hall of a Guild of the Holy Trinity up to the Reformation.

C **Great Bardfield church** has a magnificent 14th-century screen. Tie-beams above the chancel are dated 1618, and there are fine Tudor brasses.

MINIMUM WIDTHS

The Rights of Way Act 1990 stipulates minimum widths for paths on cultivated land:
- if the width of a path is recorded, then that is the minimum width
- if the width is not recorded then the minimum width is:
  - for a footpath, 1 metre across the field, 1.5 metres on the field edge
  - for a bridleway, 2 metres across the field, 3 metres on the field edge
  - for other rights of way, 3 metres across the field, 5 metres on the field edge.

SHOTTISHAM, RAMSHOLT AND THE RIVER DEBEN

T HE heart of this walk is a stretch of just over two miles along the bank of the River Deben, with wide views over this beautiful river, abundant birdlife and marsh flora. The river is approached and left by easy, pleasant tracks through parkland and farmland with a short section of quiet country road.

LENGTH 6½ miles (10.5km), 3½ hours

DIFFICULTY 1–2

START Shottisham (on B1083 south-east of Woodbridge), outside the Sorrel Horse, the village's thatched pub. Grid reference 320446

OS MAPS Landranger 169; Pathfinder 1031 (TM 24/34)

REFRESHMENTS Pub and shop at Shottisham; pub at Ramsholt

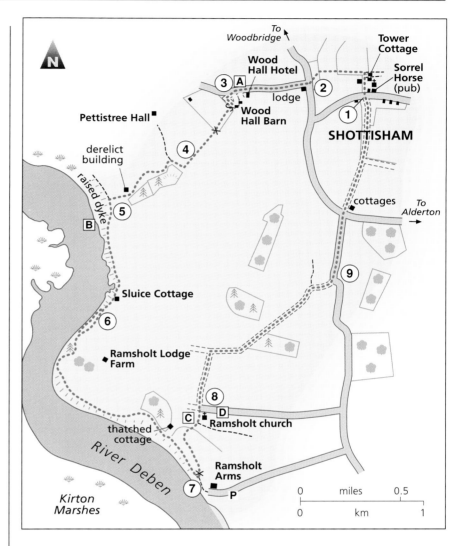

WALK DIRECTIONS

① With your back to the pub, turn right up the by-road signposted Church Lane, No Through Road. This passes the track leading up to the church on the right (ignore). Where the road ends, take the track to the left of Tower Cottage; ignore the first track on the left, but just

Ducks on crutches – a lesser-known Suffolk speciality

after, turn left at T-junction with a waymarked path, which follows the left edge of field.

From the stile in the first corner of the field (where a power line crosses overhead), the path bears half right across the next field. It crosses two shallow watercourses by footbridges with low brick abutments. Enter next field and bear left towards a prominent red-brick lodge, leaving the field by a stile in corner ②. Cross the road to the driveway of the Wood Hall Hotel opposite. Walk up the drive to the hotel and skirt to the right of the hotel grounds along a surfaced track Ⓐ.

After the hotel, ignore a track on the left to the coach house, but just after ③ turn left and immediately

fork right (left fork goes to Wood Hall Barn) on an unmade track. Just before reaching track in front of barns, take the stile on your right, and follow the left edge of field. At the end of field, find a gate just to the right of the field corner, and proceed on an enclosed track with a ditch on your right. This enters a field, where you keep forward. ④ After 250 yards the track turns right in front of a fenced area of scrub and woodland (at end of field on right), to enter right-hand field. After 100 yards, turn left at a signposted track junction, continuing with the fence of the woodland area on your left and passing to the left of a derelict building.

⑤ Turn left along the river, either at the foot of the raised dyke or on top of it if grass permits (or along shore) B. After ½ mile, where Shottisham Creek empties into the River Deben at Sluice Cottage, you are diverted on to the top of the bank. ⑥ Just after Sluice Cottage a waymark post points to the shore; if it is low tide follow the shore until the next waymark post indicates a return to the dyke; otherwise follow the landward side of the dyke, along the right edge of field with woods on your right. At the end of the field, take a path on the right through the woods and rejoin the top of the dyke, soon crossing a stile.

⑦ 50 yards before the Ramsholt Arms, turn left on a signposted bridleway, with Ramsholt church visible on the rise. Follow the grassy trodden track over the field ahead, through a gate, following a curving path round to the right to where in the hedge ahead a notice points the way through. Continue over the field beyond ignoring a path to the right C. ⑧ Soon you reach a cross-junction of tracks by the church (a small path on the right just before the junction leads into the churchyard D). Go forward.

At the end of the field, turn right at T-junction of tracks. After ¾ mile this track veers slightly right as power lines leave to left. ⑨ When you reach the road, turn left along it for 600 yards.

At T-junction, take the sandy track opposite to the left of a pair of cottages. Proceed forward along a line of Scots pines to Shottisham village (ignoring main track which bends right at the end of first field), to emerge directly opposite the Sorrel Horse pub.

ON THE ROUTE

A Note the picture on the sign of a bandaged duck on crutches: the **wildfowl** habitat can be seen in a lake beyond the hedge to the left.

B The **River Deben** draws yachters and bird-watchers to the attractive estuary. Up to the 1920s the river was busy with barges carrying coal, lime and coprolite (fossilised animal dung). The latter was shipped all over the country from quays here, including Ramsholt, for use as fertiliser. The river was also an important boat-building centre.

Near Woodbridge, the greatest Anglo-Saxon hoard of all time was unearthed in 1939 at Sutton Hoo when the Viking Treasure Ship was found. This was the burial place of King Raedwald of the East Angles (who died c625AD); the forty-oar ship was crammed with gold and jewelled items. The treasure is now displayed in the British Museum.

Cruises are available on the river from Woodbridge between April and October.

C The remains of a brick wall in this field are telling evidence that **Ramsholt** was once more substantial than it now is. Few buildings now survive and the population is around 30; in 1855 the villagers numbered 203.

D **Ramsholt church** has a simple interior with early 19th-century box pews, a harmonium and no electricity. The tower is one of only two oval ones in Suffolk and dates from Norman or possibly Saxon times. The churchyard offers a fine **view** over the Deben.

THE SUFFOLK COAST

Suffolk's coast was officially recognised as an Area of Outstanding Natural Beauty in 1969. It has the monopoly of the county's best walking and is a rich habitat for flora and animals. The immediate hinterland includes some of England's most significant expanses of lowland heath, the so-called Suffolk Sandlings; the heath once covered 80 per cent more than it does now. At the southern end of Suffolk's coast, the village of Shotley Gate makes a good starting-point for exploring the shoreline paths along the Stour and Orwell estuaries, looking across to Harwich Harbour; Shotley village, inland, is a recommended alternative starting-point for a circular walk using field-paths to link the two estuaries.

St Margaret's Church, Shottisham, set against a wintry sky

ALDEBURGH AND THORPENESS

Of special interest for bird- and plant-life. All on the level, yet varied, leading along an old railway track, through heathland, past a lake near Thorpeness and along a shingle beach. One section on road. Easy route-finding.

LENGTH *Full walk* 5½ miles (9km), 2½ hours. *Shorter walk* 4½ miles (7km), 2 hours

DIFFICULTY 1–2

START Moot Hall (brick and half-timbered building on the sea-front), Aldeburgh (north edge of town). Grid reference 466568

OS MAPS Landranger 156; Pathfinder 1009 (TM 44/45)

REFRESHMENTS Full range at Aldeburgh. Pub and cafés at Thorpeness

WALK DIRECTIONS

① Ⓐ From Moot Hall cross to the Mill Inn opposite, and take the road to left of it, signposted A12. Cross High Street and take Victoria Road opposite. Just before the church take gate into churchyard Ⓑ and follow the path to a gate on the far side. Continue along enclosed path beyond, ignoring a right turn after 100 yards. On reaching the road, cross to a gate opposite into a caravan site ②. Go right on the service road inside the site and immediately left (after toilet block) at junction of service roads. Ignore side turns in caravan site and proceed to a stile beside a prominent

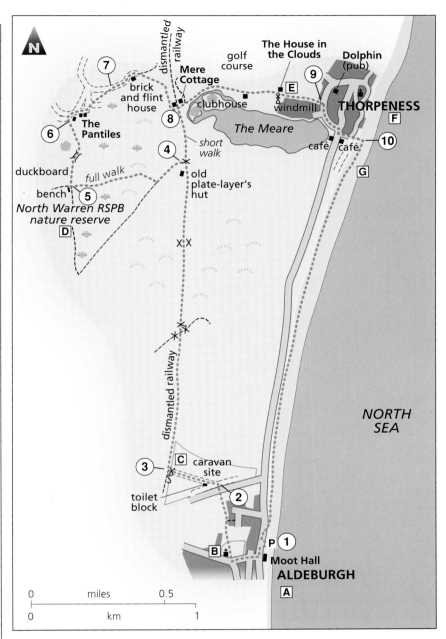

Aldeburgh's Moot Hall in its striking position on the sea front

gate, leading on to an abandoned railway line ③. Turn right along this, ignoring side turns. ④ After 1 mile it passes an old plate-layer's hut on the left and enters a wood by a gate (the course of the railway disappears here). Reach a T-junction just inside the wood.
For short walk Turn right, rejoining the old railway line and proceed to former level-crossing cottage and Mere Cottage. Turn right at staggered crossing of paths, in front of Mere Cottage, to continue. This is ⑧.
For full walk, taking in North Warren Turn left. After 200 yards turn right

at path junction. A fence later joins on the left. Follow this path for ½ mile, then ⑤ turn right at crossing of paths. This path follows duck-boards through a marshy area, and crosses a footbridge. Eventually it rises, with fence on left, to houses ⑥, with a brick and flint house (The Pantiles) on the right. Keep right, skirting the garden hedge of The Pantiles, and ignoring enclosed track descending to left towards a red-roofed house. Just after the Pantiles fork right. The track passes two houses on the right; just after it bends left, take a narrow path on the right, reaching a cross-track after

30 yards, where you go forward (the narrow path gets submerged in vegetation in summer; if you cannot see it, carry on along the track for 25 yards and turn right on another track; the path continues on the left after 15 yards). ⑦ Merge into track, turn right along it. Beyond brick and flint house, keep forward, past a garage on left, to continue on narrower path; soon ignore a minor path forking to left, but keep right as signposted. Reach the former level-crossing cottage and Mere Cottage ⑧: go straight on by turning left and immediately right.

Both routes Path soon follows right edge of a golf course and left side of Meare. Path passes to left of golf clubhouse: keep forward on track between House in the Clouds and windmill E into Thorpeness itself F. ⑨ Turn right on reaching tarmac road and walk round edge of Meare; take next road on left (opposite village sign and by cafés) and go down to the beach G ⑩. Turn right and walk either along the beach proper or the path.

ON THE ROUTE

A **Aldeburgh** A long-established fishing and ship-building centre, now doubling as a resort, and home of the Aldeburgh Festival, founded in 1948 by the composer Benjamin Britten, the tenor Peter Pears and librettist and producer Eric Crozier. Aldeburgh was the birthplace of the 18th-century poet George Crabbe, and the home of Britten, whose opera *Peter Grimes*, set on this coast, was based on a character in Crabbe's poem *The Borough*. The walk passes two buildings of particular interest, the 16th-century timber-framed Moot Hall and the church of St Peter and St Paul (largely 16th-century interior; ship auctions used to be held inside at that period). There is a characterful clutch of fishermen's shacks selling fresh fish (which can also be sampled at the town's celebrated fish and chip shop). Ye Olde Cross Keys Inn in Crabbe Street has a long gravelled garden; it is also possible to drink al fresco on the sea wall and shingle beach across the road. In winter

---

THE ALDEBURGH TOWN MARSH TRAIL

The tourist information office in Aldeburgh has a free leaflet detailing this four-mile walk south and west of the town. The trail skirts the town marshes, municipal property since the 16th century, and looks over the River Alde. Kingfishers, snipe and reed buntings are among the estuary and marshland birds that can be seen.

---

customers will prefer to stay inside in the dark beamed bar of this 16th-century atmospheric windswept retreat.

B Turn right on a gravel path at the far end of the churchyard. In 20 yards on the left of the path are the **graves of Benjamin Britten, Peter Pears and Imogen Holst**. Only after Britten's death did Pears tell the world that he and Britten were lovers. Imogen Holst, daughter of the composer Gustav Holst, knew Britten well and was his biographer.

C The **railway line** used to run from Saxmundham to Aldeburgh, via Leiston and Thorpeness; it was one of the many lines closed by the recommendation of Dr Beeching in the 1960s. The track-bed now forms a permissive path, a charming way of enjoying the heathy scenery that encompasses it. Prolific quantities of tree lupins, pale yellow flowering shrubs, grow along the path.

D **North Warren** An RSPB nature reserve of 250 acres (leaflet available from Minsmere, further up the coast towards Dunwich). It provides a varied habitat of heath, woodland and wetland, attracting a range of **birds** including willow, reed and sedge warblers, redpolls, bitterns, linnets and stonechats, with occasional marsh harriers and bearded tits. The wetter areas have marsh marigolds, meadowsweet and yellow iris; just south of Sluice Cottage a small patch of marsh orchids can be seen in season (late spring to early summer). The fen and reed bed has dried out and woodland has invaded. The RSPB is encouraging the wetland to re-establish itself and it is hoped that otters, bitterns and kingfishers will thrive in this habitat.

E The **windmill** dates from 1803 and is *open* free of charge (donations welcome). It is a post mill: that is, one built around a central post enabling the whole mill to be rotated according to the direction of the wind. Although originally built for grinding corn, its function at this site was to pump water from a well within it to the astonishing House in the Clouds, the water-tower-cum-folly adjacent (now let as holiday accommodation) to provide water for the village of Thorpeness (see below). At first a more conventional pump was used for this purpose, but this more picturesque contrivance was later preferred. The mill was moved to its present site from Aldringham, 2 miles away.

F **Thorpeness** A village built as a planned, upmarket holiday resort between 1910 and the 1930s, and remarkably well preserved. The houses are mock-rustic, with wooden garden fences and sham half-timbering, while the imposing Westgate is another disguised water-tower. The Meare is an artificial boating lake; rowing-boats and punts can be hired.

G **Birds** along the shore include terns and ringed plovers. **Flora** includes yellow-horned poppies, sea holly and sea-pea.

The startlingly eccentric House in the Clouds at Thorpeness, itself a resort village of curiosity value

MINSMERE AND DUNWICH HEATH

A ROUTE of outstanding
interest for its birdlife and
heathland vegetation. Those who
prefer the pub halfway through the
walk should start at Minsmere, but
the walk unravels more
dramatically if starting where we
have done, at Eastbridge: a section
across fields and skirting
marshland to the sea, then a walk
along the coast, looking across

LENGTH 6 miles (9.5 km), 3 hours
DIFFICULTY 1
START Eel's Foot Inn, Eastbridge,
2 miles north of Leiston. Park on the
roadside by telephone-box or just
north of the hamlet by bridge over
Minsmere New Cut. Grid reference
453662
Alternatively, start at Minsmere
National Trust car park, on the coast

south of Dunwich, by coastguard
cottages (NT shop and tea-room).
Start directions at ⑥. Grid reference
477678
OS MAPS Landranger 156;
Pathfinder 987 (TM 46)
REFRESHMENTS Eel's Foot Inn, at
Eastbridge; National Trust tea-room
by former coastguard cottages
at ⑥

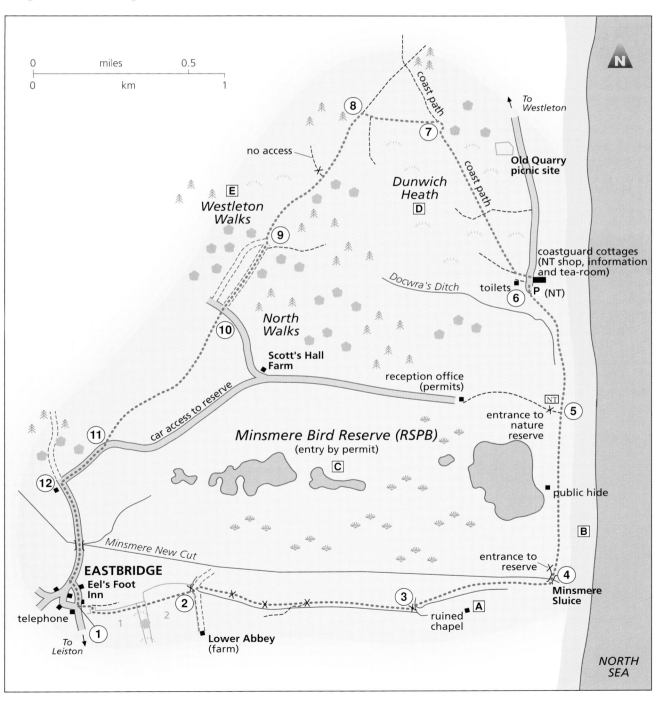

Minsmere Bird Reserve. There are opportunities to enter the reserve and follow the reserve trail (fee payable; free for RSPB members), but you can skirt the reserve without doing this. Bring binoculars if possible. Beyond a strategically sited National Trust tea-room the walk crosses Dunwich Heath and Westleton Walks, both fine examples of the Suffolk Sandlings. Easy route-finding.

WALK DIRECTIONS

① Standing with Eel's Foot Inn behind you, turn left along metalled lane and after 100 yards take track on left signposted Minsmere Sluice 1½ miles. Follow for 30 yards to footpath sign indicating enclosed footpath to right. Follow along edge of first field, through gorse bushes and through middle of second field. ② Beyond a stile beside a gate, emerge on junction of tracks; continue in same direction by turning left, over a water channel; track immediately bends right, with the channel on your right and later passes through three gates. ③ After ½ mile the track bends left through a gate and crosses channel to continue in the same direction Ⓐ. ④ Cross a brick sluice and head up to top of a grassy seawall. Turn left Ⓑ. Entrances to Minsmere Reserve are passed on the left Ⓒ, and the public hide (always open; no permit required) is also passed; ⑤ after ½ mile, by a National Trust sign, there is an optional detour through a gate

The adult tawny owl is frequently sighted at Minsmere

into the reserve (the grassy path leads to the reception, where permits are obtained). Continue, finally bending left at the bottom of the slope and rising up on main path towards prominent coastguard cottages at car park and turn left on the road ⑥. Follow the road, passing to the left of the coastguard cottages, then just after them turn left on a broad track. 80 yards later, just after a work-store building on left, fork right on to broad waymarked path (coast path) crossing Dunwich Heath Ⓓ. Ignore a cross-path and keep to the main path, which goes under power lines. ⑦ ¼ mile after the power lines the path bends right, then bends left: ignore path on right as it bends left, and ignore coast path (which also leads off to right) 20 yards later, but keep to main path. On leaving the heath, this enters semi-wooded area as it drops into a pronounced hollow at a path junction: keep forward, avoiding path to left. ⑧ 30 yards later, turn left at T-junction with broad track Ⓔ. After 400 yards, ignore track on right (marked as No Access), and ⑨ after a further 400 yards, fork left at junction (both tracks in fact go closely parallel), immediately ignoring path signposted to left. ⑩ At the road, cross over and take the bridleway opposite. This later leads through woods to a road ⑪; turn right on the road. ⑫ Keep left along road where a track goes off to the right, in front of gates to house, and proceed to Eastbridge.

ON THE ROUTE

Ⓐ A ruined **chapel** is seen to the field on the right; further away the gigantic white ball of **Sizewell B nuclear power station** exerts an eerie presence, and an unfortunate addition to an otherwise quite unspoilt landscape.
Ⓑ The concrete blocks along the seawall are **Second World War anti-tank defences**, placed in the event of enemy invasion. The **view** extends northwards to Southwold. Parts of the beach are fenced off to protect **little terns**, who nest on the

The exotic-looking but firmly native bee orchid

ground and whose eggs are camouflaged on the shingle. These are the second rarest breeding seabird in Britain; just over 2,000 pairs breed in Britain and Ireland, making up over a third of the north European population.
Ⓒ **Minsmere** is an RSPB reserve of 1,500 acres. Its freshwater marsh attracts an exceptional number of **birds**, including bitterns and bearded tits, and provides a habitat for the rare marsh sow thistle, hemp agrimony, marsh mallows and orchids. It also has heathland (a stronghold for the nightjar) and woodland, supporting nightingales, owls and all three varieties of British woodpecker. Over 280 species of bird have been recorded here, some 200 of which are seen annually. After an absence from Britain for a century, the avocet has re-established itself here; this is the graceful wader depicted on the RSPB emblem. The reserve is closed on Tuesday; fee for non-members. There is a hide for public use; entry to the rest of the reserve is by permit only.
Ⓓ **Dunwich Heath** (NT) is a fine example of the Sandlings, great coastal heathlands that were once the grazing grounds for the sheep that provided the wool on which Suffolk's prosperity was built. The sheep have gone, but the heather is still a fine sight when the gorse and ling heather are in bloom, and there are many small mammals and insects. Adders, green woodpeckers and stone chats may be seen hereabouts.
Ⓔ **Westleton Walks** Another vestige of the East Suffolk heathlands.

WALBERSWICK AND SOUTHWOLD

To the west of the River Blyth the route covers wide expanses of marshland and heath, much of it nature reserve. The eastern section of the walk crosses a breezy, open common to Southwold, whose intricate townscape and strong character make it one of the most distinguished of East Anglia's coastal towns. Easy route-finding.

WALK DIRECTIONS

① From the car park, walk back along the road towards Walberswick, passing two tea-rooms on the right and the Bell Hotel on the left-hand side. After 300 yards the road turns sharply right: just beyond this corner, take the path going left immediately before the Anchor bar and restaurant.

LENGTH 7½ miles (12km), 3½ hours (or can be shortened to 6 miles if the River Blyth ferry is in operation)

DIFFICULTY 1

START Car park at the seaward end of Walberswick village, where the B1387 terminates at the river. Grid reference 501748.
Alternatively start at the seafront at Southwold, by St James's Green, near Sole Bay Inn at end of Victoria Street. Stand with the sea on your left and start directions at ⑧. Grid reference 510762

OS MAPS Landranger 156; Pathfinder 966 (TM 47/57)

REFRESHMENTS Pubs (including the Bell) and tea-rooms in Walberswick; Harbour Inn near the footbridge at ⑥; full range in Southwold

The path ascends past allotment gardens, then turns to the right at a junction with another path coming in from left. Continue to reach a field and T-junction with another path, where you turn left. The path skirts the field and turns right at the far corner. ② 20 yards past this corner, take a smaller path diverging left through the bushes. This leads out through reed beds Ⓐ with wooden duckboards underfoot to the bank of the Dunwich River.

Turn right, along the bank. At the footbridge (do not cross), drop down off the bank and continue closer to the river edge (ignore any paths to right and keep along river). ③ Turn right at T-junction in front of the brick tower of a former drainage pump-mill.

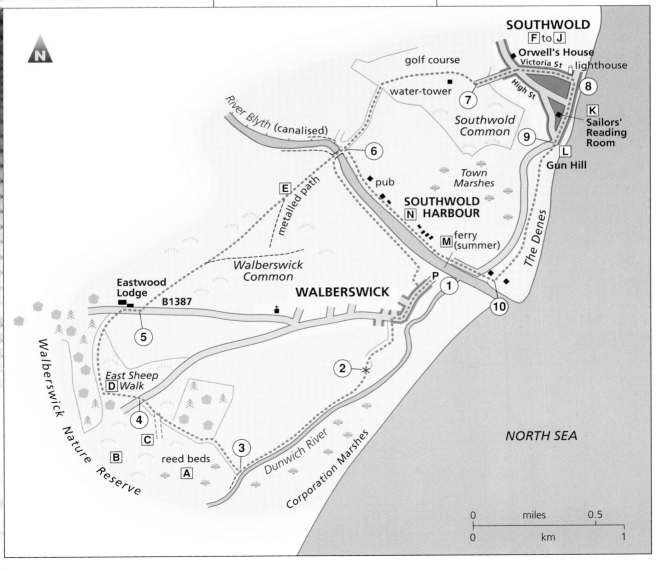

The path heads towards woods and passes Walberswick Nature Reserve B. After 300 yards, the path enters woodland: ignore minor side turns but follow main track C. Continue to reach minor road.

④ Cross the road to a notice-board with large-scale map. The walk continues behind this board, following grassy track curving left across heath towards woodland. D. When the track meets the woodland, it bears right following the edge of the trees. When the track forks keep right. This reaches a road: turn right along this for 200 yards to a house on the left-hand side. ⑤ Just pass house on left, take signposted path on left, through gate and over the common.

At cross-track, keep ahead. Continue for 500 yards to reach gate. Through the gate, take the path slightly left, going up on to old railway embankment E. This is now a sandy track, between banks with gorse: follow this to reach T-junction with a small road (closed to horses and motor vehicles). Turn left along this and cross footbridge over the River Blyth ⑥.

On far side of bridge, continue straight ahead. Alternatively, detour right for 300 yards for Harbour Inn. At beginning of gorse, where path ceases to be surfaced, take track to right (signposted Footpath over Common to Town Centre), passing golf clubhouse and tennis courts away to right, over the common and pass just to left of water-tower and church. ⑦ Beyond the water-tower, turn left on the road, into a residential area. Fork right into York Road to reach High Street F; turn right and immediately left into Victoria Street, passing Southwold Museum G and the parish church H. The green here is Bartholomew Green I.

Note here on the right a row of Victorian houses with a remarkable array of painted sculpture heads just below the eaves. Further down the street you pass Adnam's brewery and reach East Green. On the left is the Sole Bay Inn J. Just past this is Stradbroke Road, containing Southwold's lighthouse, a prominent landmark. Turn right along the sea-front.

⑧ At St James's Green, which is marked by a mast and two ornamental cannons, detour right for the High Street and Market Place. Return to this point to resume the walk. Continue along seafront: where the road bears right, go between white posts straight ahead, and continue along path following low cliff-top, passing the Sailors' Reading Room K.

The path drops down to beach level at a concrete area just behind the beach: where it does, take the path ahead going back up the slope again, keeping railings on the left, leading out on to Gun Hill L.

⑨ The path drops down again to the shore. Follow route along grass at the back of the shore, heading for a small group of houses in the distance. ⑩ Eventually you reach a wooden hut (Suffolk Wildlife Trust information centre).

Continue to the river edge and turn right. The track continues alongside the river, reaching after 400 yards the crossing-point for the Walberswick ferry M which will shorten the route back to the starting-point. Turn left on other side to reach car park. If, however, inclination or the time of year excludes the ferry, there are further pleasures still to come. Follow the track along the river: this leads through an area of boats, tarred shacks (some selling fish), a ship's chandlery offering teas, the Harbour Inn, a pleasurable stretch for those who appreciate a scene of busy marine activity N.

At the end of the stretch, take footbridge (if you started from Walberswick, you crossed this earlier) and return down the opposite bank to reach the ferry crossing-point, where a path leads away from the bank, back to the car park.

ON THE ROUTE

A The reeds are managed by cutting, with a rotational harvest which provides supplies for thatching, while keeping a suitable habitat for the bearded tit, bittern, reed warbler, water rail and other birds.

B The Walberswick Nature Reserve consists of about 1,300 acres of reed beds, mudflats, heathland and woods. Apart from its prolific bird life, it has a range of butterflies and moths.

C This is a good example of the surviving Suffolk sandlings, the areas of sandy heathland once widespread.

D East Sheep Walk is a reminder of the extent to which sheep farming and the wool trade created the economy of East Anglia in the Middle Ages.

E The Southwold Railway closed in 1929. Never a successful line, it was regarded with affectionate derision locally. The rolling stock was antiquated and odd – some claimed that it was a job lot from a failed order for a line in China.

F Directly opposite is the house where George Orwell (Eric Blair), the author of *Animal Farm* and *1984*, lived.

G Southwold Museum has displays on local topography and history. (*Open* late May to late Sept in the afternoons, plus Easter weekends and May bank holidays).

H The 15th-century church has a beautiful painted screen, dating from about 1500, and magnificent carved stalls.

I A disastrous fire in the 17th century destroyed much of Southwold: when it was rebuilt, some plots were left undeveloped as fire-breaks: these became the present-day greens.

J The name is a reminder of the Battle of Sole Bay, fought against the Dutch at Gun Hill.

K The Sailors' Reading Room is a major Southwold institution: full of paintings, photographs and models of ships. It was established in 1864 by Mrs Rayley in memory of her husband who was lost at sea, and has changed little since its doors opened. There is a satirical cartoon of the ill-fated Southwold Railway (see above), showing rails haphazardly tied together with bits of string.

L The cannon on Gun Hill provided a pretext during the 1914–18 war to regard Southwold as a fortified place, and the town was accordingly bombarded from the sea.

M The ferry operates from Whitsun to September, and occasionally at weekends at other times.

N The artist Wilson Steer was very fond of this scene.

RIVER BURE AND UPTON FEN

A BUSY boating area of the Broads contrasts with the memorable empty expanses of drained fens, with windmills dominating the landscape for miles around. South Walsham Broad and the mysterious woodlands of Upton Fen are glimpsed in the final section. Easy route-finding on level paths and tracks.

WALK DIRECTIONS

① Take the path on the left bank of Upton Dyke, a waterway, which leads out to turn left at the confluence with the River Bure.

Proceed along the river: the path keeps left at a confluence of rivers after 1½ miles, then left again at the next one, 1½ miles later ② **A**. The path later continues as a track past a

LENGTH	7 miles (11km), 3 hours
DIFFICULTY	1–2
START	Car park at end of Upton Dyke, Upton; north of Acle and east of Norwich off B1140. Grid reference 402128
OS MAPS	Landranger 134; Pathfinder 883 and 884 (TG 21/31 and TG 41/51)
REFRESHMENTS	Pub and shop at Upton; shop and toilets at South Walsham Broad

boatyard, then as a surfaced lane. Ignore right fork (Kingfisher Lane), but 30 yards later ③ take a signposted field-path on your left. This path proceeds along the left edge of a field, switching to the other side of hedge midway through

St Benet's Abbey, at about the halfway mark of the walk

field. Turn left on surfaced lane, past Tiled Cottage, then ④ fork right on to a waymarked enclosed path, soon with hedge on right only and then bending right to pass a farm, where you continue along the road **B**.

At staggered junction, turn left into private road to farm ⑤. At the

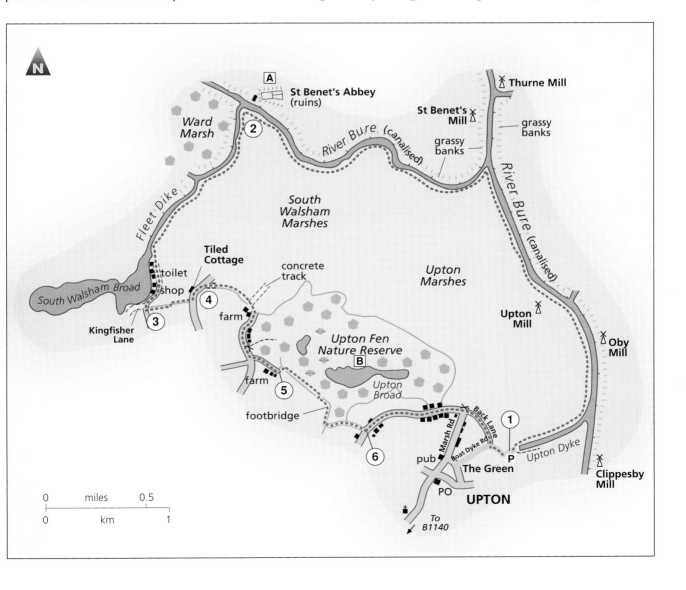

Sailing on the Norfolk Broads

THE NORFOLK BROADS

The ever-popular boating area and national park was formed from medieval peat cuttings that flooded when the sea-level rose. Reed beds and alder woods are gradually taking over the margins, forming important wetland habitats (known as 'carr'); adjacent to the Broads proper lie the great pasture lands that were drained by long cuts, or ditches; numerous ruined pumping mills punctuate the broad horizons.

Hickling and Horsey are probably the best part of the Broads for wildlife, and are notable summer haunts of marsh harriers and swallowtail butterflies.

end of farm buildings turn left on to a path along the left edge of field. The path is easily followed: it bends right at field corner to proceed inside and along edge of woods of Upton Fen. The path eventually reaches a road and houses ⑥. Turn left on the road. After ½ mile, go straight on into Back Lane. At its end turn left for the car park.

ON THE ROUTE

Ⓐ **St Benet's Abbey ruins** on the opposite bank just before the confluence of rivers. An 11th-century Benedictine foundation, of great importance in its heyday.

Ⓑ **Upton Fen Nature Reserve** To the left of the road, later skirted by a footpath. A 50-hectare area of fen and woodland, which is totally undisturbed and unpolluted and contains landlocked Upton Broad. Noted for water-lilies and other aquatic plants. Access restricted.

AROUND HORSEY

REED beds, diverse birdlife, marshland plants, sand dunes and a long sandy beach are all part of this absorbing walk which starts from one of the best-known pumping windmills on the Broads. Easy route-finding.

WALK DIRECTIONS

① A From the car park, go to the right of the thatched toilet block, then turn right along the waterway. After 100 yards, the path bends right as waterway is about to enter Horsey Mere B, and has a ditch on the right. After 200 yards, ignore footbridge on right and keep to the main path (which bends left).

② After 300 yards, the path turns right to a marker pole and footbridge, from where it cuts diagonally across a field to another marker pole and footbridge. The path continues, reaching a waterway

(Waxham New Cut) ③, and turns right along it. ④ After ½ mile, turn right at Brograve Windmill C, and follow the right edge of two fields towards trees. At the end of the second field, the path bends left in front of the trees, and, immediately after the trees end, take the footbridge on right and go forward alongside trees to a house.

LENGTH	4½ miles (7km), 2½ hours
DIFFICULTY	1
START	Horsey Mill car park, on B1159 just south of Horsey village; between Mundesley and Great Yarmouth. Grid reference 457222
OS MAPS	Landranger 134; Pathfinder 863 (TG 42)
REFRESHMENTS	Shop at Horsey Mill car park; tea-room near Horsey Corner; pub at Horsey near end of walk

Emerge on to a surfaced lane, turn right then immediately left on a track which narrows to a path after 30 yards, entering a field. The path bends left along field edge, then

Otters inhabit Horsey Mere

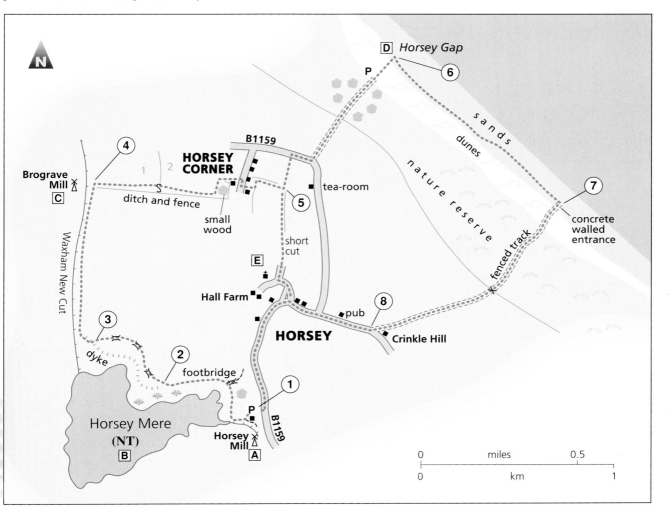

UNDERGROUND POWER

Pylons are a regrettable intrusion on the British landscape. It is now possible to refrigerate high-voltage cables and bury them. This technique is expensive, but the Countryside Commission has given grants in some places so that the power lines can be hidden from public view.

bends right at first corner, to reach a path T-junction at the far side of field (with line of electricity poles going off to the right) ⑤. Turn left here (or turn right, along the electricity poles for a short cut back to Horsey; bear left by the church and turn right on the main road),

and proceed to road.

Turn right on the road, and after 120 yards, where the road bends right, take a track on the left. This leads out through dunes and on to the beach ⑥ D. Turn right along the beach. ⑦ After ¼ mile, just after steps up on to the seawall, take an obvious concrete-walled entrance in the seawall and follow the track between fences leading inland (crossing over track which skirts inland edge of dunes).

After ½ mile, by a gate, the track ceases to be enclosed. ⑧ Keep right by lone red-brick houses, on road soon past a pub and on to the B1159. Keep forward in the direction signposted for Horsey Mill

(where road bends left, you can detour right to the church E).

ON THE ROUTE

A **Horsey Mill** (National Trust, *open* April to October). A windpump constructed to drain marshes into the waterway. Reeds from beds on **Brayden Marshes** to the west have been used for thatching for centuries.

B **Horsey Mere** is a rich habitat for wildfowl, including marsh harriers and bitterns. Otters also inhabit the 1,700-acre site which has been declared a nature reserve.

C **Brograve Mill**, an 18th-century brick tower, is named after the family who owned nearby Waxham Hall.

D **Horsey Gap** is highly vulnerable to the sea which has breached the dunes on several occasions, including during the great floods of 1953. A concrete seawall has now been built to protect the dunes.

E **Horsey church** is thatched and pleasingly simple, with nave and chancel in one, and a charming yew-shaded churchyard; note its octagonal flint tower.

The brackish water of Horsey Mere, separated from the sea by sand dunes. The windpump worked until 1947 when lightning caused severe damage to it (now restored)

RESTORING THE REEDS

In the Norfolk Broads, the cutting of reeds and sedge forms an important part of the management of some 2,500 acres of fenland. As well as providing an income from the thatching market, cutting the reeds keeps the fenland healthy and prevents its ultimate disappearance. Reeds are cut on an annual cycle; sedge every four years. The reeds are an important habitat for birdlife. The Broads Authority is encouraging farmers to reduce their acreage of cereal production and to set aside at least some of their land so that marshland can be re-established and that ultimately reeds can be harvested.

HOLKHAM HALL AND BURNHAM OVERY STAITHE

THE route starts off through parkland before following country roads and farm tracks past a water-mill and windmill to reach the small natural harbour of Overy Staithe; the return leg follows the top of a dyke overlooking the largest salt-marsh in Europe, and then takes you out on a huge sandy beach fringed with dunes and pine trees. The roads across Holkham Park are closed to pedestrians for about two hours a week in the shooting season (notices are displayed). Easy route-finding.

WALK DIRECTIONS

① From the car park Ⓐ go back to the main road, cross it and continue along the minor road opposite, through Holkham estate village and enter Holkham Hall estate via gates, beyond which you keep forward. ② ¼ mile later keep right at T-junction (left is private) and follow the estate

---

LENGTH 10 miles (16km), 5 hours
DIFFICULTY 2
START Holkham, on A149 1½ miles west of Wells-next-the-Sea. Car park on north side of road, opposite signposted entrance for Bygones Museum/Holkham Hall (fee in summer); if this is full, use the second car park in Holkham village by the estate gate. Grid reference 891446
OS MAPS Landranger 132; Pathfinder 819 (TF 84/94)
REFRESHMENTS Victoria Hotel, Holkham; The Hero at Burnham Overy Staithe

---

road past Holkham Hall Ⓑ, immediately after which road bends left by lake.

③ At the end of the lake, fork right Ⓒ (signposted to garden centre). This road soon leads over cattlegrid, shortly beyond which you keep forward at a junction, ignoring a right turn signposted to the garden centre but continuing forward to leave the estate by a lodge at West Gate. Beyond, proceed to a B-road ④. Turn left on the road and follow it for 1 mile.

⑤ At the village of Burnham Overy Town, immediately before houses begin on the right side of the road, turn right on to a farm track signposted as public footpath. At the end of the field turn left, picking up a track between hedges (signposted Norfolk Coast project circular walk).

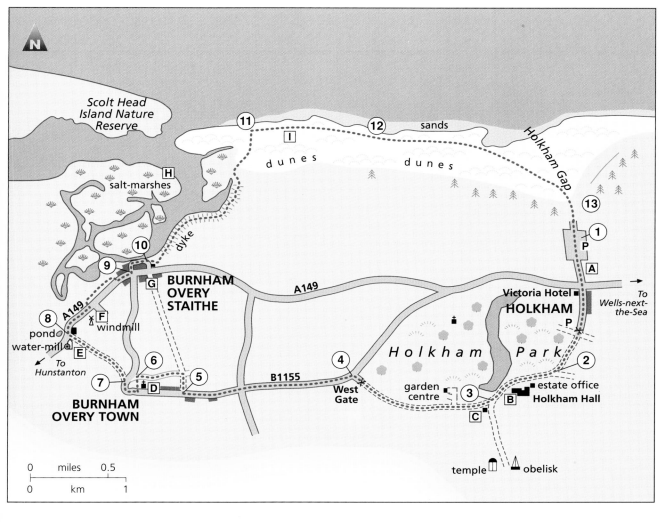

⑥ On joining the corner of the road, turn immediately left, on an enclosed path leading to the church [D], then through the churchyard to the road; turn right on the road, then after 75 yards turn right at a junction, signposted Burnham Overy Staithe.

⑦ 100 yards later, where the road bends right, turn left on to a track between hedges. On emerging through a gate into a field, keep forward alongside a hedge on your right, until reaching a road by a water-mill [E] ⑧. Turn right on the road [F], and follow it to Burnham Overy Staithe (past the windmill you can walk just inside the field to the left, closely parallel to the road; this is part of the long-distance Norfolk Coast Path; rejoin the road just before the village). ⑨ Take the first turn on the left in the village to the quayside [G] and where the road bends right inland, keep forward on a gravel path (signposted Long-Distance Path) leading to a raised dyke beyond nature reserve sign [H].

⑩ Turn left on the dyke, and follow it for 1½ miles to sand dunes, where duckboards lead through the dunes to the beach ⑪.

Turn right along the beach [I]. ⑫ Pine woods soon begin on your right; keep parallel to them and walk along the beach for 2½ miles in all until reaching Holkham Gap ⑬, a prominent V-shaped break in the corner of the woods (which now extend some way out to left). At Holkham Gap, head inland on a wide path, soon on duckboards, back to the car park.

ON THE ROUTE

[A] Just before the main road is reached, the site of little **Holkham station** is passed on the left. This used to be on the branch line from Heacham to Wells, washed out in the disastrous flood of 1953 and never reinstated.

[B] **Holkham Hall** is in the Palladian style, with gardens landscaped by Capability Brown. It was the home of Thomas Coke, the great 'improving landlord' who inspired agricultural progress in the 18th and early 19th centuries. By his experiments in breeding, by manuring and by adopting rotation farming he improved the value of his land ten-fold. His annual 'sheep-shearings' attracted agriculturalists from all over Britain and became an important means of spreading knowledge of new methods. The tall column in the park was raised as a memorial to him by his neighbours.

[C] Just after the lake, straight ahead, is a thatched 17th-century **ice house** with Dutch gables. Ice would be cut from the lake in winter and stored in it for use in the summer.

[D] **Burnham Overy Town** Its crooked **church** contains a faded wall-painting of the patron saint of travel, St Christopher, carrying the infant Jesus across the water in the flight into Egypt. In the village is the foot of an ancient cross, the former commercial centre of Burnham Overy.

[E] The **water-mill** (National Trust; *not open* to public) has a flood marker showing the depth of water in the 1953 floods.

[F] On the right is a fine six-storey **tower mill** (National Trust; *not open* to public), built in 1816 and rescued in the 1920s after it had been tail-winded in a storm and had its machinery wrecked.

[G] **Burnham Overy Staithe** Once a flourishing little harbour with a regular packet-boat from London; traces of berths and warehouses can still be seen. Nelson, born at Burnham Thorpe, sailed here as a boy. It was also the home of Captain Woodger of the *Cutty Sark*.

[H] These **marshes** are of international importance ecologically. Apart from the prolific **birds**, the area shows all the stages in establishing dense larch woods on dunes and mudflats. Away to the left are the dunes on Scolt Head Island.

[I] This great expanse of sand has been used for filming desert scenes. A beachcomber's paradise: the shells, starfish and assorted objects washed up from the sea are a constant distraction for the walker.

The walk passes right in front of Holkham Hall. Its most famous owner, 'Coke of Norfolk', started a fashion revolution by wearing country clothes at court

RUTLAND WATER

A WATERSIDE walk without rival in Central England, around the landscaped shores of the huge man-made lake of Rutland Water. Further interest is added by the waterfowl, windsurfing and sailing scene, and the varied views as you round the peninsula. Route-finding entirely straightforward.

LENGTH 3½ miles (5.5km). 1½ hours

DIFFICULTY 1

START Hambleton, east of Oakham, signposted off A606 (Oakham–Stamford); roadside parking in village centre. Grid reference 900076

OS MAPS Landranger 141; Pathfinder 896 (SK 80/90)

REFRESHMENTS Pub in Hambleton

WALK DIRECTIONS

① A Follow road in the Oakham direction, past pub on right, out of village. 150 yards after last house, take track over cattlegrid on right, and follow it close to the lakeside B.

② Cross the road and take the track opposite around the south side of peninsula C.

③ Go forward on reaching the road (left is private to Old Hall) D; at next cattlegrid, follow the road back up to the village. If desired you can proceed further along the lakeside track.

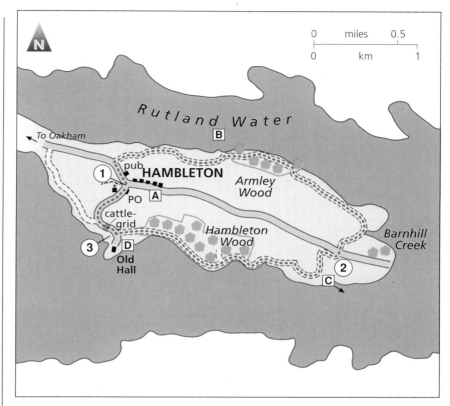

Trout fishermen are just one of many sporting groups who use Rutland Water

ON THE ROUTE

A **Hambleton** A pleasant village centre, with 'Arts and Crafts'-style estate cottages and post office (1892) opposite the restored 12th-century **church**; the village gives absolutely no hint of its remarkable peninsular site, all but surrounded by Rutland Water, under which its twin, **Nether Hambleton**, disappeared when the reservoir was constructed.

VILLAGES AND OPEN FIELDS

The Anglo-Saxons who settled in this country after the Romans departed colonised the landscape and lived in village communities, many of which have evolved into the villages found today (particularly in eastern England). These settlements were sometimes on the sites of earlier ones, but others were in new locations, particularly in the valleys.

The new villages often possessed open fields. These were divided into unenclosed strips, farmed often by different tenants. Through the Middle Ages, many areas of waste were gradually colonised, and open fields were extended. Three major factors accounted for the widespread abandonment of villages in medieval England; the Black Death of 1349, the clearance of land for royal forests, and the appearance of monastic farms.

At the peak of the wool industry in the late 15th and 16th centuries, many open fields were enclosed to make agriculture more efficient. This threatened doom to some villagers, who moved out; but other villages prospered, and much money was made from farming (many farmhouses were built, and a good deal of these survive in some form today). After the Dissolution of the Monasteries, the great monastic estates were broken up and gradually taken over by a new class of yeoman farmers. During the 15th to 17th centuries, many great parks came into being.

Between the mid-17th and 19th centuries private Acts of Parliament led to the enclosure of most of the remaining open fields and much of the wastes. The later enclosures are often distinguishable from the earlier ones by their large size and greater regularity; by comparison small, irregular fields are often quite ancient enclosures. At Chelmorton, in the Peak District, something akin to a 'fossilisation' of an open field system can be seen. The village originally had a single open field within an earth bank, and a common pasture outside. After the 1809 Enclosure Award, the dry-stone walls retained virtually the same pattern.

The village of Laxton, in Nottinghamshire, retains a fine example of an open field system.

B **Rutland Water** Covering an area of 3,500 acres, with a shoreline of 24 miles, this is the largest lowland lake in England. Its 900-million gallon capacity is an important water source for the East Midlands. After it was completed in 1977 the shore was landscaped and picnic sites laid out. Rutland Water is now a major recreational area, attracting 400,000 visitors every year. Its 350-acre nature reserve at the west end is an important site for waterfowl. Beyond the woodlands above Rutland Water you can see **Burley House**, a rebuilding (1696–1700) on a grand scale, in the Palladian style, by Daniel Finch, second Earl of Nottingham, to his own design; colonnades enclose a 650 × 500-ft piazza. Its landscaped grounds were modified by Repton; a grand avenue led to fish-ponds, now underwater.

C View of **Normanton church**, a survival of the largely underwater Normanton Estate, which belonged to Sir Gilbert Heathcote, a man of immense wealth – one-time Lord Mayor of London and in 1694 one of the founders of the Bank of England. The church, which has a baroque tower inspired by St John's, Smith Square in London (architect Thomas Cundy was surveyor of the Grosvenor Estate in Westminster), was retained as a landscape feature. It has rather ignominiously lost its proportions as its base has been lowered into rubble, but from a distance the church splendidly graces the water's edge. The church is now a **museum**.

D **Old Hall** Built 1611 in Jacobean style; an unusual design with mullions and gabled wings in an H-plan; the building has been altered over the years and now enjoys a magnificent site by the water.

Eastern England's largest lake, Rutland Water provides an important waterfowl habitat as well as a much-used recreational amenity

THE GRANTHAM CANAL AND DENTON

THE Grantham Canal towpath, followed by green tracks and part of the Viking Way are the distinctive features of this walk, which ends on a note of considerable drama. Route-finding mostly easy.

WALK DIRECTIONS

① With the pub sign on your right, follow Main Street. Go straight over at junction into Sedgebrook Road. ② ¼ mile after the end of village, fork right (by advertising sign for Rutland Arms). ③ After crossing the canal, cross a stile on right and join the canal towpath, along which

you turn left (walking with canal on right) Ⓐ. Bridges are numbered with plaques.

④ At bridge 66 (with a house up to the right), leave the canal and cross the bridge. On other side take signposted steps on right into a field. Follow the right edge of three fields, close to the canal (briefly inside woods above canal at end of second field): the third field narrows to a thin strip at its far end.

⑤ Ignore the gate beside a stile on left and proceed forward along left edge of fourth, fifth and sixth fields to reach Denton Reservoir. Turn left on waterside path. ⑥ At

the end of the reservoir, cross the water channel on the right by

LENGTH 8½ miles (14.5km), 4 hours
DIFFICULTY 2
START Woolsthorpe by Belvoir, east of Belvoir Castle and west of Grantham (do not confuse with Woolsthorpe south of Grantham). Roadside parking by sign for Chequers Inn. Grid reference 341827
OS MAPS Landranger 130; Pathfinder 835 (SK 83/93)
REFRESHMENTS Pub and shop in Woolsthorpe; pubs at Woolsthorpe Bridge and Denton

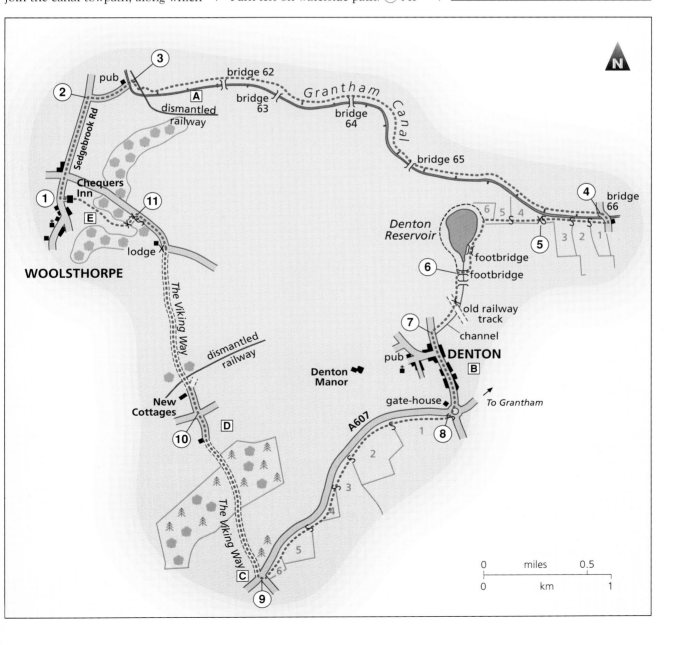

footbridge, turn left and follow track alongside the channel to a gate beside a stile giving on to track (of old railway). Take gate beside stile opposite, still with the channel alongside on your left.

⑦ Emerge on to a road, and turn left into Denton village ⒷB. Keep forward at crossroads, signposted Grantham (pub is to right), through village. ⑧ At cross-junction with A607, cross the main road and take a stile to the right of the turning opposite: continue to the right, closely parallel to A607 for 1¼ miles along the edges of six fields.

⑨ Emerge by a stile on to the road and track by the county boundary; cross A607 and take track opposite (signposted Viking Way) ⒸC. Keep straight ahead as main track bends left to a farm after 50 yards, and forward just as you enter woods (ignoring minor right fork into field) ⒹD.

⑩ Cross the road and take road opposite; go past a row of houses on your left and ignore right fork;

proceed for 1 mile to road. Turn left on the road then ⑪ after 350 yards, where road is about to descend and woodland is about to start on the right-hand side of road, take a gate beside stile on left and follow woodland track to emerge by a gate beside stile on to a strip of pasture. Turn right along this strip; the view ahead opens out ⒺE. Drop to stile into left-hand side of cricket field (which is the right-hand of two sports fields below) and follow left edge to emerge by pub in Woolsthorpe.

ON THE ROUTE

Ⓐ **Grantham Canal** runs 33 miles fron Nottingham to Grantham to the Vale of Belvoir; it was used commercially until 1797. Coal, limestone, coke and building materials from Nottinghamshire were transported eastwards; the return journey took agricultural products destined for market at Hull via Newark and the River Trent.

Ⓑ **Denton** An unspoilt L-shaped village of mellow ironstone, lying beside the estate wall of the private manor (the Tudor-style gate-house of which is passed on the walk). A minor architectural storm occurred in 1980 when 17th-century almshouses in the park, reckoned as among the most delightful in England by architectural writer Sir Nikolaus Pevsner, were demolished.

Ⓒ A long-distance path across Lincolnshire, through many settlements with Viking origins, the **Viking Way** starts at the Humber Bridge and ends 140 miles away at Oakham in Leicester.

Ⓓ **View** to right of **Harlaxton Manor**, a palatial mansion covering half the hillside. Its first owner was Gregory Gregory, a devoted collector of the arts, who commissioned 32-year-old Anthony Salvin to design it, largely to accommodate his growing collection. Not surprisingly the building work took time: Gregory, who owned the smaller 17th-century manor house, only lived here for the last three years of his life. It is likely that he took a large part in planning the design.

Ⓔ Arresting **view** of the spectacular outline of **Belvoir Castle** (pronounced 'Beaver'), against the huge Midland plain beyond. This massive pile, with its castellations, was remodelled 1801–30 by James Wyatt and Revd Sir John Thoroton. The site has Norman origins. The late 11th-century structure was built by Robert De Todeni, standard-bearer to William I (*open* March to October; closed Monday).

CANALS

Often peaceful backwaters today, canals in their heyday were a major component of the early Industrial Revolution. During the late 18th and early 19th centuries, the country was gripped by a frenzy of canal construction. It all began in the 1750s with a canal linking St Helens with the Mersey, but more significant was the waterway constructed in the next decade for the Earl of Bridgewater by the great engineer James Brindley. This, the Bridgewater Canal, eventually linked Manchester with Liverpool, halving the cost of coal in Manchester and acting as a catalyst for the town's massive industrial expansion.

The potter Josiah Wedgwood was a backer of a scheme to link the Trent and the Mersey, with canals feeding into the Thames and the Severn, connecting London, Birmingham, Hull, Bristol and Liverpool.

By 1800 there were some 1,600 miles of canals, and half a century later this had risen to 4,250 miles. But the advent of the railways spelt the beginning of the end, and motor transport precipitated the decline. The canal system is still used for carrying goods, but today they are seen as a leisure resource. The restoration of many waterways continues apace.

Since early canal barges were towed by horses, all canals have towpaths (except in tunnels, where they needed to be 'legged' by the crew, lying on their backs and pushing their legs against the brickwork), and these are accessible to walkers. The famous Pontcysyllte Aqueduct, near Llangollen in Clwyd, is one of the most spectacular canal features; there are fine flights of locks at Foxton in Leicestershire and Marple just outside Stockport (to name but two). Stoke Bruerne in Northamptonshire has an absorbing canal museum and canalside pub, and visitors can walk along the Grand Union from there to the entrance of the huge Blisworth Tunnel. In Manchester, the Castlefield urban heritage area is at an atmospheric meeting of canals (the Bridgewater and the Rochdale), near some impressive warehouses. In London, there is a fine canalside walk along the Regent's Canal from Little Venice to Camden Lock, passing London Zoo, with narrowboats at either end providing an appropriate means of returning to the start.

Belvoir Castle

LOWESBY, BAGGRAVE AND QUENBY HALLS

A TRIO of country houses, with Quenby Hall the grandest, are the main features of interest; the route crosses intimate and varied landscape in between, over parkland and farmland. Finding the way across fields requires some care in places.

LENGTH 6 miles (9.5 km), 3 hours
DIFFICULTY 1–2
START Lowesby, 9 miles east of Leicester (off B6047), limited parking by church. Grid reference 724075
OS MAPS Landranger 141; Pathfinder 895 (SK 60/70)
REFRESHMENTS Pub in Hungarton

WALK DIRECTIONS

① Standing by church gate, take road with No Through Road sign (towards estate buildings of Lowesby Hall, with churchyard on your left). At end of churchyard take gateway on right with yellow waymarker and keep left over stile to proceed along left edge of fields closely parallel to the private driveway to the hall; take gate into second field, where Lowesby Hall now appears on your left A.

Go forward, past corner of garden wall of the hall, and then proceed ahead across semi-parkland: a well-defined track between an avenue of trees proceeds straight ahead, but keep just to the left of it (aiming for the distant red-roofed barn of Portels Farm). Once you are over the rise, a road with prominent signpost can be seen ahead.

② Cross the road at this signpost and take the track opposite. Follow the waymarked route, close to left edge of three large fields, with stream close by on your left (in the second field you leave the track as it bends right just after disused pit). In the middle of fourth field, the path joins woodland fence but does not enter woods, then drops to a gate with signpost beyond. ③ Turn right, over stile, signposted Baggrave.

Again proceed along edges of fields with stream close by on left (but not always visible). ④ Where Bell Dip Farm is visible up on right, keep forward, now on farm track and still parallel to stream. Leave the track as it bends left into woods but at end of same field take stile on left into woods. Proceed along plantation fence on left to take footbridge over stream, and carry on a few yards to reach a long duck-pond. Turn right along the pond B.

⑤ Turn left along road. ⑥ After ½ mile when road bends left, turn

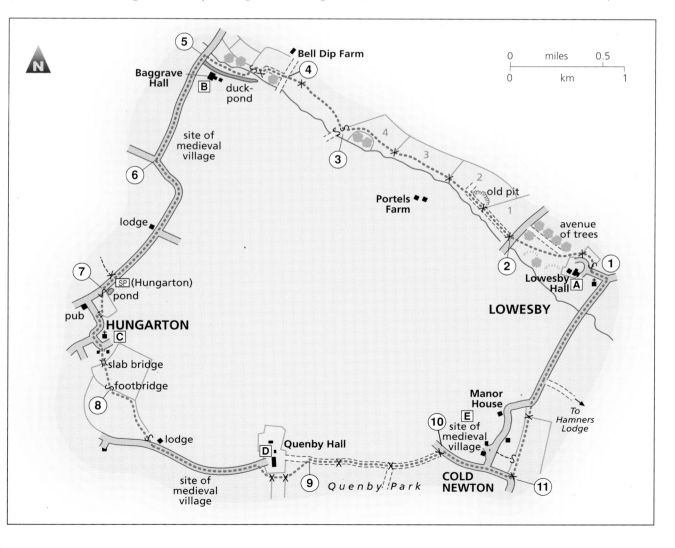

Quenby Hall, the oldest of the three country houses to be seen on the walk

left with it. Ignore a later left turning by lodge. ⑦ Just after the sign for Hungarton, take signposted stile on left (or continue along road for pub). Head towards Hungarton church to find a kissing-gate to track giving on to road, where you turn left through the village towards the church ⒞.

Fork left into Church Lane by the war memorial, pass church on your left; at end of churchyard, keep forward at junction, downhill. 30 yards later (with brick house away to right and older house on left) proceed on enclosed path to enter field. Cross slab bridge, then bear half right slightly uphill: the route is not obvious but the exit from field can be found by keeping to the left of group of trees lining right-hand side, to reach a prominent yellow marker-post by a stile and

footbridge, which you cross ⑧. From here you can see a lodge in trees up half left; you reach it by turning left alongside hedgerow at bottom of field, keeping right inside field at corner by cattle-trough. Emerge by the stile on to road, and turn left along it through entrance gate to Quenby Hall (*note* path is always open, even if hall is closed). Keep to right of hall ⒟, to take gate just to right of wall. ⑨ Beyond the hall, join unsurfaced driveway coming from the hall, and follow it ½ mile.

⑩ Turn right on road ⒠. Keep forward at next junction (left is signposted Lowesby), then after 150 yards where road bends right, ⑪ take signposted gate on left and follow left-hand hedgerow (soon ignore stile on left) to exit at end of field, then cross the grass to reach

the road. Turn right on road to Lowesby.

ON THE ROUTE

⒜ **Lowesby Hall** Isaac Wollaston built this two-storey brick mansion in the 1700s around a 17th-century core; a later wing and stable block were added by Edwin Lutyens in 1910, who was partly responsible for laying out the garden.

⒝ **Baggrave Hall** once belonged to Leicester Abbey, and was acquired by Francis Cave after the Dissolution and then by the Edwyn family in 1686. John Edwyn rebuilt the hall in the 1750s, and his work can be best seen from the road; the house retains some elegant interior features, including a Jacobean Revival drawing-room and a staircase hall with rococo stucco.

⒞ **Hungarton** Much of the village was rebuilt, 1766–75, by Shukbrugh Ashby: his work is distinguishable by yellow and red brick chequer-work and date-stones. Ashby's monument is in the **church**.

⒟ **Quenby Hall** The finest early 17th-century house in Leicestershire, built for George Ashby, and acquired by Shukbrugh Ashby in 1759; the latter was responsible for renewing the structure and décor, but its Jacobean interior was later reinstated. The house has strong similarities in design to Doddington Hall in Lincolnshire.

⒠ On the left, grassy humps mark the site of the abandoned **medieval village of Cold Newton**. Lowesby and Baggrave also have medieval village sites, although far less is visible.

BROOMSBRIGGS, BEACON HILL AND OUTWOOD

SOME of the county's highest land, with volcanic crags peeping out from the bracken, forms the attraction of this varied walk, taking in mixed woodland and farmland. The route is mostly waymarked.

WALK DIRECTIONS

① From the car park entrance, with the road behind you, take the track beyond the barrier half left, signposted Broombriggs Farm. Where, after 200 yards, the corner of a wall appears on left (just before you reach cross-junction with waymarked horse track), turn left downhill alongside wall to emerge on to a road ②.

Turn left on road and immediately right by Woodhouse Eaves sign, to pass into a field just to the left of the car park. In the second field, a well-defined path leads up to a gate in corner of woods. Turn right, immediately leaving woods to follow right-hand side of third field, alongside a wall, towards Broombriggs Farm (ignore first stile on right) A.

③ Take the stile ahead into a fourth field, where you turn left as waymarked along the bottom of fourth, fifth and sixth fields. ④ As soon as you enter the seventh field, turn right uphill (opposite gap in wall) with woodland on your right, past memorial benches and along the right edge of eighth field B, past a picnic site.

LENGTH *Short walk* 3 miles (5km), 1½ hours. *Full walk* 4½ miles (7km), 2½ hours
DIFFICULTY 1
START Beacon Hill Lower car park, south of Loughborough and west of Woodhouse Eaves; follow B591 east

from junction with B5330 and take first turning left (signposted Nanpantan); car park is on left after ¼ mile, opposite lodge for golf course. Grid reference 522148
OS MAPS Landranger 129; Pathfinder 874 (SK 41/51)

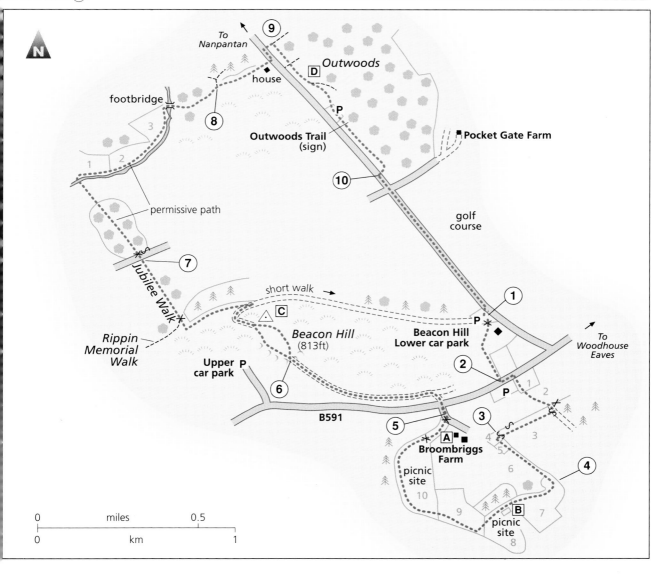

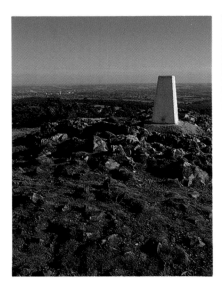

The trig point at the summit of Beacon Hill

Keep to left edge of ninth and tenth fields (you effectively follow three sides of the tenth field), then drop on an enclosed path to a farm road where ⑤ you turn left to reach the main road. Cross the road and take the gate opposite, keep left (signposted Beacon Upper car park) and left again on to a well-defined hard track, soon into open land with Beacon Hill ahead. Fork right up to the top of Beacon Hill ⓒ. Beyond view indicator, proceed, to left of trig point (summit pillar) to turn right on track, with a wall on left ⑥.

For short walk Follow this track to reach lower car park.

For full walk Follow the track, which soon bends right. Just before woods begin on left, take the path on left through a gap in the wall, proceeding over moorland and alongside the woodland wall on your right. At the edge of moorland and corner of the woodland wall, the path keeps right through a gateway (with the woodland wall still on your right).

50 yards later, take the signposted Jubilee Walk ahead (avoiding Rippin Memorial Walk on left). ⑦ Cross the road to take a gate beside a stile opposite (keep dogs on lead; this is a permissive path which may be closed without warning – in the unlikely event of closure, retrace your steps to the tracks skirting Beacon Hill and turn left to follow short walk back to lower car park).

Follow the waymarked route, down through a woodland strip, over a stream and turning right along the bottom edge of three fields, then over a footbridge to follow the path through woods and into rough land.

⑧ Fork right as soon as the woods begin on your left (left fork crosses woodland wall), proceeding alongside the wall on left to reach a house and then the road. Turn left on road and then right after 150 yards over a signposted stile.

⑨ 30 yards later turn right through the (intentional) break in fence to take the path closely parallel to the road on your right (not always in view); if the path is overgrown, take any other path leading to the right, or follow the road itself. Keep forward at cross-junction of paths where a fence comes in from the left.

At the car park, continue closely parallel to road, taking the path to the right of sign for Outwoods Trail ⒹD.

⑩ Just before a road-sign indicating a right turn, emerge by a gate on to the road. Turn left along the road and follow for ½ mile to the starting-point.

ON THE ROUTE

ⒶA **Broombriggs Farm** Owned by Leicestershire County Council and run as a 139-acre arable and stock farm. Information boards are placed around the estate in summer months to explain the working of the farm.

ⒷB As you round the hill, the view opens out over **Loughborough**, the cooling towers of **Castle Donington power station** and **Charnwood Forest**. To the left, amid the heathland of Bradgate Park, stands **Old John's Folly**, commemorating a retainer who died in a bonfire accident at the Earl of Stanford's 21st birthday party in 1786.

ⒸC **Beacon Hill** (813ft) A moorland summit with small crags; a **view indicator** identifies the panorama over the Trent and Soar valleys, with the Derbyshire hills in the distance. The rocks are volcanic, striped with layers of grey, cream and green representing successive stages of lava eruption laid down on the sea-bed 700 million years ago which was tilted by movements from within the Earth. Erosion has subsequently created a series of parallel, broken ridges which form the present-day hills of Charnwood Forest. The rocks of Charnwood harbour the oldest known evidence of life forms more complex than seaweeds.

ⒹD **Outwoods** is a 44-hectare site of oaks and conifers, mostly planted but of ancient origins; the woodland possesses a rich flora.

How many people who didn't know would guess that these crags on Beacon Hill (albeit miniature) are in Leicestershire?

EVERDON AND FAWSLEY PARK

THREE attractive villages in orange-coloured stone amid rolling farmland and parkland are the high points of this route. Mostly on waymarked paths.

WALK DIRECTIONS

① **A** Return along Church Way to High Street and take the path opposite and slightly to right through gates of Manor Farm. Go forward across the first field to the

right of the farm and, where the wall meets a fence, take a gate into second field. Go forward alongside wall, later a fence, on left to a gate.

Over the gate into a third field, go forward to a waymarked stile which is just to the left of the outline of a barn on skyline. Proceed

LENGTH 8 miles (13km), 4 hours	Street and turn left into Church Way.
DIFFICULTY 2	Grid reference 574548
START Preston Capes church; turn	**OS MAPS** Landranger 152;
off Maidford–Charwelton road at	Pathfinder 999 (SP 45/55)
Preston Capes, taking north turn	**REFRESHMENTS** Pubs at Everdon;
signposted Daventry, down High	pubs and shops at Badby

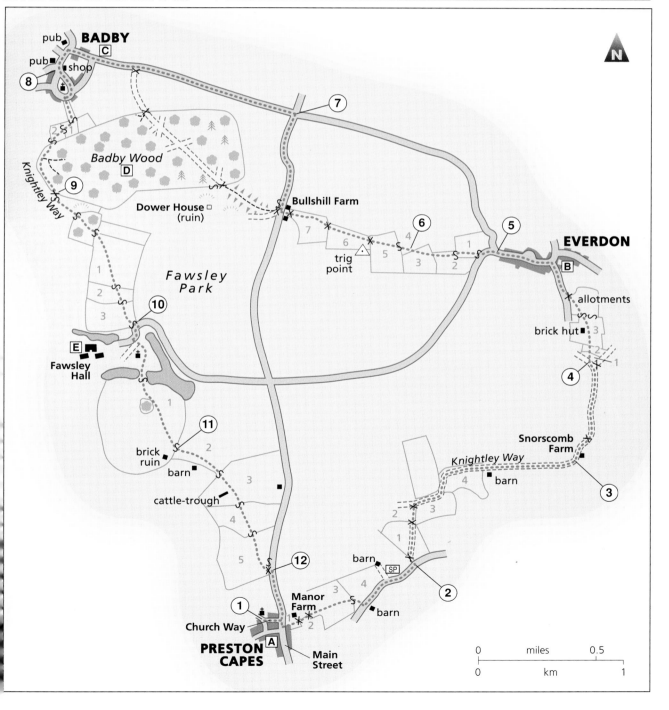

across the fourth field, bearing half right towards a barn to reach a minor road.

Turn left along the road (ignore small track on the left after 200 yards, leading to the barn) and after 400 yards ② turn sharp left alongside a hedgerow at the end of the field and at 30 yards take a gate on your right through the hedgerow.

Go forward on a track through first field and in the second field keep close to the right-hand hedgerow and after ¼ mile turn right at waymark through a large gap which leaps into a third field.

Keep the hedge on your left and shortly the track bends left through a break in the hedge to enter a fourth field. Follow the bottom side of fourth field, soon bending right at a corner, past a barn, and at field end enter an enclosed track which eventually leads to Snorscomb Farm ③. Keep to the left of farm buildings on the main track, which dips down to a gate. After the gate, turn sharp left along a tarmac track and after passing Snorscomb Mill on left, immediately fork left ④ through a gate.

Cross the bridge and immediately turn right to cross a stile. Cross a narrow second field to a stile directly ahead. Emerge into a third field, go forward and slightly left, heading well to the right of the distant church tower and passing well to the right of a red-brick hut, heading to the right of projecting hedge corner to cross the fence at the corner of field into allotments.

Proceed through the allotments on track toward Everdon Church, turning right at the road, passing the church on the left to enter the village B. Turn left into Main Street past the village green. ⑤ Towards the end of the village, fork left where signposted Fawsley. 100 yards after 30 mph speed derestriction sign, ascend steps on right to a stile into first field. Climb left alongside the hedgerow leaving by a stile in the top left-hand corner, not forgetting to enjoy the panoramic view to the rear.

Through the second field the track proceeds forward roughly 30 yards from the right-hand edge of

field to reach an opening in the hedgerow ahead. On entering a third field, head quarter right to cross right-hand hedgerow at a waymark located on a tree which is 90 yards before the right-hand corner of the field ⑥, ignoring obvious track directly ahead.

Cut diagonally across corner of fourth field to a stile in the left-hand hedgerow, some 70 yards from the left-hand corner of field. Heading slightly right towards right-hand corner of the fifth field, cross to a prominent opening in the hedge. Follow the right-hand edge of the sixth field to a gate in the far right-hand corner, turning left in seventh field downhill to Bullshill Farm in the bottom right-hand corner of field. Go through the farmyard and on to the road.

Turn right along the road, ⑦ turning left after ¾ mile at crossroads, to follow a minor road for 1 mile into Badby. Go forward into the village centre C, turning left at T-junction along Main Street. ⑧ After 200 yards turn left into Vicarage Hill. At the church follow road round to right and immediately take an enclosed path on the left, signposted Knightley Way, to Fawsley.

The path drops, rises and crosses a stile into first field where you bear right to the next waymarked stile. (From this point, the walk joins the Knightley Way which is well waymarked). Cross the second field diagonally left up to a stile at the corner of Badby Wood D. Proceed along the path at edge of woodland, keeping the ditch on your left and fence on your right. ⑨ After ¼ mile leave the woods by a gate and immediately keep left over a further waymarked gate/stile, bearing ahead and slightly right across open land to a waymarked stile into semi-open woodland.

Follow waymarks (slightly left and downhill) to a stile, and descend through three fields to waymarked stiles below and slightly left. Emerge on to an estate road, turn right and ⑩ after 50 yards where the road bends right, take the gate ahead and cross parkland, passing just to the left of Fawsley Church E.

At the church, note the direction

of the route which proceeds down between the two lakes, over a stile, and then bears half left, aiming to the left of the distant tower of Preston Capes Church. Thus keep half left after the lakes, ⑪ and leave the first field by a waymarked stile, at the point where the power line leaves the field and 100 yards left of a brick ruin. (Power line cannot be sighted until you are in the lower half of field.)

Go straight uphill in second field initially with right edge and barn 100 yards away, when the route finally veers right to leave the field by the far right-hand corner. Ascend third field slightly right, passing a drinking-trough on your right at the hill brow, then drop to stile. Preston Capes village is now in view. Head straight to a waymarked stile at the end of fourth field and continue ahead, to leave fifth field by a gate beside a stile in the far left-hand corner.

⑫ Turn right on to the road and proceed up the hill to Preston Capes village via High Street, to turn right into Church Way and the start of the walk.

ON THE ROUTE

A **Preston Capes**. Castellated brick cottages were built as 'eye-catchers' for Fawsley Hall. The 12-mile **Knightley Way** goes from Greens Norton to Badby.

B **Everdon** A broad street flanked by orange-coloured ironstone cottages and broad verges with a chestnut tree on the village green.

The **church** possesses a 15th-century traceried screen, carved box pews, an ancient roof and a rare musician's gallery.

C **Badby** In Vicarage Hill, cottages are ranged on the slope beneath the 14th-century church.

D **Badby Wood** Enchanting in spring for the spectacular shows of bluebells; also a habitat for foxes.

E **Fawsley** The **house** and the estate **church** were built for the Knightley family, and nestle amid lovely landscaped parkland with artificial lakes and ancient trees. The **Great Hall** is 16th century. The estate **church** has carved beasts on its pew-ends and monuments to the Knightleys.

HARTSHILL HAYES AND THE COVENTRY CANAL

ONE of the most impressive
viewpoints in Warwickshire sets
the mood for an absorbing short
walk in and around the woodlands
of Hartshill Hayes country park,
making use of the towpath of the
Coventry Canal. Nature trail
leaflets are available from the
visitor centre. The walk is partly
waymarked.

LENGTH 3 miles (5 km), 1½ hours
DIFFICULTY 1–2
START Hartshill Hayes country park,
west of Hartshill, and south of
Atherstone; signposted from A5
south-east of Atherstone. Fee for car
park. Grid reference 316944
OS MAPS Landranger 140;
Pathfinder 914 (SP 29/39)
REFRESHMENTS Café at visitor
centre (weekends only)

WALK DIRECTIONS

① Take the signposted path at back
of car park, behind warden's office
and to the right of fenced-off grassy
bank (reservoir). This leads to a
hillside, with the reservoir fence up
on left and woodland fence down to
the right. Proceed as you like on the
hillside (keep high up to enjoy the
view to the full) Ⓐ, to enter
woodland at a sign for St Lawrence's
Wood at the end of the grassland
Ⓑ. ② Just after entering the woods,
there is a post marked 4, indicating
a left fork (this is part of the short St

Lawrence's Wood nature trail: you
can either follow to the left, then go
down steps, or keep on the main
path; the two routes soon rejoin).

At post 5 keep forward (leaving
the nature trail, which bears right)
and fork right 20 yards later as
waymarked, to enter a field. Go
forward on a path along the right
edge of field, ③ bending left at the
first corner of the field. Midway
along next edge of the field, take a
waymarked gate on to an enclosed
path on right.

At the end of enclosed section,
turn right on to enclosed track

leading uphill. At the top, the route
continues along left edge of field
until ④ passing through a break in
the hedgerow on left (where field
beyond the hedgerow on left has
ended) to follow a well-defined cart
track down to a farm. Keep to left of
farm buildings, turn right on the
road and bear right at next road
junction.

⑤ Cross the canal, then turn
right to join the canal towpath; turn
left along towpath, walking with
canal on your right Ⓒ. (Bridges are
numbered with plaques.) ⑥
Immediately after bridge 33, turn

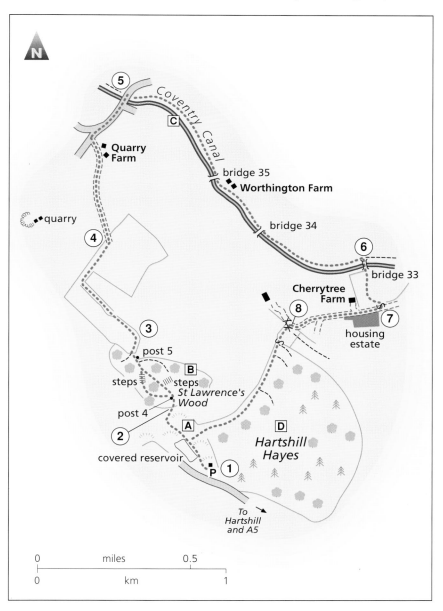

*The berries of the rowan, one of several tree
species in Hartshill Hayes*

left up the bank and cross the bridge to follow a path across a field (bisecting the rightmost two power posts in the centre of the field) to a gate in hedgerow ahead ⑦.

Turn right on farm track between hedges. Ignore right turn to Cherry Tree Farm, then soon after the houses on left end, fork right. ⑧ After 150 yards, just where the track is about to bend right to a farm, take the gate on left into a grassy area. Keep right, to take a stile in corner of woodland and follow the path leading uphill along the inside edge of wood with fence posts on right ⒟. After ⅓ mile, a playground is visible ahead: proceed straight up to reach open hillside, where you turn left into the car park.

ON THE ROUTE

Ⓐ The **view** encompasses four counties: Warwickshire, Leicestershire, Derbyshire and Staffordshire; Mancetter church, the A5, the Coventry Canal, Drakelow power station and the Peak District are all in view.

Ⓑ **St Lawrence's Wood** This was a plantation created to landscape the ground of vanished Oldbury Hall, the site of which was at the top of the hillside, just off the end of the present-day reservoir; the hall was built 1770, on the site of a medieval nunnery and was demolished in the 1950s after bomb damage. The wood contains Scots pine and sycamores, and supports a variety of mosses.

Ⓒ **Coventry Canal** Built 1771, linking Coventry with Bedworth, Nuneaton and Tamworth, it was one of the most profitable canals up to the Second World War.

Ⓓ **Hartshill Hayes** 114 acres of mixed coppiced woodland, a fragment of the ancient Forest of Arden which once covered the area. Larch predominates, but the species also include birch, hazel, holly, lime, rowan and oak; the site is a rich habitat for birds and insects.

The Coventry Canal near Hartshill

BOURTON-ON-THE-WATER AND THE SLAUGHTERS

THREE classic Cotswolds villages are linked here by paths along gently defined river valleys epitomising the quiet charm of the area. Waymarking is good throughout (part of the route follows the Windrush Way, part follows the Wardens' Way), although there is a briefly confusing section on leaving Upper Slaughter.

LENGTH 4½ miles (7km), 2½ hours

DIFFICULTY 1

START Bourton-on-the-Water village green. Parking in village. From main village car park take path at back of car park signposted to village; turn left at path T-junction, then immediately turn right. Grid reference 167207

OS MAPS Landranger 163; Pathfinder 1067 (SP 02/12)

REFRESHMENTS Full range in Bourton-on-the-Water. Washbourne Court Hotel in Lower Slaughter is open to non-residents

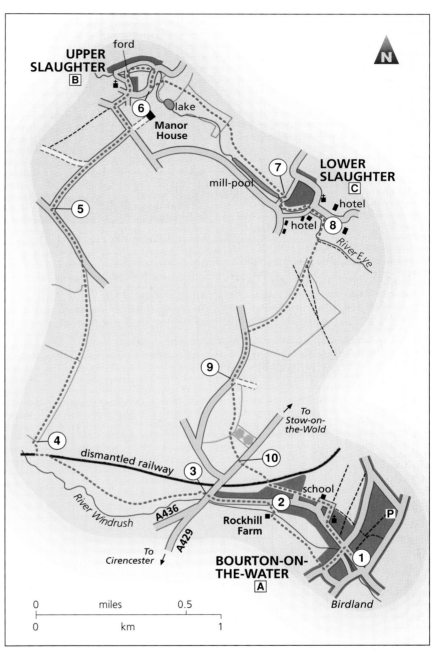

WALK DIRECTIONS

① Ⓐ From the war memorial on the village green, take Sherborne Street over low bridge. After 100 yards pass Harrington House on left and reach road fork, where you take signposted path on right. Soon emerge into pasture, where the path joins the river away to your right. The path crosses at a stone bridge to join the road ②. Turn left along the road to reach main road at T-junction ③. Take path opposite (to right of road-bridge), beginning at the stile (the Windrush Way), and follow blue arrows, roughly parallel to meandering river. Go through waymarked gate and walk alongside fence on left. Emerge on to the embankment of a defunct railway; turn left and after 40 yards fork right to leave the railway track. ④ On leaving woodland, turn right at the junction of tracks, uphill and along edge of field. In second field ignore path going off right through a gate

but continue on main track on field edge. Turn left along the road, then ⑤ right at first road junction. Turn left at T-junction in front of gateway to manor, and take first right turn into Upper Slaughter village Ⓑ. Take the road on the left in village centre, dropping to a ford, where you take footbridge and turn right on riverside path. At the end, turn right on road over river; ⑥ after 100 yards take signposted path on left (Wardens' Way), with stone wall on right. At bottom, enter field

The shallow Windrush glides beneath the bridges at the centre of Bourton-on-the-Water

and carry on forward (no path visible), leaving the stream, with a lake in view down to right; very soon a gate ahead comes into view marking the route. Maintain direction in second field, with stream down to the right; in third field take the right-hand of two field paths to reach gate. Lower Slaughter is now visible; follow the waterside path. ⑦ C At the road in the village, turn right, along river walkway; avoid two footbridges but carry on to road-bridge. Cross over road (Washbourne Court Hotel is to right) and continue along riverside path. ⑧ Where river bends right (50 yards) opposite Lower Slaughter Manor Hotel, take Wardens' Way footpath on right. Where path crosses over river ignore stile on left; continue onwards to reach a field. Keep right, along right edge of field (soon ignore a stile on the right). At end, turn left on road. ⑨ After 250 yards take waymarked path on left immediately after gravel service track on left. Follow close to left edge of field to find a stile (and plank footbridge) at far end, to the right of a small woodland (ignore entrance in hedge just before the woodland). Cross next field to stile. Cross main road to gate and stile opposite ⑩ and carry on in direction of church tower to cross over grassy embankment of old railway at the edge of Bourton-on-the-Water. On the other side immediately fork left on enclosed path. Continue past back gardens, then a primary school. Turn right in front of church to reach centre of village.

ON THE ROUTE

A **Bourton-on-the-Water** is one of the most visited of all Cotswold

Horses wade past the cottages at Lower Slaughter, delightfully set by the River Eye

villages. At its heart, a series of stone bridges spans the shallow River Windrush. The walk snakes around the back of the village, through a meadow and re-crosses the river at an exceptionally pretty point where the Windrush divides around a walled garden.

The village has a number of family attractions: the **Village Life Exhibition** features an Edwardian village shop, a smithy and period rooms and is *open* outside December to February. The **Cotswold Motor Museum** is a former water-mill crammed with vintage cars celebrating the golden age of motoring; there are motor cycles and advertising signs too. Bourton-on-the-Water has its own **Model Village**, faithfully built at 1:9 scale in authentic Cotswold stone. A **Perfumery Exhibition** has a scented garden as well as scent extraction demonstrations. Just out of the village are two bird-related

attractions: **Folly Farm Waterfowl** and **Birdland**; the latter is a garden on the river, with penguins, parrots and macaws.

The **railway line** used to run from Cheltenham Spa to Kingham. The 26-mile journey took about 50 minutes, stopping at Bourton-on-the-Water.

B **Upper Slaughter** has some fascinating old headstones in its churchyard; the **church** itself has remains of a Norman tympanum in its porch. The walk passes the entrance to the **Elizabethan manor house** and takes in a very pretty area around the ford, graced with a strategically sited bench to allure picnickers.

C **Lower Slaughter** is a delightful set piece with an old mill, by the duck-populated River Eye, crossed by small bridges and flanked by cottage gardens. The **church** was restored in the 1860s but its arcades date from the 12th century.

SHENBERROW HILL AND STANTON

THIS route unites two outstanding Cotswold villages. From Buckland it climbs quickly to follow farm tracks along the Cotswold ridge, with views of the Vale of Evesham, Bredon Hill and the Malverns. The Cotswold Way drops down through partly wooded pasture into Stanton. The finale is level and easily managed, over pasture, with views of the escarpment from below. All of the route is on defined paths and tracks. There is one ascent at the beginning.

LENGTH 5 miles (8km), 2½ hours
DIFFICULTY 2
START Buckland, 12 miles north-east of Cheltenham and 1 mile east of B4632. Park on road near Buckland Manor Hotel. Grid reference 084360
OS MAPS Landranger 150; Pathfinder 1043 (SP 03/13)
REFRESHMENTS Mount Inn, Stanton (with garden)

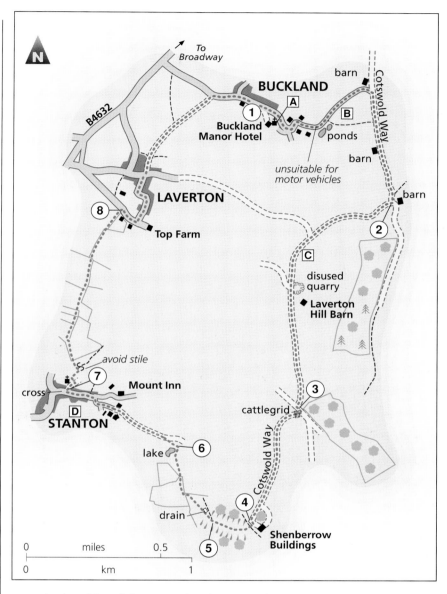

WALK DIRECTIONS

① Take road past Buckland Manor Hotel and church Ⓐ (both on your right); just after the church keep on the road as it bends sharp left, ignoring sharp right turn (back

Limestone walls and cottage gardens are classic Cotswolds features

towards church) and driveway ahead (going to Mill Close). Road bends back and rises past houses and then ponds (on right); at end of ponds ignore path signposted to right, but keep on the road. Where road levels out and becomes an unsurfaced track, keep forward (avoiding track to right) on Cotswold Way Ⓑ. ② ½ mile later ignore left turn, go through gate and turn right opposite barn. Track now proceeds with fence on right; later it is enclosed by fences on both sides (ignore forks down to right) Ⓒ. Pass abandoned quarry and Laverton Hill Barn away to left. ③ Reach T-junction of tracks with Cotswold Way signs and turn left and immediately right, over cattlegrid. Reach small group of

trees (ignore gate and bridleway to left).

④ Where main track veers left to house, continue straight ahead through gate (yellow marker). Ignore cross-track after 20 yards but make for marker post ahead; path then swings right to follow bottom of dry valley. ⑤ After 300 yards fork left (marker post), soon passing a fenced drain, and cross stile in corner of field. Keep to right side of field, passing stone outhouse after 100 yards, and cross stile (yellow marker) on your right soon after. Beyond stile, bear immediately half left on faint path, aiming to right of lake in distance, to reach stile which leads between fences to second stile ⑥.

After second stile ascend ahead for 20 yards to reach track. Turn left and follow this into and through Stanton village (Mount Inn is on first turning right) [D]. (7) Turn right by the stone cross in centre of village, follow lane for 50 yards, then turn left into churchyard. Pass around right side of church to find walled path on far side of churchyard. At end of walled section do not take stile into field but turn left on path between fences. Enter field, turn left along left edge to take stile where you go right along right edge of second field to find a stile near the field corner into a third field. Maintain the same direction across further fields to

reach the road at Laverton (8) . Turn right through village, keeping left on the road where a driveway leads ahead to Top Farm. At road T-junction take bridleway opposite and slightly to the right and follow to Buckland, ignoring side paths. Turn right at road to reach the centre of the village.

ON THE ROUTE

[A] **Buckland church** Has 13th-century arcades and 16th-century panelling. The building fortunately escaped over-restoration. The **rectory** nearby is largely medieval.
[B] To the left is seen **Broadway Tower**, on top of the escarpment, a castellated folly erected in 1800 at

an elevation of 1024 feet.
[C] The village of **Snowshill** is seen away to the left. A recommended excursion after you have completed this walk is to **Snowshill Manor**, where the eccentric and eclectic collection of Charles Wade fills the house; items are far-ranging in styles and include such diverse objects as antique bicycles, clocks and Japanese Samurai armour. (NT – *open* April to October except Monday and Tuesday; open Bank Holiday Monday.)
[D] **Stanton** A pretty example of a North Cotswold village, which owes much to the care of Sir Philip Stott, a landowner and architect. In the centre is the village cross, which has a 17th-century sundial on its medieval base.

Stone benches in the **church** date from the time when the congregation, save the weak and infirm, were expected to stand – just 'the weakest went to the wall' and were allowed to sit down. The church has traces of ancient murals. The rood screen, east window and churchyard cross were designed as First World War memorials by Ninian Comper, whose strawberry motif may be seen at the bottom right-hand corner of the east window (unusually for stained glass, these are actually easiest seen by looking from outside). Some bench ends in the nave have been grooved by the chains of attendant sheep-dogs tethered while their masters attended services.

Stanton's ancient market cross

CLEEVE COMMON AND POSTLIP WARREN

FROM the breezy hillside hamlet of Cleeve Hill, tracks lead up on to the highest point in the Cotswolds. Once up, the walker encounters easy walking on the plateau top, on tracks across springy turf. In complete contrast, the route descends into the steep-sided wooded valley of Postlip Warren. No major ascents. There are numerous track junctions around Cleeve Common, and the track from ④ to ⑥ is faint at places; route-finding may be difficult in mist.

WALK DIRECTIONS

① From car park follow road downhill for 30 yards, then turn left opposite bus shelter and phone-box, over gate/stile (signposted public path) to follow track. After 10 yards

turn right and 35 yards later ignore track forking right (towards house and wall) and immediately after ignore another track ascending sharp left; the track you take is the one which goes roughly on the level, with wall and houses a short distance down to the right. This

LENGTH 6 miles (9.5km), 3 hours
DIFFICULTY 2
START Car park on north-east side of Cleeve Hill village on B4632, 5 miles north-east of Cheltenham. Grid reference 985270. Drive past the Rising Sun and Cleeve Hill hotels; there are car parks on both sides of the road near telephone-box and toilet block. Further parking by following B4632 for a further ½ mile, then turning right to the municipal

grassy track winds below rocks and grassy hummocks on your left. ② After 400 yards reach 5-way junction of tracks and lanes with gate and cattlegrid down to right (and castellated folly, the Little Castle, just beyond); bear half left uphill on semi-metalled track; keep

golf course; ignore the golf course car park by the clubhouse to the right, carry on over cattlegrid and turn left; car park is shortly on right. Begin walk by following track downhill, keeping to left of golf clubhouse; toilet block by telephone-box later appears down to right

OS MAPS Landranger 163; Pathfinder 1066 and 1067 (SO 82/92 and SP 02/12)

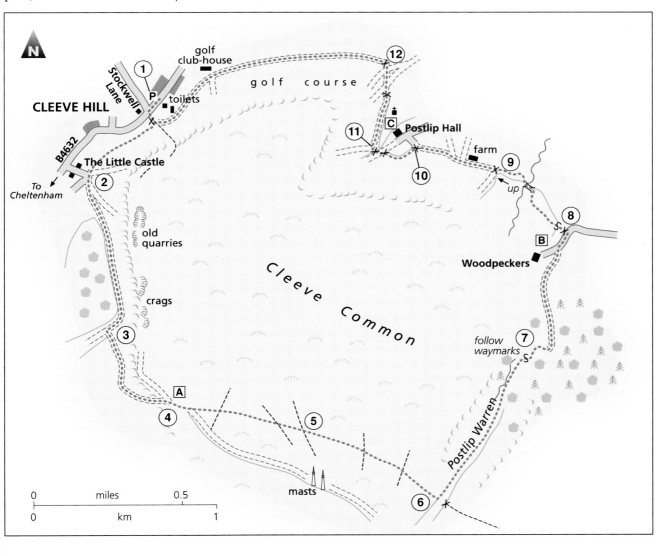

View from the top of Cleeve Hill overlooking Postlip Warren towards Breakheart Wood

to the main track, which is later joined by woodland on right. ③ At end of woodland, track bends right and just as it is about to bend left (houses suddenly appear ahead) fork left on to grassy track snaking uphill (keep to the main track all the way up), soon passing bench on your right to emerge at top of hill ④. A Do not take track to right (close to wall and fence) towards masts but take grassy track half right across the grassland. Maintain direction (ignoring cross-tracks) as track becomes fainter, heading immediately to right of prominent area of gorse ⑤, which immediately swings away half left. Carry forward over open grassland (heading for third pylon from right in far distance); once you are past the masts away to the right, the wall away to the right veers away further right; the track soon becomes well defined. At gate in stone wall after ¼ mile ⑥, do not pass through gate, but turn left, descending with wall on right. After ½ mile, cross stile (waymarked) into wood, and ⑦ 200 yards later turn right (marker-post) and 50 yards later turn sharp left on woodland track. This descends gently to emerge from woods on to track (with house, Woodpeckers, behind and to left); go forward on the track B.

⑧ 100 yards beyond Woodpeckers, where wooden railing on left ceases, turn sharp left through gate (blue arrow marker) and follow path down to stream. After crossing stream, ascend alongside fence on left, towards brow of hill. ⑨ Near top, pass through gate on left (blue marker) and maintain direction on farm track which shortly passes farm. After farm, ignore two turnings to the right C. ⑩ Just before trees and houses, take waymarked gate on left and walk alongside wall on right. Where wall bends right follow it through gate. Cross track to take gate opposite and pass through gates opposite.

⑪ Where wall on right veers right, ignore path to left but continue to follow wall, on track which leads through gate, to emerge on open land. Continue straight on and avoid all side tracks. Pass through gate at top ⑫. This track leads to starting-point – avoid right turn after 200 yards and ¼ mile later pass golf clubhouse on your right and keep forward downhill (the two right-hand tracks soon rejoin), past

abandoned quarry on your right. Soon the main road becomes visible and a small path leads to the right to the toilet block where the walk began.

ON THE ROUTE

A Water permeating through the oolitic Cotswold limestone has lubricated the impermeable clay foundations, resulting in an unstable slope and large-scale landslips. The scarp slope caused by this has been eroded back and troughs have been created – including the embayments in which Cheltenham and Winchcombe stand, and the valley of Postlip Warren. **View** west across the Severn to the Forest of Dean, with the Sugar Loaf and Black Mountains beyond. Further to the right is the jagged outline of the Malverns and, further right still, Birmingham.

B **View** of Winchcombe, with Sudeley Castle further right.

C Visible ahead is **Postlip Hall** (*not open to public*), a 16th- to early 17th-century manor house with a restored Norman chapel in its grounds.

The many-gabled façade of Postlip Hall (now divided up into separate homes), with the tithe barn in the foreground

THE THAMES AND SEVERN CANAL AND SAPPERTON

AN exploration of the narrow and secluded Stroud Valley, along the towpath of the derelict canal on the valley floor, then heading up over turfy fields towards the spire of Sapperton church. The return route is through pasture lands and woodland on the northern slopes of the valley. Be prepared for somewhat intricate route-finding from Sapperton onwards. An easily followed alternative is to take in the canal (follow sections 1–5) and return the same way. The walk may be shortened to approximately 4 miles (6.5km) by following the road from the Daneway Inn at ⑤ to ⑨ and omitting Sapperton.

> **LENGTH** 6 miles (9.5km), 3 hours
> **DIFFICULTY** 2
> **START** Church in Oakridge, 6 miles east of Stroud. Grid reference 913033
> **OS MAPS** Landranger 163; Pathfinder 1113 (SO 80/90)
> **REFRESHMENTS** Butcher's Arms (closed Mondays) and village shop (near the pub) in Oakridge; Daneway Inn, Daneway and Bell Inn, Sapperton

WALK DIRECTIONS

① Start on the small green by the entrance to church, with church immediately down to left and school on right. Take the right-hand of two footpaths at end of the green (to left of house called Stokyes Close) leading between walls to a stile with yellow waymark. Follow left edge of four fields (ignore another waymarked path to right in third field) to enter woodland ②.

After 30 yards turn left over stile, and continue downhill (avoid path coming in from right after 150 yards). Reach tarmac lane at bottom and turn left along it. ③ After ¼ mile reach junction and turn right, signposted Frampton Mansell, over a road-bridge. Immediately after, road bends left; 20 yards later take steps on left leading to footbridge; then turn right along canal towpath Ⓐ.

④ At next bridge pass to other side of old canal, taking track past cottages; 30 yards later continue ahead through kissing-gate, marked Footpath. Follow towpath for 1 mile, finally crossing to the left bank by wooden bridge, then emerging on road by the Daneway Inn ⑤.

For short version of walk, omitting Sapperton take road ahead and to the left, ascending; just after house up

The Thames and Severn Canal, now romantically overgrown

on right, take signposted stile on left (this is ⑨).

For full walk via Sapperton cross to other side of bridge and continue along other side of the towpath, signposted Sapperton; the course of the canal is now through the pub car park.

⑥ After ½ mile, path crosses over mouth of canal tunnel Ⓑ and leads up to a stile. Bear quarter right uphill across field, heading for spire

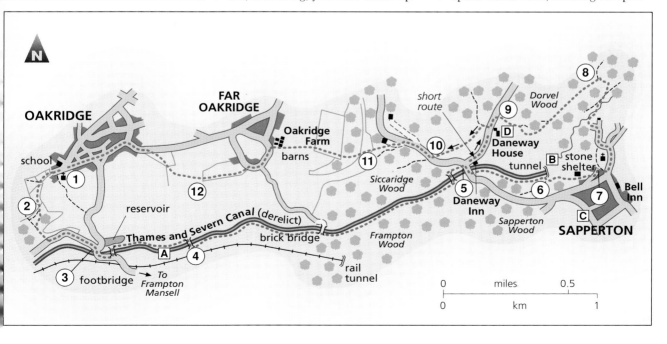

of Sapperton church and soon passing to right of stone shelter. At stile at top, path continues on left. Continue to road and turn left to reach path junction at edge of churchyard ⑦. Turn right uphill to corner of road in Sapperton village Ⓒ (Bell Inn is a short way up road, on left) and turn left downhill. After passing the church, ignore private driveways to right but keep left on road, which becomes a track. Further down, keep left (where main track leads to house ahead). Cross stream to enter woodland. 50 yards after bridge, avoid sharp left turn, and 50 yards later take fork left uphill.

⑧ After 200 yards turn left at crossing of tracks. Follow track approximately along the level, avoiding any right turns and continue until finally dropping to road Ⓓ. Turn left on road but immediately cross stile by gate on right and ⑨ follow path winding half left round side of hill with fence on left. After 50 yards cross stile by gate on left (avoid stile and gate on right) and maintain direction across grassland, with fence up on right, at far end of which emerge by stile on to road ⑩. Ignore path opposite but turn right on road, passing driveway on right after 120 yards. 100 yards later, fork left on stony driveway; ignore stile on left after only 20 yards (into Siccaridge Wood nature reserve) but carry on driveway and 30 yards later take waymarked woodland path on left. This soon drops. At edge of wood cross low stone slab and cross field to waymarker post by slab footbridge ⑪. Go forward to stile into woods,

A carved pew in Sapperton's 18th-century church

ignoring side paths. Pass through woodland to take stile/gate into field: bear half right across first field (no defined path), aiming towards buildings and heading through gate in hedge ahead on skyline. In second field head for gate immediately to left of metal barn.

Emerge on to lane and turn left along it. Avoid left turning marked Unsuitable For Motors after 200 yards, but 100 yards later, where road bends right, keep ahead through gate (yellow waymark). Path follows left edge of field and is well defined.

⑫ On far side of field, cross stile and bear quarter right (path undefined) uphill, following telegraph poles. At junction at top (with farmhouse away to right), continue forward along left edge of field to find gate leading on to road.

Turn left on road and follow road through Oakridge and to Oakridge church (turnings up on right take you through middle of village).

ON THE ROUTE

Ⓐ The derelict **Thames and Severn Canal** functioned from 1789 until 1911. Further on is one of its feeder reservoirs, followed by the Daneway Inn, a canalside pub by the site of a former flight of locks. It is a friendly old pub (1784) with a garden and a no-smoking family room. The canal and its surroundings are a wildlife sanctuary and are partly owned by the Gloucestershire Wildlife Trust.

Ⓑ **Canal tunnel** with grand embattled parapet. The tunnel leads south-west for two miles, to emerge at a pub near Coates.

Ⓒ **Sapperton** Ernest Gimson and the brothers Barnsley, followers of the Arts and Crafts movement, settled here at the beginning of this century and built a number of cottages in the village in traditional style, including Upper Dorvel House, Leasowes, Beechanger, number 40a on the Green, and the village hall. The **church** was largely remodelled in the early 18th century and contains bench-ends with Jacobean caryatids, transplanted from Sapperton House after it was demolished in the 1730s. Poet John Masefield lived at Pinbury House during the Second World War.

Ⓓ A few yards left is **Daneway House**, a medieval manor that Lord Bathurst allowed the Barnsley brothers and Ernest Gimson to use as a workshop for producing and exhibiting Arts and Crafts-style furniture.

PAINSWICK AND SLAD

A SHORT walk in Laurie Lee country, with fine views of the old wool town of Painswick and many old Cotswold-stone buildings. It makes an ideal family ramble. Some sections can be muddy. The route is moderately easy to find.

LENGTH 4½ miles (7km), 3 hours
DIFFICULTY 2
START Falcon Hotel, opposite the church in Painswick on the A46 Cheltenham–Stroud road (there is a large free car park about 20 yards on the left down the road towards Stroud). Grid reference 866097
OS MAPS Landranger 162; Pathfinder 1113 (SO 80/90)
REFRESHMENTS The Woolpack, Slad; pubs and tea-shops in Painswick

WALK DIRECTIONS

① Ⓐ With your back to the Falcon Hotel, cross road and turn right for 20 yards then left into churchyard to left of bus shelter. Keep to right of spire, and turn left behind church to pass church porch Ⓑ, then when level with end of church turn right under arch of yews to leave churchyard by Stocks Gate. Continue forward down Hale Lane Ⓒ, which narrows to an alley, then at end turn right on road.

When road forks by post-box, continue sharply downhill on Knapp

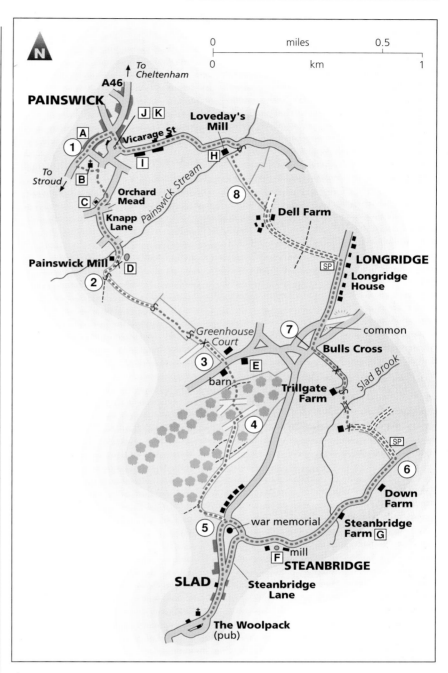

Painswick's church spire soars above a surreal churchyard of clipped yews

Lane, and when this bends round to the right continue forward and downhill on the footpath with a stone wall on left. At bottom of hill, cross road and continue forward on access road to houses Ⓓ; this becomes an unsurfaced track.

Once past the entrance to mill, follow track around to the right and uphill. After 80 yards, turn right in front of field gate, and continue on path between fences. Follow this around corner of field, then ② immediately take the fork to the left and continue uphill on

the path between the fences.

When this ends, go over stile into field and continue forward with hedge on right, then forward over stile to next field to continue along right edge. Exit through gate beside stile on to track between hedges coming in from right, and continue forward up to road Ⓔ.

③ Cross road, and take path opposite to left of barn to stile into field. At top left corner of field, go up bank to stile into wood. Ignore cross-track running just inside wood, and continue uphill on well-defined path. When path reaches complex junction of tracks, take track half left and uphill for 15 yards, then turn right on to path going directly uphill signposted by blue waymarks.

④ At top of rise, turn right on track, with wall and field on right but after 20 yards turn half left on track running downhill into wood. Go down through wood on this track, following blue waymarks and ignoring right fork after 50 yards and subsequent cross-tracks. At the bottom, the track runs just inside the edge of some woodland.

After 100 yards, fork left and further 100 yards turn left on to access road to houses. Go down this to main road at war memorial ⑤. *For Woolpack pub* turn right along main road for ⅓ mile; pub is on left opposite parish church. On leaving pub return same way along main road for 200 yards, but then fork right along Steanbridge Lane just before red-brick house. After another 200 yards, follow road around and down to the right, ignoring road uphill to the left. *For route omitting pub* go straight across main road by the war memorial and continue downhill on minor road, which bends round to the right. At the bottom of the hill turn sharp left at road junction (this is Steanbridge Lane). *Both routes* Continue down Steanbridge Lane to the bottom of the valley F. Pass pond and mill, then Steanbridge Farm G on your right, go uphill, pass Down Farm and Springbank Stables also on right, then ⑥ when road bends slightly to right, turn left into field on gravel track signposted to Trillgate. Follow track along edge of field, with wall on the left.

At end of field, bear left and downhill, ignoring track branching to right. After another 100 yards (at end of field on right), turn right through gate into field, following signposted Public Footpath to Bulls Cross. Go down across field, making for buildings of Trillgate Farm on other side of small valley; at bottom of valley, cross stream by bridge and

go through gate beside stile then ahead up slope keeping immediately to right of fence and farm buildings to find a stile by a gate.

Emerge on to farm road and turn right. Follow farm road uphill to main road ⑦. Turn right on main road, but immediately left on to minor road signposted to Sheepscombe. The road crosses a small common: ignore minor junction after 120 yards. Descend on road to group of houses (Longridge), and just after passing Longridge House on right, turn left on track between hedges, following the public footpath sign.

Follow track down to Dell Farm and go through farmyard, passing house on right and main group of buildings on left. Once through farmyard, when vehicle track ahead is about to climb slightly, turn half left towards marker-post with yellow arrow, and from there continue along left edge of field.

⑧ After another 100 yards, follow track through gap in hedge to left, again with marker-post. In next field, continue downhill with hedge on left. At bottom left corner of field turn right and continue along side of the same field for 40 yards, then go left over stile on to road.

Turn left on to road, across stream H, and follow road for ¼ of a mile uphill into Painswick. Immediately after 30mph limit signs, road joins Vicarage Street, merging in from right. Follow it I to small square before Royal Oak public house, then turn right up Bisley Street J. At crossroads, turn left along New Street to return to start K.

ON THE ROUTE

A The Falcon Hotel dates from 1711, and supposedly used to stage cockfights.

B The earliest parts of **St Mary's church** date from c.1378, and its most notable feature is the fine 17th- and 18th-century tombs, reflecting the wealth of the clothiers of Painswick; a guide to a 'Tomb Trail' around the churchyard is available in the church. The

inscriptions on many of the tombs are now unreadable, but you may be able to find, near the east end of the church, a monument, with a metal plaque, to William Hogg who died in 1800: 'he was for fifty years a much esteemed gratuitous preacher of the gospel.' The churchyard also contains 99 yew trees, mostly about 200 years old.

C On your right at this point is the **Court House**, a traditional gabled Cotswold building, built c.1604.

D The mill-pond which served **Painswick Mill** is on your left. The mill was built in 1634 and made cloth until the mid-19th century.

E Look left along the road from here, to glimpse a fantastic **stable** with castellations and strange fanlight windows.

F **Steanbridge** The house on the right at the bend is Elizabethan at the back. There was a cloth mill here until 1825, and the house figures in Laurie Lee's classic childhood novel/autobiography *Cider with Rosie* as the squire's house.

G **Steanbridge Farm** 17th century, with a fine front with parapet.

H The house on your left was **Loveday's Mill**, named after one of the principal family of clothiers. The millhouse is 17th century, the mill building early 19th century.

I **Dover House** is a perfect example of an early Georgian Cotswold house. **Yew Tree House**, shortly after this, was built c.1688 for Thomas Loveday, and one of the yew trees in the garden is thought to have been planted in the reign of Elizabeth I.

J **Bisley Street** used to be the main street of the village. Friday Street, halfway up on the left, was the site of the Friday market, and the houses on the right, The Chur and the Little Fleece, date from the 14th century.

K **New Hall**, on the left at the junction of Bisley Street and New Street, was first mentioned as a Cloth Hall in 1429. The post office on the right in New Street is the town's only exposed timber-framed house and dates from the 1400s.

MALVERN AND THE WORCESTERSHIRE BEACON

BY straddling the magnificent northern end of the Malvern Hills ridge, the walk takes in the two old counties of Worcestershire and Herefordshire, the former on the Severn plain, the latter with its rolling hills. Expect mud after prolonged rain. Part of the route is waymarked. There are two particularly steep sections (uphill past Whitman's Hill Farm and downhill after ③).

LENGTH 6½ miles (10.5km), 3½ hrs
DIFFICULTY 3
START Great Malvern town centre, at junction of A4532 (Church Street) and A449 (Belvue Terrace/Worcester Road/Wells Road), by WH Smith and near Unicorn pub. Grid reference 775459. Alternatively start at the car park at North Malvern quarry; walk back to road and join the walk at ③, turning off North Malvern Road by clock tower; grid reference 771469.
By train Malvern
OS MAPS Landranger 150; Pathfinder 1018 (SO 64/74)
REFRESHMENTS Full range in Great Malvern; New Inn, Storridge; snacks, soft drinks, perry and cider at Knight's Cider; café at St Ann's Well

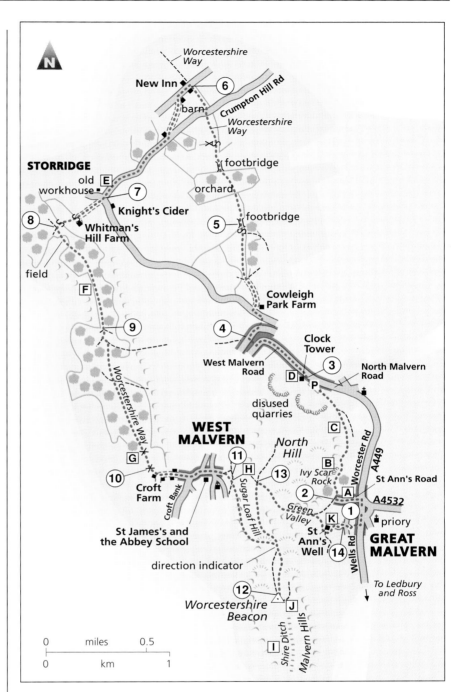

WALK DIRECTIONS

① Standing with your back to WH Smith, turn left along the A449 (in the road direction towards Bromyard on what soon becomes Worcester Road). Turn left by the Unicorn pub, up St Ann's Road Ⓐ. After 100 yards, keep forward where the principal road bends left, uphill (on small road marked by dead-end sign). Where double-yellow lines on road end and there are signs Malvern Hills Conservators – No Wheeled Vehicles, ② turn sharp right on a level path (ignore minor right fork downhill after 20 yards), which then leads slightly uphill. After 160 yards, at a five-way path junction, go forward and uphill. After 80 yards, keep right on joining a gravel path merging from left and soon pass Ivy Scar Rock on your left Ⓑ. The path now levels out.

Continue on main path, ignoring minor side turns. It eventually drops, becoming a track with abandoned workings of North Malvern quarry to the left Ⓒ, and passes a house on the right. Pass through car park and continue to the road ③. Turn left along the road, past clock tower on left Ⓓ. After ¼ mile the road makes a sharp left-hand bend and the right-hand pavement is protected by a railing; at the end of the railing, and opposite 51 West Malvern Road, take the footpath on your

right, descending very steeply between houses. ④ At the bottom, ignore footpath directly ahead and turn right on the road for 130 yards, then left over stile on to a path between fences. At the bottom, descend by steps to a road, then turn left along road for 75 yards. After the entrance to Cowleigh Park Farm, turn right on a hard track between field and farm buildings, on the Worcestershire Way (which you now follow until the New Inn at Storridge). Follow this track as it curves to the left and ascends a slight ridge. At the top of the rise, take the second path from the right, marked by a Worcestershire Way waymark. After 30 yards, turn right on a footpath running within a belt of trees; soon enter a field and continue on the path along the right edge of it (ignore a stile on right just before the end of field). At the field corner, cross a stile and immediately turn left, along a fence on left, over a stream by a footbridge ⑤. Turn right beyond the footbridge, on a field-path close to right-hand fence and following any waymarks. At the corner of field, cross stile, then go forward on a track through an orchard. On reaching a hedge at the far end of the orchard, turn left, then right after 20 yards over a footbridge. Continue across the field in same direction, to join corner of hedge and go forward, alongside the hedge on right through fields to emerge on to a minor road (if you do not wish to visit the New Inn, you can turn left up this road to reach road junction after ¾ mile at point ⑦). Take left-hand of two field entrances opposite and maintain direction, alongside a fence on your right. ⑥ At the end of the field go forward on a driveway to the main road and turn left, past the New Inn on your right, along the road. 150 yards later, where electricity lines cross the road, turn left on a track into a field. Follow this track leading half right, up to brick house (Crumpton Hill Cottage), turning left in front of it and emerging on to a road. Turn right. ⑦ Ⓔ At road junction, cross the more major road and take the track opposite marked by Public Footpath sign, ascending to Whitman's Hill Farm. At the farm, do not go left into the farm itself but take the stile ahead and ascend the steep hillside to take a stile into a wood, and follow woodland path for 50 yards to reach top of ridge ⑧.

Turn left at path junction. After 80 yards take stile on right into field but maintain direction, keeping alongside woodland fence on left. At the corner of field, return to woodland over a stile and follow the main path ahead. After 270 yards, the path now has a field

immediately on right Ⓕ. ⑨ 25 yards after fields end, ignore the left fork; fork left uphill 20 yards later, but at next fork (after a further 50 yards) keep right. Follow this path (Worcestershire Way), along the ridge, for ½ mile, ignoring a crossing-path after 400 yards. Finally go through a gate Ⓖ. ⑩ After 200 yards go through a second gate, to emerge in field at the rear of Croft Farm; take the track leading slightly left into the farm, passing between brick barns, then passing farmhouse on your right (ignoring turn to right just before) and heading for a large Victorian building (St James's and the Abbey School). Go forward along a residential road, to join a public road (Croft Bank), on which you turn left uphill (ignoring a left fork into Mathon Road). By the school, cross the road and go up a minor road opposite, forking right after 50 yards (signposted Great Malvern, etc), passing a black and white house on your right and rising alongside a wall. ⑪ Ⓗ After 100 yards, you reach an oblique path junction at foot of open hill and go forward on a rising path. As this begins to bend left, Worcestershire Beacon is in view ahead. At the top of the pass (by the stone direction indicator) Ⓘ, left is the continuation, but first detour right up to summit of Worcestershire Beacon ⑫ Ⓙ, and beyond if desired. Return to the stone direction indicator and take the main path ahead, on the level towards North Hill. ⑬ After 300 yards turn right at the first junction (there is a stone sign for The Beacon, pointing back the way you have come, on the left), descending through Green Valley to St Ann's Well; this bends left after 200 yards (keep to main path). At path junction (with St Ann's Well café visible below to the right) turn right. The path bends left to pass in front of St Ann's Well Ⓚ, between benches (left) and pond (right). This track zigzags down to the road. ⑭ Turn right on road, then almost immediately fork left. After 30 yards, as the road becomes an entrance to a house (Bello Squardo), turn left down a flight of steps. At the bottom, reach the road and turn

left along Belvue Terrace to return to the start.

ON THE ROUTE
Ⓐ The houses in **St Ann's Road** are the oldest buildings in Malvern apart from the priory. Donkey carts used to take Victorian holiday-makers up to the Worcestershire Beacon from here.
Ⓑ **Ivy Scar Rock** One of the largest natural rock faces on the Malvern Hills, used for climbing.
Ⓒ View of the antennae on the north site of the **Royal Signals and Radar Establishment** can be seen; one of the largest electronics research establishments in Europe.
Ⓓ The **clock tower** was erected by Malvern council for the coronation of Edward VII in 1901.
Ⓔ The house to your right is the former **Storridge workhouse**.
Ⓕ The path follows the ridge for some 1½ miles, and wherever the trees open out there are fine **views** to the west: the Much Marcle Ridge (with a television transmitter on top), and the high, flat tops of the Black Mountains in Powys.
Ⓖ This is a permissive path running through a **nature reserve**, owned by the Hereford & Worcester Nature Trust. The tops of old **lime kilns** are visible to the right of the path.
Ⓗ Just to your left is a **spring** which is regularly checked for drinking quality.
Ⓘ On the ridge is the **Shire Ditch** or **Red Earl's Dyke**, constructed in the Dark Ages to divide the lands of Leofric, Earl of Mercia, from those of the Bishop of Hereford; it runs the length of the Malvern Hills.
Ⓙ **Worcestershire Beacon** At 1,381ft, the highest point of the Malvern Hills. The summit offers excellent views in all directions and includes the Shropshire Hills to the north, the Welsh Marches and Offa's Dyke country to the west, the fruit-growing area of the Vale of Evesham to the east, with the escarpment of the Cotswolds rising beyond it.
Ⓚ This quaint stone pavilion houses the spring which is the source of the original **Malvern Water**. The café is *open* daily March to October and at winter weekends.

LICKEY HILLS AND BITTEL RESERVOIRS

A VARIED walk over farmland and wooded hills, with opportunities for bird-watching by the reservoirs. Only the view from the Lickey Hills reminds the walker of the proximity to Birmingham. Most field-paths are signposted and defined, but some care is needed with the numerous woodland path junctions. Part of the route follows the North Worcestershire Path.

WALK DIRECTIONS

① From the station car park proceed down to road, turn left, then right along the B4120. Take the first left (Margesson Drive). Where road bends left after 50 yards, keep straight on/slightly to left through entrance in fence, across sports club car park (signposted Bittell Farm Road). Keep to the right of the sports club buildings, behind which path follows hedge into field ②. Follow left edge of first and second fields and over a stile into third field. Bear half right in third field, passing immediately to the right of a copse in centre of field, to a gate and on to the road ③.

Continue forward along road (ignoring road on right and private road on left), past reservoirs Ⓐ and

LENGTH	5 miles (8km), 2½ hours
DIFFICULTY	1–2

START Barnt Green station, 5 miles north-west of Redditch (platform 4 exit). From Birmingham direction take B4120 to Barnt Green, turn right immediately after railway bridge, into main village street. Park at station. Grid reference 006737
OS MAPS Landranger 139; Pathfinder 953 (SO 87/97) and Pathfinder 954 (SP 07/17)
REFRESHMENTS Victoria Inn and shops in Barnt Green

uphill past a farm on right, immediately after which ④ take the gate/stile on the left, just before house (signposted Upper Bittell Reservoir), leading to a track between a fence (left) and hedge (right). Where the fence on left swings away, keep alongside the fence on right, over stile through a group of trees to next stile. Beyond stile continue forward along the reservoir until just before the boat club, where the path turns left away

The wigeon is a gregarious bird and feeds more on land than any other duck

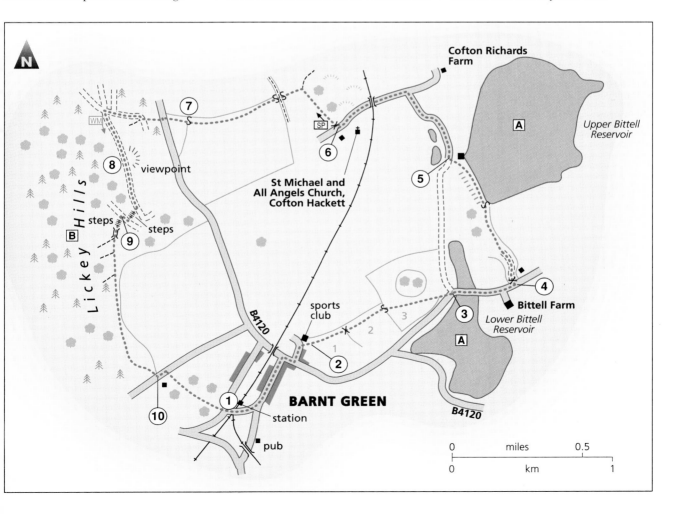

Fog in the distance seen from Beacon Hill in the Lickey Hills; much of the hillside is covered with mixed woodland

BARRIERS TO PROGRESS

Never climb a gate that you can open. Gates across rights of way that are locked or impossible to open should be climbed at the hinges to minimise damage to the gate and gatepost.

from reservoir to reach a pond 50 yards later. ⑤ Turn right on bridleway in front of pond and follow this for ½ mile to T-junction with farm road, at which you turn left. The road passes under the railway, then past church on left.

⑥ Just before the first house on the left take a gate/stile on right (signposted Barnt Green Road). Follow trees on the right side of field, at the end of which turn left uphill on a grassy path leading to a stile. Cross the tarmacked path beyond, take the stile opposite and continue forward, along fence on right edge of field. ⑦ At the end of the field cross a stile, follow the path between fences to a road. Cross the road, and take the ascending stepped woodland path opposite. After 100 yards turn right on to cross-track and ascend for 250 yards; track then levels – ignore two right turns then turn sharp left on to a wide waymarked track. Ascend gently to viewpoint B, after which ⑧ continue on the same track, soon descending.

After 350 yards, and just before the track is about to bend left, take waymarked path on the right, descending to steps. At the bottom of the steps turn right. ⑨ 30 yards later turn left by post, down steps. The path crosses a bridge after 100 yards. From here ignore all right turns and follow the path which runs roughly parallel to the edge of woodland, occasionally reaching it. ⑩ Turn left on road, then immediately right up wooded steps. Follow the woodland path back to the station (station footbridge is always open).

ON THE ROUTE

A The **reservoirs** are the habitat for **wildfowl**: tufted duck, waders, great crested grebe, pochard; in winter, wigeon, teal, snipe and golden-eye.

B **Lickey Hills** A hillside of mixed woodland, some of which is a fragment of the primeval forest that once covered this area. One side of the hill was used centuries ago as a shooting range, and ancient cannonballs have since been found. There is a fine panorama towards Birmingham.

CROFT AMBREY AND CROFT CASTLE

AN exploration of remote country between Ludlow and Leominster; much of the walk is on common land and parkland owned by the National Trust, and Croft Castle is on the route. For its few miles the walk has surprising variety and changing views most of the way. The terrain is quite hilly but not particularly steep.

LENGTH 5 miles (8km), 2½ hours

DIFFICULTY 2

START Bircher Common, Hereford & Worcester. Parking space after cattlegrid by NT sign for Bircher Common, just north of B4362 and 5 miles north-west of Leominster. Alternatively, start at NT car park for Croft Castle and start directions at ⑦.
Grid reference 466661

OS MAPS Landranger 137, 148 or 149; Pathfinder 972 (SO 46/56)

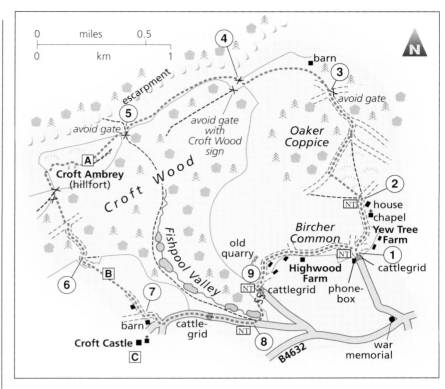

WALK DIRECTIONS

① With cattle grid behind you take the surfaced track on the right and fork first left on to another track; this bends left, uphill, past a chapel on the right. ② By the next house, fork left on a track leading up to wooden posts by NT sign Visitors Are Welcome . . .; here fork right to climb up to the centre of the

Fishpool Valley near Croft Castle

woodland on the skyline. At the trees, turn right on a track skirting the woods. ③ At a junction of tracks at corner of woods, bear left, still skirting woods. 400 yards later, keep forward at crossing of tracks (with gate to the right). After 30 yards, where main track bears left, keep forward on grassy path, and fork left 150 yards later. You enter a long field with a barn in the trees to your right: go forward, uphill and across field to the skyline, heading for right-hand field edge to find gates in far right-hand corner of field ④. Take the right-hand gate (not the left-hand one at sign for Croft Wood), which leads into open land and joins forest fence away to left, then goes along top of escarpment with views to the right; ignore minor side paths. ⑤ Eventually you drop slightly to an old beech tree: avoid gate (giving on to descending path) on left and stile to its right, but carry on uphill a further 30 yards to take next stile on left. The path climbs up to Croft Ambrey, an Iron Age hillfort with visible ramparts Ⓐ, then later drops to stile. Turn left immediately beyond, on path along top of escarpment, to reach two gates on

the left; take the right-hand gate, with sign for Croft Castle. Drop to crossing of tracks, where you go forward and ⑥ leave woods by a gate. Ignore NT path signposted to left but go forward, into parkland; track disappears, but keep to the right of a line of Spanish chestnuts Ⓑ. Track becomes defined, crosses through another line of chestnuts and drops to gate. Carry on down to T-junction of tracks in front of barn ⑦; turn left to reach castellated gateway of Croft Castle Ⓒ. Turn left on driveway (if starting from here, stand with gateway behind you and take the driveway ahead). ⑧ After ½ mile, take path half left by NT sign for Fishpool Valley, then turn left on reaching level of lake, around end of lake, then at corner avoid lakeside path to left but take narrow path ahead (ill-defined) rising through woodland strip to stile into field (with house prominent). Cross to next stile, turn left on lane to cross cattlegrid, where you fork right on track to right of NT sign. ⑨ At farm buildings fork left, keeping on main track. Keep forward, on the level, at Highwood Farm, ignoring left fork and follow to junction of tracks by cattlegrid and Bircher Common NT sign.

ON THE ROUTE

A **Croft Ambrey** An Iron Age **hillfort** with a total area of about 40 acres, which was occupied from about 450BC to its destruction, probably in AD48. The inner part of the fort was surrounded by a rampart and ditch and contained rows of rectangular wooden huts, serving as houses, granaries and other stores.

While it was inhabited it underwent many changes (excavation has revealed 15 successive sets of gateposts at one entrance) and was eventually used as a Romano-British sanctuary, after it ceased to be a fort. There is a fine **view** west to Radnor Forest, and north to the Shropshire hills.

B These **Spanish chestnuts** are about 350 years old.

C Originally a Norman border castle, **Croft Castle** (NT; *open to public*) is like a fortified manor house and is mainly 14th and 15th century, with substantial 18th-century Gothick alterations. It has been occupied by the Croft family continually since the Norman Conquest, except for the period 1750–1923. It passed to the National Trust in 1957.

The **Church of St Michael and All Angels** is close to the Great Door of the castle. It contains the exceptionally fine early 16th-century tomb of Sir Richard Croft and his wife; she was a widow of one of the Mortimers. The model for the church was at nearby Shobdon, an 18th-century church with a wedding-cake Gothic interior.

A path in the backwoods of Croft Castle

HIGHWAY AUTHORITIES' DUTIES AND POWERS

Highway authorities have the main responsibility for rights of way, and have discretionary powers too.
  Important statutory duties are:
- asserting and protecting the public's rights to use and enjoy rights of way
- ensuring that farmers comply with the law that paths over cultivated land are restored after they have been ploughed or otherwise disturbed, and thereafter remain visible on the ground, and ensuring that farmers do not allow growing crops to inconvenience right of way users
- maintaining bridges used by rights of way (landowners are responsible for gates and stiles, but highway authorities can put pressure on landowners to keep gates and stiles in usable condition)
- maintaining the surface of most rights of way
- preparing and keeping up to date a 'definite map and statement' giving a legal record of all rights of way
- signposting rights of way where they leave metalled highways and providing additional signs and waymarks along a path whenever they are necessary.
  Discretionary powers include:
- creating new paths by agreement with the landowner
- improving rights of way, for instance by providing seats and lighting
- providing footpath wardens.

GLADESTRY AND HERGEST RIDGE

A PERFECT example of the transition between the Welsh and English sides of the border: this is a walk full of interest and choice views, beginning with peaceful lanes and farm tracks before heading over common land and woodland. The finale is the scenic highlight, with a steady ascent on to Hergest Ridge, where the Offa's Dyke Path provides a spectacular conclusion along an easily managed track over turf. The route follows mostly defined tracks and paths, and there are landmarks to guide you in the short pathless sections.

WALK DIRECTIONS

① Take the dead-end road by grassy triangle in village centre, passing the church. At end of churchyard keep right and follow tarmacked lane uphill, ignoring side tracks Ⓐ. ②

LENGTH 5½ miles (9km), 3 hours
DIFFICULTY 2–3
START Gladestry village centre, on B4594 7 miles from Kington.
Grid reference 231551
OS MAPS Landranger 148; Pathfinder 993 (SO 25/35)
REFRESHMENTS Royal Oak Inn and shop in Gladestry

The lane eventually drops to T-junction of lanes with Grove Cottage on your right; turn right and follow farm road, through next gate Ⓑ, where you keep right along the power lines to Gwerndyfnant Farm Ⓒ. Turn left in farmyard in front of the farmhouse and follow the farm track winding downhill across a field; soon after the end of the field keep right at a junction of tracks ③. Drop to cross a stream;

30 yards later leave the track as it bends left uphill and keep right along the level across the field, aiming for a distant cottage. Go through gate and follow the track through a further gate on to end of lane ④. Follow the lane for 200 yards; where it bends left uphill by some houses (hamlet of Weythel) turn right on track; cross the brook

Looking east from Hanter Hill, a craggy, gorse-covered hill of igneous rock

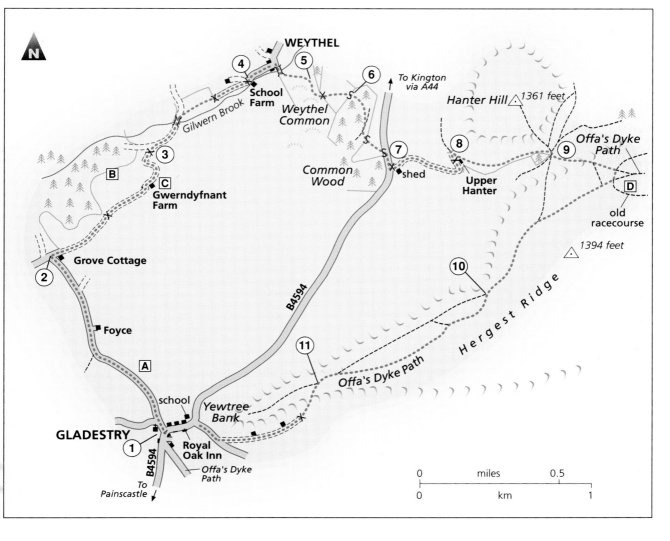

by bridge to emerge on to common.
Turn left, rising above stream and
finding a grassy path cutting
diagonally uphill over common. ⑤
This path soon reaches the edge of
the common and bends right with
slope and woods down to left; after
100 yards take gate on left and bear
half left over field to stile in middle
of woodland fence ⑥. Follow
woodland path which leads uphill,
bends right and drops to T-junction
with broad path; turn right and
immediately left on narrow path
dropping to stile. Go forward down
to stile in bottom corner of field (to
left of conifer woodland beyond
field) and on to the road. Turn right
on the road and after 75 yards ⑦
take gate on left and follow track
uphill. This bends sharp left to pass
in front of a cottage and barns
(Upper Hanter); ⑧ at the end of
buildings, go through gate and turn
right up alongside barn wall and
then fence to join a grassy track at
fence corner. Turn right along it. ⑨
At end of small conifer plantation
on right, you reach a seven-way path
junction and continue forward
uphill on path on to Hergest Ridge;
ignore right fork two-thirds the way
up. At top ⑤, turn right on broad
level grassy track (old race-course),
then in 75 yards turn half right at
junction (ignoring a track to the
left), now following Offa's Dyke
Path (waymarked with acorn
motifs). ⑩ Offa's Dyke Path forks
left when level with the valley head
immediately down on right and
house foundations on left (but both
paths later rejoin), and descends
gently. ⑪ At the final section of the
ridge, keep left as waymarked
(ignoring path climbing on to the
last part of the ridge; worth a detour
for views), dropping through gates.
Turn right at road T-junction at
bottom, and left at next road
junction into Gladestry village.

ON THE ROUTE

Ⓐ The **hedgerows** enclosing this
pretty lane may, like many in
Radnorshire, have started as dry-
stone walls. A rough guide for dating

hedgerows is to count the number of
hedgerow species for each 30 yards;
each one represents around a
century's growth – that is, it would
take around 500 years for five
species to establish themselves.
Ⓑ Down to the left, a small
plantation of trees around an
ornamental pond survives from the
headier days of Gwerndyfnant Farm.
The trees contain a **heronry**; the
herons can often be seen circling in
the sky or flying along the Gilwern
Brook.
Ⓒ **Gwerndyfnant Farm** formerly
belonged to the Hutchinson family,
into whom William Wordsworth
married. His wife Mary and his sister
Dorothy stayed here on several
occasions. Dorothy recorded taking
the children to bathe in the brook,
and wrote a poem about the farm.
As yet, no record has come to light
of William having visited the farm,
but since he is known to have stayed
at Hindwell Farm, a few miles away
at Walton, it seems likely
(considering his appetite for long
walks) that he did.
Ⓓ **Hergest Ridge** (pronounced
Harggist), half a mile wide at the
Kington end but of horse-saddle
narrowness above Gladestry, offers a
magnificent walk with ever-
changing views, on the right beyond
the prominent limestone quarries at
Dolyhir across to Radnor Forest
(topped by a tall mast), with
Titterstone Clee Hill in Shropshire
to its right in the far distance; to the
left and eastwards extends the
jagged outline of the Malvern Hills,
while southwards are the darkened
bluffs of the Black Mountains (the
reason for their name is apparent
from this side), and south-west are
the symmetrical summits of the
Brecon Beacons. Edward Elgar
walked on the Ridge, and is said to
have come here to seek inspiration
for composing *Introduction and
Allegro*. Mike Oldfield, composer of
Tubular Bells, named an album after
Hergest Ridge. The terrain on the
south side of the Ridge has been
immortalised by the diary of Francis
Kilvert, a 19th-century vicar from

*Herons have large, untidy nests on tree-tops
and frequent rivers and streams*

Clyro. Published in recent years,
Bruce Chatwin's *On the Black Hill* is
a powerful novel of rural life set in
southern Radnorshire and in Hay-
on-Wye. The circular track on the
Ridge is an old racecourse, disused
for many years but surprisingly still
prominent; at its centre is a small
plantation of monkey-puzzle trees.
The long-distance Offa's Dyke Path
takes in the length of the ridge,
although the Dyke itself, a 9th-
century earthwork marking the
western boundary of Offa's kingdom
of Mercia, is not extant here.

LOCAL STROLLS

Almost anywhere locally on the Offa's
Dyke Path will reap scenic bounties.
The easiest way on to Hergest Ridge is
at the Kington end; near the church, a
signposted road to Ridgebourne gives
access, and near the top of the road
you can also visit Hergest Croft, a
wonderful garden and tree collection
(best in May and June when the
rhododendrons are out); the Gladestry
end has more compactness and better
all-round views. In the other direction
from Kington, the Offa's Dyke Path
crosses the A44 and heads up to
Bradnor Hill (there is car access by the
golf course at Bradnor Green) and on
to Rushock Hill, where Offa's Dyke
itself is visible. Further north, towards
Knighton, the Dyke is seen as an
appreciable bank.

SYMONDS YAT AND THE WYE GORGE

SOME of the best scenery of the River Wye can be enjoyed here, in and around the wooded gorge on the England–Wales border (once a busy copper-smelting centre). The trees display magnificent colours in autumn, but the walk is enjoyable at any time of year. Mud can be a problem after rain. Link sections include field-paths, a quiet dead-end road and waymarked paths over an area of hilly common. The sections in the valley follow the waymarked Wye Valley Walk. The extension (which can be treated as

a separate walk) leads from Symonds Yat, crossing the river by ferry and walking along the bank on either side, recrossing further down by the wire suspension bridge (which creaks and bounces as you walk over it; and the river is in view directly beneath your feet).

WALK DIRECTIONS

① Ⓐ Walk back down the access road into Goodrich village, then turn left on a road signposted to

Courtfield and Welsh Bicknor, taking the road-bridge over another road below ②. When you reach road fork at triangular junction, take the path up steps on the other side of the triangle (between the two roads). Follow multi-coloured waymarks on a clear path going steeply up Coppet Hill, ignoring the path coming up from your right half-way up, to reach a trig point (summit pillar) ③ Ⓑ.

Turn left on a level path making for the end of the wood, where you

---

LENGTH 8 miles (13km), 4 hours. Can extend by a further 3 miles (5km) by walking further along the gorge from Symonds Yat East; or two separate walks of 8 and 3 miles

DIFFICULTY 3

START Goodrich Castle car park; turn off the A40 at Pencraig, 4 miles south-west of Ross-on-Wye, and turn left up access road in the centre of Goodrich; car park is free, but there is an entrance fee to castle. Grid reference 576196. The 3-mile walk can start at Symonds Yat East at ⑨; there is a car park by the Saracen's Head, by the river (grid reference 561160). Alternatively begin from the car park at Symonds Yat Rock (on B4432 3 miles north-west of Coleford; grid reference 564158) and walk down to the river by going past the refreshment kiosk by the toilet block and picking up directions at ⑨

OS MAPS Landranger 162; Outdoor Leisure 14

REFRESHMENTS Pub and shop in Goodrich; refreshment kiosks at Goodrich Castle and Symonds Yat Rock. Saracen's Head at Symonds Yat East

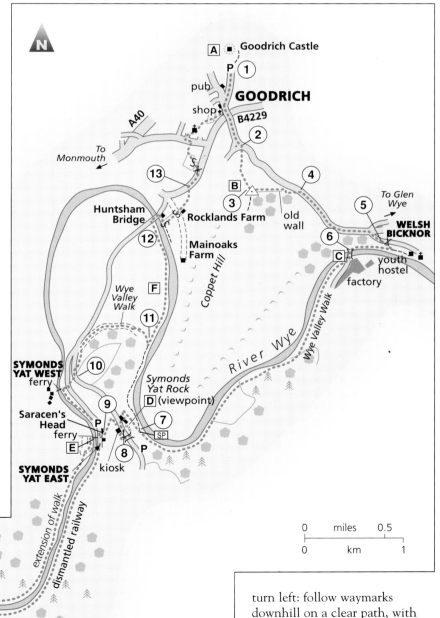

turn left: follow waymarks downhill on a clear path, with occasional constructed steps, keeping the wall and wood always on your right and soon entering woodland (ignore paths to left); where the wall ends, go forward and pick up a path leading slightly to the right, dropping gently to the road ④. Turn right along it, soon going over a cattlegrid. ⑤ Just before gateway to Welsh Bicknor Youth Hostel (80 yards after turns on left to Glen Wye and Mill Hill Fathers) fork right on to a narrow woodland path downhill. At path T-junction, with the youth hostel away to the left, turn right (on Wye Valley Walk), soon joining river. ⑥ Ⓒ Cross the river by the next bridge (reach it by forking right); on the other bank, pick up riverside path for Symonds Yat to the right by turning left and going under the bridge. Proceed for 2 miles. ⑦ After crags appear above gorge, take signposted path on left for Yat Rock (i.e. Symonds Yat Rock), climbing all the way and ignoring a descending fork. It zigzags past a cottage (Wren's Nest) and joins a road. Turn left along the road, and fork right on a path just before footbridge over road. ⑧ At the refreshment kiosk, detour over the footbridge to the Symonds Yat Rock viewpoint Ⓓ. Return to the kiosk. Follow the Wye Valley Walk (signposted) for Symonds Yat East, descending from the kiosk down steps (soon ignore a short path leading right, to road) until T-junction with track. Turn left on this and immediately right. When you reach a signposted junction just before edge of wood, go sharp left and keep left at next junction (in front of chalet-style house visible just out of woods); descend to riverside road at Symonds Yat East village and turn right to the Saracen's Head Inn ⑨ Ⓔ. (NB: there is not enough room on the map to show all these junctions.)

For 3-mile extension/short walk Locate ferryman (in Saracen's Head, or just outside), take the ferry across the river. Walk up to a surfaced lane. Go left on the lane; where it bends sharp right go forward, and follow the track alongside river to cross by a suspension bridge. Turn left and follow the path along the river back to Symonds Yat East.

To continue main walk Pass the Saracen's Head; just after toilet

block, go through the car park on left, at far end of which pick up the riverside path (Wye Valley Walk). Opposite Ye Olde Ferrie Inne (on the other bank) the path turns right, away from river, then left on road for 30 yards, then right on a rising path to another road ⑩. Turn left on the road for 50 yards then fork right on a woodland path, rising then levelling out. Keep right where this joins a hard track merging from the left. 400 yards later, as the track bends right, take the path on your left (waymarked Wye Valley Walk); this descends 20 yards to T-junction of paths, then turns right. Continue down, past a derelict cottage, to a T-junction in front of rock ⑪; turn left (leaving the Wye Valley Walk) on the riverside path, soon along field edges; Goodrich church comes into view Ⓕ. ⑫ Cross the river at Huntsham Bridge. On the other bank take the short path on your right to the river, at which turn left (thus doubling back from previous direction). After 100 yards, when garden on left ends, go forward over stile but immediately turn left up side of field. At left-hand corner of field, cross stile, cross drive to Mainoaks Farm, and continue up track immediately to left of farm buildings, passing through series of gates and along narrow enclosed strip to reach road.

Turn right along road for 180 yards, then ⑬ left through kissing-gate opposite start of track on right. Go half right across (first) field to stile just to left of top right corner, and then half right across second field, again to top right corner.

Ancient woodland graces the Wye Valley; rarities such as small-leaf limes thrive in the gorge

Proceed on enclosed track to road and turn left for 50 yards, then right on private road signposted as public footpath, starting opposite prominent black and white building.

At end of road (after 50 yards), turn half right to enter churchyard by gate, and follow surfaced footpath around right-hand end of church; at porch, keep left at fork (right fork goes to wooden gates), and exit by metal kissing-gate at far corner.

Continue same direction on path, then through gate into second field and diagonally downhill towards gate in middle of right-hand side. Cross school playing field to further gate and road, turn left, and at road junction continue forward on road signposted to Goodrich Castle, to return to start of walk.

ON THE ROUTE

Ⓐ **Goodrich Castle** (English Heritage) A magnificent and substantial sandstone ruin, built on its craggy bedrock. Of an earlier structure, built by Godric, nothing survives. The keep is 12th century and the remainder of the building a century later.

Ⓑ Fine views are seen, north to **Titterstone Clee**, west to the **Black Mountains**.

Ⓒ This bridge used to carry the **Wye Valley Railway**, but has now been repaired for use as a footbridge only and is part of the Wye Valley Walk. The line ran from Chepstow to Monmouth, part of a dense network in the Forest of Dean and Wye Valley.

Ⓓ The path over the footbridge leads on to **Symonds Yat Rock** itself, a spectacular 650-foot high **viewpoint** from which you can see the River Wye to both left and right as it curves around the deeply incised meander. Peregrine falcons have frequented this site since 1984.

Ⓔ The **ferry** at the hamlet of Symonds Yat East is operated by the ferryman hauling on an overhead cable. Boat trips are on offer here.

Ⓕ As well as waterfowl on the river, this section of the walk is memorable for the **view** ahead, across the bend in the river, of Goodrich church and spire, beautifully sited and somewhat isolated.

NEATH VALE: THE BRECON BEACONS WATERFALL COUNTRY

THE riverside path takes in a tremendous series of waterfalls, whose torrents get more violent as you proceed along the wooded Neath Gorge. The return is much quieter, along a road which has good views and only occasional (but fast-moving) traffic. The full version of the walk between ② and ④ can be very slippery and great care is needed, along with suitable footwear. Easy route-finding.

LENGTH *Full walk* 5½ miles (9km), 3 hours *Short walk* 2½ miles (4km), 1½ hours

DIFFICULTY *Full walk* 3
Short walk 1

START Pont Nedd Fechan on B4242 1 mile north-east of Glyn Neath and 11 miles north-east of Neath. Follow road for 100 yards beyond Angel Inn and over bridge for ample roadside parking. Grid reference 901077

OS MAPS Landranger 160; Outdoor Leisure 11

REFRESHMENTS Three pubs in Pont Nedd Fechan: Dinas Inn, Angel Inn and Old White Horse Inn

WALK DIRECTIONS

① Take the path immediately to the right of Angel Inn, signposted Sgwd Gwladus; it leads through an

Sgwd Gwladus (Lady Fall) slipping gracefully into the River Pyrrdin

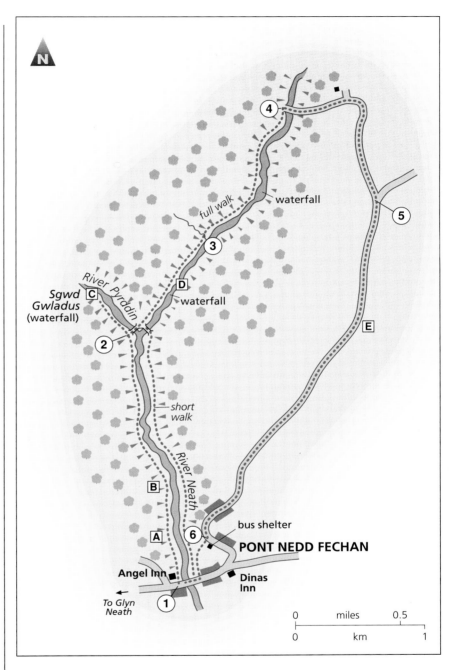

iron gate and along the river Ⓐ Ⓑ. Follow this for 1 mile. ② At the confluence of rivers, avoid (for the moment) a crossing bridge, but continue up to a viewing-platform at Sgwd Gwladus waterfall Ⓒ. Return to cross the bridge over River Pyrddin. *For short walk* Cross the second footbridge over River Neath and return along the gorge to the start. *For full walk* Turn right on the other side, to follow the river upstream. The path ascends a little

and the river becomes more dramatic Ⓓ. ③ After ½ mile take care in fording a small stream by a waterfall on the left (retrace steps to start if you don't feel confident).

④ ¾ mile later emerge from the wood and make for the road beyond a car park. Turn right on the road over a bridge. ⑤ Turn right at T-junction Ⓔ. ⑥ After 30 minutes of road-walking, you reach the edge of the village. Where the road bends left, keep forward on a signposted

One of the Ddwli falls

footpath to the right of the bus shelter. Descend to the start.

ON THE ROUTE

A Soon after the start of the walk, the path passes the ruins of an **old flour-mill**. Two quern stones can be seen. The rock that was suitable for the grinding process was millstone grit, found extensively in the Pennines. The Peak District was a major millstone-producing area.

B A crag to the left is known as **Farewell Rock**, a name conjured up by miners. It marks the end of the coal and ironstone seams. The rock itself is sandstone. The area was also busy with silica mining in the 19th century; the product was used for making fire-bricks.

C **Sgwd Gwladus** is a fine waterfall which takes its name from one of the 24 daughters of King Briychan, who lived in the 5th century. She was the mother of St Cadoc.

D The river has cut down through soft shales to the Old Red Sandstone, which forms the great hills of the Brecon Beacons and the Black Mountains, to form the **gorge**. The waterfalls were caused by geological faulting across the direction of the stream, causing sudden changes in height. Dippers may be seen on and around the rivers. Rare mosses and ferns grow in the damp gorge.

E The quiet country lane is not without compensations, and has some pleasant **views** over the Mellte valley and to the southern moorland hills of Fforest Fawr.

THE MELLTE AND HEPSTE WATERFALLS

The magnificence of the waterfalls seen on the walk is matched by those in the nearby valleys of the Mellte and Hepste rivers. There is a car park at Porth yr Ogof (reached by following the road north-east from Pontneddfechan and turning off before you reach Ystradfellte). The first mile is mild going, along a gentle track to Hendre-bolon. Sgwd Clun-gwyn is the first fall seen; notices urge walkers to keep to the upper path and not walk along the river (which can be dangerously slippery). At the fourth major fall, Sgwd yr Eira, the footpath actually goes beneath the curtain of the fall; an unforgettable, if dampening experience.

The vicinity is riddled with caves and pot-holes, including the Dan-yr-Ogof show caves.

PEN Y FAN

The highest point in South Wales is a magnet for walkers visiting the Brecon Beacons National Park. Probably the most popular ascents are from the Storey Arms, on the A470 to the west of the summit, and from the Taf Fechan valley on the south side. However, the mountain looks its shapeliest from the north. One good starting-point is from the car park at Cwm Gwdi Training Camp. Ascents are steady rather than severe, although the slopes steepen near the top (which means descents need care). In fine weather the walk along the ridges at the top is a joy, and you can connect the summits of Fan y Big, Pen y Fan and Corn Du. In clear conditions the views include Carmarthen Fan, Mynydd Eppynt, Plynlimon, Radnor Forest, the Black Mountains, the Malvern Hills, the Forest of Dean, the South Wales mining valleys and, across the Bristol Channel and into Somerset, Dunkery Beacon in Exmoor.

Einon-gan, yet another fairytale cascade in the beautiful setting of Neath Vale

NASH POINT AND ST DONAT'S CASTLE

TWO wooded combes form part of the inland sections of this walk, which offers some striking cliff scenery and views across the Bristol Channel. There is an optional there-and-back extension along the coast as far as St Donat's Castle. The cliff path is fenced on its seaward side and the route reaches sea-level at a small cove at Nash Point. Paths across fields are undefined, but route-finding is made easy by waymarking.

WALK DIRECTIONS

① From T-junction, with minor road behind you, turn left along the road towards Bridgend. After 300 yards cross a stile on left, signposted for coastal walk, opposite first right turn. Turn left beyond the stile, along the wall of a building (forge) then continue in this direction across field to a stile. In second field continue forward keeping immediately to the right of prominent ruins of a monastic grange Ⓐ, to find a stile. Continue and cross a third field to a point where the hedge meets a stone wall: cross the stile, and emerge on a track.

② Turn right on track, ford the stream then immediately turn left on a path running just above stream (or follow left edge of field – routes merge). At the end of the field cross stile and follow left edge of second and third fields. Avoid the footbridge on your left in third field but continue to a stile, through paddock and on to a tarmac lane ③.

Turn left on lane, through a gate/stile, then after 50 yards turn right on a track into Blaen-y-cwm

LENGTH 4½ miles (7km), 2½ hours *With extension to St Donat's* 7 miles (13km), 3½ hours **DIFFICULTY** 2 **START** Grass triangle in Monknash, ¾ mile north of Marcross and 4 miles west of Llantwit Major. Grid	reference 921706 **OS MAPS** Landranger 170; Pathfinder 1163 (SS 87/96/97) **REFRESHMENTS** Plough and Harrow, Monknash; kiosk sometimes in summer at Nash Point; Horseshoe Inn, Marcross

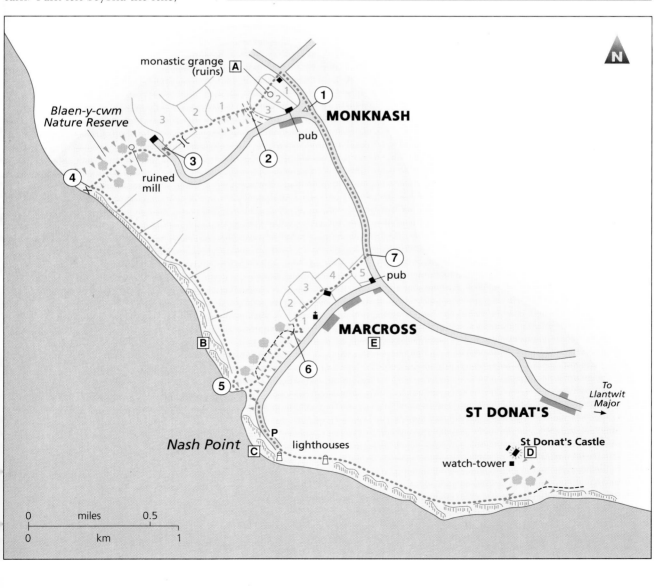

The beautiful and raucous herring gull

Nature Reserve. Follow the track through woods and then along valley towards the sea. ④ 50 yards before the gate leading to the beach, turn left up a narrow path to reach the cliff-top. Follow cliff-top alongside fence on the right, crossing stiles as necessary B.

⑤ Just before Nash Point lighthouses ahead C, the path descends into valley. Turn left along the valley to continue (or detour to lighthouses, beach and St Donat's Castle D 1½ miles beyond, via the coast path). After 150 yards you reach woods and fork right (or go left along nature trail; both paths lead to the same place). Follow the path for 600 yards until left path joins it by footbridge ⑥.

If you want to visit pub or church in Marcross E, or have had enough of field-walking, take road at this point (left on road, then left at next junction to finish). Otherwise, cross the stile ahead and follow the left edge of first field. Where the wooded bank on your left ends, cross a stile on left and turn right along the hedge in second field. Continue direction along right edge of third and fourth fields, and along left edge of fifth field. ⑦ Turn left on the road, and follow this for ¾ mile to the start.

ON THE ROUTE

A Ruins of a **monastic grange** that belonged to Neath Abbey. Still standing are several walls and a dovecot.

B These **cliffs** owe their striking candy-striped appearance to alternating horizontal beds of light grey lias limestone and dark, weaker shale. Vertical joints in the limestone have created fissures and blow-holes, some of which have enough wind being forced up them to blow away a hat placed over the top.

C **Nash Point** The two lighthouses were built in 1836 in line with the sandbank just south-west of Nash Point as a navigational aid (buoys had yet to be invented), following the wreck of the *Frolic*, in which 60 lives were lost. They still contain the original lenses for magnifying the beam. There are excellent **views** of the cliffs from the shore itself, which is well worth exploring.

D **St Donat's Castle** (*occasionally open to public*) Built c.1300 by the Stradling family and restored in the early 20th century; within the medieval castle is a 15th–17th-century country house. In the grounds are cavalry barracks and, near the cliffs, a look-out tower used as a shipwrecker's tower by a lord of Dunraven who, in the 15th century, unwittingly lured his own two sons to be wrecked on the rocks below. From 1925 the castle was owned by American newspaper millionaire William Randolph Hearst; since 1962 it has been the headquarters of Atlantic College.

E **Marcross church** dates from Norman times and has been restored. To the right of the porch is a lepers' window, through which those suffering from infectious diseases could follow the service. A pillar in the churchyard is the surviving stump of an ancient sundial.

The extraordinary layered cliffs near Nash Point, best seen from below (you can reach the shore at ⑤); from the cliff tops are views out over the Bristol Channel to Exmoor

RHOSSILI DOWN AND MEWSLADE BAY

A BREEZY moorland top, pale grey limestone cliffs and huge beaches of fine sand are packed into this astonishingly varied short walk. No problems of route-finding once you have found the turn-off point at ③.

LENGTH	4½ miles (7km), 2½ hours
DIFFICULTY	2
START	Rhossili car park, at west end of Gower peninsula (off B4247). Grid reference 414881
OS MAPS	Landranger 159; Pathfinder 1145 (SS 48/58/68)
REFRESHMENTS	Pub, tea-room and shop in Rhossili; shop in Middleton

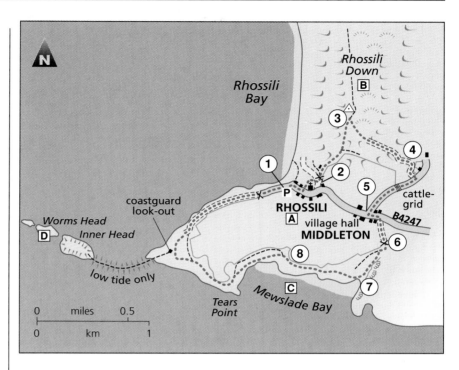

WALK DIRECTIONS

① Turn right out of the car park, into Rhossili village centre, towards the church [A]. Turn left at bus shelter and telephone-box, on to enclosed path which turns left to skirt the churchyard.

② When you reach a track (on near side of road) turn left to reach a gate and National Trust sign at foot of Rhossili Down [B]. Take the path to the right of the sign, steeply up to the top (keeping seaward slope close on your left) towards a trig point at summit.

③ 40 yards before the trig point, find a very sharp right turn (keeping straight on at a minor cross-junction after 30 yards): this is a broad grassy path which becomes a well-defined track as it descends.

④ The track turns right in front of the corner of a wall (close to houses) and 80 yards later merges into a better defined track which immediately bends left downhill to a T-junction where you turn right along a surfaced lane.

⑤ Turn left at main road at Middleton, and after 100 yards take a track on your right signposted Mewslade Bay. This soon narrows to a path enclosed between hedges.

⑥ Near the end of the enclosed section you reach a gate into an open area and by a nature reserve sign. Just after this, the hedges end: keep right, initially with wall and fence up on your right, and after 80 yards fork left on to a lower path which heads along the right-hand side of a prominent wall along valley bottom (Mew Slade), towards the sea.

⑦ After the wall ends, the path bends right and gently climbs the cliff (beware of sudden drop by overhang) and proceed along cliff-top with wall on right [C]. ⑧ In the next bay the path divides: take either the lower or upper path (lower path gets better views and upper path continues alongside wall and then leaves it to join lower path).

Continue around the cliff-top, past Worms Head [D] to reach Rhossili.

ON THE ROUTE

[A] **Rhossili** A windswept village above a superb 5-mile arc of beach

A view of Worms Head island and the jagged, contorted headland at the climax of the walk

Rhossili Down: you could extend the walk by turning off at point ③, walking its length and returning along the beach

from Burry Holm south to Worms Head. The **church** has a 12th-century doorway, perhaps transplanted from an older church which was in the warren below the down; there is a lepers' window into the chancel, so that lepers could watch services without risk of spreading infection. On fields near the church a farming practice known as the 'viel', by which the benefit of fertile land is shared out over the years, is a survival from the medieval open-strip field system.

B **Rhossili Down** Formerly a vertical cliff, but erosion has degraded the slope into a hillside, giving a most unusual juxtaposition of coast and upland. From the 632ft summit, the highest point on Gower, a magnificent view extends over the peninsula, while Lundy Island, Devon, Carmarthenshire and Pembrokeshire may also be in sight.

C **Mewslade Bay** Part of the South Gower Nature Reserve, these splendid carboniferous limestone cliffs, which have been tilted, folded and faulted by the earth's movements, are Gower's most striking coastal landforms. Below, the bay itself has another lovely sandy beach, less frequented than that at Rhossili. This coast is a noted site both for wild flowers and insect life. It is the only British habitat for yellow whitlow grass, and spring cinquefoil, spiked speedwell, clary, and hoary rock rose may also be found; the coastal site also supports populations of marbled white butterflies and the rare great green bush cricket.

D **Worm's Head** The serpentine, slender mile-long western tip of Gower is the most important bird sanctuary in the west part of the Bristol Channel: kittiwakes, razorbills, guillemots, cormorants, fulmars and shags are abundant, and there are occasional puffins. A slipway between the mainland and Inner Head is exposed at ebb tide, when you can walk across over rocks: rough but fun (but take care not to get cut off by the tide: only venture on to it 2½ hours either side of low tide).

WOOLTACK POINT AND MARLOES SANDS

A RARE phenomenon – a near-perfect round coastal walk on a narrow peninsula lined with fine cliffs, ending on a long sandy beach. Excellent for bird-watching. Very short link sections on field paths and quiet roads. It shows that a walk doesn't have to be physically demanding to be outstanding. Easy route-finding.

LENGTH 7 miles (11km), 3 hours
DIFFICULTY 1–2
START Marloes, 11 miles south-west of Haverfordwest, by Lobster Pot Inn at centre of village. Grid reference 794085
OS MAPS Landranger 157; Pathfinder 1102 (SM 70)
REFRESHMENTS Lobster Pot Inn, Marloes

WALK DIRECTIONS

① With the Lobster Pot Inn on your left, follow the village street past post office. ② 200 yards beyond the speed derestriction sign, turn right over a stile (signposted) and follow an obvious path round the edge of the field. At the end of field cross a stony track and continue towards the sea. 70 yards later fork left. ③ Emerge on to the coast path, on which you turn left. Follow this for 2 miles to a small cove. ④ Turn left uphill on a track, later surfaced. At a left bend, turn right between stone posts Ⓐ, and continue forward on an obvious path uphill. From the coastguard hut Ⓑ, with the islands in front of you, the continuation of the route is left along coast path, but first detour down on to the rocky headland (this is Wooltack Point) ⑤.

Retrace your steps downhill and fork right on to the coast path. After 1 mile along cliff-top you get close-up views of a big rocky island (Gateholm Island) Ⓒ. ½ mile beyond this, the path descends to a

Skomer Island off Wooltack Point is well known for its puffin colony

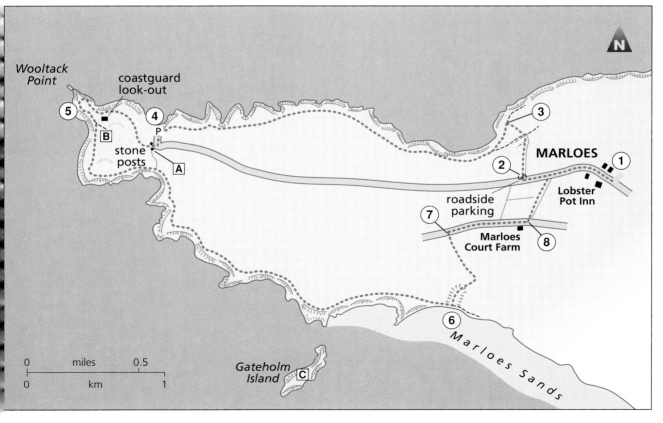

gully ⑥. Turn left on to a cross-track, and follow this to the road ⑦. Turn right on road. ⑧ After 600 yards, turn left on to a signposted path immediately after farm. Cross two fields and turn right on the road to return to the centre of Marloes.

ON THE ROUTE

A The **stone posts** are in the boundary wall for a deer park that was planned in the late 18th century but never materialised. The land belonged to the Edwardes, whose family seat was at Wolf's Castle; the estate was broken up in the 1920s.

B **View** To the right (north), St David's Head; straight ahead Skomer Island, with The Neck (just joined on to it) in front (west), and Midland Isle foremost. Further away, and to the left (south-west), is Skokholm Island. The islands are important bird habitats, supporting the largest concentration of Manx shearwaters in Britain (135,000 pairs). Skomer is also famous for puffins and Skokholm for storm petrels. Grey Atlantic seals can sometimes be seen on the rocks (breeding time is autumn). The islands and the 'deer park' are all flat-topped – the result of wave erosion when sea-level was 200ft higher than it is today.

C **Gateholm Island** At low tide remains are visible of the paddle-steamer *Albion* (the first to be bought by a Bristol Channel port), wrecked on its voyage of delivery in 1840. In the 7th century, the island was inhabited, probably by monks.

Government surveys of social, economic and consumer trends find that walking is the most popular sporting activity in the UK. The General Household Survey for 1990 found that 41 per cent of adults said that they had gone for a walk of at least two miles in the previous four weeks.

The view from Wooltack Point, with Midland Island ahead and Skomer Island beyond

ST DAVID'S HEAD AND CARN LLIDI

AN impressively rugged coastal walk with perhaps the finest seaboard hill in Pembrokeshire for the climax; the changes of direction provide an interesting sequence of views. Easy route-finding.

LENGTH 3½ or 4½ miles (5.5km or 7km), 2–2½ hours
DIFFICULTY 1–2
START Whitesands Bay car park, north-west of St David's. Grid reference 735272
OS MAPS Landranger 157; Pathfinder 1055 (SM 62/72)
REFRESHMENTS Snack kiosk in Whitesands Bay car park

WALK DIRECTIONS

① A Take the signposted coast path to the right of telephone-box. Proceed between fences; after 150 yards fork right (left goes to promontory B). Follow the coast path along top of rugged cliffs C , past National Trust sign, over a footbridge (left is optional detour to sandy beach), past promontory of St David's Head D .

Keep close to the cliff-top. ② 200 yards after St David's Head, look for a burial chamber E 30 yards off path to right but easily missed; it is just before big crags begin; inland to your right is the big hill of Carn Llidi. Continue along the coast path. ③ When you have almost passed Carn Llidi, fork right inland, heading uphill and immediately to the right of a prominent stone-walled enclosure to go up on to the left-hand shoulder of Carn Llidi.

④ At top of shoulder, where view ahead opens, a wall joins on left: you can turn right up to summit of Carn Llidi F , but the path is not defined near top. (If you want to continue along the ridge make your way slightly along the right-hand side of ridge until reaching the concrete and brick foundation of an old (wartime) radar hut, where you turn right on a concrete path, down steps, and soon between iron posts and along track; rejoin directions at ⑤). *To continue* Descend from the shoulder, on a well-defined path with a wall on your left; where the wall bends right, keep right alongside it, and soon ignore a stile on left. Turn left on reaching

Watch out for Coetan Arthur shortly after you have turned course at St David's Head

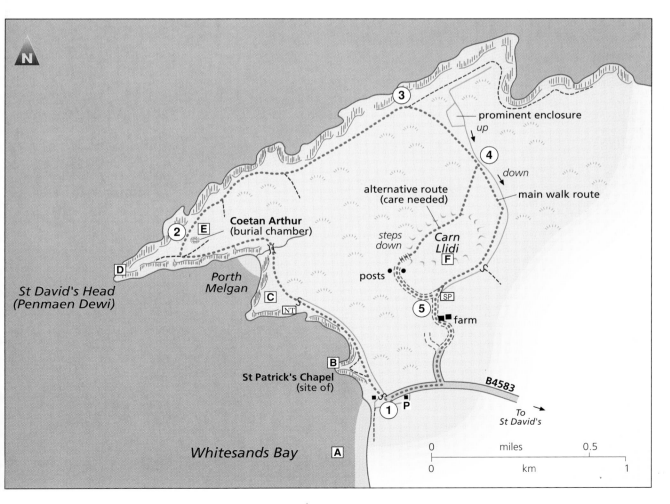

junction with hard track. ⑤ Follow the track to a farm, keeping forward as signposted in centre of farm (ignoring left fork), and descend gently to the main road. Turn right on road to reach car park.

ON THE ROUTE

A **Whitesands Bay** The mile-long beach is one of Pembrokeshire's most popular bathing places. At very low tide, remains of a forest are revealed, consisting of stumps of birch, fir, hazel and oak trees.

B The small **promontory** on the left is the site of St Patrick's Chapel (no ruin survives), built between the 6th and 10th centuries on the spot from where St Patrick is thought to have sailed for Ireland. Here sea voyagers used to pray for a safe journey and to offer thanks for their arrival.

Whitesands Bay was on a Bronze Age trade route from Stonehenge to the Wicklow Mountains in Ireland

C Views extend south-west to **Ramsey Island**, Wales' major breeding ground for Atlantic grey seals.

D **St David's Head** (Penmaen Dewi) Described in a Roman survey of the known world in AD140 as the 'Promontory of the Eight Perils', this low but rugged headland looks west towards the Bishop's and Clerk's Rocks.

E **Coetan Arthur** A 5,000-year-old burial chamber with an 8ft capstone and supports. Despite its proximity to the path, it can be easily missed, as it is well camouflaged among the rocks.

F **Carn Llidi** (595ft) A rough path leads to the summit of this miniature mountain, whose lower slopes have discernible traces of enclosures made by Iron Age farmers. From here there is a magnificent **view**, even in poorish visibility, of the nearby coast; in clear conditions the Waterford and Wicklow mountains in Ireland are visible. From the top you can continue along the seaward side (care is needed on the rocks), described above.

GARN FAWR AND STRUMBLE HEAD

A DEEPLY indented coastline makes up most of the walk; the shorter inland sections are hardly any less distinguished, and include a breezy stroll over moorland that looks over the whole peninsula, and the ascent of a craggy hill to reveal suddenly a dramatic view along the Pembrokeshire coast. The coast path itself is far from level. The paths used are well defined nearly all the way, although waymarking and signposting was absent for some of the inland paths when the walk was inspected.

WALK DIRECTIONS

① Ⓐ Stand with the sea on your left and walk back along the road. After 200 yards, where the road bends right inland, take the signposted coast path ahead. After ¼ mile, where the view opens out ahead, ignore a sharp right turn. Carry on around two bays (Pwlluog, with its cave, and Porthsychan, with its small grey beach); ② at the recess of Porthsychan bay, keep left at a signposted path junction (ignore small path on left to beach, 40 yards later), and continue along the coast path. ③ 100 yards before a lone bungalow, leave the coast path

at a signposted junction by turning right and immediately take the signposted stile on left, leading inland (effectively this means taking the stile seen a few yards to the right of the signposted junction) to enter a field with the bungalow away to

> **LENGTH** 6½ miles (10.5km), 3 hours; can be shortened to 5½ miles (9km), 2½ hours
> **DIFFICULTY** 3
> **START** Free car park at Strumble Head, overlooking the lighthouse (5½ miles north-west of Goodwick). Grid reference 895413
> **OS MAPS** Landranger 157; Pathfinder 1032 (SM 83/93)

Garn Fawr, an Iron Age fort built at the summit of a hill

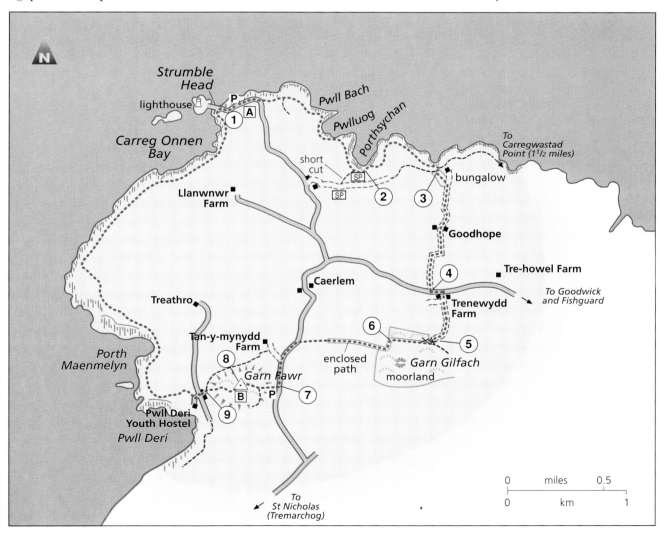

Strumble Head, the start and finish of the walk, seen from Garn Fawr

the left. Walk close to left-hand edge of field, until crossing a fence by a stile, then turn right on track and proceed, later past a farm (Goodhope), to the road ④. Turn left on road and after 50 yards take the second gate on right into Trenewydd Farm. Proceed through the farmyard to a gate opposite, leading to a rising track between hedges. ⑤ After 600 yards, where the track ends below open moorland, take the left-hand gate and emerge at the bottom of moor with crags directly above. Immediately turn right at a path T-junction, walking alongside grown-over field wall (which appears mostly as an embankment) on your right. ⑥ Once past the end of the crags, this path reaches a corner with the embankment on the right and a fence at 90 degrees to direction of travel; go through the gate, beyond which the path leads to the left but bends right after 70 yards. This path is enclosed most of the way and finally drops to a road. Turn left on the road; ⑦ where road is about to descend, enter the car park on your right and take signposted path on its right-hand side, leading up a hill known as Garn Fawr B (keep on the main path, ignoring another path to the left), passing to the right of first big crag then to left of trig point at summit ⑧ (see Shorter versions). The path then drops towards houses, crossing a stile. Go left and ⑨ immediately right (by first house) on

a metalled lane, downhill. After 50 yards cross over a small road and take the driveway for Pwll Deri Youth Hostel opposite. After only 20 yards fork right on the coast path and follow this all the way round to Strumble Head. (Note that the steep descent from the top of Garn Fawr can be avoided. Return to the road, turn left (retracing) then left again on a farm road, then left on a level path that joins the end of a lane by a house. This is point ⑨.)

ON THE ROUTE

A Strumble Head A magnificent rugged headland overlooking a lighthouse (no public access) on its own island. Among the profuse birdlife to be found on this coast are Manx shearwaters (which breed on Skomer Island), choughs, fulmars and herring gulls.

B Garn Fawr The summit of this prominent hill is capped by the site of an Iron Age fort. Ramparts and hut circles can be discerned. Views extend westwards towards St David's Head.

SHORTER VERSIONS

(a) The walk can be shortened by about a mile by turning right at ② and right at a junction with a track, leading to a farm, where you keep left, then left along the road to Garn Fawr car park, picking up the directions again at ⑦. The

drawback of this is a rather tedious distance uphill on the road; it is pleasanter to do this the other way round, making the road walking all gentle downhill, with views ahead of you. Start from Strumble Head with the sea on your right and pick up the coast path at the end of the road. Follow it to Pwll Deri Youth Hostel (where the coast path joins the drive to the hostel), turn left, cross the road and take the rising lane opposite, turning left by the house and immediately right over a stile, where a path heads up the hill of Garn Fawr. Drop to the car park and turn left on the road. Later, fork left (signposted for Strumble Head) at a road junction, then ignoring a left fork to Llanwnwr Farm. *Either* follow the road all the way back *or* turn right at Tydraw Farm, then right after 50 yards opposite the house; follow the track, forking left on to a signposted path after 250 yards, then left on reaching the coast path which can be followed to Strumble Head. (b) For a short stroll of about a mile, start at the car park at Garn Fawr. Follow the directions from ⑦ to ⑨, but on crossing the stile at the base of the hill (at ⑨) turn right on a level path, then turn right on reaching a farm track. Go up to the road and turn right to return to the start. For its length this is a marvellous little walk with tremendous views.

BRECHFA COMMON AND THE RIVER WYE

A LITTLE-KNOWN part of the Upper Wye Valley, yielding an easily followed walk with lovely views, skirting moorland in early stages then dropping to follow the River Wye. One climb, at the beginning (path may be overgrown in summer).

LENGTH 7 miles (11km), 3½ hours
DIFFICULTY 2
START Llyswen on A470 south-east of Builth Wells and north-east of Brecon; parking is easiest near church (in cul-de-sac opposite Griffin Inn and A470 to Brecon). Grid reference 133380
OS MAPS Landranger 161; Pathfinder 1038 and 1015 (SO 03/13 and SO 04/14)
REFRESHMENTS Tea-shop and three pubs in Llyswen

WALK DIRECTIONS

① Follow the A470 in the signposted Brecon direction to end of village. ② 250 yards later, and after the last house on right (by speed restriction sign), turn right on a track, which leads to a gate after only 30 yards; do not take the gate which leads into field, but pick up a path between hedges to the left of this.

The path rises steadily (it can be rather overgrown in summer) to reach the junction with a lane ③, where you continue forward on surfaced lane, over a cattlegrid. Just after the cattlegrid *either* continue along the lane *or* divert from it by forking left on to common land alongside left-hand hedge, following edge of common until reaching a track in front of Brechfa Pool Ⓐ along which you turn right to rejoin lane and turn left along the lane.

④ At T-junction, turn right: open land briefly appears on both sides of road, but then it is enclosed. Notice a farm (Whitehall) on right of road; just after, the road re-emerges on to common land – immediately ⑤ bear left to leave the road for a fence on your left making for the left-hand side of a

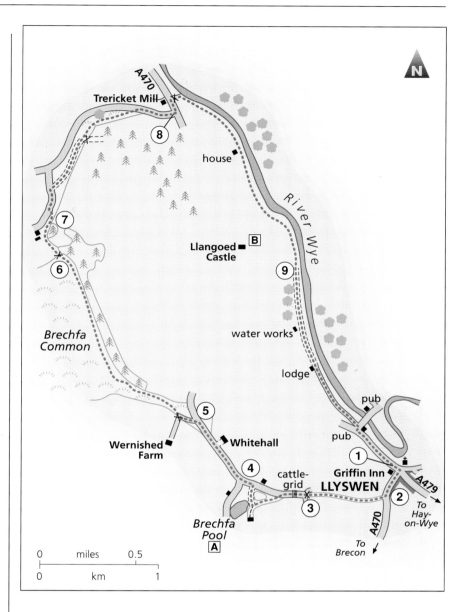

Clough Williams-Ellis's Llangoed Hall

nearby conifer plantation, where you pick up a well-defined path which runs alongside the edge of common with a woodland wall close by on your right.

⑥ After passing through a gate, field is on right; soon after, the wall bends right and the view opens up over a large valley with scattered farmsteads below. Keep right alongside wall or fence on right (now with woods on right again).

⑦ Where (after 200 yards) woods on right end, fork left on to well-defined track down to reach a surfaced lane. Turn right on the lane and after 100 yards turn right on to level track (or continue along road for easier walking – keep right at next junction, and follow the road to A470 at ⑧), which soon rejoins

woodland fence and later narrows to a path. Keep close by the woodland fence all the way until it finally drops to the road. There is some bracken to contend with, but it is generally easy to find the way. Turn right on the road.

⑧ Turn left along A470 and after 100 yards, just before road crosses a stream, take signposted gate on right. Follow left edge of field: soon the River Wye is visible immediately down to left. Follow left edge of a succession of fields. ⑨ Ⓑ After 1 mile pick up track close to the river (i.e. no longer inside field), which later becomes surfaced and then reaches the road at the edge of Llyswen. Turn right on the road and left on main road to the centre of village.

ON THE ROUTE

Ⓐ Splendid **views** of the Brecon Beacons and Black Mountains made **Brechfa Pool** a favourite haunt of 19th-century rector Francis Kilvert, whose diary of rural life in this area has become a minor classic. The pool is now a nature reserve.

Ⓑ To the right, **Llangoed Castle** is a large mansion in 17th-century style, mostly rebuilt in 1912 by Clough Williams-Ellis, architect of the Italianate village of Portmeirion in North Wales. This castle has been regarded by some as his best work.

COMMON LAND

There are 8,675 registered commons in England and Wales, covering an area about the size of Surrey, Berkshire and Oxfordshire put together. There are none in Scotland.

Despite the popular belief to the contrary, there is no automatic public right of access to all of these.

Common land is a legacy from the time when much of the country was wild and not owned by anyone, and used communally. The manorial system gave it legal owners, but the peasantry retained rights to share the land's produce, such as for grazing or for firewood. The enclosure of much of England and Wales reduced the number of commons. Of those that survive, some may be used only by commoners (who may be the residents of a village or hamlet); others have public access for all, such as the commons of London. Many commons are important wildlife sites; over one-third have been designated Sites of Special Scientific Interest (SSSIs).

Common land registers and maps are held by the relevant county council, metropolitan district council or London borough. Unfortunately, many of the common rights were not recorded when registers were assembled and legal loopholes have appeared that give means of deregistering commons so they can be used like any other private land.

The creeper-covered Griffin Inn at Llyswen, near the start and finish of the walk

WATER-BREAK-ITS-NECK AND RADNOR FOREST

PLENTY of contrasts here, with sections over open upland, as well as dense forest and a romantically sited waterfall. The finale is Harley Dingle – more a dale than a dingle, enclosed by plunging 1,000ft slopes. Mostly on defined tracks but directions require care. Approach to Water-break-its-neck is usually very wet. Ascent 1,300ft.

WALK DIRECTIONS

① Ⓐ Start in Broad Street, New Radnor, with the Radnor Arms on

your right and walk down the street, passing the tall Gothic memorial to George Cornewall Lewis. ② Turn left along the A44 for 100 yards then take the first turning on your right (past entrance to caravan site on left Ⓑ). Ignore side turnings and follow this steeply uphill through woodland. After it emerges from the woodland it passes Smatcher Cottage on your right; 150 yards later ③ turn right at T-junction with another tarmacked lane. 130 yards later, cross a cattlegrid and fork right through a gate (leaving

LENGTH 8½ miles (13.5km), 4½ hours
DIFFICULTY 3
START New Radnor village centre just off A44, 6 miles west-north-west of Kington. Grid reference 213609
OS MAPS Landranger 148; Pathfinder 970, 971, 992, and 993 (SO 16/16, SO 26/36, SO 05/15 and SO 25/35)
REFRESHMENTS Pubs and shops in New Radnor

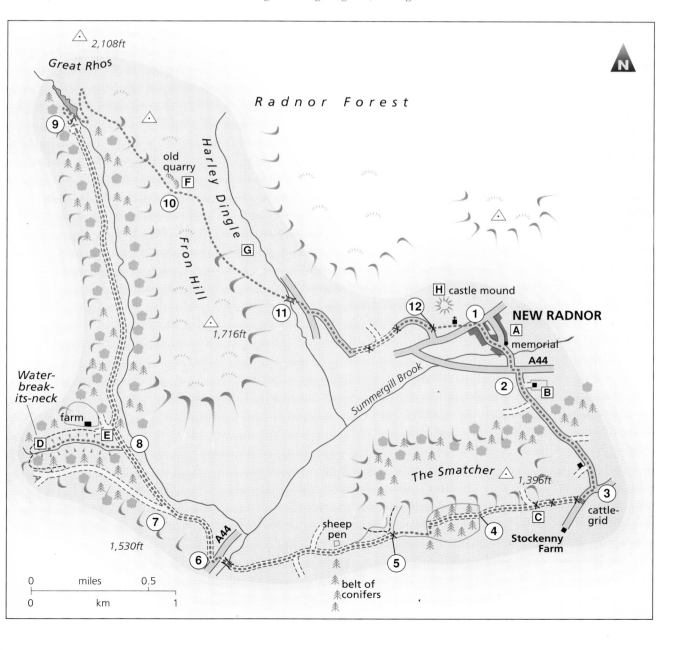

Despite its name, much of the Radnor Forest is open terrain

the lane which drops to a farm), following a grassy track along the fence on your right C. Later this becomes enclosed on both sides by fences; where the enclosed section ends, ignore the main track which bends uphill to the right but continue along the level, along a fence on left to take a gate into a conifer wood ④.

At the far end of the wood, go through a gate and immediately turn right through another gate into a field; follow left edge of field to a gate at the far end ⑤. Beyond this, the route is not marked on the ground for a few yards: continue forward to pick up a prominent track along the left side of valley, passing just below the bottom of a belt of conifers dropping from the skyline of the left-hand hillside (before you reach this point, the track is joined by a fence on right). Continue to drop all the way, avoiding side turns; where main track bends sharp right take the gate ahead. Cross a bridge over the river and follow the lane ahead to the A44. Turn left on A44 and ⑥ immediately right on a hard track. ⑦ Where the track forks near beginning of forestry plantation, keep right. ⑧ Where the track crosses a stream, detour left along

stream into the gorge to see Water-break-its-neck waterfall D. Return to the track and continue along it, immediately ignoring a sharply ascending left fork E. The track rises gradually, with stream down to the right. ⑨ After 1 mile, you reach a turning circle (NB forest may be extended in the future, although the extent of the new and old plantations should be obvious for several years); go forward to a stile out of the forest, make towards a prominent path seen across the valley that zigzags steeply uphill, first diagonally left, then right; to reach it follow the path that drops to a stile, crosses stream and turns right and then left 30 yards later. At top of slope F, the path becomes invisible; continue for 100 yards on the level, then ⑩ pick up path in old quarry (seen here as a pronounced hollow with rocks on one side), dropping into Harley Dingle G. ⑪ At the bottom, cross a footbridge and ascend to the road. Turn right on road, then left after 40 yards on a tarmacked driveway. Where this bends left take the gate ahead: follow this grassy track, contouring around the hill; as it bends left the fence on the right drops away – here take the left (upper) fork. Beyond the next gate New Radnor is in view; continue forward to next gate; track is now enclosed between hedges and bends right downhill. ⑫ Just past a house on the right at edge of village, take signposted gate, past castle mound H, on a level path to next gate; go forward to a further gate into churchyard and drop to the centre of New Radnor. Turn left to reach the start.

ON THE ROUTE
A **New Radnor** Former capital of Radnorshire (now a quiet village by-passed by the main road), laid out on a gridiron plan in the 11th century, and once a flourishing borough with a Norman castle destroyed in the Civil War and marked only by its earthworks. Some traces of the **old town wall** can still be found. On the way out of the

village, the route passes an enormous memorial to George Cornewall Lewis, Chancellor under Lord Palmerston 1855–58 and MP for New Radnor 1855–63.

B The caravans are on the site of the **station**, once the terminus of a very unprofitable branch line.

C **View** east over the vale of the River Lugg. On the hill away to the left south-east is the tower of Old Radnor, one of the finest churches in Wales. Below is the farmstead of Wolfpits, a reminder that this was a haunt of wolves until the 17th century.

D **Water-break-its-neck** Approached along a narrow, twisting ravine with trees growing out at implausible angles, and hidden from view until almost the last moment. Around the turn of the century, in the heyday of the nearby spa of Llandrindod Wells, the waterfall was a popular excursion for visitors.

E The top of the waterfall can be reached by taking this left fork and then keeping left again, keeping to the left of the garden at the farmhouse and following a faint path through the grass which shortly enters the woods and becomes well defined. High up in the ravine at the edge of the forest to the right is a cave which was occupied in the 18th century by a hermit who scratched graffiti on the rock wall. Return to the main route after exploration.

F **View** south to the Black Mountains (2,660ft); further to the right, in the far distance, are the twin peaks of the Brecon Beacons (2,906ft); further to the right still is the Carmarthen Fan (2,632ft).

G **Harley Dingle** is occasionally used for testing ammunition, but the track described is always open and provides magnificent walking in the most dramatic part of Radnor Forest.

H The short climb to the top of the **castle mound** is well worth it for those who still have the energy. This former border castle is now reduced to grassy mounds with a few remaining stones from the walls.

CASTELL Y BERE

WALK DIRECTIONS

LEVEL paths and tracks lead along an unspoilt river valley and past a ruined castle, then along the river with high hills all around. There is a slightly more ambitious finale up a narrow valley with a descent through woods; a couple of very quiet stretches of lane-walking are included. Route-finding is fairly straightforward.

WALK DIRECTIONS

① Ⓐ With Railway Inn on your right, walk along the main road through the village (towards Tywyn) for 50 yards, but immediately before the road crosses the river, turn right on to a lane (with river on left and playground and terrace of houses on right). Soon cross a footbridge over river, pick up a path leading to a house, in front of which the path bends right (it is soon briefly

undefined; ignore a faint right fork). The path soon becomes well defined as it follows the left side of the valley, on the level, with the river down to your right.

② 50 yards after waymark post, fork right (left ascends), dropping to river level and going through a gate by a house (Rhiwlas), where you pick up a track and follow it to the

LENGTH 7½ miles (12km), 3½ hours
DIFFICULTY 2
START Abergynolwyn, on B4405 south-west of Dolgellau. Grid reference 678070
By train Abergynolwyn (½ mile from village), on the Talyllyn Railway
OS MAPS Landranger 124; Outdoor Leisure 23
REFRESHMENTS Pub, cafés and shops in Abergynolwyn

road ③. Turn right on road, over the river, and turn right at a

The spectacularly sited ruins of the 13th-century Castell y Bere

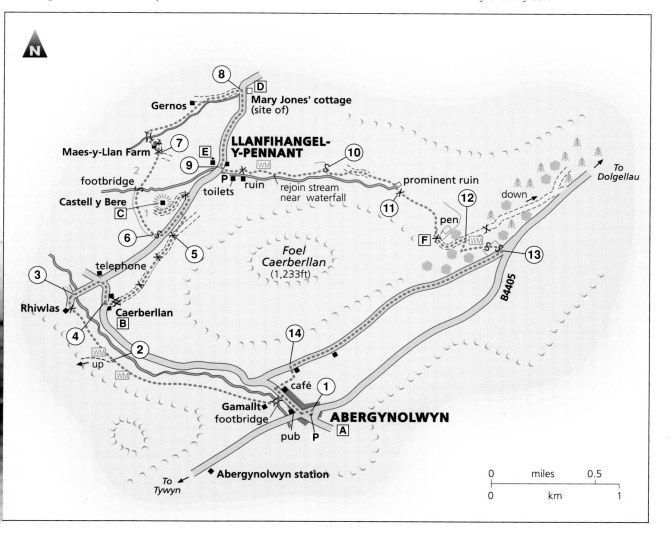

staggered junction (signposted Abergynolwyn).

④ After 150 yards, turn left through double gates into Caerberllan Farm B. Go through the farmyard and take the right-hand of two gates, leading on to a track (the left-hand gate goes to barns), which contours below a craggy slope. Soon the hill on which stands Castell y Bere is visible a short distance to your left; as soon as you are level with the beginning of it ⑤ take a metal kissing-gate on left (not the small gate just before this), and with your back to the track bear half right diagonally across field to reach a signposted stile on to the road.

Turn right if you want to reach Castell y Bere (100 yards away) C, but turn left to continue the route. ⑥ After 300 yards, just after the hill on your right ends, take the signposted stile on right into field, and follow the left edge, soon past the foot of the hill on your right, and then cross a ladder-stile beside a gate at end of field. Turn right in the next field, alongside right edge and towards a farm.

⑦ Immediately before the first barn, turn right through gate and then left, past farmhouse to reach vehicle turning-circle (where track ends). Take the gate ahead and go over a bridge over river, turning right on the other side alongside the river and soon crossing a stile. Later you join a track close to a house, and eventually reach a lane junction ⑧ D. Turn right.

⑨ At the hamlet of Llanfihangel-y-pennant, turn left opposite the church E on signposted track to the left of the post-box, to reach a gate beside a stile next to a partly ruined cottage. Proceed along the path by the stream for 50 yards, then veer left to leave it as waymarked for a short distance; the path goes up and soon rejoins the stream by a waterfall (where path forks, take either as the forks rejoin).

After the waterfall, a fence soon begins on right: follow it as it bends left away from the stream where you go over a stile (50 yards to left of stream) ⑩. Turn right on other side of this stile on to a path which rejoins the stream, and continues up the valley, merging into a stony track. The track soon ends: head forward to a gate beside a stile to the right of a prominent ruin (no path) ⑪, then continue up the valley. At the head of valley F, you reach a solid wall with a fence beyond, and cross it by a stile (close to sheep pens), at its right end. Follow the well-defined track beyond, immediately bending left and descending gently.

⑫ 100 yards after trees begin on both sides, look out for a low path sharp right at waymark post (if in doubt continue on the main track down to the road, where you turn right, and fork right at next junction after ½ mile in Llanegryn direction – this is ⑬).

Look for yellow waymark posts as you descend through the woods: after 60 yards bend sharp left, soon reaching the ends of woods where you keep left and follow ill-defined route steeply down towards the road junction at the bottom. Soon go over rough ground and cross a stile, then down the left edge of field to emerge on to road by a stile beside a gate.

Turn right on the minor road ⑬ and follow this for nearly 1 mile. ⑭ Just after a house on your left, cut off a corner by taking signposted steps on left (or you can continue on the road to next junction where you turn left to descend to Abergynolwyn), dropping down to a stile, then down a sunken path with a fence on your left, bending right at fence corner. Soon go over another stile and drop to the river, proceeding to the bridge at Abergynolwyn. Turn left on road, back to the start.

ON THE ROUTE

A **Abergynolwyn** A 19th-century village of sturdy terraces, which grew up to house workers from the Bryneglwys Slate Quarry (closed 1947), which was served by the still-functioning private Talyllyn Railway.

B **Caerberllan Farm** The handsome farmhouse, built 1755, replaced an older structure.

C **Castell y Bere** The path winds round to the top of the rock and into the shattered 13th-century castle ruins. Llewelyn the Great founded it in 1221, but after the Earl of Pembroke took it in 1283 it was rebuilt by Edward I before the Welsh recapture in 1295. Finely sited above a flat-bottomed dale under the shadow of the outliers of Cader Idris (2,927ft).

D Straight ahead as you emerge on to the road, immediately on your right, is the labelled site of **Mary Jones' Cottage.** In 1800, 16-year-old Mary took her six years of careful savings and walked barefoot 28 miles over the hills to Bala, where she hoped to buy a Welsh bible from Revd Thomas Charles, only to find he had no such bible for sale. Touched by her efforts, he gave her his own copy, and her determination inspired him to set up the British and Foreign Bible Society, which now keeps Mary's bible at its London headquarters.

E **Llanfihangel-y-pennant church** A long, low building, typical of the area, with a solid stone lych-gate and carved slate gravestones.

F The **view** ahead is of the deep valley of **Glen Iago**, with the plunging slopes of **Graig Goch** to the left.

The memorial to Mary Jones at Bala, 28 barefoot miles from her home

PEN Y CIL AND ST MARY'S WELL

THE tip of the Lleyn Peninsula, at the western extremity of North Wales, merits a special pilgrimage for its magnificent coastline; in parts this is a rough cliff-top route, but there are remarkable views all round. Route-finding is mostly obvious but there are some undefined sections across fields.

WALK DIRECTIONS

① A Make your way to the beach at Aberdaron and turn right along it. At the end of the beach, go up steps, bear left at a signpost (for Porth Meudwy), along the cliff-top. ② After ¾ mile go through a kissing-gate, descend to the cove at Porth Meudwy, ford the stream where you see steps opposite, and go straight up again to the cliff-top; take care, as the path has fallen away a little in places.

After ½ mile, past two waymark posts (remains of harbour is visible down to the left), the path then goes round the inlet of Hen Borth ③: here bear half right (leaving the

cliff-top for the moment) past a waymark to a prominent National Trust sign on the skyline for Pen y Cil; at the sign continue on level track (still following the coast, but now higher up). The track soon becomes indistinct, but make your way around the craggy cliff-top to reach a summit cairn (piled-up stones) on Pen y Cil B, and proceed past the memorial plaque to cross a ladder-stile beside a gate ④.

LENGTH *Full walk* 7 miles (11km), 3½ hours
DIFFICULTY 3
LENGTH *Short walk* 5½ miles (9km), 2½ hours
DIFFICULTY 2–3
START Aberdaron, near west end of Lleyn Peninsula; car park in village centre. Grid reference 173264
OS MAPS Landranger 123; Pathfinder 843 (SH 12/22/32)
REFRESHMENTS Pubs, shops and cafés in Aberdaron; café at Pen-bryn-bach at ⑧.

Immediately turn left for 30 yards to take gate (signposted Mynydd Mawr) and follow the right edge of the field alongside a fence (then followed by a ruined wall). At the end, cross a ladder-stile on to rough land, where you go forward on a path alongside a fence/wall on your right; this reaches a gate, and continues as an enclosed track for 100 yards to T-junction ⑤. Turn right.

For short walk Follow this lane passing a house after ¼ mile and reach a junction. Bear left along the road; after ¼ mile take a signposted path on the right, up steps and on to

St Mary's Well (Ffynnon Fair)

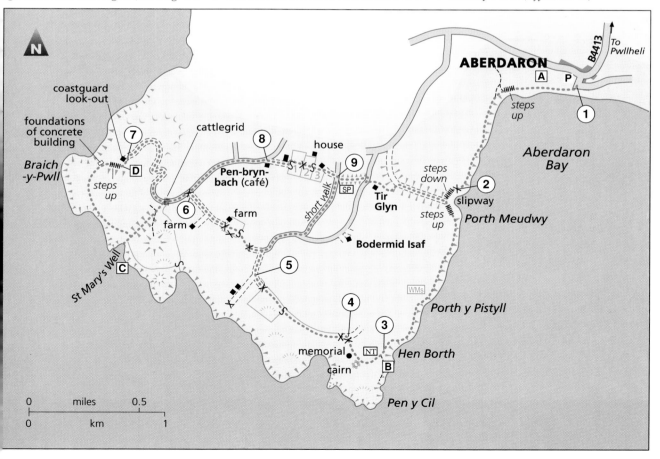

a raised path between fields; this is point ⑨.

For full walk Follow the lane and turn left after 200 yards on to an enclosed track by a waymark post. After 120 yards, at the end of enclosed section, emerge by a gate into a field and take the ladder-stile beside a gate and waymarker ahead, then go half right to take another ladder-stile beside a gate, with farm beyond.

Beyond the stile and gate turn left alongside the fence to take a waymarked gate ahead at the end of the field (not gate in fence on left by cattle-trough); a clear track leads alongside the fence and old wall on the left. Soon keep forward at the corner of a farm track (with farm down to left) and take the gate on to a surfaced lane ⑥.

Detour left along the lane. After the cattlegrid, immediately take a grassy path on left by National Trust sign for Braich-y-Pwll, initially alongside a wall on your left, then down the valley down to the sea at St Mary's Well [C] (or you can divert on the path on the left to summit of Mynydd y Gwyddel). Turn right on reaching the sea and make your way around the grassy cliffs (no path defined), ascending to Mynydd Mawr.

Near the top look to your right to find concrete steps up, which lead up to a disused coastguard look-out at the summit ⑦ [D]. Proceed on a winding concrete track, downhill, which becomes a lane and bends left over the cattlegrid crossed earlier. ⑧ 200 yards after passing a left turn (which you avoid – it is signposted No Through Road), take the track ahead where the road bends left, by Pen-bryn-bach café.

Follow the track to the next farm, take the gate to the right of farmhouse and follow the track which bends round to the left behind the farmhouse, but immediately cross rough steps on your right, over a stile and into a field. Follow the left edge of first field to a gate, go forward in second field to a ladder-stile just to the right of right-hand house, continue along the left edge of third field to a small gate, then turn right on an enclosed track which reaches a lane. Turn right on the lane for 20 yards, then left by the signpost up steps on to a raised path between fields ⑨.

Soon you emerge on a lane and turn right (if you are tired you can turn left on the lane, and keep right at the next junctions to follow roads all the way back to the start); after 50 yards take the track on the left immediately before Tir Glyn.

The track leads to a gate into a field, where you continue alongside left edge. At the end of the field you are above a valley: take the path half right, descending gently towards the valley bottom, where the path goes through a kissing-gate and joins a track. Turn right along the track to reach Porth Meudwy; turn left up steps and retrace the route along the cliff-top and on to the beach into Aberdaron.

ON THE ROUTE

[A] **Aberdaron** A fishing and resort village huddled beside a sandy beach. Y Gegin Fawr Café stands on the site of an ancient pilgrim's kitchen used *en route* for Bardsey Island. High tide laps against the seaward wall of the 12th-century **church**, which was founded as a refuge for pilgrims waiting for favourable weather before crossing Bardsey Sound.

[B] **View** of **Bardsey Island**, a pilgrimage centre from the 5th or 6th century; its earliest monastery was probably founded by St Cadfan of Brittany. A legend that 20,000 saints are buried on Bardsey is perhaps explained by a priest's tomb inscribed *Cum Multitudinem Fratrum* ('with multitude of brethren'), where 'multitudinem' became weathered and could have been misread as 20,000 in Roman numerals. The island has remains of a 13th-century Augustinian abbey, and is now an excellent area for bird-watching. Pen y Cil itself is a likely place to see choughs.

[C] **St Mary's Well** This inlet was used for the taking of holy water in the Middle Ages by pilgrims who did not want to chance the treacherous sea crossing of Bardsey Sound.

[D] **View** over the Lleyn Peninsula, described on a view indicator, including the Rivals (the highest hills on the peninsula); the Harlech area in Snowdonia and, in exceptional conditions, the Wicklow Mountains in Ireland may be seen.

The pilgrims' path to St Mary's Well, opposite Bardsey Island

ABERGLASLYN AND LLYN DINAS

NOT all of Snowdonia's best walks involve energetic mountain ascents. This route keeps to much lower ground, but is graced by views most of the way, with many of the area's best-known peaks in sight. The first stages lead along the Aberglaslyn Pass, via a defunct railway track which involves a quarter of a mile through an unlit tunnel (a torch may be useful). It is followed by 700ft of ascent before you drop down to Llyn Dinas, a lake at the south-east side of Snowdon, for a riverside return. All paths are quite well defined; easy route-finding.

LENGTH 4½ miles (7km), 2 hours
DIFFICULTY 2
START Beddgelert, at junction of A4085 and A498, 13 miles south-east of Caernarfon. Park in the village. Grid reference 590481
OS MAPS Landranger 115; Outdoor Leisure 17
REFRESHMENTS Various in Beddgelert

WALK DIRECTIONS

① Ⓐ From the road-bridge take the lane between Llewelyn's Cottage and the river, signposted Gelert's Grave. 100 yards later cross a bridge and turn right on a path following the river. Once level with the next bridge, the path emerges on to an old railway track Ⓑ, passing through a series of short tunnels, then a longer one.

The swift waters of the Glaslyn as they tumble through the Pass

② On emerging from this tunnel turn sharp left uphill (the left-hand of two paths). The path climbs steadily, and is easy to follow. After ¾ mile it follows disused mine conveyors uphill. ③ At the top, the view opens out suddenly Ⓒ: continue forward, descending gently towards a distant lake (Llyn Dinas). The final part of the descent is much steeper.

④ Turn left at the lake and after 30 yards proceed beyond footpath signpost (avoid crossing the bridge) to follow the left side of the river. ⑤ After ½ mile pass through a gate into a field, and keep quarter right (signposted) at X-junction, after 30

yards. Follow this to reach a track on which you turn left. The track immediately bends left; 10 yards after the Copper Mine car park entrance on the left Ⓓ, turn right on a grassy path which runs alongside a wall on your right. This soon reaches a gate leading on to a tarmac lane ⑥.

Follow the lane until the bridge, then ⑦ cross steps over a wall on the left just before the bridge, and take the riverside path into Beddgelert.

ON THE ROUTE

Ⓐ **Beddgelert** An attractively set, stone-built village, one of the main

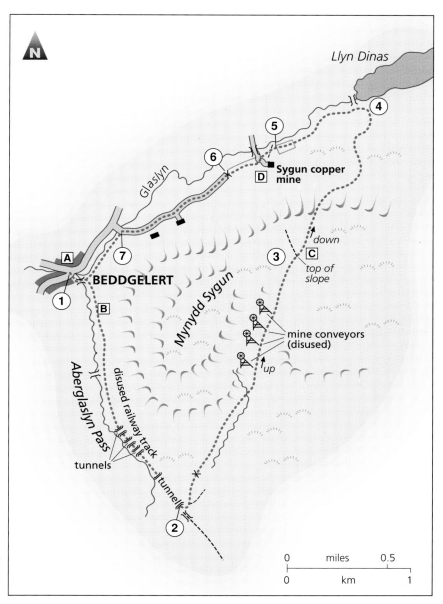

centres in Snowdonia. Its name means Grave of Gelert, for Prince Llewelyn's faithful hound was killed by its master who was under the impression that it had attacked his son, when it had in fact saved him from the jaws of a ravenous wolf. All very melodramatic stuff, and in the 18th century a local innkeeper 'discovered' Gelert's Grave (which is signposted from the path taken at the start of the walk) and he did very well out of the increased tourist trade that followed. It inspired the verse:

Pass on O tender-hearted,
Dry your eyes.
Not here a greyhound
But a landlord lies.

B **Old railway** The former North Wales Narrow Gauge Railway, which ran from Beddgelert to Dinas Junction, south of Caernarfon.
C **View** To the north is Snowdon (3,560ft); north-east are the Glyders (3,279ft); west is Moel Hebod (2,568ft); and eastwards the

pyramid-shaped Cnicht (2,265ft) may be visible.
D **Sygun copper mine** (*open to the public*) has not been mined since

1903, but has been opened as a tourist attraction, featuring an exciting underground tour and an audio-visual show.

The walk follows the course of the River Glaslyn through the Aberglaslyn Pass near the beginning of the walk

SNOWDON

Snowdon towers to 3,560 feet above sea-level and is the highest peak in England and Wales. Its Welsh name, Y Wyddfa Fawr (great tomb), refers to the legend of King Arthur killing the giant Rhita, who was buried on the summit. It may have been into Llyn Llydaw, the lake on its east side, that the sword Excalibur was hurled.

As well as a stupendous viewpoint, Snowdon is of great appeal for a number of spectacular routes up to the summit. A huge glacial corrie gouged out on its east side presents two knife-edge ridges which can be followed in the famous Horseshoe Route, generally agreed to be the most spectacular mountain walk in Wales. It is emphatically only for those with a strong head for heights and should be attempted only in good weather. The Miners' Track and Pig Track are two further easterly approaches. The first stage of the Miners' Track itself makes an excellent introduction for those who wish an easy amble without going up to the top: follow the track from the Pen-y-Pass car park at the top of the A4086 south-east of Llanberis. The track winds up past Llyn Llydaw and ruins of copper mine buildings. The next lake, Glaslyn, is about 2¾ miles from and 800 feet above the start; the track ends here, giving the option of retracing steps or tackling the much steeper path to the summit.

The Watkin Path involves more climbing than any other route, but is not especially difficult. The views are quite different from the other approaches; on the way you pass Gladstone's Rock, named after the 83-year-old Liberal prime minister who made a speech from that point in 1892. The path passes close to abandoned slate mines.

The other routes are the Snowdon Ranger Path, the path from Rhyd-Ddu and the path from Llanberis along the Mountain Railway; the last of these is the least interesting, but the steam-hauled railway itself is great fun, giving the option of travelling up and walking down.

In summer there are buses circuiting Snowdon, giving you the opportunity to ascend via one route and descend via another. There is a café at the summit.

At the height of summer, Snowdon can look something of a Sunday-school outing, with processions of walkers on the most popular paths. But the mountain must nevertheless be treated with great respect; allow plenty of time, watch the weather and wear good walking boots.

LLYN ELSI AND THE MINERS' BRIDGE

THIS route offers a steady ascent through mixed woodland, leading to a view over Llyn Elsi reservoir and some of the nearby peaks, and concludes with a path by the River Llugwy. Route-finding is generally easy, but some care is needed with directions between ③ and ⑥.

LENGTH	4½ miles (7 km), 2½ hours
DIFFICULTY	2
START	Station car park, Betws-y-coed, on A5 4 miles south of Llanrwst. Grid reference 795765
OS MAPS	Landranger 115; Outdoor Leisure 16
REFRESHMENTS	Wide range in Betws-y-coed

WALK DIRECTIONS

① With station on left, proceed forward to the A5, turn right then immediately left just before St Mary's church and just after the post office on your left. After 50 yards turn right at T-junction, and 50 yards later turn left on a path leading uphill into woods (immediately after a bungalow on the left). The path ascends steadily.
② After ½ mile, and immediately after the path crosses a stream, turn right, by a stone post, on a path which recrosses the stream by a footbridge, and zigzags uphill. Beyond the top of the slope continue straight on (following green and purple paintmarks on

rocks) at the next two cross-tracks, which appear at ¼-mile intervals. The path emerges from a forest shortly before reaching a monument by Llyn Elsi reservoir A ③.

The River Conwy at Betws-y-coed

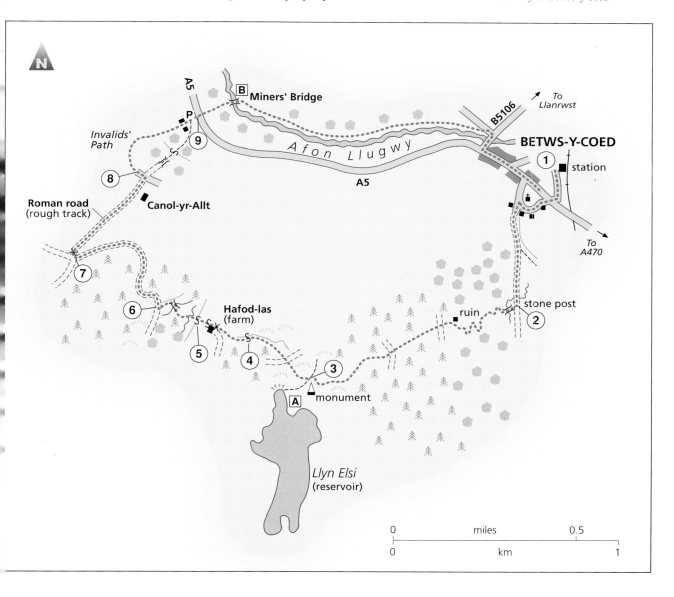

The Miners' Bridge, like a ship's gangway, spans the River Llugwy

At the monument, take the path quarter right downhill (ignore the waymark fully to the right). Ignore also turnings to the left, continue to cross a forestry track 300 yards later, and take the path opposite. ④ After 200 yards climb a ladder-stile and turn left, heading for a farmhouse ahead. Pass through the gate into the farmyard. Go through farmyard with farm on your left, leaving farmyard by a stile. Follow the path for 100 yards with the wall on the left, then enter woodland by a makeshift stile ⑤. The path in the woodland snakes a little: take care to stay on it, and 250 yards into wood (shortly after crossing a stream by stone slab), turn left on meeting a fence. The path leads out of the wood to reach a track ⑥. Turn right on the track and continue on it for 600 yards to reach a junction of tracks ⑦. Turn sharp right, through two sets of gates (blue waymark), to descend on a grassy track between walls. ⑧ Turn left on forestry track for 30 yards, passing over a bridge, then turn right and proceed for 50 yards, down through the woods to join the trail designed for disabled people (note, for instance, the Braille signs on the railings). Pass through the car park and down road to A5 ⑨. Cross the road and take the path opposite. After crossing Miners' Bridge Ⓑ, turn right and follow the river for ¾ mile back to Betws-y-coed. Cross Betws-y-coed bridge and turn left to return to the station.

EARLY ROADS

The earliest farmers created cross-country routes, and many prehistoric roads exist today, both as busy traffic routes and as quiet footpaths. The first national road network was introduced by the Romans, who built long, straight roads as a means of traversing the terrain as fast as possible. These routes formed a crucial military role and could be used in all seasons and weathers. Ditches lay alongside the roads for drainage. The Wade's Causeway in the North York Moors is the best-preserved example of a Roman road, retaining its original surface.

Many 'green lanes' were originally 'meres' or boundary lanes, along the boundaries of newly colonised land. Other roads were created as salt routes in the days before refrigeration, when salt was essential for preserving meat and fish. Cattle and sheep drovers usually used existing tracks and lanes, but sometimes created new, carefully graded ones; inns grew up along these routes. In the dry-stone wall country of the Pennines, old drovers' roads are visible as broad grassy strips between walls, giving the livestock plenty of pasture for their long journeys. Turnpike roads too mostly took over existing routes; in some hilly parts new stretches of road were built. Toll-houses survive in many places along these routes. Milestones are common too; they became a legal requirement along all turnpike roads from 1773.

ON THE ROUTE

Ⓐ **Llyn Elsi reservoir** There are fine views from this peaceful lake of the pyramidal peak of Moel Siabod (2,861 ft).

Ⓑ **Miners' Bridge** The original bridge, a rough step-ladder, was part of a miners' route to the lead mines at Rhiwddolion. The river was a favourite scene for Victorian artists, notably David Cox.

FOEL FENLLI AND MOEL FAMAU

A WALK around both sides of the Clwydian Range, a rounded upland of grass and moor giving a marvellous panorama of Snowdonia. Route-finding is quite easy (some care is needed in the early stages); the way is clearly marked once the Offa's Dyke Path has been joined.

LENGTH 6½ miles (10.5km), 3½ hours

DIFFICULTY 2–3

START Car park (fee payable) and picnic site by toilets on minor road ½ mile north-east of Moel Famau car park. From A494 (Ruthin–Mold) turn off north-east at Llanbedr–Dyffryn-Clwyd, immediately east of church, on to road called Lôn-cae-glâs, signposted Llandyrnog; this goes up steeply on to hills; ½ mile east of top point of road go into the car park on your left. From Mold turn off just south-west of Loggerheads. Grid reference 172611. There is also a free car park at ⑦.

OS MAPS Landranger 116; Pathfinder 788 and 772 (SJ 05/15 and SJ 06/16)

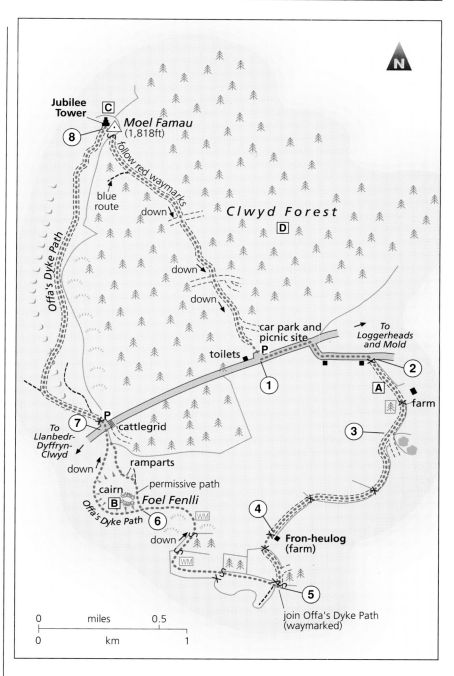

WALK DIRECTIONS

① Start on the road with the car park on your left, walk along road (in north-east direction). Take the first right after ½ mile; this bends left in front of a farmhouse. ② Immediately after the next house (Fyn y groessord) on your right, take a rising track on the right, initially between walls and then into the open, then later with a fence on your left only A.

③ After ½ mile, where the wall

Moel Famau, the highest point on this exhilarating walk

recommences, with a wood close by down to your left, ignore the left (descending) fork, but carry on along the main track (with wall now on left).

④ After ¾ mile, you reach a farm on left of track, where the track goes through two sets of gates.

70 yards later, bear left through a third gate, proceeding on the track on the left edge of field, alongside wall, under power lines and dipping down to trees, then continue up and slightly to the right for 50 yards to reach a gate beside a stile with acorn

waymarker denoting Offa's Dyke Path (which you now follow to Moel Famau) ⑤.

Turn right beyond this gate and stile, alongside a fence on right and pass a small plantation on your right and go over stile; the waymarked route continues forward, with a fence on the left (bending right alongside fence at fence corner) to take waymark stile and continue along plantation down to a stile at the foot of the hill (Foel Fenlli) ⑥.

The path leads up towards the top of the hill: halfway up, the Offa's

Dyke Path is waymarked to the left (skirting hill) but the best views are had by keeping forward to the summit B on a permissive path and then taking a path ahead (there are several, but they rejoin); whichever way you go, paths rejoin and head towards the prominent tower on Moel Famau, first dropping on to a road by prominent signpost and cattlegrid ⑦.

Cross the road into a small car park and take the gate opposite, following waymarked main track which leads half left and gradually ascends (avoid right fork after 50 yards). ⑧ C At the summit of Moel Famau at the Jubilee Tower, turn right to take a stile 70 yards to the right of trig point (summit pillar), as it is seen from the tower.

On the other side of the stile is the first of a series of red-hooped waymark posts, which you follow all the way back to the main car park: the route drops into forest D, and later is briefly joined by a blue route too, but keep straight on all the way down to reach the car park.

ON THE ROUTE

A There are good **views** east from this little-frequented track, with BBC mast on Cyrn y Brain (1,844ft) to the south-east.

B **Foel Fenlli** (1,676ft) Ramparts of an Iron Age hillfort still encircle this hill.

C **Moel Famau** A **view indicator** at the summit details one of the grandest views on the Offa's Dyke Path, with Snowdonia to the west (including Snowdon and Tryfan), Denbigh and Liverpool Bay north, Alyn valley and Stanlow Oil

Refinery east, Cader Idris and the Berwyn uplands south-west. The **tower** was built as a mock-Egyptian memorial to George III's golden jubilee in 1810 by a Thomas Harrison of Chester, who submitted grandiose schemes for triumphal arches and Grecian follies; this selected design was relatively simple, but its sheer bulk caused its downfall, for it collapsed in 1862. It was partly restored, and the viewing platform added, during European Conservation Year (1970).

D **Clwyd Forest** A mixed conifer

plantation, started in the 1950s, covering 500 hectares.

ADOPTING TRIG POINTS

The familiar British trig point is now redundant with today's cartographic surveying methods. The Ordnance Survey invited the public to adopt these important landmarks, so that someone would maintain the structures and keep them in the landscape. The scheme caught the public imagination: response was overwhelming, and virtually all the most visible trig points were adopted.

On Foel Fenlli hillfort itself, looking towards Moel Famau and the Clwydian Hills, one of the many superb views this walk offers

VALE OF LLANGOLLEN AND CASTELL DINAS BRAN

THE Vale of Llangollen, edged by the limestone terraces of the Eglwyseg escarpment and traversed by the long-distance Offa's Dyke Path, is one of the great sights of North Wales. Here it is seen at three levels: first along the Llangollen Branch of the Shropshire Union Canal, then, after a sharp haul up through forest, from the Panorama Walk (which is actually a small road), and most memorably of all from the dramatic ruins of Castell Dinas Bran. A steep descent leads back down to Llangollen. Walkers can tie this in with a boat trip along the canal to see the Horseshoe Falls or Pontcysyllte Aqueduct. Paths are generally well waymarked. The shorter version of the walk uses a quiet road to ascend to the Panorama Walk from Trevor Uchaf.

WALK DIRECTIONS

① Ⓐ Cross the bridge over the River Dee, turn right on the A539

then immediately left up a lane (called Wharf Hill but not labelled at road junction). Just before the canal bridge join the canal towpath by Llangollen Wharf Ⓑ and turn right under the bridge. Follow the towpath for 1½ miles; you pass a lift bridge, then pass under a stone bridge, then under a main-road bridge. ② Leave the canal at the next bridge after the main-road bridge, crossing the road and taking a rising minor road just to the left of the Sun public house at Trevor

---

LENGTH *Full walk* 5½ miles (9km), 3 hours *Short walk* 4 miles (6.5km), 2½ hours

DIFFICULTY 2–3

START Llangollen, by the south side of the river bridge. Grid reference 215422

OS MAPS Landranger 117; Pathfinder 806 (SJ 24/34)

REFRESHMENTS Full range in Llangollen; Sun public house, Trevor Uchaf

---

Uchaf. Follow this uphill for ¼ mile to where the road bends sharp left ③.

For short version of walk Follow the road up to reach an oblique T-junction with another minor road

The Pontcysyllte Aqueduct carries the canal high over the River Dee

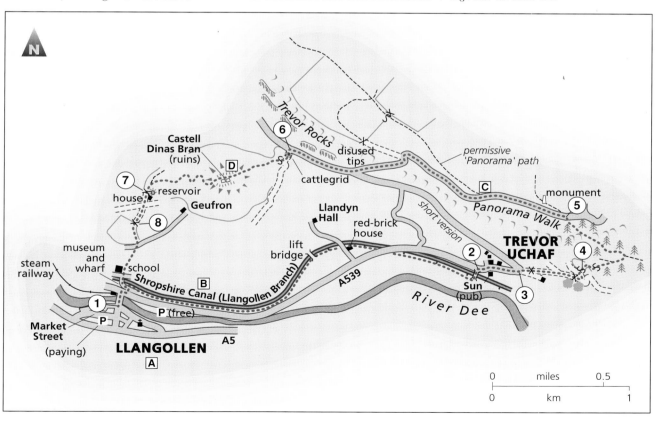

(the Panorama Walk) and turn left; resume directions at ⑥.

For full walk Continue forward on the left-hand of two tracks. The track passes through a gate, after ¼ mile it goes under power lines (where you ignore a sharp left turn uphill) and through a second gate, reaching (50 yards later) a hairpin corner of another track. Turn left. ④ 75 yards later, take a stile on the right and go forward in a field alongside fence on right. At the corner of the fence, turn right, still alongside the fence for a further 30 yards then bear half left towards a stile, behind which you enter dense forest. Ascend the path. After 300 yards you reach a junction with acorn waymark denoting Offa's Dyke Path at an open firebreak with power lines, and turn left along Offa's Dyke Path, uphill, back into forest and up to stile on to small road (the Panorama Walk) ⑤. Turn left ⒸC and follow for 1½ miles (ignore sharp left turn, downhill, after 1 mile). ⑥ When you are level with Castell Dinas Bran (the ruined castle on the isolated hill on your left), turn left over a cattlegrid, and 50 yards later take a stile on the right and follow the path to top of hill Ⓓ. Walk through the castle ruins, then descend on a zigzagging path along wooden railings, then head towards the right of a prominent house with a fenced reservoir (which appears as a grassy hump) on its right-hand side. ⑦ Just past the house, go through a gate and follow the track downhill. Go forward at a junction of tracks 100 yards later, and ⑧ at the end of the track, pass through the right-hand of two gates. Follow the path along the left edge of the field, across a lane and take the kissing-gate opposite. Emerge above the canal bridge by Llangollen Wharf and turn left back to the start.

ON THE ROUTE

Ⓐ **Llangollen** Its fame as the headquarters of the **International Musical Eisteddfod** (which takes place in July in the tent-like Royal International Pavilion) and its scenic setting in the Vale of Llangollen have made the town into a bustling tourist centre. Llangollen flourished as a meeting point of highways, including the London–Holyhead road (A5), improved by Thomas Telford in 1815, when the hairpinning Horseshoe Pass was constructed.

The bridge over which the walk crosses at the start dates from 1345 (subsequently widened) and is one of the 'Seven Wonders of Wales'. It was built by John Trevor, who became bishop of St Asaph. The 13th-century **church** of St Collen has a fine 15th-century hammer-beamed roof. In its churchyard is the burial place of the 'Ladies of Llangollen', the eccentric Irishwomen who lived at Plas Newydd just outside town, and entertained Walter Scott, William Wordsworth, the Duke of Wellington and others. Other attractions in town include the **Motor Museum, Victorian School and Museum** and the 5½-mile **Llangollen Railway**, offering steam-hauled rides.

Ⓑ **Shropshire Union Canal (Llangollen Branch)** This waterway, generally reckoned to be one of the most scenic on the entire canal network, runs 46 miles from the Shropshire Union Canal proper at Hurleston to Llantysilio, just north-west of Llangollen. At the Llantysilio end it is fed by the River Dee by means of Thomas Telford's engineered 'Horseshoe Falls'. **Llangollen Wharf** is a busy scene with narrow-boats and has a **Canal Exhibition Centre** in a former canal warehouse. A recommended add-on to this walk is to take one of the **boat trips** from here, either with a horse-drawn barge or with the *Thomas Telford* narrow-boat, which chugs its way eastwards to the spectacular **Pontcysyllte Aqueduct** – 126 feet above the valley floor and one of the marvels of the canal era.

Ⓒ The **Panorama Walk** follows this scenic high-level route, looking on to the massive crags of the Eglwyseg escarpment. Carrying along the road, about 300 yards after the woodland ends on your left and opposite a bench, a signpost points to the right for **Panorama**. This is a permissive path which gains very fine views: a worthwhile loop can be made by following it up – the return route down the side valley (and on the near side of the abandoned quarries) to the left can be seen as you climb. Take a stile beside a gate (where fence on right ends); 140 yards later, turn left at a crossing of paths (the path ahead leads towards distinct woodland); this path bends left at the head of the side valley and crosses a gate, then drops to rejoin the road. At time of inspection the second gate was locked and rather difficult to climb.

Ⓓ **Castell Dinas Bran** ('Crow Castle') There is open access to this memorable site, crowned by the jagged remains of a stone castle built around 1236. The castle was probably in ruins by 1578. On the same site have been a Norman wooden castle, and much earlier an Iron Age hillfort. Castell Dinas Bran was occupied in the 13th century by Griffith, son of Madoc, who sided with Henry III and thus betrayed his country. The **view** extends eastwards down the Dee Valley to the railway viaduct near Newbridge. To the west, in the distance, are the Berwyn Hills.

The bridge over the River Dee at Llangollen has episcopal connections

SNAILBEACH AND THE STIPERSTONES

THE focus of this exhilarating ramble is the Stiperstones, a moorland ridge capped by jagged crags, but there are wide-ranging views almost throughout the walk over the Welsh Marches and the Midlands. Despite the high-level character of much of the route, it is not particularly demanding, with one fairly gentle, if substantial, ascent at the beginning, and a steeper descent later on. There are two sections along very quiet, surfaced roads. The paths were not waymarked at the time of checking, but the route is reasonably obvious most of the way. Those who prefer an easier there-and-back stroll along the Stiperstones ridge can walk up from the car park at the top of the minor road between Shelve and The Bog to the west and Bridges and Ratlinghope to the east.

LENGTH	6 miles (9.5km), 3 hours
DIFFICULTY	2

START Snailbeach village hall (by toilet block and post-box), 1 mile south of A488 and 10 miles south-west of Shrewsbury. Grid reference 373021

OS MAPS Landranger 126 and 137; Pathfinder 808 and 909 (SJ 20/30 and SO 29/39)

REFRESHMENTS Sycamore Cottage (light snacks), on the edge of Stiperstones village; Stiperstones Inn and shop in Stiperstones village; Weighbridge Café, on edge of Snailbeach near the end of the walk

WALK DIRECTIONS

① Ⓐ With Snailbeach village hall behind you, take the rising surfaced

The peacock butterfly photographed at the Stiperstones National Nature Reserve

lane ahead, signposted Lordshill, up through the village. Keep to the

surfaced lane, ignoring unsurfaced side tracks (you pass close to a tall

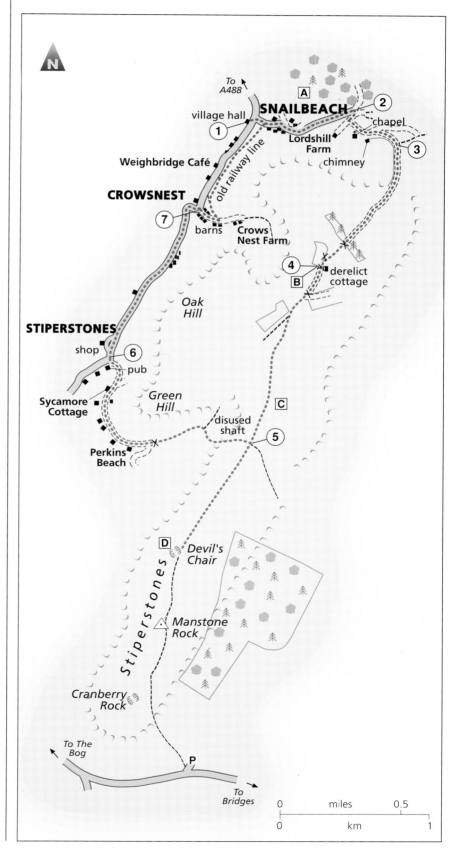

mine chimney away to the right, then house 17 on the left). After the houses end, there is a valley down to the left. ② After ½ mile (as woodland ends on your left), bear right at a fork. Ignore a track sharp left after 50 yards but take the next fork left: this track passes to the left of a chapel and its prominent graveyard. After 70 yards, ignore a left fork. The track rises steadily and a fence joins on the right; ③ the track then curves to the right (still along the fence; ignore a track coming in from the left at this point; the fence later disappears but old fence posts are visible) and under power lines, then heads to a prominent belt of trees. On the other side of the trees, enter a field, go to the left-hand gate (with a stile, to right of derelict cottage), to enter Stiperstones National Nature Reserve ④ B. Proceed up a rising track to the next gate giving on to moorland. Proceed ahead, keeping half right at a track junction after 30 yards. After 200 yards the track reaches a wall corner: ignore a minor path alongside the wall but continue on the main track up to the skyline. As the track levels out, the jagged forms of the Stiperstones are seen ahead C. ⑤ You reach a cairn (formed of piled-up stones) at a major crossing of tracks; the right turn is your eventual continuation, but first detour along the Stiperstones ridge to the Devil's Chair D, continuing further along the ridge if desired. Return to the cairn at the track crossing and go left, downhill. Ignore any minor ascending side paths; the main path bends right after 350 yards, then left; beyond a gate, ignore the track to the left but follow the track ahead, still descending, to the scattered village of Stiperstones, where you proceed down to a road ⑥. Turn right along the road (ignore immediate minor left fork). After ½ mile this passes a cluster of houses on the right, then ¼ mile later past the Snailbeach village sign

it bends right by another cluster of houses (Crowsnest): ⑦ just as the road bends to the left, take a track on the right between the houses (this is to the left of the red-brick house called '5 Crowsnest'). After 100 yards, cross a cattlegrid, then 100 yards later, at the end of barns away to your right, fork very sharp left on to a gently rising grassy path, which initially doubles back on your previous direction (this is an old railway track that served the lead mines; although it is not a public right of way there is informal public access along it); this path later has a fence on the right and goes through woods; keep right at two forks, still alongside the fence, and go forward at a staggered junction by houses, past the piers of a defunct bridge, and past a former locomotive shed to the road followed at the start; turn left to return to the village hall.

ON THE ROUTE

A **Snailbeach** The village has striking reminders of a once-thriving lead-mining industry centred on Snailbeach, The Bog in the Stiperstones and Shelve Hill. Evidence of Roman lead mining has been found in the area, and by the 12th century lead was being transported from Shelve as far as Wiltshire. The activity peaked in the 18th and 19th centuries, when landlords enticed squatters on to their common land by charging them a 6d or 1s annual rent so that the demand for mining and quarry labour could be met. Remnants of these communities can still be seen on and around the hill; rails from

The Devil's Chair, a place of lore and legend in the jagged Stiperstones

the long-since closed mineral railway to Pontesbury are still in place, and on re-entering the village at the end of the walk, the route passes a number of shafts, a derelict chimney and a locomotive shed.

B **Stiperstones National Nature Reserve** The reserve, maintained by English Nature, covers some 1,100 acres of upland moorland and coppice oak woodland. The south-western slopes harbour bell heather, which blooms in August, while a month later the ling heather makes a spectacular sea of purple. Cow wheat, crowberries and lichens flourish on the moors, which are also renowned for the edible red-berried cowberry (similar to the cranberry), best when cooked and an excellent accompaniment to game. Ravens, red grouse and buzzards are common sightings.

C In **view** to the left are the cooling towers of Buildwas power station near Ironbridge; the summit to its left is the Wrekin (1,334ft), another famous Shropshire viewing-platform. Further to the right of Buildwas is the Long Mynd with the summit of Caer Caradoc just visible beyond it.

D **The Stiperstones** The windswept ridge is here capped by a series of quartzite outcrops formed 480 million years ago. The first reached is known as the Devil's Chair, surrounded by boulders which are said to have fallen from the Devil's leather apron when its strings broke; he now sits there hoping his weight will sink the Chair into the ground, which event is supposed to bring about the immediate ruination of England. The story also says that an instant thunderstorm takes place whenever anyone sits on the Chair, and that on a hot day the wind carries a whiff of the Devil's brimstone. The **view** on a clear day encompasses points well over a hundred miles apart, including Brown Clee and Titterstone Clee hills, the Berwyns, Plynlimon, Cader Idris and Snowdon.

CAER CARADOC AND HOPE BOWDLER HILL

PICK a clear day and the views are wide-ranging, over the Marches and the West Midlands, with glimpses of the far-flung hills. This route mostly takes gently graded tracks over windswept moors, although there are two steep descents. Caer Caradoc, the walk's high point, has impressive Iron Age ramparts. Total ascent 1,000 feet.

LENGTH	6 miles (9.5km), 3 hours
DIFFICULTY	3
START	Hope Bowdler, on B4371, 1½ miles south-east of Church Stretton. Grid reference 475925
BY TRAIN	Church Stretton
OS MAPS	Landranger 137 or 138; Pathfinder 910 (SO 49/59)

WALK DIRECTIONS

① Walk along B4371 through the village away from Church Stretton. 30 yards after the last house (No 12) on left and just before Hope Bowdler sign on road (facing other way), take the signposted gate on left. Follow the track uphill, with fence on right; ignore gates in fence on right. Carry on through gate across the track, which is now fenced on both sides, then ② through another gate on to the open moor. The path leads ahead and rises gently; ignore a crossing path and cross a seasonal stream just after. ③ At the saddle of hill (Caer Caradoc is the ridge ahead: the summit is to the right, and Three Fingers Rock is at its left end), where a fence joins on right, avoid stile on right but take the path ahead, dropping steeply and leaving

The Wrekin, one of several peaks in view

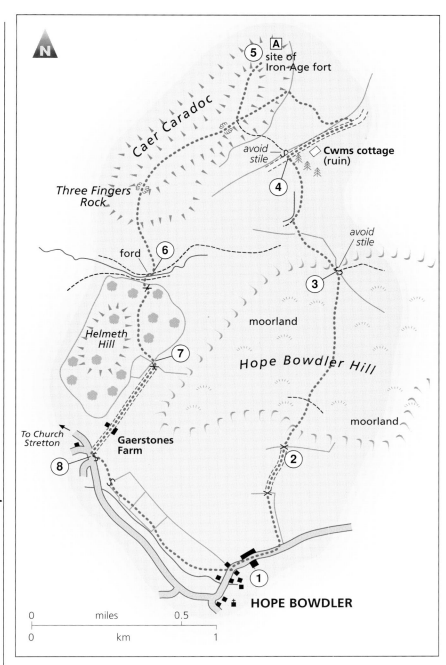

the fence to reach a gate. Go forward for 50 yards to join grassy path, along which you turn right, to reach a group of trees. ④ Beyond the trees you can either take stiles ahead for a direct but steep ascent of Caer Caradoc or (easier although slightly longer) turn right on the track, which passes a ruin (Cwms Cottage) on the right. Where the track drops slightly as the view opens out on the left, take signposted stile on left. Immediately bear sharp left on grassy track, doubling back initially, then

bending round to gate at base of Caer Caradoc. A gentle track leads up half left to bisect the two main groups of crags; at the top, going left along the entire length of the ridge to Three Fingers Rock, is the continuation, but first detour to the right to the summit ⑤ for the view Ⓐ. Return and follow the ridge beyond Three Fingers Rock, where the path drops half left and very steeply. ⑥ At the bottom, you will find two parallel tracks: cross first and turn right on second, go over a ford after 30 yards then immediately left uphill 30 yards to a gate; then on for 500 yards up to a fence crossing your direction. Turn left, walking with fence on your right for 70 yards, then ⑦ take stile beside gate on right. Go forward alongside fence on right (ignore paths ascending to moor to your left) to reach another gate giving on to a fenced track. Follow this for 600 yards. Turn left on road, then after only 30 yards ⑧ take stile on left and follow directional arrows across fields back to Hope Bowdler: go diagonally right up to a stile in corner of first field, then keep forward, initially alongside the fence on right in second field. Maintain direction in next two fields, with a stream close by on right; path becomes enclosed and emerges at village centre.

WALKS ON THE LONG MYND

Church Stretton, a short distance west of Hope Bowdler, nestles beneath the Long Mynd. This upland mass of bilberry- and bracken-covered slopes is bisected by steep-sided dales. Probably the most popular strolling ground is the Carding Mill Valley, which has a car park; Ashes Hollow, further south, is much quieter and quite unspoilt. An excellent ten-mile walk linking the two can begin from Carding Mill Valley; a pass along the bottom of the valley leads up to the high moorland plateau; tracks leading south-westwards include the Port Way, an ancient route once used by Neolithic axe traders and intermittently marked with Bronze Age tumuli. Another scenic path leads from the south side of Ashes Hollow to Little Stretton; return to the car park by following the B4370 and then taking footpaths – you'll need an OS map, Landranger 137 or Pathfinder 110 (SO 49/59).

ON THE ROUTE

[A] **Caer Caradoc** (1,506ft) Capped by the grassy ramparts of a hill fort. Caradoc is the Welsh form of Caractacus, who, according to legend, made his last stand here against the Romans in AD50 (though the account that was given by Tacitus, the Roman historian, does not tally with this).

View north to the Cheshire Plain; north-east to the Wrekin (1,334ft) and the Peak District a long way beyond; south-east to Wenlock Edge and Brown Clee Hill (1,772ft) with Titterstone Clee (1,750ft) beyond; west to the Long Mynd which blocks out anything more distant; north-north-west to Ruabon Mountain (1,677ft) near Wrexham.

PATH PROBLEMS

It is illegal to obstruct a public right of way. If you find an obstruction, such as impenetrable crops or barbed wire, across such a path you are entitled to remove it/them (or in the case of crops, walk over them). If the problem is bad, you can take an alternative route providing you do not trespass or cause damage.

It is illegal to put up a sign on a right of way that deters potential users, such as Private or Path Closed, when it refers to that route.

Waymarks and signposts have the same status as any other traffic sign, and it is an offence to remove them. If you come across hindrances like these, write to the relevant highway authority, which has the duty to sort out problems relating to rights of way. Give exact locations, with grid references, and a sketch map if possible.

Caer Caradoc seen from near Church Stretton; black and white timber-framed buildings are typical of this area

IRONBRIDGE AND THE SEVERN GORGE

A SPECTACULAR tour of the cradle of the Industrial Revolution, starting from a village and following footpaths between most of the main sights. Route-finding is intricate but not especially difficult.

WALK DIRECTIONS

① Ⓐ From Broseley High Street take turning 50 yards downhill from the Albion pub, immediately opposite Victoria Hall and the memorial garden. This road appears to be unnamed but an obscured sign on the right some 20 yards from the

junction reveals that it is Dark Lane.

After 300 yards, just beyond a red-brick lodge, turn right on to a clear track. This soon opens out to follow left-hand edge of a field, then skirting edge of small copse, fork right in meadow at the bottom to pass through a gate to road ②.

Turn right on the road, and left after 30 yards (signposted) just before Broseley village sign on to a small road that leads to Coneybury and Woodhouse Farms. On reaching a crossroads after 200 yards, continue forward on an unmade track, avoiding the fork to the right

just beyond. Pass through a wooden gate and continue forward on track, later passing between barriers to drop into a wooded dingle.

LENGTH 7½ miles (12km), 4 hours
DIFFICULTY 2–3
START High Street in Broseley (on B4375 6 miles north of Bridgnorth. Grid reference 675017
OS MAPS Landranger 127; Pathfinder 890 (SJ 60/70)
REFRESHMENTS Several pubs in Broseley, two at Coalport, several in Ironbridge. Cafés in Ironbridge

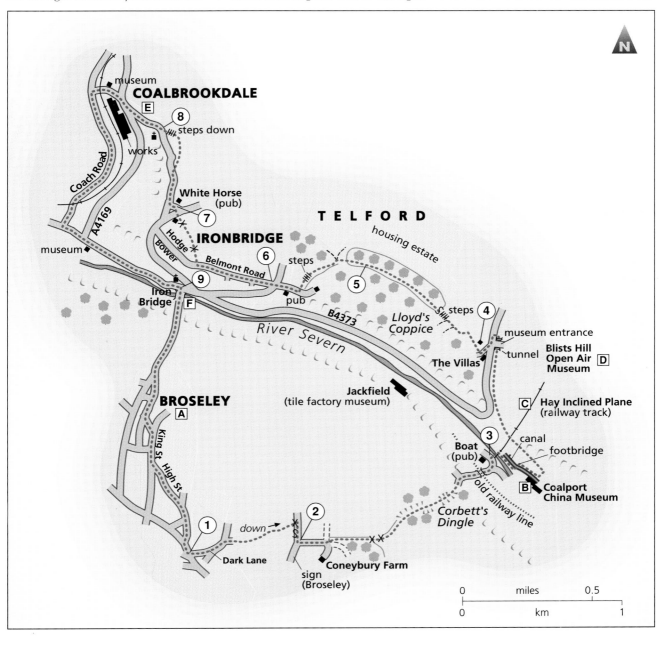

Avoid a turning to the right, and continue along the bottom of the valley with rocks rising to your left. Emerge at the bottom of wood by a small brick house, on your left, and continue forward in driveway which soon becomes metalled and passes under a railway bridge. Bear left at the bottom to reach Boat pub ③.

Turn right over the footbridge and turn right again along the narrow canal towpath. Turn left over the footbridge at the end, and continue on the far bank. On reaching the entrance to Coalport China Museum B, turn left uphill, and then immediately left on road. Just before reaching the Shakespeare pub turn right on path marked the Silkin Way, first following steps uphill and then turning left on a cross-track (marker post).

Follow this for about ½ mile C; 15 yards after passing through a tunnel turn right up steps, turn right again at the top, and turn right a third time to reach road ④ D. Turn on the road, and turn immediately right on driveway in front of The Villas.

Turn right after 20 yards on to a narrow stony path with a garden wall, later a fence, on your left and woodland on right. When the fence ends, continue forward, avoiding a path which bears away to the left, and 50 yards beyond this point fork right uphill on a clear path marked with wooden steps. Cross over the stile at top and continue in a field with the fence on your left. Keep left at fork to follow a clear path through trees.

Follow this for ½ mile, avoiding all turnings to the right and keeping close to the top of the slope, which drops away sharply to your left. ⑤ On reaching a wooden barrier, fork left past a post bearing footprint sign, and continue with fence on right. The path soon passes into a second field, and into small copse just beyond. Turn left on cross-track just inside this copse, to drop steeply downhill, soon joining a driveway which merges from the left.

Turn right on the road at the bottom, and keep left just beyond the pub (avoiding right turn up Jockey Bank). Continue on a gravel path where the road ends, to reach

the main road ⑥. Cross over into Belmont Road, which you follow for about 500 yards. Watch out for Belle Vue Road on your left (the third proper turning on the left); 30 yards beyond this ignore turning on right (named Woodlands) and continue into Hodge Bower and look out for a kissing-gate on your right leading into a meadow. Head diagonally across towards a bungalow, on the near side of which you take the kissing-gate and follow the path to a road junction ⑦. Cross the road and continue up on the far side, passing the White Horse pub on your right. 75 yards beyond the brow of the hill, fork right on a path into woods, and fork left 350 yards beyond.

On reaching a clear cross-track, turn left down wooden steps to reach a barrier with the road and Holy Trinity church beyond ⑧. Turn right on the road, and on reaching the main road take the road diagonally opposite to pass through Coalbrookdale works E.

After passing under a railway bridge, turn left on Coach Road, which you follow for ½ mile, passing under a further bridge. Turn left on main road along bank of the river on right to reach Iron Bridge ⑨ F.

Turn right across the bridge, cross the road on the far side and climb steps to continue up a surfaced path. After ¼ mile, at the top of a steep rise, turn half left (avoiding sharp left turn into Cobwell Road) on to a surfaced driveway which continues to climb steeply uphill.

A road later joins from the left, and after a further 70 yards, fork left, continuing uphill. Turn right in a larger road (King Street) to pass the

The Iron Bridge: its table of tolls is still in place

King's Head Inn on your right. Follow this road for ¼ mile avoiding turnings to left and right, and at the end turn left into Broseley High Street to return to village centre.

ON THE ROUTE
NB The **Ironbridge Gorge Museum** is spread over six sites, five of which are passed on this walk; combined entry tickets for all sites have no expiry date (*Open daily* excluding Christmas, April to late October, 10 to 6; late October to April, 10 to 5).

A **Broseley** Street names such as Foundry Street and Foundry Court are reminders of the town's busy past. Ironmaster John Wilkinson, who in 1787 built the first iron barge, lived in The Lawns, an imposing house in Church Street.

B **Coalport China Museum** The porcelain works, established in the 1790s, became world-famous; they closed 1926 when the Coalport Company moved to Stoke-on-Trent. The museum has displays of the production processes as well as much fine porcelain, and visitors can walk inside the shapely bottle-kilns.

C **The Hay Inclined Plane** (over the path) is a remarkable engineering feat. The restored double-track railway was built to transport tub boats by gravity from the Shropshire Canal (at the top of the Blists Hill Museum site) to the River Severn at Coalport.

D **Blists Hill Open Air Museum** A re-created industrial community of the type found in the local coalfield about 1890, with forge, candle factory, saw-mill, bank and locksmiths to be found in the high street, and a tollhouse, coal mine railway and furnaces elsewhere.

E **Coalbrookdale** The true birthplace of the Industrial Revolution. It was here in 1709 that Abraham Darby first smelted iron using coke instead of the traditional charcoal, a far more efficient process. Soon the world's first cast-iron wheels, bridge and rails were made in Coalbrookdale.

F **Iron Bridge** The world's first iron bridge, erected in 1779, and the most famous symbol of the Industrial Revolution. The bridge was designed by Thomas Pritchard under the direction of Abraham Darby.

MAIDEN CASTLE AND RAW HEAD

THIS walk along and beneath the Central Cheshire Ridge, which divides the Cheshire Plain, is upland in character: it is characterised by heath and woods, with extensive views from the sandstone cliff. One short rocky section on the Sandstone Trail. Easy route-finding, thanks to good waymarking throughout.

LENGTH 5½ miles (9km), 2½ hours

DIFFICULTY 2

START Copper Mine Inn, Brown Knowl, on A534, between junctions with A49 and A41 (between Wrexham and Nantwich); car park at rear of inn. Grid reference 501522

OS MAPS Landranger 117; Pathfinder 790 (SJ 45/55)

REFRESHMENTS Copper Mine Inn

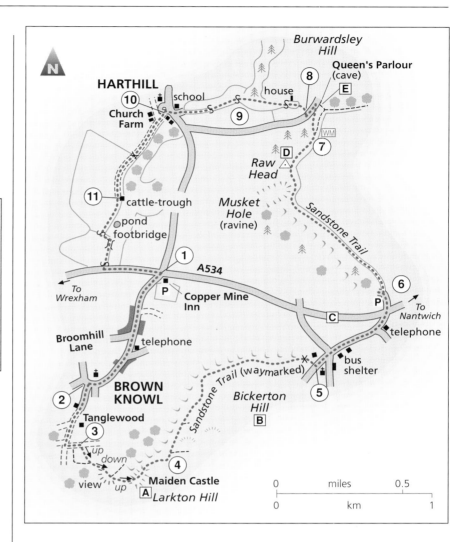

WALK DIRECTIONS

① From the main road, take the minor road to the right of pub, bearing left at the next junction, through Brown Knowl village (ignore minor turns to right and then to left by telephone-box). Past the Methodist church, the road bends right (ignore cul-de-sac ahead).

② 40 yards later, turn left into another cul-de-sac (Sandy Lane). This enters woods and becomes a track (there is a driveway to Tanglewood on your left); immediately after, keep left as waymarked (yellow arrow), where right fork ascends. Soon, you reach National Trust sign for Bickerton Hill and information board: turn left, past a children's football pitch on your left. ③ At the end of the

The start and finish of the walk, the Copper Mine Inn takes its name from mines once worked in the area

pitch, go through the gate and take the path on right uphill along power lines. At the top, turn left on a well-defined path and reach a small grassy plateau with views. Take the left path downhill to cross-routes: follow the steep path up (waymarked with yellow arrow and boot-print motifs marked with an 's' contained within a yellow circle: this denotes the Sandstone Trail); there is a steep rocky section near the top of the ridge. ④ At the top (by plaque about Maiden Castle) Ⓐ, bear left.

Follow the trail along the top edge of the hill, with big drops on your left Ⓑ (the trail briefly leaves the edge at one point but returns to it after a signpost pointing left to Beeston where ahead is private). ⑤ At the road, turn left (signposted Raw Head and Beeston) and go forward at crossroads to reach T-

junction with A534 Ⓒ. Take the cul-de-sac opposite, to the left of house. This lane rises past The Paddocks and a car park on your left, then ⑥ 50 yards later keep straight on (signposted Raw Head) where left goes to Chiflik (house).

The Sandstone Trail now proceeds as an enclosed track with woods on the left and soon narrows to a path along the top of the edge. You reach a trig point (summit pillar) at Raw Head Ⓓ and continue along the edge for 200 yards to reach a fork ⑦: bear left (waymarked with yellow arrow), leaving the top of the edge Ⓔ.

Descend through woods to a tarmacked lane. Turn left on lane, then ⑧ right after 100 yards on a waymarked path (opposite track signposted Gallantry Bank), through woods to a stile. Follow the right edge of field, past a house, then over

Bickerton Hill is one in a short chain of mainly wooded hills in the middle of the Cheshire Plain, a gently undulating landscape studded with meres

a stile into woods, where you follow either upper or lower path to reach a stile into a field ⑨. Turn left and follow left edge of field, heading towards Harthill village.

100 yards before a house, take the stile on your left, leading on to an enclosed track into village. Cross to the turning opposite and slightly to the right (signposted Brown Knowl, A534), into village square (with the church on your right). ⑩ Keep to the left, leaving the square by the far left-hand corner on a farm track which passes the barns of Church Farm on your right. Track then runs along the top of a field with woods on your left.

⑪ Where woods reach corner (near cattle-trough), go forward, with a fence on your left (do not take track to left). At bottom left-hand corner of field, cross the stile and enter the next field to follow bottom edge for 50 yards (pub visible ahead), then take footbridge on right. Follow left edge of next field, then turn left along road to reach the Copper Mine Inn.

ON THE ROUTE

Ⓐ **Maiden Castle** Two four-foot banks survive of this Iron Age hill-fort. Carbondating has put the date of its destruction by fire to 400BC. There are good **views** throughout this high-level section west to North Wales, including the Clwydian Range. On a clear day Liverpool Anglican Cathedral and the Royal Liver building may be seen.

Ⓑ **Bickerton Hill** A plateau where heathland vegetation has grown up since pasture was abandoned in the 1930s.

Ⓒ The main road is an old **salt route** between Nantwich and Wales. ½ mile north-east, by the road, is a pumping-house chimney from a long-abandoned **copper mine.**

Ⓓ **Raw Head** At 746ft, the highest point on this range; it is made more impressive by sheer sandstone cliffs whose honeycomb patterns are the result of weathering away of weaker bands of rock. A small cave by the trig point is said to have been the haunt of brigands.

Ⓔ Some 250 yards further along the ridge, and below the path to the left, is the **Queen's Parlour**, a large cave, excavated for sand (once used locally for cleaning cottage floors).

THE RIVER BOLLIN, STYAL COUNTRY PARK AND QUARRY BANK MILL

AN oasis of wooded river scenery and survivals of the Industrial Revolution just beyond the suburbs of the Manchester conurbation. There are some quite deep flights of steps on the route. There are many paths in the woodland sections, but the river assists route-finding.

WALK DIRECTIONS

① Ⓐ At the end of the car park furthest from the road, exit at the right-hand corner then turn left on to a cobbled road past Oak Cottages, and go towards the school. At small crossroads, turn left along road, across the village green to Styal Cross. Turn right to pass the Northcliffe Unitarian Chapel. Continue forward through a gate into Northern Woods. At the first fork keep left along the main path

descending in about 300 yards to the river. Keep the river on your right, to reach a footbridge ②, where you cross over to other bank and turn left. A steep stepped path can be seen straight ahead. Climb this and descend a further stepped path to the river. Continue to next footbridge ③, where you cross over the river.

After the bridge, the path rises steeply up steps, taking a route high above the river before dropping again to the riverside. The path follows riverside for 1 mile to the road at Oversley Bridge ④. Turn left to cross the bridge and take the path to the right at end of far bridge parapet. After 50 yards cross the busy A538 road, and take path opposite (signposted Castle Hill, Morley Green; soon marked by yellow arrows) over road barrier and

along the riverside. Just after the river veers right, continue forward to a stile and climb steep steps up a wooded slope to field ⑤.

LENGTH 5½ miles (9km), 2½ hours
DIFFICULTY 2
START Free NT car park (locked at dusk) near the primary school in Styal, just off B5166, 2 miles north of Wilmslow. (Do not confuse with large car park closer to chapel and cottages.) Grid reference 836835. *By train* Styal station. Turn right out of station, right at T-junction then first left into Styal village
OS MAPS Landranger 109; Pathfinder 741 (SJ 88/98)
REFRESHMENTS Ship Inn, Styal (at start); tea-room and restaurant· at Quarry Bank Mill (when mill is open)

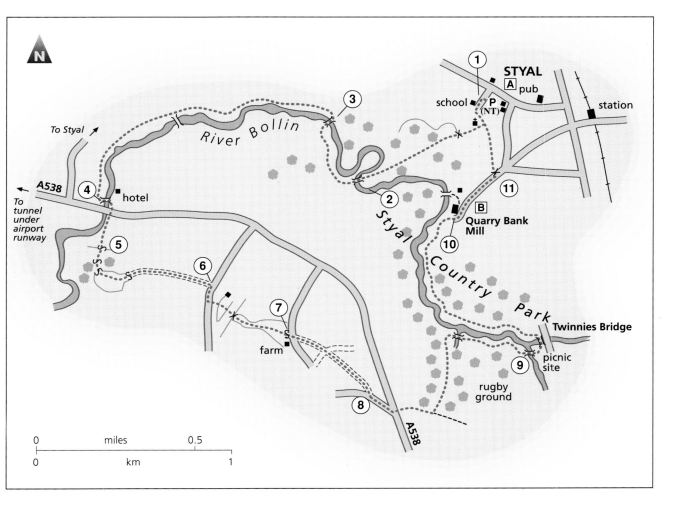

Part of the period window display in the Styal village shop

Continue forward (diagonally across field) as signposted (this is part of the Bollin Valley Way), to reach a footbridge over a small stream. Turn left on to path signposted to Morley Green, pass over stile on to a grassy track, then emerge on to the road ⑥. Turn right on the road for 100 yards then left on to a path (signposted Altrincham Road), immediately past farm entrance. The route crosses a small triangular field, runs along the left edge of field, then briefly between fences and finally bears quarter right across field to a stile in front of a farm ⑦.

Cross the road to take grassy track opposite, which runs between hedges. Continue forward at oblique junction of tracks after 200 yards and follow to the road ⑧. Turn left, and at main road cross to footpath opposite (signposted Twinnies Bridge). As soon as the path enters woods, turn left (signposted again).

Woodland path leads down to the River Bollin and turns right along it. 500 yards later the path turns right along right branch of river.

⑨ Cross the footbridge into picnic area; here there is also a car park and toilet block. Keep left, where there is a footbridge visible; this leads back into Styal Country Park. This area is a maze of paths: keep the river directly on your left until the path appears to run right: here take path keeping to left and going up a few steps to a path with a field on the right; the path goes over another footbridge and, keeping to the left, goes back to the river near to the mill dam and pool; the path turns right to the mill and visitor centre B ⑩. At the mill, follow the road uphill away from the river (path on left by mill, signposted Morley, gives a good view in front of building). ⑪ Just before the road reaches junction (Apprentices' House is ahead on left), *either* (to return to car park) turn left (signposted to Styal village),

through barrier marked No Cycles and follow clear field path to starting-point *or* (to return to the station) continue forward past Apprentices' House on a surfaced path between wooden railings and go straight on at junction of tarmac lanes. At road junction turn left; Station Road is the first on the right.

ON THE ROUTE

A **Styal village** Model dwellings built to house Samuel Greg's workforce who were employed at Quarry Bank Mill; the shop, chapel and school were built at the same time.

B **Quarry Bank Mill** (NT, *open to public*) A handsome building in a pretty woodland and river setting. Built by Samuel Greg of Belfast in 1784, for cotton spinning. It now houses a magnificent working mill museum. Weaving and spinning demonstrations are given. The Apprentices' House, now restored, can also be visited.

The beautiful Apprentices' House, part of Quarry Bank Mill, has been restored to its original state when it was home to the mill apprentices in about 1830

THREE SHIRE HEADS AND SHUTLINGSLOE

THE route mostly follows defined tracks up and along river valleys that dissect a landscape of exposed grassy moors and hills. An optional but strongly recommended ascent of Shutlingsloe is the highlight.

WALK DIRECTIONS

① Follow the surfaced track through the car park, uphill, past Clough House Farm on your right, to reach the road by grass triangle. Take the track opposite, signposted Cat and Fiddle. This ascends the valley, soon crossing a stream by footbridge where you keep right on the other side, up the valley, soon with woods on your right.

② After ¼ mile, keep close to stream, ignoring a left fork to a cottage. ③ Soon after, you reach a gate and turn right on a track around top of waterfall (signposted). ④ You reach a road ½ mile later. Cross a crash barrier opposite, go

down steps and find a stone stile in the far left-hand corner of small field. Beyond, turn left alongside the wall, downhill, to reach a track: there is now a farm away to your left.

> **LENGTH** 6 miles (9.5km), 3½ hours; 45 minutes less if avoiding ascent of Shutlingsloe
> **DIFFICULTY** 3 (with ascent of Shutlingsloe), 2 (without)
> **START** Clough House car park, Wildboarclough, north of A54 (Buxton–Congleton). Turn off A54 past Crag Inn in Wildboarclough; ¾ mile later pass a prominent signpost for path to Langley via Shutlingsloe on your left: the car park is not prominent. (There is also parking just south of Crag Inn.) Grid reference 987698
> **OS MAPS** Landranger 118 and 119; Outdoor Leisure 24
> **REFRESHMENTS** Crag Inn at Wildboarclough

Turn right on the track; ⑤ at the end of field, go through a gate, and turn left, down hill alongside a wall, towards the bottom of the valley. Soon the wall on your left bends right; keep alongside it (parallel with power lines on right), soon on a well-defined path along the valley floor, with a stream on your left. Reach bridges at Three Shire Heads

View from Wildboarclough, with Crag Hall in the middle distance

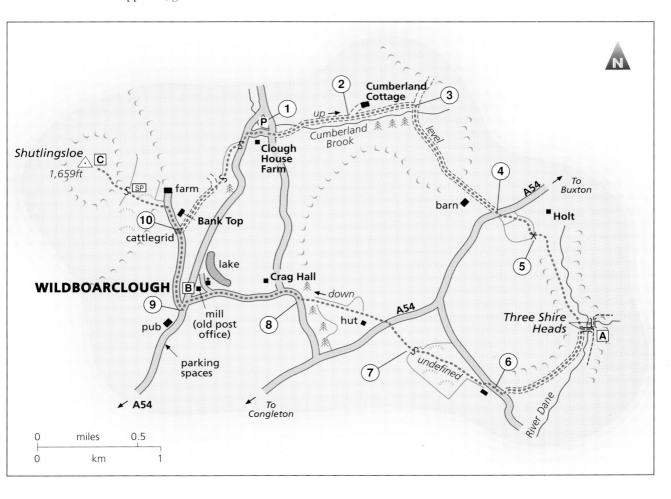

The ascent route is straightforward (100 yards before reaching next farm, leave road as waymarked for path on left and ascend via a stile visible ahead to the summit [c]; descend the same way). Follow the track past Bank Top; at the end of the next field, where wall on left ends, keep forward alongside a woodland fence, ignoring track on left which rises between walls. Soon cross a stile and proceed forward, now with wall on your left, to follow the well-defined path for ¼ mile to road. Turn left on the road and right soon after, into the car park.

ON THE ROUTE

[A] **Three Shire Heads** Two stone bridges mark an attractive meeting-point of three counties: Cheshire (near side), Derbyshire (over the first bridge) and Staffordshire (over the second).

[B] **Wildboarclough** Below Crag Hall, on the right of the road, is the handsome **old post office**, previously Crag Mill; three storeys, fine clock and a densely fenestrated facade (627 panes of glass on the front, and more at the back).

[C] **Shutlingsloe** (1,659ft) This conical grassy hill makes an excellent **viewpoint**; a view indicator points to landmarks, which include Mow Cop, Roach End, Cat's Tor, Croker Hill (with mast), the Cloud, the Cheshire plain and Macclesfield, Macclesfield Forest and Tittesworth Reservoir.

The unmistakable shape of Shutlingsloe rears above the smooth, whaleback Pennine hills of the Dark Peak

[A]. Keep on the right-hand side of the stream, on a level track. ⑥ After ⅓ mile, you reach a tarmacked lane: take the stile opposite and slightly to the right, just to the right of house. Cross small yard to enter a field: the path follows close to the wall on left heading towards Shutlingsloe (the crescent-shaped hilltop just peering over the skyline, soon disappearing from view).

Where the wall reaches a corner, the path becomes poorly defined: continue towards Shutlingsloe. The wall on your right is a useful guide; keep parallel to it, veering left as it does the same. At the top, the wall becomes dilapidated and eventually ends at top of a slightly pronounced valley. ⑦ Just before it ends, find a narrow stile in it with a clear path beyond, still heading for Shutlingsloe.

When you reach the road, cross to a signposted stile opposite and follow the well-defined path over moorland; beyond a stone hut, the path becomes grassy and descends into a wood to the road ⑧. Turn right along the road, bear left at the junction by Crag Hall [B], then past a church (ignore track forking right) to a T-junction. Turn left, then after 70 yards ⑨ sharp right (or keep on a few yards for the Crag Inn) on a rising farm road.

⑩ After ¼ mile you reach a cattlegrid: the continuation is right, on the track to Bank Top; left is *detour* to summit of Shutlingsloe.

THE STRUGGLE FOR PUBLIC ACCESS TO THE COUNTRYSIDE

Every weekend during the inter-war years, factory-workers surged from the mill and steel towns of northern England into the Peak District. Ramblers' clubs organised walks into the hills. Walking became the great working-class pastime.

But access to the hills at that time was extremely limited; no national network of rights of way existed. Much of the moorland was the preserve of game-keepers, who posted 'trespassers will be prosecuted' signs, and did everything they could to keep the ramblers out; even physical confrontations occurred. In 1923 a notorious advertisement appeared in the *Manchester Evening Chronicle*, with photographs of 'wanted' ramblers and offers of a £5 reward for any names and addresses. Three years later the ramblers responded by a public rally, calling for free access to open country and for the formation of National Parks.

In May 1932, 400 walkers publicised their deliberate mass trespass on to Kinder Scout in Derbyshire; a skirmish followed and ramblers were arrested. But the demonstrators had made their point. In 1945 John Dower published a report calling for the formation of National Parks. When the National Parks and Access to the Countryside Act was passed four years later, the machinery for surveying and definitive mapping of public rights of way was set up. In 1951 the Peak District became the first National Park in the country.

HALL DALE AND DOVE DALE

A DELECTABLE transition from the rolling plateau into secretive Hall Dale, which leads down into Dove Dale. The route avoids the most walked approach (which is from the large car park at its southern end; at peak times this can get extremely crowded) without missing any of its highlights. After a detour to see the dale's famous rock formations you continue to Milldale, then along a gently rising stone-walled lane to Alstonefield. Route-finding is generally easy, although the initial stages were not signposted or waymarked when the walk was checked.

LENGTH 4 miles, plus 1½ miles for recommended detour to Reynard's Cave in Dove Dale (6.5km plus 2km), 2 to 3 hours
DIFFICULTY 2
START Alstonefield, in the south part of the Peak; signposted free car park (with toilets) in village. Grid reference 130557
OS MAPS Landranger 119; Outdoor Leisure 24
REFRESHMENTS Pub in Alstonefield; shop (serving hot and cold drinks) at Milldale

WALK DIRECTIONS

① Ⓐ Turn right out of the village car park and right after 30 yards at a road T-junction (signposted Dove Dale), past telephone-box; turn left at T-junction in front of memorial hall, signposted Dove Dale and immediately ② take a track on the left, which soon runs between walls. Where the track bends right, take a gate ahead into a field, follow the right edge alongside a wall; ③ at the end of field, keep right into a small enclosed area, still keeping beside right-hand wall to take a gate and proceed downhill alongside the wall on your right to a road ④. Take signposted ascending track opposite.

⑤ When you reach road T-junction with grassy triangle at hamlet of Stanshope, keep left and

immediately left again on a track between walls, signposted Milldale.

After 100 yards, take gap-stile on right, signposted Dove Dale: head

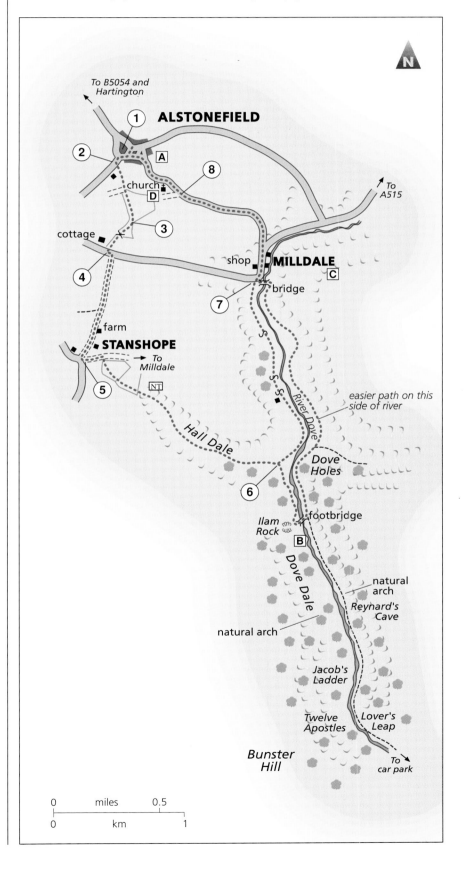

You pass this cottage in its glorious garden with dry-stone walling near the start

diagonally across the field in signposted direction to a stile in the left-hand wall; carry on in the same direction in the next field to a stile and proceed towards the valley of Hall Dale which you see directly ahead. The route goes down the centre of the dale and drops to Dove Dale ⑥: here the route continues to the left along Dove Dale (but you can detour right, crossing the river by the next bridge, to see the most famous section of the gorge – as far as Reynard's Cave, a natural arch, is recommended Ⓑ). There is a path on the near side of the river which is less crowded at peak times than the more level path on the other side, and later rises a little to get fine views (if you wish to cross the river, turn right as you reach Dove Dale, to take a footbridge at Ilam Rock, which is the first big outcrop).

⑦ At the hamlet of Milldale Ⓒ, pass in front of the shop and ignore path on left signposted Alstonefield by the telephone-box; follow the

lane to Alstonefield – ⑧ ignore a minor left turn before you reach Alstonefield church Ⓓ; in the village centre, turn left to reach the car park.

ON THE ROUTE

Ⓐ **Alstonefield** The quiet and unspoilt village stands between the Dove and Manifold dales and has some attractive corners around its green, with a number of characteristically mullioned cottages and a 16th-century hall. Alstonefield grew as a busy market centre after receiving its charter in 1308. Cattle sales took place up to the early years of the 20th century.

Ⓑ **Dove Dale** This favourite of all the Peak District dales is notable both for its towering limestone crags and its magnificent broad-leaved woodlands. Fanciful names adhere to the rock formations: beyond **Ilam Rock**, which rises to 120ft, the path southwards passes **Lion's Head Rock** (named for obvious reasons), **Reynard's Cave** (a natural arch), **Jacob's Ladder** and **Tissington Spires**. **Lover's Leap** is a 130ft high spur from which a jilted girl in the 18th century tried to hurl herself to her death, only to have her fall

---

A WALK FROM HARTINGTON

The steep-sided Wolfscote Dale, the effective northern continuation of Dove Dale, can be reached from a well-trodden path from near the toilet block at Hartington. Charles Cotton's fishing house in seen in Wolfscote Dale, close to the site of Beresford Hall, where he lived. After about 2 miles, turn left into Biggin Dale, partly designated a nature reserve for its profusion of flora characteristic of the limestone country. Further up the dale, a path leads back towards Hartington; a very quiet lane is followed for the final section.

The classic limestone scenery of Dove Dale, the Peak District's most popular dale

broken by the bushes, leaving her a little scratched and surprised. As the walk heads northwards, the shallow caves of **Dove Holes** and the crag of **Raven's Tor** are passed.

Ⓒ **Milldale** The setting inspired Izaak Walton and Charles Cotton to write the classic work on fly-fishing, *The Compleat Angler or the Contemplative Man's Recreation* (1653), a pastoral reflection on the joys of the sport as enjoyed on the rivers Dove and Lea. In the book the compact size of Milldale's packhorse bridge, known as Viator's Bridge, was immortalised: 'Why! A mouse can hardly go over it; it is but two fingers broad.'

Ⓓ **Alstonefield church** occupies a site where there has been a place of worship since 892. The present building has some Norman work, notably the south doorway and chancel arch, but principally it displays Decorated and Perpendicular styles, as well as some fine 17th-century box pews and double-decker pulpit.

AROUND CROMFORD, SITE OF THE EARLY INDUSTRIAL REVOLUTION

THIS route takes in Arkwright's historic village and mills, the track of the vanished High Peak Railway and the Cromford Canal towpath. Route-finding is easy once you are on the High Peak Trail.

WALK DIRECTIONS

① Make your way up the main street (B5036) towards Wirksworth. Opposite A5012 (Via Gellia) take the narrow lane on the left to see the sluice [A] and follow the path beyond it to the right, to reach a road. Turn right to reach North Street (tall terraced houses on either side) [B] and turn right along it to rejoin the main road.

② Turn left, uphill, [C] for 100 yards to a bus stop, then turn left into Bedehouse Lane. Immediately fork right, then right again 30 yards later by No Cycling sign on a path between walls (with houses on right and Black Rock, which you soon reach, visible on the skyline ahead). By a lamp-post [D], the path bends right and immediately left to become a lane. Follow it up to a T-junction with residential road ③, where you take the enclosed path opposite and slightly to the right.

LENGTH	5 miles (8km), 2½ hours
DIFFICULTY	1–2

START Cromford village centre, at junction of A5012 and B5036, between Matlock and Wirksworth. Grid reference 296569 *By train* Cromford

OS MAPS Landranger 119; Outdoor Leisure 24

REFRESHMENTS Cafés, pubs, shops in Cromford; café at Cromford Mill

When you reach a lane, turn left along it: the lane bends right uphill

Cromford Canal was once used for transporting goods to the North-West's industrial centres

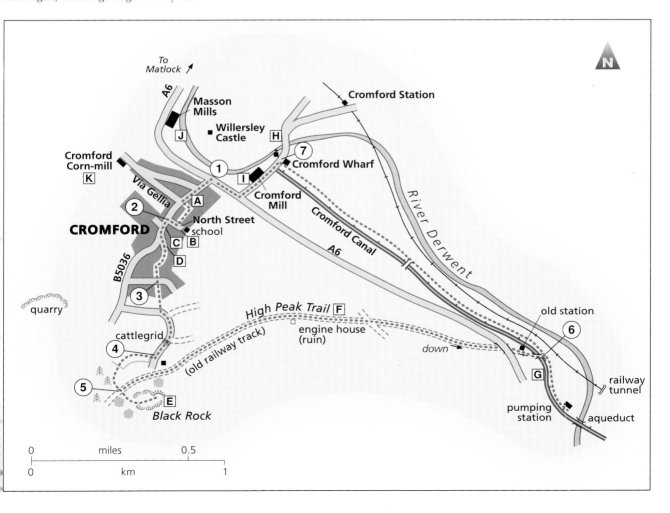

after 50 yards. 150 yards later keep right at the fork.

④ Immediately before a house, take the gate on the right and walk alongside wall (heading towards distant quarry) along the top of a field. At the end, you enter woods, bear quarter right, slightly downhill; pick up clear path ascending through woods and soon leaving fence, passing a car park away to your right. ⑤ Soon you reach an old railway track (enclosed by stone walls), at the base of Black Rock. Turn left along the railway track (the High Peak Trail) to continue, or make a detour to the top of the rocks [E].

Follow the railway track for 1½ miles [F], down a long slope and under the A6 to reach the canal ⑥ [G]. Cross to the far side, turn left along the towpath to continue the route but first turn right along towpath to detour past the pumphouse to the aqueduct; then return and follow the towpath to Cromford, emerging opposite the church ⑦ [H].

Turn left on road, past Cromford Mill on your right [I], then cross A6 (or turn right along it for ¼ mile to detour to Masson Mills [J]), into the village centre. Here you can detour to see two more mills: take the first right (before reaching Greyhound Hotel) on a narrow lane signposted to post office; at junction with main road, one mill is ahead and on left [K]. Go past a mill-pond and mill complete with water-wheel, and return to the main road.

ON THE ROUTE

[A] The semi-circular **sluice**, constructed in 1785, supplied water to local cotton-mills.
[B] **North Street**, with its model three-storey dwellings fronting directly on to a broad street, was the first planned street of its kind in industrial Derbyshire, built by Richard Arkwright (see [I]) in 1776–77 to house mill-workers.
[C] More Industrial Revolution houses front Cromford's main street.

Cromford, one of the cradles of the Industrial Revolution

Nos 9, 11, 31 and 37 (all on left as you go up the street) are good examples, retaining their original small-pane windows.
[D] At the top of Bedehouse Lane, by the lamp-post, are the single-storey 17th-century **almshouses** that give the lane its name.
[E] **View** from Black Rock: on the other side of Cromford, the neat, symmetrical mansion in honey-coloured stone is **Willersley Castle**, built for Richard Arkwright but not completed until 1792, after his death. To the left of it are **Masson Mills** (to which you can detour later in the walk). Beyond are the **Derwent Gorge, High Tor** (an inland cliff) and the cable-car line to the **Heights of Abraham; Riber Castle** is away to the right.
[F] **High Peak Trail** Follows an old railway track which operated 1831–1967, connecting the Cromford and Peak Forest canals. The 33-mile goods line rose 990 feet to a height of 1,264ft, making the sharp ascent at the Cromford Canal end via the **inclined plane** down which the walk passes; haulage for trains was provided by an engine house at the top of the incline (now partly ruined, but with an explanatory plaque). At the bottom, beyond a short tunnel with half a railway track embedded in it, is a short section of reinstated track, with two old guards' vans, by the **old station**.
[G] **Cromford Canal** Completed 1793, it runs for 14½ miles to join the Erewash Canal at Langley Mill, so linking Cromford with Manchester, Liverpool and other

major industrial centres, and used to transport raw cotton, yarn and minerals. The canal leads to the right past the **Leawood Pumphouse**, built 1849 for pumping water into the canal (still with its original beam engine; *occasionally open to the public*), to the **Wigwell aqueduct**, triple-arched and 600ft long. Returning along the canal towards Cromford, the still-extant **railway** on the right was opened in 1849 as the Manchester, Buxton, Matlock and Midlands Junction Railway. At **Cromford Wharf**, once a busy goods and passenger port, a **horse-drawn barge** for tourist traffic operates in summer.
[H] Arkwright is buried in **St Mary's church**, which was originally a private chapel in the grounds of Arkwright's home, Willersley Castle, but became the village church in 1797.
[I] **Cromford Mill** (*open* 10 to 4.30 Monday to Friday, 11 to 5 Saturday and Sunday; closes 3.30 in winter) Here in 1771 Sir Richard Arkwright established the world's first water-powered cotton-spinning mill. In the 1840s, cotton production moved to Lancashire as water power gave way to steam power. Arkwright perfected the water frame in nearby Arkwright House in 1768, and decided to use water power from the Bonsall Brook and Cromford Sough for this mill. A second mill on the site was in production by 1777. Opposite the mill entrance is the **mill manager's house**, and on the hill is **Rock House**, Arkwright's home before he moved to Willersley Castle.
[J] **Masson Mills** (off route: follow A6 towards Matlock) Another Arkwright mill, built in 1783. Its six storeys, Venetian windows, cupola and alien red brick tell of great prosperity.
[K] The mill ahead is **Cromford Corn-Mill** (being restored), which functioned from the late 18th century until about 1930; to the left is a former paint-grinding mill retaining its water-wheel.

THE RIVER DERWENT AND FROGGATT EDGE

A ROUTE with splendid variety: mixed woodlands, river banks and pasture on the valley floor, before a steep rise up on to the gritstone edge for two miles of majestic views; finishes with an abrupt descent to Calver. Not all field-paths are defined.

LENGTH 6½ miles (10.5km), 3½ hours

DIFFICULTY 2

START The Bridge pub, Calver, on A623 (north-northeast of Bakewell) at east end of village, by bridge and signpost for Froggatt and Curbar. Parking on minor road by the pub and school. Grid reference 248744

OS MAPS Landranger 119; Outdoor Leisure 24

REFRESHMENTS Pub at Calver; pub, tea-room and shop at Grindleford; Grouse Inn near ⑨

WALK DIRECTIONS

① With the pub on your left and the church on your right take road half right with speed derestriction sign and signpost for Froggatt and Sheffield. The road runs beside the river, and a mill is seen on the other side Ⓐ. 100 yards after the mill, take the signposted riverside path on the left, later passing a weir Ⓑ. ② Cross the road-bridge and turn right on the other side, on riverside path. ③ Cross next road-bridge, then turn left at T-junction, ignoring an immediate right turn called The Green; follow this through the village. ④ At next junction keep straight on, signposted Grindleford Bridge,

where right goes steeply uphill. This lane soon becomes unsurfaced, then the wall on left ends. Where the wall on right ends (and turns right up to barn) bear half right across field to entrance in wall (ahead is signposted as private) then ⑤ keep forward, with the wall on your left.

In next field, continue forward to a stile into Froggatt Woods by National Trust sign. The path through the woods may be muddy,

Part of the Bronze Age stone circle along Froggatt Edge

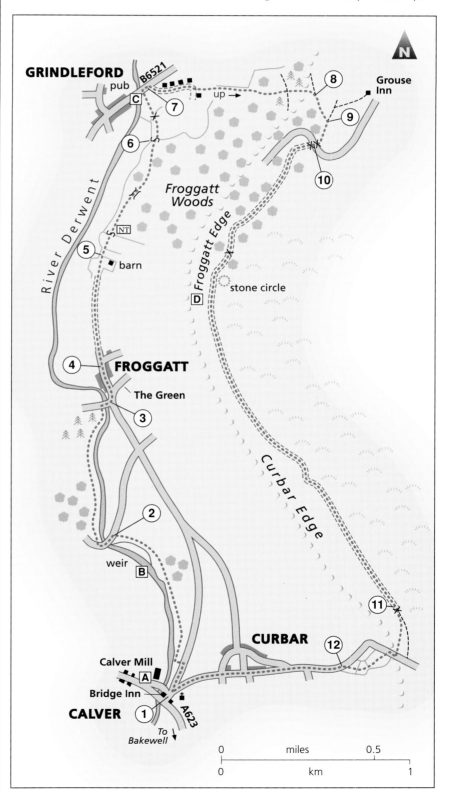

but is easy to follow – running along the wall on your left until a slab bridge then proceeding for ¼ mile to a gap-stile into field ⑥. Go forward, with wall on left; 50 yards after the wall is replaced by a fence, take the gate on left, head diagonally across the field towards the filling station (to right of bridge) at the edge of Grindleford Ⓒ.

Turn right on the road, then after 30 yards ⑦ take a track on your right. After the houses on left end, track bends right; 50 yards later, just before an isolated group of cottages, take the path on left (signposted Froggatt Edge and Grouse Inn) which climbs through woods towards the top of a slope (at first with a wall on the left; where the wall reaches a corner, continue up and slightly to the right; keep forward after 200 yards at a cross-junction by metal well-cover). ⑧ Close to the top, turn right at path T-junction, to reach a gate by power post ⑨. (*To detour to Grouse Inn*, turn left, then left again by signpost, to cross stile; 50 yards later, take a gate on your right and cross fields diagonally to the inn visible ahead – the stile on to the road is just to the right of the inn).

Turn right to continue, soon reaching a stile; the path then drops to cross a stream and rises to a road. Turn right on the road, and immediately ⑩ left through a gate by sign for Eastern Moors Estate. Follow this broad path along Froggatt Edge for 2 miles Ⓓ. ⑪ Beyond the gate by next Eastern Moors sign, turn right, down towards Curbar, to reach the road, and follow it until taking a path on the left by a National Trust sign for Curbar Gap (or simply continue

A dramatic view seen through jagged gritstone rocks that form the extensive Froggatt Edge at the climax of the walk

down the road back to the start).

The path heads through old enclosures, reaching two stone posts after 50 yards, where you continue down towards the village, with wall on right, to a National Trust sign (facing other way), then forward for 30 yards to the squeeze-stile, and along the left edge of fields to rejoin the road. ⑫ Follow the road down through Curbar and back to the start (keep straight on at crossroads by telephone-box).

ON THE ROUTE

Ⓐ **Calver Mill** across the river was built by Richard Arkwright in 1805 on the site of an 18th-century cotton-mill.

Ⓑ In the 18th century Daniel Defoe observed the **River Derwent** to be 'a fury of a river . . . a frightful creature when the hills load her current.' Banking has now reduced the risk of flooding, but the weir, old bridges and fine broad-leafed woodlands still contribute to its romantic quality. Wild geese are a common sight.

Ⓒ An antique **footpath signpost** is dated 1908. Several of this vintage survive in the Peak District.

Ⓓ **Froggatt Edge** and Curbar Edge Coppice give way to boulders, tors and overhangs along the gritstone edge, which in its entirety can be followed for a 15-mile walk. This is particularly dramatic at the south end, with an extensive view of the valley and an outcrop shaped like a lizard's head. Local **quarries** once provided many of the nation's millstones. 200 yards after the gate, just to left of path, look out for a **Bronze Age stone circle**, about 25ft in diameter, with some eight uprights (depending on what is included), three feet high.

CASTLETON AND MAM TOR

STARTING from one of the Peak's most remarkable villages, the walk heads over farmland and ascends steeply 400 feet on to the great ridge which dominates the Hope Valley – a fine 360-degree panorama for a mile is the reward, culminating at the ancient fort site on Mam Tor. The route then drops down past show caves and the entrance of Winnats Pass before returning to Castleton.

WALK DIRECTIONS

① Ⓐ Take the road opposite the Bull's Head public house in the village centre, signposted Peveril Castle and leading past the Castle and George inns and the Youth Hostel on your right, just after which you turn right (signposted Peak Cavern). Just after crossing the

river, turn right (left turn goes to Peak Cavern – it's worth the short detour to see the huge cave entrance Ⓑ) on track through the Peak Cavern car park. Turn left at the main road, then ② immediately right on to a signposted path (leaving the road just to left of house called Fairholme) between walls to enter a field: keep left along

Peveril Castle, said to have been built by an illegitimate son of William the Conqueror

the left edge of field, at the end of which cross a stile and proceed along the right edge of the next two fields (the ridge you will soon climb is in view ahead, with the summit of Mam Tor at its left end).

③ Emerge on to a farm road at a

LENGTH 5 miles (8km), 3 hours
DIFFICULTY 2–3
START Castleton village, on the A625 at the centre of the Peak District National Park. Car park and roadside parking in village. Grid reference 149829
OS MAPS Landranger 110; Outdoor Leisure 1
REFRESHMENTS Pubs, shops and cafés in Castleton; the show caves passed later in the walk each sell a limited range of snacks

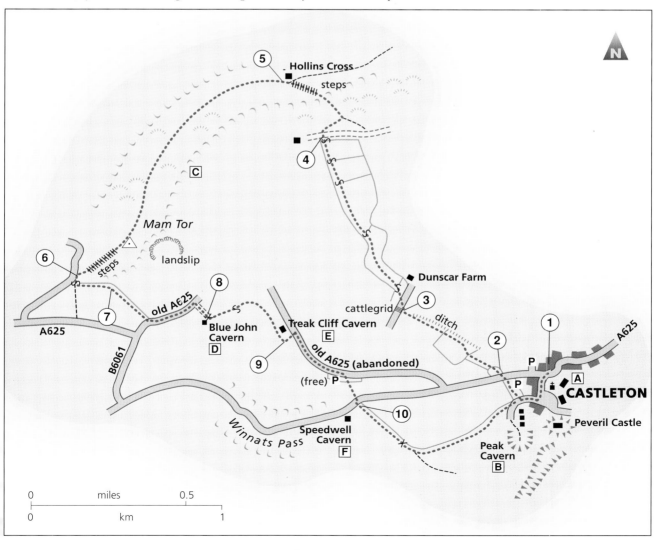

cattlegrid, turn right to cross the brook and immediately left through a gate to enter a field: the next section is marked by yellow painted fence posts – cross the first field diagonally to a stile beside a gate, follow the right edge of second field to the far right-hand corner, keep left in the third field (signposted Edale); follow the left edge of next field, then maintain the same direction to emerge on to track with a house away to your left at the limit of the cultivated land ④. Cross the stile opposite and climb the path diagonally right up moorland hill, soon joining a wider path at a T-junction, leading up left, soon up steps, to the top of the ridge at Hollins Cross ⑤. Turn left along the ridge to Mam Tor ⓒ, the summit has a trig point (summit pillar), continuing on the far side down steps.

⑥ As soon as path joins a road, turn sharp left down steps to a stile by a signpost. Turn left on path (marked with posts), signposted Blue John, proceeding close by a fence/wall on the left and soon ⑦ bending right to drop to a gate on to a road. Turn left on the road, then right on access road to the entrance of Blue John Cavern ⓓ. ⑧ Turn left at the cavern building, over a ladder-stile beside a gate. Carry on ahead (no defined path), on the level, soon dropping to take a stile in fence, then on a defined path ahead, contouring around to the right to reach Treak Cliff Cavern building ⓔ, on the far side of which turn left on a concrete path.

⑨ Continue past the cave building and descend to the road;

Castleton may be geared up for tourists but its special atmosphere still wins through

turn right along the road, then turn right through car park and follow a short path up to Speedwell Cavern ⓕ with Winnats Pass on your right. Turn left along the road for 50 yards then ⑩ take signposted gate on the right. Follow the path alongside or just above wall on left: after the next gate, this bends left and gradually drops (ignore ascending right fork) to enter Castleton. Proceed on the back road into the village centre. Just after crossing the river, turn left on a path back to the car park.

ON THE ROUTE

Ⓐ **Castleton** Lying at the geographical heart of the Peak District, Castleton is a large village dissected by a former mill brook and overshadowed by the gaunt ruins of **Peveril Castle**, dating from Norman times. Souvenir vases and trinkets made from a mauve crystalline fluorspar known as Blue John, which is only found in this area, are sold locally and can be seen in the Ollerenshaw Collection, a one-room **museum.** The **church** of St Edmund was comprehensively restored in 1837 but retains a complete set of 17th-century box pews.

Ⓑ **Peak Cavern** The awe-inspiringly vast cave entrance, Europe's largest, is sited in a narrow gorge beneath Peveril Castle. A former rope-maker's cottage, inhabited until 1830, huddles just inside the natural cavern, with surviving rope-making apparatus and a rope-walk behind. Known as the Devil's Arse until Victorian times, the cave system is the biggest in the country. Only a fraction is shown on the guided tour, but this gives a good idea of its size; there are no significant stalactite concretions.

Ⓒ **Mam Tor** The ridge walk to Mam Tor affords grandstand views, with the village of Edale visible to the right, snuggled beneath the lofty plateau of Kinder Scout; the Pennine Way begins its 270-mile route from Edale to Kirk Yetholm in the Scottish Borders. Mam Tor itself, the highest point on the walk, has ramparts of a Bronze and Iron Age hillfort. It is known as the 'Shivering Mountain', because of its tendency to succumb to landslips:

soft shale underlies harder gritstone, and when the shale is eroded, the hillside has collapsed. This has led to the closure of the A625 below the mountain, which on this side resembles a quarried slope. To the left, the huge chimney of the cement works at Bradwell dominates the Hope valley.

Ⓓ **Blue John Cavern** The guided tour passes outcrops of Blue John (see Castleton, above) and glistening 'flow rock', formed by dripping water. There are no stalactite formations of any significance, but you experience some exciting moments when unexpected narrow depths of the cavern are revealed.

Ⓔ **Treak Cliff Cavern** A short cavern that has been mined for Blue John. It has some very pretty stalactite formations; pieces of Blue John are placed over lights to show the rock's translucent quality.

Ⓕ **Speedwell Cavern** The only cave visit in the Peak District with an **underground boat trip**, which leads along a flooded tunnel blasted out by lead-miners. At the end of the tunnel is a narrow and phenomenally tall natural cavern. **Winnats Pass** is a cave that collapsed, leaving a spectacular limestone gorge. It was a rallying ground in the inter-war years when thousands of ramblers met to demonstrate for free access to open countryside.

TWO MORE CAVES

Bagshawe Cavern, on the edge of Bradwell, is the cave to visit if you want to experience some of the elements of true caving; guided tours involve scrambling, wading and crawling through chimneys and natural features with names such as the Letter Box and Agony Crawl. There is also an electrically lit show-cave with stalagmites and stalactites. **Poole Cavern**, just outside Buxton, is arguably the most beautiful of them all, and takes its name from an outlaw who is thought to have used the cavern as a hideaway in the 1440s; evidence of much earlier occupants is on display in a small museum. The concretions include stalactites, fragile 'straw formations' and unique stalagmites coloured rusty orange by the seeping of water through iron ore. At one point you look 500 feet along the longest show-cave view in Britain.

CLUMBER PARK

A GENTLE walk in a huge landscaped parkland with fine trees (predominantly oak, beech, Spanish chestnut and lime), some coniferous plantations and more open terrain. Paths and tracks are mostly well defined; route-finding is a little complicated through woodland. There is a fee to enter the park (free for National Trust members).

WALK DIRECTIONS

① Ⓐ From the car park, walk along the wide lakeside path in a clockwise direction, with the lake on your right Ⓑ. ② Cross over the footbridge above weir. After 250 yards, where the main path bears right, fork left along the track away from the lake, through woodland. In 50 yards, the path runs along the left-hand side of large field; keep the fence on your right, walking just inside the wood. At corner of field take the path ahead through scrub-woodland. Where the path becomes ill-defined, continue ahead through scrub and cross straight over the next track ③ to reach a tarmac estate road in front of dense pine forest ④.

LENGTH 4½ miles (7km), 2½ hours	Hardwick village. Take first left after houses and go downhill to the car park on the left beside lake. Grid reference 636755
DIFFICULTY 1	
START Car park close to Hardwick village, inside Clumber Park, 5 miles south-east of Worksop. Turn off A614 4½ miles north of Ollerton roundabout directly opposite Clumber Park Hotel to enter Clumber Park by Mormanton Gate; follow the park road which turns right and descends to cross a ford, then passes	**OS MAPS** Landranger 120; Pathfinder 763 (SK 67/77); Clumber Park map published by the National Trust
	REFRESHMENTS National Trust café in park, after ⑦

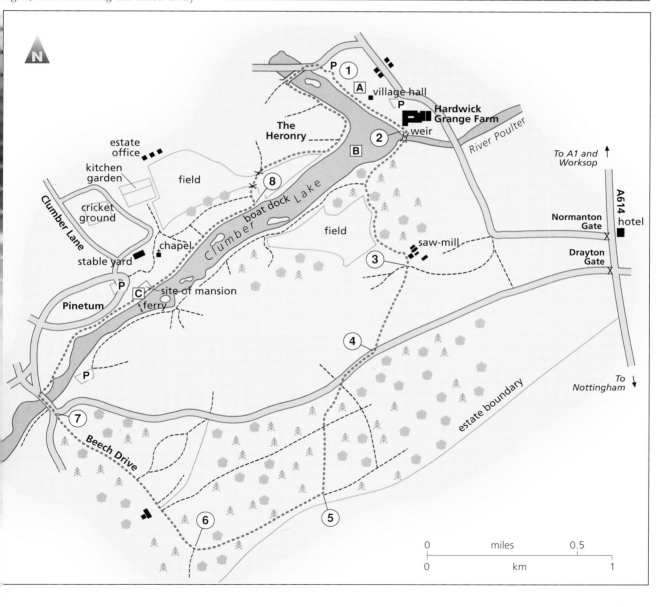

A pair of red-crested pochard, among numerous birds that live round Clumber Lake

Turn right along the road walking slightly downhill to the lowest point. Enter woodland (waymarked) via a log barrier on your left* and immediately fork right. ⑤ At T-junction with cleared area ahead turn right and follow the track with shady yew trees on your right. Where the yew trees end at log barriers ⑥, turn right and follow this track for ½ mile, ignoring side tracks, to reach roads at Clumber Bridge ⑦.

Cross over the bridge and turn immediately right on to a path near the lake. Follow the lake closely, passing the Grotto, until you are level with the site of the house, restaurant, shop and church. Visit as appropriate ☐c☐. Rejoin the lakeside path through the Lincoln Terrace to the boat dock ⑧. Turn left through the rhododendrons, bearing right to exit at a stone-arched gate. Cross the field into woodland via the kissing-gate, turning right to follow the lakeside path. Turn right over footbridge and right again to reach the start.

* NB If woodland is closed for forestry operations, continue along Drayton Road to reach Clumber Bridge at ⑦.

ON THE ROUTE

☐A☐ **Clumber Park** is the former seat of the Dukes of Newcastle and one of the four estates that constitute the Dukeries, the others being Worksop, Thoresby and Welbeck.

The park was once part of the huge Sherwood forest; in 1707 a licence was granted for its enclosure as a hunting park. When it became developed as a great estate, the lake was created and ornate lodges were erected around the park. Between the two World Wars the public was denied access to the park, and in the Second World War it was used as an ammunition dump. Happily, the National Trust has taken it over and opened it to the public. Large areas are managed forestry, and are occasionally closed during felling operations. *Open* (Park) all year during daylight hours.

☐B☐ **Birds** on the lake include Canada geese, mallards, tufted ducks, coots, moorhens, great crested grebes, swans, pochards and herons. The lake took 15 years to construct.

☐c☐ **Clumber House** Built in 1767 and demolished in 1938. John Murray, in his *Handbook for Travellers* (1892), wrote: 'The park was laid out, planted, and in fact created by the great-great-grandfather of the present Duke. The house, though of stone, is not imposing externally, from want of height; but it has comfort and splendour within. In 1879 nearly all the rooms were consumed by fire. It has been replaced by a fine Central Hall in classic style by Charles Barry. The state Dining-room will accommodate 150 guests.' Its near priceless collection of pictures, which includes works by Rembrandt, Rubens, Raphael, Van Dyck, Holbein, Dürer and Gainsborough, is on exhibition at the Nottingham Castle Museum. Its Victorian chapel of St Mary stands intact. Close by are the stable yard, palm house, kitchen garden and pleasure grounds – the latter adorned by Roman and Grecian 'temple' follies.

A classical bridge over the man-made lake in Clumber Park. The Park is also dignified by Europe's longest double lime avenue. Although Clumber House is no more, visitors are welcome between April and September (Sat, Sun, bank holiday Mon, 10 to 5) at the vineries and exhibition centre

ANSTON BROOK AND CHESTERFIELD CANAL

A WOODED valley and the tranquil towpath of the disused canal constitute something of an oasis amid agricultural landscape; the walk is pleasant throughout and the going underfoot is easy. Field-paths are well defined.

WALK DIRECTIONS

① With the church on your right and the B6060 to Dinnington on left follow Sheffield Road. Where the road bends right, take an unmade lane straight ahead, soon cross the A57 and take the track opposite (to left of filling station). At the rear of the building, bear slightly left (avoid hard-standing area) across a field, go over railway and soon over a footbridge.

② Turn right on other side of the footbridge, keeping stream on right

and ignoring left forks. Ⓐ The path leads under the railway bridge, still keeping stream on right (ignore next crossing under the next bridge 150 yards later). ③ After ½ mile, path crosses stream then under another railway bridge and has stream on left, rising to the A57 (beware of traffic) ④. Turn left along the road, then after 200 yards take road turning on right for Lindrick Dale.

⑤ After ⅓ mile fork left at footpath signpost in front of The Cottage (a house with an old-fashioned lamp-post). Keep cottage on your right. Track rises to reach a sign for Lindrick Golf Club; go forward, entering golf course and keep right along right edge of it. The path runs through a short patch of woodland and re-emerges on to golf course: keep to the right edge,

avoiding metal bridge on right, but ⑥ at three-way signpost take right-hand path over next bridge (a stone one), leading into woods.

Ignore gates on both sides just after crossing a water channel and

---

LENGTH 5 miles (8km), 2½ hours
DIFFICULTY 2
START South Anston parish church (do not confuse with Methodist church) at east side of village, at junction with B6060 and Sheffield Road, off A57/M1 junction. Roadside parking in village. Grid reference 519837
OS MAPS Landranger 111 or 120; Pathfinder 744 (SK 48/58)
REFRESHMENTS Shop, chip shop and pubs in South Anston; pub in Thorpe Salvin

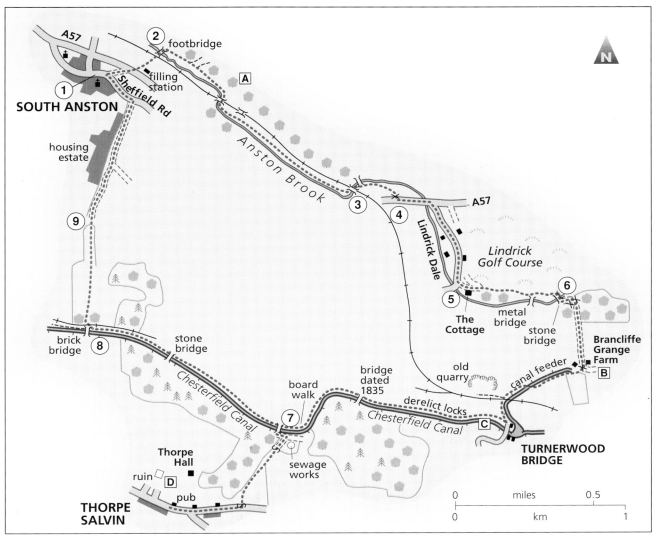

follow the track up out of woods and across a field to Brancliffe Grange Farm B. Turn right in farmyard, cross a stile beside a gate and go slightly right to next stile beside gate, then follow path beside water channel (canal feeder); path soon crosses the other side of channel.

After ¼ mile, take stile on left, and cross the railway carefully, continuing on a path beside the canal feeder. Just before a house garden, turn right to leave the feeder and reach Turnerwood Bridge, on the near side of which you turn right on to the canal towpath (walking with the canal on your left) C. *For detour to Thorpe Salvin* ⑦ Cross the next bridge but one (after ¾ mile; it is just after crossing boards over channel draining from the canal); keep left on the other side (initially doubling back) on main track; after 80 yards take waymarked steps leading to an enclosed path, passing to the right of sewage works, then along the right edge of two fields, keeping beside woodland to reach a stile on to a road. The village is to the right D; return the same way.

To continue Follow towpath from Turnerwood Bridge for 1½ miles: the third bridge you pass under is stone; ⑧ leave the canal immediately before the fourth bridge (a patched-up brick bridge), taking a stile on the right. Follow path over railway and through a wooded area then up the middle of a field (path was well defined at time of inspection: if it is obscured by crops, the route runs parallel to and 150 yards from left edge of field (close to hedge on right, then continues along narrow strip, passing between stone posts at end); ⑨ continue on track along left edge of field (hedge now on left), soon with houses on your left. At the road at the edge of village, turn left to return to the start.

ON THE ROUTE

A **Anston Stones Wood** Cowslips and bee orchids are among the flora; the woods are deep and secretive, with sandstone crags here and there, and red squirrels are sometimes seen. A cave to the left, just after you join the valley, has yielded evidence of pre-historic man: flints, reindeer and brown bear bones have been found.

The red squirrel survives in pockets where the grey squirrel has failed to invade

B **Brancliffe Grange Farm** Until the dissolution of Roche Abbey in 1538, this was a monastic grange for Cistercian monks.

C **Chesterfield Canal** Now derelict, its locks ruined and bed choked with weeds, the canal was surveyed·by James Brindley, pioneer of the canal network, in 1769 and completed after his death in 1777. It led from Chesterfield to Worksop and Retford, linking up with the River Trent at Stockwith; lead and coal were carried this way. In 1908, the half-mile long Norwood Tunnel (to the west) collapsed and the canal never reopened in its entirety.

D **Thorpe Salvin** If detouring to the pub, you may like also to visit the **church** which has some good Norman work and a fine font, and the 16th-century **hall**, built for the Sandfords and later owned by the Osbournes until 1697 when they moved to Kiveton Park, abandoning this structure to fall into ruin.

The cowslip (Primula veris), like its relative the primrose, thrives in damp soils, particularly in woods and meadows and on grassy banks

PLOUGHING UP PATHS

The Rights of Way Act 1990 lays down the requirement for farmers to reinstate public paths after ploughing has taken place. The surface must be made good and the line made apparent on the ground within 14 days of the first disturbance for that crop or 24 hours of any subsequent disturbance (unless a longer period has first been agreed by the highway authority). This applies only to paths that cross fields. Paths along field edges may not be ploughed.

BURBAGE ROCKS AND CARL WARK

T HE walk skirts a deep
moorland basin, an impressive
boulder-strewn expanse fringed by
Burbage Rocks on one side and the
summits of Higger Tor and Carl
Wark on the other. Rough and
rugged in character but reasonably
easy going, and in clear weather
the route is obvious.

LENGTH 4½ miles (7km), 2½ hours

DIFFICULTY 2

START Woodcroft National Trust car
park, Longshaw Estate, off B6055
and 200 yards south of junction with
A625 (Hathersage–Sheffield) at Fox
House Inn. Entrance on west side of
road; not very prominently
signposted. Grid reference 267801

OS MAPS Landranger 110;
Pathfinder 743 (SK 28/38)

REFRESHMENTS Fox House Inn (near
start; not on route)

WALK DIRECTIONS

① Ⓐ Start by National Trust sign,
facing into car park with its road
entrance behind you. Take the path
ahead signposted to visitor centre,
which reaches a stone bridge just
visible from car park. Beyond bridge,
turn right at T-junction with a track
near house and ② turn right on
tarmacked driveway. Cross the main
road and take a gate opposite and
slightly to right. Follow the track
through semi-wooded area, forking
right after 300 yards towards a bus
stop and Road Bends sign.

③ Ⓑ Cross the road and take the
right-hand of two signposted paths,
over a stile and rising. The shape of
walk is now apparent. You will skirt
the rim of the massive natural

hollow you see before you in an
anti-clockwise direction; the
summits of Carl Wark and Higger
Tor (beyond) are half left. Keep to
higher ground, avoiding left forks,
soon past a prominently rectangular
stone trough on to a well-defined
path along the top of the edge.

④ Where the edge ends, the path
bends left, initially along a line of
stones (former wall), passes between
cairns then along top of another
rocky edge until reaching the road
⑤. Turn left on road, over two
bridges, then left on a broad track.
⑥ Immediately take signposted stile

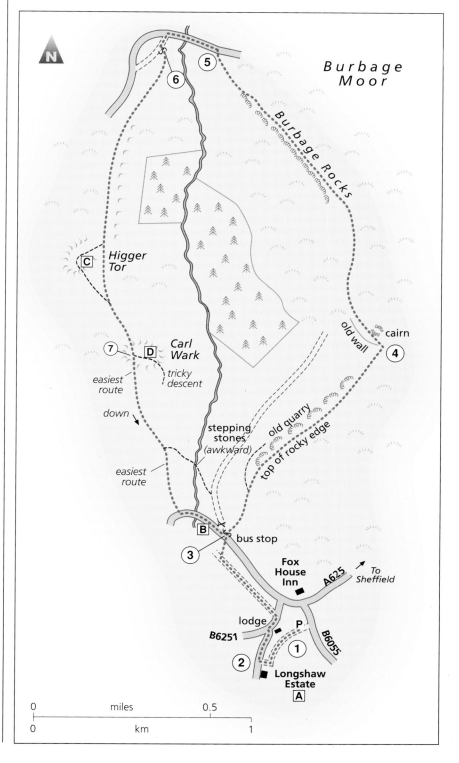

*Carl Wark, seen from the open moorland of
the National Trust's Longshaw Estate*

PLOUGHING UP PATHS

The Rights of Way Act 1990 lays down the requirement for farmers to reinstate public paths after ploughing has taken place. The surface must be made good and the line made apparent on the ground within 14 days of the first disturbance for that crop or 24 hours of any subsequent disturbance (unless a longer period has first been agreed by the highway authority). This applies only to paths that cross fields. Paths along field edges may not be ploughed.

The view from Burbage Rocks out over Burbage Moor

on the left and take the right-hand of two signposted paths, which goes along the top of the edge before proceeding to the summit of Higger Tor c.

After this proceed down to Carl Wark ⑦ D, where path turns left past remains of stone wall: the easiest route is to keep immediately right after it does this, finding a path leading directly towards the road. The stream away to the left can be forded at boulders, but it is easier to follow path on near side (skirting raised slope on your right). If in doubt, head for dip in road. Turn left on road, then right through a gate by bus stop and retrace steps (follow track to next road; cross to drive by lodge; turn left just before house, then left after 30 yards, over bridge, into the car park).

ON THE ROUTE

A **Longshaw Estate** Parkland and woodland, once belonging to the Duke of Rutland, but purchased by subscription in 1927 and donated to the National Trust. **Longshaw Lodge**, a former shooting lodge, is soon passed on the walk. This is a major venue for sheepdog trials, held in September.

B A boulder by the road at the sharp bend is known as the **Toad's Mouth**, because of its appearance (further enhanced by a man-made addition resembling an eye).

C **Higger Tor** (1,261ft) offers a wide **view** of the Hope Valley (including the chimney of the Bradwell cement works), and the bleak moors west of Sheffield.

D **Carl Wark** (1,250ft). A hillfort of unknown date, originally thought to be Bronze Age, but a more recent theory has put it around AD500–600. A splendid natural site, with cliffs on three sides and a gritstone wall along its east side (still standing to a height of 11ft).

PREHISTORIC MAN AND THE LANDSCAPE

Britain's countryside, for its many moments of rural calm and rugged grandeur, has virtually no true wilderness. Nearly all of it bears the stamp of settlers, farmers and industrialists past and present.

During the long Palaeolithic (Old Stone Age) and Mesolithic (Middle Stone Age) periods (up to around 4500BC); Man was a hunter-gatherer, living in small groups and passing a nomadic existence in a huge wilderness. They left no impression on the landscape, but the Neolithic (New Stone Age) population were the first farmers and were here from about 4500 until 2500BC. Farming space was gained by 'slash and burn', which gradually diminished some of the woodland and scrublands. The moorlands of upland Britain are a legacy from this and later removals of tree cover. Even at this time the total population was only about 20,000. The Neolithic peoples occupied the lighter soils, leaving the marshes and larger forests alone. With their stone axes these people are thought to have been able to clear the land at a rate of about half an acre a week per person.

In the Bronze Age (c2500–750BC), the tendency slowly changed from a semi-nomadic existence to a more settled way of life; the ard-plough was developed, and the field systems imposed on the landscape can still be seen today in places as distinct ridges on grassy landscapes. Settlers ensconced themselves in areas such as the Wiltshire chalklands and the granite uplands of south-west England, and left burial chambers, hut circles and mysterious standing stones and stone circles (such as Stonehenge). During the Iron Age (from 750BC to AD43) the pattern of village settlements began to establish itself. Carn Euny and Chysauster (both in Cornwall) are two outstanding survivals of villages of this period. Numerous hillforts from this period were established, and their grassy ramparts can even today be seen in many parts of upland Britain.

RIVINGTON PIKE AND LEVER PARK

THE former estate of Lord Leverhulme parkland, overgrown terraced gardens, a panoramic view from Rivington Pike, woodlands and a lakeside path lend variety. Route-finding is fairly straightforward but rather intricate in the terraced garden section. The paths in the garden may be slippery in the wet or when there are fallen leaves underfoot.

LENGTH *Full walk* 7½ miles (12km), 4½ hours

DIFFICULTY 2

START Anglezarke car park (50 yards from junction signposted to Adlington, Rivington and Anglezarke), near south-east corner of reservoir (on right if coming from White Coppice). Grid reference 620161

LENGTH *Short walk* 4½ miles (7km), 3 hours

DIFFICULTY 2

START Great House Barn visitor centre; parking on drive opposite, ½ mile south of Rivington. Grid reference 628138. To join route, walk along minor road to right of Great House Barn, keeping forward where road bends left into short-stay car park, on track beyond barrier, heading towards reservoir. Continue forward at cross-junction 50 yards later, down steps then right 50 yards later in front of barrier on path closest to reservoir and with iron railing on right; pick up walk at ⑫.

OS MAPS Landranger 109; Pathfinder 700 (SD 61/71)

REFRESHMENTS Teas available in Rivington café at Great House Barn

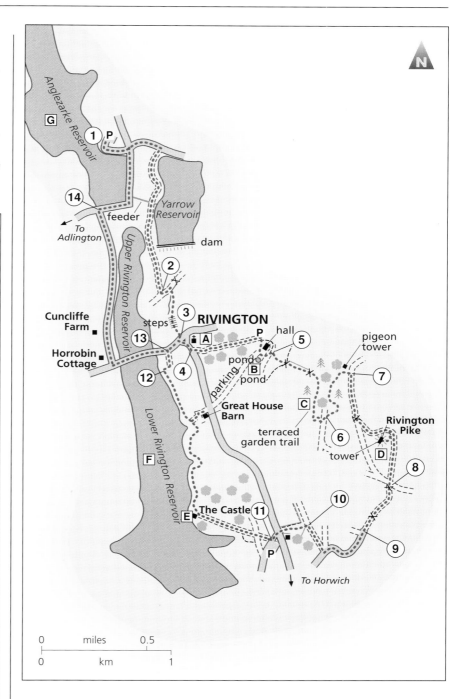

WALK DIRECTIONS

① From car park return to road and turn right to road junction 50 yards ahead; turn left (signposted Rivington and Belmont); after 300 yards, at the top of the rise, take gate on right and follow the track (signposted Concessionary Bridleway) along right-hand side of reservoir. ② After ¾ mile, you reach a gate across the track where you turn left on a stony track into wood;

100 yards later, just after crossing a channelled stream, turn right on to a waymarked path which has the stream on its right. Where the stream bends right, the path goes forward over a stile by a map, across a small field, up steps, then continues forward to the flag-pole on Rivington village green ③ Ⓐ.

Go forward to take the road signposted Horwich. ④ 150 yards later (just after last house on left) fork left on to a broad stony track (keep left after 50 yards where right

goes back to the road); follow this track to reach Rivington Hall Barn, where you turn right, passing to the right-hand side of barn and in front of the hall Ⓑ. Pick up the hall driveway for a few yards, but leave it immediately before it goes between the ponds: instead, keep left across the grass (no path here) for 50 yards to pass between stone gateposts, then turn sharp left on the track.

⑤ At the back of the hall, turn right through a gate and barrier (with red waymark for Terraced

Garden Trail, which you now follow: the trail is waymarked with red numbers and red marks on top of posts). After 140 yards, fork left (waymarked) to path junction at the bottom of a grassy slope at edge of woods, with a gate ahead: keep forward on rising path up to woods.

Follow the trail markers [C] (fork left at post 2; ignore steps to left before post 2); just past sign for Hall Barn (pointing back) take the path at this junction leading off a quarter right along the level; there is no trail post at this junction. You soon pass post 3 on your left, post 4 on your right (ignore steps here keeping forward on level path). Soon you come to a stone footbridge at post 5/6, then 30 yards later turn sharp left up steps and right at top, ignoring a minor right turn 100 yards later; path rises gently past a seat and bends sharp left to reach a track with a gate on the right and post 7 ahead ⑥. Here, take steps opposite, bear right at next junction (20 yards after post 8 on left), around the right-hand side of the pond. Turn right at next junction, up rough steps and then left by post 13; pass ruins on your right.

Turn right 20 yards after post 15 following trail signs; 20 yards later cross the track to take steps opposite up to arch, beyond which you turn left. At curved colonnaded structure on your right, take steps which lead up behind it and turn left on to path above. Follow this path keeping upwards, past post 21, up steps to top terrace. Turn left at top by post 22 along a large flattened area; ignore the sign for trail at the end, which leads down steps, but keep along top terrace (leaving the trail), soon on a narrow path to a gate near Pigeon Tower ⑦.

Turn sharp right beyond this gate, on a hard track, heading for Rivington Pike Tower. Fork left through a gate opposite toilets towards the tower – a track skirts round the base of the hillock: detour right to the tower [D]; continue on the track around the hillock, with Horwich and church in the distance ahead, descending with a wooden fence on your left. Beyond a gate, you reach a junction ⑧ and take

gate opposite to follow the track descending through a field.

⑨ At the corner of farm road keep forward (still downhill). Immediately after a small electricity sub-station (on right) take the lower of two tracks on the right, into woods. ⑩ After 150 yards, there is a break in the tree canopy overhead where domestic power lines cross the track; immediately before these, take a narrow woodland path sharp left. After 50 yards, this reaches close to the corner of a field: fork right (path is indistinct here but keep close to edge of woods, later between fences) to reach a road.

Cross to the path opposite where you bear left (ignore path to the right signposted Great House Barn). ⑪ 75 yards after, turn right on a broad track which you follow for ⅓ mile to reach the castle [E]. Walk round to the right of the castle, behind which you turn right on a path close to the water's edge of Lower Rivington Reservoir. Keep as close to the reservoir as the path allows. Follow the path close to reservoir [F] (path kinks right: 300 yards later, where metal railings appear, next right fork leads to Great House Barn for refreshments and end of short walk). To continue, keep to the path on the left of iron railings, at first with a fence on your left, later with a low stone wall on your right, until ⑫ the path bends right and reaches a track; turn left to the road ⑬.

For short walk Turn right to reach Rivington village green [A], where you turn right (signposted Horwich); continue directions at ④.

For long walk Turn left over road between reservoirs, then right on other side in front of a house on reservoir road (no entry to traffic

The curlew (and the coot, moorhen and sandpiper) are waders to be seen at Anglezarke Reservoir

but open to pedestrians) along west side of Upper Rivington Reservoir; ⑭ turn right at end, on a road along south end of Anglezarke Reservoir [G]; this bends left on other side, soon reaching car park entrance.

ON THE ROUTE

[A] **Rivington** retains stocks on the village green; the interesting 16th- or 17th-century **church** has double-decker pulpit with linenfold panelling and box-pews.

[B] **Hall Barn** and nearby **Great House Barn** are cruck structures dating from the early 18th century but altered by W.H. Lever (who later became Lord Leverhulme) after acquiring the estate in 1899. Lever had opened the Sunlight Soap works at Port Sunlight (near Birkenhead) in 1889, and built a village for the employees where there was a strong emphasis on good sanitation, clean air and landscaping. He purchased 18th-century Rivington Hall and created a country park.

[C] **Terraced gardens** (trail leaflet available from Great House Barn). Began in 1905, the gardens fell into disuse after Lord Leverhulme's death in 1925. The main features are at these stages of the trail: **5** artificial ravine; **9 to 12** Japanese Garden, with bases of Tea Houses; **14** Kitchen Garden; **19** Great Lawn; **20** Tennis court; **23** Ballroom (black and white tiled floor visible); **29** Pigeon Tower, a pigeon and dovecot built 1910, used by Lady Leverhulme as a sewing room.

[D] **Rivington Pike** Nearly 1,200ft above sea-level; an ancient site of a defensive beacon to warn of invasion. The **tower** was built in 1733 for John Andrews of Rivington, probably to show the extent of his estate. **View** south-west over north Wales and the Lancashire coast.

[E] The **castle**, a replica of 13th-century Liverpool Castle as a ruin prior to demolition in 1725, was built by Lord Leverhulme in 1912.

[F] **Lower Rivington Reservoir** Constructed in 1856, this is one of eight reservoirs in this valley to supply Liverpool.

[G] **Anglezarke Reservoir** This is a good site for wildfowl and waders.

WARTON CRAG AND LEIGHTON MOSS

THE north side of Morecambe Bay, renowned for its birdlife and flora, provides a walk of great scenic variety – limestone hills, native woodlands, marshes and parkland with several splendid features of interest. Route-finding is intricate at times, and field routes are not defined.

WALK DIRECTIONS

① With the station on your right, walk along the road; after 100 yards, go left through a signposted gate into golf course. Follow the signposted path across the course (mostly a well-defined route). Head up to rightmost house to find a signposted gate on to the lane ②; turn right on lane for 100 yards, then immediately before bungalow turn left on woodland path signposted to village and Burton Well.

After the wall on right ends, continue forward at a staggered cross-junction. Descend, down steps, to a ladder-stile into field; go forward, soon over a footbridge, then ③ immediately turn left along the edge of the field (with woods on your right) until an opening in wall at the end of field into woods Ⓐ, where you follow a well-defined and broad woodland path.

④ At the far end of the wood, path bends right to reach houses at Silverdale Green; then proceed to the road. Turn left on the road; bear right at road junction by signpost (towards Silverdale).

⑤ After 150 yards, turn left on to a signposted track between walls (for Woodwell and Gibraltar) to reach a gate into field, where you go forward over steps on an enclosed path along the right edge of field and into woods at the end. Immediately turn left on a path along the top edge of wood, gradually dropping and crossing two stiles to enter an irregularly shaped field (where path disappears): continue forward, ⑥ turning right by a signpost after 100 yards (for Hollins Lane) to find a stile in field corner.

Then continue forward along a

LENGTH   7½ miles (12km), 4 hours
DIFFICULTY   2
START   Silverdale railway station (1½ miles east of Silverdale). Grid reference 476752; if the small car park by station is full, start at Silverdale Green (½ mile south-east of Silverdale, by junction with Bottoms Lane and signpost for Arnside 4¼; Milnthorpe 6; railway station ¾; Carnforth 4; Silverdale ½); walk along road in Silverdale direction and start directions at ⑤
OS MAPS   Landranger 97; Pathfinder 636 and 637 (SD 37/47 and SD 56/57)
REFRESHMENTS   Pub at Yealand Conyers; café at Wolf House Gallery, Silverdale (near ⑦)

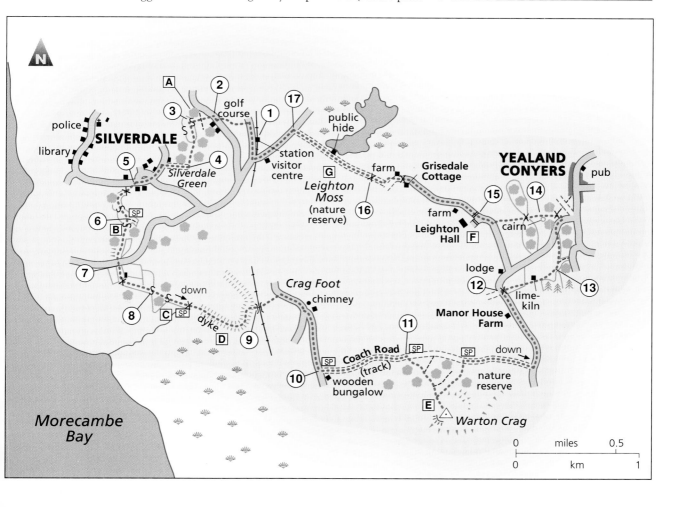

woodland path B, soon with a vertical drop on your right and a field on your left, to reach a road ⑦. Take the signposted path opposite and slightly to right (for Heald Brow and Crag Foot), through a gate; beyond, pick up an enclosed path (to left of field-gate), and follow to end of enclosed section. Turn left through gate, then over stile immediately ahead. Continue through two fields alongside stone wall on right.

⑧ At the end cross a stile. 30 yards later, fork right as soon as woods begin (follow the yellow waymarks, ignoring right fork after just 15 yards) C, soon over a stile and steeply downhill with a fence on your right. At the bottom, turn right through a gate and immediately left (signposted Crag Foot) along a raised grassy dyke D.

⑨ Just before the railway bridge, take a gate on the right to cross a canalised river, then left under the bridge (the gate is difficult to open) and go on to reach the road. Turn right along road, and left at the next junction, signposted Warton. ⑩ At the top of rise, turn left by a wooden bungalow on to an enclosed track (signposted Coach Road, Warton).

⑪ After ½ mile, turn right on to path (signposted Concessionary Path to Warton Crag), keeping right after 300 yards at next signpost, and follow main path to next signpost 300 yards later – left is the continuation but first detour right a few yards to the viewpoint at the top of Warton Crag E; return to signpost and follow the path (soon forking left as waymarked where right goes through section of wall) to rejoin the enclosed track (coach road) where you turn right; this eventually drops to a road.

Turn left on the road. ⑫ 200 yards after Manor House Farm (on left) and just before the road bends right, turn right through a gate: gate is not signposted but is opposite a woodland track (*note* if Leighton Hall is open (times below) you can continue on the road and take the drive on the left down to the hall to rejoin route at ⑮).

Go forward along the right edge of field. At the end, exit between stone posts and follow a faint track ahead, gently downhill, past the old lime-kiln on your left, then past the corner of some woods on your right; the track now becomes better defined. 200 yards after the lime-kiln, a woodland wall begins on right; ⑬ 40 yards later, fork left (opposite a gap-stile – two stone posts and gap between, in the wall), walking along the level with a wall on your right, to reach a stile, then continue forward across a small semi-open area to emerge on a road by 20% gradient sign. Turn right.

To continue, omitting pub After 100 yards, where road bends right, take a stile beside a gate on the left, into woods and bear left following power lines uphill.

For pub in Yealand Conyers Follow the road to bottom, turn left at T-junction for pub, passing the return route on the way – look for steps and railing on left, opposite The Old Post House (house No 29–30), into a field, and bear half left up to a stile at top left-hand corner of field (passing prominent signpost on driveway then past a copper beech tree). Then, in woods, follow power lines up hill.

Both routes ⑭ At the top of slope, emerge into a field by a small cairn, just to left of power lines; continue forward across the field, towards a line of trees (with power lines now 80 yards away to right) to find a gate in the wall F. Descend to Leighton Hall, picking up estate driveway before the hall itself.

⑮ At the entrance to the hall, keep to the right fork (left goes into hall grounds), on tarmacked estate farm road. After ¾ mile, after second farm, take the gate ahead

Leighton Hall, Georgian but gothicised in 1810 by the Gillow family (furniture-makers)

(continuing now on a stony track, and forking right across grass after 30 yards, to join track at a break in the fence). Continue forward, to enter the nature reserve by gate ⑯ G, and follow the main track ahead, past the public birdwatching hide, to reach the road ⑰. Turn left on road, then turn right after crossing railway, to Silverdale station.

ON THE ROUTE

A An eerily dark wood of **yews**.

B A large, natural **limestone pavement** can be seen in these woods.

C Views over **Morecambe Bay**, famous for its 200,000 wader population; tides here are among the fastest in Britain, and reveal a huge expanse of sand and mudflats at low tide. Inland are the **Forest of Bowland** and (further away) the **Pennines**, including the summit of Ingleborough.

D Chimneys on either side of this marshy bay are remains of old **lime-kilns**.

E **Warton Crag** Recent concessionary paths (not marked on current OS maps) lead out to this viewpoint, which overlooks **Morecambe Bay**, the **Cumbrian Fells** (including Black Combe, Fairfield and High Street), **Heysham Power Station** on the coast and the **Forest of Bowland**.

F Probably the best possible view of **Leighton Hall** (*open* May to September 2 to 5), in a landscaped parkland setting with glimpses of southern Cumbria beyond. Gillow family furniture and antique clocks are displayed inside; **eagle flying** display (weather permitting) at 3.30 when the house is open.

G **Leighton Moss** RSPB reserve (day permits are available from the visitor centre passed later in the walk; this main path, a public right of way through the reserve, is always open). This fenland, wetland and woodland site is a habitat for **otters**, **red deer**, profuse **birdlife** in its meres and reed beds and diverse **flora**. The birds, which include water rail, bearded tits and the only breeding colony of bitterns in northern England, can be watched from a public hide on the path.

HEPTONSTALL AND COLDEN CLOUGH

THE distinctive Pennine landscape characterises this walk, with its numerous reminders of Calderdale's textile industry. A steep 650-foot ascent out of Hebden Bridge to Heptonstall is followed by astonishing cliff-top views (not for vertigo sufferers) on the descent into Colden Clough, ending with a walk along the canal towpath. An intricate route, but for the most part visible on the ground.

WALK DIRECTIONS

① Ⓐ From A646 take the turning by the tourist information centre and Yorkshire Bank, called Bridge Gate. 80 yards later, opposite the White Swan, cross stone packhorse bridge on your left Ⓑ. On the other side, take the steep cobbled lane opposite, which is signposted Footpath to Heptonstall Ⓒ.

② At the top turn left on the road Ⓓ then 30 yards later half right on a lane signposted Access Only, Breeze Mount and Delph House (avoiding the road sharper right). 130 yards later, and 30 yards past

the last house (with double garage doors) on the right, the lane ends 20 yards before a power-post: take an unprominent path very sharp right rising between walls, passing a house (this is a right of way) and reaching the road where ③ you turn left up into Heptonstall. Follow the cobbled street up through the village Ⓔ.

(If you do not follow the detour described in On The Route, turn left off the main street just after the Cross Inn, signposted to the museum; just past the museum, do not go through the gates into the

> **LENGTH** 4½ miles (7km), 3 hours
> **DIFFIULTY** 2–3
> **START** Hebden Bridge town centre (on A646 between Burnley and Halifax), Calderdale. Grid reference 992272.
> *By train* Hebden Bridge
> **OS MAPS** Landranger 103; Outdoor Leisure 21
> **REFRESHMENTS** Full range in Hebden Bridge; pubs and shop in Heptonstall; pub at Jack Bridge (off route)

churchyard but turn left down a few steps, then right along a lane called West Laithe, which skirts the churchyard on your right).

At the end of the churchyard keep left ④, go over at the cross-junction 50 yards later then immediately fork right by the Calderdale Way signpost (you follow the Calderdale Way until ⑨). Follow the track between walls to reach the top of precipice ⑤ Ⓕ: turn right on the path which follows the top of the rim of Colden Clough. ⑥ Emerge on a lane, turn left, downhill on it, then 100 yards later fork right on to a track (with a wall on your right; there are yellow arrow waymarks in the next few stages).

⑦ After 250 yards, ignore a right fork but take the path just to the right of a seat: the stone flagged path leads along the top of a field to a stile, then past a barn. 60 yards past the barn, take next fork left (waymarked Calderdale Way and descending on to track between walls). ⑧ 100 yards later fork right (still between walls) to enter a field

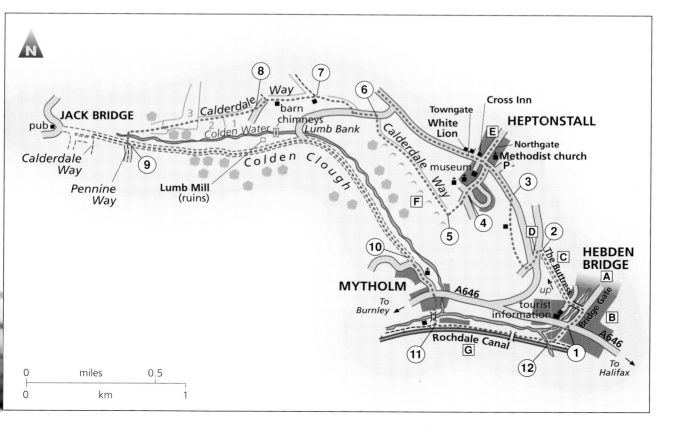

– path follows the top edge of two fields, then continues on a flagstoned path along the edge of a third field, at the end of which you turn left to a gap in the wall by a metal post and follow flagstoned path diagonally across a field into woods, where you turn right. The path soon leaves woods and drops to cross a stone bridge: take the steps up to reach a track ⑨, where you turn left (ignoring the path ahead ascending between walls; *note* for the pub at Jack Bridge detour right here). Follow the track for 1 mile, along the level and ignoring minor side turns (ignore sharp left signposted Lumb Bank after ½ mile).

⑩ When you reach the edge of Mytholm village, turn left on a residential road, down past the church to the main road. Cross to a deliberate gap in the wall opposite (with railings beyond) just to the left of the bus stop. Follow the stream-side path, to cross the river bridge then continue forward up a few steps to reach the canal after 50 yards ⑪.

⑥ Turn left on the canal towpath. ½ mile later, the canal crosses the river: ⑫ turn left just after (at the bridge) and follow the road in to the centre of Hebden Bridge.

ON THE ROUTE

Ⓐ **Hebden Bridge** is a mill town which grew in the 18th and 19th centuries, finely situated at the confluence of two deep valleys, with terraces stacked up the slopes and mill chimneys below giving a precarious and intriguing appearance to the whole. It has become a commuter satellite town for Leeds and Bradford but much has been carefully preserved; a good town trail is available locally. Britain's last remaining clog-mill is on the edge of town, near the station. Horse-drawn boat trips can be taken from the centre of Hebden Bridge.

Ⓑ **Old bridge** This gives the town its name. James Grenewode of Heptonstall left 3s 4d 'to the fabric of Hebden Bridge' in 1508, replacing a wooden bridge. The bridge has

stone inscriptions detailing repairs from 1602.

Ⓒ **The Buttress** This very steep cobbled lane is the original packhorse road from the bridge to Heptonstall and is part of an old route from Halifax to Burnley.

Ⓓ Note the old **milestone** by the road to Slack Colden and Blackshaw Head.

Ⓔ **Heptonstall** The hilltop village predates Hebden Bridge, and contains a maze of fascinating streets and alleys. Heptonstall prospered in the 18th century as a hand-loom weaving centre. As you enter the village, detour into the car park on the right, where the **village lock-up** can be seen. Continue up along the street (Towngate); the first turning on the right is **Northgate**, where a short distance along and to the left the decorative gateway to Whitehall bears the date 1578 and the initials of owner John Bentley. Further along Northgate, on the right, the eight-sided **Methodist church** is the oldest in the world to be in continuous use. Erected in 1764 as a preaching house after John Wesley's preaching had attracted large crowds to the village, the building deliberately avoided the traditional church shape in an attempt to avoid confrontation with the church authorities. Northgate forks by Stocks Villas; Northwell Lane to the right has a milestone made from part of the village stocks.

Returning to Towngate and turning right up the main village street, you pass the Cross Inn on the

right. Just after, the Cloth Hall on the left was the market-place for woollen cloth produced by villagers from the 16th century until the opening of the Piece Hall in Halifax in 1779. The street rises past the White Lion pub, passing the Mechanics Institute (set up in 1868) on the left.

Return past the Cloth Hall, then turn right. This path skirts the ruins of the **old church**, first built in 1260 but dating mostly from the 15th century. It was damaged in a storm in 1847 and never repaired. Cragg Vale coin forger 'King David' Hartley, hanged at York in 1770, is buried here. You then pass the **Grammar School Museum**; the school was founded in 1642 and rebuilt in 1771; after closure in 1889 the building was occupied by the Yorkshire Penny Bank; the old wooden desks and flagged floor can still be seen.

Immediately turn left down steps into West Laithe, where you turn right, past the **Chantry House**, where human bones were stored. West Laithe bends slightly left after the churchyard and goes across the entrance to a modern development called The Courtyard Becketts Close. Beyond is the **'new' church**, consecrated in 1854, which contains relics from the old church, including a table, settle and chair, and the coat of arms of George III. In the overflow graveyard opposite the new church is the burial place of poet Sylvia Plath.

Keep to the left of the new church and resume walk directions at ④.

Ⓕ Spectacular views into **Colden Clough**, with a dizzy 500-foot drop. The **Calderdale Way** makes a scenic 50-mile circuit around this area.

Ⓖ **Rochdale Canal** An absorbing section of the 33-mile, 92-lock canal, through a slice of early industrial landscape. When the canal opened in 1804, it was the catalyst for the expansion of Hebden Bridge (and hastened the decline of the fortunes of Heptonstall). The canal is a cross-Pennine route, climbing 521ft from Lancashire, and 358ft from Yorkshire.

The Rochdale Canal as it passes through Hebden Bridge

FLAMBOROUGH HEAD

JUTTING out far into the ocean, Flamborough Head is one of the most prominent features on the map of the East Coast. From Flamborough village, the walk soon joins the coast and follows a level cliff path to Flamborough Head, where the drama starts; the transition to rugged clifflands is a spectacular one. Binoculars are highly recommended, as this is a renowned place for sea birds. Paths can be muddy after rain. Beware of sheer cliff drops. Easy route-finding.

WALK DIRECTIONS

① From the memorial Ⓐ in the village centre, follow main street southwards, signposted Lighthouse and Bridlington Ⓑ. At road junction, cross over to take the path through the churchyard Ⓒ; on other side take Church Lane ahead and

---

LENGTH 7½ miles (12km), 4 hours
DIFFICULTY 2
START Flamborough village centre, by prominent memorial (north-east of Bridlington); parking in the village. Grid reference 226702
OS MAPS Landranger 101; Pathfinder 646 (TA 26/27)
REFRESHMENTS Cafés by lighthouse, at North Landing and Thornwick Bay; shops and pubs at Flamborough

---

slightly to the left; the road bends right after 130 yards; 80 yards later at junction take a track on your left into Beacon Farm, signposted as footpath to Beacon Hill. The track goes through the farmyard, along the

The puffin breeds in cliff-top burrows; its flight is fast for a heavy bird

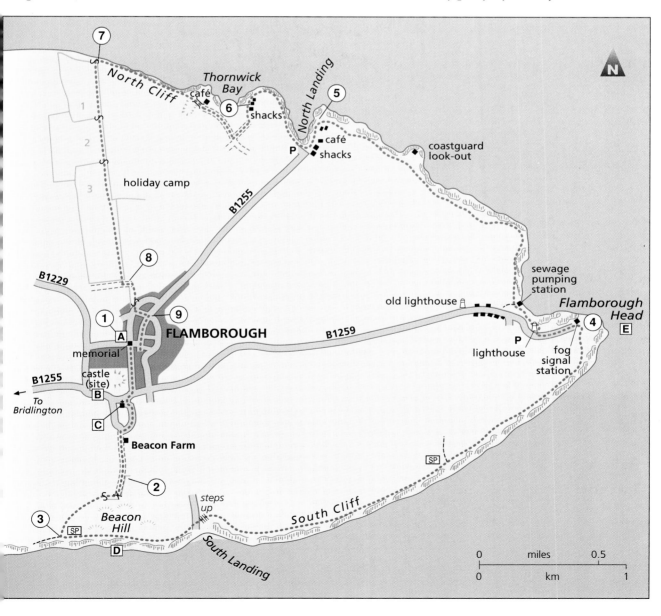

BEMPTON CLIFFS

West of Flamborough, the B1229 passes through Bempton; a lane north from here leads to Bempton Cliffs, an RSPB reserve harbouring the only gannetry in England, as well as nesting sites for puffins, and numerous other species.

edge of fields, soon ② with a hedge on the left and proceeding slightly uphill to a gate: do not pass through this but take the path just to the right of it to proceed with fence on your left.

Proceed towards the sea, where you ③ turn left on the coast path by a signpost [D]. At South Landing (which is a beach) drop to sea-level via steps to a road; take steps opposite, turn right at the top to regain the cliff-top. ④ At Flamborough Head (where there is access to the shore via steps) [E], pass side of fog signal station (square white building), following road. Just before the lighthouse, leave the road to skirt around the right side of the lighthouse, on the other side of which the cliff path continues down steps. Descend to a life-belt (ahead goes down steps to beach), where the coast path turns left up; just after a small brick building (sewage pumping station) turn right along the cliff-top path. ⑤ Eventually you reach a big bay at the shacky development of North Landing; continue through the car park and pick up the cliff path.

⑥ At Thornwick Bay (the next cluster of bungalows), join a stony track around the top of the cliff, then go beyond a low café building, to resume along the coast path (which drops steeply to a bridge over an inlet then ascends). ⑦ ½ mile later take a stile over corner of a fence on your left to leave the coast path: follow the path along the left edge of three large fields.

⑧ Emerge on to a track, turn left then right after 50 yards (with fence on your right) towards houses at the edge of Flamborough, to reach a stile. Cross the main road to take a narrow semi-metalled lane opposite to emerge by the Rose and Crown pub, where ⑨ you turn right along

Flamborough Head: a virtually detached and extremely exposed promontory where it is possible to walk on decent days

High Street; turn right by the Ship Inn to the memorial at the centre of the village.

ON THE ROUTE

[A] **Memorial** Erected at the centre of Flamborough, this structure is dedicated to the crew of the coble (a local open-decked, flat-bottomed fishing-boat) *The Two Brothers*, who were killed in 1909 while attempting to rescue another crew.

[B] **Flamborough Castle** On the right, after the houses end, grassy humps and a portion of masonry of the castle is visible; here lived the Constable family, lords of the manor for nearly 500 years until 1537.

[C] **Flamborough church** has a Norman chancel arch, a 16th-century carved rood screen, and a memorial to Sir Marmaduke Constable, who died in 1520 from eating a toad.

[D] **View** From here until Flamborough Head there is a sweeping curve of coast to the south, from Bridlington to Spurn Head (far left: a thin spit of shingle and sand,

moved inshore on a 250-year cycle). [E] **Flamborough Head** This exposed eastern headland has been the scene of many shipwrecks. **Views** open out dramatically to the north, and include Filey Brigg and the coast towards Scarborough. The deeply indented cliffs, precipitous inlets and ledges are rich in **birdlife**; echoing cries of kittiwakes are immediately noticeable; also here are fulmar, guillemot, gull, razorbill and puffin.

The **lighthouse** was built 1806, and stands 85ft high; the nearby **fog signal station** emits a loud electronic bleep when needed, but when built in 1859 used a cannon signal. Inland, the **old lighthouse** was built in 1674.

DANES' DYKE

Just under a mile west of Flamborough village, a huge earthwork cuts north to south across the peninsula. Known as Danes' Dyke, this two-mile ditch is of uncertain origin. One theory is that it is pre-Roman; another that it is a boundary marker constructed at the time of the Viking invasions.

ROBIN HOOD'S BAY

THE walk opens with a gentle stroll along the former railway line to Robin Hood's Bay – which ranks among England's prettiest seaside villages. The return leg is both more dramatic and more energetic, taking the Cleveland Way along the tops of high sandstone cliffs. The Whitby–Robin Hood's Bay–Ravenscar–Scarborough bus service can be used to split the walk in two (and see the box overleaf). All paths are well defined and signposted or waymarked; easy route-finding.

LENGTH 7½ miles (12km), 3½ hours
DIFFICULTY 2
START Car park (free) at Ravenscar (large demarcated verge by road, by entrance drive to Raven Hall Hotel), midway between Scarborough and Whitby.
Grid reference 980016

OS MAPS Landranger 94; Outdoor Leisure 27
REFRESHMENTS Hotel and café at Ravenscar; plenty of pubs and tea-rooms in Robin Hood's Bay; a house on the old railway track (1 mile from start) occasionally serves tea – look out for notice-boards

WALK DIRECTIONS

① Ⓐ From the road/car parking area, with the entrance to Raven Hall Hotel behind you, take the second path on the right, signposted Cleveland Way and leading past National Trust shop/information centre. Ignore a right turn after 100 yards by National Trust sign. ② 100 yards later, turn left by a geological trail post, to lead on to the old railway track Ⓑ. Follow this for 2½ (easy) miles Ⓒ.

③ Descend to a road by steps and take the steps opposite to regain the old railway (avoid immediate path fork on left). ④ After 1 mile cross a road and continue on the old railway opposite. ⑤ 500 yards later take a ladder-stile on the right, signposted Public Footpath. Bear half left across a field to a gate in the left-hand corner. Proceed alongside the fence on left through two fields: the path becomes clearly trodden and leads after ¼ mile into Robin Hood's Bay Ⓓ Ⓔ.

⑥ *If it is high tide* take the right turn immediately before the road ends at rocky foreshore in village, leading up stone steps, then 50 yards later keep right (signposted Cliff Path). In the first mile, path descends to two inlets. *Note: This section of coast is subject to erosion and the Cleveland Way may be diverted from time to time: please follow the signposts and acorn waymarks.*

If it is low tide (this route is more

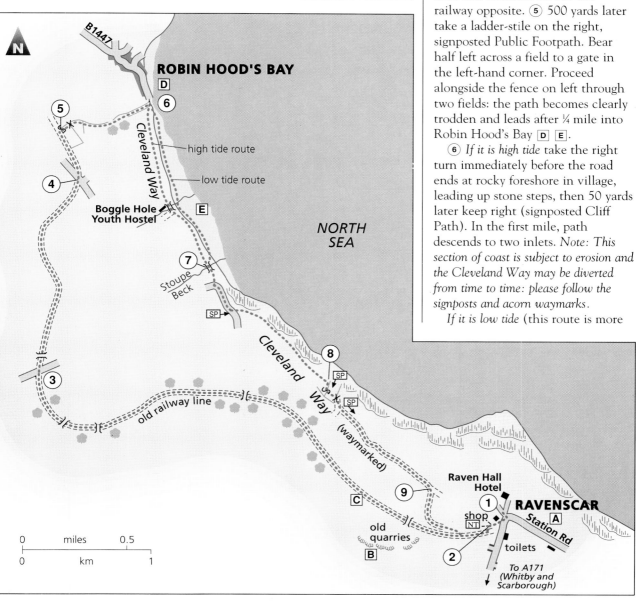

Each cottage in Robin Hood's Bay jostles for a view over the roofs of its neighbours

interesting) descend to the foreshore/beach and turn right along it. After ½ mile you pass Boggle Hole Youth Hostel and a footbridge at inlet on right; 500 yards later leave the beach for the next foot-bridge in next inlet, to maintain direction up a path with a handrail.

Both routes ⑦ The path ascends to a road. Continue forward along it for 300 yards then go left over a stile (Cleveland Way signpost) on to the cliff-top. ⑧ After ½ mile, turn right as signposted, to leave the cliff-top, walking alongside a fence on your left. 50 yards before the end of field, go left over a stile. A clear path follows the right edge of the field to reach a gate, then go forward on the track, keeping left 50 yards later (signposted Cleveland Way). ⑨ ½ mile later, fork right as waymarked and follow signs up to Ravenscar.

ON THE ROUTE

[A] **Ravenscar** was planned as an Edwardian seaside resort. Pavements, roads and drains were laid out, but the distance to the beach and the unstable ground deterred developers from building

villas. There is even a failed parade of shops in Station Road. The Raven Hall Hotel, built on the site of a Roman signal station, dates from 18th century.

[B] Old **alum quarries** and overgrown **spoil heaps** are visible on the left, and it is possible to make out lines of shale, sandstone and ironstone. The alum, processed with human urine shipped from London beer-houses, was used as a fixer for dyes. Good place for fossil-collecting.

[C] The **old railway line** used to run along the Yorkshire coast, from Seamer Junction, near Scarborough, to Whitby and beyond, to Saltburn. Opened in 1885, closed in 1965.

[D] **Robin Hood's Bay** is so steep that the window of one house looks on the roof of its neighbours. It was one of the most notorious spots for

smuggling on the East Coast, and many of the houses have smugglers' cupboards – recesses between the party walls for hiding in when the excise men were at large. Robin Hood is said to have kept his boats here for use as getaways, and he is also supposed to have seen off some marauding Danish pirates at the request of Abbot Richard of Whitby, in the mid 12th century. Some houses in the village have curious bow windows, called coffin windows, built so that passers-by could pay their last respects. The Laurel Inn, occupying a tall building on a bend halfway down the slope, is one of the smallest pubs in Yorkshire. Its beamed bar was carved from solid rock and it makes a memorable setting for pub games and a pint.

[E] **Beach** Another excellent place for fossils.

THE CLEVELAND WAY

The 93-mile route takes in much of the finest walking in the North York Moors. Beginning from Helmsley it crosses rolling pasture and high moors, with a magnificent finale along sea-cliffs. Other coastal highlights of the walk include Skinningrove to Staithes (4 miles), ending at a picturesque fishing-village (the path only follows the cliff-edge for part of the way, however); Staithes to Sandsend (8 miles), taking in Runswick Bay; Whitby to Robin Hood's Bay (6 miles); Robin Hood's Bay to Scarborough (13 miles). Apart from the route described here, the coast does not lend itself to round walks, as the hinterland is unexceptional farmland. However, walkers can make use of buses between Robin Hood's Bay, Whitby, Sandsend, Runswick Bay and Staithes. Services are less frequent on Sundays.

The view across the top part of Robin Hood's Bay towards Ravenscar

HOLE OF HORCUM AND LEVISHAM

WIDE open moorland expanses as far as Levisham, seen from the easiest of level tracks, followed by a path along a deeply incised valley which gives contrast. Easy route-finding.

LENGTH 5½ miles (9 km), 2½ hours

DIFFICULTY 1

START Car park at the AA box above Hole of Horcum, south of Saltergate Inn and on A169 (Whitby–Pickering). Grid reference 853937

OS MAPS Landranger 94 or 100; Outdoor Leisure 27

REFRESHMENTS Pub and shop at Levisham

Heather adorns the moorland at the Hole of Horcum

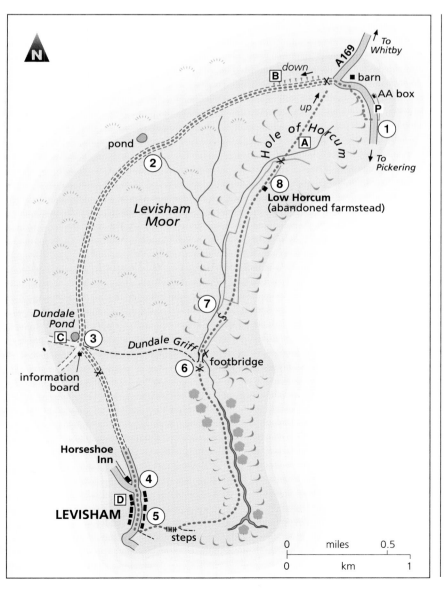

WALK DIRECTIONS

① From the car park, cross the main road, turn right on a path that runs closely parallel to the road in Whitby direction, along the top of the Hole of Horcum Ⓐ. Where the road is about to bend sharply right, take the gate beside a stile on left on to moorland track (not ladder-stile on left just before this, which leads to a descending path) Ⓑ.

② You pass a pond (on right) after 1 mile. ③ 1 mile later, the track dips down to reach Dundale Pond Ⓒ at track junction: take the ascending track to the left, leading up to a gate to continue as an enclosed track (which becomes a lane) to Levisham ④ Ⓓ. Proceed along the village street to the far end of village, then ⑤ turn left (where road is about to bend right) on to a signposted path by bench, immediately forking left.

Path drops a little, then rises up steps and continues along the top left edge of dale (ignore minor right descending fork soon after steps) gradually curving round to the left. The path descends gradually to reach a gate just above level of stream.

⑥ 100 yards later, step over a subsidiary stream and ignore path to left up side valley of Dundale Griff: go forward to footbridge, after which do not go through the gate ahead but follow the path which keeps left along the valley, now with stream on your left and a wall on right.

(7) Beyond the next stile, the path continues along the valley in the same direction. (8) When you reach Low Horcum (abandoned farmstead), pass to the left of it: proceed alongside hawthorn hedgerow on right down to gate, then head up to a prominent path ascending slope (to the left of the barn on the skyline). Emerge on to the road; turn right to reach car park, or take gate beside the stile on left if you started from Levisham.

ON THE ROUTE

A To the left, the **Hole of Horcum** is a great hollow, with an extensive view beyond over the Howardian Hills, and the eastern part of the North York Moors; moorland and commercial forestry dominate the landscape. Below, steam and diesel trains run along the bottom of the valley along the private **North Yorkshire Moors Railway**.

B Two dykes here are prehistoric **earthworks** (one is by a sign for Levisham Moor; the other is along the right of the track), probably boundary markers.

C **Dundale Pond** Probably artificially created for cattle; in medieval times this was part of a grazing pasture belonging to Malton Priory.

D **Levisham** A broad green runs the length of its street, with the Horseshoe Inn at its top end. The church has two fragments of an Anglo-Danish gravestone c. 1000, marked with a dragon.

Goathland Station on the North Yorkshire Moors Railway; the line passes through Levisham (on this walk). There's another excellent walk from Grosmont to Goathland along the abandoned earlier 'deviation' line

CAPTAIN JAMES COOK

It is hard to pay a visit to the North York Moors without coming across a mention of Captain Cook, the great explorer and very much the local hero. He was born in Marton in 1728; the village is now engulfed into the suburbs of Middlesbrough, and a museum there honours his life. He spent his childhood in and around Great Ayton, attending school in the village (now set up as a small museum) and working at Airey Home Farm. In 1745 he took up an apprenticeship at a shop at Staithes; he soon realised that his ambitions lay at sea, and his master arranged an apprenticeship with a Quaker ship-owner called John Walker, from Whitby (the house he stayed at is another absorbing museum).

After joining the Royal Navy, Cook rose meteorically through the ranks, and in 1758 became master of HMS *Pembroke* in the campaign against France in America. But it is for his three exploratory voyages on collier ships known as Whitby Cats in the South Pacific that he is remembered. In the course of these he charted the east coast of Australia, became the first white man to set foot in New Zealand and discovered a number of islands. The first expedition was undertaken for astronomical observations, but Cook had secret instructions to seek for a southern continent that was thought to exist; but he narrowly failed to discover Antarctica. He was clubbed to death by natives in Hawaii in 1779.

HUTTON-LE-HOLE AND LASTINGHAM

TWO picture-book villages linked by a route with changes in height and varied views. The route is obvious for much of the way, but is invisible at ④.

LENGTH 4½ miles (7km), 2½ hours

DIFFICULTY 1–2

START Village street, Spaunton (easy roadside parking), ¾ mile south-west of Lastingham, and north-east of Kirkbymoorside. Grid reference 725899. (There is also a paying car park in Hutton-le-Hole, but this often is full at peak times)

OS MAPS Landranger 94 or 100; Outdoor Leisure 26

REFRESHMENTS Pub, tea-room and shop in Hutton-le-Hole and Lastingham

WALK DIRECTIONS

① Start with the telephone-box on your right and walk west along the street; keep on the road as it bends right (ignoring semi-surfaced track on left), then 30 yards later take signposted farm road on the left (with cattlegrid) into Grange Farm; fork right as signposted after 30 yards, in front of barn. At the end of the farm, track bends right, then left. ② At the end of two fields on left, track bends left. At the end of field on right, turn right at track junction Ⓐ.

③ ⅓ mile later, the view opens out suddenly ahead: turn left here

(signposted), continuing along the enclosed track. 50 yards later, turn right by a signpost where the track ends, to follow an enclosed path, soon descending along a belt of trees. ④ 20 yards after path crosses a stile, take a stile on the right (leaving the enclosed path) to

The beck that runs down the middle of the green, straddled by several footbridges, makes Hutton-le-Hole one of the prettiest of Yorkshire villages

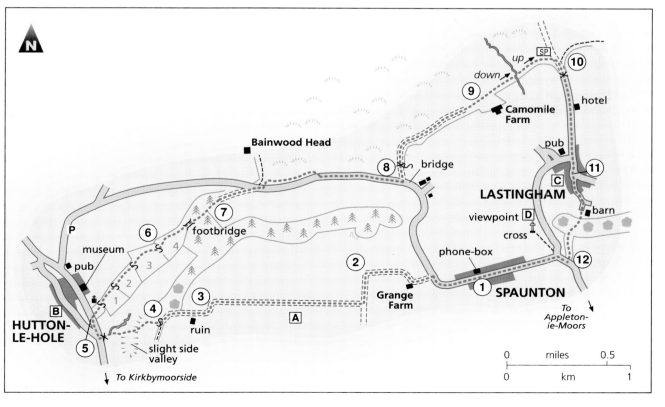

The wheelwright's shop, one of several evocative reconstructions of rural life in times past at the Ryedale Folk Museum in Hutton-le-Hole

emerge at top of grassy slope with Hutton-le-Hole visible ahead.

Turn left downhill (leaving fence which is on your left) and soon reaching the bottom of a slight side-valley coming down from left (route-finding is a little tricky here; if you find yourself at the top of a steep wooded bank you are too far to the right). Turn right, soon picking up a clear descending path. At the bottom, a stream appears on right: proceed to a gate and stile, then forward to road at bottom of Hutton-le-Hole where you turn right for a few yards B. ⑤ Take a signposted gate on right opposite post-box (30 yards before St Chad's church) and follow the enclosed path past a bowling-green to a gate (church ahead): turn right into field. The route across fields is waymarked with yellow arrows, as it leads along the left edge of the first two fields, then keeps forward in third field to gate beside stile ⑥, and finally follows the left edge of fourth field

to cross footbridge and enter a wood. ⑦ On leaving the wood, continue along grassy track (with fence on right) to reach the road. Turn right along road (or walk along grass just to left of it).

⑧ 50 yards before road junction by houses and bridge, take a signposted track on left, soon through a gate beside a stile on to moorland: keep on track which runs close to wall on your right along edge of moor. ⑨ Beyond farm on right, the track is no longer defined; continue along edge of moor always with wall or fence on right. The route descends, over a stream by stepping-stones (easy), then ascends to a bench by a signpost ⑩: turn right on track which soon becomes a surfaced lane, dropping into Lastingham.

At bottom C, turn left in the centre of the village (signposted Pickering), then ⑪ take the first right turn (with No Through Road sign). Just after the road metalling

ends, turn right in front of barns as signposted uphill, on a broad enclosed path which soon narrows to ascend through a wood, then reaches road junction ⑫. Detour right (on level grassy path above Lastingham road) to see Victoria Cross viewpoint D. Continue route along the road signposted to Spaunton.

ON THE ROUTE

A The **view** to the south extends to the **Howardian Hills** and the **Vale of Pickering**.

B **Hutton-le-Hole** A sheep-nibbled green runs the length of its broad main street, with a stream down the middle crossed by a series of footbridges, lined by characteristic cottages of local yellow stone and red roofs. The village became a refuge for persecuted Quakers in the 17th and 18th centuries; Quaker Cottage (1695) is the oldest surviving building. **Ryedale Folk Museum** records rural and village life over 400 years, and includes a smithy, a medieval glass furnace from Rosedale, tools, furniture and a gypsy caravan.

C **Lastingham** On a hillock on the edge of this compact village stands the **church.** The Norman crypt, and Norman and Early English building was part of an abbey founded by Abbot Stephen of Whitby in 1078, but never completed. This in turn was built on the site of a monastery founded by Cedd (whose remains are said to be in the crypt) in 655, but destroyed by the Danes. Repeated attacks caused the abbot to move to York, where he founded St Mary's Abbey. The partly completed abbey became a church about 1230.

D A bench by this 19th-century stone cross is a memorable **viewpoint** over the Lastingham area.

COLD MOOR AND WHITE HILL

This is a horseshoe-shaped arrangement of moorland ridges, making exhilarating walking once the haul on to them has been achieved. The best of the views occurs in the Cleveland Way section, 1½ miles along the top of a steep escarpment. Easy route-finding, although it can be boggy at ⑧ and the going underfoot can be tough after rain.

LENGTH 6½ miles (10.5 km), 3½ hours
DIFFICULTY 3
START Chop Gate (on B1257 north-west of Helmsley and south of Stokesley and Middlesbrough; car park at south end of hamlet). Grid reference 559994.
Alternatively start at Clay Bank Forestry Commission car park by the turn-off from B1257 signposted

Ingleby Greenhow; turn left out of the car park and walk along B1257 towards Helmsley, then after 200 yards turn left through a gate with a signpost for the Cleveland Way; start walk directions at ⑤. Grid reference 573035
OS MAPS Landranger 93; Outdoor Leisure 26
REFRESHMENTS There is a pub at Chop Gate

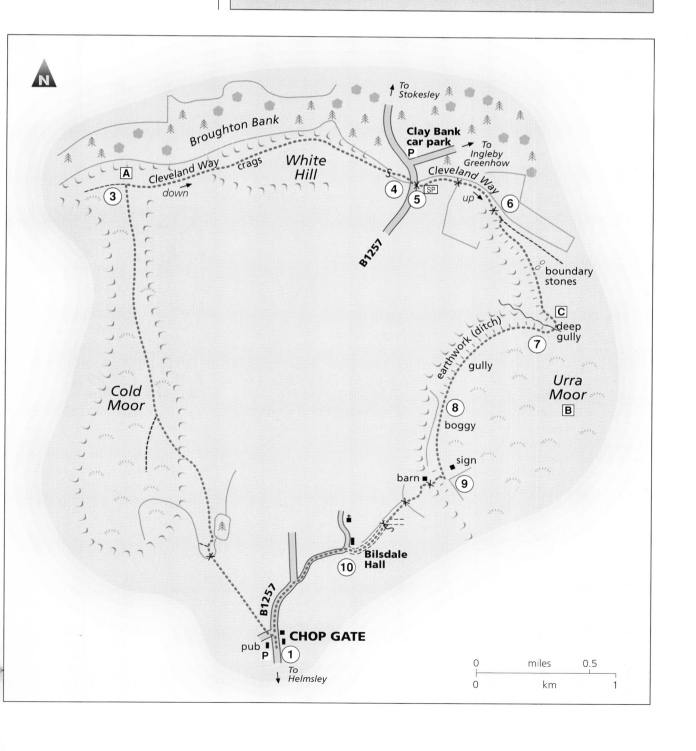

Cairns are unofficial ways of showing the routes of many upland paths in the North York Moors

WALK DIRECTIONS

① With the Buck Inn pub on your left, follow the main road but soon turn left by a signpost for Carlton (opposite war memorial), immediately forking right on to a rising enclosed track (signposted Bridleway).

② After ½ mile, you reach a gate on to moorland: keep right on path close to right-hand wall. As soon as the path reaches a small conifer plantation on your right it leaves the wall, climbing steadily up on to Cold Moor ridge; the path is well defined all the way and soon heads along the centre of the ridge with big views opening ahead.

③ When you reach end of ridge [A], turn right by a cairn (piled-up stones) at T-junction with broad path (Cleveland Way; semi-paved with rocks and slabs), walking close to the top of edge and dropping to a gate before climbing up to the top of a craggy hill (White Hill). The path levels and then drops to cross a stile at edge of forest ④: keep right as signposted alongside wall, to reach a road. Cross to the gate opposite.

⑤ Follow Cleveland Way which ascends with a wall on your left, soon passing through a gate in fence just before the forest on left ends [B]. Beyond next gate (in wall, at end of steepest section of ascent) continue up the main path for 30 yards then ⑥ fork right (leaving Cleveland Way) on to a path that initially runs parallel to wall on your right but soon bends left away from it. The path is well defined and marked by a slight ditch (ancient earthwork) on right side [C]; it contours the moors (with the mast in far distance roughly ahead for much of the way). ⑦ After ½ mile, cross a deep gully (with stream), bear sharp right on the other side on the path (still marked by the ditch). ⑧ Where a wall appears on your right, the path is less well defined: keep alongside wall (boggy in places after rain). After the wall ends, path is well defined again; ⑨ 200 yards later turn right downhill at path junction (when walk was researched this was at point level with a large, rather old sign on the left about behaviour on moorland).

Very soon, a gate in the wall comes into view; beyond it, follow obvious snaking path down to a further gate then proceed down track to tarmacked lane by Bilsdale Hall (farm) ⑩. Turn left on lane, then left at main road to return to Chop Gate.

ON THE ROUTE

[A] A wide view suddenly appears to the north; to the left is **Teesside** (including the Tees Transporter Bridge) and to the right is the hook-shaped **Roseberry Topping**; the **Durham Pennines** stretch out in the far distance.

[B] Ahead is **Urra Moor**, the highest point in the North York Moors at 1,491 ft.

[C] The **Bilsdale West Moor TV transmitter** is directly ahead in the distance; there are **views** over nearby **Bilsdale**. The **earthwork** you are following is an ancient boundary marker; **standing stones** seen close by are more recent boundary stones erected to show the limit of landowners' estates.

Roseberry Topping, famous for its views and ironstone and whinstone quarries

---

NATIONAL TRAILS

Official long-distance paths, created by the Countryside Commission, are one of the most popular methods of exploring the country on foot. They make a good basis for day walks for those who don't want to tackle the whole route. Many miles of new paths were made in the process of establishing the National Trails. To date, the following have been opened in England and Wales.

Northern England Pennine Way (250 miles/400km), Cleveland Way (108 miles/172km), Wolds Way (79 miles/127km)

Wales and the Marches Offa's Dyke Path (168 miles/270km), Pembrokeshire Coast (167 miles/ 268km)

Southern England The Ridgeway (85 miles/136km), South Downs Way (106 miles/ 171km), North Downs Way (141 miles/227km), South-West Coast (515 miles/824km), the Thames Path (156 miles/251km)

Eastern England Peddars Way and Norfolk Coast Path (93 miles/150km)

Additionally, there are numerous unofficial long-distance routes which use the existing path network (such as the Heart of England Way). The Southern Upland Way (212 miles/340km) and the West Highland Way (95 miles/153km) are the two official long-distance paths established in Scotland.

FOUNTAINS ABBEY AND STUDLEY ROYAL

THIS route deliberately avoids the most-frequented approach to Fountains Abbey, instead beginning from the village of Studley Roger, which gives no hint of what follows. The walk keeps its surprises well concealed until the curtains are suddenly and dramatically lifted. It starts by crossing parkland, taking in the remarkable estate church, and drops into the valley graced by Britain's finest abbey ruin. A tour of the adjacent Studley Royal parkland ensues, and before the charming Seven Bridges Walk into less tamed terrain is one of the most memorably sited National Trust tea-shops to be found anywhere. The going is easy, all on defined tracks. There is an entrance fee for Fountains Abbey and Studley Royal (free for National Trust members), which can be paid at the visitor centre or at the gate-house to Studley Royal Park; it is possible to cut out this section by taking the estate drive to the lake by the gate-house and picking up the directions at ⑤.

LENGTH 5 miles (8km), 3½ hours
DIFFICULTY 1
START Studley Roger, off B6265 west of Ripon. Roadside parking in village.
Grid reference 290703
OS MAPS Landranger 99; Pathfinder 641 and 653 (SE 27/37 and SE 26/36)
REFRESHMENTS Tea-room at entrance to Studley Royal at ⑤

WALK DIRECTIONS

① Take signposted path to left of house No 24, forward along right edge of field to gate into estate by National Trust sign, and continue forward across parkland on grassy path Ⓐ. ② Join parkland road; keep right along it to church. On the way you pass a left turn signposted to the car park; you may wish to return to this point. ③ Ⓑ When you reach the church, there is a choice of routes.

For approach along meadows to abbey (which many visitors feel is the most beautiful approach, with the abbey in view in the distance as you approach it), return to the above-mentioned turning to the car park and go down to the car park; pay admission at the gate-house and continue for the abbey. For approach via visitor centre (where there is an exhibition on the abbey; the approach reveals the abbey suddenly and dramatically), go beyond the church and out through the gate and turn left on path signposted to visitor centre (where tickets must be obtained for admission to the abbey and grounds). Walk into the visitor centre and leave by its far end, fork left (on the signposted Scenic Route), approaching abbey from above. (It is worth diverting right to Fountains Hall.)

④ Ⓒ Carry on along estate road to left of abbey (if you approached via the gate-house and meadows you will initially be retracing your steps), then along the river. ⑤ Ⓓ Cross

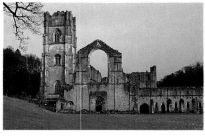

Fountains Abbey, once the wealthiest abbey in the north of England

the river at next bridge, turn right on other side, then fork left uphill. The track bends left (in front of fixed gate) at top of woods; passes pavilion with Surprise View, and continues past the Temple of Fame and Octagon Tower, before heading through tunnel. At bottom, bear right to cross weir at footbridge (the first on the Seven Bridges Walk, which you now follow) Ⓔ. Turn right again at T-junction with estate road, past gate-house/ticket office and tea-room. Where estate road bends left uphill, go forward on lakeside path, over another bridge ⑥. Continue along the riverside path, re-crossing river by five further bridges. Leave the estate by a National Trust sign at a gate in the estate wall. The track continues forward (ignore ascending path on the left, and a bridge soon after). ⑦ The track ascends to leave river, passes a farm (where you ignore a right turn). ⑧ Where the estate road goes off to left (to the church) F, go forward to Studley Roger.

ON THE ROUTE

A This side of the Studley Royal estate is crossed by public rights of way and is always open to walkers free of charge. It includes a **deer park**, home to some 350 red, fallow, Manchurian and sika deer. Studley Royal house itself belonged to the Aislabie family and was gutted by fire in 1946. The stable-block remains. Both Studley Royal and Fountains Abbey now belong to the National Trust.

B The **estate church** (*open* May to September inclusive, 1 to 5pm), which has to be manned because of its precious interior, was built 1871–78 to the design of William Burges. This extraordinarily ornate creation features depictions of angelic musicians and carved parrots against a rich background of gold and red. Elsewhere in Britain Burges is best remembered for his eye-catching alterations to Cardiff Castle, and for building the Rhenish-style Castell Coch on the outskirts of Cardiff; both of the latter were constructed for the Marquess of Bute.

C **Fountains Abbey** (National Trust; admission includes abbey and the follies and ponds of Studley Royal Park; *open* daily except Christmas and Friday November to January). In 1132 Cistercian monks founded the abbey on the banks of the River Skell. In its heyday, up to the Dissolution, Fountains was the wealthiest abbey in northern England, owning vast tracts of lands and scores of grange farms; it is still the largest abbey ruin in the country. In the 18th century, the ruins became regarded as the ultimate garden embellishment for Studley Royal.

Fountains Hall, near the abbey, is being restored by the National

Trust, and contains an exhibition. The slender Jacobean mansion was originally separate from Studley Royal; stones from the abbey were used for its construction in 1611.

D **Studley Royal** is the finest example of an 18th-century water park, begun by John Aislabie of Studley Royal house after expulsion from Parliament in 1720 for his role in the South Sea Bubble scandal. Fortunately he had the taste to keep the abbey vistas folly-free. His son William completed the landscaping. Viewed from above the ponds take on the form of items in a school geometry set. The walk rises to pass Anne Boleyn's seat, a whimsical mock-Gothic conceit giving a surprise view of the abbey and looking tailor-made for a romantic tryst. From the Octagon Tower, which gives an aerial view of the

ponds and looks across to the Banqueting House, the track heads into a drippy tunnel that deliberately twists into momentary, complete darkness – perhaps to excite the ladies on their carriage drive around the estate.

E The narrow board over the weir is the start of the **Seven Bridges Walk** (if you find crossing it unnerving, use the larger bridge crossed earlier, to the left). The five final bridges are quaint stone rustic affairs; the valley narrows and crags appear as the path encounters a tamed wilderness.

F At this point the **vista** of the church to the left is deliberately aligned with Ripon cathedral, in the far distance to the right. The cathedral has a striking early English west front, but is probably more renowned for its Saxon crypt.

Fountains Hall, built partly of stones from the Abbey, is being restored by the National Trust

RICHMOND AND THE SWALE

A TOWN and country walk, first making a tour of Richmond – a medieval-planned, fortified town whose castle, square and street layout betray a strong Continental influence – then along the River Swale, in one direction to the abbey, and in the other out into rural Swaledale, finishing with an exciting high-level section. Take care with directions after ⑩.

to join street, take steps on left (by a sign for Castle Terrace), proceed along cobbled street passing entrance to the castle keep to reach main square again.

Go to the other side of the square, taking narrow lane called Friars Wynd just to right of Finkle Street E. ④ At end F turn right along Victoria Road and go forward at

roundabout, along Ryders Wynd G. At end, turn left into Frenchgate, follow uphill H, and at top ⑤ turn right into a narrow alley called Lombards Wynd, descending.

Near the bottom, pass end of churchyard, where you keep straight on (ignoring right turn); ⑥ 50 yards later, the path on right to river is continuation, *but first detour ahead*

LENGTH 8½ miles (13.5km), 4½ hours; can shorten by 1½ miles (2.5km) by omitting detour to abbey, or can be restricted to a short stroll around the town
DIFFICULTY 2 (rather boggy underfoot in one field; one climb)
START Main square, Richmond. Grid reference 171009
OS MAPS Landranger 92; Pathfinder 609 (NZ 00/10)
REFRESHMENTS Full range in town

WALK DIRECTIONS

① A From main square (Trinity Church Square), by church tower, take Finkle Street (just to right of National Westminster Bank). Turn left at T-junction by the Unicorn Inn into Newbiggin B, then left again down Bargate. ② Turn left opposite the Oak Tree pub, up Cornforth Hill C to archway, just after which bear right (left is The Bar), then right again along Castle Walk which skirts the curtain wall of castle D. ③ Just as you are about

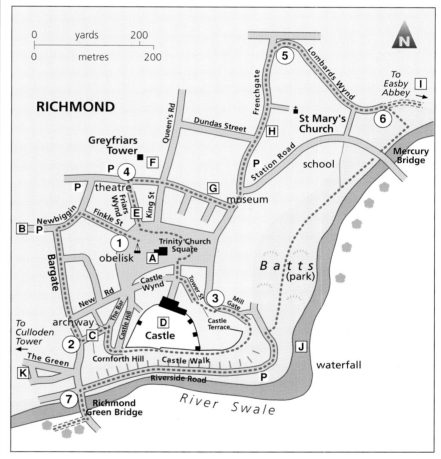

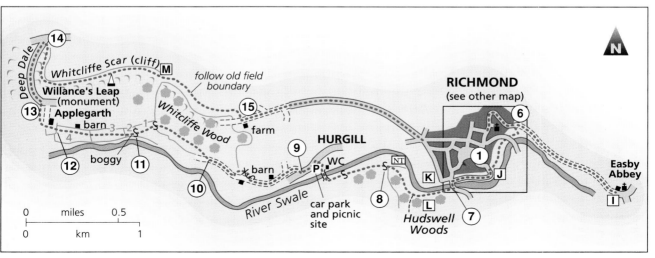

on track ¾ mile to Easby Abbey (at boathouse sign, fork right on to riverside path) I. Retrace your steps from Abbey to ⑥ and turn along the riverside path, under bridge, past a school on your right, just after which you bear left over grass to continue along river J. Later, you join road and reach Richmond Green Bridge ⑦. *Detour right:* immediately on your left is The Green, with the Culloden Tower behind K. *To finish walk* continue up Bridge Street into town centre. *To continue* return to bridge and cross it; and turn right on riverside path L. Soon fork left, uphill: keep to the main path (edged with narrow logs), ignoring side turns; by a footbridge in woods, ignore a right descending path. The main path soon descends, leaving woods by a stile ⑧ at National Trust sign for Hudswell, then proceed through meadow alongside River Swale. Just after passing Hurgill on the outskirts of Richmond on other bank, cross a footbridge over river. Continue forward, past toilet block, bearing left up the road to join the main road, where you turn left.

⑨ Take an enclosed track on right (after 130 yards), before Road Liable to Subsidence sign. This goes along the level; just before a farm take gate on right (waymarked with yellow arrow), turn left, to by-pass the farm, through gate and stile to follow left edge of field, then over stile; keep forward beyond on a path (soon a track) into woods.

⑩ 100 yards after River Swale comes into view, turn right (waymarked) on to woodland path, to reach a stile into a field. Turn left, to cross bridge over channel and go forward to take stile in fence. Turn right to follow fence and then reach section of dilapidated wall. Here turn left to river, and right along riverside path. ⑪ In second field continue along river, then into third field by a gate beside a stile: keep to left of the tree-lined water channel. Enter fourth field, continue up close to right edge, past a barn then through a gateway.

⑫ In fifth field there is a farm, Applegarth, on right: bear half right to the field corner, finding an

unprominently waymarked track, which proceeds through a gate. Just after, leave track as it bends round in front of Applegarth; and go forward, uphill, following scant remains of a wall, which immediately bends right, above the track. Where track below emerges on to a tarmacked lane, turn left, now with a solid wall on your right, up to a stile on to lane by cattlegrid (ignore waymarking for Coast to Coast Path).

⑬ Turn left uphill on the lane, up Deep Dale. ⑭ Just before cattlegrid on to road at top, turn very sharp right (doubling back) on to a grassy path heading to a wall.

The path proceeds on the level along top of edge M, with dramatic views on the right, past a monument and later just above top of woods. Soon after, path switches to the other side of fence, to proceed just inside a field with fence on right: at end of field, keep to left of gorse area finding a gateway a short distance to left of edge of slope. In next field, with Richmond directly ahead, path runs down along a prominent grassy hump to a farm. ⑮ At farm turn left along a stony track (later becomes surfaced lane) and follow this to Richmond.

ON THE ROUTE

A **Trinity Church Square** A clear indication of Richmond's prosperity in the 15th and 16th centuries as a trading place, and in the 18th century as a wool centre. The **church** of Holy Trinity (founded 1135) is a rarity in having shops built into it; the building has also been a prison, courthouse and granary, and is now the **Regimental Museum** of the Green Howards (*open* Easter to Oct, 11 to 5 daily).
B **Newbiggin** This broad cobbled street lies outside the old town walls.
C **Cornforth Hill** One of a number of alleys or 'wynds' in the town, leading steeply up through one of two surviving town wall gateways.
D The path skirts the huge curtain wall of the **castle** (English Heritage, *open* Easter to Sept, 10 to 6 daily), occupying a natural defensive position with precipitous drops to the Swale. The building was begun in 1071 as the Normans

strengthened their hold on northern England. Its 12th-century keep soars to 100 feet, and has 11-foot thick walls; the herring-bone masonry is a characteristic Norman feature.
E In Friars Wynd, the **gateway** in the town wall gave access to the Franciscan friary (see F). At the end of the Wynd on the right, **Richmond Theatre** conceals the oldest theatrical interior in its original form in Britain. Built by actor-manager Samuel Butler in 1788; *open* Easter to October, 11 to 4.45 Monday to Saturday, 2.30 to 4.45 Sunday.
F **Greyfriars Tower** (opposite). One of only three Franciscan bell-towers left in England; the foundation dates from 1258 but the Perpendicular tower is 15th century.
G **Richmondshire Museum** (on left in Ryders Wynd; *open* Easter to October 11 to 5 daily) has exhibits on the history of the area.
H **Frenchgate** French followers of the first Earl of Richmond were originally housed here.
I **Easby Abbey** (English Heritage; *open* 9.30 to 4 or 6.30 daily; closed Sunday am). A foundation of about 1152 which belonged to the Premonstratensians (or 'white canons', because of the colour of their habits).
J There are waterfalls and a weir along this fast-flowing stretch of the **Swale.**
K The Green has a view of **Culloden Tower,** a Georgian Gothic folly (not open).
L **Hudswell Woods** Best in spring and autumn, covering steep slopes on the south side of the Swale.
M **Whitcliffe Scar,** a limestone feature, provides a level walk high above Swaledale, looking towards the Vale of York and the North York Moors.

England's largest market place at Richmond

SWALEDALE AND ARKENGARTHDALE

THE route follows moorland tracks over high ground for the most part, but low-level sections in lush river valleys make this a richly varied walk, not to be hurried.

WALK DIRECTIONS

(1) [A] Start at the bottom end of the green and take the lane just to right of Congregational church. At T-junction after 60 yards, turn right. After 100 yards keep straight on at junction taking lane with No Through Road sign. You soon reach a gate at end of lane. (2) Turn left (*note* this section can get flooded; if so, use directions given at end to reach (3)), signposted Grinton, down between walls to a gate, then over the footbridge; bear right in

direction of signpost to gate, then proceed to a suspension bridge. Do not cross the bridge but turn right along the riverside path [B].

Soon the path passes a big flat meadow on your right; Healaugh village comes into view ahead and to right.

(3) Turn right (signposted; this is ½ mile after the suspension bridge), alongside wall on right to reach gate at right-hand end of Healaugh [C]. Turn left on the road through the village. Take the second road turn on right, by a telephone-box, immediately bear left at junction. 50 yards later, turn left on grassy track between walls (by power post).

(4) At the end of walled track, take stone steps on left (rather hidden; do not take either gate to

the right of this) and turn right in the field, alongside wall on your right, passing a barn and going through a gap-stile (a deliberate gap in the wall). In the second field, go half right heading for another barn, and taking gap-stile 40 yards away. In the third field turn left to find stile just to left of (same) barn.

LENGTH 10 miles (16km), 4½ hours
DIFFICULTY 3
START Village green, Reeth (on B6270 west of Richmond); roadside parking. Grid reference 038993
OS MAPS Landranger 92 and 98; Outdoor Leisure 30
REFRESHMENTS Full range in Reeth; pub (Red Lion) and shop in Langthwaite

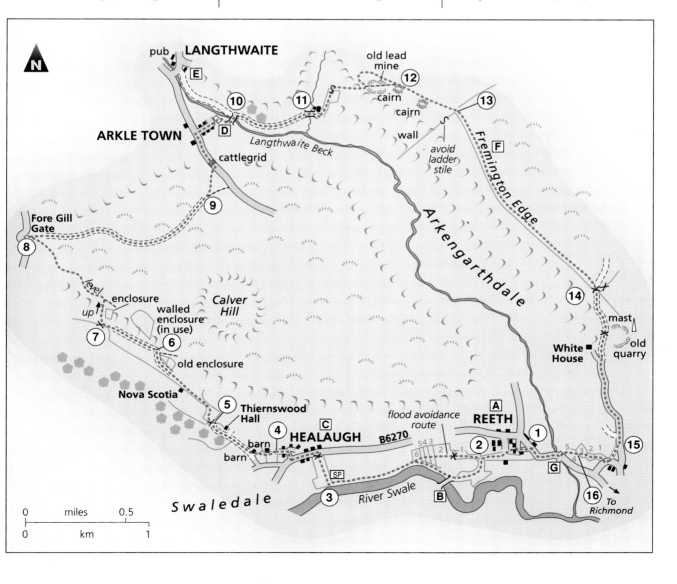

Emerge on unmade track and turn right along it; in front of the next house (Thiernswood Hall), ignore the right turn but continue on into woods; the track contours around the top of the woods, soon bending right to a gate out of woods (5).

Beyond this gate keep left (no path defined), alongside wall, up to a stile. Follow this wall as it bends right and then left uphill. At a point level with house close by on left (Nova Scotia), the route picks up defined track, leaving wall on left and heading up immediately to left of an old enclosure.

(6) 100 yards after the old enclosure, turn left at T-junction with track (100 yards before an enclosure which is still in use ahead). You then reach stone wall on left around another enclosure. (7) 100 yards later, the track ends: turn right (opposite gate in the wall) heading up over pathless moor to a moorland ridge 200 yards away to pick up a prominent grassy path gently rising to the left over the shoulder of the ridge.

(8) After ½ mile, just before the gate giving on to road, reach corner of wall on left; turn sharp right on a well-defined track (almost doubling back; a small valley on left and Arkengarthdale are visible ahead in the distance); follow this for 1¼ miles.

(9) Shortly before reaching the road, fork left to cut off a small corner, towards cattlegrid. Turn left on road. 250 yards after the cattlegrid, turn right opposite post-box, along a cul-de-sac. After 200 yards, just as road is about to bend left, keep straight on through a signposted small gate, crossing field (old graveyard) (D) to a stile in corner, then bear right on path dropping to a footbridge over river. (10) On other side, you turn right for the continuation, but first detour left to reach Langthwaite village and pub (E). Return to point (10) and proceed along track (which leaves

The hardy Swaledale sheep can survive the harsh Pennine winters

river), into a wood where you soon fork left; the track crosses a field then bends right (signposted Fremington) to cross a footbridge (11). Pass a farm (Strothwaite Hall) on your left then, immediately after, turn left uphill between walls (signposted Hurst). Where the wall on right ends, continue up alongside wall on left (blue paint waymarks here) to a gate; then bear right, heading up to an obvious breach in the top of Fremington Edge (old lead workings), with a prominent cairn (piled-up stones) on top (12).

Turn right along the top of the Edge: there is no defined path initially, but there is a small cairn shortly – keep slightly away from the very edge (F). (13) When you reach a wall across the path, cross via (gateless) gateway (if you reach a ladder-stile you are 200 yards too far to the right), and proceed now with the wall on your right for 1¼ miles. (14) You eventually reach a gate beside a stile over fence at right angles to the path, with a track coming in from left: take the gate on right and follow the well-defined track downhill. Reeth is in view, but the track heads to the left of it; track later becomes surfaced.

(15) After ¾ mile, ignore track on right signposted Arkengarthdale, but 50 yards later take grassy track on right to reach T-junction with lane. Turn right then after 30 yards, where lane bends left, fork right through gate. Follow left edge of three fields, alongside the wall. (16) Halfway through third field, take

gate on left and cross fourth field towards 30mph signs by bridge (G). Cross bridge and follow road into Reeth.

Flood avoidance route: continue forward (as approaching from Reeth), signposted Healaugh, through gate, and proceed with wall on left in (first) field; in second field go forward (along grassy hump marking former field boundary) to leave by gate; proceed across three small fields heading for stile or gate ahead; in sixth field, river is close by on left. Go forward 50 yards then drop down to stile by river; turn right along riverside path. Resume directions at (3).

ON THE ROUTE

(A) **Reeth** A large village at the junction of Swaledale and Arkengarthdale, with a large, irregular green as its focal point. This was a flourishing lead-mining area in the 18th and 19th centuries; in the 1880s decline set in with the availability of cheap lead from overseas.

(B) The **Swale** is reputedly England's swiftest-flowing river; floods are frequent, and it has been canalised in places. Swaledale's stone barns are very much a landscape feature.

(C) **Healaugh** A one-street hamlet, which grew in the 19th-century lead-mining boom.

(D) A few tombstones are all that remains of **Arkle Town's old church**, built 1145 and demolished 1818.

(E) The **bridge** at **Langthwaite** is featured in the opening sequence of *All Creatures Great and Small*, the TV series based on James Herriot's books.

(F) **Fremington Edge** is littered with evidence of lead-mining, but offers a splendid walk along the top of its escarpment, high above Arkengarthdale. Halfway along, **views** open out east to the North York Moors.

(G) **Reeth Bridge** Built in 1773 by John Carr, architect of Harewood House.

UPPER SWALEDALE AND KISDON HILL

FINE river scenery and waterfalls feature in the landscape here which is mellow rather than rugged, in spite of the steepness of the Swaledale slopes. After a modest ascent from Keld, the return is on grassy tracks over Kisdon Hill (or by the easier Pennine Way). Paths and tracks are generally well defined; route-finding is quite easy.

LENGTH	5½ miles (9km), 3 hours
DIFFICULTY	2
START	Muker, 20 miles west of Richmond on B6270; roadside parking. Grid reference 909978
OS MAPS	Landranger 98 and 91, or 98 and 92; Outdoor Leisure 30
REFRESHMENTS	Shop and pub in Muker; water tap in square at Keld

WALK DIRECTIONS

① From the B6270 take the minor road uphill into the village centre and keep to the right of the post office Ⓐ. 30 yards later turn right, signposted Gunnerside. This leads into a field where a clear path leads through five fields, then cross the bridge over the Swale and turn left ②. Walk along the turf or track to follow the river upstream. ③ After 1 mile, reach Swinner Gill with its deep gorge, waterfalls and foot-bridge Ⓑ. Cross the bridge, immediately forking right on the upper track rising out of Swinner Gill Ⓒ.

④ After ¾ mile pass through a gate, and 100 yards later fork left downhill to cross two bridges, the second crossing the Swale itself. ⑤ 200 yards later, reach the Pennine Way sign at T-junction of paths. Turn right to continue (or detour left for views of Kisdon Force Ⓓ, forking left again as signposted after ¼ mile, then retrace your steps; you can continue back to Muker along the Pennine Way for easy route-finding, but then you miss the view from Kisdon Hill).

The path soon enters the square at Keld ⑥ Ⓔ. Turn left through the village, take first left fork and turn left again at T-junction by the phone-box.

⑦ After 300 yards fork left on to a track (signposted Muker) by the side of a barn. Follow this walled track which very soon turns uphill and becomes more gradual after passing a farmhouse up on your left Ⓕ. ⑧ At the end of the second (long) field after passing that farm, continue half left (signposted Muker) to pick up a track between walls on the other side of the pasture. ⑨ Where the walled section ends, continue forward on a grassy track and on reaching the corner of a wall proceed with the wall on your left down towards Muker Ⓖ. Join a surfaced lane further down, and continue down to the start.

ON THE ROUTE

Ⓐ **Muker** Tightly clustered around its Elizabethan church. Pioneer botanists Cherry and Richard Kearton, who were born nearby at Thwaite, went to school here (there

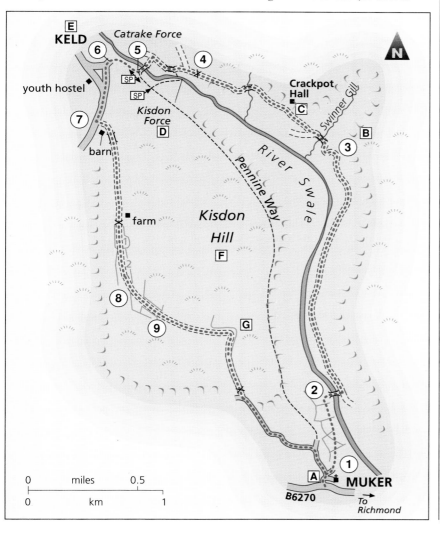

The River Swale, the fastest-flowing river in the Dales

THE PENNINES PAY

The Countryside Commission carried out a survey on the Pennine Way, and estimated that over 12,000 long-distance walkers and over 250,000 day ramblers use the Pennine Way every year; between them they spend about £2 million along the route, which helps create or support 156 jobs.

The Swale at perhaps its most scenic stretch as it flows between the villages of Muker and Keld

are commemorative tablets on either side of the school door). They were the first to use photographs for illustrating botanical books.

B The hillside on the right is dotted with relics – shafts, workings and spoil heaps – of the Swaledale **lead-mining industry**; it once accounted for most of Yorkshire's lead output (see box). When the industry (which dated from medieval times) declined at the end of the last century, huge depopulation followed. Just after crossing **Swinner Gill** you will pass a ruined **smelt mill**, part of the Beldi Hill mines; a little further on a leat (channel) runs close to the path: this comes down the hill from the old workings, and used to operate a water-wheel in the mine dressing works.

C **Crackpot Hall** The ruin up on the hill on the right was named after the Norse for 'hole of the crows', although the meaning of its name was not fully appreciated until the 1950s, when a cave entrance to Fairy Hole (Crackpot Cave) was discovered.

D **Kisdon Force** Well worth the short detour from the route, not so much for the **waterfall** itself as for its situation, deep in a rocky gorge.

E **Keld** On the other side of the square an entrance leads into a farmyard, at the far end of which is a good view down into another **waterfall, Catrake Force**.

F **Kisdon Hill** Its name means 'little detached (hill)'. It was cut off from the main upland mass to the east when glacial ice blocked the Swale and diverted it to cut its present course around the east side of the hill. **View** ahead south is towards Lovely Seat (2,213ft) and, away to the right (south-west), Great Shunner Fell (2,349ft).

G The final part of the walk into Muker follows the old **corpse way**. This was the route coffin-bearers used from Muker to the church at Grinton, before the church at Muker was built in 1580. Stone slabs were placed at intervals.

SWALEDALE AND THE LEAD-MINING INDUSTRY

Swaledale may be less visited than some other parts of the Dales, but its beauties are no less considerable or varied. The landscape here is traditional, with Swaledale sheep, now widespread in northern England for their hardy qualities, stone barns in profusion and a great number of uncultivated meadows; these present a blaze of yellow in June when buttercups, globe flowers, meadow vetchling and birdsfoot-trefoil are out, with thistles providing splashes of purple.

Yet the dale also bears the scars of its time before 1840 as the major lead-mining area in the Dales. The process was first carried out by surface digging, then levels (or 'adits') were driven horizontally into the hillsides and shafts were sunk. The ore went to the smelting-mills. An unusual feature of mining in the dale was the use of 'hushes', where streams were dammed to make ponds, from which torrents of water would be released to wash down and break up any lead-rich veins ('orebodies') in the rock. Today the hushes of Gunnerside Gill (a couple of miles east of this walk) and heaps of orange-grey spoil make spectacular gashes on the scene, and stone-arched entrances to adits and eerie ruins of smelting- and crushing-mills haunt the landscape. After 1840 the industry began to decline with cheaper ore available from overseas and the population, 8,000 in 1801, dwindled to the 2,000 or so inhabitants here today.

NORTHERN WHARFEDALE

A ROUTE memorable for its views. It follows the side of the dale before joining the valley floor at Hubberholme and ending along the Wharfe. Route-finding is mostly easy. Stepping stones at Cray can be tricky after prolonged rain.

LENGTH 4½ miles (7km), 2 hours
DIFFICULTY 2
START Buckden (car park next to post office). Grid reference 942774
OS MAPS Landranger 98; Outdoor Leisure 10
REFRESHMENTS Shop, tea-rooms and pub in Buckden; pub in Cray and in Hubberholme

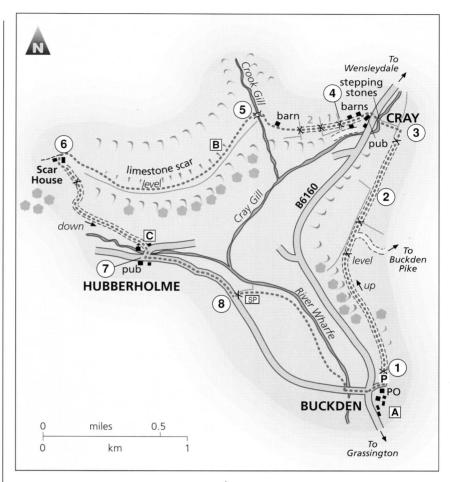

WALK DIRECTIONS

① Ⓐ From B6160 by post office, take signposted bridleway from Buckden Pike, at entrance to car park, passing toilets, then through the gate at the far end of car park by signpost for Buckden Pike and Cray High Bridge. Follow the track that rises gently, soon through trees. Beyond the trees, the track is joined by a wall on your left and now levels out (ignore right turn up to Buckden Pike by gate). ② Where the wall ends, proceed along level grassy track. After next gate, a wall on left begins.

③ 50 yards later turn left through gate signposted Cray, heading down towards the pub at right end of village and crossing a ford. Cross the road and take the track to right of pub; behind pub keep to right (upper) fork, passing through farmyard by barns, then keep forward through a gate, passing further barns and picking up a stony track.

④ 100 yards later, keep to right of last barn, through signposted gate for Yockenthwaite (avoiding lower track signposted Stubbing Bridge). A stony track crosses the first field (yellow paint waymarks in the following section make route-finding simple; these directions are given in case of problems). In second field (where track ends) keep forward to gate. In third field, continue slightly right, aiming just to left of barn, then continue along the level, with wall up on right, and cross footbridge over Crook Gill ⑤.

On the other side, bear slightly left, still along the level, with the wall (later a fence) on left Ⓑ. ⑥ After 1 mile, you reach a farm (Scar House) on left, by signpost. Turn left, through farmyard, and follow track down to emerge on road by Hubberholme church ⑦ Ⓒ. Turn right on road, over the river bridge, then left on the other side, by the George Inn.

⑧ ⅓ mile later, take the gate on left by signpost for Buckden Bridge. Keep left, alongside the wall and turn right on reaching the river; follow river to Buckden Bridge. Cross the bridge and follow the road up to the post office and the car park.

ON THE ROUTE

Ⓐ **Buckden** Named after deer, a herd of which survived until recent

YORKSHIRE DALES PASTURE LANDS

The sheep that features on the Yorkshire Dales National Park emblem is a Swaledale tup, a black-and-white faced creature which grazes throughout the northern Dales. In the southern Dales, the Dalesbred (identifiable by its black face with two white patches) is common, while the irregularly marked Rough Fell sheep wander the Howgill Fells. Cattle, too, are widespread; Wensleydale cheese is a household name.

After the Dissolution of the Monasteries, the great monastic estates were sold off, and between 1630 and 1730 a new class stratum of yeomen farmers appeared. Sitting tenants gradually took over the freeholds. The farms were rebuilt, but the dimensions of the earlier buildings were retained.

A particular feature of Swaledale is the predominance of stone barns, built as winter byres. Nearly every field has one. Changed farming practices mean that many of these structures have become redundant, and their long-term future is by no means assured.

times; the antlers from the last to be shot hangs at the White Lion in Cray (on this route). Buckden housed foresters in Norman times, when Langstrothdale Chase was a hunting forest.

B Large **limestone pavement**, with a long limestone scar on the right; this natural terrace provides a magnificent viewing platform for admiring Wharfedale.

C **Hubberholme** The **church** is 12th and 16th century and contains a rare roof loft of 1558, used as a musicians' gallery before the organ was installed. Pews and stalls have a carved trademark in the form of a mouse, signifying the maker, Thompson of Kilburn, near Helmsley, who died in 1955. The Thompson company still makes furniture and other wooden items with the carved mouse. Across the Wharfe, the **George Inn** is the venue for an ancient dale 'land letting' custom, in which the tenancy of the 'poor field', which belongs to the church, is auctioned to local farmers on New Year's Eve; the vicar places a candle on the bar and waits in the other room while the auction is under way. The ensuing sing-song includes the *Song of Wharfedale*. The main bar of the pub has a timeless air with a stone-flagged floor, oak beams and a huge log fire in a leaded iron grate; toilets are outside and are labelled 'ewes' and 'tups'.

The classic limestone scenery of the River Wharfe

GORDALE SCAR AND MALHAM COVE

A MUCH-VISITED area (best avoided at summer weekends). Three remarkable natural features: Gordale Scar, the limestone pavement and Malham Cove; also takes in some wooded river scenery at Janet's Foss. Short sections of field-paths undefined, but route-finding quite easy. Watch your footing as you cross the limestone pavement.

LENGTH 4 miles (6.5km), 2 hours
DIFFICULTY 1–2
START Malham, 11 miles north-west of Skipton. Large car park (fee) at information centre in village. Grid reference 900626
OS MAPS Landranger 98; Outdoor Leisure 10
REFRESHMENTS Pub, café and hotel at Malham. Occasionally, refreshment van at entrance to Gordale Scar (high season)

WALK DIRECTIONS

① Turn left out of car park and into village, turning right over bridge opposite Buck Inn. After bridge immediately turn right again, doubling back on track, alongside river, leading to stile. Follow this well-trodden path across two fields, then turn left on path signposted Janet's Foss (ignoring path signposted Pennine Way, half right). Path is well signposted and after two fields proceeds alongside river on right. ② After ½ mile path enters Janet's Foss (wooded gorge) by kissing-gate and NT sign Ⓐ. After passing waterfall it continues up to road ③.

Rainwater seeps through the porous limestone at the top of Malham Cove to emerge as a stream at its foot

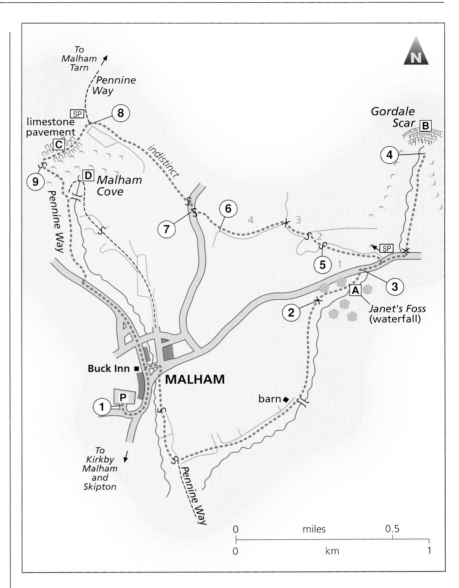

Turn right along road and 150 yards later turn left through gate, signposted Gordale Scar (avoiding, for the moment, first path on left, signposted Malham Cove). Follow up to waterfalls Ⓑ ④. After viewing Gordale Scar retrace steps to road, turn right, then after 50 yards cross bridge on right and stile beyond it, signposted Malham Cove. Bear immediately half left across first field to corner of wall (yellow marker posts) then continue forward with wall on right to ladder-stile ⑤. In second field, continue forward to cross ladder-stile in top right-hand corner and turn left to proceed on clear path with wall on left.

⑥ ¼ mile later, at corner of wall on left, path continues forward to wall ahead, turns right, then crosses

ladder-stile on left 50 yards later, to emerge on road ⑦. Turn right on road, then immediately left over stile signposted Malham Cove. The route (not always defined on the ground) ascends quarter right over a small rise then joins wall on left. Proceed alongside the wall on left to a signpost ⑧ where keep forward (ignoring Pennine Way, signposted to right). Proceed towards limestone pavement Ⓒ), crossing wall by gap or stile, then forward over the pavement (take great care: it may be easier to skirt it to the right) to reach stiles at far side of the pavement ⑨, beyond which descend steps steeply to foot of Malham Cove Ⓓ. At bottom turn left to view cove, then retrace steps and *either* follow well-marked track across fields to lane at edge of Malham (this track teems with visitors at peak times) *or* (if you want more seclusion) 30 yards before Cove, cross stream by stones and follow the left bank. At stile continue forward uphill, cross two fields in direction of signposts heading for ladder-stiles, and in third field continue forward to wall at top (left side) of field and follow easy path back to Malham.

ON THE ROUTE

[A] **Janet's Foss** Wooded gorge, rich in insect, bird and plant life, leading to the Foss (or force) itself, a modest waterfall flowing over a very fine cone of tufa (a limestone incrustation). The cave just behind is the home of Janet, queen of the fairies.

[B] **GordaleScar** Remains hidden until the last moment. Gordale Beck performs a double jump from a stone 'window'. The limestone cliff, standing on the Mid-Craven Fault, was eroded by the stream, which then disappeared underground. The roof of the cavern, which was gouged out, has now collapsed, exposing the stream once more. The scene made a strong impression on early Romantic English landscape artists, including James Ward, whose painting of the Scar (1815) is now in the Tate Gallery.

[C] **Limestone pavement** Britain's finest example of such a feature, caused by the dissolving effect of rainwater; often likened to an outsized bar of white chocolate. The fissures are 'grykes' and the blocks are 'clints'. The grykes harbour a number of plants (some rare), including hart's tongue, geranium, wood sorrel, rue, asplenium, enchanter's nightshade and wood garlic.

[D] **Malham Cove** 250ft high at its highest point, an inland cliff of limestone, representing one stage before what has happened at Gordale Scar; the cliff has been eroded by the stream, which has now vanished underground, but its cavern has not collapsed yet. The stream re-emerges at the foot of the cove. Probably most of the rock at the bottom was scoured away by glacial action.

One of the cove's most significant visits was that made by Charles Kingsley, who joked that the black lichen marks on the rock could have been caused by a chimney sweep falling over the edge. He later enlarged this idea into the plot of *The Water Babies*, in which Tom, the sweep, meets the water babies in the River Aire. Ruskin and Wordsworth wrote about Malham Cove and in 1786 John Hurtley recorded the excellence of its five-fold echo: 'a most pleasing effect in a calm and clear evening from a French horn or any other instrument'.

Part of Malham's spectacular limestone pavement viewed from just above the Cove itself

PEN-Y-GHENT

THE lowest of the Three Peaks, involving a mild scramble to reach its flat summit. In addition to the vast panorama over the central and southern dales, the route passes close to two pot-hole entrances before taking a stone-walled green lane back down to Horton. The paths are well defined to a point of serious erosion, although much repair work has been done.

WALK DIRECTIONS

① Turn right out of the car park on the main road, past the information centre; 80 yards later, turn left on to a track signposted Pennine Way. At a fork, bear right (signposted Three Peaks Walk) Ⓐ. ② Emerge at farms and buildings, turn right on a surfaced road, then immediately left over a footbridge and turn left on the other side to follow the road

past the primary school. ③ At the beginning of the hamlet of Brackenbottom take a signposted gate on the left, through enclosure to a gate beside a stile; the route up Pen-y-ghent is obvious: proceed along the wall on the left; after a ladder-stile with a signpost pointing back to Brackenbottom, you are at the foot of the final part of the ascent – the route leads up to the left and needs care on loose rocks.

LENGTH	5 miles (8km), 2½ hours
DIFFICULTY	3
START	Horton in Ribblesdale car park (B6479 north of Settle). Grid reference 808727
OS MAPS	Landranger 98; Outdoor Leisure 2
REFRESHMENTS	Café and pub at start

④ Ⓑ At the trig point (summit pillar) at the top, go left over a ladder-stile and take the Pennine Way (signposted PW Horton), which is obvious all the way back Ⓒ: it drops and later reaches a ladder-stile (just after, look for Hunt Pot, a few yards off the path to the

Ribblesdale harbours some of the most dramatic rock shapes in the Dales

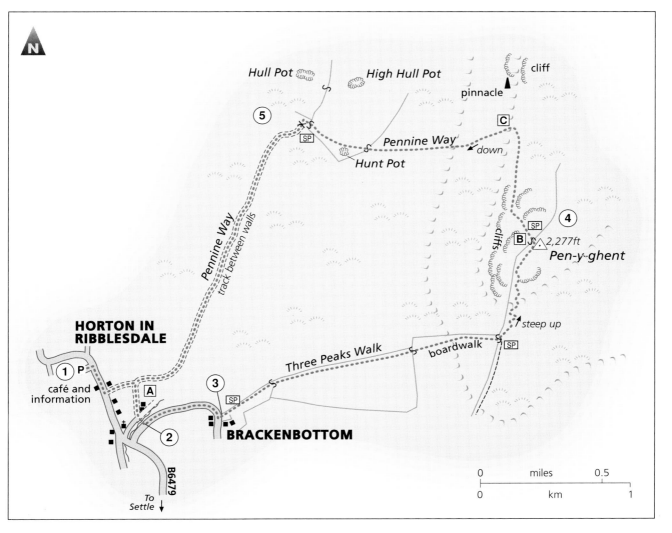

left). ⑤ After the next ladder-stile you soon continue (to the left) between walls (a 300-yard detour to the right brings you to the spectacular entrance to Hull Pot). At the fork reached near start, keep right to enter the village.

ON THE ROUTE

[A] **The Three Peaks Walk** The famous challenge walk begins from Horton in Ribblesdale and takes in the three Yorkshire giants – Pen-y-ghent, Ingleborough and Whernside. Virtually every weekend throughout the year, walkers can be seen making their way around it. The challenge is to complete the 22-mile route within eight hours, but anyone who manages it within twelve qualifies for membership of the Three Peaks of Yorkshire Club (based at the Pen-y-ghent café in Horton).

[B] **Pen-y-ghent (2,277ft)** The

INGLEBOROUGH AND WHERNSIDE

Of the other mountains that comprise the Three Peaks, **Ingleborough** (2,372ft) is probably the more interesting to the walker. Of its many caves and pot-holes, White Scar Cave and Ingleborough Cave are open to the public; both have fine **stalactite formations.** A fascinating walk leaves Clapham village and follows the Reginald Farrer Trail, for which a small toll is payable, passing the **tree collection** gathered by Farrer on his travels in Asia (he introduced Farrer's Gentian and scores of other species to Europe, including about twenty varieties of rhododendron). Carry on past Ingleborough Cave and ascend past **Gaping Gill**, the best-known pot-hole in the Dales; on certain days the public may descend into it by a winched chair – definitely not an experience for vertigo-sufferers or claustrophobics. There is a huge chamber within, large enough to swallow a decent-sized cathedral comfortably (if the opportunity ever arose . . .). The summit is now obvious; on top there are traces of an Iron Age camp. The view extends far into Yorkshire and Cumbria. It is possible to ascend from or descend into Ingleton via another path; there is a good bus service linking Ingleton and Clapham.

Whernside is reckoned by some as the boring one of the three, which is perhaps a little harsh as it offers a magnificent ridge section up to Yorkshire's highest point (2,414ft), right on the Cumbria boundary. The obvious starting-point is Ribblehead Viaduct.

rockiest and steepest part of the 270-mile Pennine Way, although not its highest point. **Views** extend over Ribblesdale, Littondale, Langstrothdale, Ingleborough and Whernside.

[C] The Pennine Way now follows a former miners' track. **Hunt Pot** and the more spectacular **Hull Pot** are characteristic limestone features: they are all the non-caver can see of the extremely dangerous pot-holes and cave systems which riddle this area.

ENVIRONMENTALLY SENSITIVE AREAS (ESAs)

At the time of writing there were 22 such areas in Britain (the Lake District being the largest); in 1994 almost 5,000 farmers held such agreements. Under the scheme, farmers receive grants for maintaining traditional farming practices. By bolstering the hill-farming economy, there is an increasing likelihood that sheep pastures and meadows full of wild flowers will continue to be the norm in these areas; without a financial incentive, scrubland would take over the meadows, and pesticides and fertilisers might predominate at the expense of wild flora. Under the ESA agreement, a farmer might call for breeding ewes to come off the hills in winter to reduce pressure on grazing, or harrowing and harvesting of hay meadows might be carried out in such a way as to maximise the varieties of wild flowers and minimise disturbance to ground-nesting birds. The ESAs should also help to revive traditional crafts such as hedging and walling.

A walker surveys the south face of Pen-y-ghent

MORECAMBE BAY AND ARNSIDE KNOTT

THIS walk follows the sandy and rocky shores edging the huge mud-flats of Morecambe Bay (rich in birdlife) and ascends Arnside Knott, a wooded hill with fine views over the bay and into the Lake District. Paths and tracks are mostly well defined; route-finding is quite easy. Rocks on the shore can be slippery.

LENGTH 6½ miles (10km), 3 hours

DIFFICULTY 2

START Arnside, Morecambe Bay; free car park (grid reference 454786) at end of B5282. Follow the B-road through Arnside, keeping right at end at No Through Road sign by Albion Hotel. *By train* Arnside station, on the Lancaster to Barrow line. Turn right out of station, and after 50 yards turn left on the path signposted to church. Keep forward at the church, on path signposted Silverdale Road. 300 yards later, cross road and take path opposite to emerge at T-junction opposite police station. Turn right to esplanade road and turn left along it.

OS MAPS Landranger 97; Pathfinder 636 (SD 37/47)

REFRESHMENTS Pubs and cafés in Arnside

WALK DIRECTIONS

① Follow esplanade road to the end, then go forward on path signposted New Barns Bay, alongside the beach Ⓐ. ② After ½ mile path reaches the bay with a house on other side. Cross to far side, pass to the right of house on beach, then either follow the beach or pick up the path just inside woods above the beach, 150 yards after house. ③ At the next bay, pick up the path climbing to top of low cliffs on the far side of bay.

④ ¾ mile later pass through a gate. After 150 yards take the track (signposted Arnside and Silverdale). This track soon leads into a caravan site; avoid side turns; follow lane through hamlet of Far Arnside. ⑤ At T-junction with road take the path opposite, signposted Silverdale,

proceeding with a wall on your right across first field then forward and up to pass through a small gate at the far side of second field. Bear slightly left through trees for 50 yards, making your way to a service road in caravan site. Turn left along it. ⑥ Opposite a sharp right turn with another service road (with No Entry road-sign), take grassy track on left by wooden electricity pole (waymarked with yellow arrow). Follow this for ¼ mile to ruined tower Ⓑ ⑦.

Turn left in front of the tower on track down to farm. Pass through a gate by the farm, signposted Arnside, taking the farm road to reach a road ⑧. Cross this road and pass through a gate opposite, with NT sign for Arnside Knott Ⓒ. Follow woodland bridleway gently uphill for ½ mile, then turn right on path marked 'This is a footpath, not

a bridleway; walkers only please'. Ascend to T-junction of paths by a bench, then right to viewpoint Ⓓ.

⑨ 300 yards after the viewpoint take stile on left on to grassy hillside. Go downhill to join wall on your right, then follow it down to a ladder-stile. Cross the ladder-stile

The handsome black and white oystercatcher

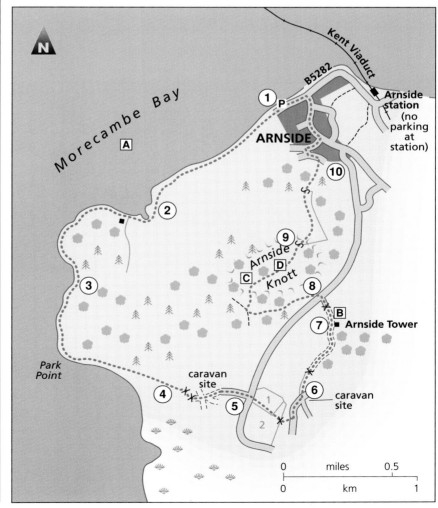

and almost immediately turn left into Redhills Wood (signposted); bear left on track to emerge on to the road. (10) Turn left on the road, which soon bends sharp right. Turn right at next junction and follow to Silverdale Road (signposted).

For car park Turn left and follow back to waterfront.

For railway station Turn right and after ¼ mile take path on left by Our Lady of Lourdes Chapel and descend to a road. Turn left to reach the station.

ON THE ROUTE

[A] **Morecambe Bay** One of the fastest incoming tides in Britain crosses this vast expanse of sand and mudflats. Though extremely dangerous to walk across without a detailed knowledge of the tides, it can be safely crossed, with a guide, from Kents Bank near Grange-over-Sands to Hest Bank, between Camforth and Morecambe (about 8 miles in all). Ask at local tourist offices if you are interested in trying it.

Over 200,000 waders (the largest estuary population in Britain): mallard, curlew, shoveller, redshank, shelduck, oystercatcher, ringed plover, dunlin, diver, pink-footed goose, merlin, knot, godwit, eider, wigeon.

In spring, wild daffodils and lily of the valley are seen along the coast here, while summer flora includes bloody cranesbill, centaury and rock rose.

[B] **Arnside Tower** A ruined peel tower – a four-storey building with what was a five-storey tower. Remains of the parapet are visible, but the internal floors have collapsed. Probably 15th century, built as a defence.

[C] **Arnside Knott** Has a yew grove and some uncommon grasses and ferns, among them adder's tongue. **Birds** that can be seen are redwing, woodcock, greenfinch, hawkfinch and fieldfare.

[D] **View** Over Morecambe Bay, with Grange-over-Sands to the west; the north-west are the southern fells of the Lake District, including the Old Man of Coniston; eastwards lie Shap Fell, the Howgills and the Forest of Bowland.

Treacherous to venture across at any time of year, Morecambe Bay has a dangerous beauty, especially in winter

---

WAYMARKS

Footpaths are sometimes marked with yellow arrows; bridleways (for walkers, cyclists and horse-riders) are shown by blue arrows; red arrows indicate byways (open to all traffic). National Trails are waymarked with acorn motifs.

WANSFELL PIKE, TROUTBECK AND AMBLESIDE

AN opportunity to climb a minor peak at the north end of Windermere, set somewhat apart from the main Lakeland fells hence giving superlative views. Pasture tracks and some road-walking for the link sections. The route is all on defined paths, most signposted; it is quite easy to find the way. Ascent 400ft through Skelghyll Wood and 1,000ft from Troutbeck to summit; then a very steep descent.

WALK DIRECTIONS

① From the car park, cross the river by the Bridge House and turn right into the town. Follow the main road past shops (one-way in your direction) and fork left into Old Lake Road. Keep forward past left turns (Blue Hill Road and Fisherbeck Lane) and past the other car park ②. Just before the Old Lake Road rejoins the main road,

---

LENGTH 6 miles (9.5km), 3½ hours
DIFFICULTY 3
START Ambleside, either just north of town centre (car park opposite Charlotte Mason College), at ①, (grid ref. 374048) or car park at end of town, opposite Hayes Garden Centre, at ② (grid ref. 377039). Parking at both points (fee).
OS MAPS Landranger 90; Outdoor Leisure 7
REFRESHMENTS Plenty at Ambleside; Post Office and Stores, Troutbeck (drinks can be enjoyed on a bench outside); the Mortal Man, Troutbeck

---

turn left up a steep narrow lane signposted to Jenkin Crag, Skelghyll and Troutbeck. Follow this lane avoiding turns into private houses. ③ After ½ mile, where the lane finally bends left, keep forward on a track. ④ The track enters woodlands Ⓐ and passes National

Trust signs; go forward over a bridge and uphill to a NT sign for Jenkin's Crag and Robin Lane; divert to the crag for fine views of Windermere and the hills to the south and west ⑤.

Return to the woodland path and follow it out of the wood, through farmland and through a farm (High Skelghyll). ⑥ 200 yards after the farm, cross a stream by a bridge, then immediately turn left through a gate signposted Troutbeck. Ignore minor left fork after 30 yards and by keeping right follow the path which rises to join a walled track: turn right along it. ⑦ After ¼ mile ignore the right fork by a wooden seat and continue until reaching the road at Troutbeck Ⓑ ⑧. For detour to Townend house, turn right for 200 yards Ⓒ.

To continue, turn left along the road for ½ mile. ⑨ Immediately after Hogarth's Cottage (on right),

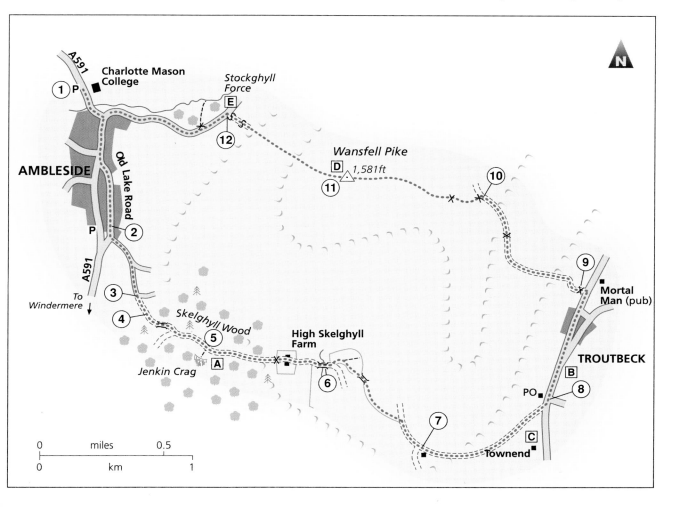

take the lane on your left between Lanefoot farmhouse and farm buildings. Follow the track uphill, passing through a gate after ½ mile, then ⑩ 220 yards later turn left through a gate signposted Ambleside via Wansfell, which gives access to a path over peaty ground (very clearly marked with cairns, and soon well defined) leading to the summit of Wansfell Pike ⓓ ⑪. Continue ahead to cross the wall by a stile, and descend carefully on a steep, well-defined path leading towards Ambleside. At the bottom cross two stiles within 200 yards to emerge on to a tarmac lane ⑫.

Turn left, towards Ambleside: shortly after the lane passes through a gate, look out for a metal turnstile on your right, the entrance to Stock ghyll Force ⓔ. After viewing the falls, continue on the lane back to the start. Turn right for car park at ①; left for car park at ②.

ON THE ROUTE

ⓐ **Skelghyll Wood** Mixed woodland of oak and exotic firs (including Sequoia and Hondo Spruce). **View** from Jenkin Crag over Windermere.

ⓑ **Troutbeck** A scattered village

Bridge House straddles Stockghyll at Ambleside; it once housed a family of six, and is now the National Trust's oldest information centre and smallest shop

Townend, 370 years old, retains the accumulated belongings of a family that kept everything and modernised nothing

with a number of **roadside wells**, each given a saint's name and a Victorian stone surround. The **inn sign** of Mortal Man (a rather grand Lakeland inn), with its jingle, was painted by Julius Caesar Ibbetson, who lived in the village 1801–05.

*O mortal man that lives by bread
What is it makes thy nose so red?
Thou silly fool that looks so pale,
'Tis drinking Sally Birkett's ale.*

ⓒ **Townend** (NT; *open to public*) A marvellously unspoilt yeoman's house (*c.* 1626), the home of the Browne family for over 300 years until it was handed over to the Trust in 1944. The house is full of evocations of the past; the family's hand-carved furniture and domestic utensils have been handed down through generations. Nothing has been modernised, and even today the building does not have electricity.

ⓓ **View** down Windermere, with Grizedale Forest on the west side and, south-west, standing on its own, the small conical hill of Latterbarrow (803ft); beyond it, Hawkshead village – further right is the Old Man of Coniston (2,633ft), Crinkle Crags (2,816ft) Bowfell (2,960ft) and the Langdale Pikes (2,403ft), Rydal Water and Grasmere; north-west Fairfield (2,863ft), north the Kirkstone Pass; north-east across the Troutbeck valley.

ⓔ **Stockghyll Force** A popular beauty spot, with pretty falls in a fine woodland setting.

RYDAL AND GRASMERE

A LITERARY pilgrimage, taking in two of Wordsworth's homes and his burial place, and encircling two lakes joined by the River Rothay. The area is very popular with visitors, but the setting remains practically unchanged since Wordsworth's time. All tracks and paths are well defined and signposted; easy route-finding.

WALK DIRECTIONS

① A With the church on your left follow the road over bridge through Grasmere. ② Cross the main road to the lane opposite, signposted Dove Cottage B. Follow the lane, avoiding side turns. ③ After 600 yards continue forward (No Through Road to Motors). ¼ mile later, the lane becomes a track. Follow this through pasture and woodland (the track forks after ½ mile, with the left fork ascending along a high stone wall: forks rejoin)

to village of Rydal ④.

Turn right on the tarmac lane (Rydal Mount C is soon on your right) and follow this to the main road. Turn right along it, then 300 yards later turn left through a gap in wall on to footbridge. The path immediately swings right ⑤. The path follows river, then the side of the lake D.

⑥ After the path ascends away from Rydal Water, ignore path entering woods on your right, but continue forward towards Grasmere,

> **LENGTH** 5 miles (8km), 2 hours
> **DIFFICULTY** 1
> **START** Grasmere, just off A591, 4 miles north-west of Ambleside. Grid reference 337074
> **OS MAPS** Landranger 90; Outdoor Leisure 7
> **REFRESHMENTS** Pubs and tea-rooms in Grasmere and a pub/hotel in Rydal

soon bearing right, down towards lake (the path up to the left, along Loughrigg Terrace, is a highly recommended detour for the marvellous views of the dale). Follow shore of Grasmere (lake) E.

⑦ The path turns away from the lake by a stone boathouse. Emerge on to tarmac lane and turn right into Grasmere.

Rydal Water from White Moss

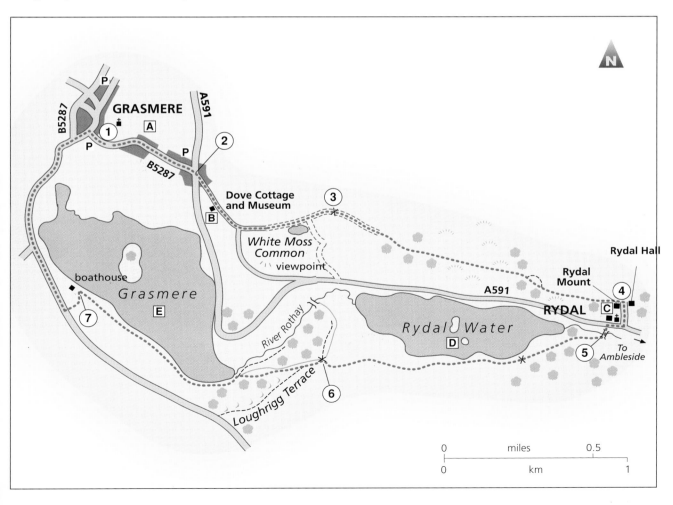

ON THE ROUTE

A **Grasmere (village)** Wordsworth described it as 'the loveliest spot that man hath ever found'. He lived in the village for 14 years, first at Dove Cottage (1799–1808), then at Allan Bank, later at the Rectory and finally at Rydal Mount, until his death in 1850. He, his wife, Mary, and sister, Dorothy, are all buried in Grasmere churchyard.

Grasmere is also famous for its **annual sports** (which include Cumberland wrestling and races up Butter Crag), its **gingerbread** (on sale at Sarah Nelson's Grasmere gingerbread shop: a Lakeland institution) and its St Oswald Day **rush-bearing procession** on 5 August – a north country tradition of bringing rushes into the church for strewing on the floor.

B **Dove Cottage** (*open to the public*; fee) The home of the Wordsworths until 1808, then of their friend De Quincey, author of *Confessions of an English Opium Eater*. The museum next door contains several of Wordsworth's possessions, including his buckles, his silk umbrella and his 'ww' monogrammed socks.

C **Rydal Mount** Wordsworth's home for the last 37 years of his life (*open to the public*; fee).

D **Rydal Water** Good for watching **wildfowl.** Along the banks of the River Rothay, which connects the two lakes, grows alder buckthorn, a species local to the Lakes. Across Rydal Water is Nab Cottage, where De Quincey used to visit Margaret Simpson, to the strong disapproval of the Wordsworths, who thought her too low-born. Beyond is Heron Pike (2,003ft).

E **Grasmere (lake)** The island in the middle is a drumlin, a hillock of boulder debris left behind by glaciation. Butterwort (insect-eating) and enchanter's nightshade are among the wild flowers found around the lake. Birds include dippers, grey and pied wagtails and sandpipers.

PLAIN LIVING AND HIGH THINKING

William Wordsworth lived at Dove Cottage from 1799 to 1808, his most productive years and the first six years of his married life. The first three of his children were born here, and during this time he wrote *The Daffodils, To the Cuckoo, The Rainbow, The Leech Gatherer, Immortality Ode*, and completed his autobiographical poem *The Prelude*.

The cottage dates from the early 17th century and was originally a pub called the Dove and Olive Bough; Wordsworth never knew it as Dove Cottage.

The Wordsworths – William, his wife Mary and sister Dorothy – had a spartan lifestyle, going for long walks, gardening and doing housework. Sir Walter Scott paid a visit and found it a little too bleak, and secretly climbed out of his bedroom window so he could get a decent meal at the Swan Hotel. The children's room was damp and needed to be papered with newspaper.

Rydal Mount, on the other hand, is distinctly grander. Wordsworth was a famous man by the time he lived here, from 1813 until his death in 1850. He derived an income as Distributor of Stamps for Westmorland and as Poet Laureate (although for all his years as Poet Laureate he never wrote a line of official verse). The garden was one of his great joys.

The garden of Dove Cottage was a beloved place for the Wordsworths, who transplanted local flora picked from the lakeside and the neighbouring fells, farmland and woodland

AROUND LANGDALE

FEW places in Britain have such an enchanting mix of upland and lowland: this route encircles Lingmoor Fell and shows off the best of the dale at low level. Some moderate short ascents; the route is not always defined.

WALK DIRECTIONS

① Take the gate at the back of the car park (to left of toilets) leading on to an enclosed path. After 50 yards this emerges into a small meadow: keep forward on a well-defined path, after 50 yards passing the corner of a fence on your left where ② you fork left on to a path alongside wall on left (right fork rises up Stickle Ghyll and then up to the Langdale Pikes) Ⓐ.

Continue along until ③ you are just past a house on the left, where the wall on left ends: here turn left to take the right-hand of two gates, and follow the enclosed path down to the road. Keep forward, over the bridge, to reach the main valley road. Turn right along the road; keep left with the principal road after 50 yards at cross-junction, then ④ after 150 yards (just after crossing a stream) take the signposted stile on your left into wooded area (National Trust campsite). Keep alongside the right-hand wall, bearing right after 50 yards as the wall bends right; where wall ends, cross a small grassy area to take kissing-gate into a wood. The path leads through the wood, through

LENGTH 8½ miles (13.5km), 4½ hours

DIFFICULTY 2–3

START National Trust car park, Dungeon Ghyll New Hotel, Langdale. Turn off A593 (Coniston to Ambleside) at Skelwith Bridge, and follow B5343 into Langdale; the car park is on the right just past sign for Sticklebarn Tavern. Grid reference 295064. (Additional parking is available at Elterwater and above Blea Tarn)

OS MAPS Landranger 90; Outdoor Leisure 6

REFRESHMENTS There is a café at the start; a pub and shop at Elterwater and Chapel Stile; and a pub at Little Langdale

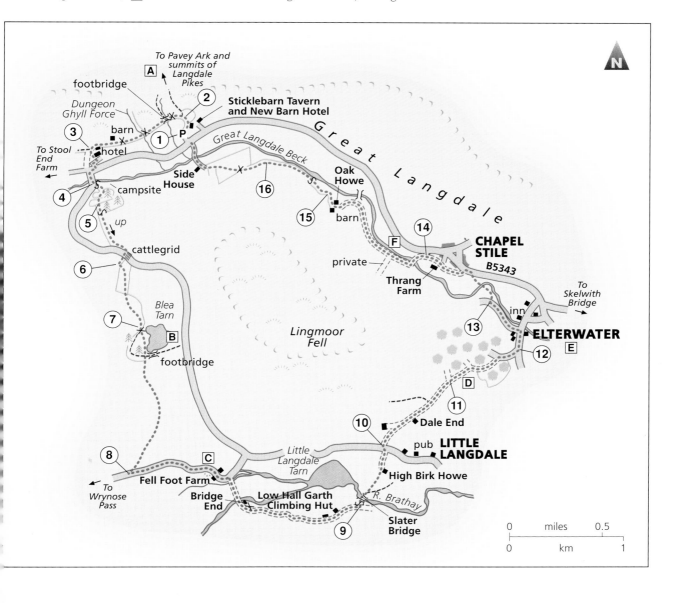

another kissing-gate, to emerge between stone gateposts into a field, where you continue forward and slightly to the right (no path), heading for an obvious gap with stile 50 yards ahead ⑤. Pick up the woodland path and on leaving the wood, keep forward alongside the wall on your right, ascending steadily. Where a road appears on other side of wall, do not cross stile to join it but continue uphill (closely parallel to the road) until crossing the next ladder-stile at a cattlegrid over the road. Cross the road (do not go over cattlegrid) and go forward alongside the wall on your left (Blea Tarn is down to your left), and after 20 yards ⑥ turn left on a well-defined path down to Blea Tarn Ⓑ.

⑦ Go through the kissing-gate and into woods, forking left after 20 yards; follow the path, ignoring a footbridge on the left, and keeping to the higher ground to avoid Blea Moss and to reach a road. ⑧ Turn left along the road for ½ mile, passing Fell Foot Farm Ⓒ, then turn right over Fell Foot Bridge to Bridge End. Follow the track along the valley to Low Hall Garth and after 300 yards ⑨ take a stone step stile (beside gate) on the left. Cross the river Brathay by Slater Bridge (a traditional packhorse bridge), and fork left on a rising path, alongside wall on right, to High Birk Howe. Continue on an enclosed track to a road ⑩. Turn left and immediately right on a track to Dale End and Elterwater.

⑪ Keep to the right fork on entering a tarmacked lane where you keep forward Ⓓ. ⑫ At T-junction, turn left and follow road towards Elterwater village. Turn left immediately before the road crosses the river (thus route does not quite go into the village Ⓔ), on to a road. ⑬ After 350 yards, fork right on to a signposted path, which leads down to the river. Cross the footbridge and emerge on the road at Chapel Stile village. Turn left on the road, past Wainwright's Inn, 50 yards after which you turn left on to a stony track (by School road-sign), now with a wall on your right. 250 yards later turn left on to a tarmacked lane, past houses (including Thrang

A Langdale stile

Farm); after 75 yards, the lane ends; go forward on a signposted path between walls.

⑭ After 60 yards, where walls open out, fork left (right goes to road) on a track which soon bends left and crosses a bridge over Great Langdale Beck, and turn right on the other side (along the river) Ⓕ. Eventually the track bends left to leave the river; on rejoining it, ignore the footbridge, but follow the track to reach a house (Oak Howe). Turn right immediately after the house to pass between a barn (left) and the house itself and pick up a level path with a dilapidated wall on your left.

⑮ Where the wall bends left, keep left alongside it; soon the path is well defined and has a wall on the right. ⑯ Take a gate with a stile alongside (avoid another stile just to the right of these, which leads on to the riverside path), and follow the path ahead, later through a kissing-gate and down to a farmhouse 300 yards ahead (Side House). In the farmyard, turn right on the tarmacked farm road, to reach the road. Take the road turning opposite.

ON THE ROUTE

Ⓐ Views west along Langdale, with the **Langdale Pikes** (2,415ft) on the right (perhaps the best-known mountain shape in the Lake District, with the cliff feature of Pavey Ark on the top); the slopes are littered with vestiges of a Neolithic stone axe 'factory', not discovered until this century. The rock was worked with granite hammers and shipped for export. Ahead, **Crinkle Crags** (left, 2,816ft) and **Bow Fell** (2,960ft) seal off the dale.

Ⓑ **Blea Tarn** (see the photograph on the title page of the *Guide*) is a memorably sited small lake, beneath

Wrynose Fell; a plantation of mixed trees and rhododendrons on its west side make a small oasis of civilisation in an otherwise wild place.

Ⓒ The road is the eastward end of the exciting **Wrynose Pass**, part of an ancient route used by the Romans into Eskdale and to the Cumbrian coast. A mound near **Fell Foot Farm** is a 'thing mound', or ancient meeting place for an annual Viking parliament. East of the farm lies **Little Langdale Tarn**.

Ⓓ **View** (to right) of **Elter Water** (the smallest lake in the district, according to some; but much depends on what you classify as a lake and what a tarn) and across to Loughrigg Fell.

Ⓔ **Elterwater** has a tiny, informal village green which almost doubles as a garden to the rambling old Britannia Inn, a magnet for ramblers and visitors to Langdale with all-day opening Monday to Saturday. The white-painted inn has a typically Cumbrian interior, with spartan country furnishings, exposed beams, real fires and a welcoming atmosphere. The village cottages were mostly built for workers in nearby gunpowder works, which grew up to supply local quarries and mines; the site of the works is now a timeshare complex, but slate continues to be quarried locally.

Ⓕ A pretty section of **Great Langdale Beck**, and along Great Langdale with **Bow Fell** in the distance. The old **bridge** is dated 1818, with the name of the builder and his wife. The beck features on some older maps as the River Elter (hence Elter Water).

The Langdale Pikes, a hugely popular goal for fell-walkers in this south-west area of the Lake District

BUTTERMERE AND HAYSTACKS

A figure-of-eight-shaped route which can be treated as two separate short walks. The first section is the circuit of Buttermere, one of the most satisfying lake circuits in the Lake District and just about the easiest: all on the level and with no real problems of route-finding. The surrounding fells give the lake its appeal, with the high wall of the Red Pike–High Crag ridge on one side and the milder green slopes of High Snockrigg on the other. The walk goes through a short section of tunnel. Expect crowds on fine days.

Haystacks is a dark, jagged fell above the valley. Although of modest height compared with the likes of Scafell Pikes and Helvellyn, it has a compact, well-defined summit and is particularly rewarding to climb. It should only be attempted in clear, settled weather; the ascent is 1,350 feet.

WALK DIRECTIONS

① A From Buttermere car park, take the road past the Fish Inn to B5289 by the Bridge Hotel, and turn right along the road. After 50 yards, turn right through farm (signposted as lake shore path). ¼ mile later, turn right in front of a gate, as signposted for lakeside. The path follows the lake and later goes through a short tunnel. ② At the road, continue forward along it to reach Gatesgarth ③.

For short route, circuiting Buttermere Take the track by post-box opposite car park, for Buttermere. Pass

---

Buttermere circuit
LENGTH 3½ miles (5.5km), 1½ hours
DIFFICULTY 1
Complete walk taking in Haystacks
LENGTH 8 miles (13km), 4 hours
DIFFICULTY 3
START Buttermere village car park, south-west of Keswick; turn off

B5289 by Bridge Hotel. Grid reference 173169. Alternatively start from Gatesgarth car park; begin walk at ③; grid reference 195150
OS MAPS Landranger 97; Outdoor Leisure 4
REFRESHMENTS Bridge Hotel, Fish Inn and snack bar, all in Buttermere

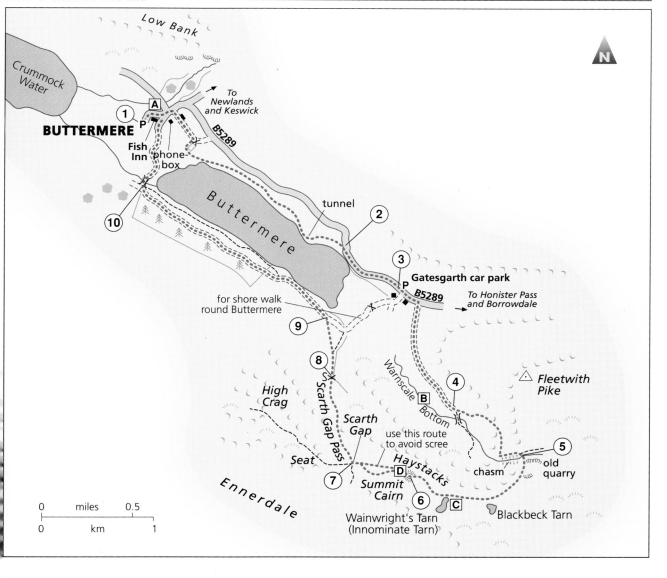

Buttermere, with Loweswater and Crummock Water, forms a small chain of three lakes

through farm then immediately fork right on a track that heads towards a stone wall. At the wall, turn right: the next path joining from the hillside on the left is at point ⑨. *For full walk via Haystacks* Carry on along the road, past the car park (if you started from here, turn left out of car park, towards Honister Pass, to begin the walk) for 100 yards. Just after house on right, leave the road for a signposted bridleway on the right. This track leads into Warnscale Bottom ⑧. ④ At the beginning of the ascent, take the path well marked by cairns (piles of stones) some way to the left of the stream (Warnscale Beck): its route up is visible from the bottom – it can be seen bending right halfway up, towards the stream, where it turns left and follows the stream (which at this point cuts into a small chasm; do not cross the stream at the start of the chasm).

⑤ At the top of chasm, cross the stream via easy natural stepping-stones and take the well-defined path on other side. At the top of the main ascent, keep right and follow cairns, past two tarns (small lakes) ⓒ, then climbing to a summit cairn on Haystacks (by old metal fence posts) ⑥ ⓓ. Descend by crossing a slight depression to the right of the summit cairn and follow the well-

cairned zigzag stony path to a prominent junction of paths at saddle of Scarth Gap ⑦, where you turn right. Skirt the next summit (Seat) on your left; the path soon descends.

After a gate beside stile ⑧, continue down the path with a broken wall on right (this later becomes a fence). At the junction of paths, fork left (leaving the fence) to reach the bottom. This is ⑨. Turn left.

⑨ *Both routes* Follow the path, soon reaching a point level with lake; proceed, ignoring all left forks, and keep as close as possible to the lakeside. ⑩ At the end of the lake, head for a footbridge 50 yards away to the right. Then follow the path, which later becomes a track, to Buttermere village.

ON THE ROUTE

Ⓐ **Buttermere** The tiny village has been popular with visitors for many years. Back in 1795 one J. Budworth published *A Fortnight's Ramble in the Lakes*, in which he made the innkeeper's daughter, 15-year-old Mary Robinson, into a tourist attraction. ('She looked an angel, and I doubt not she is the reigning lily of the valley'.) One who came was someone claiming to be Colonel the Hon. Alexander Augustus Hope; he married her before he was discovered to be James Hatfield bigamist and impostor. He was tried and hanged; Mary gave birth to a still-born child. But the sightseers still came to gawp at her. Coleridge wrote up the case, and in recent years Melvyn Bragg made her the subject of a novel, *The Maid of Buttermere*. She married, more happily, and spent her remaining days in Caldbeck, in the northern fringes of the Lake District. The Bridge Hotel, located between Buttermere and Crummock Water and formerly known as the Bridge Inn and later as the Queen and the

Victoria, is built on a site which has been inhabited for over 1,000 years. It was first licensed in 1735 and despite alterations still has something of a country rectory about it.

Ⓑ **Warnscale Bottom** The track is an old road serving the now-vanished Dubs slate quarry, once sited at the south-east end of this valley. Haystacks is the foreboding jagged-looking fell directly ahead.

Ⓒ The second major **tarn** to the left was once called Loaf Tarn, but lost its name when its loaf-shaped islets sank. It then became known as Innominate Tarn (surely a contradiction in terms). More recently, the great Alfred Wainwright, author of perhaps the most idiosyncratic walk-books ever published, has had it named after him. Haystacks was one of Wainwright's favourite fells.

Ⓓ **Haystacks** The summit has a magnificent **view** over Buttermere, Crummock Water and continuing along Lorton Vale, with Ennerdale the next valley to the left. Major peaks in sight include Pillar, to the south-west; Pillar Rock is a rock-climbers' favourite (Wasdale, the dale beyond Ennerdale, was the birthplace of British rock-climbing). To the right and left of Crummock Water are, respectively, Grasmoor and Mellbreak. To the north-east Skiddaw is just in view and Helvellyn may be seen to the east.

Haystacks, one of the Lake District's most popular fell walks

NEWLANDS BECK AND BARROW

A RIVERSIDE walk in the Newlands Valley, followed by a gradual 1,250ft rise on to a low fell called Barrow, keeping the finest section down a long, turfy ridge, for the end. Most paths quite easy to find, though turn-off at ⑥ requires care.

WALK DIRECTIONS

① Ⓐ Start at the road-bridge at village centre (by village shop) and take signposted turn for Keswick 2½. After 50 yards, take a path on the right signposted for Little Braithwaite, and keep alongside the river (Newlands Beck), crossing it ② at the next footbridge ¼ mile on Ⓑ. Continue along the riverside until reaching Little Braithwaite

Farm, in front of which you leave river, as waymarked, to pass above barn and below farmhouse.

Turn left on the road, then after 100 yards (after crossing Newlands

LENGTH 5½ miles (9km), 3½ hours
DIFFICULTY 3
START Braithwaite, on B5292 west of Keswick; as roadside parking in village centre is limited, it may be easier to park by housing estates on north side of village or in lay-by on A66 by junction with B5292. Grid reference 231236
OS MAPS Landranger 89 or 90; Outdoor Leisure 4
REFRESHMENTS Hotel bar and shop in Braithwaite

Beck) ③ take riverside path on right signposted Stair. ④ After ½ mile, cross a stone bridge over the river and pick up a farm track, past Lower Uzzicar (on right) and

Newlands Valley, now a peaceful dale, was once a busy mining area

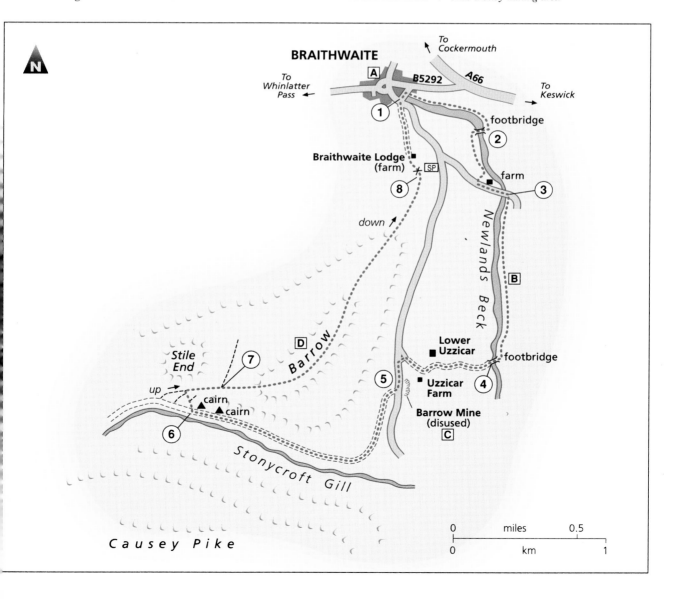

turning right at Uzzicar Farm; the track bends right just after to reach a road. Turn left on road ⓒ, then ⑤ after 200 yards fork right on to a signposted stony track. Follow it up valley with a stream (Stonycroft Gill) down on your left, later with a distinctive pointed summit (Causey Pike) to the left.

⑥ After one mile from road, where the valley and track are about to bend markedly left, turn right 40 yards after cairn (piled-up stones), to pick up a rising narrow path (ignore minor right fork after a further 30 yards). This path soon levels out. ⑦ After the hillock of Stile End on left, ignore the left fork (which descends) but keep forward along the path which soon reaches the top of Barrow ridge ⒹⒹ and then descends along the middle of it for its entire length. ⑧ At the bottom, go forward to a farm, where you keep forward at crossing of tracks to return to Braithwaite.

ON THE ROUTE
Ⓐ **Braithwaite** was the original site of the Cumberland Pencil Factory, which was established 1868. After a fire in 1898 the firm moved to Keswick.
Ⓑ **Newlands Beck valley** The 'new lands' were reclaimed after the draining of Husaker Tarn. It is now a green and pastoral dale, but it teemed with mining activity from the time of Elizabeth I until this century. Copper was the first mineral to be mined, with lead, silver and barites worked later. Plunging grassy slopes surround the valley: Cat Bells and Maiden Moor are to the left; Barrow is close by on the right and Causey Pike beyond; Dale Head is due south at the end of the valley.
Ⓒ Vestiges of spoil heaps of the old **Barrow Mine** are visible on the left of the road.
Ⓓ **View** from Barrow (1,494ft) north-west over Braithwaite and Thornthwaite Forest; north is Bassenthwaite Lake (the only body of water in Lakeland actually called a lake; the lake inspired the scene for the death of Arthur in

Beatrix Potter's illustration for the frontispiece of The Tale of Tom Kitten: *Mrs Tabitha Twitchit takes the kittens back to the house (modelled on Beatrix Potter's own house, Hill Top)*

BEFRIENDING THE LAKE DISTRICT

Beatrix Potter's love affair with the Lake District is to the eternal benefit of all who visit it. After a series of family holidays in the Lakes, she discovered that Hill Top, a typical Cumbrian farmhouse at Near Sawrey, was for sale. She had already published the children's book, *The Tale of Peter Rabbit*, and her income from the book's royalties was sufficient to enable her to buy the house. Thereafter Hill Top became her sanctuary; happily immersed in country life, she wrote more of the now famous books, almost all her illustrations being inspired by her lakeland surroundings. During the last 30 years of her life she bought over 4,000 acres of land with many houses and farms. On her death she left everything to the National Trust and in this way the Trust became the major landowner in the Lake District, safeguarding all property held in perpetuity.

Another person instrumental in the Lake District's salvation was Canon Rawnsley, co-founder of the National Trust and Lake District Defence Association. Although the latter society failed to prevent the expansion of Thirlmere into a reservoir, it attracted support on a nationwide scale. On the 'Rock of Names' by the lake, Coleridge and Wordsworth had carved their initials: somewhat symbolically this was blasted to bits when reservoir construction began, but Rawnsley gathered the pieces and they are now cemented together behind Dove Cottage in Grasmere.

Tennyson's *Idylls of the King*); north-east is the huge mass of Skiddaw (3,054ft); east north-east Keswick; east south-east is the distant Helvellyn range (3,116ft, the third highest peak in the Lake District).

WALLA CRAG AND ASHNESS BRIDGE

A GENTLE woodland track, an exhilarating moorland edge and a brief stroll by Derwent Water form three sharply contrasting sections to this route. Reasonably straightforward route-finding; 1,000ft of ascent.

LENGTH 4½ miles (7km), 3½ hours
DIFFICULTY 2–3
START Great Wood National Trust car park (pay and display), signposted on east side of B5289 1 mile south south-east of Keswick. Grid reference 271212
OS MAPS Landranger 89 or 90; Outdoor Leisure 4

WALK DIRECTIONS

① Take the gate out of the car park (with sign for Ashness Bridge and Walla Crag just beyond). Keep right at junction after 50 yards, but 20 yards later turn left signposted Walla Crag via Rakefoot. Follow this woodland track Ⓐ, ② forking right after ½ mile by a signpost for Rakefoot and Walla Crag, to reach a stile out of the wood, and follow fenced path.

At path T-junction, turn right over a stile, on a path running on the right-hand side of stream in wooded dingle. At the end of wood,

cross a footbridge and follow the path to a small gate, emerging on to a tarmac lane ③. Turn right on the lane, fork right after 100 yards (signposted Walla Crag). Where lane ends (100 yards later), cross a footbridge, ascend track with a wall on your immediate right; ④ where the wall bends right, keep alongside it.

⑤ Near the top of hill, turn right through a kissing-gate and follow the path along the top of Walla Crag Ⓑ. After the cairn on the last crag, the path leads to a stile: cross the stile, turn right alongside wall, but then immediately go left at cairn on to a broad grassy path leading across moorland and away from wall. The path is well defined and curves around to the right, crossing two streams Ⓒ and eventually dropping to cross a ladder-stile ⑥. Continue

forward and turn right before the stream to reach a small road at Ashness Bridge Ⓓ.

Turn right along the road, and descend to B5289. Cross road to take wooden steps opposite, and ⑦ turn right along the shore of Derwent Water Ⓔ. Just after the shore veers half left, there is a footbridge away to your right (do not cross it). 150 yards later ⑧ leave the shore to take track on right and rejoin B5289. Cross to the road opposite (No Entry sign refers to vehicles) and follow this up to Great Wood car park.

ON THE ROUTE

Ⓐ **Great Wood** A few oaks of the original wood remain but otherwise larches predominate; frequented by red squirrels.

Ⓑ **Walla Crag** A series of

Walla Crag, in fact a series of rugged peaks above Derwent Water

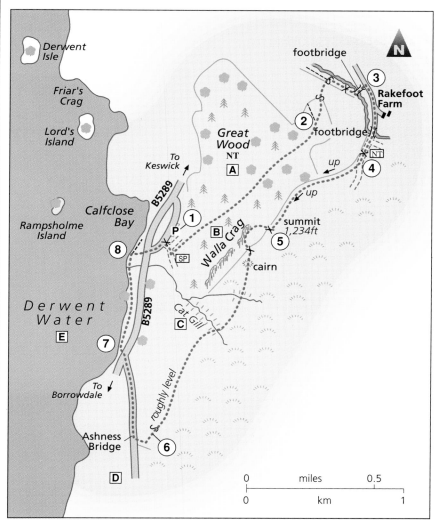

precipitous crags high above Derwent Water, giving a grandeur of view belying its modest height (1,234ft). Across the lake are Cat Bells and Grisedale Pike; to the north-west is Bassenthwaite Lake, a breeding ground for over 70 bird species; south south-west is the entrance to Borrowdale; Skiddaw (3,053ft) towers to the north; Brandelhow Park in the south-west corner of the lake is an area of woodland which in 1902 was the first Lake District property to be acquired by the National Trust.

C The deeply incised stream, **Cat Gill**, owes its name to wild cats which are thought to have lived here in the mid-18th century although half a century later they had disappeared from England. Cat Bells (the fell on the west side of Derwent Water) may be a corruption of 'cat bields' (cat shelters).

D **Ashness Bridge** The little packhorse bridge over the stream provides a much-photographed scene, with Derwent Water and Skiddaw beyond.

E **Derwent Water** Its site among the fells mentioned above is further enhanced by its islands, the four largest being at its north end: Rampsholme Island, St Herbert's Island (the southernmost; named after a hermitage established here in 685), Lord's Island (formerly the site of the Earl of Derwentwater's house) and Derwent Isle (which was home to a colony of German miners in the 16th century).

Ashness Bridge with Skiddaw (one of four 3,000-foot summits in the Lake District) beyond. This is one of the most famous lakeland views. The road winds up to the remote hamlet of Watendlath

GOWBARROW PARK AND AIRA FORCE

THIS is a remarkably compact walk, considering its scenic variety, with magnificent views of Ullswater and of the countryside towards Great Mell Fell; it makes the most of the woods and a series of waterfalls culminating at Aira Force. The going is easy underfoot, and route-finding poses no problems.

LENGTH 4 miles (6.5km), 2 hours
DIFFICULTY 2
START Aira Force car park (pay and display) on A592, just east of junction with A5091
OS MAPS Landranger 90; Outdoor Leisure 5
REFRESHMENTS National Trust café close by Aira Force car park

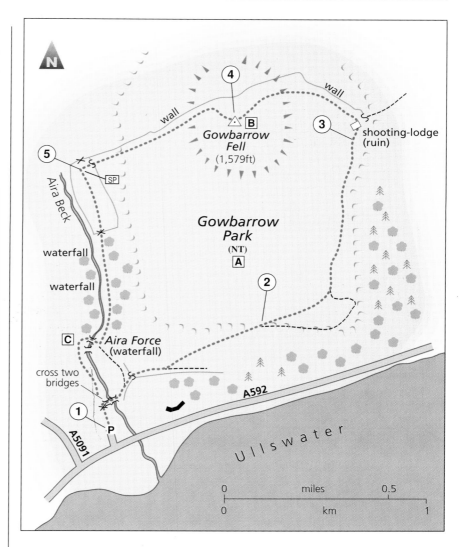

WALK DIRECTIONS

(1) From Aira Force car park take the gate into woods at the back of car park soon crossing a river by two bridges. The path rises and follows a wooden fence. Take the next fork right which continues along fence. Just after the wooden fence is replaced by wire take the right fork over a stile. The path, now in open ground, soon forks left, ascending the front of Gowbarrow Park (the hill straight ahead).

(2) A Fork left again higher up. The path levels and skirts the hillside curving away from the lake.

(3) After crossing a wooden bridge, the path drops towards a ladder-stile over a wall by a ruined shooting-lodge; do not cross the stile but fork left by the lodge. The path becomes less distinct but the wall away to your right is a guide. Keep on upwards, curving left and aiming for a trig point on Gowbarrow Fell – the tallest, craggy hillock on this hummocky ground.

(4) B The best way to the top is to work your way around the back. From the summit, pick up a clear path by wall away to the right. The path soon descends steeply. When you eventually reach the corner of wall, cross a stone stile by a signpost,

heading for another signpost 90 yards away.

(5) Turn left at the second signpost and follow the path back to the car park via woods and waterfalls C keeping the river to your right.

ON THE ROUTE

A **Gowbarrow Park**, the hillside beneath Gowbarrow Fell, is perhaps best known for its abundance of wild daffodils, which inspired William Wordsworth to write one of the most famous poems in the English language:

I wandered lonely as a cloud
That floats on high o'er vales and hills,
When all at once I saw a crowd,
A host, of golden daffodils;
Beside the lake, beneath the trees,
Fluttering and dancing in the breeze.

The common buzzard preys on rabbits, small mammals such as mice, and earthworms and beetles

Dora's Field at Rydal (a few miles to the south of this walk), named after William and Mary Wordsworth's daughter. Despite appearances, Wordsworth actually found inspiration for his famous poem here at Gowbarrow Park

DEATH OF THE VILLAGES

In 1348 the Black Death wiped out between a third and a half of the country's population (a loss of some 1½ million people). A major effect of this was that villages in the marginal lands – heaths, woods and hills – were abandoned as there was now plenty of land. Some villages were re-sited; today lonely churches adjacent to humpy fields where a village once stood are testimony to this, the modern village now perhaps half a mile or so away. Some villages had already been on the point of collapse, and the Black Death was the final blow. Many villages ultimately became enclosed pasture lands owned by laymen farmers or monastic houses.

OTHER ULLSWATER WALKS

Those who want to keep at **shore level** can start at Howtown Pier, on the eastern side of Ullswater, and follow the much-tramped path south-westwards; the route is easy to find, but not entirely level. The delightful little rises and dips make for constantly changing views. The return route is by steamer from Glenridding. To be on the safe side, you may prefer to check operating times with the steamer companies before you set out on the walk, or to take the steamer first, then walk back.

An optional add-on at the Howtown end is to ascend **Hallin Fell**, a prominent knob-shaped hill by the lake, with an obvious track leading up it from its southern side. A magnificent circular route taking in the Ullswater shore path can begin at Patterdale and ascending 2,154-foot high **Place Fell** via the pass known as Boredale Hause. From the summit, a gentle path leads down over springy turf to the north-east; then one can turn north just after a ruined sheepfold to join the lakeside. In all, this walk is 6½ miles.

B **Gowbarrow Fell**, at 1,579 ft, is a superb viewpoint, notably over Ullswater, the Lake District's second longest lake, after Windermere. The shores are rich in birdlife. Species include ring ouzel, meadow pipit, whinchat, wagtail, redpoll, raven, sandpiper, kestrel, buzzard, peregrine, raven, woodpecker, spotted flycatcher, goldcrest and jackdaw. Both the lake steamers are Victorian: *Lady of the Lake* was launched in 1877 and *Raven* in 1880. They were converted from steam to oil in the 1930s. In season, they run from Glenridding to Pooley Bridge and back, via Howtown.

C **Aira Force** The Aira Beck tumbles down this waterfall, which can be admired from the bridge. It is perhaps the best-known fall, or force, in the Lake District, although Scale Force (near Buttermere) is the tallest.

HULNE PARK, ALNWICK

AN easily managed tour of parkland owned by Alnwick Castle. All on tracks; easy route-finding. No public rights of way in the park, but public access is allowed on its drives and tracks, 11am until dusk. No dogs.

LENGTH	8 miles (13km), 3½ hours
DIFFICULTY	1–2
START	Entrance, Alnwick Castle; alternatively, park on wide roadside verges outside gate-house. Grid reference 186136
OS MAPS	Landranger 81; Pathfinder 488 (NU 01/11)
REFRESHMENTS	Full range in Alnwick

WALK DIRECTIONS

① A With castle entrance behind you, follow the street ahead (Bailiffgate). 30 yards after passing Northumberland Street on your left, keep left into a no-through road, soon to reach gate-house, then follow the estate drive for ½ mile. ② 50 yards after lodge on left, turn half right on a track downhill (not sharp right, signposted Park Cottage).

③ Turn left at triangular T-junction. (To view Abbey Gate B look out for a bridge on right after ¼ mile, approached by a narrow path. Cross the bridge, turn right on track on other side through parkland with the river on your right. Retrace steps from gateway.)

Alnwick on market day

④ ½ mile later (¼ mile after diversion to Abbey Gate) turn half right at an oblique T-junction, into parkland by a gate after 100 yards. The track leads past a bridge: do not cross, but follow for ¼ mile to next bridge ⑤. Cross bridge, fork left. Track follows close to river for 1½ miles. ⑥ Hulne Priory C comes into view up on the right, but no track leads to it from the river; therefore ignore straight track ahead and keep to the riverside (Hulne Priory is not open to the public, though you are welcome to walk outside the walls at weekends).

⑦ Take the next bridge on the left after passing the priory. The track ascends gently. ⑧ Reach a tarmac estate drive (farm visible away to left) and turn right. After 50 yards turn right at a triangular T-junction. ⑨ Take the next left turn (opposite sentry hut). Ignore next left turn and ascend gently to Brizlee Tower (just to right of track) D .

⑩ Continue forward, on the track, soon passing a viewpoint with a stone bench/standing stone E . ⑪ 150 yards after the viewpoint turn left at a crossing of tracks, in woods: follow this round past a cave F to rejoin the point reached earlier ⑫. Turn right on the track, downhill. ⑬ Turn right on the tarmac drive; follow this back to the start G .

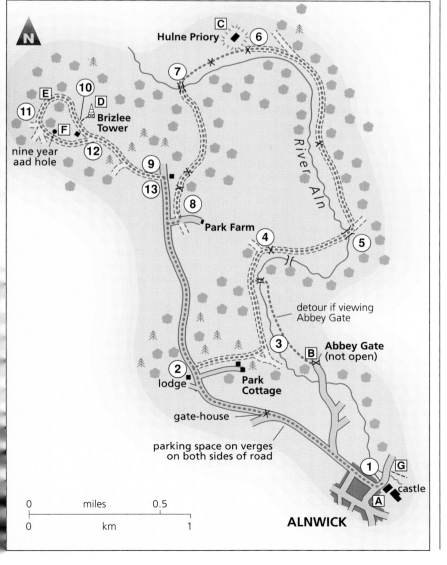

The splendour of Alnwick Castle reflected in the River Aln

ON THE ROUTE

A **Alnwick** By the river is the huge castle (*open to public*; fee), Norman with 18th- and 19th-century restoration. There are two town gates (the one with the Percy Lion is 15th century), an 18th-century market hall and bridge of the same period.

B **Abbey gate-house** The only visible remnant of the abbey, a 14th-century archway under four projecting towers, highly ornamented on its side. Heraldic shields are visible just below the castellations.

C **Hulne Priory** A Carmelite foundation of c. 1240, with a 15th-century tower and a handsome 18th-century farmhouse inside its curtain wall. The Carmelite monks eked out a stark existence: their own coffins furnished their cells and they were required to dig daily a shovelful of earth for their graves. The principal church in the priory has a rare pre-Christian Tau cross.

D **Brizlee Tower** A Gothick folly erected in 1781 by the first Duke of Northumberland. On it is inscribed in Latin, 'Look around yourself; I have measured out everything here: my commands and my planting; I have even planted many of the trees with my own hands'.

E **View** Over the Cheviots, with the coast beyond Alnwick to the right.

F **Cave** Known as the 'nine year aad hole', a natural cave with the stone figure of a hermit placed by its entrance. Three robbers allegedly once hid here with their booty; two killed each other off, then the third died, leaving the whereabouts of the treasure (and the provenance of the story) uncertain.

G If you have time, turn left at the end of the walk, down to the river bridge; a path on the right on the far side of the river gives a good view of the **castle**.

NATIONAL TRAILS

Official long-distance paths, created by the Countryside Commission, are one of the most popular methods of exploring the country on foot. They make a good basis for day walks for those who don't want to tackle the whole route. Many miles of new paths were made in the process of establishing the National Trails. To date, the following have been opened in England and Wales.

Northern England Pennine Way (250 miles/400km), Cleveland Way (108 miles/172km), Wolds Way (79 miles/127km)

Wales and the Marches Offa's Dyke Path (168 miles/270km), Pembrokeshire Coast (167 miles/ 268km)

Southern England The Ridgeway (85 miles/136km), South Downs Way (106 miles/171km), North Downs Way (141 miles/227km), South-West Coast (515 miles/824km), the Thames Path (156 miles/251km)

Eastern England Peddars Way and Norfolk Coast Path (93 miles/150km)

  Additionally, there are numerous unofficial long-distance routes which use the existing path network (such as the Heart of England Way). The Southern Upland Way (212 miles/340km) and the West Highland Way (95 miles/152km) are the two official long-distance paths established in Scotland.

HOLY ISLAND

A SHORT sea-level walk of great historic, natural and scenic interest. At its best in winter when the only crowds encountered are of wildfowl and waders. Time your visit to coincide with low tide.

WALK DIRECTIONS

① Turn left out of car park main entrance, and left again into Sandham Lane, soon to reach a farm where you keep forward (now on unsurfaced track). ② At nature reserve sign Ⓐ, continue forward, cross a large area of dunes to reach the beach where you turn right. Follow the coast past marker obelisk at Emanuel Head.

③ After the next nature reserve sign, the path runs south along the coast Ⓑ, to reach a castle Ⓒ ④. After the castle, pick up the road Ⓓ; where the road bends right, keep left along coast to pick up a track, leading to a low wooden building ⑤, in front of which you turn right (left goes to jetty).

Soon take a turnstile on your right and follow tarmac path towards priory ruins; turn left at the Crown and Anchor Hotel to enter the square (detour ahead and to left if you want to see the priory Ⓔ), where ⑥ the first street on the right leads to the car park (turn right at T-junction by the Northumberland

Arms and first left into Sandham Lane).

LENGTH 3½ miles (6km), 2 hours
DIFFICULTY 1
START Holy Island car park, signposted on the left as soon as you enter village from mainland (from which you turn off A1 between Berwick and Belford). Tide times are displayed at mainland and in car park; at high tide the island is cut off for five hours. Grid reference 126422
OS MAPS Landranger 75; Pathfinder 452 (NU 04/140)
REFRESHMENTS Pubs, shops, cafés in Holy Island village

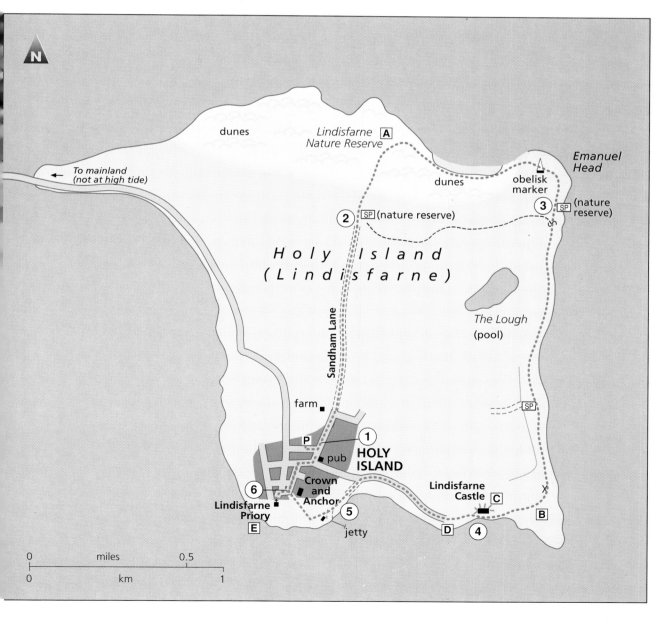

ON THE ROUTE

A **Lindisfarne Nature Reserve** Tidal mudflats attract great numbers of **waders** and **wildfowl** in winter. This is Britain's most important coastal site for wigeon (whose population here peaks at 25,000), and the only wintering ground for pale-bellied Brent Goose. Among the wild flowers is a fine seasonal show of orchids. In the dunes is a huge rabbit colony, once an important resource for the island. From the obelisk on Emanuel Head is a good **view** north along the coast towards Berwick and St Abb's Head.

B The **view** extends southwards to the mainland, including **Ross Back Sands** and 12th-century **Bamburgh Castle**, with the **Cheviot Hills** further inland. To the left are the **Farne Islands**, whose 15 isles are a haunt of seabirds and seals; monastic hermits from Lindisfarne had cells there up to 1246.

C **Lindisfarne Castle** was built in 1550 soon after Henry VIII's dissolution of the monasteries, marking the island's new role as a military base rather than a religious centre; stone taken from the abandoned priory was used as building material. Edward Hudson, founder of *Country Life* magazine, bought the ruined castle in 1903 and commissioned Edwin Lutyens to convert it into a comfortable home (National Trust, *open* April to October, daily except Friday, but open Good Friday; 1 to 5.30). The **lime-kiln** (labelled), just before the castle is reached, produced fertiliser which was transported to Scotland.

D **Lobster** and **crab** pots are much in evidence, and these shellfish are on sale locally. Notice the **sheds** made out of upturned boats.

E **Lindisfarne Priory** The English cradle of Christianity, where Aidan, a missionary from Iona, arrived in 635 at the invitation of King

Lindisfarne Castle in its extraordinary position looking out over the North Sea

Oswald of Northumbria and founded a monastery (then a simple wooden structure), with the aim of spreading Christianity across northern England. It became a Benedictine monastery in 1082, and despite its exposure to the elements since its ruination in the Reformation, much of the fine stone decoration and arches survive. In the adjacent **museum** are inscribed stones and an historical display. (English Heritage, *open* 1 April, or Good Friday if earlier, to 31 October 10 to 6; rest of year 10 to 4. Closed 24 to 26 December and 1 January.) The celebrated **Lindisfarne Gospels**, a superb illuminated manuscript made about 700, is in the British Museum.

Aidan came from Iona with other Irish monks as a Christian missionary

TWO FURTHER WALKS

- From the fishing village of Craster (famous for its kippers), an enjoyable 1½-mile walk extends northwards along the coast to Dunstanburgh Castle, the largest of the Northumbrian castles. The immediate hinterland is flat and agricultural; it is best to return the same way.
- Ross Back Sands is a huge and lonely beach, giving sweeping views of the coast and Holy Island to its immediate north.

BERWICK AND THE TWEED

A route along both banks of the river and around the town walls, with the first glimpse of Berwick from its three great bridges.

WALK DIRECTIONS

① Walk from car park and picnic site towards River Tweed, to find a stile in corner of fence (50 yards to right of A1), giving access to a path dropping to river. Just before reaching ruin, turn right over wooden bridge and continue upwards (path is overgrown but discernible in summer).

The path soon continues along edge of fields, above river ☐A. ② Keep left on reaching the corner of road and 20 yards after, where road bends right into sewage works, keep left through gate into field. Follow track for 40 yards, then fork right on to a narrow path (track goes to river and ends) alongside fence to follow right edge of this and next field,

then along river. After passing under a railway viaduct ☐B, ③ you reach a residential road at edge of Tweedmouth but leave it immediately for the riverside path, passing under Royal Tweed Bridge ☐C (road-bridge). Cross (low-arched) Berwick Bridge ☐D. ④ Turn right on the other side to join level walkway, with town wall on right (here doubling as quayside wall).

Make a complete circuit of town walls. ☐E to ☐T. ⑤ Immediately before Royal Tweed Bridge, turn right down steps to riverside where you turn right ☐U. Pass under the railway viaduct. ⑥ Path becomes unsurfaced as it enters woods, where it rises, then levels. Turn left at T-junction with stony track.

⑦ As soon as woods on the left end, cross a ladder-stile on left and go towards the river (with woods on left), thus doubling back towards the railway viaduct. Just before the river,

cross footbridge on right over channel and follow waymarked posts across field to ladder-stile 150 yards short of the A1 road-bridge.

⑧ Beyond the stile, a narrow path bends right then left up steps on to the bridge itself. Cross the A1 road-bridge (there is a pavement) to return to the car park.

ON THE ROUTE

☐A The **River Tweed** is famous for its salmon, fished since the 9th century. Mute swans are common.

LENGTH 5 miles (8km), 3 hours
DIFFICULTY 1
START East Ord picnic site, by A1/A698 roundabout just south of A1 bridge over River Tweed. Grid reference 975515
OS MAPS Landranger 75; Pathfinder 75 (NT 95/NU 05)
REFRESHMENTS Full range in Berwick

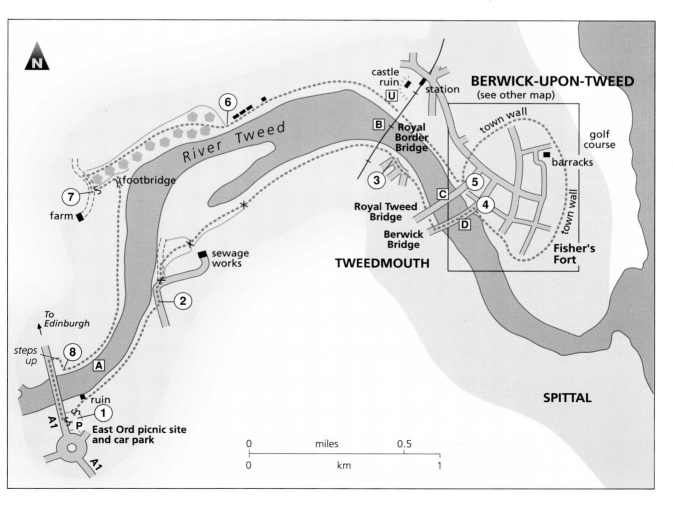

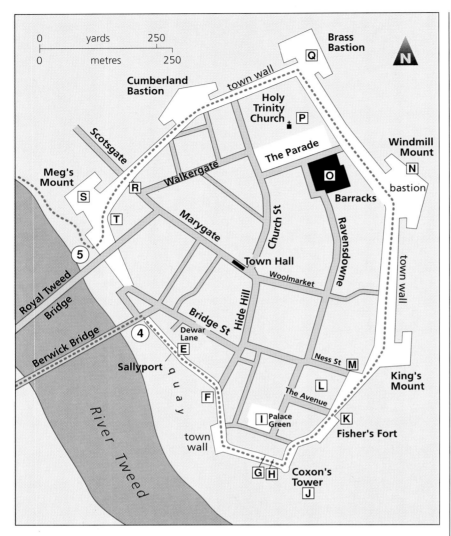

The fifteen arches of Berwick Bridge

B **Royal Border Railway Bridge** A 28-arched railway viaduct designed by Robert Stephenson and opened by Queen Victoria in 1850.

C **Royal Tweed Bridge** Road-bridge opened 1928.

D **Berwick Bridge** Early 17th century; 15 arches span the river. This was the fifth bridge, earlier structures having been washed away. *Berwick town walk* The following route follows the well-preserved **town walls**, first fortified by Edward I and then Henry VIII, but what

remains is the great Elizabethan fortification, Britain's most complete surviving example of its period.

E Handsome 18th- and 19th-century houses line the **quay**. Steps lead down by No 5, at the bottom of which is **Sallyport**, one of the original passages or 'ports' connecting Bridge Street with the quay. Steps on left after No 9 descend to a car park, where **Dewar Lane**, to left, has the area's last surviving old warehouses.

F View up **Hide Hill**, which was a major route into Berwick before the Royal Tweed Bridge opened.

G **Customs House**, a former dispensary, is part of an attractive Georgian group with Nos 19–23.

H **No 1 Wellington Terrace** has replica harpoon heads on its door and railings, indicating the town's connection in the early 19th century with the whaling industry.

I **Palace Green**, a former bowling-green on left at end of Quay Walls, includes the early 18th century

Governor's House on the east side of the green. The **guard house** (labelled) is 18th century and was moved here in 1815 from Marygate.

J Thirteen gun emplacements sit along **Saluting Battery**. Coxon's Tower is a two-storey **watch-tower**.

K **Fisher's Fort** Six gun-ports guard the harbour entrance. A Russian cannon placed here was taken in the Crimea. **View** of **pier** and **lighthouse** (both constructed in the 1820s) and **Holy Island**.

L **The Avenue** The grass rectangle was a rope-walk used by the rope industry in the 18th century.

M Detour left into Ness Street to see **Ravensdowne**, the finest Georgian street in town.

N **Windmill Mount** Across the moat are earthworks of the Great Bulwark in the Snook, part of Henry VIII's fortification.

O **Berwick Barracks** (entrance from the Parade; English Heritage, *open* 10 to 6, daily except Monday; closes at 4 October to Easter). Built 1717–21, Britain's first purpose-built barracks, used until 1964, housed 600 men and 36 officers. Inside are a **regimental museum**, a museum of army life, and a part of the **Burrell Collection** (**art, porcelain** and **glass**).

P **Parish church of Holy Trinity** A rare Commonwealth church of 1652: altar-piece by Edwin Lutyens. As you return to the wall, look for **Cow Port**, the only surviving Elizabethan gate under the wall.

Q At **Brass Bastion**, at the wall corner, part of the original sentry walk above the west flanker has been uncovered.

R **Marygate** View down market street to the **town hall**, built 1750–61, with Tuscan columns beneath a portico and 150-foot high tower; a **museum of local history** is upstairs.

S **Meg's Mount**, a good **viewpoint**, is named after a large gun placed here called Roaring Meg.

T The old **Corporation Academy** (with clock) was founded for children of Freemen. Just below the Royal Tweed Bridge, an **ice house** once supplied ice for the packing of Tweed salmon.

U The **castle**, dating from at least the 12th century, is up on the right. A tower over the river path was built 1539–42 for artillery.

MELROSE AND THE EILDON HILLS

T HE landscape beloved of Walter
Scott is explored from Melrose and
by the banks of the Tweed before a
900ft ascent on to the Eildons, one
of the best-known natural features
of the Borders and an outstanding
viewpoint. On defined tracks and
paths, the route is waymarked
some of the way. The section along
a raised wall by the river has a six-
foot drop and may not appeal to
vertigo sufferers.

LENGTH 4½ miles (7km), 3 hours
DIFFICULTY 3
START Melrose; car park in St
Dunstan's Park (road name), on west
side of town opposite rugby ground.
Grid reference 546342
OS MAPS Landranger 73; Pathfinder
461 (NT 43/53)
REFRESHMENTS Full range in
Melrose

WALK DIRECTIONS

① A From the cark park, turn left
along the main road, then turn right
into St Mary's Road; take tarmacked
path to pass to the right of the
church and reach the river ② where
you turn right on a tarmacked path
B. Pass a suspension bridge (do not
cross), then after 120 yards take gate
on left and go up the side of a small
field. Turn right through another
gate, on to path running along the
top of a walled bank ③. Follow the
path along the river. After a stile ④
the path runs along top of a wall
(the Battery Dyke). After leaving
the wall, follow the broad path to a
footbridge, then up a lane into
Newstead village C.

Turn right on the main village
street, and immediately left into

Claymires Lane and turn right at T-
junction with Back Road
(unsurfaced) ⑤. 50 yards later, turn
left under old railway bridge D, and
follow track up to the main road.
Turn right on main road, then after
100 yards, turn left on a rising track.

⑥ You reach a gate on to open
moorland at foot of North Hill,
where you continue forward,
initially alongside woods on left and
picking up yellow arrow waymarks
to ascend Eildon Hill North by a
well-defined path. ⑦ E From the
summit cairn, go down right to
reach saddle between Eildon Hill
North and Eildon Mid Hill ⑧
(where you can continue up an
obvious path for detour to Eildon

Mid Hill and along ridge to Eildon
Wester Hill).

To continue route back to
Melrose, take care to pick up the
waymarked route (*not* the path
marked by prominent red and white
marker-posts): find Eildon Walk
marker-post on the saddle and
follow the path to the right which
drops slightly and then contours
round the lower slopes of North Hill
with Melrose away to your left.

⑨ Reach path junction with
waymarker (pointing the way you
have come) and turn left down past
MOD sign (facing other way) and
towards abbey in distance, crossing a
stile, following the right-hand side
of a field to reach a stile on to an

*The Eildon Hills to the south of Melrose –
natural or the work of wizardry?*

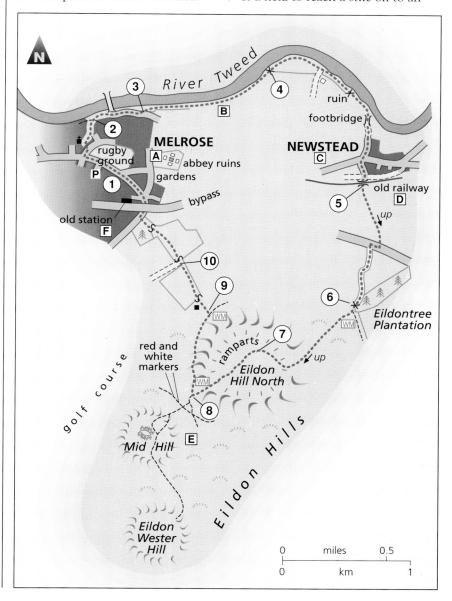

Melrose Abbey is widely agreed to be Scotland's finest Gothic building, with stone carving to rival the best in Britain

enclosed track ⑩; cross the track and take stile opposite, go down left-hand side of field to find a waymarked stile in the bottom corner and beyond it take a path down steps to reach the road. Turn right on road to reach the town square ⒡; turn left to reach the car park.

ON THE ROUTE

Ⓐ **Melrose** Perhaps the most attractive of the small towns in the Borders, nestling at the foot of the Eildon Hills. The **abbey** (*open Monday to Saturday 9.30 to 7; Sun 2 to 7*), founded in 1136 by David I for Cistercian monks from Rievaulx Abbey in Yorkshire and in its time probably the wealthiest abbey in Scotland, suffered destruction from English incursions in the 14th century; most of what remains is post 1385 – nave, transepts, tower, chancel, south nave. It is noted for its outstanding stone carving. Adjacent is **Priorswood Gardens** (National Trust for Scotland), which has ancient apple varieties and where flowers are cultivated for drying. The **rugby ground** is the birthplace of Rugby 'sevens', first played here in 1883.

Ⓑ The fertile farmland by the River Tweed was a prime attraction for the Cistercians at Melrose, who were renowned for their farming skills. The long-distance Southern Upland Way branches off here and crosses the bouncy suspension bridge.

Ⓒ Near Newstead, the Romans set up **Trimontium** ('the camp of the three hills').

Ⓓ Part of the much-lamented **Waverley Line** which used to run from Edinburgh to Carlisle, scenically comparable to the Settle to Carlisle line. It operated 1849–1969.

Ⓔ The three-peaked ridge of the **Eildon Hills** is volcanic, but legend has it that it was the work of 13th-century wizard Michael Scott (a real person, who features in Dante's *Inferno* as Michele Scoto). North Hill is ringed with ancient ramparts: here up to 2,000 years ago the Segolvae tribe kept an Iron Age hillfort; from the 1st century the hill was used as a Roman signal station. A view indicator on Mid Hill (10 minutes' walk up from this route) identifies Melrose, Cheviots and Peniel Heugh Monument to the south-east; eastwards is Smailholm Tower and to the north-east the Moorfoots and Lammermuir Hills.

Ⓕ Just before reaching the town square, a signposted turn on the left leads to the handsome **Melrose station** (*open daily*, free), built in Jacobean style with Dutch gables; although the line has closed (see above) the station was restored in 1986 and now contains a **railway museum**, **craft shop** and **restaurant**.

EYEMOUTH TO ST ABB'S HEAD

A COASTAL walk with several variants: do the whole coastal stretch, looping round inland and finishing at the visitor centre for the bus back, or start a shorter walk from Coldingham (walking back along the road or taking the bus). Try the shortest route from St Abb's visitor centre, or split the full walk into two separate excursions. The scenic highlight is St Abb's Head, but there are also good beaches (popular in summer) at ② and ④. There is a frequent bus service on weekdays, less frequent on Sundays (when you are advised to park by the visitor centre and take the bus to Eyemouth before starting the walk).

WALK DIRECTIONS

① Ⓐ Facing Eyemouth seafront, turn left along the esplanade,

LENGTH *Eyemouth to St Abb's Head visitor centre* 6½ miles (10.5km), 3½ hours
Coldingham to St Abb's Head visitor centre 4½ miles (7km), 2½ hours
Round walk from St Abb's Head visitor centre 3 miles (5km), 1½ hours
DIFFICULTY *Full walk* 3, *Shorter walks* 2
START *6½-mile walk* On the seafront at Eyemouth, grid reference 946645
4½-mile walk Coldingham (car park in village centre opposite war memorial, grid reference 902659; take B6438 signposted St Abb's, turning right at end of village on road signposted Sands ¾; opposite Unsuitable for Motors sign take path parallel on left-hand side of road and follow this to the beach where you

turn left to start walk directions at ④)
3-mile walk St Abb's nature reserve visitor centre (turn off by sign by St Abb's Head; to start the walk, go to right of coffee shop to reach road, and take waymarked path opposite, on the left-hand side of road and parallel to it to reach 30 mph road-sign, where you turn left on path signposted St Abb's Head); grid reference 913675
OS MAPS Landranger 67; Pathfinder 432 (NT 86/96)
REFRESHMENTS Full range in Eyemouth; pubs and shops at Coldingham; café and hotel at Coldingham Bay; shop at St Abb's; coffee shop at the St Abb's Head visitor centre

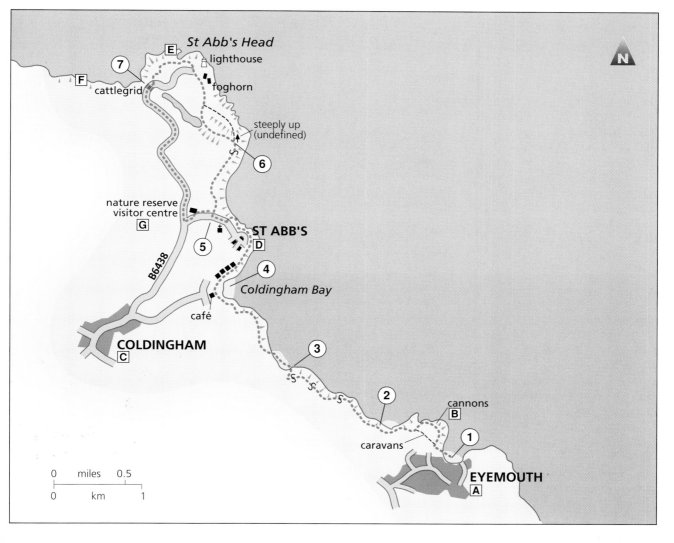

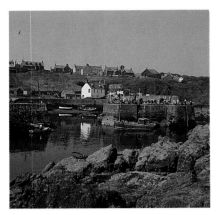

The walk takes you through St Abb's before you carry on along the cliff-top

joining the beach at Dolphin Hotel (which is to your left); leave the beach by a prominent path up on to the cliff-top, and then keep along top of cliffs (ignoring left forks), with a caravan site on your left and soon diverting out to the headland (with cannons) B.

② After going around a series of bays (ignoring path descending to beach), the path keeps to edge of fields on the seaward side (in some places cutting off headlands); ③ just after waymarked stile, the path goes over a footbridge and drops down on to the shore, where you turn left. 500 yards later the path climbs up at the far end of the bay to regain cliff-top. The path fairly soon descends into a small stony bay and climbs a hillock to reach Coldingham Bay (with beach huts and café).

For Coldingham C Turn left inland on a tarmacked track between the café and lifeguard hut and follow the road (a signposted path runs parallel to it on right-hand side for a distance to avoid road-walking).

④ *To continue main walk* After the beach huts, take steps up (behind the rocks) on to the cliff and follow the path to St Abb's village D, where you keep as close as possible to the coast, to drop down into the harbour; take the steps between the last two cottages in harbour (with red-tiled roofs) and ascend on path to a road where you turn right, past church to the end of village.

⑤ Turn right by 30mph speed derestriction sign, on an enclosed

path signposted St Abb's Head, soon going along the cliff-top E. The path falls to a pair of small, stony bays, then rises to where a wall meets a fence. ⑥ Cross a stile – the path goes left, around a hillock and along a valley (becoming less defined towards top), but there are much better views by ascending the steep hillock on right and walking along cliff-top; meanwhile the main path route goes up the valley until sea reappears (where these two routes merge).

Continue along the coast soon keeping to the left of the lighthouse buildings at St Abb's Head; briefly join lighthouse road, but it is best almost immediately to divert off it and rejoin the cliff-top for more sea views F.

Eventually you drop steeply to reach the corner of the road ⑦. *Either* retrace your steps to St Abb's *or* (easier) keep right along the road, over a cattlegrid to reach the nature reserve visitor centre G (which is on the left just before road junction). At B6438, you can get the bus back to Eyemouth via Coldingham; to the latter it's an easy, though unexciting, 15-minute walk along the road to the right.

ON THE ROUTE

A **Eyemouth** is a busy fishing port specialising in shellfish; lobster tanks and fish-smoking sheds can be seen in town, and a **fish market** operates Monday to Thursday when catches are landed. A tight cluster of terraces and yards adjoins the quay; the town's **museum** (fishing, local history and rural life) is housed in the Auld Kirk, close by. In the 18th century smuggling was rife, and the town was riddled with underground passages for the purpose (some reputedly still exist).

B The **cannons** are 32-pounders cast about 1830, probably placed as a defence against a possible French invasion in the 1850s. They are on the site of a **fort** which existed 1547–60 and was built by the Duke of Somerset, protector to the boy king Edward.

C **Coldingham** (off route) is the site of an 11th-century Benedictine

priory, largely destroyed by Cromwell's men in 1648, but foundations and a south aisle arch are visible, and north and east walls of the 12th- and 13th-century choir have been incorporated into the adjacent parish church.

D **St Abb's** is a quiet fishing village with a picturesque harbour; crabs and lobsters are often unloaded. At Castle Rock (the house on the cliff) lived 19th-century landscape artist Gemmel Hutchison.

E **St Abb's Head** Some of the best **cliff scenery** on the Scottish east coast; stacks, deep inlets and precipitously sited ledges provide nesting places for some 50,000 **birds**, including guillemots, razorbills, fulmars, herring gulls, kittiwakes, shags and a few puffins; offshore are sooty and Manx shearwater. The greatest concentrations of birds are near the lighthouse. Varied soils (acid and mineral rich) result in rich **flora** and **insect** life, including the Camberwell Beauty butterfly and death's head hawkmoth. St Abb's is a corruption of Ebba, a Northumbrian princess who was shipwrecked here and founded a nunnery.

F Just beyond St Abb's itself, a rugged coastline is revealed to the north; you are now looking towards **East Castle**, a shattered cliff-top ruin used by Walter Scott as the model for Wolf Crags in *The Bride of Lammermoor*. Close to the lighthouse road is **Mire Loch**, a haunt of waders.

G The **nature reserve visitor centre** for St Abb's has a small exhibition and a café.

Eyemouth is a mixture of fishing port and seaside resort

GULLANE BAY AND THE EAST LOTHIAN COAST

A LINEAR walk along an unspoilt sand and rock coast a few miles east of Edinburgh, becoming increasingly remote and ending on a long golden beach leading to the fishing-cum-resort town of North Berwick. Good views across the estuary to Fife; excellent for bird-watching. Route-finding is straightforward. Return by bus; frequent daily service North Berwick to Edinburgh; there is also a daily train service from North Berwick to Edinburgh.

WALK DIRECTIONS

None needed, once you have found the coast. Keep to the path as

LENGTH *Full walk* 9 miles (14.5km), 4½ hours
From Gullane 6½ miles (10.5km), 3 hours
From Dirleton 2½ miles (4km), 2 hours
DIFFICULTY 1–2
START Aberlady Bay Nature Reserve. From Edinburgh, take A198 through Aberlady village; ¼ mile after village, park on a lay-by on the left by a long wooden footbridge marking the entrance to the nature reserve. The bus will drop you here. Grid reference 471805
Gullane village. From the bus stop

walk along the main road towards Edinburgh for 50 yards then turn right up a road signposted To The Beach. Park in village or drive up this road to the beach car park (fee payable). Grid reference 477831 · *Dirleton* village. If coming from Edinburgh, take the last turning on the left, signposted Yellow Craig. Car park (fee payable) just before beach. Grid reference 515855
OS MAPS Landranger 66; Pathfinder 396 (NT 48/58/68)
REFRESHMENTS Tea-shops and pubs in Gullane, North Berwick and Dirleton; Waggon Inn, Aberlady

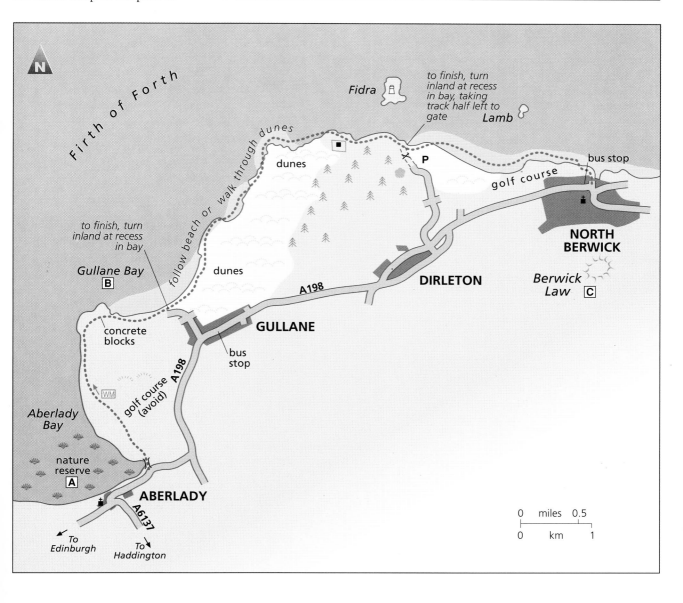

signposted from Aberlady Bay; avoid turning inland on to the golf course. If you want to finish at Gullane or Dirleton, see the map for where to turn inland; if finishing at North Berwick, keep on the beach, and strike inland when level with the church tower.

ON THE ROUTE

A **Aberlady Bay Nature Reserve** Notable for its **birds**; 55 species are recorded as breeding here. In winter, thousands of scoter can be seen just out of the bay. Other species include eider, shelduck, ringed plover,

A large section of the walk involves walking along the sands or through the dunes of Gullane Bay

The distinctive pied plumage of the eider drake

grebes, divers, wigeon, mallard, dunlin and godwit. **Plants** found here include lichen, grasses, saltmarsh mosses, marsh orchids, bog pimpernel and moonwort.

B **Gullane Bay** This too is notable for **birds**, including large flocks of sea-duck and scoter. There are sweeping **views** across to Fife. The nearest island is Fidra, which supports a colony of terns. The towering island further east is **Bass Rock**, a famous place for gannets; puffins live here, too. There are daily **boat trips** in summer to Bass Rock from North Berwick.

C Inland, the abrupt and distinctive hill is **Berwick Law** which, like Bass Rock, is a volcanic plug. There is a path to the top.

ANOTHER WALK IN THE FIRTH OF FORTH

The Firth of Forth's other indisputably magnificent walk is from **Cramond to South Queensferry**, returning by bus (frequent services, continuing back to Edinburgh), on the west side of Edinburgh. Buses from Edinburgh stop on the A90 by the Cramond Brig Hotel from which it is a pleasant stroll along the River Almond (go past the hotel, then fork left along the track by the river) to the estuary at Cramond, itself a village of great character, with whitewashed cottages, old maltings and lots of boats. Cramond is the best starting-point for those arriving by car.

The next part is the most problematic in our experience! You need to cross the river by ferry. In theory this operates 9 to 7 April to September and 10 to 4 the rest of the year, with an hour off for lunch at 1 to 2 pm. There's a half-hourly service on Sundays. However, our researchers have twice come a cropper with this and had to return another day. Once over the Almond, the rest of the walk offers no difficulties: turn right once you have alighted from the ferry and follow the path or track that is closest to the coast. Shortly there is access to the shore and **Eagle Rock**, where a plaque records the rock's doubtful provenance: it might or might not be Roman, and bears something that might or might not be a carving of something that might or might not be an eagle . . . Dalmeny House comes into view a little later; built in 1815 for the Earls of Rosebery, who married into the Rothschilds, this was the very first example of Tudor-Gothic revival style in Scotland; the house is *open* on some summer afternoons. The path also passes close to Barnbougle Castle (private).

At **Hound Point**, the path and coastline change direction and the first views of the formidable **Forth Bridges** appear. The **Forth Railway Bridge**, built 1882–89, was the engineering wonder of its age, with a total span of 1 mile and 1,005 yards, 135 acres of painted surface (requiring continuous repainting on a four-year cycle) and carrying the railway 157 feet above the water. The cantilever design was by John Fowler and Benjamin Baker. Below it is the islet of Inchgarvie, with its fort; this was defended against Cromwell and rebuilt in 1779.

When the **Forth Road Bridge** opened in 1964 its 512-foot towers, 3,300-foot central span, 39,000 tons of steel and 150,000 cubic yards of concrete made it the world's largest suspension bridge. North and South Queensferry lost their 900-year status as ferry landing stages.

The walk concludes as you go through the Queensferry Gate and pass directly beneath these gigantic structures. Summer **boat trips** from both South Queensferry and North Queensferry head out to Inchcolm Island, which has a well-preserved abbey and a grey seal colony.

The whole walk is 5½ miles (9km) and takes about 2½ hours, plus stops.

BALCARY POINT

BEYOND Loch Mackie a track leads down to the shore to pick up a coast path which rises gently on to cliffs and around Balcary Point, the finest part of this short walk. Easy route-finding.

LENGTH 3½ miles (5.5 km), 2 hours
DIFFICULTY 2
START Balcary Bay Hotel. Turn off the A711 at east end of Auchencairn (signposted Balcary); just past the hotel entrance, park on the right-hand side of road in small (free) car park and just beyond the signpost on right for Right of Way Past Loch Mackie to Rascarrel Bay. Grid reference 821495
OS MAPS Landranger 84; Pathfinder 555 (NX 85/95)
REFRESHMENTS Balcary Bay Hotel

WALK DIRECTIONS

① Ⓐ Take the signposted track for Loch Mackie and Rascarrel Bay. Just before a house, continue forward (ignoring left turn), to pass house on your left, then a derelict cottage on the right ②. The track then goes along the edge of two fields to reach Loch Mackie Ⓑ. ③ As soon as you reach the loch, take signposted gate

The shag, a 20th-century immigrant to Britain, scarcely ventures inland

on the left (do not carry along loch edge) and follow the grassy track along the right edge of the field. After the next gate, enter rough land and follow main track to a gate by the coast ④.

Beyond it, path leads to the left to reach the shore by chalets. ⑤ Later the path ascends to reach the cliff-top. Continue along the cliff path all the way (to avoid the high cliff-edge walk, some walkers may prefer to turn left inland at a signpost after ½ mile) past Balcary Point Ⓒ, then later into woods, eventually reaching a gate into a field ⑥, where you follow the right (bottom) edge, past a house. Then go right, through a gate and continue forward on an enclosed path to reach the road, where you continue forward to reach the starting-point.

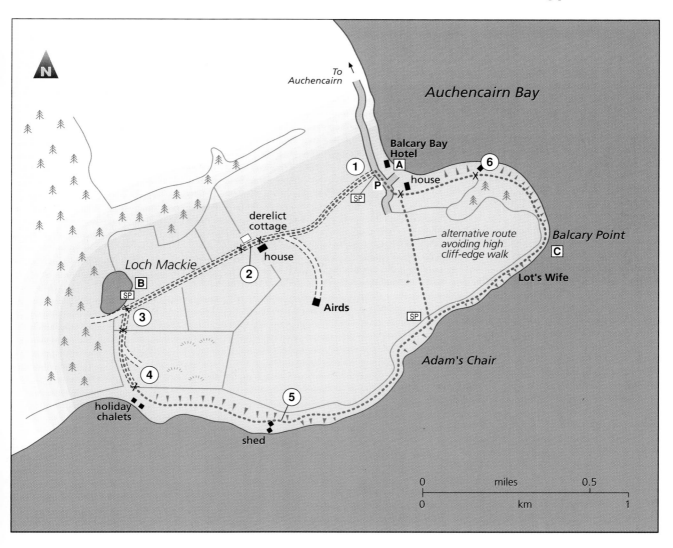

ON THE ROUTE

A **The hotel** was built by the notorious Solway smugglers for their headquarters.

B In summer, the loch is the haunt of colourful **dragonflies.**

C These are good cliffs for watching **sea birds**, whose cries echo on the sheer cliffs far below. You might see buzzards and kestrels, perhaps two of the most attractive birds; also fulmars, parrot-beaked puffins and herring gulls. There is a charming view across **Auchencairn Bay**, which appears almost land-locked, hemmed in to the east by Hestan Island (the site of an ancient manor house).

RIGHTS OF WAY IN SCOTLAND

There is no officially registered network of rights of way in Scotland (unlike England and Wales), and a tradition of informal access for walkers (except in shooting and stalking seasons) has developed. However, many local authority planning departments keep records of rights of way; the Scottish Rights of Way Society publishes maps of some of these routes for its members.

Rights of way are not distinguished from other paths on OS maps, but many are signposted by the Scottish Rights of Way Society, and by local authorities.

The creation of a right of way depends primarily on common law. The requirements for a route to become a right of way are:

1 It must run from one public place (where the public are entitled to be, such as a road or church) to another.
2 It must follow a consistent and generally defined line (although it need not be visible on the ground and may make minor deviations).
3 It must have been used openly and peaceably by the public as of right, without the express or implied permission of the landowner.
4 It must have been used without substantial and effective interruption for a period of at least 20 years.

Balcary Points juts out into the Solway Firth, the great estuary dividing lowland Scotland and Cumbria. It offers a fine opportunity for watching sea birds

CULZEAN

A GREAT castle estate (now a country park), with much to see and many quiet tracks in delightful mixed woodland with occasional patches of more open parkland. The walk begins and ends with a stroll along a big sandy beach. Park facilities are closed in winter, but there is free pedestrian access all year round.

WALK DIRECTIONS

① Take path from car park past toilets to reach the beach where you turn right A. ② Just after last house visible (by caravan site) turn right inland and immediately left on a track to reach a gate by a lodge where you continue forward to enter the estate on a track.

Soon pass a cottage, then 100 yards later go through a barrier where you continue forward. The track becomes a surfaced park road,

---

LENGTH *Full walk* 4½ miles (7km), 2½ hours. *Short walk* (omitting old railway track) 3½ miles (5.5km), 2 hours

DIFFICULTY 1

START Maidens village, south-west of Ayr. Turn off A77 north-east into Ardlochan Road (which runs along the seafront) and start from unsignposted car park on left just before No Through Road sign, after the speed derestriction sign and opposite house No 99. Grid reference 216083

Alternatively start in Culzean Country Park and park at Swan Pond car park at ③ (fee for cars, free for pedestrians; start the walk with the car park on your left). Grid reference 225095

OS MAPS Landranger 70; Pathfinder 479 and 491 (NS 21/31 and NS 20/30); estate maps available at visitor centre in Culzean Country Park

REFRESHMENTS Restaurant at visitor centre and snack bar by main car park in Culzean Country Park

---

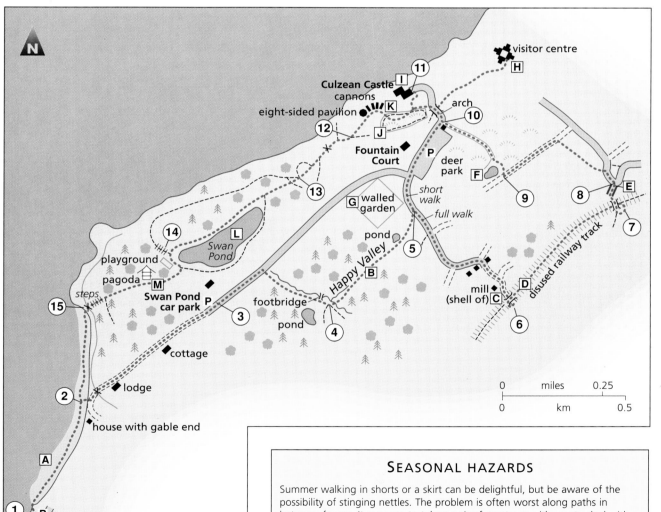

SEASONAL HAZARDS

Summer walking in shorts or a skirt can be delightful, but be aware of the possibility of stinging nettles. The problem is often worst along paths in between fences. It may pay to take a pair of secateurs with you to deal with high-summer vegetation. July and August bring out the midges, notably around the lochs of Scotland.

In autumn, woodland paths often get obscured by fallen leaves. Mud can be a problem at any time of year, especially along bridleways where horses may churn up the path surface.

passing Swan Pond car park on your left ③ (with a pavilion-like Gothic building close by); 150 yards after the track has become a surfaced park road, turn right on a broad path with a pond and channelised stream on your left.

Avoid a footbridge on the left after 250 yards, but 50 yards later ④ turn left at a cross-junction. Follow this path through semi-exotic woodland B to reach a T-junction with surfaced driveway ⑤.

For short walk Turn left, then turn right at the gateway of a walled garden G on the left, and follow the driveway past Camellia House and the main car park (tourist information) at ⑩ then turn left through an archway into Culzean Castle. Pick up directions at ⑪.

For full walk Turn right and take the surfaced road uphill; the road bends left at an estate house. Turn right immediately after the house on an unsurfaced track. Ignore left turn after 100 yards (the remains of a mill are seen to the right of the track C), and proceed to reach an old railway bridge over the track ⑥.

Ascend one of the steep, narrow paths up to the old (dismantled) railway, and turn left along it (or, for a gentler climb, go under the bridge and immediately turn right), turning sharp right on reaching the old railway track D.

⑦ After ⅓ mile, just after bridge overhead, take steps on the right and turn right again to cross the bridge. After 100 yards, you reach a surfaced drive where you keep left E; ⑧ 100 yards after, turn left on a gravel track down the edge of a field to T-junction, where you turn left on a level track.

⑨ Immediately on reaching woods take a path on the right, down the right edge of the woods and around the right-hand side of the Fire Pond F. After 50 yards, just after the path bends left (continuing to encircle pond) take steps on the right to a stile, then descend on a path between high fences enclosing the deer park.

Emerge by the tourist information and main car park ⑩. There is an optional detour to the left past Camellia House (right) to the walled garden G; but the route

continues to the right, then left through an archway into Culzean Castle. As you go over the bridge beyond the archway, notice the track underneath: the detour to the right along the track to the visitor centre is recommended H.

⑪ Take the gateway to the left of the castle I to a terrace with cannons, with Fountain Court (gardens) J down on your left and the castle on your right. Pass the cannons, then take steps down on the left into Fountain Court and turn right at the bottom past a conservatory. Just after, take a small gate on the right and cross the grass towards the sea to find a row of cannons K ranged along a gravel path; turn left along this path which bends left by an octagonal pavilion, then ⑫ soon bends right into woods, with the sea away to right.

Avoid minor side turns and reach a barrier; ⑬ 350 yards later you reach a fork (the right fork, which you might like to try as a variant, descends and continues along cliffs before dropping down steps to T-junction by lake, where you keep right at ⑭). Keep forward and ignore side turns, until immediately before the lake (just visible through the trees, ahead) fork right on a broad path marked by a log border along its left-hand side and pass around the right-hand side of the lake L, turning left at the end ⑭. Follow the lakeside path round to reach an adventure playground.

If you started from Swan Pond car park, carry on; otherwise turn right on the track, past a ruined pagoda M and continue forward to reach a view over the beach ⑮, then go down steps on to the beach where you turn left. At the toilet block turn inland to reach the car park.

ON THE ROUTE

A **View** of two islands: **Arran** and **Ailsa Craig**; the latter is 1,114ft high and just 2 miles round, with a sheer fall on its west side; once occupied by a monastic community and now a bird sanctuary.

B Part of Culzean's magnificent **woodlands**, which are home to 155 **bird species**. Many trees near this path and around Happy Valley Pond are exotic specimens, including palm

trees and bamboo.

C Shell of **Sunnyside Mill**, used until 1900; its wheel was removed for scrap in the last war.

D The **old railway** ran from Maidens to Dunure; it opened in 1906 and carried passenger traffic until 1930.

E From here is a particularly fine **view** of **Culzean Castle** and **Arran**.

F The **Fire Pond** was created to supply water for fire-fighting, and now feeds the castle fountain. Just below, the **deer park** contains red deer which have been re-introduced.

G The **walled garden** includes kitchen and pleasure gardens; its corners are at the points of the compass.

H The **park visitor centre** is within the well-restored Home Farm, a design of Robert Adam (1777).

I **Culzean Castle** (National Trust for Scotland; *open* April to October 10 to 5 daily) One of Robert Adam's greatest designs, built in three phases, 1777–92, for the 10th Earl of Cassillis on the site of 16th-century Scots Tower House. Among the internal masterpieces are the oval staircase and round drawing-room.

Culzean Castle was given to Eisenhower for his lifetime

J **Fountain Court** Two parallel terraces, ornamental fountain and herbaceous borders; at its best in July and August.

K The **battery** was placed here against a possible Napoleonic invasion.

L **Swan Pond** (13 acres), set in woods, has 700 ducks in winter, moorhens, herons and coots as well as mute swans.

M The **pagoda** was built as a romantic landscape feature.

SOUTH BUTE SHORES AND ST BLANE'S CHAPEL

THIS route takes a grand sequence of island views, following the coast before rising past the remote ruins of a monastery. The final sections, including the modest summit of Suidhe Hill (but steep descent at end), can be avoided in poor visibility by using the road. The ground is generally firm, with patches of uneven terrain; the route is not always defined.

WALK DIRECTIONS

① **A** Continue to the end of the shoreside road and pick up the track ahead; beyond a gate, this narrows to a path, leading along grass just above shore level **B**. ② Near the lighthouse, keep around the shoreline (path scarcely defined), around Glencallum Bay **C**. ③ At the west side of the bay, take the upper of the two paths, that zigzags up the hillside, and continues through bracken above the marshy depression on the far side of the ridge. The path rises gently and a view opens up of Loch na Leighe, a

> **LENGTH** 5½ miles (9km), 3½ hours
> **DIFFICULTY** 3
> **START** South end of Kilchattan, on Isle of Bute at end of road; roadside parking. Grid reference 105546
> **OS MAPS** Landranger 63; Pathfinder 428 (NS 05/15)
> **REFRESHMENTS** Hotel and shop at Kilchattan

The tufted duck is very active, constantly diving down and bobbing up again

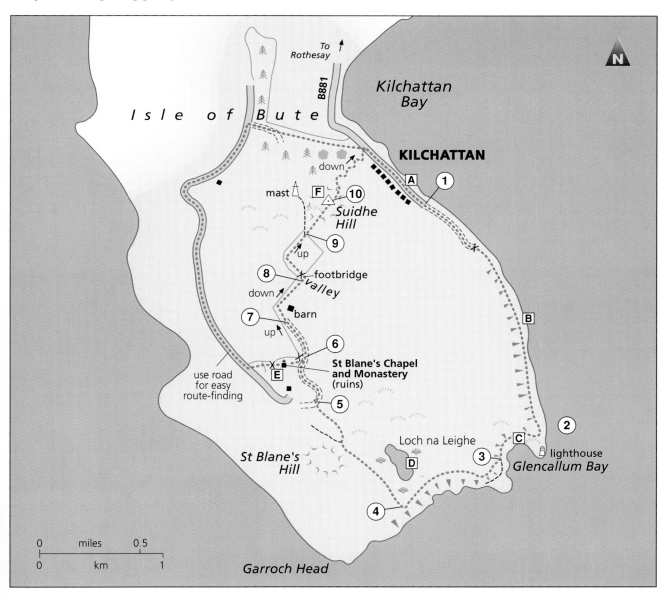

small lake down to the right.

④ Immediately after passing the loch, turn right to proceed close to its left side. Beyond the loch do not go too far left but soon pick up a track heading towards Plan Farm. Do not go as far as the farm – instead, ⑤ pick up a well-defined stony track 100 yards to the right, which can be seen curving round along a valley to the right of, and a short distance before, the farm, then heading up towards trees. ⑥ As soon as the fence begins on left-hand side of track, make a detour left through gate to see St Blane's Chapel E.

Route back to Kilchattan via road, avoiding hill walk Descend hill from the chapel to reach a kissing-gate, then follow path down edge of fields until a gate gives access on to road; turn right along the road. After 2 miles, woodland begins on your right. 150 yards later, soon after a milestone on the left, turn right on a woodland track, initially following power lines. The track narrows to path width and continues along left edge of wood to reach the road at Kilchattan. Turn right to reach the starting-point.

Route back via Suidhe Hill (steep descent at end; route-finding quite easy in good visibility) Return to the track, turn left along it to continue uphill. ⑦ At the top of the slope, the track ends (a barn is visible close by to right): here, continue forward, alongside fence on left, soon bending right as the fence does the same, and drop into a slight valley ⑧.

Here continue to keep alongside fence, which now bends left; soon cross a footbridge and go through a gate. 100 yards later, at the end of enclosure, turn right uphill (alongside fence on left); a mast soon comes into view. ⑨ At the top of enclosure enter open land at fence corner and head for the top of Suidhe Hill (the obvious hill to the right of the mast). It is easiest to ascend by keeping to the right. At the top, cross a stile to reach trig point (summit pillar) ⑩ F.

RIGHTS OF WAY IN SCOTLAND

There is no officially registered network of rights of way in Scotland (unlike England and Wales), and a tradition of informal access for walkers (except in shooting and stalking seasons) has developed. However, many local authority planning departments keep records of rights of way; the Scottish Rights of Way Society publishes maps of some of these routes for its members.

Rights of way are not distinguished from other paths on OS maps, but many are signposted by the Scottish Rights of Way Society, and by local authorities.

The creation of a right of way depends primarily on common law. The requirements for a route to become a right of way are:

1 It must run from one public place (where the public are entitled to be, such as a road or church) to another.
2 It must follow a consistent and generally defined line (although need not be visible on the ground and may make minor deviations).
3 It must have been used openly and peaceably by the public as of right, without the express or implied permission of the landowner.
4 It must have been used without substantial and effective interruption for a period of at least 20 years.

Return to the stile and continue to follow the path, leading steeply down to Kilchattan, skirting woods and dropping to the road and rear of houses. Turn right on road, to starting-point.

ON THE ROUTE

A **Kilchattan** was named after Cattan, a 6th-century saint.

B This grassy strip is one of the many examples of a Scottish west coast **raised beach**, now just above sea-level. Excellent **views** of Great Cumbrae Island close up, Little Cumbrae Island to the right; to the south, the lone granite island of Ailsa Craig towers 1,114ft; later the Isle of Arran should be visible, with Goat Fell (2,866ft) its highest point.

C A striking **sill** of hard, grey rock protrudes across the bay; overgrown ruins remain here of an **old inn.**

D The loch is rich in wildlife, including **teal** and **tufted duck.**

E Remains of the splendidly sited **St Blane's Chapel and Monastery** in a sheltered glade looking down to the coast. Founded in the 6th century, its last church minister was ordained in the 18th century. The ruined **Norman chapel** with its archway is the most prominent feature.

F **Suidhe Hill** gives a spectacular view over Arran, Kintyre, the Cumbraes, Bute and the mainland.

A peaceful scene at Kilchattan Bay

KELBURN AND FAIRLIE GLENS

A NICELY varied route taking in two glens, each with a waterfall and castle linked by a high-level section along the edge of the moors looking down over the coast and islands. The moorland section may be boggy in places, but the paths up and down the glens are well maintained.

The Kelburn Country Centre grounds are *open all year* (11 to 5 winter, 10 to 6 Easter to October) except Christmas and Boxing Day, and Saturdays from November to January. The Centre organises pony-trekking, trails and has a ranger service. The entrance fee is reduced in winter, when some facilities, such as the shop and the adventure course, are closed.

LENGTH 4½ miles (7km), 2½ hours
DIFFICULTY 2
START Kelburn Country Centre car park (admission fee), just east of A78 and south of Largs. Grid reference 215564
By train Fairlie. Leave the station, turn right by the station sign on to an enclosed tarmacked path, soon passing over a stream (Fairlie Burn) then immediately turn right (at a cottage), to cross over the railway.

Carry on up the path close to the stream to reach Fairlie Castle; continue up the track to the left of the castle to reach a gate on left with stone gateposts (one of which has fallen). This is point ⑩.

OS MAPS Landranger 63; Pathfinder 429 (NS 25/35); path map of Kelburn estate from Country Centre
REFRESHMENTS Café at Country Centre

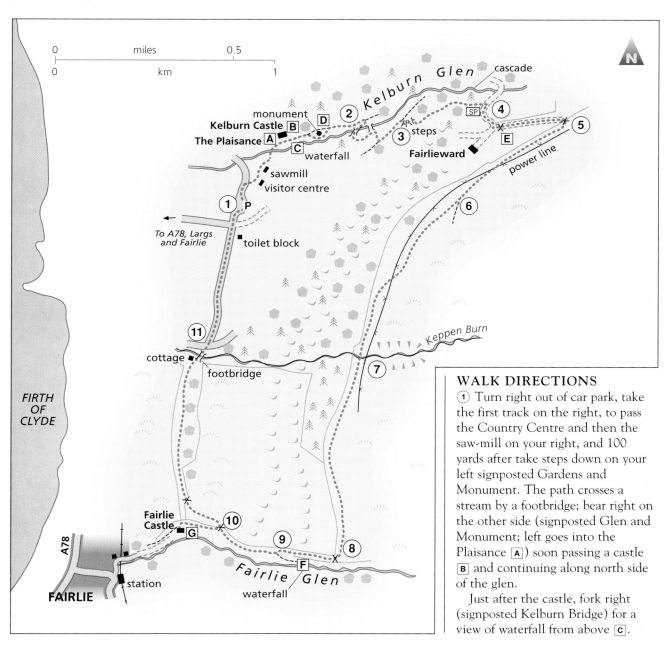

WALK DIRECTIONS

① Turn right out of car park, take the first track on the right, to pass the Country Centre and then the saw-mill on your right, and 100 yards after take steps down on your left signposted Gardens and Monument. The path crosses a stream by a footbridge; bear right on the other side (signposted Glen and Monument; left goes into the Plaisance A) soon passing a castle B and continuing along north side of the glen.

Just after the castle, fork right (signposted Kelburn Bridge) for a view of waterfall from above C.

Immediately before the footbridge fork left on to path to rejoin the northern glen path, and, 20 yards later, fork right (left goes up steps) to pass a monument Ⓓ.

② 200 yards later, fork right down steps down to a footbridge; do not cross it but turn right downstream to another footbridge. After 100 yards, by a wooden railing, turn left at path junction to follow path along south side of glen with a view of the glen down on your left; keep left at T-junction 250 yards later, and 100 yards further on ③ fork right up steps.

④ When you reach a broad track at top of glen and stone bridge, turn right (signposted Upper Estate Road South). At a cross-junction out of the woods with a house visible ahead, turn sharp left, through gate and proceed alongside fence on left to reach double gate ⑤. Turn sharp right on a well-defined track alongside fence and wall on right Ⓔ.

The track eventually leaves the wall, and goes under power lines; then ⑥ forks right. Track narrows to a path, rejoins the wall and power lines and later disappears (it can be boggy here), but the wall is your guide. Later ⑦, step across the stream (deeply incised into hillside). ⑧ Soon after forest on right ends, cross fixed gate (Fairlie Glen is immediately ahead) and immediately turn right through a gate to follow a well-defined path down the right-hand side of Fairlie Glen, initially with a wall on your left.

⑨ Just before power lines, the path enters woods: here it is worth detouring left a few yards, on a streamside path up glen, to reach a waterfall Ⓕ. Proceed on path down, soon past a bench then past a gateway on your right with stone gateposts (one has fallen). After

Kelburn Castle at the start of the walk through Kelburn Glen, with architectural features typical of grand Scottish houses

detouring ahead to see Fairlie Castle Ⓖ, go through this gateway.

⑩ Immediately turn left downhill alongside a wall on your left until you are level with the castle to reach a strip of trees at bottom of this field. Turn right, with the strip of trees on your left, soon giving access to path within this strip. Pass a cottage close on your left: continue forward to reach a footbridge, then ⑪ continue forward again at a three-way road junction (along the level) and follow to reach the car park.

ON THE ROUTE

Ⓐ **The Plaisance**, a formal part-walled garden, contains two 1,000-year-old yews. Just before entering, look on the left for the 100-ft tall **Monterey Pine**, the oldest and tallest of its kind in Scotland, and the **weeping larch**, a unique mutant whose branches touch the ground and reseed, sprawling across an impressively large area.

Ⓑ **Kelburn Castle**, home of the Earls of Glasgow, was originally a Norman keep but has been adapted; the door was moved to the south side in 1581 (date-stone is visible from the path, with the initials of the then baird John Boyle). It is open to the public on afternoons in spring.

Ⓒ The **waterfall** drops 20ft into a chasm with sandstone overhangs.

Ⓓ **Monument** of 1775 to the third Earl of Glasgow, placed at his favourite spot and designed by Robert Adam.

Ⓔ Wide **views** in this section, of Great and Little Cumbrae (islands), Toward Point, Bute, Arran, Kintyre and Ailsa Craig.

Ⓕ Fine **waterfall** in wooded Fairlie Glen.

Ⓖ **Fairlie Castle**, a small 16th-century keep, stands over 30ft high. There is no way over the wall from the castle, hence the need to retrace your steps back to the stone gateposts.

CRAIGEND AND MUGDOCK CASTLES

THE route leads from suburban Glasgow straight into remote-feeling moorland; further on are mixed woods, three lochs, two ruined castles, a reservoir path and a view of Glasgow, which feels miles away. All paths and tracks are well defined and mostly signposted. Route-finding is quite easy; the first half of the walk follows the initial stages of the West Highland Way (see Walk 144).

LENGTH *Full walk* 8 miles (13km), 4 hours; *short walk* 5½ miles (9km), 2½ hours

DIFFICULTY 1–2 (short walk 1)

START Milngavie (pronounced 'Mulguy') station, about 25 minutes by train from Glasgow Central. Large car park. Sundays: bus services only (to station). Grid reference 555745

OS MAPS Landranger 64; Pathfinder 403 (NS 47/57)

REFRESHMENTS Full range in Milngavie

WALK DIRECTIONS

① With the station entrance behind you, turn left, under a pedestrian tunnel. The West Highland Way (WHW) begins here (map displayed), and is clearly signposted or waymarked with thistle motifs; Allander Way signposts are also followed. Follow Station Road beyond the tunnel, down the main pedestrian street in Milngavie, turning right just after

The common buzzard's preferred habitat is open woodland

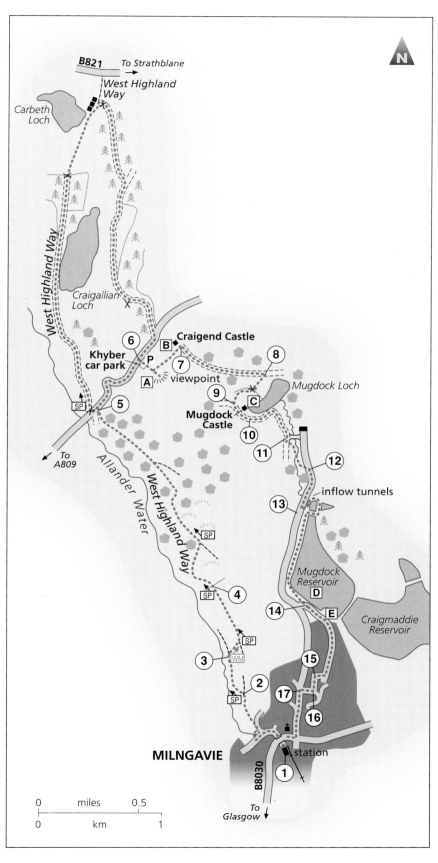

crossing the river (signpost), down a ramp, then right on a side road then immediately left on a tarmac path parallel to the main road.

② Follow waymarked route ahead for 300 yards, then turn left as

A WALK ALONG GREENOCK CUT

To the west of Glasgow, the industrial town of Greenock occupies a spectacular site at the mouth of the Clyde. Just above the town, a water channel known as Greenock Cut threads a level course through open country, gaining magnificent views of the south-west Highlands. The cut, built in 1827 as a scheme for solving Greenock's water shortage, has a footpath along it. The cut is no longer used, but is designated an Ancient Monument.

Walkers should begin from the Clyde Muirshiel Regional Park Centre car park at Cornalees Bridge (grid reference 247722), south of Greenock; follow signs to Loch Thom from the A78. A short nature trail takes in Kelly Cut and a wooded glen. From the visitor centre, head north on the reservoir road, past Compensation Reservoir and Loch Thom; about a mile later the track reaches a cottage by Greenock Cut, which can be followed round to the left: this eventually reaches Kelly Cut and the visitor centre. The total walk is seven miles and takes about three hours.

signposted (yellow arrow), then after 50 yards turn right, along the riverside (waymarked). ③ WHW turns right to leave the river after 500 yards (waymark), turning left 300 yards later at a T-junction (waymarked). ④ Carry straight on after ¼ mile at junction. Follow this to reach a road after ¾ mile ⑤.

For full walk Turn left on the road, then right after 30 yards over a stile, continuing on WHW; the track passes a lake after ½ mile and later the WHW takes a waymarked right turn. On reaching a lake on the left, keep forward on the track past cabins, reaching a turning-circle after 100 yards. 50 yards later, turn sharp right over a ladder-stile, signposted to Mugdock Country Park (Khyber Pass Road), to leave WHW, and follow this for ½ mile to T-junction. Turn right; follow signposts to a road. Turn right on the road, then first left into Khyber car park. Resume route at ⑥.

For short walk Turn right on the road, to leave WHW. Turn right after ½ mile, into Khyber car park ⑥; note a kissing-gate on your left after 30 yards (signposted Craigend Castle), but before passing through it, detour ahead a few yards for a view of Glasgow Ⓐ. Return to the kissing-gate and proceed to Craigend Castle Ⓑ. ⑦ Turn right at Craigend Castle (signposted Mugdock Castle) and follow the

track for ½ mile. ⑧ Turn right (signposted Mugdock Castle) on to a path, which leads into and across a field to a gap in fence, beyond which you fork right. ⑨ When you reach T-junction with track (castle on left), turn left to pass in front of the castle Ⓒ.

⑩ 200 yards later, keep on the main track as it bends left down to the lochside. The track soon bends right into woods. ⑪ Just after passing level with a house (visible away to left), avoid a stone bridge on left leading to iron gates, but fork left 20 yards later on to a narrow path which crosses the stream and follows it, then reaches a road ⑫. Turn right on the road.

⑬ At the bottom of hill, pass through a gateway in the reservoir wall on the left, turning immediately left to follow the path parallel to the road. This loops round in front of ornate inflow tunnels that feed the reservoir. Opposite the entrance, turn right and cross the walkway over the reservoir, then turn left along the path between the reservoir and the road Ⓓ; follow the path to buildings. ⑭ Keep forward on road coming in from the right at the far end, past waterworks building on the left Ⓔ, then turn right at the ornamental garden into driveway. ⑮ 200 yards before (usually locked) gates ahead, and 60 yards after a short section of metal railings, turn

right through a small gate, then left along a residential road parallel to the drive. ⑯ Turn right at road junction at the bottom, into Moor Road. ⑰ Turn left at T-junction (Buchanan Street); follow this back to the start.

ON THE ROUTE

Ⓐ **View** Glasgow city centre ahead; in the other direction can be seen the Campsie Fells (1,897ft).

Ⓑ **Craigend Castle** This sinister ruin of a Gothic revival country house was built *c.*1816 by James Smith.

Ⓒ **Mugdock Castle** A 14th-century ruin (being restored at time of writing) previously belonging to the Earl of Lennox, David de Grahame and the Montrose family. It adjoins a pleasant lily-covered loch. The castle, loch and woods were proposed in the 1970s as a site for a leisure and sports complex, to include night-club, cinema, angling loch and housing. The plan failed.

Ⓓ **Mugdock** and **Craigmaddie Reservoirs** were opened in 1859 and later extended. The pipeline comes from Loch Katrine, 26 miles away, to supply water for Glasgow.

Ⓔ **Memorial** (where you turn right at the ornamental garden) to one of the Water Board's founders, 1904. In the art-nouveau style, the lettering and bronze basin show the influence of Charles Rennie Mackintosh, designer of the Glasgow School of Art.

The Craigmaddie Reservoir in Mugdock Country Park

DUNARDRY AND THE CRINAN CANAL

A SHORT exploration of the northern fringe of Knapdale Forest, using easily followed tracks (partly waymarked): the canal towpath provides the return route.

WALK DIRECTIONS

① With the canal on your left, follow the B841 towards Lochgilphead. ② After ¼ mile, where the road bends slightly left, take a forest track on the right, which winds up to reach a junction after 200 yards: turn left (through a gate) Ⓐ. ③ 300 yards later turn left at the next junction (soon joined by power lines on the left).

④ After 600 yards, turn right at the next junction (oblique T-junction), still with power lines on your left. ⑤ Emerge between a barn

(on left) and a house (Dunans) and continue forward on a hard forestry track. Ignore later side turns to the right and then to left (at the latter there is a yellow footprint waymarker indicating Dunardry Forest Walk which you now follow until the main road).

⑥ The track bends right in front

of a quarry: here detour left up the waymarked path to reach a viewpoint Ⓑ. Return to the track, which becomes tarmacked. ⑦ Keep left at the next junction (keeping to the main track); there is now a stream on your right. Look for a yellow waymarker on the left after 150 yards (just before track crosses

---

LENGTH 5 miles (8km), 2½ hours *with extension to Crinan 9 miles (14.5km) 4 hours*

DIFFICULTY 1

START Bellanoch (signposted on road), by junction of B841 and B8025, north-west of Lochgilphead; there is limited roadside parking near garage, or park on the other side of B8025 bridge (you can also start

from the car park for the signposted Dunardry Forest Walk, ½ mile west of Cairnbaan, and follow the canal section at the start of the walk; return to the road to begin directions at ⑧). Grid reference 804924

OS MAPS Landranger 55; Pathfinder 377 (NR 79/89)

REFRESHMENTS Shop at Bellanoch; hotel at Crinan

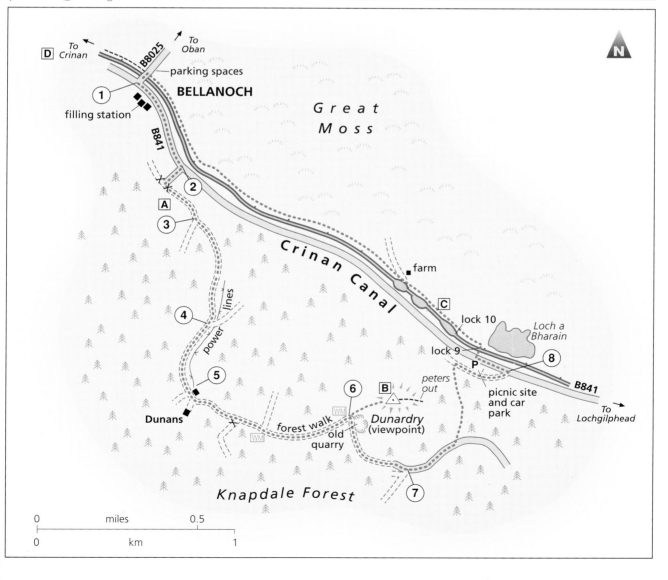

the stream), and take the path through woods, soon dropping to a track where you turn right to reach a car park and go down to the road ⑧.

Turn left on the road, then just after the first house on the right, cross a footbridge away to the right and go over the canal lock. Turn left on the canal towpath (avoid a track which goes closely parallel initially, as it soon veers to right, away from the canal) Ⓒ. Eventually you reach a road-bridge, and turn left to cross it and return to the starting-point (*or* continue along the canal for 2 miles to Crinan Ⓓ; return the same way).

ON THE ROUTE

Ⓐ **Knapdale Forest** One of the Forestry Commission's vast Argyll plantations, at the north end of the Kintyre peninsula; occasional views of lochs within the forest.

Ⓑ **Dunardry** gives an extensive view north over **Moine Mhor** (or Great Moss), a raised bog of green fields, densely strewn with prehistoric burial sites, forts and other antiquities. Northwards is the great rock of **Dunadd**, where Fergus landed in AD498; the hillock was the site of the first recorded British coronation in AD574; Dunadd was the capital of the ancient kingdom of Dalriada until around AD900.

Ⓒ The 9-mile **Crinan Canal**, opened in 1801, avoids an 80-mile trip around the Mull of Kintyre, and connects Loch Gilp at Ardrishaig to the sea at Crinan. There are 15 locks on it; the **Dunardry Rolling Bridge** at lock 11, installed in 1900, is wound by hand and something of a rarity.

Ⓓ At **Crinan** there is a pleasant boating scene with yachts and fishing craft.

Crinan basin

Although the engineer of the Crinan Canal was Sir John Rennie, Thomas Telford was called in to sort out early snags and often gets all the credit

ARCHAEOLOGY AT KILMARTIN

A few miles north of the Crinan Canal, the village of Kilmartin reveals an archaeological bounty. The church itself, although uninteresting architecturally, contains a 10th-century Celtic cross bearing one of Britain's oldest images of Christ. In the churchyard, under a cover, are a fine selection of carved medieval tombstones.

A track leading south from the village passes a linear Bronze Age cemetery, about a mile in length. The burial cairns along it have been plundered, but what survives is none the less remarkable. The North Cairn (the first cairn encountered) has a reconstructed exterior and is entered by a trapdoor, under which a ladder leads into a chamber. There is a tomb and carved slab inside. Walk on past the Middle Cairn, which bears cup and axehead marks on a cist (a box made of stone slabs), to the South Cairn, at 134 feet long one of the largest ancient burial sites in Britain. The chamber is 19 feet long and is entered by an opening between stone slabs; graves of the Beaker Folk were excavated here in the 19th century. A short walk brings you to the Templewood Circles; the main stone circle comprises 17 uprights, with one orange-coloured stone with a carved spiral motif thought to be connected with sun worship.

LISMORE

AN exploration of the north end of this island, unsurpassed for views of Loch Linnhe and many of the western isles and peninsulas; two castle ruins add interest. This is one of the very finest low-level walks in Scotland, but requires both careful timing to avoid missing the last ferry and good boots to cope with the rocky shore.

WALK DIRECTIONS

① Ⓐ From the jetty, turn right along the turf, just above low cliffs and the shore. Follow the coast in this way (no path but easy going), later past a small cave to reach a disused lime-kiln on your left Ⓑ, just after which ② take the gate on your right.

Continue now along the track along the shore to cottages (Port Ramsay). At the end of the main row of cottages, turn left (inland) on surfaced lane by a telephone-box. ③ After 50 yards turn right on a gravel track, later passing houses, to reach the end of the track where you continue forward (no path) along the turf just above the shore.

Eventually you pass two ruined cottages; ④ immediately after, turn left away from the shore (this avoids a tricky scramble on rocks around headland), head up across grass keeping a craggy hill immediately on your left. Soon the view opens westwards over bay: locate a big cliff on the opposite side – your objective is to follow the grassy valley just to the left of this.

Head across the bay, crossing a wall and low fence on the way. It is

---

LENGTH 8 miles (13km), 5 hours (minimum); can shorten to 6 miles (9.5km), 4 hours by following the road back from ⑨

DIFFICULTY 3

START Ferry jetty at north-east tip of isle of Lismore, reached by passenger ferry from Port Appin (north of Oban; NB Oban ferries for Lismore do not go to this jetty). Make a note of the ferry times and time the walk carefully (times are displayed at jetties, also available from Oban tourist office); there are about seven services each day; crossing takes 10 minutes. Grid reference 894462

OS MAPS Landranger 49; Pathfinder 318 (NM 84/94)

REFRESHMENTS Pub with restaurant on mainland at Port Appin; snacks and meals sometimes at Isle of Lismore Guest House at ⑨

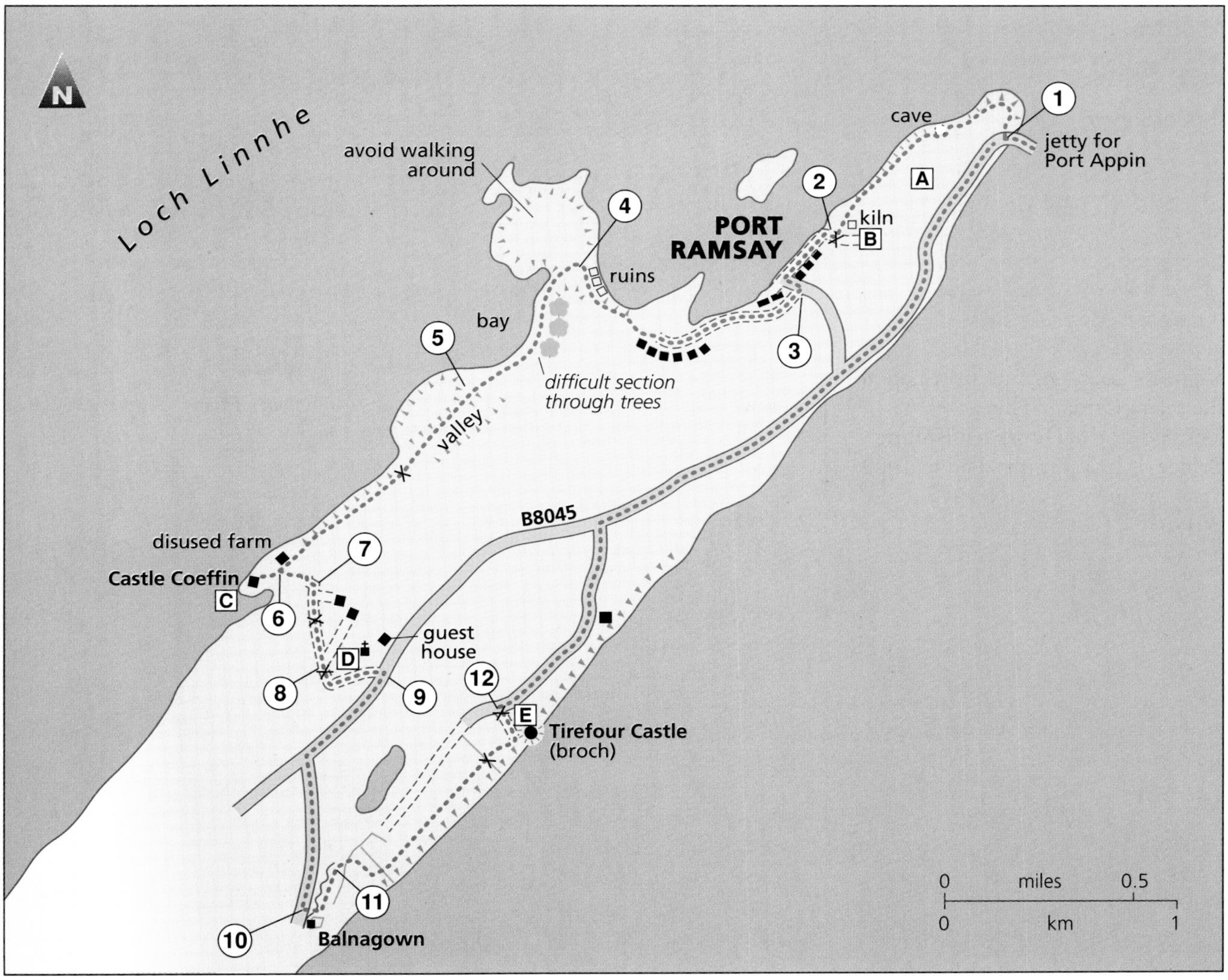

Lismore's church, medieval in parts

rough-going initially but manageable, and gets easier. ⑤ Leave the bay by a ruin to enter the grassy valley; soon it is easy to divert up to higher ground on your right, and walk along the grass.

Castle Coeffin comes into view; just before you reach it, pass an abandoned farm, where you can detour ahead to see the castle [C]. The continuation of the route is 50 yards after passing the abandoned farm; ⑥ turn left inland, on a path leading towards a prominent zigzagging (rising) track.

Follow the track up to reach a gate: the track then bends left, by a power post, but 50 yards later ⑦ turn sharp right on a faint grassy track (as main track continues to go through a wall and heads for a hut where it peters out), immediately crossing a stream. Keep high ground (a grassy and craggy slope) immediately on your left, soon reaching a gate, then continue forward along the right edge of field. ⑧ At the end of field, join a well-defined track (go through gate) and follow it ahead. Beyond next gate, track bends left, soon reaching a farm then on to a road ⑨ [D].

Easy way back Turn left along the road: an hour's brisk walking along this road will bring you to the ferry jetty. Alternatively, if you want to see the Broch and don't mind some road-walking, take the road turning on the right after ½ mile signposted for Broch (this also avoids the somewhat complex route-finding given below). Follow the road for another ¾ mile, then take gate on right up to the Broch; return same way and follow road back to ferry jetty. *Route avoiding (some) road-walking (route-finding less easy)* Turn right on the road; after ½ mile turn left, signposted Balnagown. ⑩ One

field before reaching the farm, take the gate on your left signposted to Broch and walk with a fence on your right. After 50 yards turn left and walk between a wall on right and water channel on left; soon cross channel via a plank-bridge.

⑪ 20 yards before the loch, take stile over wall on right to emerge on to open land, and continue uphill towards the coast (*or* keep down just to the right of loch and pass pens to pick up a track, which soon becomes a surfaced farm road, until detouring through a gate on right once near Broch; return to the road and proceed to a junction where you turn right to reach the ferry jetty; this is easier but misses sea views), then turn left towards the Broch (prominent circular walled structure on hillock).

To reach this, it is necessary to cross a wall (it is easiest to go down the slope towards the sea, where wall is lower and not topped with barbed wire). At Broch [E], turn left on a track down to a gate to the farm road, where ⑫ you turn right to reach T-junction with the principal island road. Turn right and follow the road back to the jetty.

ON THE ROUTE

[A] **Lismore** 'Ieis More' translates from Gaelic as 'great garden'. The nine-mile-long island is green and fertile, with scattered farmsteads, and its highest point only 416ft. Vertical tilting of rock strata has formed a series of valleys parallel to the sea; on a smaller scale, much of the razor-edged rock above the shore is tilted the same way. Legend has it that there was a boat race between St Moluaig and St Mulhac in the 6th century for the possession of Lismore. The former, seeing that he was trailing, cut off his finger and threw it ashore, thus winning the race; he later founded a monastery here. **Views** are complex and ever-changing as the walk progresses: north are the mountains of Kingairloch; north-east is **Ben Nevis** (4,408ft) and nearby Shuna Island; south and west the islands of the Firth of Lorn and Mull; immediately west is Morvern (with a prominent quarry); in view later to

the east are Loch Creran and Benderloch.

[B] The **lime-kiln** is a survival of the Lismore lime trade; there, from Port Ramsay, lime used for agricultural fertiliser was shipped out.

[C] **Castle Coeffin** was a 13th-century Viking stronghold, looking over to Mull and Morvern.

[D] To the left by the road is Lismore's tiny **church** which incorporates parts of the choir of a medieval cathedral, the seat of the diocese of Argyll from the 13th century until 1507.

[E] **Broch (Tirefour Castle)** Neatly walled circular fort guarding the sea approach about 25ft across.

Lismore seen from the jetty at Port Appin

THE RIVER LEVEN GLEN

THE route rises gently up a majestic valley, broad and sinuous, loosely dotted with broad-leaved trees mingled with rushing waterfalls. Beyond two lochans you reach the valley head and vast bleak expanses of moorland surrounding the Blackwater Reservoir; return the same way. The terrain may be boggy briefly after ③, but otherwise this is a good path.

WALK DIRECTIONS

(Make a mental note of the outward route, as you will return the same way.)

① Ⓐ With houses on your left, follow the road to the end. 100 yards after the last house, the road becomes an unsurfaced track (by a shed); immediately after, turn left at track junction. Soon you pass an electricity sub-station on your right; just 20 yards after, take a rising path on the right and 35 yards later ② turn right (along level) at an oblique cross-junction of paths Ⓑ.

The path leads through a semi-wooded area, eventually crossing a footbridge ③, beyond which the path keeps left, initially with the river on left (but soon the river bends away to the left). The path leads up a semi-wooded valley – boggy for a short section, but soon

Loch Leven (not on the route but just west of the start) at sunset; this is a fine walk for majestic views

LENGTH 8 miles (13km), 4½ hours there and back
DIFFICULTY 2
START Kinlochmore (on B863 at east end of Loch Leven, south-east of Fort William). Turn off at the signpost for Grey Mare's Tail Waterfall, turn right at T-junction in front of St Paul's church to follow a long road with a housing estate on left and woods on right; park on roadside at the far end. Grid reference 192619
OS MAPS Landranger 41; Pathfinder 290 and 291 (NN 06/16 and NN 26/36)
REFRESHMENTS Pubs and shops in Kinlochleven (¼ mile from start, but not on route); shop in Kinlochmore

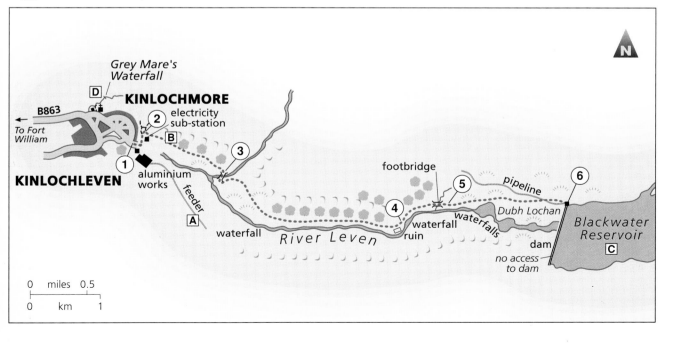

gets easier and very well defined as it climbs gently.

④ The path crosses a small stream at a waterfall (care needed). ⑤ After a footbridge, the path emerges into the open, and finally heads towards Blackwater Dam, following the reservoir pipeline for the final stage [C]. ⑥ From the reservoir, retrace your steps to the starting-point [D].

ON THE ROUTE

[A] The **feeder** for water supplying hydroelectric power from Blackwater Reservoir for the aluminium works at Kinlochleven is across the valley.
[B] For much of the following sections there are fine **views** of major peaks: west south-west is shapely Garbh Bheinn (2,835ft); northwards are Mamore Forest, including (left to right) Am Bodach (3,382ft), Binnein Mor (3,700ft), Sgurr Eilde Mor (3,279ft) and Glas Bheinn (2,587ft); to the south are the northern Glencoe group.
[C] **Blackwater Reservoir**, 8 miles long, was constructed 1905–09 in a bleak setting – a total contrast from the valley from which you have just emerged.

[D] On the return to Kinlochmore, it is worth taking in the **Grey Mare's Tail Waterfall.** Signposted from the

car park by St Paul's church, there is a path leading 200 yards to a viewing point.

The Grey Mare's Tail Waterfall – how could it be called otherwise?

THE WEST HIGHLAND WAY

Beginning from Milngavie, in the suburbs of Glasgow, the West Highland Way gets increasingly dramatic as it heads north. For that reason it is best walked south to north, carrying past Loch Lomond and Glen Coe, through Kinlochleven and taking in Glen Nevis.

Despite the grandeur of the scenery through which it passes, the Way generally keeps quite low throughout its 95 miles (152km) and offers one of the less challenging opportunities for a week's walking in the West Highlands. Signposting and waymarking is thorough, and the paths are easy to follow.

An excellent two-day sample of the Way can be had by starting at Kingshouse Hotel and walking to Fort William, with an overnight bed-and-breakfast stop at Kinlochleven or Kinlochmore (arrange this in advance). The return is by public transport: begin by taking the train or car to Bridge of Orchy and catch any bus going via Glen Coe; alight at White Corries ski slope, near the Kingshouse Hotel at the eastern end of Glen Coe. On completing the walk there are buses and trains from Fort William to Bridge of Orchy. For bus information telephone Buchanan Street Bus Station in Glasgow; tel (0141) 332 9191.

Just to the east of Glen Coe lies Rannoch Moor – a huge and desolate expanse studded with lochans and remains of stumps of the great Caledonian Forest that disappeared in the Highland Clearances. Glen Coe itself is impressively austere: a classic example of post-glacial scenery. From here, the Way follows General Caulfeild's military road, constructed for strategic purposes after the 1745 rising. At Altnafeadh it zigzags up the Devil's Staircase, gaining views of the famous Three Sisters of Glen Coe, a trio of lofty peaks. You may spot peregrines and golden eagles hereabouts.

Beyond Kinlochleven and Kinlochmore the Way continues on a lonely route into Glen Nevis, perhaps the finest of all Scottish glens, overlooked by Ben Nevis, Britain's tallest mountain. For a short, totally straightforward but spectacular there-and-back walk, Glen Nevis can hardly be bettered. From Fort William, drive into Glen Nevis, park at the end of the road and just follow the well-tramped track for a mile or so. The Glen assumes almost Alpine grandeur before widening out.

LOCH MOIDART AND CASTLE TIORAM

A MOORLAND route using a reasonably well-defined path (often boggy, so good footwear is essential) past two small lochs, before dropping towards Loch Moidart; the route then follows a low-level coastal path, with a classic highland view near Castle Tioram. Dogs must be on a lead. There is no access to the moorland part of the walk in stalking season (1 Sept to 21 Oct).

> **LENGTH** 6 miles (9.5km), 3 hours
> **DIFFICULTY** 2
> **START** By a turning off the A861 signposted Dorlin, 18 miles south-west of Lochailort (where the A861 joins the A830 Fort William to Mallaig road) and 3 miles north of Salen; roadside parking nearby. Grid reference 675692
> **OS MAPS** Landranger 40; Pathfinder 288 and 275 (NM 66/76 and NM 67/77)

WALK DIRECTIONS

① From the road junction, with the Dorlin road to your left, walk along the A861 in the direction signposted Lochailort. After 250 yards, where the road bends right, take a stony track on your left which rises gently through woods until reaching a gate into moorland ②: here keep to the main track which first bends right and then narrows to path width.

Pass a lochan (small lake) on your left. ③ Path continues around the left side of a second lochan, just after the end of which you turn sharp right at a path junction (continuing around the lochan) –

The ruins of Castle Tioram are accessible except at very high tide

there was a lone tree at this junction when the walk was inspected. ④ The path soon bends left away from lochan (initially with a stream on the right).

Where the path begins to level out, it very briefly becomes ill-defined (at the time of inspection, there was another small lone tree near this point) – bear slightly left, soon picking up a clear path again, which later passes two cairns (piled-up stones) Ⓐ and drops steadily towards Loch Moidart, veering right as it does so, and entering a semi-wooded area. ⑤ A short distance above the coast, turn sharp left at a path junction by a cairn and follow this coast path to reach Castle Tioram Ⓑ. ⑥ Continue along the

coast, eventually joining a road which you follow back to the starting-point. ⑦ Just after a car park and bollards on the road, you can take a 'private road' on your right for better coastal views; this rejoins the principal road later.

Castle Tioram seen from near the jetty at Dorlin

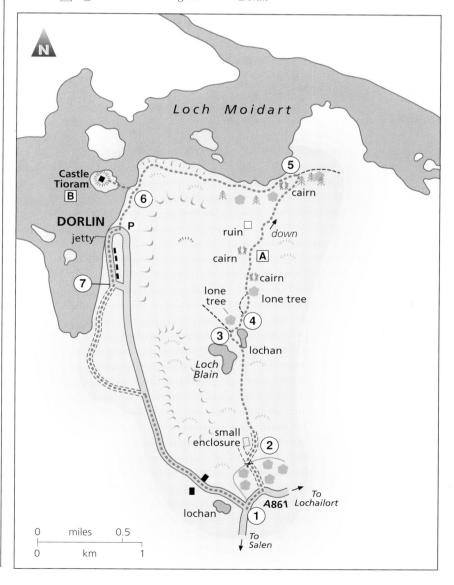

ON THE ROUTE

[A] There is a good **view** from the highest cairn over Loch Moidart and its islands.

[B] **Castle Tioram** (always *open* although not accessible at high tide) stands on a tidal promontory watching over the sea loch. This five-sided 14th-century keep, standing to its original height, was the seat of the Macdonalds of Clan Ranald. It was burned by its chief in 1715 when he was afraid that the Campbells would take the castle. The castle's lack of seaward windows was probably intended as a defensive measure against sea attacks.

Loch Moidart, cutting inland from the sea, is studded with islands, heavily wooded and may have seals basking on its skerries. This is Riska, viewed between points ⑤ and ⑥

WAYMARKS

Footpaths are sometimes marked with yellow arrows; bridleways (for walkers, cyclists and horse-riders) are shown by blue arrows; red arrows indicate byways (open to all traffic). National Trails are waymarked with acorn motifs.

SEASONAL HAZARDS

Summer walking in shorts or a skirt can be delightful, but be aware of the possibility of stinging nettles. The problem is often worst along paths in between fences. It may pay to take a pair of secateurs with you to deal with high-summer vegetation. July and August bring out the midges, notably around the lochs of Scotland.

In autumn, woodland paths often get obscured by fallen leaves. Mud can be a problem at any time of year, especially along bridleways where horses may churn up the path surface.

LOCH NA CREITHEACH AND THE EASTERN CUILLINS

A THERE-AND-BACK route along the coast path, leading straight to one of Britain's most challenging mountain ranges. The walk reaches a climax at Loch na Creitheach, where you will look into the rugged magnificence of the Cuillin Hills, one of Scotland's finest areas for mountaineering. A good walk for one of Skye's many inclement days, as the coast is often sheltered and quite low, and the going underfoot is easy. Easy route-finding.

LENGTH 8 miles (13km), 4 hours (4 miles each way)

DIFFICULTY 2

START Elgol, at the end of the A881, 14 miles south-west of Broadford. Small car park opposite signposted turning to Glasnakillie. Grid reference 518136

OS MAPS Landranger 32; Outdoor Leisure 8

REFRESHMENTS Shop at Elgol

WALK DIRECTIONS

① From the car park follow the road uphill for 300 yards to a cluster of cottages near the top of a steep portion of road, then turn left on a stony track which passes a two-storey house after 100 yards. Do not keep on the track to the second house, but change to the far side of the fence on your right, where path leads along the bottom (left) edge of two fields to a gate ②. The path ahead is easy to find as it contours above the coast Ⓐ.

③ After descending into the first large bay, the path continues up on the far side, along the edge of low cliffs. Ⓑ ④ At the next bay, follow the path to prominently placed Camasunary farmhouse Ⓒ (noting the way you have come, as you will come back along the same route). Cross the stream by a bridge below a waterfall.

⑤ Turn right just before reaching Camasunary (a working farm, partly

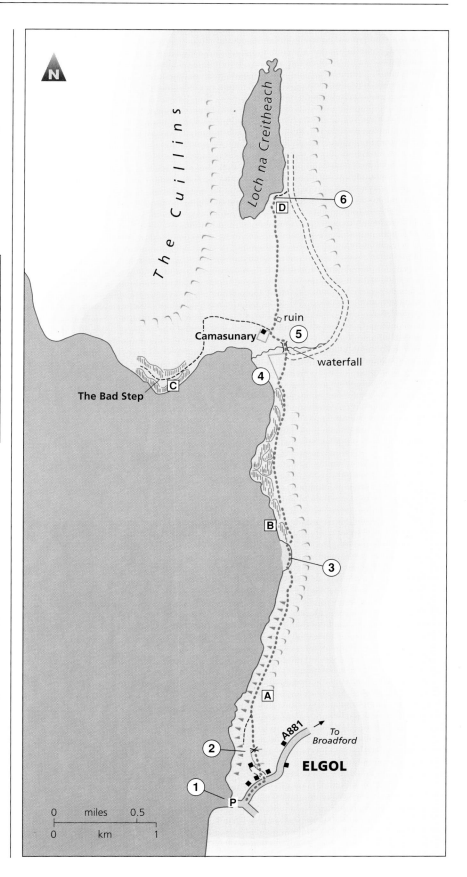

surrounded by a ruined one), to pick up a stony path leading past a second ruin. Proceed to Loch na Creitheach [D] (6). Retrace steps from the loch.

ON THE ROUTE

[A] ½ mile out of Elgol, on a promontory, is a small **cave** where Bonnie Prince Charlie hid before leaving Skye for ever. The promontory, known as Sharp Seat, used to be a haunt of childless women who came here in the hope that they would become fertile.

[B] **View** westwards is the nearby island of Soay (4 miles), and north of it are the Cuillins, including Gars Bheinn (2,934ft) and Sgurr Alasdair (3,257ft); 12 miles south-west is the island of Rhum.

[C] **View** The continuation of the

A solitary croft huddles at the foot of the stark Cuillin Hills

coast path beyond Camasunary follows the aptly named Bad Step (more of a climbing route than a path) to the entrance of Loch Coruisk. It requires walking on a high ledge, with a sheer drop on the seaward side and little more than a narrow cleft to hang on to; a slip on

the wet rocks is usually fatal.

[D] The **view** reveals some of the brutal beauty of the Cuillins. Left to right: Trodhu (1,623ft); Marsco (at the far end of the loch, 2,414ft); Bla Bheinn (3,044ft).

TWO OTHER WALKS ON THE ISLE OF SKYE

Skye is an island of many moods. Much of its terrain is strictly for experienced mountain-walkers and climbers, but the **Neist peninsula**, at its western tip, is easily accessible on foot. The drive to it encounters views of the extraordinary flat-topped mountains of Healabhal Mhor and Healabhal Bheag (Macleod's Table North and Macleod's Table South).

A small road branches off the B884 south-west to end at a car park. From here the path heads south-west around the rocky lump known as the Stallion. At the lighthouse there are views across Moonen Bay to nearby Waterstein Head, the next coastal summit to the east, and further out at the end of the bay is the headland, both of which can be included in a more energetic excursion. To the west over the water are the Outer Hebrides: sunsets here are certainly worth the long drive.

Retrace your steps to the car park and follow the cliffs for an easy half-mile to the coastguard look-out for a phenomenal view of Biod Ban, a 645-foot cliff. Another path cuts directly across the moor to the car park. The length of this walk is 3 miles (5 km).

One of the most spectacular landforms in Scotland is the **Quiraing**, a breathtaking series of cliffs, stone towers and pinnacles surrounding a huge chasm caused by geological faulting. This bizarre moonscape can be enjoyed by a rugged, but (in good weather) reasonably manageable path leading north-east from a car park on the road between Uig and Brogaig. The path heads beneath the 120ft tall Needle. After about a mile, retrace your steps back.

A covey of canoeists near Elgol; across the water can be seen the jagged form of the Cuillins, skirted by the Bad Step

KINNOULL HILL AND THE TAY VALLEY

A WOODED hill on the edge of Perth, flat on top but precipitous on one side, and capped by two stone follies. The walk contains one stretch of road-walking, though the road is quiet and there are good views beyond Kinfauns Castle to the Tay. The full walk is a figure-of-eight route; the short version takes the southern loop via Kinnoull Tower. Trail leaflets are available from Perth Tourist Office. Thoroughly waymarked; easy route-finding.

WALK DIRECTIONS

① From information board adjacent to car park follow path signposted Tower Walk. Follow the yellow marker-posts, past a viewpoint and forking right by a house, then turning left 150 yards later into woods. Many paths exist in the woods: follow further yellow marker-posts. Just before reaching a wider track, the path passes a red marker post (for 'nature walk', which here duplicates Tower Walk) ②. Turn left on this track and follow it to a gate leading on to a road ③.

LENGTH *Full walk* 6 miles (9.5km), 3 hours
Short walk 3½ miles (5.5km), 1½ hours
DIFFICULTY 1
START Quarry car park, Kinnoull Hill, 1 mile east of Perth. From Perth town centre cross the river by either bridge. At the other side turn right (Dundee Road) then just after Isle of Skye Hotel turn left into Manse Road. At the end of the road turn right at crossroads into Hatton Road. Car park is 150 yards after the end of the built-up area, signposted on the right of the road. Grid reference 134235
OS MAPS Landranger 53 or 58: Pathfinder 350 (NO 02/12)

For short walk Turn sharp right immediately before reaching road, signposted Tower Walk; this is ⑧.
For full walk Turn right on road, and look out soon for Binnhill Tower in woods ahead, just to the right of the road. ④ For detour to Binnhill Tower A turn right on track leading into woods, take left fork through a wicket gate and follow to tower. Retrace your steps

The Tay at Perth, said to have reminded Roman soldiers of home when they first saw its site

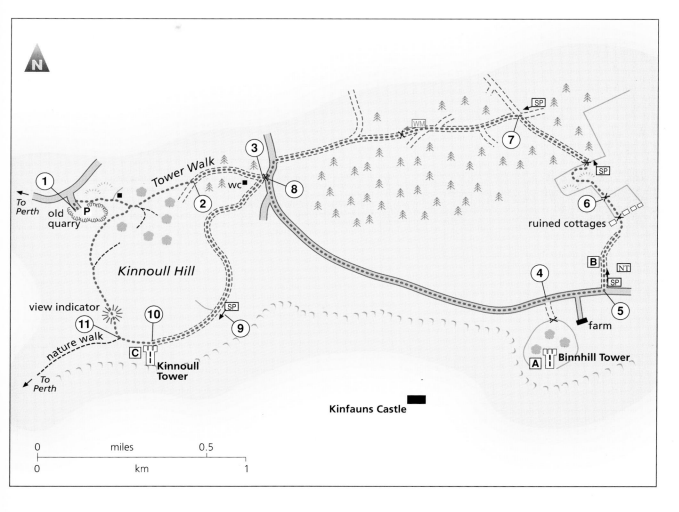

to the road. Turn right to continue along the road for 250 yards. ⑤ Turn left on a track, signposted Coronation Road B. The track leads to deserted cottages, and bends left through a gate between them. Follow the left edge of field ahead, to a gate in the far left-hand corner.

⑥ Keep forward beyond the gate, at first with a fence on your left, and then continue ahead uphill on a faint path for 200 yards, through a clump of gorse to find a signpost for Coronation Road. Turn left through a gate into the forest.

⑦ After ¼ mile turn left, following sign to Jubilee car park and Corsie Hill. Keep forward after 250 yards, ignoring track sharp left. Keep forward after a further 200 yards, ignoring track sharp right, then fork right 50 yards later (after a green marker-post). Continue to a barrier then follow the track along the edge of woods gently downhill to the road. Turn left on the road then 100 yards later right to Forestry Commission board ⑧. Fork left before a gate (signposted for Tower Walk). ⑨ After ¾ mile turn left, signposted Kinnoull Tower C. ⑩ Go forward at the tower along the cliff-top path to a viewpoint ⑪. (If you started on foot from Perth, you can follow the cliff path all the way back; keep left at ⑪, ignore all subsequent right turns). From the viewpoint pick up the yellow marker-posts (Tower Walk) to a view indicator. Here fork right and follow yellow waymarks through woods to the car park (ignoring a final waymarked turn on the right).

ON THE ROUTE

A **Binnhill Tower** The stone tower was built in the 18th century as a picturesque imitation ruin. Lord Gray and the ninth Earl of Kinnoull decided after a trip up the Rhine that the Tay could do with its own romantic castles, and built Binnhill and Kinnoull Towers at the top of the cliffs above the river.

B **Coronation Road** Also known as the King's Highway, the road connected the former royal city of Scone and Abernethy, another Pictish capital, from AD 700 to 1050 (the road may be older than this).

Kinnoull Hill and the River Tay in summer

C **Kinnoull Tower** and **Hill** The tower, like Binnhill, is a folly. Near it is a stone table where the ninth Earl of Kinnoull used to picnic and enjoy the view over the Tay and to the Ochils. An excellent panorama extends in all directions from the summit of the hill.

MORE WALKS NEAR PERTH

The Lomond Hills, Fife These hills (which are nowhere near Loch Lomond) overlook much of southern Scotland, including Ben Lomond, Ben More, the Trossachs, Ben Lawers, the Fife coast, Edinburgh and the Pentland Hills. There is easy walking along an almost level track from the car park from a road leading south-west from the attractive town of Falkland, dominated by its Renaissance palace; it is about ¾ mile each way. You can lengthen the walk by heading along the ridge in the other direction to West Lomond (just over a mile each way). Those who prefer to earn their view rather than to drive up to the car park can take a steep path up from Falkland to East Lomond.

Knock of Crieff, Tayside This small wooded sandstone protuberance does not rise to any great height, but makes a fine viewpoint by virtue of its position. From the north side of Crieff, near the Strathearn Hydro (established in 1868 for those who wished to take the waters), paths ascend to the summit. The woods briefly open out at the top, giving an outlook encompassing many of the peaks of the south-east Highlands, including Ben Vorlich and Ben Chonzie. This is a very short stroll, but can be extended by following the nearby Crieff Nature Trail, which makes a 1½-mile circuit.

Callander Crags, Central From the west side of Callander, a stepped path ascends steadily through dense forest before emerging into the open at the end of Callander Crags. The Crags are lined along a narrow ridge that makes a particularly enjoyable mile-long walk north-eastwards. There are exhilarating views of the Trossachs, Campsie Fells and the Forth plain.

Castle Campbell, Central This must be one of the most enthralling half-miles in all Scotland: around the base of this fairy-tale castle (National Trust for Scotland), a specially constructed walkway threads beneath improbable rock overhangs, past dripping ferns and along a chasm gushing with fast-flowing water. Extend the walk by a mile by starting from Dollar and heading up Dollar Glen. The castle is perched most dramatically on the edge of the Ochils, a range of smooth, green hills that rise abruptly from the lowland plain and give phenomenal views as well as some invigorating (though largely pathless) walking.

KENMORE AND THE BANKS OF THE TAY

THIS walk begins along the River Tay and passes along a fine avenue of trees before leading up through forest to take a track giving good views of Taymouth Castle and Loch Tay. There is one very leisurely 300ft climb, otherwise the route is all on the level. Easy route-finding.

LENGTH 4½ miles (7km), 2 hours
With detour to viewpoint at end
5½ miles (9km), 2½ hours
DIFFICULTY 1
START Kenmore village square, at east end of Loch Tay. Park here; larger car park at lakeside near south end of village (both car parks free). Grid reference 773455
OS MAPS Landranger 51 or 52; Pathfinder 322 (NN 64/74)
REFRESHMENTS Kenmore Hotel, Kenmore

WALK DIRECTIONS

① A With the church away to the left, follow the main road out of the village. Immediately after crossing bridge turn right through an opening in wall to join the riverside path B. ② The path passes through a deer-gate into woods, soon passing a stone folly (which you can climb by steps) and continues, as a track, along an avenue of beeches. ③ When level with a bridge down on the right you can detour down the bank and across bridge to castle C (but you will get a good view of the castle later).
④ The track turns left by castellated parapet. Turn right on reaching the road. ⑤ 250 yards later go left on forest track. Go left after ¼ mile at first fork, follow the track for 1½ miles D.

View out over Loch Tay

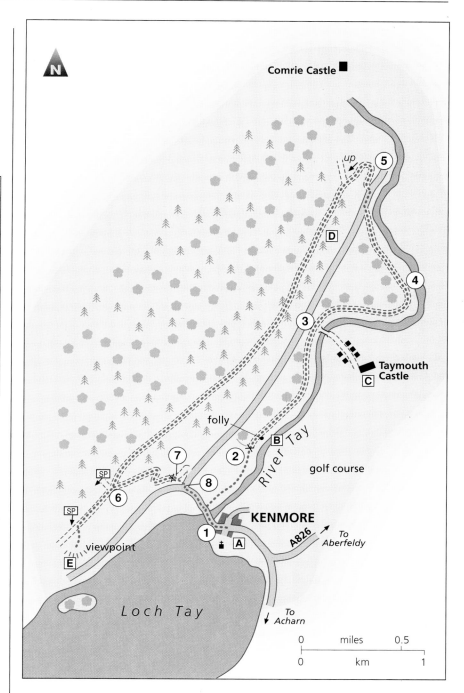

⑥ To detour to viewpoint keep forward at staggered junction of tracks (signposted Viewpoint) and fork left ½ mile later to viewpoint (signposted) E. Retrace your steps.
To continue the walk turn left downhill at staggered junction (right if retracing steps from viewpoint), and turn sharp left at next junction. ⑦ Just after the barrier/forestry map turn right on path. ⑧ Turn right on reaching the road and follow this back into Kenmore, avoiding right turns.

ON THE ROUTE

A **Kenmore** Its present location is due to landowner Colin Campbell of Glenorchy who, in the 16th century, decided that the village, its church and inhabitants should be moved from a few miles further up the Tay. His plan was not realised fully, however, until 1760, when the present estate village of model dwellings was built. Tenants lived here rent-free on condition that they carried on a trade and kept their houses clean. The Kenmore

The eighteenth-century model village of Kenmore at the head of Loch Tay

Hotel, dating from 1572, claims to be Scotland's oldest inn. The hotel has its own boats and resident gillie, and boasts a delightful riverside garden.

B **River Tay** A ceremony every January marks the start of the salmon season, and an annual raft race from Kenmore is held in June.

C **Taymouth Castle** A Gothick steel-blue extravaganza, begun in 1801 for the Earl of Breadalbane and finished in 1842 just in time for the visit of Queen Victoria, who remarked that it was 'princely and romantic'. Unfortunately, it is now somewhat run-down.

D **View** Over Taymouth Castle and the east end of Loch Tay.

E **View** Below is the wooded Isle of Loch Tay, one of many artificial islands in the loch, built by the Celts as a defensive site and originally approached by a causeway that is now under water (except in very dry weather). When, in 1122, the wife of King Alexander I died there, the King granted the island to Scone Abbey, so that the site could be consecrated. Over the next 200 years the island was used as a monastery garden and later housed a nunnery. The Campbells of Glenorchy (who were responsible for moving Kenmore village) had a castle on it.

FALLS OF ACHARN

The walk described here can be coupled with a visit to the Falls of Acharn. Drive or walk south-west on the road along the south side of Loch Tay for 1¼ miles. At Acharn village, follow the road across a stream then turn left by a bus shelter on a track rising up the right-hand side of Acharn Glen. This leads past a man-made 'hermitage cave' giving on to a viewpoint over the waterfall: the viewpoint was a 19th-century creation made by the estate owner. Either go back the same way or carry on up: the track soon bends left and levels out; beyond Balmacnaughton (a house and barn), the track gains panoramic views over the loch. Eventually it reaches a minor road which leads to the left down towards Kenmore.

BLAIR CASTLE AND GLEN TILT

AN exploration along woodland and pasture tracks of the Atholl estates. Although the route effectively goes up one side of Glen Tilt and comes down the other, there is enough variation in landscape to sustain interest throughout. There is a short, quiet road section at the end. The riverside route used in the full walk is not visible on the ground, but other tracks are well defined. There is a rifle range near ⑧ on the route; if it is in use, warning signs will be displayed. Route-finding is quite easy. The short version of the walk omits sections ⑨ and ⑩.

LENGTH *Full walk* 11 miles (17.5km), 5½ hours

DIFFICULTY 3

Short walk 7 miles (11km), 3½ hours

DIFFICULTY 2

START Atholl Arms Hotel (by station), Blair Atholl, off A9 6½ miles north-west of Pitlochry. Roadside parking. Grid reference 870654

OS MAPS Landranger 43; Pathfinder 294 (NN 86/96)

REFRESHMENTS Hotels in Blair Atholl

WALK DIRECTIONS

① With the Atholl Arms on your right follow the main road, then take the first left up the main drive to the castle Ⓐ. ② Just beyond the castle turn half right on to a path (signposted Diana's Grove) leading through woods Ⓑ. Ignore side turnings, and follow the path to a

Blair Atholl, the village at the confluence of the Rivers Tilt and Garry

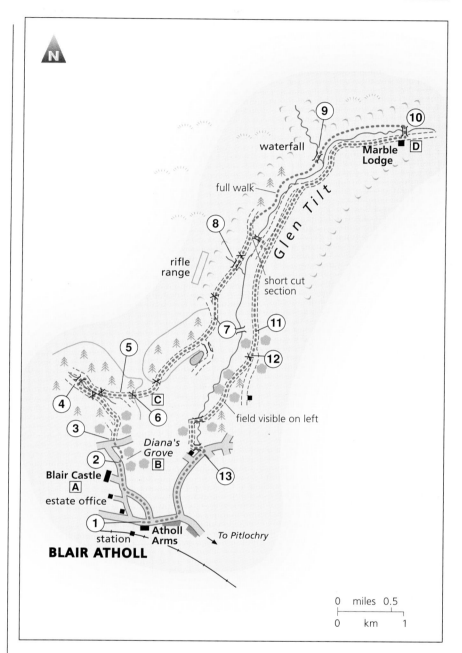

gateway and on to the road ③. Cross the road to a woodland track opposite, follow this for ¾ mile (passing through a gate on the way). ④ Turn right over a bridge, fork right on the other side, soon to reach a deer-gate. ⑤ Fork left 50 yards after deer-gate; the track ascends gently. Keep left at the next fork, 100 yards later.

⑥ Leave the woods by a gate Ⓒ, and continue on a grassy track along the top of the hill. Re-enter woods by a gate and descend gently past a large pond on your right. Ignore sharp right turn over a bridge soon

after the pond. ⑦ Take the next fork right and descend to a small stream by bridge. ⑧ Just after a bridge pass through a gate.

For short walk Take next fork right, cross the river bridge, then fork right over a cattlegrid. 200 yards later turn left on to a narrow path indicated by marker-posts (blue arrows), ascend to a stile, then to a track. Turn right on the track for ¾ mile, to reach point ⑪.

For full walk Fork left up the forestry track and after 150 yards fork on to a narrow path just to the right of, and initially parallel to, forest track (easily missed, but soon becomes very distinct). The path leads into a forest (fork right as waymarked after 100 yards), eventually out of the forest, through fields and then to a bridge over a waterfall ⑨. Beyond the waterfall the route along the river is obvious but the path is a little rougher, sometimes indistinct. ⑩ Cross river at next bridge, then turn right on track Ⓓ. Fork left after ¾ mile.

⑪ The track enters woods. ⑫ ¼ mile into woods fork right through a gate. Track descends gently, bending right after ¾ mile. Follow it over a bridge then forward to emerge on the road ⑬. Turn right on the road, then left at next junction, signposted Blair Atholl ½.

ON THE ROUTE

Ⓐ **Blair Castle** (*open to the public; fee*) is the chief residence of Earls and Dukes of Atholl, and the mustering ground of the Duke's private army, the only one allowed in Britain. The Atholl Highlanders were the product of a moment's romantic weakness by Queen Victoria, who visited the castle in 1844. Other house guests have included Edward III and Mary Queen of Scots. The best parts of the interior are the Georgian conversions of older rooms, the

drawing-room ceiling being especially elaborate and beautiful. Although there are masses of interesting family portraits, this is primarily a stately home for lovers of odds and ends: on the lowest floor is a miscellany of Victoriana, which consists of everything from reticules to mourning brooches, and the castle also boasts a number of Jacobite relics. The grounds are both ducal and welcoming.

Ⓑ **Diana's Grove** This collection of trees, including some fine conifers (described by notice on gate) was planted in 1737. The grove contains a statue of Diana (1861).

Ⓒ **View** Over the sizeable Atholl estates, an area of forest plantation and moorland used for grouse-shooting and deer-stalking. The valley was farmed, in narrow strips, until the last century by tenant farmers, remains of whose crofts can be seen in places.

Ⓓ By the bridge is **Marble Lodge**, named after a nearby outcrop of green marble that also went to make the fireplace in the castle's great hall.

It is not easy to tell from the outside which parts of Blair Castle are 13th century and which are Victorian (though the castellations are certainly the latter)

CULLEN TO PORTSOY

A COASTAL route, first at shore level then along cliff-tops, linking three particularly appealing fishing ports and two sandy beaches. The path is well defined (up and down) as far as Sandend, then there is an undefined but mostly level route along cliff-tops to Portsoy. Return by bus (frequent service Monday to Saturday; about five a day on Sunday).

LENGTH *Full walk* 7 miles (11km), 3½ hours. *Cullen to Sandend* 4 miles (6.5km), 2 hours

DIFFICULTY 2–3

START Cullen harbour, on A98 between Banff and Elgin. Grid reference 511673

OS MAPS Landranger 29; Pathfinder 148 (NJ 56/66)

REFRESHMENTS Full range in Cullen and Portsoy

WALK DIRECTIONS

① A With the harbour on your left, follow the shoreside road which soon becomes an unsurfaced track and later narrows to a path, which is well defined as it runs along the shore below cliffs B. ② At Logie Head, the path goes up and then down steps at a rock buttress. ③ Cross a stile on entering Sunnyside Bay C: the path then leads up to the top of the cliff, where it turns left with a fence on the right: ignore track leading to right inland, and keep along the cliff-top D, soon past Findlater Castle (on promontory) E and continue along cliff-tops over a series of stiles (the path is not defined, but the route is obvious).

④ Enter Sandend Bay (stiles still mark the route) to reach Sandend village F; the path goes to the right of the highest-placed house in the village to reach a road. *To finish walk here* Turn right and proceed to the main road for the bus service back to Cullen.

To continue Walk across the beach, beside dunes, to climb steps at the far side of the bay ⑤, on to the cliff-top, and soon through a kissing-gate: from here, proceed on level cliff-top alongside a fence on the right (the path is undefined but the route is obvious).

⑥ After you round Redhythe Point, you pass a concrete wartime bunker on your right; the fence on right ends soon after, then pick up a well-defined track which bends inland after 100 yards to reach T-junction with farm track after 300 yards, where ⑦ you turn left.

Proceed to reach the road, turn

Cullen, famous for its smoked haddock soup, also boasts a long stretch of sand and a fine golf course

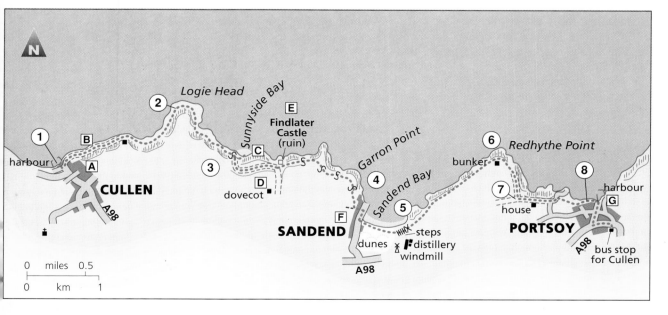

SEASONAL HAZARDS

Summer walking in shorts or a skirt can be delightful, but be aware of the possibility of stinging nettles. The problem is often worst along paths in between fences. It may pay to take a pair of secateurs with you to deal with high-summer vegetation. July and August bring out the midges, notably around the lochs of Scotland.

In autumn, woodland paths often get obscured by fallen leaves. Mud can be a problem at any time of year, especially along bridleways where horses may churn up the path surface.

Portsoy's harbour is a rewarding sight at the end of the walk

left on it; after 100 yards, where the road bends left (dropping to the shore) continue forward on a tarmac path. (8) On reaching the road at the edge of Portsoy, keep left on a grassy path around the cliff-top, soon reaching the harbour G.

Turn right into North High Street, cross a square into South High Street to reach the main street in town; the bus stop for Cullen is to the left (just beyond the Bank of Scotland).

ON THE ROUTE

A **Cullen** gives its name to a local haddock broth called 'Cullen skink'. The upper town has a broad main street with a market cross at the centre and a disused railway viaduct at the bottom end; below is the harbour. The Bayview Hotel is a small country hotel with outstanding views across the Moray Firth. Off the route, ½ mile south, the **Auld Kirk** has a sculptured tomb to Alexander Ogilvie, carved panels and a 16th-century sacrament house.

B **Views** to the peninsula of the Black Isle.

C **Sunnyside Bay** has a secluded sandy beach set beneath rugged cliffs; at its west side is a recess known as 'Charlie the Rock's Cave', inhabited by a Frenchman until the 1930s.

D Inland is a prominent 19th-century **dovecot** ('doocot').

E Scant remains of **Findlater Castle**, a three-storey structure built by the Ogilvies in 1455 and abandoned in the 17th century (take great care – sheer drops).

F The fishing village of **Sandend** lies huddled beneath the slope on the west side of the bay; its quaint cottages and lanes are on toytown scale. Fresh fish are often on sale. The large and popular beach has attracted holiday development. Inland are a distillery and the tower of sailless Glasslaugh Windmill (built 1761), nicknamed the 'cup and saucer' and built on the site of a prehistoric burial mound.

G **Portsoy** has a wealth of fine 18th-century buildings, particularly around its harbour, which prospered as a major port trading with the Low Countries and Scandinavia. The old harbour dates from 1692, the 'new' one from 1839. Portsoy marble is still produced (there's a workshop as you enter the harbour). A famous product of green and red serpentine colour, it was used in many European palaces, including Versailles.

RIGHTS OF WAY IN SCOTLAND

There is no officially registered network of rights of way in Scotland (unlike England and Wales), and a tradition of informal access for walkers (except in shooting and stalking seasons) has developed. However, many local authority planning departments keep records of rights of way; the Scottish Rights of Way Society publishes maps of some of these routes for its members.

Rights of way are not distinguished from other paths on OS maps, but many are signposted by the Scottish Rights of Way Society, and by local authorities.

The creation of a right of way depends primarily on common law. The requirements for a route to become a right of way are:

1 It must run from one public place (where the public are entitled to be, such as a road or church) to another.
2 It must follow a consistent and generally defined line (although need not be visible on the ground and may make minor deviations).
3 It must have been used openly and peaceably by the public as of right, without the express or implied permission of the landowner.
4 It must have been used without substantial and effective interruption for a period of at least 20 years.